Law and the Technologies of the Twenty-First Century

Law and the Technologies of the Twenty-First Century provides a contextual account of the way in which law functions in a broader regulatory environment across different jurisdictions. It identifies and clearly structures the four key challenges that technology poses to regulatory efforts, distinguishing between technology as a regulatory target and as a tool, and guiding the reader through an emerging field that is subject to rapid change. By extensive use of examples and extracts from the texts and materials that form and shape the scholarly and public debates over technology regulation, it presents complex material in a stimulating and engaging manner. Co-authored by a leading scholar in the field with a scholar new to the area, it combines comprehensive knowledge of the field with a fresh approach. This is essential reading for students of law and technology, risk regulation, policy studies, and science and technology studies.

Roger Brownsword is Professor of Law at King's College London. He has been teaching in university law schools since 1968 and currently teaches Law and the Technologies of the Twenty-First Century to students at both King's College London and Singapore Management University. He is a co-founding editor of the journal *Law, Innovation and Technology*, and a member of the editorial board of the *Modern Law Review*. He has published extensively in the fields of contracts and the common law, legal theory, bioethics and the regulation of technology.

Morag Goodwin is a senior lecturer of European and international law at the School of Law, Tilburg University. Between 2008 and 2011 she worked at the Tilburg Institute for Law, Technology and Society (TILT). She is a member of the editorial board of the *German Law Journal* and a member of the editorial committee of *Rechtstheorie & Rechtsfilosofie* (*Netherlands Journal of Legal Philosophy*).

The Law in Context Series

Editors: William Twining (University College London),
Christopher McCrudden (Lincoln College, Oxford) and
Bronwen Morgan (University of Bristol).

Since 1970 the Law in Context series has been at the forefront of the movement to broaden the study of law. It has been a vehicle for the publication of innovative scholarly books that treat law and legal phenomena critically in their social, political and economic contexts from a variety of perspectives. The series particularly aims to publish scholarly legal writing that brings fresh perspectives to bear on new and existing areas of law taught in universities. A contextual approach involves treating legal subjects broadly, using materials from other social sciences, and from any other discipline that helps to explain the operation in practice of the subject under discussion. It is hoped that this orientation is at once more stimulating and more realistic than the bare exposition of legal rules. The series includes original books that have a different emphasis from traditional legal textbooks, while maintaining the same high standards of scholarship. They are written primarily for undergraduate and graduate students of law and of other disciplines, but most also appeal to a wider readership. In the past, most books in the series have focused on English law, but recent publications include books on European law, globalisation, transnational legal processes, and comparative law.

Books in the Series
Anderson, Schum & Twining: *Analysis of Evidence*
Ashworth: *Sentencing and Criminal Justice*
Barton & Douglas: *Law and Parenthood*
Beecher-Monas: *Evaluating Scientific Evidence: An Interdisciplinary Framework for Intellectual Due Process*
Bell: *French Legal Cultures*
Bercusson: *European Labour Law*
Birkinshaw: *European Public Law*
Birkinshaw: *Freedom of Information: The Law, the Practice and the Ideal*
Cane: *Atiyah's Accidents, Compensation and the Law*
Clarke & Kohler: *Property Law: Commentary and Materials*
Collins: *The Law of Contract*
Cowan: *Housing Law*
Cranston: *Legal Foundations of the Welfare State*
Dauvergne *Making People Illegal: What Globalisation Means for Immigration and Law*
Davies: *Perspectives on Labour Law*
Dembour: *Who Believes in Human Rights?: The European Convention in Question*
de Sousa Santos: *Toward a New Legal Common Sense*

Diduck: *Law's Families*
Fortin: *Children's Rights and the Developing Law*
Glover-Thomas: *Reconstructing Mental Health Law and Policy*
Goldman: *Globalisation and the Western Legal Tradition: Recurring Patterns of Law and Authority*
Gobert & Punch: *Rethinking Corporate Crime*
Harlow & Rawlings: *Law and Administration*
Harris: *An Introduction to Law*
Harris, Campbell & Halson: *Remedies in Contract and Tort*
Harvey: *Seeking Asylum in the UK: Problems and Prospects*
Hervey & McHale: *Health Law and the European Union*
Holder and Lee: *Environmental Protection, Law and Policy*
Kostakopoulou: *The Future Governance of Citizenship*
Lewis: *Choice and the Legal Order: Rising above Politics*
Likosky: *Transnational Legal Processes*
Likosky: *Law, Infrastructure and Human Rights*
Maughan & Webb: *Lawyering Skills and the Legal Process*
McGlynn: *Families and the European Union: Law, Politics and Pluralism*
Moffat: *Trusts Law: Text and Materials*
Monti: *EC Competition Law*
Morgan & Yeung: *An Introduction to Law and Regulation: Text and Materials*
Norrie: *Crime, Reason and History*
O'Dair: *Legal Ethics*
Oliver: *Common Values and the Public–Private Divide*
Oliver & Drewry: *The Law and Parliament*
Picciotto: *International Business Taxation*
Reed: *Internet Law: Text and Materials*
Richardson: *Law, Process and Custody*
Roberts & Palmer: *Dispute Processes: ADR and the Primary Forms of Decision-Making*
Rowbottom: *Democracy Distorted: Wealth, Influence and Democratic Politics*
Scott & Black: *Cranston's Consumers and the Law*
Seneviratne: *Ombudsmen: Public Services and Administrative Justice*
Stapleton: *Product Liability*
Stewart: Gender, Law and Justice in a Global Market
Tamanaha: *Law as a Means to an End: Threat to the Rule of Law*
Turpin and Tomkins: *British Government and the Constitution: Text and Materials*
Twining: *Globalisation and Legal Theory*
Twining: *Rethinking Evidence*
Twining: *General Jurisprudence: Understanding Law from a Global Perspective*
Twining: *Human Rights, Southern Voices: Francis Deng, Abdullahi An-Na'im, Yash Ghai and Upendra Baxi*
Twining & Miers: *How to Do Things with Rules*
Ward: *A Critical Introduction to European Law*
Ward: *Law, Text, Terror*
Ward: *Shakespeare and Legal Imagination*
Wells and Quick: *Lacey, Wells and Quick: Reconstructing Criminal Law*
Zander: *Cases and Materials on the English Legal System*
Zander: *The Law-Making Process*

Law and the Technologies of the Twenty-First Century: Text and Materials

ROGER BROWNSWORD
Professor of Law, King's College London

MORAG GOODWIN
Senior lecturer, Tilburg Law School

CAMBRIDGE
UNIVERSITY PRESS

University Printing House, Cambridge CB2 8BS, United Kingdom

One Liberty Plaza, 20th Floor, New York, NY 10006, USA

477 Williamstown Road, Port Melbourne, VIC 3207, Australia

314-321, 3rd Floor, Plot 3, Splendor Forum, Jasola District Centre, New Delhi - 110025, India

79 Anson Road, #06-04/06, Singapore 079906

Cambridge University Press is part of the University of Cambridge.

It furthers the University's mission by disseminating knowledge in the pursuit of education, learning and research at the highest international levels of excellence.

www.cambridge.org
Information on this title: www.cambridge.org/9780521186247

© Roger Brownsword and Morag Goodwin 2012

This publication is in copyright. Subject to statutory exception and to the provisions of relevant collective licensing agreements, no reproduction of any part may take place without the written permission of Cambridge University Press.

First published 2012

A catalogue record for this publication is available from the British Library

ISBN 978-1-107-00655-3 Hardback
ISBN 978-0-521-18624-7 Paperback

Cambridge University Press has no responsibility for the persistence or accuracy of URLs for external or third-party internet websites referred to in this publication, and does not guarantee that any content on such websites is, or will remain, accurate or appropriate.

Contents

Acknowledgements	*page*	ix
List of abbreviations		xi
Tables of cases		xiii
Table of statutes and other public documents		xvi

PART I   GENERAL INTRODUCTION — 1

1 **Introduction** — 3

2 **The regulatory environment: UK Biobank, eBay and *Wikipedia*** — 24

3 **Four key regulatory challenges** — 46

4 **Technology as a regulatory tool: DNA profiling and *Marper*** — 72

PART II   REGULATORY PRUDENCE AND PRECAUTION — 109

5 **Regulatory prudence I: health, safety and environment: GM crops, nanoparticles and sound science** — 111

6 **Regulatory prudence II: precaution** — 137

PART III   REGULATORY LEGITIMACY — 167

7 **The legitimacy of the regulatory environment: basic ideas** — 169

8 **Key boundary-marking concepts** — 188

9 **Human rights as boundary markers** — 225

10 **A look at procedural legitimacy: the role of public participation in technology regulation** — 246

PART IV   REGULATORY EFFECTIVENESS — 269

11 **Regulatory effectiveness I** — 271

12 **Regulatory effectiveness II: failure by regulators** — 296

13	**Regulatory effectiveness III: resistance by regulatees**	318
14	**Regulatory effectiveness IV: third-party interference and disruptive externalities**	342
	PART V REGULATORY CONNECTION	369
15	**Regulatory connection I: getting connected**	371
16	**Regulatory connection II: disconnection and sustainability**	398
	CONCLUDING OVERVIEW	421
17	**From law to code: the surveillance society and *Marper* revisited**	423
	Index	453

Acknowledgements

The writing of this book has benefited significantly from the input of others. Drafts of this book were inflicted on several cohorts of students – at King's College London in 2009 and 2010, at the University of Singapore in 2010, and at Tilburg University in the course ICT and Law offered as part of the School of Law's Research Master in 2010 and 2011. Not only were these courses fun to teach, but the feedback of the students has helped us to tighten certain arguments and rethink how we present others. We are particularly grateful for their input. Also to colleagues at faculty seminars in Tilburg where various chapters have been presented for their useful suggestions and questions.

The authors thank the many copyright holders of the texts and materials cited for their permission to reproduce them here. Thanks are also due to Sinead Moloney, Sarah Roberts, Martin Barr and Helen Francis of CUP, who have ably assisted the authors throughout the process of this book's production.

The Tilburg Institute of Law, Technology and Society (TILT) provided a home to Morag Goodwin for the three years in which the book was conceived, materials collected and chapters written. The book has benefited greatly from discussions with TILT colleagues about both structure and content. She wishes to acknowledge a particular debt to Paul de Hert, Bert-Jaap Koops and Han Somsen, who read and commented on various chapters and who have been her tutors in the field of law and technology.

RB & MG

London and Tilburg, December 2011

Every attempt has been made to secure permission to reproduce copyright material in this title and grateful acknowledgement is made to the authors and publishers of all reproduced material. In particular, the publishers would like to acknowledge the following for granting permission to reproduce material from the sources set out below:

Stuart Biegelspace, 'Beyond Our Control? Confronting the Limits of Our Legal System in the Age of Cyberspace' (2003), pp 359–364. Reprinted with permission by The MIT Press.

Owen Boycott, 'CCTV boom has failed to slash crime, say police' (2008). Reprinted with permission by Guardian News and Media Limited.

D J Galligan, 'Citizens' Rights and Participation in the Regulation of Biotechnology' in Francesco Francioni (ed.), *Biotechnologies and International Human Rights* (2007). Reprinted with permission by Hart Publishing.

Gregory Mandel, 'Regulating Emerging Technologies' (2009) 1 *Law, Innovation and Technology* 75. Reprinted with permission by Hart Publishing.

Gary Marx, *Foreword* in David Wright, Serge Gutwirth, Michael Friedewald, Elena Vildjiounaite (eds.), *Safeguards in a World of Ambient Intelligence* (2008). Reprinted with permission by Springer.

Chris Reed, 'The Law of Unintended Consequences – Embedded Business Models in IT Regulation', JILT (2), 2007: part 2.1. Reprinted with permission from the author.

Han Somsen, 'Regulating Technologies: Legal Futures, Regulatory Frames and Technological Fixes' (2008), pp 221, 224–231. Reprinted with permission by Hart Publishing.

Abbreviations

ANPR	automatic number plate recognition
BMA	British Medical Association
BSE	bovine spongiform encephalopathy
BT	British Telecom [British Telecommunications plc]
CCTV	closed-circuit television
CII	critical information infrastructure
Cm/Cmd	[UK Parliament] Command Paper
CNR	cell nuclear replacement
DA	[US] Department of Agriculture
DC	deliberative–constitutive
DDoS	(distributed) denial-of-service
DNA	deoxyribonucleic acid
EC	European Community
ECHR	European Convention on Human Rights
ECJ	European Court of Justice
ECNH	Swiss Federal Committee on Non-Human Biotechnology
EctHR	European Court of Human Rights
EEC	European Economic Community
EFSA	European Food Safety Authority
EGC	[UK] Ethics and Governance Council
EGE	European Group on Ethics in Science and New Technologies
EGF	[UK] Ethics and Governance Framework [document]
EPA	[US] Environmental Protection Agency
EPC	European Patent Convention
EPO	European Patent Office
ESRC	[UK] Economic and Social Research Council
EU	European Union
FAO	[UN] Food and Agricultural Organization
FDA	[US] Food and Drug Administration
FIND	[UK] Facial Identification National Database
fMRI	functional magnetic resonance imaging
FSA	[UK] Food Standards Agency
GA	[UN] General Assembly
GATT	General Agreement on Tariffs and Trade

GC	Grand Chamber [*of EctHR*]
GM	genetically modified
GMO	genetically modified organism
HC	[UK] House of Commons Paper
hESC	human embryonic stem cells
HFEA	[UK] Human Fertilisation and Embryology Authority
HL	[UK] House of Lords Paper
HSE	[UK] Health and Safety Executive
IBC	International Bioethics Committee [*of UNESCO*]
ICCPR	International Covenant on Civil and Political Rights
ICJ	International Court of Justice
ICT	information and communication[s] technology
IP	Internet Protocol
ISP	internet service provider
IVF	in vitro fertilisation
LICRA	Ligue Internationale Contre le Racisme et l'Antisémitisme [*League Against Racism and Antisemitism*]
LMO	living modified organism
NGO	non-governmental organisation
OECD	Organization for Economic Cooperation and Development
OFCOM	[UK] Office of Communications
OSHA	[US] Office of Safety and Health Administration
PC	personal computer
PETs	privacy-enhancing technologies
PGD	pre-implantation genetic diagnosis [*of human embryo*]
PNDT	[1994 Indian] Pre-natal Diagnostic Techniques Regulation and Prevention of Misuse Act
PTT	pre-implantation tissue-typing
REACH	Registration, Evaluation, Authorisation and Restriction of Chemicals [*European Regulation on the*]
RFID	radio frequency identification
RI	rational–instrumental
SC	[UN] Security Council
SEC	[US] Securities and Exchange Commission
SPS	Sanitary and Phytosanitary [Agreement]
SWAMI	Safeguards in a World of Ambient Intelligence [project]
TSCA	[US] Toxic Substances Control Act
UN	United Nations
UNCED	UN Conference on Environment and Development
UNESCO	United Nations Educational, Scientific and Cultural Organization
USDA	Unites States Department of Agriculture
VoIP	Voice over Internet Protocol
WHO	World Health Organization
WTO	World Trade Organization

Table of cases

Note: Where a case is quoted in full or extensively, the page reference appears in **bold**.

A & M Records, Inc. v. *Napster, Inc.* 239 F 3d 1004 (9th Circuit, 2001) 328, 332–3

Amann v. *Switzerland* [GC] no. 27798/95, § 69, ECHR 2000-II 89, 90, 94

Asan Rushiti v. *Austria*, no. 28389/95, 21 March 2000 99

Association for European Integration and Human Rights and Ekimdzhiev v. *Bulgaria*, no. 62540/00, 28 June 2007 95

Attorney General's Reference (No. 3 of 1999) 29 [2001] 2 AC 91 77

Bensaid v. *United Kingdom*, no. 44599/98, § 47, ECHR 2001-I 88

Biotech Products case, see: *European Communities Measures Affecting the Approval and Marketing of Biotech Products*

Bismarck, RGZ 45, Judgment of 28 December 1899, 170 235–6

Brüstle v. *Greenpeace eV*, Case C 34–10, Judgment given by the European Court of Justice, 18 October 2011 13-14

Burghartz v. *Switzerland*, 22 February 1994, § 24, Series A no. 280-B 89

BVerfGE 45, 187, 229 (1977) (German Federal Constitutional Court) 196

Campbell (Naomi) v. *Mirror Group Newspapers Ltd* [2002] EWCA Civ. 1373 305–6, 393, 428, 429

Capital Records v. *Thomas Rassett* 579 F Supp 2d 1210 (DC Minnesota 2008) 329

Cassis de Dijon, see: *Rewe-Zentral AG* v. *Bundesmonopolverwaltung für Branntwein*

Chief Constables of West Yorkshire, South Yorkshire and North Wales Police v. *the Information Commissioner* [2005] UK IT EA 2005 0010 87

Commission v. *Italy*, Case C-420/01 [2003] ECR I-6445 362

Connors v. *United Kingdom*, no. 66746/01, 27 May 2004 96

Conseil Constitutionnel, Decision no. 2009–580 of 10 June 2009 215

CORE case, see: *R (Quintavalle on behalf of Comment on Reproductive Ethics)*

Coster v. *the United Kingdom* [GC], no. 24876/94, 18 January 2001 96

DaimlerChrysler AG v. *Land Baden-Württemberg*, Case C-324/99 [2001] ECR I-9897 362

Dassonville, see : *Procureur du Roi* v. *Dassonville*

Davis v. *Davis* 842 S.W.2d 588 (Tenn. 1992) 240

Deutscher Apothekerverband eV v. *0800 DocMorris NV and Jacques Waterval*, Case C-322/01 [2003] ECR 1-14887 **360–7**

Diamond v. *Chakrabarty*, US SCR 65 L Ed 2d (1980) 144 6–7

Dickson v. *United Kingdom* [GC], no. 44362/04, § 78, ECHR 2007-XIII 96

Doodeward v. *Spence* [1908] HCA 45; (1908) 6 CLR 406 221, 222

Edwards (Jocelyn); Re the estate of the late Mark Edwards [2011] NSWSC 478 220

European Communities – Measures Affecting the Approval and Marketing of Biotech Products, WT/DS291/23 (United States), WT/DS292/17 (Canada), and WT/DS293/17

(Argentina), 8 August 2003 15–16, 115, 124–5, 129, 268

European Communities – Measures Concerning Meat and Meat Products (Hormones), Report of the Appellate Body WT/DS26/AB/R, WT/DS48/AB/R, 16 January 1998 137, 140–1, 146

European Parliament and Denmark v. *Commission* [2008] ECR-I-1649 407

Evans v. *United Kingdom* [GC], no. 6339/05, § 77, ECHR 2007-IV 96, 237–43, 246–7

Fairchild v. *Glenhaven Funeral Services* [2002] 3 WLR 89 300

Familiapress, see: *Vereinigte Familiapress Zeitungsverlags*

Friedl v. *Austria*, judgment of 31 January 1995, Series A no. 305-B 89, 91, 432

Gambelli, Case C-243/01, 6 November 2003 367

Gourmet International Products, Case C-405/98 [2001] ECR I-1795 363

Grokster, see: *MGM Studios, Inc.* v. *Grokster Ltd*

Hasan and Chaush v. *Bulgaria* [GC], no. 30985/96, § 84, ECHR 2000-XI 95

Hormones case, see: *European Communities – Measures Concerning Meat and Meat Products*

Howard Florey/Relaxin [1995] EPOR 541 11

Hünermund v. *Landesapothekerkammer*, Case C-292/92 [1993] ECR I-6787 362–3

Japan – Measures Affecting Agricultural Products, WT/DS76/R, 1998, modified by Appellate Body 19 March 1999 141

Katz v. *United States* 389 US 347 (1967) 393

Keck and Mithouard, Joined Cases C-267/91 and C-268/91 [1993] ECR I-6097 362

Kinnunen v. *Finland*, no. 24950/94, Commission decision of 15 May 1996 91

Klas Rosengren and Others v. *Riksäklagaren*, Case C-170/4 [2007] ECR 1–04071 367

Konsumentombudsmannen (KO) v. *De Agostini (Svenska) Förlag AB and TV-Shop i Sverige AB*, Cases C-34/95, C-35/95 and C-36/95 [1997] ECR I-3843 363

Kruslin v. *France*, 24 April 1990, Series A no. 176-A 95

Leander v. *Sweden*, 26 March 1987, § 48, Series A no. 116 89

Leclerc-Siplec v. *TF1 Publicité*, Case C-412/93 [1995] ECR I-179 362–3

Leeds Teaching Hospitals NHS Trust v. *A* [2003] 1 FLR 1091 415

Legality of the Threat of the Use of Nuclear Weapons, Advisory Opinion, ICJ Reports 1996 232

Liberty and Others v. *United Kingdom*, no. 58243/00, 1 July 2008 95

LICRA v. *Yahoo! Inc. & Yahoo! France*, Tribunal de Grande Instance, Paris, 22 May 2000 358

Lindqvist, Case C-101/01 [2003] All ER (D) 77 308, 309–10

McVeigh, O'Neill and Evans, nos. 8022/77, 8025/77 and 8027/77, Report of the Commission of 18 March 1981, DR 25 91, 103

Malone v. *United Kingdom* (1985) 7 EHRR 14 94, 434

Meechie v. *Multi-Media Marketing* 94 LGR 474 375

MGM Studios, Inc. v. *Grokster Ltd* 125 S.Ct 2764 (2005); 545 US 913 (2005) 332–5

Mikulić v. *Croatia*, no. 53176/99, § 53, ECHR 2002-I 88

Monsanto, Case C-236/01, ECR 2003 I-08105 157–8

Moore v. *Regents of the University of California* (1988) 249 Cal Rptr; (1990) 271 Cal Rptr 146, (1990) 793 P2d 479; cert denied (1991) 111 SCt 1388 222

Mosley v. *United Kingdom*, Judgment of 10 May 2011, application no. 48009/08 236

Murray v. *Express Newspapers plc* [2007] EWHC 1908 (Ch); [2008] EWCA Civ. 446 393–4, 428, 430

Nachmani v. *Nachmani* 50(4) PD 661 (Isr.) 241

Napster, see: *A & M Records, Inc.* v. *Napster, Inc.*

Onco-mouse/Harvard, Decision of 14 July 1989, OJ EPO 11/1989, 451; [1990] 1 EPOR 4 6–7, 8, 9, 10–11, 209

Peck v. *United Kingdom*, no. 44647/98, § 57, ECHR 2003-I 88, 89

Pfizer [2002] ECR II-3305 138

P. G. and J. H. v. *United Kingdom*, no. 44787/98, § 59–60, ECHR 2001-IX 91–2

Pirate Bay, see: *Sweden* v. *Neij et al.*

Plant Cells/PLANT GENETIC SYSTEMS, EPO Case T 0356/93. 10–11, 15

Pretty v. *United Kingdom*, no. 2346/02, § 61, ECHR 2002-III 88

Pro-Life Alliance case, see: *R* v. *Secretary of State for Health*

Procureur du Roi v. *Dassonville*, Case 8/74 [1974] ECR 837 362

R (on the application of GC) (FC) v. *Commissioner of Police of the Metropolis*, and *R (on the application of C) (FC)* v. *Commissioner of Police of the Metropolis* [2011] UKSC 21, 423

R (Gillan) v. *Commissioner of Police for the Metropolis* [2006] 2 AC 307 429, 432, 434

R (Quintavalle on behalf of Comment on Reproductive Ethics) v. *Human Fertilisation and Embryology Authority* [2005] UKHL 28 402, 407, 409–10, **413–18**

R v. *Fellows and Arnold* [1997] 2 All ER 548) 375

R v. *Plant* [1993] 3 SCR 281 86

R v. *RC* [2005] 3 SCR 99, 2005 SCC 61 86

R v. *Secretary of State for Health ex parte Quintavalle (on behalf of Pro-Life Alliance)* [2001] EWHC 918 (Admin.); [2002] EWCA Civ. 29; [2003] UKHL 13 407, 409–13

Relaxin Opposition, see: *Howard Florey/Relaxin*

Rewe-Zentral AG v. *Bundesmonopolverwaltung für Branntwein (Cassis de Dijon)*, Case C-120/78 [1979] ECR 649 362

Roche v. *Douglas* [2000] WASC 146 221

Roe v. *Wade*, 410 US 113 (1973), 162 242

Roper v. *Simmons* 543 US 551 (2005) 9, 389

Rotaru v. *Romania* [GC], no. 28341/95, ECHR 2000-V 94–5

S and Marper v. *United Kingdom* [2002] EWCA Civ. 1275 (CA); [2004] UKHL 39 (HL) 5, 73–4, 75–7

S and Marper v. *United Kingdom (No. 2)* (2009) 48 EHRR 50 5, 74, **77–105**, 107–8, 274, 346, 423, 426, 428, 433, 434, 436, 440

Sciacca v. *Italy*, no. 50774/99, § 29, ECHR 2005-I 89

S. H. and Others v. *Austria*, Judgment given by the Grand Chamber of the European Court of Human Rights, 3 November 2011 106–7, 345

Sony Corp. of America v. *Universal City Studios, Inc.*, 464 US 417 (1984) 333–5

State of Missouri ex rel Nixon v. *Coeur d'Alene Tribe* 164 F. 3d 1102 (8th Cir. 1999) 373

State of Washington v. *Athan*, 160 Wn.2d 354, 380,158 P.3d 27 (2007) 107

Sweden v. *Neij et al.*, Stockholms Tingsrätt, no. B 13301-06, 17 April 2009 ('Pirate Bay') 332, 335

T. v. *United Kingdom* [GC], no. 24724/94, 16 December 1999 100

Ünal Tekeli v. *Turkey*, no. 29865/96, § 42, ECHR 2004-X 89

Vanacker and Lesage, Case C-37/92 [1993] ECR I-4947 362

Van der Velden v. *Netherlands* (dec.), no. 29514/05, ECHR 2006-XV 89–90

Vereinigte Familiapress Zeitungsverlags- und vertriebs GmbH v. *Heinrich Bauer Verlag*, Case C-368/95 [1997] ECR I-3689 362

Vo v. *France*, application no. 53924/00 [2005] 40 EHRR 259 242

Von Hannover v. *Germany*, application no. 59320/00 [2004] ECHR 294 175, 428, 430

Wackenheim v. *France*, CCPR/C/75/D/854/1999, 26 July 2000 196

WARF case, see: *Wisconsin Alumni Research Foundation*

Weber and Saravia v. *Germany* (dec.), no. 54934/00, ECHR 2006-XI 95

Western Sahara Case, Advisory Opinion, ICJ Reports (1975) 248

Williams v. *Williams* [1882] 51 LJ Ch 388 220

Wisconsin Alumni Research Foundation, EPO Case T 1374/04 (OJ EPO 2007, 313); G 0002/06, 25 November 2008 5, 12, 13

Wood v. *Commissioner of Police for the Metropolis* [2009] EWCA Civ. 414 424, 426

Yearworth and Others v. *North Bristol NHS Trust* [2009] EWCA Civ. 37; [2010] QB 1 221–2

Y. F. v. *Turkey*, no. 24209/94, § 33, ECHR 2003-IX 88

Z. v. *Finland*, 25 February 1997, § 71, *Reports of Judgments and Decisions* 1997-I 89, 96

Table of statutes and other public documents

Note: Where a statute, or part thereof, is quoted in full or extensively, the page reference appears in **bold**.

United Nations
Conventions and agreements
Aarhus Convention on Access to Information, Public Participation in Decision-making and Access to Justice in Environmental Matters 1998 146, 251, 258–63
> Preamble 251, 263
> Art. 6 259–61
>> (4) 260
>> (6) 260
>> (7) 260
>> (8) 260, 261
>> (9) 260
> Art. 8 258–9

Biodiversity Convention 1992 206, 247
> Preamble 139
> Art. 1 215
> Art. 7(j) 255
> *see also* Cartagena Protocol

Cartagena Protocol on Biosafety 2000 140
> Preamble 206
> Art. 1(6) 140

Climate Change Convention 1992
> Art. 3 139–40

Convention on the Rights of the Child 1989 82
> Art. 40 86–7, 100

Declaration on Human Cloning 2005 14

Declaration on the Rights of Indigenous Peoples 2007 255

International Covenant on Civil and Political Rights 1966
> Art. 1 248
> Art. 19 235
> Art. 25 248–9
>> (5) 248
>> (6) 249
>> (7) 249
>> (8) 249, 262

International Covenant on Economic, Cultural and Social Rights 1966

Art. 1 248
International Declaration on Human Genetic Data 2003 52, 225
Rio Declaration on Environment and Development 1992 139
Principle 15 47, 137–8, 139, 154
Universal Declaration on Bioethics and Human Rights 2005 **52–8**, 195, 225, 226, 257
Art. 1 52
Art. 2 52–3
Art. 3 53
Art. 4 53
Art. 5 53
Art. 6 53–4
Art. 7 54
Art. 8 54
Art. 9 54
Art. 10 55
Art. 11 55
Art. 12 55
Art. 13 55
Art. 14 55
Art. 15 55–6
Art. 16 56
Art. 17 56
Art. 18 56
Art. 19 56
Art. 20 56
Art. 21 57
Art. 22 57
Art. 23 57
Art. 24 57–8
Art. 25 58
Art. 26 58
Art. 27 58
Art. 28 58
Universal Declaration on Human Rights 1948 248
Art. 1 195
Art. 19 225
Universal Declaration on the Human Genome and Human Rights 1997 52, 195, 225
Art. 11 4
World Summit on the Information Society Declaration of Principles 225

Resolutions

GA Resolution 1514 (1960) 248
SC Resolution 421 (1977) 178
SC Resolution 473 (1980) 178
SC Resolution 558 (1984) 178
SC Resolution 591 (1986) 178

Other international agreements
World Trade Organization

GATT (General Agreement on Tariffs and Trade)
Art. XX(b) 125
Sanitary and Phytosanitary (SPS) Agreement 1994 15, 128, 149

Art. 2 **125**
  (1) 125
  (2) 182–3
Art. 5 **125–7**
  (7) 125, 127, 140–1, 149
  Annex C1(a) 127
TRIPs (Trade-Related Intellectual Property Rights) Agreement 1994
  Art. 27(2) 14
WTO Agreement 1994
  Preamble 140

Miscellaneous

Cairo Declaration of Human Rights in Islam
  Art. 2 198
Ministerial Declaration of the Second International Conference on the Protection of the North Sea 1987 139
Ministerial Declaration of the Third International Conference on the Protection of the North Sea 1990 139
Paris Convention for the Protection of the Marine Environment of the North-East Atlantic 1992 (OSPAR Convention) 140

Europe
Agreements and conventions

Charter of Fundamental Rights and Freedoms 2000 226
  Art. 8 308
Council of Europe Convention on Cybercrime 2001 352–4
  Art. 2 352
  Art. 3 352–3
  Art. 4 353
  Art. 5 353
  Art. 6 345, 353
  Art. 7 354
  Art. 8 354
  Art. 9 354–5
  Art. 10 355
  Art. 11 355
  Art. 23 355
  Art. 25 356
    (4) 352
  Art. 27 352, 356–8
Data Protection Convention 1981 82–3, 86, 89
  Art. 5 82, 96
  Art. 6 82, 96
  Art. 7 82–3, 96
  Art. 9 96
EC Treaty
  Art. 28 360–2, 364
  Art. 29 360–2
  Art. 30 360–2, 364, 366–7
European Convention on Human Rights 1950 234
  Art. 2 239
  Art. 8 85, 87, 100–1, 102–4, 223, 239, 242, 246, 423, 427

(1) 75–7, 88, 91, 239, 427
(2) 75–6, 95, 97, 239, 427, 429, 433
Art. 14 100–1, 239
European Patent Convention 1973
Art. 53
(a) 6, 7, 9, 10–11, 14
(b) 6
Art. 83 6
Lisbon Treaty 2007 183
Oviedo Convention on Human Rights and Biomedicine 214, 227
Art. 6 196
Art. 17 196
Art. 21 221
Art. 28 247
Prüm Convention on the stepping up of cross-border cooperation 86
Art. 34 86
Art. 35 86
Treaty on the Functioning of the European Union
Art. 19 214

Directives

Directive 65/65/EC on the approximation of provisions relating to proprietary medicinal products
Art. 3 361
Directive 90/220/EC on the deliberate release into the environment of genetically modified
organisms 169–70
Directive 95/46/EC (Data Protection Directive) 85–6, 174–5, 304, 375–6, 403
Recital 3 308
Recital 7 308
Recital 26 306–7
Art. 8 309
(1) 309
Directive 96/9/EC (Database Directive) 3, 404
Directive 97/7/EC on the protection of consumers in respect of distance contracts 374
Art. 14 362
Directive 98/44/EC (Biotechnology Directive) 10, 374
Recital 38 10
Art. 6 12–22
(1) 10
(2) 10, 12
(c) 12, 13–14
Directive 99/93/EC (e-Signatures Directive) 404
Directive 2001/83/EC (Community code relating to medicinal products for human use)
Art. 6(1) 361
Art. 71(1) 365
Art. 88(1) 367
Directive 2002/58/EC on privacy and electronic communications 376
Electronic Money Directive (proposed) 408

Regulations

European Regulation on the Registration, Evaluation, Authorisation and Restriction of Chemicals
(REACH) 313–14

Communications, recommendations, etc.

Council framework decision of 24 June 2008 on the protection of personal data processed in the
framework of police and judicial cooperation in criminal matters

Art. 5 86
European Commission Communication on the Precautionary Principle **142–51**, 152–3, 157
  Annex II **138–41**
Recommendation No. R(87)15 regulating the use of personal data in the police sector 1987 83, 86
  Principle 2 83
  Principle 3 83
  Principle 7 83, 96
Recommendation No. R(92)1 on the use of analysis of DNA within the framework of the criminal
    justice system 1992 83, 96
  Explanatory Memorandum 84
  para. 3 83
  para. 4 83
  para. 8 83

National legislation
Germany
Arzneimittelgesetz (AMG, Law on medicinal products)
  para. 43(1) 361, 363–4, 367
  para. 73(1) 361
Hacker Tool Law (Penal Code s 202(c)) 345
India
Pre-natal Diagnostic Techniques (Regulation and Prevention of Misuse) Act (PNDT)
  Preamble 214
United Kingdom
Computer Misuse Act 1990 3
Coroners and Justice Act 2009
  s 52 393
Criminal Justice and Immigration Act 2008
  s 63 297
Criminal Justice and Police Act 2001
  s 82 79–80
Criminal Procedure Act of Scotland 1995 81
  s 18A 81
Criminal Procedure Act of Scotland 2006
  s 82 81
Data Protection Act 1998 80, 88, 89, 304, 310
  s 1 80
  s 2 80
  s 13 80
  s 29 80
  s 40 80
  s 47 80
  s 55 80
  Schedule 1 80
  Schedule 2 80
  Schedule 3 80
Digital Economy Act 2010 330–2
  s 3 330–1
  s 9 331–2
Freedom of Information Act 2000 332
Human Fertilisation and Embryology Act 1990 321, 400, 401–2
  s 1(1) 410–13

s 2(1) 413
s 3(3) 410–13, 414
Schedule 2 323
   para. 1(1) 414–16
   para. 1(3) 413
   para. 3(3) 323
Human Fertilisation and Embryology Act 2008 3, 65, 67, 213–14, 272, 273, 323, 374–5, 405–6,
   409–10
s 1(5) 405, 406
s 7 61
s 14(4)(9) 213
s 26 405–6
Schedule 3 238–9
   para. 1 238
   para. 4(1) 238
   para. 4(2) 238
   para. 6(1) 238
   para. 6(2) 238
   para. 8(1) 239
   para. 8(2) 239
Explanatory Notes 213
Human Fertilisation and Embryology (Research Purposes) Regulations 2001 322
Human Reproductive Cloning Act 2001 410, 411
Human Rights Act 1998 234
Human Tissue and Embryos Bill 2007 (abandoned draft)
s 65(2) 406
Misuse of Drugs Act 1971 337
Police and Criminal Evidence Act 1984 79–80
s 61 79
s 63 79
s 64 79–80, 88, 93, 95
   (1A) 79, 87–8
   (3) 100
Police and Criminal Evidence Order of Northern Ireland 1989 81
Protection of Children Act 1978 375
Protection of Freedoms Act 2012 423, 425, 426
Retention Guidelines for Nominal Records on the Police National Computer 2006 80–1
Video Recordings Act 1984 375

United States

Constitution
   8th Amendment 9
Consumer Products Safety Act 1972 314
Federal Food, Drug and Cosmetic Act 1938 315
Federal Hazardous Substances Act 1960 314
Indian Gaming Regulatory Act 1988 373
Patriot Act 2001 344
Toxic Substances Control Act 1976 314–15

Part I
General introduction

1

Introduction

1 Introduction

This book is an introduction to law (and, more broadly, regulation) and the technologies of the twenty-first century. At present, the particular technologies that attract our interest are information and communication technologies, biotechnologies (whether applied to humans or to plants and animals), nanotechnologies and neurotechnologies. However, science and technology is a rapidly shifting scene and it is perfectly possible that, as the decades pass, our interest will be engaged by other technologies that emerge. Similarly, although these technologies are presently on the radar in a number of legal areas – for example, biotechnologies are of interest to property lawyers, to environmental lawyers, to medical lawyers, to torts lawyers, to patent lawyers, to international trade lawyers, to human rights lawyers, to data protection lawyers, and so on[1] – the pattern is constantly changing.[2]

Any introduction must start somewhere, but where should we start our introduction to law, regulation and technology? To the extent that this is a novel field for legal inquiry, there is no settled point of entry. Helpfully, Bert-Jaap Koops has highlighted ten dimensions of what he calls 'technology regulation research', these dimensions mapping on to the three focal regions of technology, regulation and research.[3] In the region of technology, we need to think about the different *types* of technology (for example, whether or not they build on the life sciences); the extent to which a technology is *innovative*; the *place* in which we find the technology (including whether it is in cyberspace); and how mature a particular technology is relative to the temporal development cycle (the dimension of *time*). In the region of regulation, we need to be sensitive to the variety of *regulatory types* as well as the *normative outlook* of the community

---

[1] Compare Roger Brownsword, W. R. Cornish and Margaret Llewelyn (eds.), *Law and Human Genetics: Regulating a Revolution* (Oxford: Hart, 1998).

[2] There are also various bespoke legal regimes, such as the UK Computer Misuse Act 1990, Directive 96/9/EC (on the legal protection of databases) and the Human Fertilisation and Embryology Act 2008, that make provision for a particular technology.

[3] Bert-Jaap Koops, 'Ten Dimensions of Technology Regulation', in Morag Goodwin, Bert-Jaap Koops and Ronald Leenes (eds.), *Dimensions of Technology Regulation* (Nijmegen: Wolf Legal Publishers, 2010), 309.

in which regulatory action is to be taken and the *knowledge* that we have with regard to the characteristics of the technology. Finally, in the region of research, the critical dimensions relate to the particular *discipline* in which we are conducting our research, the nature of our research questions (that is, the *problem* as we specify it), and the way in which our research might be shaped by a certain *frame* of inquiry. In one way or another, these dimensions will feature in our discussion. However, before we contemplate the different kinds of technologies, or the array of strategies that are available to regulators, or the like, we can start with an innocent question: why is it that the development and application of modern technologies is a matter of interest and concern for the law?

One rather obvious reason is that some of these technologies might be thought to be dangerous in the sense that they present risks to humans and to their natural environment. For example, how confident can we be that genetically modified (GM) crops will present no risk to humans who consume GM foods; and can we be sure that these crops will not degrade their environments? Or, again, can we be confident that nanoparticles, such as those used in some sunscreens and cosmetic products, will not be harmful to humans? It follows that, where we entertain concerns of this kind, it falls to the law to regulate for the relevant risks, by putting in place such prohibitions, or licensing arrangements, or compensatory provisions as are judged to be appropriate.

Concerns about health, safety and the environment, however, are not the only reasons why emerging technologies might prompt calls for regulatory intervention. For example, there are persistent concerns about privacy, confidentiality and data protection. Some such concerns are acute – witness, for example, the flood of cautionary and critical comments provoked by social networking sites and by Google's Street View mapping service; other such concerns are chronic, the thesis being that, in the information (and surveillance) society, equipped with CCTV, RFID, GSP devices, and so on, there is a silent but steady erosion of our privacy; and, with the development of powerful brain-imaging technologies, some see an even more worrying future – for, if we can no longer keep our innermost thoughts to ourselves, what is left of our privacy? However, thus far, it is modern biotechnologies that have most conspicuously raised deeper cultural and ethical concerns, especially concerns that draw on the elusive idea of human dignity; and in the almost universal rejection of human reproductive cloning we have the outstanding expression of this sense that there are limits to acceptable technological innovation. Articulating this particular concern, Article 11 of the UNESCO Universal Declaration on the Human Genome and Human Rights (1997) provides:

> Practices which are contrary to human dignity, such as reproductive cloning of human beings, shall not be permitted. States and competent international organizations are invited to co-operate in identifying such practices and in taking, at national or international level, the measures necessary to ensure that the principles set out in this Declaration are respected.

It follows, as Henk ten Have has rightly remarked, that regulators need to engage with the view 'that unbridled scientific progress is not always ethically acceptable';[4] and, in the next section of this chapter, we will sketch some of the debates about the ethics of patentability that modern biotechnologies have generated in this sector of intellectual property law.

There is also another, quite different, reason why the development of these technologies is relevant to the law. It is not simply that we need legal frameworks to regulate these technologies, it is that these technologies themselves might play a part in the regulatory framework. In other words, these technologies might themselves operate as regulatory tools. Sometimes their role might be supportive of traditional legal forms of regulation, in the way, for example, that DNA profiling, the use of CCTV surveillance and possibly brain imaging,[5] might be supportive of the criminal law; but, with greater technological sophistication, it is conceivable that these technologies might function as front-line regulatory instruments.

In line with these remarks, we will consider the technologies of the twenty-first century both as regulatory targets and as regulatory tools. In Chapter 3, we will outline four key challenges that must be met if a regulatory framework is to be adequate: namely, the challenges of regulatory prudence, regulatory legitimacy, regulatory effectiveness and regulatory connection. Each of these challenges then serves as an organising focus for the subsequent parts of the book. Hence, in Part II (Chapters 5–6) we focus on regulatory prudence and precaution; in Part III (Chapters 7–10) our focus is on regulatory legitimacy; in Part IV (Chapters 11–14), we focus on regulatory effectiveness; and in Part V (Chapters 15–16) our focus is on regulatory connection. We will also consider the questions raised by the use of these technologies as regulatory tools, most urgently questions concerning legitimacy and effectiveness; and our discussion of DNA profiling in the criminal justice system, together with *S. and Marper v. United Kingdom*[6] and its after-effects (in Chapters 4 and 17), is particularly designed to bring these latter issues into focus.

Finally, we will endeavour to do all of this in a way that we take to be consonant with the spirit of 'contextual' inquiry. First, we will try to place specifically *legal* (so to speak, 'hard law') interventions in the broader context of what we call 'the regulatory environment'. This is a concept that we elaborate in Chapter 2; but, stated shortly, the regulatory environment is constituted

---

[4] Henk ten Have, 'UNESCO and Ethics of Science and Technology', in UNESCO, *Ethics of Science and Technology: Explorations of the Frontiers of Science and Ethics* (Paris, 2006), 5–16, at 6.

[5] See, e.g., Michael Freeman (ed.), *Law and Neuroscience* (Oxford: Oxford University Press, 2011); and, for some very watchable presentations given at the Second Raymond and Beverley Sackler USA–UK Scientific Forum (on neuroscience and the law) (held 2–3 March 2011, at Irvine, California), see: http://sites.nationalacademies.org/PGA/stl/PGA_062477 (last accessed 12 June 2011).

[6] (2009) 48 EHRR 50. For the domestic UK proceedings, see [2002] EWCA Civ. 1275 (Court of Appeal), and [2004] UKHL 39 (House of Lords).

by those signals that are intended to bear on the way in which people actually behave. Sometimes the signals might be recognisably legal (as when they express and communicate a statutory requirement or the decision of a court); but, often, the legal signals are in the background and we act in the way that we do because we are responding to much stronger foreground signals emanating from our peers. To relate this to one of the standard contextual puzzles, if we want to understand why it is that there is sometimes a 'gap' between the law-in-the-books and the law-in-action, then we need to view the law-in-the-books as just one signal in a more complex signalling environment. Second, our approach is 'cosmopolitan' in the sense that it takes into account the various spheres of regulation (i.e., national, regional and international).[7] In other words, it is not simply a matter of viewing law within a larger regulatory environment, we must also take into account the way in which multilevel regulatory regimes operate. Third, our discussion is 'nested' in the sense that our discussion of the regulation of (and by) particular technologies is set in the context of the generic challenges and opportunities presented by regulating technologies which, in turn, is set in the context of our larger understanding of law and regulation. Or, to turn this round, our introduction moves from a general idea of a regulatory environment to the regulation of emerging technologies to particular regulatory issues arising in connection with particular technologies.

2 Of mice and men

Twenty years ago, there were demonstrations outside the European Patent Office (EPO) in Munich. Students from the nearby Max Planck Institute, some of them dressed as white mice, carried banners protesting that there should be 'no patents on life'. Inside the EPO, the examiners were uncertain about how to treat an application to patent the so-called Harvard Onco-mouse, a mouse that was genetically engineered to serve as a test animal for cancer research.[8] Should the mouse be treated as patentable? There was no doubt that the process associated with the genetic engineering – the method by which the oncogene was inserted into the embryonic mouse – was innovative; there was no doubt that the product, the mouse itself, was innovative; and there was no doubt that the researchers and developers expected the mouse to have a practical utility as well as reaping a commercial dividend. In some patent law regimes – notably,

---

[7] Compare the jurisprudential manifesto in William Twining, *General Jurisprudence* (Cambridge: Cambridge University Press, 2009).

[8] Decision Onco-mouse/Harvard, 14 July 1989 (OJ EPO 11/1989, 451; [1990] 1 EPOR 4). Initially, the examiners did not see the application as raising an issue under Article 53(a). Rather, they rejected the application on the grounds: (a) that there had not been sufficient disclosure of the working of the invention (as required by Article 83 of the European Patent Convention); and (b) that Article 53(b) excluded the patenting of 'animal varieties'. It was only when the case was referred to the Board of Appeal that the centrality of Article 53(a) was recognised: see EPO Decision T 19/90 (OJ EPO 12/1990, 476; [1990] 7 EPOR 501).

in the United States where, in *Diamond* v. *Chakrabarty*,[9] the majority of the US Supreme Court laid the basis for a liberal approach to patenting – such innovation and utility would be sufficient; and, in fact, applying this liberal spirit, the US Patent Office had already cleared the mouse as patentable subject matter. However, in Europe, such features, although necessary, are not sufficient; for, in Article 53(a) of the European Patent Convention (EPC), there was (and, broadly speaking, there still is) a provision to the effect that processes and products, no matter how innovative, should not be considered to be patentable if their commercial exploitation would be contrary to *ordre public* or morality. Until the Harvard Onco-mouse application, patent examiners and intellectual property lawyers had paid little attention to Article 53(a). However, the application was a wake-up call that, with innovative work under way in plant, animal and human genetics, the patent regime would need to come to terms not only with the underlying science of modern biotechnologies but also with their ethical and cultural dimensions.

At the same time that the protests were taking place in Munich, the European Commission in Brussels was trying to develop a new legal regime for the patenting of biotechnological inventions.[10] Ostensibly, the regime was a trade measure, designed to harmonise patenting rules across the European single market. However, as soon as the proposed directive reached the European Parliament, it was clear that the issues could not be confined in this way. In Europe, parliamentarians were alive to the possibility that the work under way in sequencing the human genome might lead to patent applications. Like the students from the Max Planck, an alliance of politicians protested that the Commission's quest for a common position went far beyond matters of trade. As Gerard Porter captures the mood of the time:

> [T]he slogan *'no patents on life'* began to gain a degree of political currency within the Parliament during the 1990s. This umbrella term crystallized a wide range of concerns about the proliferation of intellectual property rights in the life sciences. The concerns voiced included the fear that biotech patents would stifle scientific research by inhibiting access to key technology; unease about the degree of social power granted to private organizations through monopoly rights over key life science technologies; objections to the instrumentalization and commodification of living things (particularly the human body and the human genome) on the grounds that living matter is part of the 'Heritage of Humanity and Nature in general' and should not be 'classified as private property'; animal rights and welfare; environmental safety; the interests of

---

[9] US SCR 65 L Ed 2d (1980) 144.

[10] For the background, see Deryck Beyleveld, Roger Brownsword and Margaret Llewelyn, 'The Morality Clauses of the Directive on the Legal Protection of Biotechnological Inventions: Conflict, Compromise, and the Patent Community', in Richard Goldberg and Julian Lonbay (eds.), *Pharmaceutical Medicine, Biotechnology and European Law* (Cambridge: Cambridge University Press, 2000), 157.

European farmers; and, finally, anxieties over the impact of 'bio-piracy' and 'bio-colonialism' on the developing world.[11]

At core, though, politicians objected that the question of whether a particular sequence of the human genome might be treated as patentable subject matter was not so much economic as fundamentally ethical and cultural. If there should be no patents on mice, neither should there be patents on men.

Patent law thus found itself in the eye of a political storm.[12] One view (favoured by many political and industrial interests) was that Europe has too large a commercial stake in the biotechnology sector to be putting obstacles in the way of patentability. In other words, it was argued that the patent regime needed to be geared to encouraging research and development in modern biotechnologies and, crucially, investment in the European-based biotechnology sector. For their own reasons, patent practitioners, too, aligned themselves with the view that patent law should stick to the usual technical questions of originality, innovation, and the like, leaving moral debates to others. However, ranged against these views, a variety of constituencies – animal welfarists, environmentalists, dignitarians, and others – joined forces to insist that the law should not facilitate the biotechnological revolution without taking a hard look at the ethical and cultural implications of genetic engineering.[13]

Back at the EPO, at a symposium held to survey the issues raised by the Harvard Onco-mouse application, the influential British philosopher, Mary Warnock, offered a measured view of how Europeans might reason their way through their difficulties. She said:

> Technology has made all kinds of things possible that were impossible, or unimaginable in an earlier age. Ought all these things to be carried into practice? This is the most general ethical question to be asked about genetic engineering, whether of plants, animals or humans. The question may itself take two forms: in the first place, we may ask whether the benefits promised by the practice are outweighed by its possible harms. This is an ethical question posed in strictly utilitarian form ... It entails looking into the future, calculating probabilities, and of course evaluating outcomes. 'Benefits' and 'harm' are not self-evidently identifiable values. Secondly we may ask whether, even if the benefits of the practice seem to outweigh the dangers, it nevertheless so outrages our sense of justice or of rights or of human decency that it should be prohibited whatever the advantages.[14]

---

[11] Gerard Porter, 'The Drafting History of the European Biotechnology Directive', in Aurora Plomer and Paul Torremans (eds.), *Embryonic Stem Cell Patents* (Oxford: Oxford University Press, 2009) 3, at 13.

[12] See Deryck Beyleveld and Roger Brownsword, *Mice, Morality and Patents* (London: Common Law Institute of Intellectual Property, 1993); and Edward Armitage and Ivor Davis, *Patents and Morality in Perspective* (London: Common Law Institute of Intellectual Property, 1994).

[13] For the politics associated with the rival framings of European patent law (i.e., 'economy' versus 'ethics'), see Ingrid Schneider, 'Can Patent Legislation Make a Difference? Bringing Parliaments and Civil Society into Patent Governance', in Sebastian Haunss and Kenneth C. Shadlen (eds.), *Politics of Intellectual Property* (Cheltenham: Edward Elgar, 2009), 129.

[14] Baroness Mary Warnock, 'Philosophy and Ethics', in C. Cookson, G. Nowak and D. Thierbach (eds.), *Genetic Engineering – The New Challenge* (Munich: European Patent Office, 1993), 67 at 67.

Taking our lead from Warnock, we should start with a calculation of, on the one side, the prospective benefits and, on the other side, the possible harms (very much in line with a standard utilitarian approach). If the harms outweigh the benefits, if the technology is simply too risky, then we should not proceed. If, by contrast, the calculation indicates a net benefit, then we ought to proceed provided that there is not some overriding consideration of justice, rights or human decency, or the like.

Generally speaking, when new technologies are in their infancy, there is likely to be a good deal of uncertainty about both sides of the calculation, about both the benefits and the harms. And, again generally speaking, we will find that, while those who have a commercial, medical or political interest in the technology will talk up the anticipated benefits, those who are opposed to it will highlight the risks and advocate a precautionary approach. Some of the opposition, however, might go beyond concerns about human health and safety or even about environmental integrity; for such opponents, where their deeper concerns are engaged, the fact that the benefit–harm calculation clearly shows an overall net benefit is irrelevant – the technology should not be taken forward. For such opponents, as Warnock recognises, if the technology transgresses a 'sense of justice or of rights or of human decency' that sets limits to the technological applications that we judge to be permissible, then we simply should not proceed. For example, there might be some advantages in allowing a couple to use reliable technologies for human reproductive cloning but, for most societies, this kind of cloning is simply off limits. Or, to take a non-technological case, the jurisprudence associated with the prohibition against cruel and unusual punishments in the Eighth Amendment to the US Constitution suggests that, even if a particular form of punishment were to be effective in deterring crime, it should not be used where this would be contrary to human dignity or decency.[15]

When the examiners duly addressed the interpretation and application of Article 53(a) in the *Harvard Onco-mouse* case, they proceeded in a thoroughly utilitarian way.[16] On the one hand, the mouse promised to be an important test animal for cancer research, prospectively improving our understanding of tumour development and, with that, advancing the development of effective therapies. The anticipated benefits for humans could scarcely be greater. There was also some anticipated benefit to future mice to the extent that fewer mice would be needed for testing. On the harm side, the examiners accepted that there was pain and suffering for the mice, particularly the females, which were bred and manipulated as research tools. In short, then, the calculation showed prospective life-saving benefits for a great many humans and certain pain and suffering (and eventual sacrifice) for a limited number of mice. Quite how utilitarians do their sums is never entirely clear, but the examiners were satisfied that it would not be immoral to treat the claimed processes and product as patentable.

---

[15] For a recent example, see *Roper* v. *Simmons* 543 US 551 (2005).
[16] OJ EPO 10/1992, 588, esp. at 593.

Even if the interests of mice could not resist the surge of modern biotechnologies, the interests of men are rather more weighty – at any rate, they tend to be so when it is men themselves who are judging the matter. At the European Parliament, the opponents of the proposed directive regarded some matters as non-negotiably off-limits. For the Commission, at the first attempt, this proved an insuperable problem; they simply could not find a form of words that both permitted and prohibited patenting parts of the human genome and the proposed directive fell. However, at a second attempt, a compromise was achieved, and a revised version of the directive was agreed.[17] Significantly, it was conceded to the objectors that there are some moral outer limits to patentability. First, Article 6(1) of the Directive (in language that very closely resembles that of Article 53(a) of the EPC) provides:

> Inventions shall be considered unpatentable where their commercial exploitation would be contrary to *ordre public* or morality; however, exploitation shall not be deemed to be so contrary merely because it is prohibited by law or regulation.

Second, and critically for present purposes, Article 6(2) provides:

> On the basis of paragraph 1 [Article 6(1)], the following, in particular, shall be considered unpatentable:
>
> (a) processes for cloning human beings;
> (b) processes for modifying the germ line genetic identity of human beings;
> (c) uses of human embryos for industrial or commercial purposes;
> (d) processes for modifying the genetic identity of animals which are likely to cause them suffering without any substantial medical benefit to man or animal, and also animals resulting from such processes.

Article 6(2) draws on a number of Recitals, one of which, Recital 38, makes it clear not only that the list of four processes/uses is not intended to be exhaustive but also that inventions should simply be regarded as unpatentable where they compromise human dignity. Hence, while the examiners in the *Harvard Onco-mouse* case did not proceed beyond the first stage of Warnock's advice, we see in the Directive some indications as to where Europeans draw the lines on patentability.

In the wake of the *Harvard Onco-mouse* case, the EPO was called upon to adjudicate on the application of Article 53(a), first, to GM plants (herbicide-resistant crops)[18] and, then, to copies of a human gene sequence that codes for a muscle relaxant.[19] In the first of these applications, the *PLANT GENETIC SYSTEMS* case (the *PGS* case), the Technical Board of Appeal ruled that there was no clear moral objection to patentability. However, unlike the examiners

---

[17] Directive 98/44/EC on the Legal Protection of Biotechnological Inventions. For the politics of the renegotiation, see Schneider, 'Can Patent Legislation Make a Difference?', 139–42.

[18] *Plant Cells/PLANT GENETIC SYSTEMS* Case T 0356/93.

[19] Howard Florey/Relaxin [1995] EPOR 541.

in the *Harvard Onco-mouse* case, the Board in the *PGS* case did not conduct a benefit–harm calculation before concluding that the utilities favoured patentability. Rather, in *PGS*, the question asked was whether, in Europe, there was a clear moral consensus against the patentability of a GM crop; and, failing such an overwhelming view against patentability, it was held that there should be no exclusion on moral grounds. In this way, the *PGS* case vastly reduced the significance of Article 53(a) and, to all intents and purposes, returned the patent regime to its technical focus on inventiveness and originality. In the second application, the *Relaxin Opposition*, the opponents argued that, irrespective of the utilities, some products and processes simply should not be treated as patentable subject matter because this would be to compromise human dignity. To this extent, the opponents echoed the sentiments expressed by the students from the Max Planck Institute as well as the European parliamentarians who, having resisted the initial version of the Directive, held out for the concessions to dignitarianism that now appear in the Directive; they also reflected the second level of ethical thinking that Mary Warnock highlighted. Despite this, the members of the Opposition Division (at the EPO) seemingly (mis)interpreted the objections lined up under Article 53(a) as essentially human rights issues, hinging on whether the pregnant women who had donated the tissues used by the researchers had given a proper informed consent. This put the parties at cross purposes; for, one of the most significant features of dignitarian thinking (as advanced by the opponents) is that consent is irrelevant – if patenting a copy of a human gene sequence compromises human dignity (because, for example, it commodifies human life, or even commercialises it), then it matters not one jot that the relevant parties have consented to the research that was a prelude to the patent application.[20]

It would be premature to suggest that Article 53(a) has been marginalised, that dignitarianism has been tamed, and that the dust has now settled on these disagreements. Technological innovation is such that patent applications are constantly being made with a view to gaining protection for leading-edge research. Most recently, the EPO has been agonising about the patentability of the processes and products associated with human embryonic stem cell research.[21] Applying the EPO's standard approach, the question is whether there is an overwhelming consensus in Europe that the use of human embryos for stem cell research is immoral. To which, the answer is that there is no such consensus – indeed, there is a spectrum of opinion across Europe ranging from the view that the creation or use of human embryos as research tools is categorically wrong, to the view that such creation or use may be legitimate provided that

---

[20] For commentary, see Roger Brownsword, 'The *Relaxin Opposition* Revisited', *Jahrbuch für Recht und Ethik*, 9 (2001), 3.

[21] See, e.g., Graeme Laurie, 'Patenting Stem Cells of Human Origin', *European Intellectual Property Review*, [2004] 59; and, for a general overview, see Plomer and Torremans, *Embryonic Stem Cell Patents*.

the researchers act responsibly.[22] Given such diverse views, it is arguable that the EPO should decline to rule against the patentability of innovative human embryonic stem cell work. On the other hand, the EPO also has to contend with the prohibitions listed in Article 6(2) of the Directive (now incorporated in the EPC). Arguably, prohibitions (a) and (c) might cover stem cell work;[23] and, even if they do not fit, there is still the background question of whether the relevant processes and products should be declared unpatentable on the ground that they compromise human dignity.

In the *Wisconsin Alumni Research Foundation* case (the *WARF* case),[24] the Enlarged Board of Appeal (EBA) at the EPO was asked by the Technical Board of Appeal[25] to rule on four questions of law – one of which was whether Article 6(2)(c), as incorporated in the EPC Rules, forbids the patenting of a human embryonic stem cell culture which, at the time of filing, could be prepared only by a method that necessarily involved the destruction of human embryos (even though the method in question is not part of the claim). Treating this as an exercise in the interpretation of a particular rule, rather than a more general essay in European morality, the EBA said:

> On its face, the provision ... is straightforward and prohibits the patenting if a human embryo is used for industrial or commercial purposes. Such a reading is also in line with the concern of the legislator to prevent a misuse in the sense of a commodification of human embryos ... and with one of the essential objectives of the whole Directive to protect human dignity.[26]

Then, responding to the argument that this prohibition applies only where the use of human embryos is within the terms of the claim, the EBA says:

> [T]his Rule ... does not mention claims, but refers to 'invention' in the context of its exploitation. What needs to be looked at is not just the explicit wording of the clause but the technical teaching of the application as a whole as to how the invention is to be performed. Before human embryonic stem cell cultures can be used they have to be made. Since in the case referred ... the only teaching of how to perform the invention to make human embryonic stem cell cultures is the use (involving the destruction) of human embryos, this invention falls under the prohibition of [the Rule] ... To restrict ... the application of [the Rule] to what an applicant chooses explicitly to put in his claim would have the undesirable consequence of making avoidance of the patenting prohibition merely a matter of clever and skilful drafting of such claim.[27]

---

[22] See, e.g., Samantha Halliday, 'A Comparative Approach to the Regulation of Human Embryonic Stem Cell Research in Europe', *Medical Law Review*, 12 (2004), 40; Rosario M. Isasi and Bartha M. Knoppers, 'Towards Commonality? Policy Approaches to Human Embryonic Stem Cell Research in Europe', in Plomer and Torremans, *Embryonic Stem Cell Patents*, 29; and Josef Kuře, 'Human Embryonic Stem Cell Research in Central and Eastern Europe: A Comparative Analysis of Regulatory and Policy Approaches', *ibid.*, at 57.

[23] For the national implementation of this provision, see Åsa Hellstadius, 'A Comparative Analysis of the National Implementation of the Directive's Morality Clause', *ibid.*, at 117.

[24] Case G 0002/06, 25 November 2008.   [25] T 1374/04 (OJ EPO 2007, 313).

[26] Case G 0002/06, para. 18.   [27] *Ibid.*, at para. 22.

Finally, rejecting the argument that human embryos were not actually being used for commercial or industrial purposes, the EBA held that, where the method of producing the claimed product necessarily involved the destruction of human embryos, then such destruction was 'an integral and essential part of the industrial or commercial exploitation of the claimed invention';[28] and, thus, the prohibition applied and precluded the patent.

Critics of the EBA's decision in the *WARF* case will see this as an unacceptably broad interpretation of the prohibition against patenting inventions that involve the use of human embryos for industrial or commercial purposes.[29] And, although the EBA tries to present its decision as a technical exercise in interpretation, there is no avoiding the backdrop of contested moral viewpoints. How, then, should the EBA have decided the question? If we side with the critics, we will say that the EBA should have noted that there is no agreement among members as to the morality of using human embryos for research purposes; that to exclude the patent on moral grounds would be to privilege the dignitarian views of those members who already have domestic prohibitions against the destruction of human embryos for research purposes; and that the EBA has no warrant for such partiality. But, of course, we might turn this argument on its head. If, in the absence of a common moral position among members, the EBA declines to exclude the patent on moral grounds, then it privileges the libertarian view of those members that already have permissive domestic regimes with regard to human embryo research. Again, partiality is implicated and we might ask what warrant the EBA has for this. Neither approach looks satisfactory.

To the consternation of the critics of the *WARF* decision, the error (as the critics see it) made by the EBA has now been compounded. For, in a parallel development at the European Court of Justice, in *Brüstle* v. *Greenpeace eV*,[30] it has been ruled that Article 6(2)(c) of the Directive excludes the patenting of inventions that involve the destruction of human embryos. In his Opinion (which the Court duly followed), Advocate General Bot, fully aware of the many different views as to both the meaning of a human embryo and the degree to which such embryos should be protected, insisted that the legal position as settled by the Directive is actually perfectly clear. Within the terms of the

---

[28] *Ibid.*, at para. 25.

[29] See, e.g., Paul L. C. Torremans, 'The Construction of the Directive's Moral Exclusions under the EPC', in Plomer and Torremans, *Embryonic Stem Cell Patents*, at 141. There is also the question of how coherently the *WARF* reading of the exclusion fits with other EC legal measures that license human embryonic stem cell research: see, Aurora Plomer, 'Towards Systemic Legal Conflict: Article 6(2)(c) of the EU Directive on Biotechnological Inventions', *ibid.*, at 173. Nevertheless, this broad interpretation was foreshadowed in EDINBURGH/Animal Transgenic Stem Cells (Patent App. No. 94 913 174.2, 21 July 2002, Opposition Division), on which, see Shawn H. E. Harmon, 'From Engagement to Re-engagement: The Expression of Moral Values in European Patent Proceedings, Past and Future', *European Law Review*, 31(2006), 642.

[30] Case C 34–10 (Judgment given 18 October 2011). The full text of the Advocate General's Opinion is available online at the ECJ's website: http://curia.europa.eu/jurisp (last accessed 11 June 2011).

Directive, the concept of a human embryo must be taken as applying from 'the fertilisation stage to the initial totipotent cells and to the entire ensuing process of the development and formation of the human body'.[31] *In themselves*, isolated pluripotent stem cells would not fall within this definition of a human embryo (because they could not go on to form a whole human body). So, did it follow that the use of such cells in the inventive work in question (which involved the development of precursor cells for neural disorders such as Parkinson's disease) was unproblematic? The Advocate General held that it did not. Crucially, the history of these particular cells was tainted – they were isolated only at the cost of destroying the original human embryo; or, to put this another way, the research and invention amounted to 'using human embryos as a simple base material'.[32] In short, as the Advocate General summarised the point:

> [An] invention must be excluded from patentability ... where the application of the technical process for which the patent is filed necessitates the prior destruction of human embryos or their use as base material, even if the description of that process does not contain any reference to the use of human embryos.[33]

With the Court's endorsement of the lead given by the Advocate General, the European patent courts have expressed a very clear view that, at the regional level, they do not wish to give any encouragement to research (having commercial or industrial purposes) that involves the destruction of human embryos.

Sadly, we cannot take European differences to a higher tribunal. For one thing, Article 27(2) of the GATT/TRIPs Agreement permits members to exclude inventions from patentability on grounds of *ordre public* or morality. In other words, the international view is that provisions such as Article 53(a) of the EPC and Article 6 of Directive 98/44/EC are optional. Even if this were not so, the cultural disagreements that we find in Europe are replicated internationally. As we have said, there is pretty much universal agreement that human reproductive cloning is off-limits – indeed, all then-191 members of the United Nations support an appropriate prohibition. However, there is no such consensus in relation to so-called therapeutic cloning (of the kind practised by human embryonic stem cell researchers). At the United Nations, after four years of deliberation, during which time major efforts were made to achieve a consensus covering the regulation of all uses of cloning technology (reproductive and therapeutic) in humans, the nations (including many of the European nations) remained divided.[34]

---

[31] *Ibid.*, at para. 115.   [32] *Ibid.*, at para. 110.   [33] *Ibid.*, at para. 117.

[34] On 18 February 2005, the Legal Committee voted 71 in favour, 35 against, with 43 abstentions, to recommend to the General Assembly that members should be called on 'to prohibit all forms of human cloning inasmuch as they are incompatible with human dignity and the protection of human life' (UN press release GA/L/3271: www.un.org/News/Press/docs/2005/gal3271.doc. htm). On 8 March 2005, the General Assembly accepted this recommendation, 84 members voting in favour of the (non-binding) UN Declaration on Human Cloning, with 34 against and 37 abstentions (UN press release GA/10333: www.un.org/News/Press/docs/2005/ga10333. doc.htm).

3 Europe and GM crops

As we have seen, in the *Plant Genetic Systems* case, the EPO found no European consensus holding that it would be immoral to patent a GM plant. Nevertheless, at least some Europeans believe that it is unethical to interfere with nature in this way; and a great many Europeans are concerned about the safety of GM crops, added to which they see little compensating benefit (for Europeans) in GM food products. These latter concerns have generated a long-running dispute between the European Community and a number of GM crop-growing nations who want to export GM soya to Europe. The question of whether the European Community had denied market access for GM products and, if so, whether this was permissible under international trade law, eventually came to a head before a Disputes Panel of the World Trade Organization (WTO) in *European Communities – Measures Affecting the Approval and Marketing of Biotech Products.*[35]

In a case such as *Biotech Products*, the relevant GATT provisions (especially in the Sanitary and Phytosanitary (SPS) Agreement) channel the disputants towards arguments based on scientific evidence.[36] Where, as in *Biotech Products*, the science relating to the safety of GM crops is contested, how is the matter to be resolved? An innocent response is that the question should be determined by reference to the view supported by 'sound science', this being taken to be a neutral and reliable arbiter. However, for many commentators on the practice and politics of science, this is a naïve view. Science just is not like that; and this is a matter to which we will have to return. Here, it is enough to understand that scientists reasonably disagree with one another, not just about the bottom-line questions, but about matters of methodology, relevance and focus. Science is never going to be theory neutral (that is the whole point of the enterprise) and we might wonder whether it can ever be 'value neutral'. There is, for example, a fundamental divide between a regulatory approach that focuses on the safety of the end product (as tends to be the case in North America) and one that focuses on the safety of the process (as tends to be the case in Europe). Hence, if scientists on one side of the Atlantic make safety judgements by reference to the end product while scientists on the other side of the Atlantic make (different) safety judgements by reference to the process used, and if both practices are regarded in their own territories as sound science, then 'sound science' simply cannot serve as a neutral court of appeal – and, in consequence, we cannot expect there to be a straightforward answer to the question of whether, say, GM crops, or meat from cloned cattle, or novel nanofoods are 'safe'.

---

[35] WT/DS291/23 (United States), WT/DS292/17 (Canada) and WT/DS293/17 (Argentina), 8 August 2003.

[36] See, e.g., Robert Lee, 'GM Resistant: Europe and the WTO Panel Dispute on Biotech Products', in Jennifer Gunning and Søren Holm (eds.), *Ethics, Law and Society* (Aldershot: Ashgate, 2005), vol. 1, 131.

That said, it should be recognised that, in the case of GM crops, European attitudes involve a mix of prudential and precautionary judgements together with some profound moral concerns.[37] Irrespective, then, of whether disputes such as that in *Biotech Products* are remitted to the court of 'sound science', the question remains of how far the international trading community can permit local culture to create its own special rules for market access? In *Biotech Products*, the Panel's line is that, where there is a level of scientific uncertainty that leaves room for legitimate disagreement, those states that prefer to take a risk-averse approach are allowed, at least provisionally, to do so; on the other hand, where there is little room for scientific doubt, members are not to be encouraged to dress up their moral objections as if they are concerns about safety. Objecting that one does not want to gamble on GM crop safety is one thing; objecting against GM crops on moral grounds is something else.

Yet, for some commentators on regional governance, this is not good enough. Thus, in the concluding remarks to her extended discussion of the EU and WTO regulation of genetically modified organisms (GMOs), Maria Lee says:[38]

> Another constant tension observed ... is between different levels of regulation. The democratic pressures are most intense at a local or national level, and it is increasingly difficult for 'the public' to be heard as we internationalise decision making ... [T]o argue [as Lee does pervasively] that the full breadth of concerns should be addressed by regulation means also that the democratic will should be acknowledged and respected in decision making. This in turn means that a way needs to be found to accommodate national perspectives in a process of international governance. This is extraordinarily difficult within the terms of the trade systems so laboriously built up in recent decades ... New technologies raise questions about the social purposes of free trade, at regional and global levels. Whilst the surrendering of control over certain issues is accepted for the benefits of membership, the benefits of trade, it should not be used to discipline 'irrational' politics ... Domestic actors are not the hapless pawns of globalisation, and debate over the content and application of the rules makes for a continuous process of contestation, a constant dynamism and change.

She continues:

> Extending the scope of decisions on GMOs and enhancing the domestic role in those decisions go together. These changes are not easy and not without risks. But the opposite risk is fracturing national authority, and hence of the democracy that we currently enjoy. This in turn creates risks for the international trading system. EU and WTO systems enjoy only fragile authority and have no deep reserves of legitimacy to call on in tough times. GMOs are already something of a

---

[37] See Lee, 'GM Resistant'. For the possibility that compensatory regimes might recognise that the harm caused by GM crops is not just physical or economic but also might encompass impairment to the claimant's ethical values, see Stuart J. Smyth, A. Bryan Endres, Thomas P. Redick and Drew L. Kershen, *Innovation and Liability in Biotechnology* (Cheltenham: Edward Elgar, 2010), at 55.

[38] Maria Lee, *EU Regulation of GMOs* (Cheltenham: Edward Elgar, 2008), at 244.

cipher for public anger, and if they are pushed onto unwilling publics through the highest-profile institutions of globalisation, the harm could be serious.[39]

Clearly, there is much more to be said about this. On the one hand, to be generous in allowing local exceptions to the ground rules for international trade is to invite opportunism and abuse (the exceptions being a pretext for economic protectionism); on the other hand, as Lee emphasises, to leave no room for local exception is to threaten the perceived legitimacy of the trade regime.

What short lessons should we draw from this first encounter with the regulation of modern biotechnologies? First, whether we check out the regulatory position internationally, regionally or locally, in legislative or judicial arenas, we find that modern biotechnologies have drawn out deep disagreements. Some of these disagreements are purely matters of risk assessment (as with different judgements about the safety and the environmental impact of GM crops); some of the differences are essentially ethical and cultural (as highlighted by the cases at the EPO); and some are a cocktail of concerns that relate to both safety and ethics. As has rightly been observed:

> Ultimately an intellectual property rights system is not just about patents and plant biotechnologies, but depends upon societal attitudes towards science and technology and the 'patenting of life'. Some nations, like Argentina, may approve commercialisation of biotech crops promptly enough through science-based regulation, but have barriers in patent policy that may discourage innovation. Other sovereigns may protect biotech innovation but restrict cultivation (for example, the European Union). Finding the right balance in a changing political and social environment is difficult.[40]

Second, where the differences are of an ethical kind, there are a number of competing approaches in play. Protagonists can agree that it is important to do the right thing but disagree about the ultimate criterion of ethical action. Third, where dignitarian views are engaged, there is little possibility of compromise; and regulators, without consensus or options for compromise, face an impossible challenge. Fourth, we can see that the interface between patent law and emerging technologies is a critical one. Patent offices might try to restrict the examination of a patent application to the technical question of whether the process or product for which patent protection is claimed is truly original and innovative. However, as the recent jurisprudence of the EPO illustrates, it is difficult to sidestep the moral issues when the technology conspicuously raises ethical concerns. Finally, the rapid developments in modern biotechnology alert us to the regulatory challenges facing a body of law, such as patent law, that tries to adapt itself to a constantly changing technological scene.

---

[39] *Ibid.*, at 245.

[40] Smyth *et al.*, *Innovation and Liability*, at 101. For an interesting analysis of the Argentinian regulatory environment with regard to 'red' biotechnology, see Shawn H. E. Harmon, 'Regulation of Stem Cell and Regenerative Science: Stakeholder Opinions, Plurality and Actor Space in the Argentine Social/Science Setting', *Law, Innovation and Technology*, 2 (2010), 95.

If we want to glimpse the kinds of challenges presented to regulators by emerging technologies, biotechnologies in general and the patent cases in particular are a helpful introduction. However, biotechnologies are not the only novel technologies, and the challenges presented by biotechnologies might not exhaust the difficulties faced by regulators. We need to cast our net wider, to draw in other emerging technologies, so that we can see what further challenges there might be for the law.

4 Technologies and technologies

According to the (US) President's Council on Bioethics:[41]

> we have entered upon a golden age for biology, medicine, and biotechnology. With the completion of (the DNA sequencing phase of) the Human Genome Project and the emergence of stem cell research, we can look forward to major insights into human development, normal and abnormal, as well as novel and more precisely selected treatments for human disease.[42]

However, this is by no means the full story. Alongside developments in biotechnology, there have been important developments in both nanotechnologies and in neurotechnology. Thus, the Council continues:

> Advances in neuroscience hold out the promise of powerful new understandings of mental processes and behavior, as well as remedies for devastating mental illnesses. Ingenious nanotechnological devices, implantable into the human body and brain, raise hopes for overcoming blindness and deafness, and, more generally, of enhancing native human capacities of awareness and action ... In myriad ways, the discoveries of biologists and the inventions of biotechnologists are steadily increasing our power ever more precisely to intervene into the workings of our bodies and minds and to alter them by rational design.[43]

When we add developments in information and communication technology into this mix, developments that have already rapidly penetrated our daily lives, we might think that this golden age is also an age of revolutionary proportions, that the twenty-first century is an age of technological revolution.

As with many revolutionary developments, the impact of these emerging technologies is highly disruptive. Many of these technologies have significant economic implications, some jobs are created but many jobs are lost, some new communities are created but many more traditional communities are destroyed.[44] This is nothing new. As Mathias Klang[45] has observed:

---

[41] President's Council on Bioethics, *Beyond Therapy* (New York: Dana Press, 2003).
[42] *Ibid.*, at 5–6. [43] *Ibid.*
[44] Compare, Monroe E. Price, 'The Newness of New Technology', *Cardozo Law Review*, 22 (2001), 1885.
[45] Mathias Klang, *Disruptive Technology* (Göteborg: Göteborg University, 2006).

Printing presses replaced the scriptoria and also changed the role of the scribe. Railways replaced canals and also changed the way in which social organization around the canals functioned. Railroads did not only make an impact on the barge pilot but also on the bargeman, lock keeper, canal owners, canal-side innkeepers, barge builders, waterway engineers and the horse trade (most barges were horse drawn). This process is not only one of historical interest. Examples of disruptive technologies are all around us. It is, in fact, a continual process. Digital cameras are replacing photographic film, flash drives replace floppy disks, DVD players replace VHS players. Each change brings social and economic effects to a larger or smaller degree. This disruption brings with it new possibilities of communication and control as well as disruption.[46]

Moreover, as we have seen, some of the developments in the biotechnologies are *ethically* disruptive, drawing out profound cultural differences – and, to the extent that new technologies (particularly work in the new brain sciences and developments in information technology) challenge the assumption that we, as humans, are autonomous and in control of our actions, these disruptions and differences are set to strike not only at our self-understanding (at both an individual and a community level) but also at the heart of legal practice.

By contrast to biotechnology, modern information and communication technology arrived without quite such an *ethical* fuss. The Californian community that had been responsible for much of the research and development of the Net took a libertarian view – an approach that had served well in accelerating the innovative work. According to such so-called cyberlibertarians, regulators would not be able to control online innovation or restrict online content and nor should they try to do so.[47] This did not stop regulators trying to exercise some control over online content that was judged inappropriate for children; and it did not silence some cyberpaternalists who warned that *private* proprietary interests were the real cause for concern as well as anticipating the use of both hardware and software as a regulatory tool.[48] For the most part, though, the early regulatory priority was to facilitate e-commerce, thereby opening much larger markets to consumers and smaller enterprises. This engendered some concerns about privacy and data protection in these new distributed networked communities but, by and large, the popular view was that there was little over which we should lose sleep.

Reflecting this sanguine assessment, Francis Fukuyama,[49] referring to personal computers and the internet, said:

[T]hese new forms of information technology (IT) promised to create wealth, spread access to information and therefore power around more democratically,

---

[46] At 8.

[47] See David R. Johnson and David Post, 'Law and Borders – The Rise of Law in Cyberspace', *Stanford Law Review*, 48 (1996), 1367.

[48] Seminally, see Lawrence Lessig, *Code and Other Laws of Cyberspace* (New York: Basic Books, 1999).

[49] Francis Fukuyama, *Our Posthuman Future* (London: Profile Books, 2002).

and foster community among their users. People had to look hard for downsides to the Information Revolution; what they have found to date are issues like the so-called digital divide (that is, inequality of access to IT) and threats to privacy, neither of which qualify as earth-shaking matters of justice or morality.[50]

With the wisdom of hindsight, however, we might be rather less confident about the downsides; indeed, some might argue that our concerns about information technology should be no less intense than the concerns that Fukuyama famously entertains about biotechnology.[51] For example, we should be concerned about the relative 'lawlessness' of the online world where the 'Internet separatists', as Joel Reidenberg calls them,[52] seem to think that the rule of law (and national rules of law) simply do not apply to their online activities. Hence:

> The defenses for hate, lies, drugs, sex, gambling, and stolen music are in essence that technology justifies the denial of personal jurisdiction, the rejection of an assertion of applicable law by a sovereign state, and the denial of the enforcement of decisions … In the face of these claims, legal systems engage in a rather conventional struggle to adapt existing regulatory standards to new technologies and the Internet. Yet, the underlying fight is a profound struggle against the very right of sovereign states to establish rules for online activity.[53]

Similarly, we should be concerned about the exposure of Net users, whether governmental, corporate or individual, to various kinds of cybercrime;[54] and we can hardly be sanguine about the extent to which malware of one kind and another threatens the integrity of the system. The concerns about privacy that Fukuyama rightly noted (concerns that are now intensified by the rapid development of social networking sites, and the like) should be seen as part of a much larger concern about what Jonathan Zittrain calls the sustainability of the 'generative' (flexible and open) design of the end-to-end Net, coupled with a parallel flexibility and openness in the design of PCs.[55]

Fukuyama, too, seems to underestimate the significance of high-powered information technology in the hands of the state. As John Gibb has remarked:

> Once identity card information is pooled and cross-referenced with other personal data, including Inland Revenue and Customs and Excise records, Criminal Records, the new and fast-growing [national DNA database], the NHS database,

---

[50] Ibid., at 182.

[51] See Roger Brownsword, 'What the World Needs Now: Techno-Regulation, Human Rights and Human Dignity', in Roger Brownsword (ed.), Human Rights, Global Governance and the Quest for Justice (Oxford: Hart, 2004), vol. 4, 203.

[52] Joel R. Reidenberg, 'Technology and Internet Jurisdiction', University of Pennsylvania Law Review, 153 (2005), 1951.

[53] Ibid., at 1953–4.

[54] For an indication of the problems across the board of Net use, see, e.g., the Foresight Report, Cyber Trust and Crime Prevention Project (London: Office of Science and Technology, 2004); Susan W. Brenner, Cyberthreats: The Emerging Faults Lines of the Nation State (New York: Oxford University Press, 2009); and Saul Levmore and Martha C. Nussbaum (eds.), The Offensive Internet (Cambridge, MA: Harvard University Press, 2010).

[55] Jonathan Zittrain, 'The Generative Internet', Harvard Law Review, 119 (2006), 1974.

Introduction

the huge amount of knowledge gained and stored from smart cards and credit cards, immigration records, the Department for Education database, the Passport Office, driving licences, bank records, library records and the National Register of Births, Marriages and Deaths, everything about us will be known – and that's probably more than we know about ourselves.[56]

Even if this prospect does not evoke Orwellian concerns, we might at least be concerned that so many of our routine transactions and interactions are being migrated to an online world where there seem to be few friendly faces to talk to when things go awry. As Daniel Solove has famously remarked, the problem with information and communication technologies actually might be less one of Orwellian surveillance than one of Kafkaesque opacity.[57]

We also need to anticipate the convergence of information and communication technologies with other technologies. In this future, we can imagine – and, actually, it takes very little imagination – the development of environments that are technologically enabled so that they became smarter, more intelligent, more anticipatory and more responsive to our (supposed) needs. What kind of world would this be? According to the team that led the SWAMI project on ambient intelligence, one such world would be constituted by

an Internet of things, where radio frequency identification (RFID) tags are attached to all products. It is a world of smart dust with networked sensors and actuators so small as to be virtually invisible, where the clothes you wear, the paint on your walls, the carpets on your floor, and the paper money in your pocket have a computer communications capability. It is a 4G world where today's mobile phone is transformed into a terminal capable of receiving television, accessing the Internet, downloading music, reading RFIDs, taking pictures, enabling interactive telephony, and much more. It is a world of convergence, where heterogeneous devices are able to communicate seamlessly across today's disparate networks, a world of machine learning and intelligent software, where computers monitor our activities, routines and behaviours to predict what we will do or want next.[58]

This is a world that gives rise to a host of concerns, to concerns about privacy, security, trust, reliability, and the like. It is also a world in which there are concerns about whether there is a future for agents, particularly whether there is any room for agent autonomy and any role for agent responsibility.[59]

---

[56] John Gibb, *Who's Watching You?* (London: Collins and Brown, 2005), 236.

[57] See Daniel J. Solove, *The Digital Person: Technology and Privacy in the Information Age* (New York: New York University Press, 2004), ch. 3. Solove sums up, 'We are not just heading toward a world of Big Brother or one composed of Little Brothers, but also toward a more mindless process – of bureaucratic indifference, arbitrary errors, and dehumanization – a world that is beginning to resemble Kafka's vision in *The Trial*' (*ibid.*, at 55).

[58] David Wright, Serge Gutwirth, Michael Friedewald, Elena Vildjiounaite and Yves Punie (eds.), *Safeguards in a World of Ambient Intelligence* (Dordrecht: Springer, 2008), at 1. See, too, the various (not so futuristic) scenarios sketched in Susan W. Brenner, *Law in an Era of 'Smart' Technology* (New York: Oxford University Press, 2007), ch. 1.

[59] See Jos de Mul and Bibi van den Berg, 'Remote Control', in Mireille Hildebrandt and Antoinette Rouvroy (eds.), *Autonomic Computing and Transformations of Human Agency*

5 First impressions

In this chapter, our first impression is that there are many reasons for lawyers to be interested in, and for regulators to respond to, a range of issues arising from the development and application of new technologies. This might be a 'golden age' of technological innovation. However, if the health, safety and environmental risks presented by new technologies are to be controlled, and if distinctive cultural and social values are to be protected, technologies cannot be given a free rein. Even (or, especially) in the most innovative of times, legal and regulatory oversight is an essential element in modern high-tech societies.

However, if our introduction simply highlighted the negatives, the risks and the resistance, it would be woefully one-sided; we should also accentuate the positive, the potentially beneficial impacts of technology. Indeed, Matt Ridley has gone so far as to suggest that, by and large, what improves the quality of life is invention rather than legislation.[60] There is some plausibility in this view. After all, is it GM crops or the European moratorium on GM that is more likely to respond to the shortage of food in the developing world? Is it state-of-the-art research on stem cells or the restrictions on patentability in Article 6 of the Directive on the Legal Protection of Biotechnological Inventions that is more likely to lead to therapies for cancer, diabetes and a range of degenerative diseases? Was it the largely unregulated – or, more accurately, the largely *legally* unregulated – research of the internet pioneers or the legal responses that followed that offered a new world of economic and cultural opportunity? Thus, when scientists argue, as they commonly do, that they need more funding, more time and less regulation, they have a point.

Yet, even if we have a balanced view of the positives and negatives, our introductory comments caution against thinking that regulatory oversight of modern technology is plain sailing. Judgements as to risk and safety, like judgements as to whether a particular technology is transgressive relative to fundamental values such as respect for human rights and human dignity, are contestable and complex. It is one thing to say that the law should take a position, or that regulatory intervention is required; but we should not assume that the terms of the appropriate legal or regulatory response are straightforward and unproblematic.

To compound these difficulties, we need to be careful that the law, in its efforts to tame the scientists and technologists, does not become too powerful. Famously, Bill Joy,[61] himself a leader in the field of information technologies, has warned:

(London: Routledge, 2011); and Roger Brownsword, 'Autonomy, Delegation, and Responsibility: Agents in Autonomic Computing Environments', *ibid.*, at 64.

[60] Matt Ridley, 'We've never had it so good – and it's all thanks to science', *Guardian Life*, 3 April 2003, 8.

[61] Bill Joy, 'Why the Future Doesn't Need Us', *Wired*, 8(4) (2000) (www.wired.com/wired/archives/8.04/joy_pr.html) (last accessed 19 June 2006).

Each of these technologies also offers untold promise: The vision of near immortality … drives us forward; genetic engineering may soon provide treatments, if not outright cures, for most diseases; and nanotechnology and nanomedicine can address yet more ills. Together they could significantly extend our average life span and improve the quality of our lives. Yet, with each of these technologies, a sequence of small, individually sensible advances leads to an accumulation of great power and, concomitantly, great danger.[62]

Whether technological power is held in private or public hands, in the final analysis, we look to the law to guard against its abusive, dangerous or illegitimate exercise.

In the light of a range of multifaceted technological developments, our introductory remarks indicate that the challenges facing the law run both broad and deep. First, the law needs to maintain continuity and stability notwithstanding a rapidly changing technological scene. Second, the law must do what it can to minimise the risks presented by the technologies as well as taking steps to maximise the benefits. Third, it falls to the law to safeguard the fundamental values of communities – values such as respect for human rights and human dignity – and to ensure that there is no technological transgression of the outer limits drawn by society. Fourth, national legal systems must try to meet these challenges in a context of transnational technological activity as well as international, regional and local regimes of governance. Finally, where there is a temptation to resort to a rule of technology, the law must ensure that the values of the rule of law are preserved.[63] It is challenges of these different, but related, kinds that form the backdrop for this book; and it is the regulatory environment, to which we turn in the next chapter, that bears the burden of addressing these challenges.

---

[62] *Ibid.*, at 4.

[63] For a seminal discussion, see Mireille Hildebrandt and Bert-Jaap Koops, 'The Challenges of Ambient Law and Legal Protection in the Profiling Era', *Modern Law Review*, 73 (2010), 428; and see Chapter 17.

2

The regulatory environment: UK Biobank, eBay and *Wikipedia*

1 Introduction

The idea that the law can do all the work in creating the right kind of environment for the development and application of new technologies is unrealistic. The power of the law to confine and channel conduct is limited. If the law is to succeed in rising to the challenges presented by today's emerging technologies, it needs some cultural assistance. Or, to put this another way, if we are to understand the effectiveness of law, just as if we are to have an effective understanding of law, we need to set its rules, doctrines and decisions in the larger context of the regulatory environment.

In this chapter, having dealt with some terminological matters, we introduce the general idea of a regulatory environment and the particular idea of a regulatory mode or modality. To earth and to illustrate these ideas, we then sketch three particular environments in which the regulatory role of law is fairly low-key. These are the regulatory environments that we find at UK Biobank, for the use of eBay, and for the development and sustainability of *Wikipedia*. In each of these cases, it is clear that informal community norms play an important part in shaping the conduct of the parties.

2 Terminology: regulation, law and governance

In our opening chapter, we talked about 'regulation', 'law' and 'governance'. Are these terms merely synonyms? Or, do they, when used with discrimination, pick out distinctive forms of channelling and control? The context for the application of these terms is that of the 'regulatory environment'; however, before we introduce that concept (and context), we can make some short clarifying remarks about the meaning of each of the terms.

(a) Regulation

Although some regulatory theorists might have their own particular take on the matter, it is generally accepted that the term 'regulation' signifies:

> the sustained and focused attempt to alter the behaviour of others according to standards or goals with the intention of producing a broadly identified outcome

or outcomes, which may involve mechanisms of standard-setting, information-gathering and behaviour-modification.[1]

Nevertheless, regulation is an unwieldy concept.[2] It is unclear who counts as a regulator and what counts as regulation. For our purposes, we can take a broad approach. Hence, we can treat 'regulation' as encompassing any instrument (legal or non-legal in its character, governmental or non-governmental in its source, direct or indirect in its operation, and so on) that is designed to channel group behaviour; and we can treat as a 'regulator' any person or body who initiates regulation in this broad sense. Most importantly, we should not assume that 'regulation' is co-extensive with 'law'; and we should not assume that 'regulators' are only those who are authorised to issue legal directives.

(b) Law

The most formal contribution to the regulatory environment is made by the 'law'. By this term, we mean that set of posited instruments – treaties, constitutions, codes, legislation, and the like – as well as particular precedents laid down by courts that are conventionally taken to be the sources that are relevant to the determination of the 'legal' position. Admittedly, this suffers from some circularity; in effect, it says little more than that, for present purposes, we are using the term in pretty much the (positivistic and 'high law') way that many readers would take to be the conventional usage. Such a usage would not withstand serious jurisprudential scrutiny, failing to reflect either the moral discrimination and depth that is characteristic of legal idealist conceptualisations[3] or the breadth that is characteristic of legal pluralism.[4] However, we can bracket off the difficult jurisprudential issues: for present purposes, it suffices to say that we are treating 'law' as a particular class of normative signals that take their place in the larger regulatory array.

How, then, does 'law' relate to 'regulation'? If regulation is primarily about channelling behaviour, then legislation is certainly a species of regulation. However, to the extent that regulators rely on instruments and strategies other than legislation in their sustained and focused attempts to alter the behaviour of others, regulation is broader than law. On the other hand, to the extent that

---

[1] Julia Black, 'What Is Regulatory Innovation?', in Julia Black, Martin Lodge and Mark Thatcher (eds.), *Regulatory Innovation* (Cheltenham: Edward Elgar, 2005), 1, at 11. For two background visions of regulation (one as an infringement of private autonomy justified only by considerations of economic efficiency, the other as a much broader collaborative enterprise), see Tony Prosser, *The Regulatory Enterprise* (Oxford: Oxford University Press, 2010), ch.1.

[2] See, e.g., Julia Black, 'De-centring Regulation: Understanding the Role of Regulation and Self-Regulation in a "Post-Regulatory" World', *Current Legal Problems*, 54 (2001), 103.

[3] See, e.g., Deryck Beyleveld and Roger Brownsword, *Law as a Moral Judgment* (London: Sweet & Maxwell, 1986).

[4] See, e.g., William Twining, *General Jurisprudence* (Cambridge: Cambridge University Press, 2009); and Roger Brownsword, 'Framers and Problematisers: Getting to Grips with Global Governance', *Transnational Legal Theory*, 1 (2010), 287.

regulation does not encompass such tasks as constitution-making and dispute resolution (at any rate, when individual disputes do not raise questions that are of more general significance relative to regulatory objectives), then law is broader than regulation.[5] We might infer, therefore, that while law and regulation intersect with one another, they are not coextensive.

(c) Governance

Finally, there is the term 'governance'. According to Lewis Kornhauser, we should treat legal systems as a particular kind of governance structure, from which it follows that disputes concerning the concept of law should be understood as disputes 'concerning the property or properties that distinguish legal systems from other types of governance structures'.[6] Whatever we think that the particular distinguishing property or properties might be, the clear implication is that governance is a more inclusive category than law. If governance is to be given a broad sweep, we might use this term to cover the steering or guiding of conduct – in which case, it seems to be almost a synonym for regulation;[7] or perhaps we might treat governance as referring to all forms of regulation that are not legal (as in the locution 'law and governance'). Arguably, however, what the lexicon of regulation most needs is a term that highlights those regulatory inputs that are non-governmental. For, beyond those regulatory activities that are carried out by, or on behalf of, government and its agents, there are the activities of those many non-governmental agencies (including religious and professional associations, technical standard setting bodies, advisory bodies, and a host of others) that seek to impose a pattern of behaviour on their membership or who order group relationships.[8] It is the normative signals transmitted by this important class of agents that we take to represent the distinctive sphere of 'governance'.

To summarise, when we put together the different strands of (governmental) law, (governmental) regulation, and (non-governmental regulatory) governance, we have the ingredients – ingredients that are still largely normative – that make up the particular 'regulatory environment'.

---

[5] Here, we are drawing on the standard functional analysis of 'law-jobs' theory: see Karl N. Llewellyn, 'The Normative, the Legal, and the Law-Jobs: The Problem of Juristic Method', *Yale Law Journal*, 49 (1940), 1355.

[6] Lewis A. Kornhauser, 'Governance Structures, Legal Systems and the Concept of Law', *University of Chicago-Kent Law Review*, 70 (2004), 355, at 381.

[7] But, compare Julia Black, 'Constructing and Contesting Legitimacy and Accountability in Polycentric Regulatory Regimes', LSE Working Papers, 2/2008, at 8: 'Regulation is a particular form of governance. All forms of regulation are governance, but not all forms of governance are regulation. Regulation is a distinct activity which engages with a particular social problem: how to change the behaviour of others.'

[8] Compare the diagrammatic representations of Internet governance in Andrew D. Murray, *The Regulation of Cyberspace* (Abingdon: Routledge-Cavendish, 2007), at 93 and 99.

3 The idea of a regulatory environment

When we say that emerging technologies should be understood as being situated in a particular regulatory environment, the essential idea is that, when we act – whether we act as developers and commercial exploiters, or as users and appliers, of particular technologies – we do so in a context that has a certain coding for action, a coding that signals whether various acts are permitted (even required) or prohibited, whether they will be viewed positively, negatively or neutrally, whether they are incentivised or disincentivised, whether they are likely to be praised or criticised, even whether they are possible or impossible, and so on. Institutions acting in a regulatory capacity, likewise, do so in ways that reflect their own organisational culture and, more generally, the legal, political and social environment within which they are embedded. Institutional responsiveness to these various types of coding is crucial for understanding regulatory outcomes that, if measured against the yardstick of technological logic and efficiency, otherwise may often appear incomprehensible.[9]

To be more specific about the characteristics of a regulatory (or regulated) environment is not entirely straightforward because, while some environments are regulated in a top-down fashion (with regulators clearly distinguishable from regulatees), others are more bottom-up (in the sense that they are self-regulatory). Whereas, in top-down regulatory environments, there is likely to be a significant formal legal presence, in bottom-up self-regulatory environments, this is less likely to be the case. For convenience, we can mark this distinction by referring to 'Type 1' (top-down with significant hard law elements) and 'Type 2' (bottom-up with fewer hard-law elements) regulatory environments. However, this is by no means the end of the matter. For, while some regulatory environments are reasonably stable and well formed, others are unstable, overlapping, conflictual, polycentric, and so on[10] – indeed, the multi-level regulatory environment represented by the European Union combines many if not all of these different characteristics.

This complexity and variation notwithstanding, by way of an initial attempt to specify the characteristics of a regulatory environment, we can highlight the following three matters, namely: the variety of regulatory instruments or modalities; the bearing of the environment on the practical reason of regulatees (and the nature of the regulatory registers); and the underlying regulatory intention and effect.

First, regulators can employ a range and variety of signals that are designed to channel the conduct of their regulatees. For lawyers, there is a temptation to overlook the extent of this range and variety as a result of which two framing

---

[9] J. Fountain, *Building the Virtual State: Information Technology and Institutional Change* (Washington, DC: Brookings Institution Press, 2001).

[10] See, further, Black, 'Constructing and Contesting Legitimacy'; and see David G. Post, *In Search of Jefferson's Moose* (Oxford: Oxford University Press, 2009), ch. 11.

mistakes are liable to be made.[11] One is *the mistake of legal exclusivity* – which makes the assumption that the only signals in the regulatory environment are formal legal signals. However, as Lawrence Lessig has famously highlighted, the modes of channelling that make up a particular regulatory environment can range from law and social norms through to market signals and architecture, from the law of trespass (prohibiting entry) to a locked door or a password-protected website.[12] Indeed, in some future world, coding might not end at this, regulatees being designed so that they are genetically predisposed to favour certain kinds of (acceptable) conduct. The other framing error is *the mistake of normative exclusivity* – which makes the assumption that the only signals in the regulatory environment are normative (that is, signals that prescribe what ought, or ought not, to be done). While law and social norms are certainly normative, and while this might also be the case with market signals, it is not necessarily the case with product design or architecture. Where regulators rely on design (for example, filters to intercept spam) or architecture (for instance, in the way that the Egyptians constructed their pyramids to deter tomb-raiders, or that roads in urban areas are constructed to deter high-speed driving) these technological fixes speak (non-normatively) to the practicability or possibility of action rather than what ought or ought not to be done. This is not to say that the regulatory environment will not include legal signals or normative signals; rather, the point is that the regulatory repertoire also includes non-legal and non-normative signals and that we should allow for this in our thinking about the regulatory environment.

If we were to develop these points, we might construct a typology highlighting three generations of regulatory environment. In a first-generation regulatory environment, regulators would rely exclusively on normative signals. In a second-generation regulatory environment, regulators would rely on both (first generation) normative signals and second-generation design of products and places (architecture). Where regulators rely on such a design strategy, the signal is no longer normative; instead, as we will emphasise shortly, the design features signal what is practicable or possible. Finally, in a third-generation regulatory environment, regulators would go beyond traditional normative signals and design of products and places by incorporating the regulatory design within regulatees themselves (for example, by controlling their genetic coding). Where design is embedded in regulatees in such a way that it channels their behaviour, it is likely to be much less apparent to regulatees that they are being regulated – if the design is reliable, regulatees will simply behave (like products) in accordance with their specification.

---

[11] See, Roger Brownsword, 'Responsible Regulation: Prudence, Precaution, and Stewardship', *Northern Ireland Legal Quarterly*, 62 (2011), 573.

[12] Lawrence Lessig, *Code and Other Laws of Cyberspace* (New York: Basic Books, 1999), ch. 7; and Lessig, 'The Law of the Horse: What Cyberlaw Might Teach', *Harvard Law Review*, 113 (1999), 501, at 507–14.

This typology gives us plenty of food for thought. However, in the here and now, we can assume that regulatory environments will continue to rely primarily on normative instruments, albeit with the support of various technological devices as well as a willingness to make use of design instruments. We will return to the question of regulatory modalities in the next section of the chapter and to the implications of non-normative regulatory management in the final chapter of the book.

Second, the strategy of regulators – that is, the strategy of regulators in shaping the conduct of their regulatees – is to engage with the practical reason (in the broad and inclusive sense of an agent's reasons for action)[13] of regulatees. In pursuing this strategy, regulators employ one or more of the following three key registers:

1 the moral register: here, the coding signals (normatively) that some act, x, categorically ought or ought not to be done relative to standards of right action – regulators thus signal to regulatees that x is, or is not, the right thing to do; or,

2 the prudential register: here, the coding signals (still normatively) that some act, x, ought or ought not to be done relative to the prudential interests of regulatees – regulators thus signal to regulatees that x is, or is not, in their (regulatees') self-interest; or

3 the register of practicability/possibility: here, the signalling is no longer normative, the environment being designed in such a way that it is either not reasonably practicable or even impossible to do some act, x – in which case, regulatees reason, not that x ought not to be done, but that x cannot be done.

In an exclusively moral environment, the primary normative signal (in the sense of the reason for the norm) is always moral; but the secondary signal, depending upon the nature of the sanction, might be more prudential. In traditional criminal law environments, the signals are more complex. While the primary normative signal to regulatees can be either moral (the particular act should not be done because this would be immoral) or paternalistically prudential (the act should not be done because it is contrary to the interests of the regulatee), the secondary signal represented by the deterrent threat of punishment is prudential.[14] As the regulatory environment relies more on

---

[13] In this broad sense, 'practical reason' encompasses both moral and non-moral reasons for action.

[14] Compare Alan Norrie, 'Citizenship, Authoritarianism and the Changing Shape of the Criminal Law', in Bernadette McSherry, Alan Norrie and Simon Bronitt (eds.), *Regulating Deviance* (Oxford: Hart, 2009), 13. Norrie highlights three broad developments in recent British criminal law and justice, namely: (a) an increasing emphasis on notions of moral right and wrong and, concomitantly, on individual responsibility ('responsibilisation'); (b) an increasing emphasis on dangerousness and, concomitantly, on the need for exceptional forms of punishment or control ('dangerousness'); and (c) an increasing reliance on preventative orders and new forms of control ('regulation') (*ibid.*, at 15). While the first of these developments is in line with the aspirations of moral community, it is the second and the third that such a community needs to monitor with

technological management, the strength and significance of the moral signal fades; initially, the signals to regulatees accentuate that the doing of a particular act is contrary to their interests (the likelihood of detection becomes more pronounced); and, this is taken a step further when the technology is embedded in such a way that an act is either not reasonably practicable or simply not possible (for example, think about the regulatory environment at a modern security-sensitive airport).[15] Where the signal is that a particular act is no longer a possible option, regulatee compliance is, so to speak, fully determined; in all other cases, and especially so in the normative range, the conduct of regulatees is underdetermined.

Third, there is the matter of regulatory intention and effect. If we are to hold regulators to account, then the paradigm case is one in which they have self-consciously put in place a range of signals that are intended to direct or channel behaviour in a particular way. In such a case, the regulatory environment is purposively produced. However, designs might have regulatory effects even though such effects are not ones that the regulators (designers) intended. So, for example, there has been a long-running debate about whether the design of Robert Moses' bridges on the New York parkways was intended to have the (racially discriminatory) effect of making it more difficult for the poor, mainly black, population to reach the beaches on Long Island.[16] From the point of view of prospective beach-users, it made little difference whether the bridges had been designed with this intent – in practice, the bridges had the regulative effect of making the beaches more difficult to access. Nevertheless, if we are to hold regulators (designers) to account, is it not the case that their intentions remain important?

The paradigm, as we have said, is one in which regulators have certain channelling purposes, and they put in place a rule framework or a design that is intended to have a particular effect. In such a case, it is perfectly fair to ask regulators to justify both their purposes and the instruments (the rules or the designs) that they have adopted. However, even the best-laid regulatory plans can go awry and, as we will see in a later chapter,[17] a common problem with regulatory interventions is that they generate unintended effects. Clearly, when regulators are held to account, they must answer for both the intended and the unintended effects of the regulatory environments that they have put in place.

Having said this, the case of the New York parkway bridges might seem rather different. In defence of the bridge designers, it might be argued that there

---

care. In this light, see, in particular, Lucia Zedner, 'Fixing the Future? The Pre-emptive Turn in Criminal Justice', in McSherry *et al.*, *Regulating Deviance*, 35.

[15] Compare Bert-Jaap Koops, 'Technology and the Crime Society: Rethinking Legal Protection', *Law, Innovation and Technology*, 1 (2009), 93.

[16] See Noëmi Manders-Huits and Jeroen van den Hoven, 'The Need for a Value-Sensitive Design of Communication Infrastructures', in Paul Sollie and Marcus Düwell (eds.), *Evaluating New Technologies* (Dordrecht: Springer, 2009), 51, 54.

[17] See Chapter 11.

was no regulatory plan as such, simply an attempt to strengthen the bridges. To be sure, in practice, the newly constructed bridges might have had a regulative impact, but this was an unintended effect of the design. Once upon a time, such a defence might have been adequate; but, nowadays, regulators will not get off the hook quite so easily. For, as it becomes increasingly clear that design can matter (potentially, having both negative and positive effects), so it is no longer acceptable for regulators to plead a lack of intent, or attention, with regard to such technical details. While inattention may lead to regulatory environments that are detrimental to, say, the health or the privacy of regulatees, smart regulatory action can have the opposite impact (for example, by requiring or encouraging architects and technologists to default to health-promoting or privacy-enhancing designs).[18] In short, although the paradigmatic regulatory environment is the product of intentional design, regulators need to answer for both the intended and the unintended channelling effects of their actions as well as for their omissions.

To sum up: we can draw a crude contrast between Type 1 and Type 2 regulatory environments. However, in both types of regulatory environment, a range of normative and non-normative instruments may be employed; and, in both types, we can find the three key registers (the moral, prudential and practicable) in play. We have also suggested that the movement from normative to non-normative signals may be tracked through three generations of regulatory environment: from first-generation norms, to second-generation design of products and places, to third-generation design of regulatees themselves. Figure 2.1 shows how we would plot the type of regulatory environment if we tracked the type of register being used (moral, prudential, practicable/possible) and which generation of signals and design was applicable. Finally, we can distinguish between an environment that is regulatory by intent and one that is simply regulatory in effect. Although the former is paradigmatic, issues of regulatory accountability can be raised even where the particular regulatory effect is unintended – and even where the effect is associated with a particular architectural or design feature.

4 Regulatory modes or modalities

In the Orwellian dystopia, Oceania, 'actions are not regulated by law or by any clearly formulated code of behaviour. In Oceania, there is no law'.[19] If law is not the regulatory mode, then how are the citizens of Oceania regulated? As is well known, the answer is that Oceania is a certain kind of surveillance society:

---

[18] See, e.g., Manders-Huits and van den Hoven, 'Need for a Value-Sensitive Design'; and Peter-Paul Verbeek, 'The Moral Relevance of Technological Artifacts', in Paul Sollie and Marcus Düwell (eds.), *Evaluating New Technologies* (Dordrecht: Springer, 2009), 63.

[19] George Orwell, *Nineteen Eighty-Four* (London: Penguin Books, 1989), 219–20. For a modern version of the surveillance society, see Kirstie Ball, David Lyon, David Murakami Wood, Clive Norris and Charles Raab, *A Report on the Surveillance Society* (September 2006); and Chapter 17.

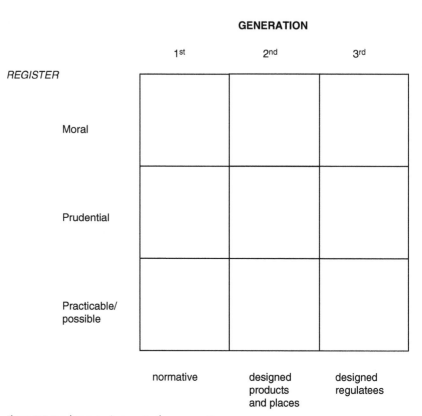

Figure 2.1 Regulatory environments: three generations

A Party member lives from birth to death under the eye of the Thought Police. Even when he is alone he can never be sure that he is alone. Wherever he may be, asleep or awake, working or resting, in his bath or in bed, he can be inspected without warning and without knowing that he is being inspected. Nothing that he does is indifferent. His friendships, his relaxations, his behaviour towards his wife and children, the expression of his face when he is alone, the words he mutters in sleep, even the characteristic movements of his body, are all jealously scrutinised. Not only any actual misdemeanour, but any eccentricity, however small, any change of habits, any nervous mannerism that could possibly be the symptom of an inner struggle, is certain to be detected. He has no freedom of choice in any direction whatever.[20]

In part, the pressure for conformity comes from fellow members. As Julia, Winston Smith's soul mate confesses, she knows that the Two Minutes Hate, the denials and contradictions of Newspeak, and all the rest of the repressive apparatus is a lot of nonsense; but she also knows 'when to cheer and when to boo'.[21] However, it is the intrusive presence of the telescreens that ensures

[20] Orwell, *Nineteen Eighty-Four*, at 219.   [21] *Ibid.*, at 163

round-the-clock monitoring; and, although Oceania is depicted as a society that has gone backwards rather than forwards technologically speaking, it is this aspect of its regulatory approach that has given it such a bad name. In other words, it is the modality of regulation in Oceania that agitates our concern.

Seminally, Lawrence Lessig has identified four regulatory modalities (or modes of regulation), that characterise the activities of regulators back in the real world. These four modalities are: the law, social norms, the market and architecture (or code).[22] The wearing of seatbelts is one of Lessig's illustrative examples, thus:

> The government may want citizens to wear seatbelts more often. It could pass a law to require the wearing of seatbelts (law regulating behavior directly). Or it could fund public education campaigns to create a stigma against those who do not wear seatbelts (law regulating social norms as a means to regulating behavior). Or it could subsidize insurance companies to offer reduced rates to seatbelt wearers (law regulating the market as a way of regulating behavior). Finally, the law could mandate automatic seatbelts, or ignition-locking systems (changing the code of the automobile as a means of regulating belting behavior). Each action might be said to have some effect on seatbelt use; each has some cost. The question for the government is how to get the most seatbelt use for the least cost.[23]

When a smart regulatory style is adopted, then regulators will consider direct and indirect strategies, choosing and combining strategies in whichever way promises the optimal ratio of regulatory input to desired regulatory output.

In a helpful paper that extends and elaborates on Lessig's four regulatory modes, Andrew Murray and Colin Scott consider the best terms in which to identify the four modalities, they discuss how the modalities might be (optimally) combined and, most importantly for present purposes, they highlight three dimensions that are fundamental to whatever strategy is adopted.[24]

On the first point, Murray and Scott reclassify the modality of law as one of 'hierarchy', that of social norms as one of 'community', that of markets as one of 'competition', and that of architecture as one of 'design'. There is more at stake here than terminological nicety, particularly where theorists are seeking out a classificatory scheme that will cover the maximum range of regulatory instruments or strategies. However, a map of this kind is not the object of the present exercise. For present purposes what matters is a distinction between two ideal-typical regulatory regimes. One ideal-typical regime operates very much like a traditional legal normative order, using a mix of the moral and prudential registers (more or less successfully) to engage the practical reason of regulatees. The other ideal-typical regime, however, secures a regulated pattern of behaviour

---

[22] Lawrence Lessig, *Code and Other Laws of Cyberspace* (New York: Basic Books, 1999), ch. 7; and Lessig, 'The Law of the Horse: What Cyberlaw Might Teach', *Harvard Law Review*, 113 (1999), 501, 507–14.

[23] *Code*, at 93–4.

[24] Andrew Murray and Colin Scott, 'Controlling the New Media: Hybrid Responses to New Forms of Power', *Modern Law Review*, 65 (2002), 491. See, too, Murray, *Regulation*.

without any such normative engagement with the practical reason of regulatees – in other words, it relies exclusively on the register of practicability/possibility. In these terms, the first three of Lessig's modalities, whether classified in Lessig's own terms or in accordance with Murray and Scott's reclassification, are variations on the former ideal-type; and the fourth of Lessig's modalities, again whether classified in Lessig's own terms or in accordance with Murray and Scott's reclassification, is characteristic of the latter.[25]

Second, other things being equal, it must make sense to aspire to identifying the optimal mix of regulatory modalities. David Garland describes a number of modern crime prevention strategies in such terms:

> The key phrases of the new strategy are terms such as 'partnership', 'public/private alliance', 'inter-agency co-operation', 'the multi-agency approach', 'activating communities', creating 'active citizens', 'help for self-help', and the 'co-production of security'. The primary objective is to spread responsibility for crime control onto agencies, organizations and individuals that operate outside the criminal justice state and to persuade them to act appropriately.[26]

However, recognising that smart regulation invites working towards the optimal mix of regulatory approaches does not have real bite until we take on board the third point made by Murray and Scott.

Following a cybernetic model, Murray and Scott present each regulatory modality as having three components (or dimensions), namely: some goal, standard, rule or norm to which the system refers; some mechanism for monitoring or feeding back information about performance; and some mechanism for realigning the system when its operation deviates from its intended goal. The importance of this third point is that it enables us to see precisely where and how a particular ingredient in the regulatory mix is intended to contribute to the total regulatory impact. For example, it is not just that regulators might employ the traditional legal mode in conjunction with, say, social pressure; rather, the strategy might be to use the traditional legal mode to set the standard but then leave it to social pressure (the community) to monitor compliance (performance) and possibly even to respond to non-compliance (deviation).

For those who are used to thinking in traditional regulatory terms, it is easy enough to relate to the three dimensions identified by Murray and Scott, but the habits of a lifetime in the law offer some resistance to adopting their cybernetic language. Far from being unhelpful, this tension paves the way for a necessary sharpening up of the contrast between a traditional regulatory approach and one that is reliant on technology. If we are operating with the latter, we will think purely in terms of a designed environment (and/or controlled regulatees)

---

[25] Compare Murray, *Regulation*, at 37, where he divides the modalities of regulation into two families, one socially mediated, the other environmental. While, within the former family, we have law, markets and norms, within the latter family, we have architecture.

[26] David Garland, *The Culture of Control* (Oxford: Oxford University Press, 2001), at 124–5.

with a required pattern of behaviour. In one dimension, regulators identify the required pattern (this is what they want their regulatory targets to do or not to do); in a second dimension, they monitor whether the control system is producing the required pattern; and, in a third dimension, they respond (by fixing the problem) where the system needs to be adjusted. If, instead, we express these three dimensions in the more familiar language of the traditional legal ideal-type, we revert to a fundamentally different paradigm. Stated in such traditional terms, the first dimension is to adopt and declare a regulatory position; the second is to monitor responses to that position and to exert pressure for compliance; and the third is to take enforcement steps against regulatees who do not comply.

Finally, it is worth emphasising that we need to be careful when we treat architecture or code as part of the (normative) regulatory environment. Some technologies function in a normative way; others simply design out what would otherwise be an option. This point is very clearly drawn out in Mireille Hildebrandt's distinction between 'regulative' and 'constitutive' technological features.[27] By way of an illustrative example, Hildebrandt invites readers to imagine a home that is enabled with a smart energy meter:

> One could imagine a smart home that automatically reduces the consumption of energy after a certain threshold has been reached, switching off lights in empty rooms and/or blocking the use of the washing machine for the rest of the day. This intervention [which is a case of a 'constitutive' technological intervention] may have been designed by the national or municipal legislator or by government agencies involved in environmental protection and implemented by the company that supplies the electricity. Alternatively [this being a case of a 'regulative' technological intervention], the user may be empowered to program her smart house in such a way. Another possibility [again, a case of a 'regulative' technological intervention] would be to have a smart home that is infested with real-time displays that inform the occupants about the amount of energy they are consuming while cooking, reading, having a shower, heating the house, keeping the fridge in function or mowing the lawn. This will allow the inhabitants to become aware of their energy consumption in a very practical way, giving them a chance to change their habits while having real-time access to the increasing eco-efficiency of their behaviour.[28]

Whether we are considering smart cars, smart homes or smart regulatory styles, we need to be sensitive to the way in which the regulatory environment engages with regulatees, whether it directs normative signals at regulatees enjoining them to act in particular ways, or whether the technology of regulation simply imposes (non-normatively) a pattern of conduct upon regulatees whether or not they would otherwise choose to act in the prescribed way.

---

[27] Mireille Hildebrandt, 'Legal and Technological Normativity: More (and Less) than Twin Sisters', *Techné*, 12(3) (2008), 169.

[28] *Ibid.*, at 174.

5 Three particular regulatory environments

In this section of the chapter, we give three illustrations of particular regulatory environments. Each is associated with emerging technologies (biotechnology in the case of UK Biobank, and the internet in the case of both eBay and *Wikipedia*); each departs from a simple top-down hierarchical model; each displays large elements of self-regulation; and, in each case, although the hard-law signals are not entirely absent, they are not predominant. Stated shortly, these examples approximate to Type 2 regulatory environments (albeit with Type 1 background features).

(a) UK Biobank

In company with a number of countries, the UK has seen the potential healthcare benefits that might flow from an improved understanding of the way in which a person's genetic make-up, their lifestyle and their environment interact.[29] Against this background, UK Biobank[30] is one of the largest public health initiatives of its kind, aiming to construct a research resource that can be used to throw light on the causes of common diseases and, with that, facilitating the development of more effective strategies for prevention and treatment. By summer 2010, the target group of 500,000 volunteers (aged 40–69)[31] had been enrolled; and, in 2012, the resource (comprising the participants' biological samples and their lifestyle data, linked to their medical records) was opened to bona fide researchers around the world, both commercial and non-commercial, for the purpose of conducting health-related research. Typically, participants will stay active with the project until their death (in some cases, many years after they have been first enrolled). Indeed, even after the death (or mental incapacitation) of participants they will maintain a passive involvement because UK Biobank will retain and continue to make use of their samples and data.[32]

It falls to the Ethics and Governance Council (EGC) to set the framework for, *inter alia*, UK Biobank's relationship with participants as well as to supervise

---

[29] For a helpful overview and critical comparative survey of the various governance structures applicable to biobanks in Europe, see Susan M. C. Gibbons, 'Are UK Genetic Databases Governed Adequately? A Comparative Legal Analysis', *Legal Studies*, 27 (2007), 312.

[30] See www.ukbiobank.ac.uk; Jean V. McHale, 'Regulating Genetic Databases: Some Legal and Ethical Issues', *Medical Law Review*, 12 (2004), 70; Alastair V. Campbell, 'The Ethical Challenges of Biobanks: Safeguarding Altruism and Trust', in Sheila A. M. McLean (ed.), *First Do No Harm* (Aldershot: Ashgate, 2006), 203; Roger Brownsword, 'Biobank Governance: Property, Privacy and Consent', in Christian Lenk, Nils Hoppe and Roberto Andorno (eds.), *Ethics and Law of Intellectual Property* (Aldershot: Ashgate, 2007), 11.

[31] The reason for selecting this particular age group is that these are the persons most likely to succumb to common serious illnesses such as diabetes, cancers of various kinds, heart disease and stroke.

[32] *UK Biobank Ethics and Governance Framework* (version 2.0, July 2006), 22, para. I.B.7. Available online at www.ukbiobank.ac.uk/docs/EGF_Version2_July%202006.pdf. If potential participants express the view that they would want to be withdrawn on death or mental incapacity, they will not be recruited.

the way in which the Biobank operates (primarily to ensure that access to the resource is regulated in a way that respects the interests of both participants and the larger public). Broadly speaking, the Ethics and Governance Framework (EGF) document designs in provisions that are relatively strong on consent (albeit wide and unspecific in the sense that the authorisation is simply for health-related research purposes), weak on property (participants being informed of 'the fact that UK Biobank will be the legal owner of the database and the sample collection, and that participants will have no property rights in the samples'),[33] and reasonably protective of participants' interests in privacy and confidentiality.[34]

The EGF, however, needs periodic review and revision as the project evolves. For example, it is highly likely that steps will be taken to enhance the resource by inviting participants to undertake brain and body scans. As is well known, when researchers carry out scans of this kind, they sometimes identify an apparent pathology that might be of clinical relevance to the particular participant. But, what are the responsibilities of researchers in relation to such so-called 'incidental findings'?[35] Should they inform participants of their findings? What if the finding is a false alarm (a false positive), or if the participant would prefer not to know, or if there is no treatment, or if the researchers have made it clear to participants that there will be no clinical feedback? If the finding is not disclosed, would the researchers be liable to the participant for a breach of contract or for a tort? Would any guidance to researchers be susceptible to judicial review? For UK Biobank, these questions are particularly acute because the policy initially (a policy, it should be said, that had its critics)[36] was to give no clinical feedback; participants were told that this was purely a research project. However, there is now much less confidence in such a strict 'no feedback' position and the EGF will need to reflect the balance of opinion on the EGC not only in relation to findings derived from scanning, but also from other kinds of tests undertaken.

There is much that could be said about the balance of interests struck in the EGF (both as originally drafted and as revised), including the terms on which

---

[33] *Ibid.*, at 6, para. I.B.1.

[34] Thus, we read: 'UK Biobank will maintain strict measures to protect confidentiality, and will ensure that data and samples are (reversibly) anonymised, linked and stored to very high standards of security. The same protection will be extended under contract for any handling or analysis of data or samples by third parties engaged to provide services necessary for developing the resource' (*ibid.*, at 12, para. I.C.1).

[35] For an excellent overview of participants' expectations together with the range of ethical and legal issues, see Jasper Bovenberg, Tineke Meulenkamp, Ellen Smets and Sjef Gevers, *Always Expect the Unexpected: Legal and Social Aspects of Reporting Biobank Research Results to Individual Research Participants* (Radboud University Nijmegen: Centre for Society and Genomics, 2009). See, too, Nikolaus Forgó, Regine Kollek, Marian Arning, Tina Kruegel and Imme Petersen, *Ethical and Legal Requirements for Transnational Genetic Research* (Munich and Oxford: Beck with Hart, 2010).

[36] See, e.g., Carolyn Johnston and Jane Kaye, 'Does the UK Biobank Have a Legal Obligation to Provide Feedback about Individual Findings to Participants', *Medical Law Review*, 12 (2004), 239.

access to the resource is granted to researchers;[37] but that is not presently the point at issue. The question is whether the regulatory environment (including the supervisory role of the EGC) will be sufficiently robust to ensure that the Biobank adheres to its EGF commitments.

In one of its annual reviews of its own activities,[38] the EGC addresses this frequently asked question (and implicit criticism)[39] head-on. Is there a problem about the EGC's apparent lack of teeth? In response, the EGC says:

> The EGC is an advisory committee and as such has no formal power of veto over UK Biobank's actions. It can, however, make public statements of concern about the project.
>
> The Council normally communicates its reflections informally to UK Biobank and a Memorandum of Understanding is in place which lays out the respective obligations of both parties. These obligations require UK Biobank to respond to all reasonable requests from the EGC. If the Council were not satisfied with UK Biobank's response, it would make a formal statement of concern (e.g., to the UK Biobank Board of Directors or the funders) or, if necessary, it would make a public statement about UK Biobank's conduct and recommend that certain actions should or should not be taken.[40]

Yet, some might remain sceptical about the EGC's chances of playing an effective role as the keeper of UK Biobank's conscience. Anticipating such scepticism, the EGC continues:

> The power and impact of a public statement from an independent body such as the EGC should not be underestimated. Such a statement would have the possibility to undermine the trust participants place in the project, possibly resulting in withdrawals from the project or a serious down-turn in recruitment. Given that the success of UK Biobank depends on long-term participation, it is in the UK Biobank's interest to maintain and strengthen the trust relationship between it and the participants and for this relationship to remain healthy.[41]

This point is well made. If we isolate the EGC's lack of formal enforcement powers from the rest of the regulatory environment in which UK Biobank operates, we might well think that this represents a design weakness. However, once we reintroduce the key features of the regulatory environment, we will see that, in the background, there are a number of relevant legal provisions (for example, concerning the privacy, confidentiality and data protection rights of

---

[37] For a helpful discussion of a range of access issues, together with some common responses, see S. Fortin, S. Pathmasiri, R. Grintuch and M. Deschênes, '"Access Arrangements" for Biobanks: A Fine Line between Facilitating and Hindering Collaboration', *Public Health Genomics*, 14 (2011), 104.

[38] UK Biobank EGC, *Review 2008*.

[39] See, e.g., Susan M. C. Gibbons, 'Governance of Population Genetic Databases: A Comparative Analysis of Legal Regulation in Estonia, Iceland, Sweden and the UK', in Matti Häyry, Ruth Chadwick, Vilhjálmur Árnason and Gardar Árnason (eds.), *The Ethics and Governance of Human Genetic Databases* (Cambridge: Cambridge University Press, 2007), 132.

[40] UK Biobank EGC, *Review 2008*, at 4.   [41] *Ibid.*

participants, as well as their contractual, tortious and proprietary entitlements) that reinforce the EGC's mandate to oversee the proper conduct of the facility. Moreover, as the EGC itself emphasises, so long as UK Biobank relies on the cooperation of participants (who need to be recontacted from time to time), the regulatory environment presents both ethical and prudential reasons for going about the biobanking business in the right kind of way.

That said, the jury is still out on whether the regulatory environment for the operation of UK Biobank is, as Susan Gibbons has argued, 'a disorganized, fragmented, confusing array of overlapping, potentially relevant but also potentially inconsistent statutory and common law rules, decisions and non-binding guidelines',[42] or a clever instantiation of a trust model of governance. At all events, if the regulatory framework proves effective by virtue of its particular mix of background law together with foreground pressure from the EGC, the funders and participants, this mix featuring both moral and prudential reasons, then it might be treated as an exemplar for 'smart' or 'responsive' regulation.

To follow up this idea briefly, the modern view is that smart or responsive regulation presupposes that regulators become more imaginative, breaking the deadlock between those who advocate more regulation and those who advocate less, that they abandon any idea that 'one regulatory size fits all', that they develop a sensitivity to the differing motivations and attitudes of regulatees, and that they recognise the limits of single instrument approaches.[43] Thus, it needs to be appreciated that traditional command and control interventions are not always an effective form of response. Having taken this first step towards an intelligent approach, the next step is for regulators to be aware of the range of regulatory instruments and the importance of putting in place an optimal mix. Hence, writing in relation to environmental protection, Neil Gunningham and Peter Grabosky argue that single-instrument 'approaches are misguided, because all instruments have strengths and weaknesses; and because none are sufficiently flexible and resilient to be able to successfully address all ... problems in all contexts'.[44] Instead, Gunningham and Grabosky maintain that 'a better strategy will seek to harness the strengths of individual mechanisms while compensating for their weaknesses by the use of additional and complementary instruments. That is ... that in the large majority of circumstances (though certainly not all), a mix of instruments is required, tailored to specific policy goals.'[45]

However, the idea that regulation will be effective if only regulators are smarter in selecting and combining their instruments falls a long way short of

---

[42] Gibbons, 'Governance', at 134.
[43] Generally, see Neil Gunningham and Peter Grabosky, *Smart Regulation* (Oxford: Clarendon Press, 1998); and Ian Ayres and John Braithwaite, *Responsive Regulation* (Oxford: Oxford University Press, 1992).
[44] Gunningham and Grabosky, *Smart Regulation*, at 14.
[45] *Ibid.*, at 14–15.

what our regulatory intelligence already tells us. For example, more recently, Robert Baldwin and Julia Black, conclude:[46]

> Regulation is really responsive when it knows its regulatees and its institutional environments, when it is capable of deploying different and new regulatory logics coherently, when it is performance sensitive and when it grasps what its shifting challenges are.

While, *other things being equal*, a smart selection will deliver a more effective intervention than a single-instrument approach, there are many other factors – not least, the rapid development and application of new technologies, with their socially disruptive effects – to hold steady under the *ceteris paribus* clause.[47]

(b) eBay

At its inception, eBay was perceived by its founder, Pierre Omidyar, as no more than a local 'find and buy' site. It was a facility for the Eagle Bay community who could be expected to deal with one another in a decent and proper way. It was social pressure rather than the law of contract that channelled parties towards fair dealing. Thus, when Omidyar introduced the 'Feedback Forum' in February 1996, he posted a message applauding the honesty of users and encouraging the eBay community to use the feedback (reputational) system to name and chase out the few dishonest or deceptive dealers. Omidyar concluded his message by enjoining users to deal with others in the spirit of the golden rule (in other words, to deal with others in the way that you would have them deal with you).

Sadly, with the rapid growth of eBay, its users were no longer tied to the local Bay community and it became a locus for online fraud. This was a cue for the utilisation of the criminal law (and cooperation with the FBI), contract law only assuming real significance when the (limited) scope of eBay's liability to its users needed to be formalised. However, it would be rash to assume from this that e-commerce can always flourish without the background support of the law of contract. As Jack Goldsmith and Tim Wu[48] say in relation to the eBay experience:

> [W]hat would eBay look like in the absence of government-enforced contract law? One might think, based on the Feedback Forum ... that eBay could continue to run much of its ordinary business. In the absence of law, though, eBay would need something to make up the difference that the legal threat now provides. It is

---

[46] Robert Baldwin and Julia Black, 'Really Responsive Regulation', *Modern Law Review*, 71 (2008), 59, at 94.

[47] Compare Graeme Laurie, 'Reflexive Governance in Biobanking: On the Value of Policy Led Approaches and the Need to Recognise the Limits of Law', *Human Genetics* (2011) DOI 10.1007/s00439–011–1066-x.

[48] Jack Goldsmith and Tim Wu, *Who Controls the Internet?* (Oxford: Oxford University Press, 2006).

true that eBay itself might possibly provide greater security for buyers and sellers. And eBay might guarantee that *it* would make sure that the contracts would be honoured. But ... the result wouldn't be eBay as we know it, but rather some very different business – and a much more expensive and less popular business. What has made eBay successful and profitable since day one is its hands-off, self-executing, low-cost nature. That, in turn, depends on a robust system of community norms and, also, underneath that community, the rule of law and government coercion.[49]

In other words, if the benefits and efficiencies of online trading are to be fully realised, we probably need law (both criminal law and contract law) in the regulatory mix; but we constantly need to remind ourselves that what we are after is not just this or that bit of law but an overall regulatory environment that best supports e-commerce.

Although the significance of community pressure declined somewhat with the growth of eBay, it can still have occasional regulatory effect. For example, in June 2005, there was a rapid community reaction when tickets for the Live 8 concert were offered for sale on eBay. The sellers, who had been lucky in obtaining the tickets via a lottery allocation, had not paid for them and the indications were that a pair of tickets would fetch as much as £1,000. Bob Geldof, the organiser of the concert, was damning in his criticism of such entrepreneurialism; but the initial reaction from the eBay management team was that it respected the right of individuals to sell and buy as they wished. Andrew Murray takes up the story:[50]

> [a]n open dispute between Geldof, eBay members and eBay could be followed by anyone accessing the eBay.co.uk website. While Geldof threatened legal action and generally blustered to the press about the moral corruption of all those involved, a far more concerted campaign began. A group of eBay members formed themselves into a small group, calling themselves 'tickettoutscum'. The group was organised through listings on the eBay.co.uk site and quickly set out to wreck the sale of Live 8 tickets by making hoax bids on all Live 8 ticket sales ... While tickettoutscum was taking direct action against the listings, the wider eBay community was making itself heard. Both through direct emails to eBay.co.uk, and through postings on eBay message fora ... many among the community expressed a strong dissatisfaction with eBay's approach to the problem ... [D]iscussion fora buzzed with debate between the majority of eBay members who saw the sale as immoral and damaging to eBay's reputation and a vocal and vociferous minority who argued that the tickets should be treated as similar to any other goods, and who drew comparisons with charity wristbands, which are freely on sale on the eBay co.uk. site.

The eBay management team responded by doing a U-turn, the managing director of eBay (UK) Ltd announcing that, even though there was no illegality involved in selling the tickets, the users' community had clearly signalled its

---

[49] *Ibid.*, at 139.   [50] Murray, *Regulation*, at 155–6.

disapproval; accordingly, all Live 8 ticket listings would be removed from the site. Murray concludes:[51]

> The community had spoken, and the eBay team had been forced to take action. What is perhaps most important about this tale is that it was not the actions of Bob Geldof, or the response of the media which forced the change, although no doubt eBay.co.uk was concerned about its public image. Neither was it the direct action of the tickettoutscum group which caused this change in policy; it was the concerns and complaints from the wider eBay community. Throughout, eBay handled the issue with perfect balance, and the ultimate decision it appears rested with the community.

If this seems a somewhat surprising story, what could be more surprising than our third example of a regulatory environment, that of *Wikipedia*?

(c) *Wikipedia*

Wikipedia, the free online encyclopaedia, is one of the most consulted of websites, receiving hundreds of millions of visits each month. Of course, like any encyclopaedia, *Wikipedia*'s content might not be perfectly accurate; even expert editors can make mistakes. However, for the most part, the distinctive characteristic of *Wikipedia* is that it dispenses with experts and simply leaves it to individuals to make their edits and entries. By removing the usual obstacles to adding copy, *Wikipedia* was able to assume encyclopaedic proportions in a relatively short time; but, by the same token, it opened itself to vandalism and abuse. Famously, for example, *Wikipedia* was relied on to settle a difference between the then UK Prime Minister, Gordon Brown, and the leader of the Opposition, David Cameron, as to the lifespan of the artist Titian. Although the *Wikipedia* entry, which was revised shortly after the difference arose, seemingly vindicated the view of the latter, it was covered with suspicion when the change was traced to an IP address at Conservative Central Office.[52] Nevertheless, the rise and the routine reliance on *Wikipedia* is remarkable and it belies the apparently rule-free regulatory environment in which it was conceived and constructed. What can we learn from this story?

According to Jonathan Zittrain, the regulatory environment in which *Wikipedia* was developed and now operates provides some important clues as to how we might encourage creativity (generativity) without it descending into chaos.[53] He starts by reminding readers about the unexpected success that was experienced in the Dutch city of Drachten when traffic signs, parking meters and parking spaces were removed. The sign-free (*verkeersbordvrij*) environment, far from inducing dangerous and disorderly driving, generated

---

[51] *Ibid.*, at 156–7.

[52] See Tim Glanfield, 'Shifting sands offer poor foundation for a dependable truth' *The Times*, 25 November 2009, 7.

[53] Jonathan Zittrain, *The Future of the Internet* (London: Penguin Books, 2008).

responsible and communicative conduct on the part of motorists, cyclists and pedestrians. What general regulatory lessons might we draw from this? According to Zittrain:[54]

> More generally, order may remain when people see themselves as part of a social system, a group of people – more than utter strangers but less than friends – with some overlap in outlook and goals. Whatever counts as a satisfying explanation, we see that sometimes the absence of law has not resulted in the absence of order. Under the right circumstances, people will behave charitably toward one another in the comparative absence or enforcement of rules that would otherwise compel that charity.
>
> In modern cyberspace, an absence of rules (or at least an enforcement) has led to both a generative blossoming and to a new round of challenges at multiple layers. If the Internet and its users experience a crisis of abuse … it will be tempting to approach such challenges as ones of law and jurisdiction. This rule-and-sanction approach frames the project of cyberlaw by asking how public authorities can find and restrain those it deems to be bad actors online …
>
> The [*verkeersbordvrij*] experiment highlights a different approach, one potentially as powerful as traditional rule and sanction … When people can come to take the welfare of one another seriously and possess the tools to readily assist and limit each other, even the most precise and well-enforced rule from a traditional public source may be less effective than that uncompelled goodwill. Such an approach reframes the project of cyberlaw to ask: What are the technical tools and social structures that inspire people to act humanely online? How might they be available to help restrain the damage that malevolent outliers can wreak?

On the face of it, *Wikipedia*, like the streets without traffic signs, sounds like an unlikely project. At least the people of Drachten had some prior experience of traffic movements regulated by signs; but, in the case of *Wikipedia*, there had been nothing like this.

Zittrain argues that the regulatory environment in which *Wikipedia* began had three key attributes. First, akin to *verkeersbordvrij*, there were few rules – the Wiki community simply had a licence to author and edit pages; but there was a technical (back)tracking feature that limited the damage that could be occasioned by mistaken, malicious, or offensive editing. Second, there was a page for discussion and debate alongside each main page. Where a main page entry was suspect, the absence of any explanation on the discussion page would invite caution. Moreover, the availability of the discussion pages helped new users to graduate from simply reading entries 'to making changes and to understanding that there was a group of people interested in the page on which changes were made and whom could be engaged in conversation before, during, and after editing the page'.[55] The third feature was that the core of initial editors shared a common ethos (prioritising the writing of articles rather than deciding who was or was not qualified or authorised to write) as well as some expertise.

---

[54] *Ibid.*, at 129.   [55] *Ibid.*, at 134.

Chiming in with this analysis, Saul Levmore argues that *Wikipedia* involves an elaborate mix of identifiability (those who contribute copy do not remain anonymous) coupled with central control.[56] Thus:

> [*Wikipedia*] thrives through a combination of informed posts, or entries, followed by numerous modifications, or comments, made by many readers ... The product reflects both the wisdom of crowds as well as the hard work of more skilled labor than a conventional encyclopedia can possibly employ ... Wikipedia does attract vandals and ideologues, but their marks can be expunged by subsequent improvers, some of whom seem to take responsibility for selected topics. The good soldiers are remarkably vigilant. Apparently, juvenile or noisy posts are commonly excised on weekends, suggesting that much of the 'central control' is accomplished by volunteers, numbering perhaps 75,000, who are otherwise occupied on workdays. But there is more than a dedicated workforce behind the site's success. Even when it was more hospitable to vandals or juveniles, Wikipedia flourished; it has improved by eliminating anonymity in ingenious fashion.[57]

With the growth of Wiki, it seems that it is the Wiki community, like the eBay community, that has set the standard (such as the rule against individuals creating or editing articles about themselves) as well as keeping things in check. As Zittrain summarises it:

> Wikipedia's generativity at the content level – soliciting uncoordinated content from tens of thousands of people – provides the basis for [vulnerability] now that it is so successful. It has weathered the most obvious perils well. Vandals might be annoying but they are kept in check with a critical mass of Wikipedians who keep an eye on articles and quickly revert those that are mangled. Some Wikipedians even appear to enjoy this duty, declaring membership in the informal Counter-Vandalism Unit and, if dealing with vandalism tied to fraud, perhaps earning the Defender of the Wiki Barnstar. Still others have written scripts that detect the most obvious cases of vandalism and automatically fix them. And there remains the option of locking those pages that consistently attract trouble from edits by new or anonymous users.[58]

In every sense, *Wikipedia* and its governance is a work in progress, the success of which 'is attributable to a messy combination of constantly updated technical tools and social conventions ... Together these tools and conventions facilitate a notion of "netizenship": belonging to an Internet project that includes other people, rather than relating to the Internet as a deterministic information location and transmission tool or as a cash-and-carry service offered by a separate vendor responsible for its content.'[59] In short, what makes Wiki tick is the existence of community standards 'that encourage contributors to do the right thing rather than the required thing or the profitable thing.'[60]

---

[56] Saul Levmore, 'The Internet's Anonymity Problem', in Saul Levmore and Martha C. Nussbaum (eds.), *The Offensive Internet* (Cambridge, MA: Harvard University Press, 2010).

[57] *Ibid.*, at 59.   [58] Zittrain, *Future of the Internet*, at 137–8.

[59] *Ibid.*, at 142.   [60] *Ibid.*, at 195.

4 Closing thoughts

Speaking in the House of Lords in April 2006, Baroness Susan Greenfield remarked that 'the 21st century is offering society an unprecedented raft of challenges'.[61] The reason for this is that:

> [a]ll at once science is now delivering a diverse range of information technology, nanotechnology and biotechnology, with a speed and convergence that we could never have predicted even a decade ago.[62]

To this list of rapidly emerging technologies, Baroness Greenfield – indeed, of all people, the Baroness with her background in the neurosciences – might have added neurotechnology. The Baroness might also have said that, viewing this constellation of modern technologies from a regulatory perspective, we can detect not only a raft of challenges but also a range of opportunities. From such a perspective, the new technologies represent both regulatory targets as well as regulatory tools.

In so far as these technologies are regulatory targets, it is important not only that the law, but the law in the context of a larger regulatory environment, is right – it will not do, for example, to expend a great deal of resource in crafting the details of a piece of data protection legislation, if the broader regulatory environment is not conducive to compliance. In our opening chapter, we indicated that the regulatory environment will not be right unless it meets a number of concerns about the safety, reliability and ethical acceptability of these novel technologies; and, in this present chapter, we have highlighted the significance of the non-legal elements (community standards, technical design features, and the like) that, together with the formal legal elements, contribute towards a functional regulatory environment. With these preparatory remarks, we can now proceed to look more closely at these criteria that define the regulatory challenge presented by the technologies of the twenty-first century.

---

[61] Hansard, 20 April 2006, col. 1219.   [62] *Ibid.*

3

Four key regulatory challenges

1 Introduction

If law and technology are to work together to improve the basic conditions of human social existence – for example, to improve the conditions of public health and security, to ensure an adequate, safe and stable supply of food and water, to safeguard the physical environment, and so on – this presupposes a regulatory environment that supports the development, application and exploitation of technologies that will contribute to such an overarching purpose, an environment properly geared for risk management and benefit sharing.[1]

Relative to such a project, regulators are liable to be called to account if:

- they fail to take sensible precautionary measures relative to the risks presented by emerging technologies;
- the purposes or objectives that they are pursuing (or, the manner and means by which they pursue those objectives) are judged to be illegitimate;
- their interventions are ineffective and not fully fit for purpose; or
- they have failed to make an initial targeted and sustainable regulatory connection; or, where regulation has become disconnected, they have failed to make an appropriate reconnection.

To create the right kind of regulatory environment for the promotion and application of beneficial technologies, regulators need to address each of these challenges. However, the tec hnologies themselves might also be integrated into the environment as regulatory instruments. Where this is the focus of concern, regulators are called to account, not so much for their failure to create the right kind of environment for new technologies, but for their over-reliance on technological tools.

In this chapter, we introduce each of the four criteria that are critical to any evaluation of the adequacy of a regulatory environment where emerging technologies are either the targets for regulators or the tools that they are utilising.

---

[1] Compare Hailemichael Teshome Demissie, 'Is Beneficent Regulation the New Better Regulation? Nano-Regulation in the Wake of the "New Better Regulation" Movement', *Law, Innovation and Technology*, 2 (2010), 115.

2 Regulatory prudence and precaution

In many cases, new technologies are something of an unknown quantity, inviting a degree of suspicion and mistrust. For example, some people fear that mobile phones present a risk to human health; or, that, where mobiles distract the attention of motorists, they might present a risk to human safety; or, that, if they are not disposed of properly, they can cause environmental damage. A similar account could be given of many technologies, old and new – they give rise to concerns about human health and safety as well as the integrity of the environment. Some communities will be more risk averse than others; and, in most communities, there will be a range of views as to an acceptable level of risk. Regulators might not be able to satisfy all views but they will be open to criticism if they do not take a suitably prudent approach.

In many cases, there will be a degree of uncertainty about just how risky a new technology is. For example, it is unclear whether nanoparticles in products such as cosmetics and sun screens present a risk to human health, just as it is unclear whether such particles might be environmentally damaging when they are introduced into waterways. Where there is no consensus among scientific experts, the community's judgements as to acceptable risk are necessarily more complex. How should regulators respond in such a context of uncertain risk?[2]

One view, most famously articulated in Principle 15 of the Rio Declaration (June 1992) holds that: 'Where there are threats of serious or irreversible damage [to the environment], lack of full scientific certainty should not be used as a reason for postponing such measures.' While one might argue that regulators should take no chances at all where there is no more than the merest hint of possibly serious or irreversible damage to the environment, it is not clear that it is sensible to generalise this precautionary approach. To return to the case of mobile phones, would we support regulators who took all phones out of circulation for fear that they might be injurious to human health? As Adam Burgess concludes in his study of precautionary responses to the perceived hazards presented by mobile phones and cellphone towers, there is a worrying tendency to create risk shadows and then commit large resources to chasing them – thus, 'In the elusive quest to establish a risk-free existence, our autonomy, intelligence, and capacity for change and enlightenment stand in danger of being compromised and diminished.'[3]

A knee-jerk precautionary response is also open to the criticism – a criticism very effectively mounted by Cass Sunstein[4] – that it fails to take into account the benefits that are forgone by imposing a prohibition or a moratorium. If

---

[2] For discussion, see Roger Brownsword, 'Regulating Nanotechnologies: A Matter of Some Uncertainty', *Politeia*, 25(94) (2009), 11–28.

[3] Adam Burgess, *Cellular Phones, Public Fears, and a Culture of Precaution* (Cambridge: Cambridge University Press, 2004), 281. But, the elusive quest continues: see, e.g., Geoffrey Lean, 'Wi-Fi: the backlash', *Independent on Sunday*, 15 July 2007, 14 (Haringey council resolving to adopt a precautionary approach to wi-fi technology in schools).

[4] Cass Sunstein, *Laws of Fear* (Cambridge: Cambridge University Press, 2005).

regulators were to prohibit the use of nanoparticles in cosmetics, this might be justified on a harm–benefit calculation (even in a context of uncertain risk); but, if the prohibition applied to nanomaterials that were key components in life-saving medical devices, the balance of arguments might look rather different. At all events, it is one thing for regulators to carry out a harm–benefit calculation and make their best prudential judgement and quite another for regulators mechanically to apply a precautionary prohibition.

To avoid any misunderstanding, it should be emphasised that the only calculation here is one of prudence – that is to say, one of acting in a way that is designed to serve our own interests (individually and collectively). Having weighed the prospective benefits against the feared harm to humans and the environment, we make a judgement about where our interests lie. We are not yet grappling with *ethical* concerns, where we only do the right thing when we give proper consideration to the legitimate interests of others (in the way, for example, that Mary Warnock introduces other-regarding considerations of harm and benefit). However, even where regulators are making purely prudential judgements, the fact that they often do so in a context of scientific disagreement and uncertainty, puts them on the horns of several dilemmas. In particular, should more weight be given to the *probability* of harm ensuing or to the *seriousness* of the harm? Which is the greater risk, a low probability of serious harm or a high probability of less serious harm? And, how are these calculations affected by the probability of the technology at issue generating a benefit where, once again, there is no simple arithmetic that accords a non-controversial weight to the *probability* and to the *nature of the benefit*? Needless to say, these are dilemmas that become all the more complex and acute when ethical concerns are added to the mix.

3 Regulatory legitimacy

Assuming that the authority of regulators is recognised as legitimate, we might ask (a) whether the right kind of procedures have been adopted before the determination of the regulatory position; (b) whether the regulatory position is legitimate; and (c) whether the means employed for the implementation of that regulatory position are legitimate.

(a) Procedural legitimacy

Regulators (particularly so, governmental regulators) are expected to operate in ways that are transparent and accountable and that involve appropriate measures for stakeholder and public participation. Hence, where a legislative framework is agreed for the application of a new technology, this will usually be preceded by public consultation, media debate, parliamentary debate, and so on. However, it is not always the case that the operative rules regulating the use of a technology – especially a technology in its embryonic stage – have been publicly debated and transparently agreed in this way. Quite possibly, all that we have are informal codes or guidelines that are self-regulatory coupled with fall-back general legal provisions such as those found in the criminal law and the law of torts. This, however, might not be thought to be adequate.[5]

Quite simply, as David Bazelon pointed out a long time ago, although '[s]cientists *are* uniquely competent to address scientific/factual issues', and although 'science *is* elitist', it does not follow that scientists have a special competence in relation to values; indeed, when it comes to value choices, 'the opinions of scientists are entitled to no greater weight than those of the rest of us'.[6] Hence, experts should advise on their best guess as to the nature and probability of the apprehended risks, but the public should be fully engaged in characterising which risks are material, which risks are acceptable and, where there are conflicting interests involved, which priorities should be set. Echoing Bazelon's thinking, Ronald Sandler and W. D. Kay (writing about the regulation of nanotechnologies) argue:[7]

> [S]cience and industry experts have an important role to play … They are well positioned to see what is possible, what is feasible, and what is required to achieve certain economic and technological ends. They thereby play a crucial informational role. But knowledge of what can and cannot be done, and of what is and is not required to do it, is quite different from knowledge of what ought and ought not to be done. What ends should be prioritised, how resources should be allocated in pursuit of those ends, and constraints on how those ends ought to be pursued are ethical and social questions to be addressed in the public sphere, not economic and technological ones to be worked out in boardrooms or laboratories … So while scientists and industry leaders may be 'elite' in their knowledge of the science and business of nanotechnology, this status does not imply that they are 'elite' with respect to the [social and ethical] issues associated with nanotechnology.[8]

These sentiments resonate with the idea that regulators need to engage their regulatees (*all* their regulatees) at an early stage. Even in the embryonic stages of technological development, public engagement needs to be inclusive.

However, even where the need for public participation is enthusiastically endorsed, even where regulators are committed to informed and inclusive public decision-making with regard to the development and application of new technologies, we should not jump to too many comfortable conclusions. As

[5] Compare Rainer Kattel, 'Genetic Databases and Governance', in Matti Häyry, Ruth Chadwick, Vilhjálmur Árnason and Gardar Árnason (eds.), *The Ethics and Governance of Genetic Databases* (Cambridge: Cambridge University Press, 2007), 236: 'Governance brings, perhaps paradoxically, the need for better government in order to resist the inherent dangers in the concept of governance: loss of governmental authority, legitimacy and responsibility' (*ibid.*, at 239).

[6] David L. Bazelon, 'Coping with Technology through the Legal Process', *Cornell Law Review*, 62 (1977), 817, 826–7.

[7] Ronald Sandler and W. D. Kay, 'The National Nanotechnology Initiative and the Social Good', *Journal of Law, Medicine and Ethics*, 34 (2006), 675.

[8] *Ibid.*, at 679.

Andy Stirling has put it, 'there can be no automatic presumption that [participatory processes] will necessarily be sufficient, or even always positive, in their effects'.[9] For one thing, participation will delay decision-making and absorb regulatory resource; and, of course, there is no guarantee that the process will generate a consensual outcome – in which event, regulators will have to hope that the legitimacy of the outcome is recognised by the minority on the basis that it at least had a fair hearing.[10]

Procedural legitimacy, we can surmise, is no soft option for regulators. Where the potential risks and benefits of emerging technologies are far from clear and settled, how is there to be a meaningful public debate? For example, if there were to be a public consultation in relation to emerging nanotechnologies or synthetic biology, where the risks are profoundly uncertain, how might a meaningful debate and decision be taken about the level of 'acceptable' risk? And, where emerging technologies provoke ethical concern, how can regulators ensure that there is a level playing field for public consultation (especially so in multicultural societies)?[11]

As an example of the limited product of public engagement where there is little lay familiarity with the science and where the scientists themselves are feeling their way, consider the public dialogue on synthetic biology that was conducted by the Royal Academy of Engineering.[12] Having found that awareness of synthetic biology (of both the terminology and the concept) in the UK was low and that there was some inconsistency in the answers given, it is suggested that participants (and, in general, members of the public) could be placed within one of four attitudinal types as follows:[13]

1 Those who may or may not have understood the science behind synthetic biology but explicitly decided that they did not need to understand the details and instead focused on the outputs and decided that the benefits outweighed the risks.

2 Those who were at least somewhat confident that synthetic biologists would be in control of their creations especially in controlled conditions, and consequently that the risk was very low. However, some had concerns over the consequences of an environmental release (accidental or intentional) and felt that the risk was too high.

3 Those that were more cautious and who needed more convincing that the outputs would be safe and wanted to see more testing before products were released to the market.

---

[9] Andy Stirling, '"Opening Up" and "Closing Down": Power, Participation, and Pluralism in the Social Appraisal of Technology', *Science, Technology, and Human Values*, 33 (2008), 262, at 286.

[10] Compare Julia Black, 'Regulation as Facilitation: Negotiating the Genetic Revolution', in Roger Brownsword, W. R. Cornish and Margaret Llewelyn (eds.), *Law and Human Genetics: Regulating a Revolution* (Oxford: Hart, 1998), 49.

[11] Compare James Tully, *Strange Multiplicity* (Cambridge: Cambridge University Press, 1995).

[12] Royal Academy of Engineering, *Synthetic Biology: Public Dialogue on Synthetic Biology* (London, 2009).

[13] *Ibid.*, at 39.

4 Lastly, there was a group who struggled to understand synthetic biology, appearing at some points to have grasped it and at others not to have done so. This group's attitude fluctuated and was influenced in the same direction as the general 'gist' of the discussions, although on balance did seem to be more positive than negative.

Given such an honest assessment of the very different characteristics of people, one wonders how the public can be adequately engaged. This is a question to which we will return in Chapter 5.

(b) The legitimacy of regulatory purposes and standards

One of the first questions that we should ask about any particular regulatory environment is whether it meets whatever standards of legitimacy we might apply. We can pose this question in relation to the environment as a whole or in relation to a particular part or parts of it (whether a particular standard or the application of that standard in a particular case, such as the Harvard Oncomouse application that we discussed in our opening chapter). More importantly, in posing this question, we can adopt a variety of more or less demanding standards of legitimacy.

The least demanding standard is one that simply insists that regulators act within their agreed competences. That is, do regulators have the legal power or authorisation to act in a particular way? For example, the European Commission might like to take greater control over the advertising of tobacco, but it is doubtful that it has the competence to act in this way.[14] However, we are interested in the kind of tests that we saw Mary Warnock highlighting in a previous chapter.[15] Are the purposes adopted by regulators ethically defensible? Are the standards set ethically appropriate? Have regulators transgressed any of the ethical limits set by the community; and how, for that matter, do they know what those limits are?

Different ethical constituencies will make their own particular demands on regulators. In modern pluralistic societies, the dilemma for regulators is that they have to answer to many constituencies, each with their own criterion of right action, each with their own view of what regulators should be doing if they are to do the right thing. For example, if we are utilitarians, we will expect regulators to select the option that comes out best in terms of net utility (benefits) over disutility (harm); while, if we demand respect for human rights or human dignity, there are likely to be some red lines that we insist should not be crossed. Is there any possibility of finding some shared ethical principles in this plurality of views?

---

[14] See Case C-376/98 *Germany* v. *Council*, where the European Court of Justice annulled a directive which banned the advertisement and sponsorship of tobacco.

[15] See p. 8 above.

Responding to the concern that the research, development and exploitation of technologies should be ethically acceptable, the International Bioethics Committee (IBC) of UNESCO has been in the vanguard of attempts to forge a worldwide bioethical consensus, publishing three major instruments, namely: the Universal Declaration on the Human Genome and Human Rights in 1997, the International Declaration on Human Genetic Data in 2003 and most significantly – or, at any rate, certainly most ambitiously – the Universal Declaration on Bioethics and Human Rights in 2005.[16] Although the latest of these Declarations is addressed specifically to 'ethical issues related to medicine, life sciences and associated technologies',[17] it presents us with a starting point for thinking about the legitimacy not only of regulation directed at biotechnology but also of the regulation of neurotechnology and nanotechnology (at any rate, in its biomedical applications).

The UNESCO Universal Declaration on Bioethics and Human Rights 2005

Article 1 – Scope

1. This Declaration addresses ethical issues related to medicine, life sciences and associated technologies as applied to human beings, taking into account their social, legal and environmental dimensions.
2. This Declaration is addressed to States. As appropriate and relevant, it also provides guidance to decisions or practices of individuals, groups, communities, institutions and corporations, public and private.

Article 2 – Aims

The aims of this Declaration are:

(a) to provide a universal framework of principles and procedures to guide States in the formulation of their legislation, policies or other instruments in the field of bioethics;

(b) to guide the actions of individuals, groups, communities, institutions and corporations, public and private;

(c) to promote respect for human dignity and protect human rights, by ensuring respect for the life of human beings, and fundamental freedoms, consistent with international human rights law;

---

[16] For commentary and analysis, see, Henk A. M. J. ten Have and Michèle S. Jean (eds.), *The UNESCO Universal Declaration on Bioethics and Human Rights* (Paris: UNESCO, 2009); Abdulqawi A. Yusuf, 'UNESCO Standard-Setting Activities on Bioethics: Speak Softly and Carry a Big Stick', in Francesco Francioni (ed.), *Biotechnologies and International Human Rights* (Oxford: Hart, 2007), 85; and, for a valuable analysis that draws out the organising values of both Universal Declarations (1997 and 2005), see Shawn H. E. Harmon, 'Ethical Rhetoric: Genomics and the Moral Content of UNESCO's "Universal" Declarations', *Journal of Medical Ethics*, 34(11) (2008), e24. Recognising that the notion of human dignity is pervasively implicated in these Declarations, Harmon suggests that the core organising values (or nodes) are: autonomy, solidarity, equality, sanctity of life and democracy.

[17] UNESCO *Universal Declaration on Bioethics and Human Rights* (adopted by acclamation on 19 October 2005 by the 33rd session of the General Conference), Article 1.

(d) to recognize the importance of freedom of scientific research and the benefits derived from scientific and technological developments, while stressing the need for such research and developments to occur within the framework of ethical principles set out in this Declaration and to respect human dignity, human rights and fundamental freedoms;

(e) to foster multidisciplinary and pluralistic dialogue about bioethical issues between all stakeholders and within society as a whole;

(f) to promote equitable access to medical, scientific and technological developments as well as the greatest possible flow and the rapid sharing of knowledge concerning those developments and the sharing of benefits, with particular attention to the needs of developing countries;

(g) to safeguard and promote the interests of the present and future generations;

(h) to underline the importance of biodiversity and its conservation as a common concern of humankind.

Principles

Within the scope of this Declaration, in decisions or practices taken or carried out by those to whom it is addressed, the following principles are to be respected.

Article 3 – Human dignity and human rights

1. Human dignity, human rights and fundamental freedoms are to be fully respected.
2. The interests and welfare of the individual should have priority over the sole interest of science or society.

Article 4 – Benefit and harm

In applying and advancing scientific knowledge, medical practice and associated technologies, direct and indirect benefits to patients, research participants and other affected individuals should be maximized and any possible harm to such individuals should be minimized.

Article 5 – Autonomy and individual responsibility

The autonomy of persons to make decisions, while taking responsibility for those decisions and respecting the autonomy of others, is to be respected. For persons who are not capable of exercising autonomy, special measures are to be taken to protect their rights and interests.

Article 6 – Consent

1. Any preventive, diagnostic and therapeutic medical intervention is only to be carried out with the prior, free and informed consent of the person concerned, based on adequate information. The consent should, where appropriate, be express and may be withdrawn by the person concerned at any time and for any reason without disadvantage or prejudice.
2. Scientific research should only be carried out with the prior, free, express and informed consent of the person concerned. The information should be

adequate, provided in a comprehensible form and should include modalities for withdrawal of consent. Consent may be withdrawn by the person concerned at any time and for any reason without any disadvantage or prejudice. Exceptions to this principle should be made only in accordance with ethical and legal standards adopted by States, consistent with the principles and provisions set out in this Declaration, in particular in Article 27 and international human rights law.

3. In appropriate cases of research carried out on a group of persons or a community, additional agreement of the legal representatives of the group or community concerned may be sought. In no case should a collective community agreement or the consent of a community leader or other authority substitute for an individual's informed consent.

Article 7 – Persons without the capacity to consent

In accordance with domestic law, special protection is to be given to persons who do not have the capacity to consent:

(a) authorization for research and medical practice should be obtained in accordance with the best interest of the person concerned and in accordance with domestic law. However, the person concerned should be involved to the greatest extent possible in the decision-making process of consent, as well as that of withdrawing consent;

(b) research should only be carried out for his or her direct health benefit, subject to the authorization and the protective conditions prescribed by law, and if there is no research alternative of comparable effectiveness with research participants able to consent. Research which does not have potential direct health benefit should only be undertaken by way of exception, with the utmost restraint, exposing the person only to a minimal risk and minimal burden and, if the research is expected to contribute to the health benefit of other persons in the same category, subject to the conditions prescribed by law and compatible with the protection of the individual's human rights. Refusal of such persons to take part in research should be respected.

Article 8 – Respect for human vulnerability and personal integrity

In applying and advancing scientific knowledge, medical practice and associated technologies, human vulnerability should be taken into account. Individuals and groups of special vulnerability should be protected and the personal integrity of such individuals respected.

Article 9 – Privacy and confidentiality

The privacy of the persons concerned and the confidentiality of their personal information should be respected. To the greatest extent possible, such information should not be used or disclosed for purposes other than those for which it was collected or consented to, consistent with international law, in particular international human rights law.

Article 10 – Equality, justice and equity

The fundamental equality of all human beings in dignity and rights is to be respected so that they are treated justly and equitably.

Article 11 – Non-discrimination and non-stigmatization

No individual or group should be discriminated against or stigmatized on any grounds, in violation of human dignity, human rights and fundamental freedoms.

Article 12 – Respect for cultural diversity and pluralism

The importance of cultural diversity and pluralism should be given due regard. However, such considerations are not to be invoked to infringe upon human dignity, human rights and fundamental freedoms, nor upon the principles set out in this Declaration, nor to limit their scope.

Article 13 – Solidarity and cooperation

Solidarity among human beings and international cooperation towards that end are to be encouraged.

Article 14 – Social responsibility and health

1. The promotion of health and social development for their people is a central purpose of governments that all sectors of society share.
2. Taking into account that the enjoyment of the highest attainable standard of health is one of the fundamental rights of every human being without distinction of race, religion, political belief, economic or social condition, progress in science and technology should advance:
   (a) access to quality health care and essential medicines, especially for the health of women and children, because health is essential to life itself and must be considered to be a social and human good;
   (b) access to adequate nutrition and water;
   (c) improvement of living conditions and the environment;
   (d) elimination of the marginalization and the exclusion of persons on the basis of any grounds;
   (e) reduction of poverty and illiteracy.

Article 15 – Sharing of benefits

1. Benefits resulting from any scientific research and its applications should be shared with society as a whole and within the international community, in particular with developing countries. In giving effect to this principle, benefits may take any of the following forms:
   (a) special and sustainable assistance to, and acknowledgement of, the persons and groups that have taken part in the research;
   (b) access to quality health care;
   (c) provision of new diagnostic and therapeutic modalities or products stemming from research;
   (d) support for health services;

(e) access to scientific and technological knowledge;
(f) capacity-building facilities for research purposes;
(g) other forms of benefit consistent with the principles set out in this Declaration.

2. Benefits should not constitute improper inducements to participate in research.

Article 16 – Protecting future generations

The impact of life sciences on future generations, including on their genetic constitution, should be given due regard.

Article 17 – Protection of the environment, the biosphere and biodiversity

Due regard is to be given to the interconnection between human beings and other forms of life, to the importance of appropriate access and utilization of biological and genetic resources, to respect for traditional knowledge and to the role of human beings in the protection of the environment, the biosphere and biodiversity.

Application of the principles

Article 18 – Decision-making and addressing bioethical issues

1. Professionalism, honesty, integrity and transparency in decision-making should be promoted, in particular declarations of all conflicts of interest and appropriate sharing of knowledge. Every endeavour should be made to use the best available scientific knowledge and methodology in addressing and periodically reviewing bioethical issues.
2. Persons and professionals concerned and society as a whole should be engaged in dialogue on a regular basis.
3. Opportunities for informed pluralistic public debate, seeking the expression of all relevant opinions, should be promoted.

Article 19 – Ethics committees

Independent, multidisciplinary and pluralist ethics committees should be established, promoted and supported at the appropriate level in order to:

(a) assess the relevant ethical, legal, scientific and social issues related to research projects involving human beings;
(b) provide advice on ethical problems in clinical settings;
(c) assess scientific and technological developments, formulate recommendations and contribute to the preparation of guidelines on issues within the scope of this Declaration;
(d) foster debate, education and public awareness of, and engagement in, bioethics.

Article 20 – Risk assessment and management

Appropriate assessment and adequate management of risk related to medicine, life sciences and associated technologies should be promoted.

Article 21 – Transnational practices

1. States, public and private institutions, and professionals associated with transnational activities should endeavour to ensure that any activity within the scope of this Declaration, undertaken, funded or otherwise pursued in whole or in part in different States, is consistent with the principles set out in this Declaration.
2. When research is undertaken or otherwise pursued in one or more States (the host State(s)) and funded by a source in another State, such research should be the object of an appropriate level of ethical review in the host State(s) and the State in which the funder is located. This review should be based on ethical and legal standards that are consistent with the principles set out in this Declaration.
3. Transnational health research should be responsive to the needs of host countries, and the importance of research contributing to the alleviation of urgent global health problems should be recognized.
4. When negotiating a research agreement, terms for collaboration and agreement on the benefits of research should be established with equal participation by those party to the negotiation.
5. States should take appropriate measures, both at the national and international levels, to combat bioterrorism and illicit traffic in organs, tissues, samples, genetic resources and genetic-related materials.

Promotion of the Declaration

Article 22 – Role of States

1. States should take all appropriate measures, whether of a legislative, administrative or other character, to give effect to the principles set out in this Declaration in accordance with international human rights law. Such measures should be supported by action in the spheres of education, training and public information.
2. States should encourage the establishment of independent, multidisciplinary and pluralist ethics committees, as set out in Article 19.

Article 23 – Bioethics education, training and information

1. In order to promote the principles set out in this Declaration and to achieve a better understanding of the ethical implications of scientific and technological developments, in particular for young people, States should endeavour to foster bioethics education and training at all levels as well as to encourage information and knowledge dissemination programmes about bioethics.
2. States should encourage the participation of international and regional intergovernmental organizations and international, regional and national non governmental organizations in this endeavour.

Article 24 – International cooperation

1. States should foster international dissemination of scientific information and encourage the free flow and sharing of scientific and technological knowledge.

2. Within the framework of international cooperation, States should promote cultural and scientific cooperation and enter into bilateral and multilateral agreements enabling developing countries to build up their capacity to participate in generating and sharing scientific knowledge, the related know-how and the benefits thereof.
3. States should respect and promote solidarity between and among States, as well as individuals, families, groups and communities, with special regard for those rendered vulnerable by disease or disability or other personal, societal or environmental conditions and those with the most limited resources.

Article 25 – Follow-up action by UNESCO

1. UNESCO shall promote and disseminate the principles set out in this Declaration. In doing so, UNESCO should seek the help and assistance of the Intergovernmental Bioethics Committee (IGBC) and the International Bioethics Committee (IBC).
2. UNESCO shall reaffirm its commitment to dealing with bioethics and to promoting collaboration between IGBC and IBC.

Final provisions

Article 26 – Interrelation and complementarity of the principles

This Declaration is to be understood as a whole and the principles are to be understood as complementary and interrelated. Each principle is to be considered in the context of the other principles, as appropriate and relevant in the circumstances.

Article 27 – Limitations on the application of the principles

If the application of the principles of this Declaration is to be limited, it should be by law, including laws in the interests of public safety, for the investigation, detection and prosecution of criminal offences, for the protection of public health or for the protection of the rights and freedoms of others. Any such law needs to be consistent with international human rights law.

Article 28 – Denial of acts contrary to human rights, fundamental freedoms and human dignity

Nothing in this Declaration may be interpreted as implying for any State, group or person any claim to engage in any activity or to perform any act contrary to human rights, fundamental freedoms and human dignity.

Many will view the Declaration as a heroic attempt to find common ground that transcends the differences of ethical pluralism. Even if this strategy does not quite succeed, might regulators appeal to the integrity of the process itself as a reason for treating the outcome as legitimate? Championing such an approach, when Professor Amy Gutmann was appointed to chair the (US) Presidential Commission for the Study of Bioethical Issues (and first tasked to report on the implications of synthetic biology), she declared her intention to promote informed debate in the spirit of deliberative democracy.[18] According to Professor Gutmann, deliberative democracy, in contrast to 'sound-bite democracy', is about engaging the public:

> Deliberative democracy is about ... listening to competing points of view, considering opposing arguments and coming to a decision that ideally finds common ground – or at least respects competing points of view.[19]

On the face of it, this is a promising strategy; for deliberative democracy, as elaborated by Professor Gutmann,[20] decrees that all freely expressed views are to be heard and that, so long as they are not wholly unreasonable, they are to be accorded equal consideration. At the end of the process, differences should have been minimised and regulators should be in a position to act on reasons that are at least acceptable to all persons who are committed to fair terms for political and social cooperation. To be sure, this does not quite guarantee that the eventual outcome will attract everyone's vote; but, because the decision in question will be supported by acceptable reasons, reasonable people should respect it. Moreover, it is characteristic of Professor Gutmann's version of deliberative democracy that debates can be reopened; decisions are, thus, reviewable, which means that the time might still come for today's dissenting views. In this way, the life sciences can proceed and pluralistic societies can settle their differences in a civilised way.

Yet, is it so simple? Where the problem is one of prudential pluralism, deliberative democracy seems to be an appropriate response. However, where we are dealing with ethical pluralism, matters are less straightforward. We should distinguish between 'closed' and 'open' types of ethical pluralism.[21] In the case of the former, fundamental ethical principles are agreed and it is in the interpretation and application of those principles that we encounter different views. In the latter, the differences reach back to the baseline principles. While deliberative democracy is an appropriate response to closed ethical pluralism, it is much less clear that it can handle open ethical pluralism in a satisfactory way. Sometimes, in conditions of open ethical pluralism, positions will converge such that parties can sign up to an agreed regulatory position (even though the underlying reasons for agreement are varied); here, we have the basis for a workable accommodation of the competing ethical views. However, where there is no such convergence, we seem to reach the limits of deliberative democracy and it is unclear how regulators are to enjoin respect for the position that is taken.[22]

---

[18] See, Meredith Wadman, 'Bioethics Gets an Airing', *Nature* (7 July 2010) (available online at www.nature.com/news/2010/070710/full/news.2010.340.html).

[19] *Ibid.*

[20] See Amy Gutmann and Dennis Thompson, *Why Deliberative Democracy?* (Princeton: Princeton University Press, 2004).

[21] See Roger Brownsword, 'Framers and Problematisers: Getting to Grips with Global Governance', *Transnational Legal Theory*, 1 (2010), 287.

[22] See, further, Roger Brownsword, 'Regulating the Life Sciences, Pluralism, and the Limits of Deliberative Democracy', *Singapore Academy Law Journal* (2010), 801.

(c) The legitimacy of the regulatory means

As we pointed out in Chapter 2, much attention has been given to whether and how regulators can make smart choices, selecting the optimal mix of regulatory instruments. The legitimacy test, however, is not about whether the selected instruments will be effective. The test is one of whether the instruments are legitimate. Where regulators rely on law, peer pressure, market signals and the like, there might well be (case-specific) questions about the acceptability of the particular regulatory mode employed. For example, if a regulator, in pursuit of public health purposes, passes a law that requires commuters to walk or to bike to their nearest railway station, rather than driving their cars there or taking the bus, some might challenge the legitimacy of the (legal) instrument used. In this instance, let us suppose, the legitimacy issue is not that regulators should not pursue policies of public health, or encourage commuters to walk or to use their bikes; nor is the objection that regulators should never resort to the use of legal instruments; rather, the objection is that it is not acceptable to back these particular policies with legal sanctions. By contrast, where regulators turn to a technical fix of some kind, there is a more pervasive concern about the acceptability of such an approach. Here, there might well be legitimacy issues concerning, for instance, the autonomy or privacy of regulatees; but there might also be questions that reflect the more subtle concern that the technology should not be applied in ways that function to corrode the conditions for practices that we value.

In 1966, when England played Germany in the World Cup final, one of the English goals was hotly disputed, the German players (and their supporters) maintaining that the ball had not actually crossed the goal line. In the 2010 final rounds, when England again played Germany, history almost repeated itself. On this occasion, televised replays showed very clearly that the ball had crossed the German goal line and yet the referee, without any technological assistance, signalled 'no goal'. We do not know whether the 1966 decision was correct; but we do know that the 2010 decision was incorrect; and it would be relatively simple to build cameras into goalposts so that goal-line decisions could be made correctly. Yet, football's governing body remains reluctant to follow other sports down the road of technological support, arguing that it would change the character of the game. Some simply prefer the game as it is.

To take a more serious example, consider the case of brain imaging. Suppose that brain imaging is introduced in the courtroom as an aid to assessing the credibility of witnesses. Where does this leave the traditional fact-finding role of judges and jurors? And, what if brain-imaging technology is routinely embedded and employed for security and criminal justice purposes? If this happens, it is likely to be in the context of a much more technologically empowered regulatory approach.[23] With developments of this kind – where brain imaging

---

[23] Compare Mark A. Rothstein and Meghan K. Talbott, 'The Expanding Use of DNA in Law Enforcement: What Role for Privacy?', *Journal of Law, Medicine and Ethics*, 34 (2006), 153.

becomes part of the apparatus of a profiling and surveillance society, where preventive detention or secured channelling is the order of the day – there is a radical change in the regulatory environment. In such a setting, it is more than the traditional role of the jury that is challenged, it is the golden thread of traditional models of criminal justice that is broken, namely the presumption of innocence.

4 Regulatory effectiveness

According to the wisdom of new public management, to be fully fit for purpose, a regulatory intervention should be effective (it should have the intended effect), economical (there should be no resource that is surplus to regulatory requirement), and efficient (there should be an optimal gearing between regulatory input and output). In this spirit, section 7 of the Human Fertilisation and Embryology Act 2008 provides that the Human Fertilisation and Embryology Authority must carry out its statutory functions 'effectively, efficiently and economically'. If we knew how to ensure that regulation was effective, we might have some prospect of delivering regulatory interventions that were also economical and efficient. It is a fact of regulatory life, however, that we simply do not know all the keys to effective regulation.

In general, we can say that, where there is regulatory failure, the locus of the problem has to be (a) with the regulators themselves, or (b) with the response (including the resistance) of regulatees, or (c) with some disruptive factors external to the regulators and regulatees – and, quite possibly, the problem will be found to lie in more than one of these loci.

So, first, the locus of the problem might be with the regulators themselves, with their integrity and competence, as well as with the adequacy of their resources. Where regulators lack integrity, they are prey to corruption or capture. Granted, corruption or capture implies a lack of integrity, too, on the part of regulatees; but the root of the problem is with the weakness of regulators. Where regulators are not corrupt but simply incompetent, they might be unclear about their regulatory purposes; or the standards that they set (where this is their regulatory strategy) might fail to give workable guidance to regulatees. As Lon Fuller highlighted many years ago,[24] a workable legal (regulatory) order implies that the rules are published and clearly articulated, that the provisions are not over complex, that the rules are not constantly subject to revision, and so on. In short, regulatees need to know where they stand. Where the resources available to regulators are inadequate, they might act on poor policy advice – for example, they might seriously miscalculate the consequences and indirect effects of their intervention;[25] and their ability to monitor compliance

[24] See, Lon L. Fuller, *The Morality of Law* (New Haven: Yale University Press, 1969).
[25] Compare, e.g., Marcus Radetzki, Marian Radetzki and Niklas Juth, *Genes and Insurance* (Cambridge: Cambridge University Press, 2003) in which the authors argue against red-light

and correct for non-compliance might be severely limited.[26] Of course, where there is a strong culture of compliance among regulatees, detection and correction are less important regulatory activities; but there is no counting on such a culture being in place.

Second, it is critical for the effectiveness of a regulatory intervention that regulatees respond in the right way. It can hardly surprise regulators that some regulatees respond in exactly the wrong way, that they have to contend with professional and habitual criminal classes as well as occasional acts of criminality. However, an important part of our regulatory intelligence is to account for, and to anticipate, non-compliance in what we might assume to be generally law-abiding sections of the regulatee population. In some cases, it might simply be that regulators have failed to give regulatees clear guidance – in which event, the remedy lies with a more competent regulatory performance. In other cases, regulatees know precisely where they stand but they also know how to respond in a way that protects their self-interest. Again, regulators should not be surprised that regulatees (particularly regulatees with business interests) should think that a calculation of rational economic interest is the appropriate way to determine how to respond to a regulatory intervention. Similarly, regulators should not be surprised that those who are opposed to the particular regulatory position might actively pursue whatever avenues for challenge and review are lawfully available (and anticipate that, while such challenges are under way, this might operate as a chill factor). There are, however, cases where regulatees know where they stand and yet they defy the regulatory position, whether openly (as in the case, say, of peer-to-peer file-sharing) or covertly (as might be the case with the use of cognition enhancers). Unless regulators are in the fortunate position of facing wholly compliant regulatees, they must either try to minimise resistance *ex ante* or have a strategy for dealing with it *ex post*.

Third, it is perfectly possible that the relationship between regulators and regulatees is aligned for effectiveness and yet a regulatory intervention fails. For example, a regulator might initiate a highly effective strategy that encourages investment in new technologies; but, then, there is a global economic crisis, funding for research and development dries up, employees in infant hi-tech businesses lose their jobs, and what was a highly successful intervention is now

---

regulatory regimes ('total regulation') that prohibit insurance companies from either requiring genetic tests to be taken or, where test information is already available, requiring disclosure of the results. The authors' principal contention is that such regimes are unlikely to have the intended effect of shielding those whose genetic make-up would otherwise disadvantage them in the insurance market; and, indeed, the consequences of adopting such regulatory approaches might be so counter-productive that the market itself collapses when it can no longer bear the weight of its high-risk burden. For another example of regulatory miscalculation (this time, concerning electronic signatures), see Chris Reed, 'Taking Sides on Technology Neutrality', *SCRIPTed*, 4 (2007), 263.

[26] Where regulatory agencies, such as the Human Fertilisation and Embryology Authority, or the Office of the Information Commissioner, are operating with fairly limited resources, their supervision is inevitably a bit patchy.

a failure. Or, again, a regulator that is in the process of rolling out an expensive (but regulatee-supported and prospectively effective) scheme of biometric identification cards might be forced by such a crisis to cut the budget for the project (with negative consequences for its reliability and success) or even to abandon it.[27] The locus of this failure, however, is neither the regulators nor the regulatees. Rather, the problem here is that of a disruptive externality. Such disruptive externalities may or may not be lawful relative to the regulator's own recognised standards of legality;[28] and there might be cases where acts that are unlawful relative to the regulator's own recognised standards of legality are not unlawful relative to the third-party's local law (i.e. cases of hybrid legality).[29] While the disruptive externality might be a single act, it might also be an accumulation of acts (of the kind precipitating a global financial crisis) or a natural disaster (for example, a pandemic or a tsunami) that creates an unanticipated emergency situation for the regulator.[30]

5 Regulatory connection

Characteristically, new technologies 'do not arrive fully mature';[31] and, once having arrived, they move on very rapidly. For regulators, this presents a triple challenge: first, there is the challenge of getting connected (that is, of making a regulatory connection); second, as knowledge, understanding and use of the technology spreads, there is the challenge of staying connected; and, third, there is the challenge of getting reconnected. In Type 1 regulatory environments, where law is the favoured regulatory instrument – and, where there is an expectation that legal measures will be clear and calculable – the challenge is at its greatest.

---

[27] Of course, where there is a lack of regulatee support for such a project, as was the case with the UK government's proposed ID card scheme, the squeeze on funding fuels opposition but it also offers sponsors of the scheme a face-saving reason for abandonment: see Nigel Morris and Colin Brown, 'Scrap ID cards now say cabinet rebels', *The Independent*, 28 April 2009, 1–2. On the same day, it was reported that the UK government had rejected the idea of a centralised super database collecting the traffic data for e-mails, phone calls and Internet use. Ostensibly, this decision was made in the light of privacy concerns about 'a super Big Brother database': see Robert Verkaik, 'Phone bills "will rise" to pay for database', *The Independent*, 28 April 2009, 2. However, the government's urgent need to find savings surely must have aided the decision.

[28] Examples of lawful decisions might be those made by the WTO, European Court of Human Rights (EctHR), European Court of Justice (ECJ), and the like. Examples of disruptive externalities that are doubly unlawful (relative to both the regulator's home country law and the third-party's local law) include the activities of online fraudsters, cybercriminals, bio-terrorists, and the like.

[29] For example, spam sent from outside the EU, not in conformity with EU regulation but not necessarily in violation of home country regulation; online hate speech; offensive trade of the kind highlighted by the *Yahoo* case, and so on.

[30] Compare the discussion in Philip Bobbitt, *Terror and Consent* (London: Allen Lane, 2008).

[31] James H. Moor, 'Why We Need Better Ethics for Emerging Technologies', in Jeroen van den Hoven and John Weckert (eds.), *Information Technology and Moral Philosophy* (Cambridge: Cambridge University Press, 2008) 26, at 27.

(a) Getting connected

When a new technology is emerging, there needs to be an early stocktaking of existing regulation (as well as of the appropriateness of the existing configuration of regulatory agencies). In the case of emerging technologies that are either thought to be high risk or that are surrounded by uncertainty about their risk profile, such an inquiry will tend to focus on the existing regulation concerning health, safety and the environment – as is the case, currently, in relation to developing nanotechnologies.[32] Where the technology is thought to have an acceptable risk profile, the inquiry will focus on the regulation of (compensatory) liability.[33] And, where the regulation is thought to be risk free, the focus will be on the adequacy of the relevant facilitative regulation – whether this is patent law or contract law (as was the case with the early debates about the regulation of e-commerce). Although there might be no part of the regulatory array that is specifically dedicated to the emerging technology, and although there might be gaps in the array, it will rarely be true to say that an emerging technology finds itself in a regulatory void. So, for example, although there is much discussion about the need to introduce a dedicated regulatory framework for nanotechnologies, some laws (such as patent law and product liability law) already engage with this emerging technology.

We can say a bit more about the regulatory array. Let us suppose that the regulatory environment is designed to minimise the negative effects of the technology, to maximise the positive effects, and to guard against any transgressive effects. This implies three key divisions within the regulatory array. In one division, the regulatory purpose is to regulate against negative effects. Here, the principal regulatory segments will be designed (a) to assess the health, environmental and safety risks presented by an emerging technology; (b) to authorise the particular and specific applications of a technology once it has achieved general regulatory clearance under (a) – whether this is a bespoke authorisation process or a general default principle such as that of informed consent; (c) to penalise dangerous and abusive acts related to the technology (through the criminal law); and (d) to provide for compensation in the event of injury or damage to an agent's protected interests (as is the case with tort, product liability, data protection regimes, and the like). In a second division, the principal regulatory segments will be designed (e) to incentivise the development of beneficial technologies (as is the case with patent law and, possibly,

---

[32] See, e.g., Albert C. Lin, 'Size Matters: Regulating Nanotechnology', *Harvard Environmental Law Review*, 31 (2007), 349, at 361–74 (for the view that US regulatory provisions are inadequate); Giorgia Guerra, 'European Regulatory Issues in Nanomedicine', *Nanoethics*, 2 (2008), 87 (for the view that EC regulation does not fit very well with potential nanomedical applications), and, generally, Trudy A. Phelps, 'The European Approach to Nanoregulation', in Nigel M. de S. Cameron and M. Ellen Mitchell (eds.), *Nanoscale* (Hoboken, NJ: Wiley, 2007), 189.

[33] See, e.g., Stuart J. Smyth, A. Bryan Endres, Thomas P. Redick, and Drew L. Kershen, *Innovation and Liability in Biotechnology* (Cheltenham: Edward Elgar, 2010).

some elements of tax law);[34] (f) to facilitate the circulation and exploitation of the technology (for example, by refining contract law); and (g) to ensure fair access (as with competition law). Finally, in a constitutive division, there will be overarching provisions (for example, concerning respect for human rights and human dignity) that will apply across the array to monitor compliance with the community's fundamental values.

(b) Staying connected

How does regulation (or, at any rate, regulation that is in a legal form) become disconnected? Sometimes, the difficulty lies in a lack of correspondence between the form of words found in the regulation and the form that the technology now takes; at other times, the difficulty is that the original regulatory purposes no longer provide clear justificatory cover for the uses to which the technology is now put.[35] For example, in 1990, after a period of considerable debate, the Human Fertilisation and Embryology Act put in place a comprehensive regulatory framework for assisted reproduction and the use of human embryos as research tools. The Act was drafted in a form that fitted with the science as it then stood. Very rapidly, however, there were developments in both the technology of assisted reproduction and in the generation and screening of embryos. To some extent, the regulatory authority was able to stay abreast of these developments by rewriting its code of practice, but it was simply a matter of time before it was necessary to overhaul the legislation. Here, we might note a certain irony: the more that regulators (in an attempt to let regulatees know where they stand) try to establish an initial set of standards that are clear, detailed and precise, the more likely it is that the regulation will lose connection with its technological target (leaving regulatees unclear as to their position).

Such is the challenge; what is the answer? How are we to keep the regulation connected to the technology? Ideally, we want regulation to bind to the technology and to evolve with it. In pursuit of this ideal, regulators face a choice between taking a traditional hard-law approach or leaving it to self-regulation and, concomitantly, a softer form of law. Where the former approach is taken, the hard edges of the law can be softened in various ways – especially by adopting a 'technology neutral' drafting style,[36] by delegating regulatory powers to

---

[34] For possible incentivisation within tax law, see Roger Brownsword, 'Tax Exemption, Moral Reservation, and Regulatory Incentivisation', *European Journal of Risk Regulation*, 3 (2010), 211.

[35] See, further, Roger Brownsword, *Rights, Regulation and the Technological Revolution* (Oxford: Oxford University Press, 2008), ch. 6.

[36] As advocated, for instance, in relation to electronic signatures (see e.g., Pamela Samuelson, 'Five Challenges for Regulating the Global Information Society', in Christopher T. Marsden (ed.), *Regulating the Global Information Society* (London: Routledge, 2000), 316, at 320–1) and electronic money. For a comprehensive analysis of technological neutrality, see Bert-Jaap Koops, 'Should ICT Regulation Be Technology-Neutral?', in Bert-Jaap Koops, Miriam Lips, Corien Prins and Maurice Schellekens (eds.), *Starting Points for ICT Regulation – Deconstructing Prevalent Policy One-Liners* (The Hague: TMC Asser Press, 2006), 77.

the relevant minister and by encouraging a culture of purposive interpretation in the courts. Conversely, where self-regulation and softer law is preferred, the regime can be hardened up by moving towards a form of co-regulatory strategy. However, no matter which approach is adopted, there is no guarantee that it will be effective and the details of the regulatory regime will always reflect a tension between the need for flexibility (if regulation is to move with the technology) and the demand for predictability and consistency (if regulatees are to know where they stand). To this extent, therefore, there is no straightforward generic lesson to be drawn; it is not as though, having identified the problem, we now have a template for responding. In this respect we are, as Michael Kirby has aptly observed, experts without a great deal of expertise.[37]

Consider, again, the case of brain-imaging technology. Currently, we are probably somewhere between the stage of introduction (when the technology is expensive, known about only by a few specialists, and not in general circulation) and the stage of permeation when, as James Moor describes it:

> The number of users grows. Special training classes may be given to educate more people in the use of the technology. The cost of application drops, and the development of the technology begins to increase as the demand for its use increases. [Nevertheless, the] integration into society will be moderate, and its overall impact on society becomes noticeable as the technological devices are adopted more widely.[38]

As the technology moves towards the stage of permeation, the need for dedicated regulatory attention begins to be seriously considered. Even if brain imaging is not being conducted in a regulatory void, the question of whether a more bespoke regulatory connection is called for is likely to become a real issue. At this juncture, there is a risk that we might repeat the kind of mistake that regulators made when they first addressed the issue of data protection in an age of big mainframe computers. In that age, it made sense to require the registration of data-processing activities (these were still exceptional) and to place obligations on data controllers (they were visible). Notoriously, though, such first generation data protection laws were outstripped by the development of much smaller and cheaper computing equipment together with distributed networks. In the same way, in an age of large expensive brain-imaging technologies, it might be tempting to think that we can operate with a regulatory scheme that is based on registration, inspection and institutional responsibility. However, as the technologies assume much less expensive micro formats, we might find that the regulation has become disconnected.[39]

---

[37] Michael Kirby, 'New Frontier – Regulating Technology by Law and "Code"', in Roger Brownsword and Karen Yeung (eds.), *Regulating Technologies* (Oxford: Hart, 2008), 367.

[38] Moor, 'Why We Need Better Ethics', at 28.

[39] Compare Henry T. Greely, 'The Social Effects of Advances in Neuroscience: Legal Problems, Legal Perspectives', in Judy Illes (ed.), *Neuroethics* (Oxford: Oxford University Press, 2006), 245, at 254–5.

(c) Dealing with disconnection

Where a regulatory framework becomes disconnected, there is no denying that this might be undesirable relative to considerations of regulatory effectiveness and/or regulatory economy. With regard to the former (regulatory effectiveness) the problem is that, once regulation becomes disconnected, regulatees cannot be quite sure where they stand – and this will create difficulties irrespective of whether the regulatory environment is intended to support and promote certain activities (for example, human embryonic stem cell research) or to prohibit them (for example, human reproductive cloning). With regard to regulatory economy, the point is that, where regulation becomes formally disconnected, it is wasteful to expend either legislative or judicial resource simply to declare, albeit expressly and for the avoidance of doubt, that the regulatory position is as it was clearly intended to be. That said, we should not assume that (*ex post*) regulatory disconnection is necessarily and inevitably a bad thing and that, when it happens, every effort should be made to close the gap. The patches applied to the Human Fertilisation and Embryology Act by the regulatory authority (in its Codes of Practice) were not always made in a way that conform to democratic and participatory ideals; and, to rely on the courts to rescue legislation can sometimes undermine the integrity of legal reasoning. In the interests of regulatory legitimacy and democracy, where a technology has outrun its regulatory framework, it might be important to take time out to debate the developments that have taken place and to determine how the regulatory framework should be adjusted.

(d) Overview

Even if there are no simple prescriptions for effective and legitimate regulatory connection, there is a growing awareness that there is a serious problem that requires attention. So, for example, in the United Kingdom, it has been proposed that 'the Chief Scientific Advisor should establish a group that brings together the representatives of a wide range of stakeholders to look at new and emerging technologies and identify at the earliest possible stage areas where potential health, safety, environmental, social, ethical and regulatory issues may arise and advise on how these might be addressed'.[40] Such a group should ensure, not only that regulators are forewarned but also, as experience is gathered, that regulators are forearmed. Regulators, too, are waking up to the fact that sustainability is a problem and there are encouraging signs of imaginative solutions being sought. So, for example, in the House of Commons Science and Technology Select Committee's report on hybrid and chimera embryos,[41] it was

---

[40] The Royal Society and the Royal Academy of Engineering, *Nanoscience and Nanotechnologies: Opportunities and Uncertainties* (London: Royal Society, 2004) (RS Policy document 19/04), para. 9.7.

[41] House of Commons Science and Technology Select Committee, *Government Proposals for the Regulation of Hybrid and Chimera Embryos* (Fifth Report of Session 2006–7) (HC 272-I, 5 April 2007).

suggested that the regulatory agency should be given a broad licensing power to authorise the use of inter-species embryos as research tools but that, if a particularly controversial use or wholly uncontemplated type of embryo were to be proposed, the regulatory framework should 'contain a provision to enable the Secretary of State to put a stop to the procedure for a limited period while deciding whether or not to make regulations'.[42] Such an idea (albeit not eventually taken up) contemplates a constructive exercise in joint regulation, with the breadth of the agency's licensing powers being geared for flexibility and connection, and the Secretary of State's stop-and-review powers designed for both clarity and legitimacy.

6 Cross-checking the challenges

The four regulatory challenges that we have identified as fundamental are not canonical. This is not a field of inquiry in which there is a received wisdom about the criteria of regulatory adequacy. Quite possibly, we have missed some matters of regulatory importance or we might have overstated the significance of some matter. By way of a cross-check, we can compare a list of twenty questions that Gary T. Marx has put forward, saying that he finds this list useful 'amidst the rapidity and constancy of technical innovation'.[43] It is important, though, to appreciate that Marx offered this list in the context of a book exploring the implications of 'a world of convergence, where heterogeneous devices are able to communicate seamlessly'.[44] In other words, the questions that are identified by Marx sometimes tend to betray a more particular concern with information and communications technologies (ICTs).

Marx, 'Foreword', in Wright *et al.*, *Safeguards*, at xv

1. *Goals* – Have the goals been clearly stated, justified, and prioritised? Are they consistent with the values of a democratic society?
2. *Accountable, public and participatory policy development* – Has the decision to apply the technique been developed through an open process and, if appropriate, with participation of those to be subject to it? This involves a transparency principle.
3. *Law and ethics* – Are the means and ends not only legal, but also ethical?
4. *Opening doors* – Has adequate thought been given to precedent creation and long-term consequences?

---

[42] *Ibid.*, at para. 100. Compare, too, Academy of Medical Sciences, *Inter-Species Embryos* (London, July 2007), at 39; and the House of Lords House of Commons Joint Committee on the Human Tissue and Embryos (Draft) Bill, *Human Tissue and Embryos (Draft) Bill*, HL Paper 169-I, HC Paper 630-I (London: Stationery Office, 1 August 2007), where a regime of 'devolved regulation' is favoured.

[43] Gary T. Marx, 'Foreword', in David Wright, Serge Gutwirth, Michael Friedewald, Elena Vildjiounaite and Yves Punie (eds.), *Safeguards in a World of Ambient Intelligence* (2008), vii, at xiv.

[44] Wright *et al.*, *Safeguards*, at 1.

5. *Golden rule* – Would the controllers of the system be comfortable in being its subject, as well as its agent? Where there is a clear division between agents and subjects, is reciprocity or equivalence possible and appropriate?
6. *Informed consent* – Are participants fully apprised of the system's presence and the conditions under which it operates? Is consent genuine (i.e., beyond deception or unreasonable seduction or denial of fundamental services) and can 'participation' be refused without dire consequences for the person?
7. *Truth in use* – Where personal and private information is involved does a principle of 'unitary usage' apply, whereby information collected for one purpose is not used for another? Are the announced goals the real goals?
8. *Means–end relationships* – Are the means clearly related to the end sought and proportional in costs and benefits to the goals?
9. *Can science save us?* – Can a strong empirical and logical case be made that a means will in fact have the broad positive consequences its advocates claim (the does-it-really-work question)?
10. *Competent application* – Even if in theory it works, does the system (or operative) using it apply it as intended and in appropriate manner?
11. *Human review* – Are automated results with significant implications for life chances subject to human review before action is taken?
12. *Minimization* – If risks and harms are associated with the tactic, is it applied to minimize these showing only the degree of intrusiveness and invasiveness that is absolutely necessary?
13. *Alternatives* – Are alternative solutions available that would meet the same ends with lesser costs and greater benefits (using a variety of measures, not just financial)?
14. *Inaction as action* – Has consideration been given to the 'sometimes it is better to do nothing' principle?
15. *Periodic review* – Are there regular efforts to test the system's vulnerability, effectiveness and fairness and to review policies and procedures?
16. *Discovery and rectification of mistakes, errors and abuses* – Are there clear means for identifying and fixing these (and, in the case of abuse, applying sanctions)?
17. *Right of inspection* – Can individuals see and challenge their own records?
18. *Reversibility* – If evidence suggests that the costs outweigh the benefits, how easily can the means (e.g., extent of capital expenditures and available alternatives) be given up?
19. *Unintended consequences* – Has adequate consideration been given to undesirable consequences, including possible harms to agents, subjects and third parties? Can harm be easily discovered and compensated for?
20. *Data protection and security* – Can agents protect the information that they collect? Do they follow standard data protection and information rights as expressed in documents such as the Code of Fair Information Protection Practices and the expanded European Data Protection Directive?

Of the four challenges that we have flagged up, it is questions of legitimacy and effectiveness that dominate Marx's list. Thus, in questions 1–3, 5–7, 11, 15, 17 and 20 we see a concern with regulatory legitimacy. However, it needs to be borne in mind that there might be a practical connection between legitimacy and effectiveness; for, if regulatees do not judge the regulatory position to be legitimate, their willingness to comply is likely to be reduced. In other words, a concern with legitimacy might have implications for the effectiveness of the regulatory scheme. Having said that, in Marx's list, the question of effectiveness is raised directly in points 8–10 (albeit that 9 is directed more at the science and technology than the regulatory intervention), 14–16 and 19; and we can take question 13 as one about regulatory efficiency or economy. This leaves questions 12 and 18, which pick up matters of regulatory prudence and question 4 which can be interpreted in a number of ways, possibly implicating effectiveness, legitimacy and connection.

It is reassuring that Marx's list highlights so many particular facets of the challenges of regulatory legitimacy and regulatory effectiveness. On the other hand, why are questions that clearly relate to regulatory prudence and regulatory connection less in evidence? Where a technology is perceived to be a threat to the health and safety of agents, or damaging to the environment, prudential considerations tend to be top of the list; conversely, where a technology is not seen as risky in this way – and the technological array that forms the setting for Marx's comments is not seen as being risky in this way – then prudential concerns tend to have a lower profile. This leaves regulatory connection, a challenge that we believe to be one of the most distinctive in the field. Indeed, some commentators would pick out the rapid development of ICT as a textbook challenge for those who are trying to construct regulatory environments that move with the technology; and Susan Brenner has argued that it is precisely the kind of ambient technology that is the context for Marx's questions that will compel regulators to rethink their connecting strategies.[45] At all events, there is ample confirmation in the questions that Marx lists for us to proceed with a degree of confidence; in suggesting that an adequate regulatory environment needs to attend to matters of prudence, legitimacy, effectiveness and connection, we are not ploughing a lone furrow.

7 Summary

In this chapter, we have highlighted four questions that need to be addressed before we can judge the adequacy of a particular regulatory environment that engages with new technologies.

First, there is the question of whether the regulators have properly assessed the risks to health, safety and the environment that might be presented by these

---

[45] Susan W. Brenner, *Law in an Era of 'Smart' Technology* (New York: Oxford University Press, 2007).

technologies; and then, if there are risks, whether the regulatory arrangements for risk management are acceptable.

Second, there is the question of whether regulators are trying to do the right kind of thing and whether they are going about it in the right kind of way. Here, it might not be enough for regulators to 'legitimate' their activities by pointing to a general competence – for example, a competence to act with a view to protecting public health or preventing crime; for we also need to be satisfied that regulators are defending and respecting the deepest values that constitute a particular society.

Third, there is the question of whether the strategy adopted by regulators will work, whether it will be effective in achieving its intended objectives. Where there is a dawning realisation that legal interventions represent a litany of failure, the attractions of a more responsive technological approach are obvious. However, one of the regulatory dilemmas that will need to be confronted in the twenty-first century is precisely the tension between strategies that are acceptable and strategies that work.

Fourth, there is the question of whether regulation is properly connected to a target technology. Again, traditional legal interventions (particularly where they are found in Type 1 regulatory environments) have their limits and one of the challenges for regulators is to develop smarter ways of getting and staying connected.

4

Technology as a regulatory tool: DNA profiling and *Marper*

1 Introduction

On a particular day in June 2006, *The Times* featured two stories that are indicative of the way in which regulators might turn to technological tools. The first story,[1] running over two pages, announces a proposed network of new generation synchronised speed cameras; if a car is driven too fast through a restricted speed zone, the cameras will pick this up, the car number plate will be identified, the information is centrally processed and penalty notices issued within minutes of the offence. The second story,[2] taking up a whole page, reports that a 58-year-old architect, having been interviewed but not charged in connection with a complaint about theft, and having had a DNA sample routinely taken, was found to have a DNA match with samples taken from crime scenes where young girls had been indecently assaulted many years earlier. In both cases, these reports are implicit endorsements, indeed a celebration, of the relevant technologies.

There is more to this than mere newspaper talk. A few months later, a report for the (UK) Information Commissioner[3] predicted that, as the technologies of surveillance[4] become increasingly sophisticated, less obtrusive and embedded, citizens will not always be aware that they are being monitored and regulated. Thus:

> [The] continuous software-sorting of people and their life chances in cities is organised through myriad electronic and physical 'passage points' or 'choke points', negotiated through a widening number of code words, pass words, PIN numbers, user names, access controls, electronic cards or biometric scans. Some are highly visible and negotiated willingly (a PIN credit card purchase or an airport passport control). Others are more covert (the sorting of internet or call centre traffic). On still other occasions, the passage point is clear (a CCTV camera

---

[1] B. Webster, 'Cameras set to catch side-street speeders' *The Times*, 15 June 2006, 1–2.
[2] S. Bird, 'Architect who dressed as tramp to attack girls trapped by DNA', *The Times*, 15 June 2006, 3.
[3] Kirstie Ball, David Lyon, David Murakami Wood, Clive Norris and Charles Raab, *A Report on the Surveillance Society* (London, IC, September 2006).
[4] For a review of the range of such technologies, see *ibid.*, at paras. 9.3ff.

on a street or a speed camera on a motorway), but it is impossible to know in practice if one's face or car number plate has actually been scanned.[5]

More generally, the 'combination of CCTV, biometrics, databases and tracking technologies can be seen as part of a much broader exploration ... of the use of interconnected "smart" systems to track movements and behaviours of millions of people in both time and space'.[6]

What should we make of this? The authors of the report for the Information Commissioner are not alarmist. There are causes for concern – most obviously, concerns about privacy and autonomy – but the development of the surveillance society is not so much a conspiracy as 'a part of just being modern'.[7]

In the courts, too, we see a positive attitude towards technological innovations that assist the regulatory enterprise. Notably, in *R* v. *Chief Constable of South Yorkshire, ex parte LS and Marper*[8] (a case that we consider in detail in this chapter), we find Lord Woolf CJ, appreciating the benefits of DNA sampling and profiling for forensic purposes, refusing to rule out the possibility of a national comprehensive collection. According to the Lord Chief Justice:

> So far as the prevention and detection of crime is concerned, it is obvious the larger the databank of fingerprints and DNA samples available to the police, the greater the value of the databank will be in preventing crime and detecting those responsible for crime. There can be no doubt that if every member of the public was required to provide fingerprints and a DNA sample this would make a dramatic contribution to the prevention and detection of crime. To take but one example, the great majority of rapists who are not known already to their victim would be able to be identified.[9]

Similarly, Lord Steyn is enthusiastic about the state making use of new forensic technologies. Thus:

> It is of paramount importance that law enforcement agencies should take full advantage of the available techniques of modern technology and forensic science. Such real evidence has the inestimable value of cogency and objectivity ... It enables the guilty to be detected and the innocent to be rapidly eliminated from enquiries. Thus in the 1990s closed circuit television [was] extensively adopted in British cities and towns. The images recorded facilitate the detection of crime and prosecution of offenders ... The benefits to the criminal justice system [of DNA profiling] are enormous. For example, recent ... statistics show that while the annual detection rate of domestic burglary is only 14%, when DNA is successfully recovered from a crime scene this rises to 48% ... [A]s a matter of policy it is a high priority that police forces should expand the use of such evidence where possible and practicable.[10]

With several million profiles now held on the National DNA Database and with the average person being caught 300 times a day on CCTV, we might see the

---

[5] *Ibid.*, at para. 9.10.2.   [6] *Ibid.*, at para. 9.10.3.   [7] *Ibid.*, at para. 1.6.

[8] [2002] EWCA Civ. 1275, [2004] UKHL 39.

[9] [2002] EWCA Civ. 1275, at para. 17; similarly Sedley LJ, at para. 87.

[10] [2004] UKHL 39, at paras. 1–2.

United Kingdom as a pilot for profiling-led criminal justice. The question is whether we judge that a regulatory environment that takes a technological turn of this kind is acceptable.

In this chapter, we start by plotting a range of concerns about the use of technology as a regulatory tool together with the depth of the regulatory reliance on such a strategy. This paves the way for a consideration of the *Marper* case, first in the UK domestic courts and then before the European Court of Human Rights.

2 Concerns about technology as a regulatory tool

Imagine that we construct a grid to plot our concerns about the use of emerging technologies as regulatory tools. Along one axis, we have a list of particular concerns; and, along the other, we measure the depth of the use. In this way, we can begin to locate the issues to which the use of DNA profiling, CCTV, and the like, might give rise.

On the first axis, our concern might be whether the technology will work (think about traffic lights failing at a busy road intersection), whether it will be accurate (whether, for example, DNA profiling and matching is as accurate as some portray it), whether it will have unanticipated and unintended effects (think about the added anxiety aroused by teenage 'hoodies' defying the CCTV cameras, or the way that joy riders use speed bumps as speed ramps), whether it will be respectful of privacy (in the way that is debated in *Marper*) and autonomy,[11] whether it will be capable of simulating the flexibility, discretion, and common sense that we find in legal rules and their human enforcers,[12] and so on.

Along the second axis, we take stock of the nature of the technological intervention and we measure the depth of the regulator's technological reliance – in other words, as we discussed in Chapter 2, we consider whether the regulatory environment is first-, second- or third-generation relative to the movement from normative to non-normative signals. Where the technology is used to support what is primarily a traditional (normative) criminal justice system (think about lie-detectors, fingerprinting, CCTV and now DNA profiling), then reliance is still relatively shallow. Already though, with the (perceived) probability of detection increasing, the tendency is for regulatees to comply, not because they judge that this is the right thing to do, but simply because they judge that this is the prudent thing to do. Moreover, even in a technologically assisted first generation regulatory environment, there may be design features that make

---

[11] See Roger Brownsword, 'Autonomy, Delegation, and Responsibility: Agents in Autonomic Computing Environments', in Mireille Hildebrandt and Antoinette Rouvroy (eds.), *Autonomic Computing and Transformations of Human Agency* (London: Routledge, 2011), 64.

[12] See Roger Brownsword, 'So What Does the World Need Now? Reflections on Regulating Technologies', in Roger Brownsword and Karen Yeung (eds.), *Regulating Technologies* (Oxford: Hart, 2008), 23.

it impracticable or impossible to deviate from the desired regulatory pattern. On this axis, as we move into second-generation regulatory environments, the register of practicability/possibility intensifies, regulators increasingly seeking out technologies that are of a kind that altogether design-out any possibility of non-compliance (or that design-in compliance). At this point, compliance no longer reflects a judgement by regulatees of what ought to be done; compliance is now the only thing that can be done.

In our concluding chapter, we will revisit the question of the significance and the acceptability of changes to the complexion of the regulatory environment. However, in the present chapter, our focus is on the *Marper* case and the question of how far, in a community that is committed to human rights, regulators may go in authorising the use of DNA evidence for forensic purposes.

3 DNA profiling and *Marper*

In the years leading up to the *Marper* case, the authorities in England and Wales built up the largest per capita DNA database of its kind in the world, with some 5 million profiles on the system. At that time, if a person was arrested then, in almost all cases, the police had the power to take a DNA sample from which an identifying profile was made. The sample and the profile could be retained even though the arrest (for any one of several reasons) did not lead to the person being convicted. These sweeping powers attracted considerable local criticism – particularly on the twin grounds that there should be no power to take a DNA sample except in the case of an arrest in connection with a serious offence, and that the sample and profile should not be retained unless the person was actually convicted.[13] In *R* v. *Chief Constable of South Yorkshire Police, ex parte LS and Marper*,[14] the legal framework that authorised the taking and retention of samples, and the making and retention of profiles, was challenged as incompatible with the UK's human rights commitments.

In the local courts, while the judges were not quite at one in deciding whether the right to informational privacy was engaged under Article 8(1) of the European Convention on Human Rights, they had no hesitation in accepting that the state could justify the legislation under Article 8(2) by reference to the compelling public interest in the prevention and detection of serious crime.

In the Court of Appeal, Lord Woolf CJ suggested that, whether or not retention is seen as engaging the privacy right, 'depends very much on the cultural traditions of a particular State'.[15] If fingerprints are viewed as personal information, so too is DNA. This is not to deny that there might be a certain shading of opinions. As Lord Woolf put it:

---

[13] See, e.g., Nuffield Council on Bioethics, *The Forensic Use of Bioinformation: Ethical Issues* (London: September 2007).
[14] [2002] EWCA Civ. 1275, [2004] UKHL 39.
[15] [2002] EWCA Civ. 1275, para. 32.

> There are no doubt a rainbow of reactions which are possible to intrusions of this nature, but at least for a substantial proportion of the public there is a strong objection to the State storing information relating to an individual unless there is some objective justification for this happening.[16]

Sedley LJ explicitly agreed, relying on the 'strong cultural unease in the United Kingdom about the official collection and retention of information about individuals'.[17]

In passing, however, we might wonder whether Sedley LJ was correct. The DNA profiles held in the National DNA Database are identifying metrics which can be employed to gather information about a particular individuated agent. Where there is no match (between a profile and a crime scene sample), we can say that the individuated agent probably was not at the scene of the crime; where there is a positive match, we can say the opposite. Contrary to the views of the Court of Appeal, one might doubt whether there is a cultural unease in the United Kingdom about the state having the capacity to draw on such locating information; but, more importantly, one might question whether contingent cultural ease or unease is the right way to distinguish between privacy engagement and non-engagement.[18]

When *Marper* was appealed, the House of Lords took a rather different approach to the engagement of privacy, distancing themselves from the culturally contingent view espoused by the Court of Appeal. Giving the leading speech, Lord Steyn said:

> While I would not wish to subscribe to all the generalisations in the Court of Appeal about cultural traditions in the United Kingdom, in comparison with other European states, I do accept that when one moves on to consider the question of objective justification under article 8(2) the cultural traditions in the United Kingdom are material. With great respect to Lord Woolf CJ the same is not true under article 8(1) ... The question whether the retention of fingerprints and samples engages article 8(1) should receive a uniform interpretation throughout member states, unaffected by different cultural traditions.[19]

Having rejected a custom-based approach, and having reviewed the essentially identifying metric nature of a DNA profile (the profile, as such, tells you nothing about the physical make-up, characteristics, health or life of the individuated agent), Lord Steyn concluded that retention either does not engage Article 8(1) at all or engages it only very modestly (whatever modest engagement might mean).[20]

The strongest support for the engagement of Article 8(1) was given by Lady Hale. For example, she said:

---

[16] *Ibid.*, at para. 34.   [17] *Ibid.*, at para. 68.

[18] See, further, Roger Brownsword, 'Consent in Data Protection Law: Privacy, Fair Processing, and Confidentiality', in Serge Gutwirth, Yves Poullet, Paul de Hert, Cécile de Terwangne and Sjaak Nouwt (eds.), *Reinventing Data Protection?* (Dordrecht: Springer, 2009), 83.

[19] [2004] UKHL 39, para. 27.   [20] *Ibid.*, at para. 31.

> It could be said that the samples are not 'information' … But the only reason that they are taken or kept is for the information which they contain. They are not kept for their intrinsic value as mouth swabs, hairs or whatever. They are kept because they contain the individual's unique genetic code within them. They are kept as information about that person and nothing else. Fingerprints and profiles are undoubtedly information. The same privacy principles should apply to all three.[21]

While the points made about the rich information-bearing potential of the DNA *samples* are extremely well taken, it is not so clear that the same applies to the *profiles*. Arguably, the profiles, which are on non-coding regions of DNA, are not so much 'information about that person' but information that enables us to identify who 'that person' is. In so far as the profiles, in conjunction with crime-scene samples, simply yield information about an individuated agent's location, we might question whether the privacy right is engaged.[22] And, indeed, this was one of the issues to be addressed by the Strasbourg Court.

4 *Marper* at the European Court of Human Rights

With the domestic courts satisfied that the local regulatory position was in line with the state's human rights commitments, *Marper* moved to Strasbourg for the consideration of the European Court of Human Rights. Here, the Grand Chamber took a very different view, concluding that the sweeping powers for the taking and retention of DNA profiles of persons suspected, but not actually convicted of, offences constituted a disproportionate interference with the right to respect for private life and could not be considered to strike a fair balance between the competing public and private interests. The key parts of the Court's judgment, which was handed down at Strasbourg on 4 December 2008, follow.

S. and Marper v. *The United Kingdom*

(Applications nos. 30562/04 and 30566/04)

PROCEDURE

1. The case originated in two applications (nos. 30562/04 and 30566/04) against the United Kingdom of Great Britain and Northern Ireland lodged with the Court under Article 34 of the Convention for the Protection of Human Rights

---

[21] *Ibid.*, at para. 70.

[22] It should be noted that there is also an interesting privacy issue arising from so-called familial DNA profiling. In some cases, although DNA samples taken from a crime scene might not fully match any profile held in the database, they might be a near match to a particular profile. In such a case, there is a possibility that a close genetic relative of the person who has the near-match profile will be a full match. This was so, for example, in the 'Shoe Rapist' case where the rapist was identified when a near match showed up between crime-scene samples and the DNA profile of the rapist's sister (the sister's profile being taken in connection with a drink-driving offence): see A. Norfolk, 'Shoe rapist is trapped by sister's DNA 20 years after serial attacks' *The Times*, 18 July 2006, 3. Quite apart from the investigative potency of familial DNA profiling, there is obviously the possibility that researching the DNA of family members might uncover embarrassing (and privacy-engaging) secrets about a person's genetic pedigree. See, further, Sheldon Krimsky and Tania Simoncelli, *Genetic Justice* (New York: Columbia University Press, 2011), ch. 4.

and Fundamental Freedoms ('the Convention') by two British nationals, Mr S. ('the first applicant') and Mr Michael Marper ('the second applicant'), on 16 August 2004. The President of the Grand Chamber acceded to the first applicant's request not to have his name disclosed (Rule 47 § 3 of the Rules of Court).

2. The applicants, who were granted legal aid, were represented by Mr P. Mahy of Messrs Howells, a solicitor practicing in Sheffield. The United Kingdom Government ('the Government') were represented by their Agent, Mr J. Grainger, Foreign and Commonwealth Office.

3. The applicants complained under Articles 8 and 14 that the authorities had continued to retain their fingerprints and cellular samples and DNA profiles after the criminal proceedings against them had ended with an acquittal or had been discontinued.

4. The applications were allocated to the Fourth Section of the Court (Rule 52 § 1 of the Rules of Court). On 16 January 2007 they were declared admissible by a Chamber of that Section composed of the following judges: Josep Casadevall, *President*, Nicolas Bratza, Giovanni Bonello, Kristaq Traja, Stanislav Pavlovschi, Ján Šikuta, Päivi Hirvelä, and also of Lawrence Early, Section Registrar.

5. On 10 July 2007 the Chamber relinquished jurisdiction in favour of the Grand Chamber, neither party having objected to relinquishment (Article 30 of the Convention and Rule 72).

6. The composition of the Grand Chamber was determined according to the provisions of Article 27 §§ 2 and 3 of the Convention and Rule 24 of the Rules of Court.

7. The applicants and the Government each filed written memorials on the merits. In addition, third-party submissions were received from Ms Anna Fairclough on behalf of Liberty (the National Council for Civil Liberties) and from Covington and Burling LLP on behalf of Privacy International, who had been granted leave by the President to intervene in the written procedure (Article 36 § 2 of the Convention and Rule 44 § 2). Both parties replied to Liberty's submissions and the Government also replied to the comments by Privacy International (Rule 44 § 5).

8. A hearing took place in public in the Human Rights Building, Strasbourg, on 27 February 2008 (Rule 59 § 3).

THE FACTS

I. THE CIRCUMSTANCES OF THE CASE

9. The applicants were born in 1989 and 1963 respectively and live in Sheffield.

10. The first applicant, Mr S., was arrested on 19 January 2001 at the age of eleven and charged with attempted robbery. His fingerprints and DNA samples[1] were taken. He was acquitted on 14 June 2001.

11. The second applicant, Mr Michael Marper, was arrested on 13 March 2001 and charged with harassment of his partner. His fingerprints and DNA samples were taken. Before a pre-trial review took place, he and his partner had become reconciled, and the charge was not pressed. On 11 June 2001, the Crown Prosecution Service served a notice of discontinuance on the applicant's solicitors, and on 14 June the case was formally discontinued.

12. Both applicants asked for their fingerprints and DNA samples to be destroyed, but in both cases the police refused. The applicants applied for judicial review of the police decisions not to destroy the fingerprints and samples. On 22

March 2002 the Administrative Court (Rose LJ and Leveson J) rejected the application [[2002] EWHC 478 (Admin.)].

13. On 12 September 2002 the Court of Appeal upheld the decision of the Administrative Court by a majority of two (Lord Woolf CJ and Waller LJ) to one (Sedley LJ) [[2003] EWCA Civ. 1275]. [The reasoning of the Court of Appeal is then summarised] …

15. On 22 July 2004 the House of Lords dismissed an appeal by the applicants. [The reasoning of the House of Lords is then summarised]

II. RELEVANT DOMESTIC LAW AND MATERIALS

A. England and Wales

1. Police and Criminal Evidence Act 1984

26. The Police and Criminal Evidence Act 1984 (the PACE) contains powers for the taking of fingerprints (principally section 61) and samples (principally section 63). By section 61, fingerprints may only be taken without consent if an officer of at least the rank of superintendent authorises the taking, or if the person has been charged with a recordable offence or has been informed that he will be reported for such an offence. Before fingerprints are taken, the person must be informed that the prints may be the subject of a speculative search, and the fact of the informing must be recorded as soon as possible. The reason for the taking of the fingerprints is recorded in the custody record. Parallel provisions relate to the taking of samples (section 63).

27. As to the retention of such fingerprints and samples (and the records thereof), section 64 (1A) of the PACE was substituted by Section 82 of the Criminal Justice and Police Act 2001. It provides as follows:

'Where – (a) fingerprints or samples are taken from a person in connection with the investigation of an offence, and (b) subsection (3) below does not require them to be destroyed, the fingerprints or samples may be retained after they have fulfilled the purposes for which they were taken but shall not be used by any person except for purposes related to the prevention or detection of crime, the investigation of an offence, or the conduct of a prosecution. …

(3) If – (a) fingerprints or samples are taken from a person in connection with the investigation of an offence; and (b) that person is not suspected of having committed the offence, they must except as provided in the following provisions of this Section be destroyed as soon as they have fulfilled the purpose for which they were taken.

(3AA) Samples and fingerprints are not required to be destroyed under subsection (3) above if (a) they were taken for the purposes of the investigation of an offence of which a person has been convicted; and (b) a sample or, as the case may be, fingerprint was also taken from the convicted person for the purposes of that investigation.'

28. Section 64 in its earlier form had included a requirement that if the person from whom the fingerprints or samples were taken in connection with the investigation was acquitted of that offence, the fingerprints and samples, subject to certain exceptions, were to be destroyed 'as soon as practicable after the conclusion of the proceedings'.

29. The subsequent use of materials retained under section 64 (1A) is not regulated by statute, other than the limitation on use contained in that provision. In *Attorney General's Reference (No 3 of 1999)* [2001] 2 AC 91, the House of Lords had to consider whether it was permissible to use in evidence a sample which should have been destroyed under the then text of section 64 the PACE.

Law and the technologies of the twenty-first century

The House considered that the prohibition on the use of an unlawfully retained sample 'for the purposes of any investigation' did not amount to a mandatory exclusion of evidence obtained as a result of a failure to comply with the prohibition, but left the question of admissibility to the discretion of the trial judge.

2. Data Protection Act 1998

30. The Data Protection Act was adopted on 16 July 1998 to give effect to the Directive 95/46/EC of the European Parliament and of the Council dated 24 October 1995 (see paragraph 50 below). Under the Data Protection Act 'personal data' means data which relate to a living individual who can be identified – (a) from those data, or (b) from those data and other information which is in the possession of, or is likely to come into the possession of, the data controller, and includes any expression of opinion about the individual and any indication of the intentions of the data controller or any other person in respect of the individual (section 1). 'Sensitive personal data' means personal data consisting, *inter alia*, of information as to the racial or ethnic origin of the data subject, the commission or alleged commission by him of any offence, or any proceedings for any offence committed or alleged to have been committed by him, the disposal of such proceedings or the sentence of any court in such proceedings (section 2).

31. The Act stipulates that the processing of personal data is subject to eight data protection principles listed in Schedule 1. Under the first principle personal data shall be processed fairly and lawfully and, in particular shall not be processed unless – (a) at least one of the conditions in Schedule 2 is met, and (b) in case of sensitive personal data, at least one of the conditions in Schedule 3 is also met. Schedule 2 contains a detailed list of conditions, and provides *inter alia* that the processing of any personal data is necessary for the administration of justice or for the exercise of any other functions of a public nature exercised in the public interest by any person (§5(a) and (d)). Schedule 3 contains a more detailed list of conditions, including that the processing of sensitive personal data is necessary for the purpose of, or in connection with, any legal proceedings (§6(a)), or for the administration of justice (§7(a)), and is carried out with appropriate safeguards for the rights and freedoms of data subjects (§4(b)). Section 29 notably provides that personal data processed for the prevention or detection of crime are exempt from the first principle except to the extent to which it requires compliance with the conditions in Schedules 2 and 3. The fifth principle stipulates that personal data processed for any purpose or purposes shall not be kept for longer than is necessary for that purpose or those purposes.

32. The Information Commissioner created pursuant to the Act (as amended) has an independent duty to promote the following of good practice by data controllers and has power to make orders ('enforcement notices') in this respect (section 40). The Act makes it a criminal offence not to comply with an enforcement notice (section 47) or to obtain or disclose personal data or information contained therein without the consent of the data controller (section 55). Section 13 affords a right to claim damages in the domestic courts in respect of contraventions of the Act.

3. Retention Guidelines for Nominal Records on the Police National Computer 2006

33. A set of guidelines for the retention of fingerprint and DNA information is contained in the Retention Guidelines for Nominal Records on the Police National

Computer 2006 drawn up by the Association of Chief Police Officers in England and Wales. The Guidelines are based on a format of restricting access to the Police National Computer (PNC) data, rather than the deletion of that data. They recognise that their introduction may thus have implications for the business of the non-police agencies with which the police currently share PNC data.

34. The Guidelines set various degrees of access to the information contained on the PNC through a process of 'stepping down' access. Access to information concerning persons who have not been convicted of an offence is automatically 'stepped down' so that this information is only open to inspection by the police. Access to information about convicted persons is likewise 'stepped down' after the expiry of certain periods of time ranging from 5 to 35 years, depending on the gravity of the offence, the age of the suspect and the sentence imposed. For certain convictions the access will never be 'stepped down'.

35. Chief Police Officers are the Data Controllers of all PNC records created by their force. They have the discretion in exceptional circumstances to authorise the deletion of any conviction, penalty notice for disorder, acquittal or arrest histories 'owned' by them. An 'exceptional case procedure' to assist Chief Officers in relation to the exercise of this discretion is set out in Appendix 2. It is suggested that exceptional cases are rare by definition and include those where the original arrest or sampling was unlawful or where it is established beyond doubt that no offence existed. Before deciding whether a case is exceptional, the Chief Officer is instructed to seek advice from the DNA and Fingerprint Retention Project.

B. Scotland

36. Under the 1995 Criminal Procedure Act of Scotland, as subsequently amended, the DNA samples and resulting profiles must be destroyed if the individual is not convicted or is granted an absolute discharge. A recent qualification provides that biological samples and profiles may be retained for three years, if the arrestee is suspected of certain sexual or violent offences even if a person is not convicted (section 83 of the 2006 Act, adding section 18A to the 1995 Act). Thereafter, samples and information are required to be destroyed unless a Chief Constable applies to a Sheriff for a two-year extension.

C. Northern Ireland

37. The Police and Criminal Evidence Order of Northern Ireland 1989 was amended in 2001 in the same way as the PACE applicable in England and Wales. The relevant provisions currently governing the retention of fingerprint and DNA data in Northern Ireland are identical to those in force in England and Wales (see paragraph 27 above).

D. Nuffield Council on Bioethics' report[2]

38. According to a recent report by the Nuffield Council on Bioethics, the retention of fingerprints, DNA profiles and biological samples is generally more controversial than the taking of such bioinformation, and the retention of biological samples raises greater ethical concerns than digitised DNA profiles and fingerprints, given the differences in the level of information that could be revealed. The report referred in particular to the lack of satisfactory empirical evidence to justify the present practice of retaining indefinitely fingerprints, samples and DNA profiles from all those arrested for a recordable offence, irrespective of whether they were

subsequently charged or convicted. The report voiced particular concerns at the policy of permanently retaining the bioinformation of minors, having regard to the requirements of the 1989 UN Convention on the Rights of the Child.

39. The report also expressed concerns at the increasing use of the DNA data for familial searching, inferring ethnicity and non-operational research. Familial searching is the process of comparing a DNA profile from a crime scene with profiles stored on the national database, and prioritising them in terms of 'closeness' to a match. This allowed identifying possible genetic relatives of an offender. Familial searching might thus lead to revealing previously unknown or concealed genetic relationships. The report considered the use of the DNA data base in searching for relatives as particularly sensitive.

40. The particular combination of alleles[3] in a DNA profile can furthermore be used to assess the most likely ethnic origin of the donor. Ethnic inferring through DNA profiles was possible as the individual 'ethnic appearance' was systematically recorded on the data base: when taking biological samples, police officers routinely classified suspects into one of seven 'ethnical appearance' categories. Ethnicity tests on the data base might thus provide inferences for use during a police investigation in order for example to help reduce a 'suspect pool' and to inform police priorities. The report noted that social factors and policing practices lead to a disproportionate number of people from black and ethnic minority groups being stopped, searched and arrested by the police, and hence having their DNA profiles recorded; it therefore voiced concerns that inferring ethnic identity from biological samples might reinforce racist views of propensity to criminality.

III. RELEVANT NATIONAL AND INTERNATIONAL MATERIAL

A. Council of Europe texts

41. The Council of Europe Convention of 1981 for the protection of individuals with regard to automatic processing of personal data ('the Data Protection Convention'), which entered into force for the United Kingdom on 1 December 1987, defines 'personal data' as any information relating to an identified or identifiable individual ('data subject'). The Convention provides *inter alia*:

'Article 5 – Quality of data
Personal data undergoing automatic processing shall be:
…
b. stored for specified and legitimate purposes and not used in a way incompatible with those purposes;
c. adequate, relevant and not excessive in relation to the purposes for which they are stored;
…
e. preserved in a form which permits identification of the data subjects for no longer than is required for the purpose for which those data are stored.

Article 6 – Special categories of data
Personal data revealing racial origin, political opinions or religious or other beliefs, as well as personal data concerning health or sexual life, may not be processed automatically unless domestic law provides appropriate safeguards …

Article 7 – Data security
Appropriate security measures shall be taken for the protection of personal data stored in automated data files against accidental or unauthorised

destruction or accidental loss as well as against unauthorised access, alteration or dissemination.'

42. Recommendation No. R(87)15 regulating the use of personal data in the police sector (adopted on 17 September 1987) states, *inter alia*:

Principle 2 – Collection of data

2.1 The collection of personal data for police purposes should be limited to such as is necessary for the prevention of a real danger or the suppression of a specific criminal offence. Any exception to this provision should be the subject of specific national legislation ...

Principle 3 – Storage of data

3.1. As far as possible, the storage of personal data for police purposes should be limited to accurate data and to such data as are necessary to allow police bodies to perform their lawful tasks within the framework of national law and their obligations arising from international law ...

Principle 7 – Length of storage and updating of data

7.1. Measures should be taken so that personal data kept for police purposes are deleted if they are no longer necessary for the purposes for which they were stored.

For this purpose, consideration shall in particular be given to the following criteria: the need to retain data in the light of the conclusion of an inquiry into a particular case; a final judicial decision, in particular an acquittal; rehabilitation; spent convictions; amnesties; the age of the data subject, particular categories of data.'

43. Recommendation No. R(92)1 on the use of analysis of deoxyribonucleic acid (DNA) within the framework of the criminal justice system (adopted on 10 February 1992) states, *inter alia*:

'3. *Use of samples and information derived therefrom*

Samples collected for DNA analysis and the information derived from such analysis for the purpose of the investigation and prosecution of criminal offences must not be used for other purposes ...

Samples taken for DNA analysis and the information so derived may be needed for research and statistical purposes. Such uses are acceptable provided the identity of the individual cannot be ascertained. Names or other identifying references must therefore be removed prior to their use for these purposes.

4. *Taking of samples for DNA analysis*

The taking of samples for DNA analysis should only be carried out in circumstances determined by the domestic law; it being understood that in some states this may necessitate specific authorisation from a judicial authority ...

8. *Storage of samples and data*

Samples or other body tissue taken from individuals for DNA analysis should not be kept after the rendering of the final decision in the case for which they were used, unless it is necessary for purposes directly linked to those for which they were collected.

Measures should be taken to ensure that the results of DNA analysis are deleted when it is no longer necessary to keep it for the purposes for which it was used. The results of DNA analysis and the information so derived may, however, be retained where the individual concerned has been convicted of serious offences against the life, integrity or security of persons. In such cases strict storage periods should be defined by domestic law.

Samples and other body tissues, or the information derived from them, may be stored for longer periods:

– when the person so requests; or
– when the sample cannot be attributed to an individual, for example when it is found at the scene of a crime;

Where the security of the state is involved, the domestic law of the member state may permit retention of the samples, the results of DNA analysis and the information so derived even though the individual concerned has not been charged or convicted of an offence. In such cases strict storage periods should be defined by domestic law … '

44.	The Explanatory Memorandum to the Recommendation stated, as regards item 8:

'47.	The working party was well aware that the drafting of Recommendation 8 was a delicate matter, involving different protected interests of a very difficult nature. It was necessary to strike the right balance between these interests. Both the European Convention on Human Rights and the Data Protection Convention provide exceptions for the interests of the suppression of criminal offences and the protection of the rights and freedoms of third parties. However, the exceptions are only allowed to the extent that they are compatible with what is necessary in a democratic society …

49.	Since the primary aim of the collection of samples and the carrying out of DNA analysis on such samples is the identification of offenders and the exoneration of suspected offenders, the data should be deleted once persons have been cleared of suspicion. The issue then arises as to how long the DNA findings and the samples on which they were based can be stored in the case of a finding of guilt.

50.	The general rule should be that the data are deleted when they are no longer necessary for the purposes for which they were collected and used. This would in general be the case when a final decision has been rendered as to the culpability of the offender. By 'final decision' the CAHBI thought that this would normally, under domestic law, refer to a judicial decision. However, the working party recognised that there was a need to set up data bases in certain cases and for specific categories of offences which could be considered to constitute circumstances warranting another solution, because of the seriousness of the offences. The working party came to this conclusion after a thorough analysis of the relevant provisions in the European Convention on Human Rights, the Data Protection Convention and other legal instruments drafted within the framework of the Council of Europe. In addition, the working party took into consideration that all member states keep a criminal record and that such record may be used for the purposes of the criminal justice system … It took into account that such an exception would be permissible under certain strict conditions:

– when there has been a conviction;
– when the conviction concerns a serious criminal offence against the life, integrity and security of a person;
– the storage period is limited strictly;
– the storage is defined and regulated by law;
– the storage is subject to control by Parliament or an independent supervisory body'

B. Law and practice in the Council of Europe member States

45.	According to the information provided by the parties or otherwise available to the Court, a majority of the Council of Europe member States allow the compulsory taking of fingerprints and cellular samples in the context of criminal proceedings. At least 20 member States make provision for the taking of DNA information and storing it on national data bases or in other forms (Austria, Belgium, the Czech Republic, Denmark, Estonia, Finland, France, Germany, Greece, Hungary, Ireland,[4] Italy,[5] Latvia, Luxembourg, the Netherlands, Norway, Poland, Spain, Sweden and Switzerland). This number is steadily increasing.

46. In most of these countries (including Austria, Belgium, Finland, France, Germany, Hungary, Ireland, Italy, Luxembourg, the Netherlands, Norway, Poland, Spain and Sweden), the taking of DNA information in the context of criminal proceedings is not systematic but limited to some specific circumstances and/or to more serious crimes, notably those punishable by certain terms of imprisonment.

47. The United Kingdom is the only member State expressly to permit the systematic and indefinite retention of DNA profiles and cellular samples of persons who have been acquitted or in respect of whom criminal proceedings have been discontinued. Five States (Belgium, Hungary, Ireland, Italy and Sweden) require such information to be destroyed *ex officio* upon acquittal or the discontinuance of the criminal proceedings. Ten other States apply the same general rule with certain very limited exceptions: Germany, Luxembourg and the Netherlands allow such information to be retained where suspicions remain about the person or if further investigations are needed in a separate case; Austria permits its retention where there is a risk that the suspect will commit a dangerous offence and Poland does likewise in relation to certain serious crimes; Norway and Spain allow the retention of profiles if the defendant is acquitted for lack of criminal accountability; Finland and Denmark allow retention for 1 and 10 years respectively in the event of an acquittal and Switzerland for 1 year when proceedings have been discontinued. In France DNA profiles can be retained for 25 years after an acquittal or discharge; during this period the public prosecutor may order their earlier deletion, either on his or her own motion or upon request, if their retention has ceased to be required for the purposes of identification in connection with a criminal investigation. Estonia and Latvia also appear to allow the retention of DNA profiles of suspects for certain periods after acquittal.

48. The retention of DNA profiles of convicted persons is allowed, as a general rule, for limited periods of time after the conviction or after the convicted person's death. The United Kingdom thus also appears to be the only member State expressly to allow the systematic and indefinite retention of both profiles and samples of convicted persons.

49. Complaint mechanisms before data-protection monitoring bodies and/or before courts are available in most of the member States with regard to decisions to take cellular samples or retain samples or DNA profiles.

C. European Union

50. Directive 95/46/EC of 24 October 1995 on the protection of individuals with regard to the processing of personal data and on the free movement of such data provides that the object of national laws on the processing of personal data is notably to protect the right to privacy as recognised both in Article 8 of the European Convention on Human Rights and in the general principles of Community law. The Directive sets out a number of principles in order to give substance to and amplify those contained in the Data Protection Convention of the Council of Europe. It allows Member States to adopt legislative measures to

restrict the scope of certain obligations and rights provided for in the Directive when such a restriction constitutes notably a necessary measure for the prevention, investigation, detection and prosecution of criminal offences (Article 13).

51. The Prüm Convention on the stepping up of cross-border cooperation, particularly in combating terrorism, cross-border crime and illegal migration, which was signed by several members of the European Union on 27 May 2005, sets out rules for the supply of fingerprinting and DNA data to other Contracting Parties and their automated checking against their relevant data bases. The Convention provides *inter alia*:

'Article 35 – Purpose
2. ... The Contracting Party administering the file may process the data supplied ... solely where this is necessary for the purposes of comparison, providing automated replies to searches or recording ... The supplied data shall be deleted immediately following data comparison or automated replies to searches unless further processing is necessary for the purposes mentioned above].'

52. Article 34 guarantees a level of protection of personal data at least equal to that resulting from the Data Protection Convention and requires the Contracting Parties to take into account Recommendation R (87) 15 of the Committee of Ministers of the Council of Europe.

53. The Council framework decision of 24 June 2008 on the protection of personal data processed in the framework of police and judicial cooperation in criminal matters states *inter alia*:

'Article 5
Establishment of time-limits for erasure and review
Appropriate time-limits shall be established for the erasure of personal data or for a periodic review of the need for the storage of the data. Procedural measures shall ensure that these time-limits are observed.'

D. Case-law in other jurisdictions

54. In the case of *R* v. *RC* [[2005] 3 SCR 99, 2005 SCC 61] the Supreme Court of Canada considered the issue of retaining a juvenile first-time offender's DNA sample on the national data bank. The court upheld the decision by a trial judge who had found, in the light of the principles and objects of youth criminal justice legislation, that the impact of the DNA retention would be grossly disproportionate. In his opinion, Fish J. observed:

'Of more concern, however, is the impact of an order on an individual's informational privacy interests. In *R*. v. *Plant*, [1993] 3 SCR 281, at p. 293, the Court found that s. 8 of the Charter protected the 'biographical core of personal information which individuals in a free and democratic society would wish to maintain and control from dissemination to the state'. An individual's DNA contains the 'highest level of personal and private information': SAB, at para. 48. Unlike a fingerprint, it is capable of revealing the most intimate details of a person's biological makeup ... The taking and retention of a DNA sample is not a trivial matter and, absent a compelling public interest, would inherently constitute a grave intrusion on the subject's right to personal and informational privacy.'

E. UN Convention on the Rights of the Child of 1989

55. Article 40 of the UN Convention on the Rights of the Child of 20 November 1989 states the right of every child alleged as, accused of, or recognised as having infringed the penal law to be treated in a manner consistent with the

promotion of the child's sense of dignity and worth, which reinforces the child's respect for the human rights and fundamental freedoms of others and which takes into account the child's age and the desirability of promoting the child's reintegration and the child's assuming a constructive role in society.

IV. THIRD PARTIES' SUBMISSIONS

56. [Third-party submissions made by The National Council for Civil Liberties ('Liberty') and by Privacy International were noted]

THE LAW

I. ALLEGED VIOLATION OF ARTICLE 8 OF THE CONVENTION

58. The applicants complained under Article 8 of the Convention about the retention of their fingerprints, cellular samples and DNA profiles pursuant to section 64 (1A) of the Police and Criminal Evidence Act 1984 ('the PACE'). Article 8 provides, so far as relevant, as follows:
'1. Everyone has the right to respect for his private ... life ...
2. There shall be no interference by a public authority with the exercise of this right except such as is in accordance with the law and is necessary in a democratic society ... for the prevention of disorder or crime...'

A. Existence of an interference with private life

59. The Court will first consider whether the retention by the authorities of the applicants' fingerprints, DNA profiles and cellular samples constitutes an interference in their private life.

1. The parties' submissions

(a) **The applicants**

60. The applicants submitted that the retention of their fingerprints, cellular samples and DNA profiles interfered with their right to respect for private life as they were crucially linked to their individual identity and concerned a type of personal information that they were entitled to keep within their control. They recalled that the initial taking of such bio-information had consistently been held to engage Article 8 and submitted that their retention was more controversial given the wealth of private information that became permanently available to others and thus came out of the control of the person concerned. They stressed in particular the social stigma and psychological implications provoked by such retention in the case of children, which made the interference with the right to private life all the more pressing in respect of the first applicant.

61. They considered that the Convention organs' case-law supported this contention, as did a recent domestic decision of the Information Tribunal (*Chief Constables of West Yorkshire, South Yorkshire and North Wales Police* v. *the Information Commissioner,* [2005] UK IT EA 2005 0010 (12 October 2005), 173). The latter decision relied on the speech of Baroness Hale of Richmond in the House of Lords (see paragraph 25 above) and followed in substance her finding when deciding a similar question about the application of Article 8 to the retention of conviction data.

62. They further emphasised that retention of cellular samples involved an even greater degree of interference with Article 8 rights as they contained full genetic information about a person including genetic information about his or her

relatives. It was of no significance whether information was actually extracted from the samples or caused a detriment in a particular case as an individual was entitled to a guarantee that such information which fundamentally belonged to him would remain private and not be communicated or accessible without his permission.

(b) The Government

63. The Government accepted that fingerprints, DNA profiles and samples were 'personal data' within the meaning of the Data Protection Act in the hands of those who can identify the individual. They considered, however, that the mere retention of fingerprints, DNA profiles and samples for the limited use permitted under section 64 of the PACE did not fall within the ambit of the right to respect for private life under Article 8 § 1 of the Convention. Unlike the initial taking of this data, their retention did not interfere with the physical and psychological integrity of the persons; nor did it breach their right to personal development, to establish and develop relationships with other human beings or the right to self-determination.

64. The Government submitted that the applicants' real concerns related to fears about the future uses of stored samples, to anticipated methods of analysis of DNA material and to potential intervention with the private life of individuals through active surveillance. It emphasised in this connection that the permitted extent of the use of the material was clearly and expressly limited by the legislation, the technological processes of DNA profiling and the nature of the DNA profile extracted.

65. The profile was merely a sequence of numbers which provided a means of identifying a person against bodily tissue, containing no materially intrusive information about an individual or his personality. The DNA database was a collection of such profiles which could be searched using material from a crime scene and a person would be identified only if and to the extent that a match was obtained against the sample. Familial searching through partial matches only occurred in very rare cases and was subject to very strict controls. Fingerprints, DNA profiles and samples were neither susceptible to any subjective commentary nor provided any information about a person's activities and thus presented no risk to affect the perception of an individual or affect his or her reputation. Even if such retention were capable of falling within the ambit of Article 8 § 1 the extremely limited nature of any adverse effects rendered the retention not sufficiently serious to constitute an interference.

2. The Court's assessment

(a) General principles

66. The Court recalls that the concept of 'private life' is a broad term not susceptible to exhaustive definition. It covers the physical and psychological integrity of a person (see *Pretty* v. *the United Kingdom*, no. 2346/02, § 61, ECHR 2002-III, and *Y.F.* v. *Turkey*, no. 24209/94, § 33, ECHR 2003-IX). It can therefore embrace multiple aspects of the person's physical and social identity (see *Mikulić* v. *Croatia*, no. 53176/99, § 53, ECHR 2002-I). Elements such as, for example, gender identification, name and sexual orientation and sexual life fall within the personal sphere protected by Article 8 (see, among other authorities, *Bensaid* v. *the United Kingdom*, no. 44599/98, § 47, ECHR 2001-I with further references, and *Peck* v. *the United Kingdom*, no. 44647/98, § 57, ECHR 2003-I). Beyond a person's name, his or her private and family life may include

other means of personal identification and of linking to a family (see *mutatis mutandis Burghartz* v. *Switzerland*, 22 February 1994, § 24, Series A no. 280-B; and *Ünal Tekeli* v. *Turkey*, no. 29865/96, § 42, ECHR 2004-X (extracts)). Information about the person's health is an important element of private life (see *Z.* v. *Finland*, 25 February 1997, § 71, *Reports of Judgments and Decisions* 1997-I). The Court furthermore considers that an individual's ethnic identity must be regarded as another such element (see in particular Article 6 of the Data Protection Convention quoted in paragraph 41 above, which lists personal data revealing racial origin as a special category of data along with other sensitive information about an individual). Article 8 protects in addition a right to personal development, and the right to establish and develop relationships with other human beings and the outside world (see, for example, *Burghartz*, cited above, opinion of the Commission, p. 37, § 47, and *Friedl* v. *Austria*, judgment of 31 January 1995, Series A no. 305-B, opinion of the Commission, p. 20, § 45). The concept of private life moreover includes elements relating to a person's right to their image (*Sciacca* v. *Italy*, no. 50774/99, § 29, ECHR 2005-I).

67.   The mere storing of data relating to the private life of an individual amounts to an interference within the meaning of Article 8 (see *Leander* v. *Sweden*, 26 March 1987, § 48, Series A no. 116). The subsequent use of the stored information has no bearing on that finding (*Amann* v. *Switzerland* [GC], no. 27798/95, § 69, ECHR 2000-II). However, in determining whether the personal information retained by the authorities involves any of the private-life aspects mentioned above, the Court will have due regard to the specific context in which the information at issue has been recorded and retained, the nature of the records, the way in which these records are used and processed and the results that may be obtained (see, *mutatis mutandis, Friedl*, cited above, §§49–51, and *Peck* v. *the United Kingdom*, cited above, § 59).

(b) Application of the principles to the present case

68.   The Court notes at the outset that all three categories of the personal information retained by the authorities in the present cases, namely fingerprints, DNA profiles and cellular samples, constitute personal data within the meaning of the Data Protection Convention as they relate to identified or identifiable individuals. The Government accepted that all three categories are 'personal data' within the meaning of the Data Protection Act 1998 in the hands of those who are able to identify the individual.

69.   The Convention organs have already considered in various circumstances questions relating to the retention of such personal data by the authorities in the context of criminal proceedings. As regards the nature and scope of the information contained in each of these three categories of data, the Court has distinguished in the past between the retention of fingerprints and the retention of cellular samples and DNA profiles in view of the stronger potential for future use of the personal information contained in the latter (see *Van der Velden* v. *the Netherlands* (dec.), no. 29514/05, ECHR 2006- ...). The Court considers it appropriate to examine separately the question of interference with the applicants' right to respect for their private lives by the retention of their cellular samples and DNA profiles on the one hand, and of their fingerprints on the other.

(i) Cellular samples and DNA profiles

70.   In *Van der Velden*, the Court considered that, given the use to which cellular material in particular could conceivably be put in the future, the systematic

retention of that material was sufficiently intrusive to disclose interference with the right to respect for private life (see *Van der Velden* cited above). The Government criticised that conclusion on the ground that it speculated on the theoretical future use of samples and that there was no such interference at present.

71. The Court maintains its view that an individual's concern about the possible future use of private information retained by the authorities is legitimate and relevant to a determination of the issue of whether there has been an interference. Indeed, bearing in mind the rapid pace of developments in the field of genetics and information technology, the Court cannot discount the possibility that in the future the private-life interests bound up with genetic information may be adversely affected in novel ways or in a manner which cannot be anticipated with precision today. Accordingly, the Court does not find any sufficient reason to depart from its finding in the *Van der Velden* case.

72. Legitimate concerns about the conceivable use of cellular material in the future are not, however, the only element to be taken into account in the determination of the present issue. In addition to the highly personal nature of cellular samples, the Court notes that they contain much sensitive information about an individual, including information about his or her health. Moreover, samples contain a unique genetic code of great relevance to both the individual and his relatives. In this respect the Court concurs with the opinion expressed by Baroness Hale in the House of Lords (see paragraph 25 above).

73. Given the nature and the amount of personal information contained in cellular samples, their retention *per se* must be regarded as interfering with the right to respect for the private lives of the individuals concerned. That only a limited part of this information is actually extracted or used by the authorities through DNA profiling and that no immediate detriment is caused in a particular case does not change this conclusion (see *Amann* cited above, § 69).

74. As regards DNA profiles themselves, the Court notes that they contain a more limited amount of personal information extracted from cellular samples in a coded form. The Government submitted that a DNA profile is nothing more than a sequence of numbers or a bar-code containing information of a purely objective and irrefutable character and that the identification of a subject only occurs in case of a match with another profile in the database. They also submitted that, being in coded form, computer technology is required to render the information intelligible and that only a limited number of persons would be able to interpret the data in question.

75. The Court observes, nonetheless, that the profiles contain substantial amounts of unique personal data. While the information contained in the profiles may be considered objective and irrefutable in the sense submitted by the Government, their processing through automated means allows the authorities to go well beyond neutral identification. The Court notes in this regard that the Government accepted that DNA profiles could be, and indeed had in some cases been, used for familial searching with a view to identifying a possible genetic relationship between individuals. They also accepted the highly sensitive nature of such searching and the need for very strict controls in this respect. In the Court's view, the DNA profiles' capacity to provide a means of identifying genetic relationships between individuals (see paragraph 39 above) is in itself sufficient to conclude that their retention interferes with the right to the private life of the individuals concerned. The frequency of familial searches, the safeguards attached thereto and the likelihood of detriment in a particular case are immaterial in this respect (see *Amann* cited above, § 69).

This conclusion is similarly not affected by the fact that, since the information is in coded form, it is intelligible only with the use of computer technology and capable of being interpreted only by a limited number of persons.

76. The Court further notes that it is not disputed by the Government that the processing of DNA profiles allows the authorities to assess the likely ethnic origin of the donor and that such techniques are in fact used in police investigations (see paragraph 40 above). The possibility the DNA profiles create for inferences to be drawn as to ethnic origin makes their retention all the more sensitive and susceptible of affecting the right to private life. This conclusion is consistent with the principle laid down in the Data Protection Convention and reflected in the Data Protection Act that both list personal data revealing ethnic origin among the special categories of sensitive data attracting a heightened level of protection (see paragraphs 30–31 and 41 above).

77. In view of the foregoing, the Court concludes that the retention of both cellular samples and DNA profiles discloses an interference with the applicants' right to respect for their private lives, within the meaning of Article 8 § 1 of the Convention.

(ii) Fingerprints

78. It is common ground that fingerprints do not contain as much information as either cellular samples or DNA profiles. The issue of alleged interference with the right to respect for private life caused by their retention by the authorities has already been considered by the Convention organs.

79. In *McVeigh*, the Commission first examined the issue of the taking and retention of fingerprints as part of a series of investigative measures. It accepted that at least some of the measures disclosed an interference with the applicants' private life, while leaving open the question of whether the retention of fingerprints alone would amount to such interference (*McVeigh, O'Neill and Evans* (no. 8022/77, 8025/77 and 8027/77, Report of the Commission of 18 March 1981, DR 25, p.15, § 224).

80. In *Kinnunen,* the Commission considered that fingerprints and photographs retained following the applicant's arrest did not constitute an interference with his private life as they did not contain any subjective appreciations which called for refutation. The Commission noted, however, that the data at issue had been destroyed nine years later at the applicant's request (*Kinnunen* v. *Finland*, no. 24950/94, Commission decision of 15 May 1996).

81. Having regard to these findings and the questions raised in the present case, the Court considers it appropriate to review this issue. It notes at the outset that the applicants' fingerprint records constitute their personal data (see paragraph 68 above) which contain certain external identification features much in the same way as, for example, personal photographs or voice samples.

82. In *Friedl*, the Commission considered that the retention of anonymous photographs that have been taken at a public demonstration did not interfere with the right to respect for private life. In so deciding, it attached special weight to the fact that the photographs concerned had not been entered in a data-processing system and that the authorities had taken no steps to identify the persons photographed by means of data processing (see *Friedl* cited above, §§ 49–51).

83. In *P. G. and J. H.*, the Court considered that the recording of data and the systematic or permanent nature of the record could give rise to private-life considerations even though the data in question may have been available in the public domain or otherwise. The Court noted that a permanent record of a person's voice for further analysis was of direct relevance to identifying that

person when considered in conjunction with other personal data. It accordingly regarded the recording of the applicants' voices for such further analysis as amounting to interference with their right to respect for their private lives (see *P. G. and J. H.* v. *the United Kingdom*, no. 44787/98, § 59–60, ECHR 2001-IX).

84. The Court is of the view that the general approach taken by the Convention organs in respect of photographs and voice samples should also be followed in respect of fingerprints. The Government distinguished the latter by arguing that they constituted neutral, objective and irrefutable material and, unlike photographs, were unintelligible to the untutored eye and without a comparator fingerprint. While true, this consideration cannot alter the fact that fingerprints objectively contain unique information about the individual concerned allowing his or her identification with precision in a wide range of circumstances. They are thus capable of affecting his or her private life and retention of this information without the consent of the individual concerned cannot be regarded as neutral or insignificant.

85. The Court accordingly considers that the retention of fingerprints on the authorities' records in connection with an identified or identifiable individual may in itself give rise, notwithstanding their objective and irrefutable character, to important private-life concerns.

86. In the instant case, the Court notes furthermore that the applicants' fingerprints were initially taken in criminal proceedings and subsequently recorded on a nationwide database with the aim of being permanently kept and regularly processed by automated means for criminal-identification purposes. It is accepted in this regard that, because of the information they contain, the retention of cellular samples and DNA profiles has a more important impact on private life than the retention of fingerprints. However, the Court, like Baroness Hale (see paragraph 25 above), considers that, while it may be necessary to distinguish between the taking, use and storage of fingerprints, on the one hand, and samples and profiles, on the other, in determining the question of justification, the retention of fingerprints constitutes an interference with the right to respect for private life.

B. Justification for the interference

1. The parties' submissions

(a) The applicants

87. The applicants argued that the retention of fingerprints, cellular samples and DNA profiles was not justified under the second paragraph of Article 8. The Government were given a very wide remit to use samples and DNA profiles notably for 'purposes related to the prevention or detection of crime', 'the investigation of an offence' or 'the conduct of a prosecution'. These purposes were vague and open to abuse as they might in particular lead to the collation of detailed personal information outside the immediate context of the investigation of a particular offence. The applicants further submitted that there were insufficient procedural safeguards against misuse or abuse of the information. Records on the PNC were not only accessible to the police, but also to 56 non-police bodies, including Government agencies and departments, private groups such as British Telecom and the Association of British Insurers, and even certain employers. Furthermore, the PNC was linked to the Europe-wide 'Schengen Information System'. Consequently, their case involved a very

substantial and controversial interference with the right to private life, as notably illustrated by ongoing public debate and disagreement about the subject in the United Kingdom. Contrary to the assertion of the Government, the applicants concluded that the issue of the retention of this material was of great individual concern and the State had a narrow margin of appreciation in this field.

88. The applicants contended that the indefinite retention of fingerprints, cellular samples and DNA profiles of unconvicted persons could not be regarded as 'necessary in a democratic society' for the purpose of preventing crime. In particular, there was no justification at all for the retention of cellular samples following the original generation of the DNA profile; nor had the efficacy of the profiles' retention been convincingly demonstrated since the high number of DNA matches relied upon by the Government was not shown to have led to successful prosecutions. Likewise, in most of the specific examples provided by the Government the successful prosecution had not been contingent on the retention of the records and in certain others the successful outcome could have been achieved through more limited retention in time and scope.

89. The applicants further submitted that the retention was disproportionate because of its blanket nature irrespective of the offences involved, the unlimited period, the failure to take account of the applicants' circumstances and the lack of an independent decision-making process or scrutiny when considering whether or not to order retention. They further considered the retention regime to be inconsistent with the Council of Europe's guidance on the subject. They emphasised, finally, that retention of the records cast suspicion on persons who had been acquitted or discharged of crimes, thus implying that they were not wholly innocent. The retention thus resulted in stigma which was particularly detrimental to children as in the case of S. and to members of certain ethnic groups over-represented on the database.

(b) The Government

90. The Government submitted that any interference resulting from the retention of the applicants' fingerprints, cellular samples and DNA profiles was justified under the second paragraph of Article 8. It was in accordance with the law as expressly provided for, and governed by section 64 of the PACE, which set out detailed powers and restrictions on the taking of fingerprints and samples and clearly stated that they would be retained by the authorities regardless of the outcome of the proceedings in respect of which they were taken. The exercise of the discretion to retain fingerprints and samples was also, in any event, subject to the normal principles of law regulating discretionary power and to judicial review.

91. The Government further stated that the interference was necessary and proportionate for the legitimate purpose of the prevention of disorder or crime and/or the protection of the rights and freedoms of others. It was of vital importance that law enforcement agencies took full advantage of available techniques of modern technology and forensic science in the prevention, investigation and detection of crime for the interests of society generally. They submitted that the retained material was of inestimable value in the fight against crime and terrorism and the detection of the guilty and provided statistics in support of this view. They emphasised that the benefits to the criminal-justice system were enormous, not only permitting the detection of the guilty but also eliminating the innocent from inquiries and correcting and preventing miscarriages of justice.

Law and the technologies of the twenty-first century

92. As at 30 September 2005, the National DNA database held 181,000 profiles from individuals who would have been entitled to have those profiles destroyed before the 2001 amendments. 8,251 of those were subsequently linked with crime-scene stains which involved 13,079 offences, including 109 murders, 55 attempted murders, 116 rapes, 67 sexual offences, 105 aggravated burglaries and 126 offences of the supply of controlled drugs.

93. The Government also submitted specific examples of use of DNA material for successful investigation and prosecution in some eighteen specific cases. In ten of these cases the DNA profiles of suspects matched some earlier unrelated crime-scene stains retained on the database, thus allowing successful prosecution for those earlier crimes. In another case, two suspects arrested for rape were eliminated from the investigation as their DNA profiles did not match the crime-scene stain. In two other cases the retention of DNA profiles of the persons found guilty of certain minor offences (disorder and theft) led to establishing their involvement in other crimes committed later. In one case the retention of a suspect's DNA profile following an alleged immigration offence helped his extradition to the United Kingdom a year later when he was identified by one of his victims as having committed rape and murder. Finally, in four cases DNA profiles retained from four persons suspected but not convicted of certain offences (possession of offensive weapons, violent disorder and assault) matched the crime-scene stains collected from victims of rape up to two years later.

94. The Government contended that the retention of fingerprints, cellular samples and DNA profiles could not be regarded as excessive since they were kept for specific limited statutory purposes and stored securely and subject to the safeguards identified. Their retention was neither warranted by any degree of suspicion of the applicants' involvement in a crime or propensity to crime nor directed at retaining records in respect of investigated alleged offences in the past. The records were retained because the police had already been lawfully in possession of them, and their retention would assist in the future prevention and detection of crime in general by increasing the size of the database. Retention resulted in no stigma and produced no practical consequence for the applicants unless the records matched a crime-scene profile. A fair balance was thus struck between individual rights and the general interest of the community and fell within the State's margin of appreciation.

2. *The Court's assessment*

(a) **In accordance with the law**

95. The Court recalls its well established case-law that the wording 'in accordance with the law' requires the impugned measure both to have some basis in domestic law and to be compatible with the rule of law, which is expressly mentioned in the preamble to the Convention and inherent in the object and purpose of Article 8. The law must thus be adequately accessible and foreseeable, that is, formulated with sufficient precision to enable the individual – if need be with appropriate advice – to regulate his conduct. For domestic law to meet these requirements, it must afford adequate legal protection against arbitrariness and accordingly indicate with sufficient clarity the scope of discretion conferred on the competent authorities and the manner of its exercise (see *Malone* v. *the United Kingdom*, 2 August 1984, §§ 66–68, Series A no. 82; *Rotaru* v. *Romania* [GC], no. 28341/95, § 55, ECHR 2000-V; and *Amann* cited above, § 56).

96. The level of precision required of domestic legislation – which cannot in any case provide for every eventuality – depends to a considerable degree on the content of the instrument in question, the field it is designed to cover and the number and status of those to whom it is addressed (*Hasan and Chaush v. Bulgaria* [GC], no. 30985/96, § 84, ECHR 2000-XI, with further references).

97. The Court notes that section 64 of the PACE provides that the fingerprints or samples taken from a person in connection with the investigation of an offence may be retained after they have fulfilled the purposes for which they were taken (see paragraph 27 above). The Court agrees with the Government that the retention of the applicants' fingerprint and DNA records had a clear basis in the domestic law. There is also clear evidence that these records are retained in practice save in exceptional circumstances. The fact that chief police officers have power to destroy them in such rare cases does not make the law insufficiently certain from the point of view of the Convention.

98. As regards the conditions attached to and arrangements for the storing and use of this personal information, section 64 is far less precise. It provides that retained samples and fingerprints must not be used by any person except for purposes related to the prevention or detection of crime, the investigation of an offence or the conduct of a prosecution.

99. The Court agrees with the applicants that at least the first of these purposes is worded in rather general terms and may give rise to extensive interpretation. It reiterates that it is as essential, in this context, as in telephone tapping, secret surveillance and covert intelligence-gathering, to have clear, detailed rules governing the scope and application of measures, as well as minimum safeguards concerning, *inter alia*, duration, storage, usage, access of third parties, procedures for preserving the integrity and confidentiality of data and procedures for its destruction, thus providing sufficient guarantees against the risk of abuse and arbitrariness (see, *mutatis mutandis, Kruslin* v. *France*, 24 April 1990, §§ 33 and 35, Series A no. 176-A; *Rotaru*, cited above, § 57–59; *Weber and Saravia* v. *Germany* (dec.), no. 54934/00, ECHR 2006-... *Association for European Integration and Human Rights and Ekimdzhiev* v. *Bulgaria*, no. 62540/00, §§ 75–77, 28 June 2007; *Liberty and Others* v. *the United Kingdom*, no. 58243/00, § 62–63, 1 July 2008). The Court notes, however, that these questions are in this case closely related to the broader issue of whether the interference was necessary in a democratic society. In view of its analysis in paragraphs 105–126 below, the Court does not find it necessary to decide whether the wording of section 64 meets the 'quality of law' requirements within the meaning of Article 8 § 2 of the Convention.

(b) Legitimate aim

100. The Court agrees with the Government that the retention of fingerprint and DNA information pursues the legitimate purpose of the detection, and therefore, prevention of crime. While the original taking of this information pursues the aim of linking a particular person to the particular crime of which he or she is suspected, its retention pursues the broader purpose of assisting in the identification of future offenders.

(c) Necessary in a democratic society

(i) General principles

101. An interference will be considered 'necessary in a democratic society' for a legitimate aim if it answers a 'pressing social need' and, in particular, if it is

proportionate to the legitimate aim pursued and if the reasons adduced by the national authorities to justify it are 'relevant and sufficient'. While it is for the national authorities to make the initial assessment in all these respects, the final evaluation of whether the interference is necessary remains subject to review by the Court for conformity with the requirements of the Convention (see *Coster* v. *the United Kingdom* [GC], no. 24876/94, § 104, 18 January 2001, with further references).

102. A margin of appreciation must be left to the competent national authorities in this assessment. The breadth of this margin varies and depends on a number of actors including the Convention right in issue, its importance for the individual, the nature of the interference and the object pursued by the interference. The margin will tend to be narrower where the right at stake is crucial to the individual's effective enjoyment of intimate or key rights (see *Connors* v. *the United Kingdom*, no. 66746/01, § 82, 27 May 2004, with further references). Where a particularly important facet of an individual's existence or identity is at stake, the margin allowed to the State will be restricted (see *Evans* v. *the United Kingdom* [GC], no. 6339/05, § 77, ECHR 2007- …). Where, however, there is no consensus within the Member States of the Council of Europe, either as to the relative importance of the interest at stake or as to how best to protect it, the margin will be wider (see *Dickson* v. *the United Kingdom* [GC], no. 44362/04, § 78, ECHR 2007- …).

103. The protection of personal data is of fundamental importance to a person's enjoyment of his or her right to respect for private and family life, as guaranteed by Article 8 of the Convention. The domestic law must afford appropriate safeguards to prevent any such use of personal data as may be inconsistent with the guarantees of this Article (see, *mutatis mutandis*, Z., cited above, § 95). The need for such safeguards is all the greater where the protection of personal data undergoing automatic processing is concerned, not least when such data are used for police purposes. The domestic law should notably ensure that such data are relevant and not excessive in relation to the purposes for which they are stored; and preserved in a form which permits identification of the data subjects for no longer than is required for the purpose for which those data are stored (see Article 5 of the Data Protection Convention and the preamble thereto and Principle 7 of Recommendation R(87)15 of the Committee of Ministers regulating the use of personal data in the police sector). The domestic law must also afford adequate guarantees that retained personal data was efficiently protected from misuse and abuse (see notably Article 7 of the Data Protection Convention). The above considerations are especially valid as regards the protection of special categories of more sensitive data (see Article 6 of the Data Protection Convention) and more particularly of DNA information, which contains the person's genetic make-up of great importance to both the person concerned and his or her family (see Recommendation No. R(92)1 of the Committee of Ministers on the use of analysis of DNA within the framework of the criminal justice system).

104. The interests of the data subjects and the community as a whole in protecting the personal data, including fingerprint and DNA information, may be outweighed by the legitimate interest in the prevention of crime (see Article 9 of the Data Protection Convention). However, the intrinsically private character of this information calls for the Court to exercise careful scrutiny of any State measure authorising its retention and use by the authorities without the consent of the person concerned (see, *mutatis mutandis*, Z. cited above, § 96).

(ii) Application of these principles to the present case

105. The Court finds it to be beyond dispute that the fight against crime, and in particular against organised crime and terrorism, which is one of the challenges faced by today's European societies, depends to a great extent on the use of modern scientific techniques of investigation and identification. The techniques of DNA analysis were acknowledged by the Council of Europe more than fifteen years ago as offering advantages to the criminal-justice system (see Recommendation R(92)1 of the Committee of Ministers, paragraphs 43–44 above). Nor is it disputed that the member States have since that time made rapid and marked progress in using DNA information in the determination of innocence or guilt.

106. However, while it recognises the importance of such information in the detection of crime, the Court must delimit the scope of its examination. The question is not whether the retention of fingerprints, cellular samples and DNA profiles may in general be regarded as justified under the Convention. The only issue to be considered by the Court is whether the retention of the fingerprint and DNA data of the applicants, as persons who had been suspected, but not convicted, of certain criminal offences, was justified under Article 8, paragraph 2 of the Convention.

107. The Court will consider this issue with due regard to the relevant instruments of the Council of Europe and the law and practice of the other Contracting States. The core principles of data protection require the retention of data to be proportionate in relation to the purpose of collection and insist on limited periods of storage (see paragraphs 41–44 above). These principles appear to have been consistently applied by the Contracting States in the police sector in accordance with the Data Protection Convention and subsequent Recommendations of the Committee of Ministers (see paragraphs 45–49 above).

108. As regards, more particularly, cellular samples, most of the Contracting States allow these materials to be taken in criminal proceedings only from individuals suspected of having committed offences of a certain minimum gravity. In the great majority of the Contracting States with functioning DNA databases, samples and DNA profiles derived from those samples are required to be removed or destroyed either immediately or within a certain limited time after acquittal or discharge. A restricted number of exceptions to this principle are allowed by some Contracting States (see paragraphs 47–48 above).

109. The current position of Scotland, as a part of the United Kingdom itself, is of particular significance in this regard. As noted above (see paragraph 36), the Scottish Parliament voted to allow retention of the DNA of unconvicted persons only in the case of adults charged with violent or sexual offences and even then, for three years only, with the possibility of an extension to keep the DNA sample and data for a further two years with the consent of a sheriff.

110. This position is notably consistent with Committee of Ministers' Recommendation R(92)1, which stresses the need for an approach which discriminates between different kinds of cases and for the application of strictly defined storage periods for data, even in more serious cases (see paragraphs 43–44 above). Against this background, England, Wales and Northern Ireland appear to be the only jurisdictions within the Council of Europe to allow the indefinite retention of fingerprint and DNA material of any person of any age suspected of any recordable offence.

111. The Government lay emphasis on the fact that the United Kingdom is in the vanguard of the development of the use of DNA samples in the detection of

crime and that other States have not yet achieved the same maturity in terms of the size and resources of DNA databases. It is argued that the comparative analysis of the law and practice in other States with less advanced systems is accordingly of limited importance.

112. The Court cannot, however, disregard the fact that, notwithstanding the advantages provided by comprehensive extension of the DNA database, other Contracting States have chosen to set limits on the retention and use of such data with a view to achieving a proper balance with the competing interests of preserving respect for private life. The Court observes that the protection afforded by Article 8 of the Convention would be unacceptably weakened if the use of modern scientific techniques in the criminal-justice system were allowed at any cost and without carefully balancing the potential benefits of the extensive use of such techniques against important private-life interests. In the Court's view, the strong consensus existing among the Contracting States in this respect is of considerable importance and narrows the margin of appreciation left to the respondent State in the assessment of the permissible limits of the interference with private life in this sphere. The Court considers that any State claiming a pioneer role in the development of new technologies bears special responsibility for striking the right balance in this regard.

113. In the present case, the applicants' fingerprints and cellular samples were taken and DNA profiles obtained in the context of criminal proceedings brought on suspicion of attempted robbery in the case of the first applicant and harassment of his partner in the case of the second applicant. The data were retained on the basis of legislation allowing for their indefinite retention, despite the acquittal of the former and the discontinuance of the criminal proceedings against the latter.

114. The Court must consider whether the permanent retention of fingerprint and DNA data of all suspected but unconvicted people is based on relevant and sufficient reasons.

115. Although the power to retain fingerprints, cellular samples and DNA profiles of unconvicted persons has only existed in England and Wales since 2001, the Government argue that their retention has been shown to be indispensable in the fight against crime. Certainly, the statistical and other evidence, which was before the House of Lords and is included in the material supplied by the Government (see paragraph 92 above) appears impressive, indicating that DNA profiles that would have been previously destroyed were linked with crime-scene stains in a high number of cases.

116. The applicants, however, assert that the statistics are misleading, a view supported in the Nuffield Report. It is true, as pointed out by the applicants, that the figures do not reveal the extent to which this 'link' with crime scenes resulted in convictions of the persons concerned or the number of convictions that were contingent on the retention of the samples of unconvicted persons. Nor do they demonstrate that the high number of successful matches with crime-scene stains was only made possible through indefinite retention of DNA records of all such persons. At the same time, in the majority of the specific cases quoted by the Government (see paragraph 93 above), the DNA records taken from the suspects produced successful matches only with earlier crime-scene stains retained on the data base. Yet such matches could have been made even in the absence of the present scheme, which permits the indefinite retention of DNA records of all suspected but unconvicted persons.

117. While neither the statistics nor the examples provided by the Government in themselves establish that the successful identification and prosecution

of offenders could not have been achieved without the permanent and indiscriminate retention of the fingerprint and DNA records of all persons in the applicants' position, the Court accepts that the extension of the database has nonetheless contributed to the detection and prevention of crime.

118. The question, however, remains whether such retention is proportionate and strikes a fair balance between the competing public and private interests.

119. In this respect, the Court is struck by the blanket and indiscriminate nature of the power of retention in England and Wales. The material may be retained irrespective of the nature or gravity of the offence with which the individual was originally suspected or of the age of the suspected offender; fingerprints and samples may be taken – and retained – from a person of any age, arrested in connection with a recordable offence, which includes minor or non-imprisonable offences. The retention is not time-limited; the material is retained indefinitely whatever the nature or seriousness of the offence of which the person was suspected. Moreover, there exist only limited possibilities for an acquitted individual to have the data removed from the nationwide database or the materials destroyed (see paragraph 35 above); in particular, there is no provision for independent review of the justification for the retention according to defined criteria, including such factors as the seriousness of the offence, previous arrests, the strength of the suspicion against the person and any other special circumstances.

120. The Court acknowledges that the level of interference with the applicants' right to private life may be different for each of the three different categories of personal data retained. The retention of cellular samples is particularly intrusive given the wealth of genetic and health information contained therein. However, such an indiscriminate and open-ended retention regime as the one in issue calls for careful scrutiny regardless of these differences.

121. The Government contend that the retention could not be considered as having any direct or significant effect on the applicants unless matches in the database were to implicate them in the commission of offences on a future occasion. The Court is unable to accept this argument and reiterates that the mere retention and storing of personal data by public authorities, however obtained, are to be regarded as having direct impact on the private-life interest of an individual concerned, irrespective of whether subsequent use is made of the data (see paragraph 67 above).

122. Of particular concern in the present context is the risk of stigmatisation, stemming from the fact that persons in the position of the applicants, who have not been convicted of any offence and are entitled to the presumption of innocence, are treated in the same way as convicted persons. In this respect, the Court must bear in mind that the right of every person under the Convention to be presumed innocent includes the general rule that no suspicion regarding an accused's innocence may be voiced after his acquittal (see *Asan Rushiti v. Austria*, no. 28389/95, § 31, 21 March 2000, with further references). It is true that the retention of the applicants' private data cannot be equated with the voicing of suspicions. Nonetheless, their perception that they are not being treated as innocent is heightened by the fact that their data are retained indefinitely in the same way as the data of convicted persons, while the data of those who have never been suspected of an offence are required to be destroyed.

123. The Government argue that the power of retention applies to all fingerprints and samples taken from a person in connection with the investigation of an offence and does not depend on innocence or guilt. It is further submitted that the fingerprints and samples have been lawfully taken and that their retention

is not related to the fact that they were originally suspected of committing a crime, the sole reason for their retention being to increase the size and, therefore, the use of the database in the identification of offenders in the future. The Court, however, finds this argument difficult to reconcile with the obligation imposed by section 64(3) of the PACE to destroy the fingerprints and samples of volunteers at their request, despite the similar value of the material in increasing the size and utility of the database. Weighty reasons would have to be put forward by the Government before the Court could regard as justified such a difference in treatment of the applicants' private data compared to that of other unconvicted people.

124. The Court further considers that the retention of the unconvicted persons' data may be especially harmful in the case of minors such as the first applicant, given their special situation and the importance of their development and integration in society. The Court has already emphasised, drawing on the provisions of Article 40 of the UN Convention on the Rights of the Child of 1989, the special position of minors in the criminal-justice sphere and has noted in particular the need for the protection of their privacy at criminal trials (see *T. v. the United Kingdom* [GC], no. 24724/94, §§ 75 and 85, 16 December 1999). In the same way, the Court considers that particular attention should be paid to the protection of juveniles from any detriment that may result from the retention by the authorities of their private data following acquittals of a criminal offence. The Court shares the view of the Nuffield Council as to the impact on young persons of the indefinite retention of their DNA material and notes the Council's concerns that the policies applied have led to the over-representation in the database of young persons and ethnic minorities, who have not been convicted of any crime (see paragraphs 38–40 above).

125. In conclusion, the Court finds that the blanket and indiscriminate nature of the powers of retention of the fingerprints, cellular samples and DNA profiles of persons suspected but not convicted of offences, as applied in the case of the present applicants, fails to strike a fair balance between the competing public and private interests and that the respondent State has overstepped any acceptable margin of appreciation in this regard. Accordingly, the retention at issue constitutes a disproportionate interference with the applicants' right to respect for private life and cannot be regarded as necessary in a democratic society. This conclusion obviates the need for the Court to consider the applicants' criticism regarding the adequacy of certain particular safeguards, such as too broad an access to the personal data concerned and insufficient protection against the misuse or abuse of such data.

126. Accordingly, there has been a violation of Article 8 of the Convention in the present case.

II. ALLEGED VIOLATION OF ARTICLE 14 TAKEN TOGETHER WITH ARTICLE 8 OF THE CONVENTION

127. The applicants submitted that they had been subjected to discriminatory treatment as compared to others in an analogous situation, namely other unconvicted persons whose samples had still to be destroyed under the legislation. This treatment related to their status and fell within the ambit of Article 14, which had always been liberally interpreted. For the reasons set out in their submissions under Article 8, there was no reasonable or objective justification for the treatment, nor any legitimate aim or reasonable relationship of proportionality to the purported aim of crime prevention, in particular as regards

the samples which played no role in crime detection or prevention. It was an entirely improper and prejudicial differentiation to retain materials of persons who should be presumed to be innocent.

128. The Government submitted that as Article 8 was not engaged Article 14 of the Convention was not applicable. Even if it were, there was no difference of treatment as all those in an analogous situation to the applicants were treated the same and the applicants could not compare themselves with those who had not had samples taken by the police or those who consented to give samples voluntarily. In any event, any difference in treatment complained of was not based on 'status' or a personal characteristic but on historical fact. If there was any difference in treatment, it was objectively justified and within the State's margin of appreciation.

129. The Court refers to its conclusion above that the retention of the applicants' fingerprints, cellular samples and DNA profiles was in violation of Article 8 of the Convention. In the light of the reasoning that has led to this conclusion, the Court considers that it is not necessary to examine separately the applicants' complaint under Article 14 of the Convention.

[The Court then dealt with some residual matters concerning compensation for the applicants' distress and anxiety and the extent of their recovery of legal costs and expenses]

FOR THESE REASONS, THE COURT UNANIMOUSLY

1. *Holds* that there has been a violation of Article 8 of the Convention;
2. *Holds* that it is not necessary to examine separately the complaint under Article 14 of the Convention;
3. *Holds* that the finding of a violation constitutes in itself sufficient just satisfaction for the non-pecuniary damage sustained by the applicants;
4. *Holds*
   (a) that the respondent State is to pay the applicants, within three months, EUR 42,000 (forty two thousand euros) in respect of costs and expenses (inclusive of any VAT which may be chargeable to the applicants), to be converted into pounds sterling at the rate applicable at the date of settlement, less EUR 2,613.07 already paid to the applicants in respect of legal aid;
   (b) that from the expiry of the above-mentioned three months until settlement simple interest shall be payable on the above amount at a rate equal to the marginal lending rate of the European Central Bank during the default period plus three percentage points;
5. *Dismisses* the remainder of the applicants' claim for just satisfaction.

Done in English and in French, and delivered at a public hearing in the Human Rights Building, Strasbourg, on 4 December 2008.

1   DNA stands for deoxyribonucleic acid; it is the chemical found in virtually every cell in the body and the genetic information therein, which is in the form of a code or language, determines physical characteristics and directs all the chemical processes in the body. Except for identical twins, each person's DNA is unique. DNA samples are cellular samples and any sub-samples or part samples retained from these after analysis. DNA profiles are digitised information which is stored electronically on the National DNA Database together with details of the person to whom it relates.

2   The Nuffield Council on Bioethics is an independent expert body composed of clinicians, lawyers, philosophers, scientists and theologians established

by the Nuffield Foundation in 1991. The present report was published on 18 September 2007 under the following title 'The forensic use of bioinformation: ethical issues'

3 Allele is one of two or more alternative forms of a particular gene. Different alleles may give rise to different forms of the characteristic for which the gene codes (*World Encyclopedia. Philip's, 2008. Oxford Reference Online. Oxford University Press*).

4 The law and practice in Ireland are presently governed by the Criminal Justice (Forensic Evidence) Act 1990. A new Bill has been approved by the Government with a view to extending the use and storage of DNA information in a national database. The Bill has not yet been approved by Parliament.

5 The Legislative Decree of 30 October 2007 establishing a national DNA database was approved by the Italian Government and the Senate. However, the Decree eventually expired without having been formally converted into a Statute as a mistake in the drafting was detected. A corrected version of the decree is expected to be issued in 2008.

5 Reflections on *Marper*

Marper was widely hailed as a landmark decision in the days that followed the publication of the Court's judgment; indeed, the Court itself had already acknowledged the importance of the case in deciding to hear it before the Grand Chamber.[23] This case provided the Court with an opportunity to deal with a number of the most important questions at issue in the retention of DNA in the form of a national DNA database: the question of *what* should be retained (only profiles or also actual samples); the question of *who* should be in a DNA database; the question of *why* (for the purpose of criminal investigation or more broadly for government activities); the question of *when* (after arrest, in the course of an investigation or only after conviction); and, finally, the question of *how long* the samples should be retained for. We will briefly reflect on the decisions the Court came to.

The Court tried in *Marper* to strike a balance between two competing interests, that of security and that of liberty, that is, between the public good of the detection and prevention of crime and the individual's rights to protection of his or her private life.[24]

The Court has traditionally viewed 'private life' extremely broadly and had no hesitation in reaffirming its earlier case law that the mere storing of personal data constitutes an interference within the meaning of Article 8 (para. 67).

---

[23] The Grand Chamber comprises seventeen judges rather than the usual seven for a Section (the President of the Court, the Vice-Presidents and the Section Presidents, plus twelve other judges chosen on a rotational basis) and is used to hear only those cases that either raise a serious issue regarding interpretation of the Convention or where a decision in the case may be inconsistent with previously established case law. In this case, the Chamber relinquished jurisdiction and thus the case was understood to raise issues vital to the interpretation of the Convention (see para. 5 of the judgment).

[24] As is usual in cases in which the Court finds a substantive violation, it did not bother to consider the case under Article 14 (non-discrimination) in conjunction with Article 8.

However, the Court did not stop there, but went on to distinguish between the level or degree of interference constituted by the retention of cellular samples, of DNA profiles and of fingerprints. The Court was most uncomfortable with the retention of cellular samples for the reason that retention of a sample, as opposed to a DNA profile, would potentially allow governments to extract vast amounts of information about an individual at a later date, as the technologies of genetics further developed. Thus, the Court was concerned not only with the issue of privacy in the present but with the possible repercussions for privacy in the future.

The Court's concerns with DNA profiles were rooted in the present, however. It accepted that DNA profiles contained less information than cellular samples, but nonetheless found that they contained 'substantial amounts of unique personal data' sufficient to constitute an interference (para. 75). In particular, the Court expressed concern about the use of DNA profiles for familial searching and the possibility of extracting information related to ethnicity from a DNA profile – a concern exacerbated by the fact that UK police investigations had already made use of such a possibility.[25] On the question of whether the storing of fingerprints constituted an interference with one's rights under Article 8, the Court tightened up on earlier case law. While in the case of *McVeigh*[26] the Court had refused to be drawn on whether the retention of fingerprints was sufficient in and of itself (as opposed to the use made of them) to constitute an interference, here the Court drew a firm, if slightly hesitant, conclusion that it does.

Thus in answering the question of 'what', the Court concluded that all three forms of data at issue – cellular samples, DNA profiles and fingerprints – are sufficient in themselves to constitute an interference.

As is usual in cases that fall under the second part of the Convention (Articles 8–11), the Court easily found that the retention of samples was in accordance with the law and pursued a legitimate aim, in this case the detection and prevention of crime. The important part of the decision comes in consideration of whether a given interference can be justified as necessary in a democratic society – in other words, consideration of whether the actions of the state have struck an appropriate balance between, in this case, crime detection and prevention and the right to privacy. In finding that the UK government's actions were disproportionate, the Court considered the remainder of the questions outlined above.

---

[25] What was not raised before the Court but has been the subject of public debate for a number of years is the apparent racially discriminatory nature of the collection of DNA. A 2009 report by the UK government advisory body, the Human Genetics Commission contained the information that three-quarters of black men between the ages of 18 and 35 are included in the database, despite being statistically no more likely to commit a serious crime. See Human Genetics Commission, *Nothing to Hide, Nothing to Fear? Balancing Individual Rights and the Public Interest In the Governance and Use of the National DNA Database*, November 2009; available online from www.hgc.gov.uk (last accessed 30 January 2012).

[26] *McVeigh, O'Neill and Evans v. UK* (1981), 25 DR 15.

The Court did not provide definitive answers to these questions. Instead, it provided a guiding framework for when given actions will fall foul of the right to private life under Article 8. Moreover, the questions cannot be considered in isolation from one another. The questions of who and when are particularly bound up together, as when the samples are taken determines in part the answer to the question of who (namely, someone convicted of a serious criminal offence or someone simply interviewed in the course of an investigation). In this regard, the Court was particularly concerned by the UK government's disregard for the age of the person whose information was being stored. Although the Court did not rule that storage of the data of a minor was in itself sufficient to tip the balance, its concerns about the particularly harmful effect on a child of inclusion in the database (para. 124) suggests that anything less than a child convicted of a very serious offence will fall foul of Article 8. Similarly, the Court was damning of the failure to differentiate between taking samples from those who had been arrested, those convicted and those convicted of a serious offence. Although the Court did not give clear indications on what the appropriate standard was, that is, when precisely it is acceptable to take samples, it is clear that the failure to differentiate will constitute a breach of Article 8. Moreover, the Court's concern about the stigmatisation of innocent people (para. 122) by inclusion in the database, and thus the failure to respect the principle of the presumption of innocence, is suggestive that it considers that the retention of such personal data from anyone who has not been convicted of an offence will cross the threshold and constitute a violation.

Turning to the question of the purpose, when asked in 2006 about possible restrictions to the national DNA database, the then-Prime Minister, Tony Blair, commented that 'The number on the database should be the maximum number you can get'.[27] The position of the Blair administration was unashamedly that the importance of as large a database as possible in the investigation of crime outweighs any possible infringement of the right to privacy. However, the Strasbourg Court's findings as to the disproportionality of the system of DNA retention was not affected by the statistical data presented by the UK government (and which was influential in the House of Lords ruling in favour of the government) that showed that the indiscriminate retention of DNA data was an important factor in the solving of crime, particularly in so-called cold cases. Thus, the purpose and usefulness of the data collected will not be sufficient to justify an interference of this type. Yet, the restriction of the use of such a database to the stated aim – that of fighting crime – did not form, somewhat surprisingly, a central element of this case, despite the applicants bringing attention to the fact that the UK database is accessible to fifty-six non-police bodies (para. 87). It may well be influential in future cases, however, where a violation is not quite so clear-cut.

[27] 'Blair champions expanding DNA database', 23 October 2006; available online at www.politics.co.uk/news/domestic-policy/crime/crime/blair-champions-expanding-dna-database-$455527.htm (last accessed 16 September 2009).

This left the question of the length of time for which samples may be retained. Once again, the Court did not consider a maximum nor give any indication of what maximum length of time might be acceptable under the Convention. What it did was note that the retention of data in the present case was not time-limited – that regardless of the question of who and of why that information was taken, data was to be stored indefinitely. This, coupled with the fact that the Court found that the English and Welsh system contained no provision for independent review where an individual wished to have his or her data removed from the system, is probably sufficient in itself to breach Article 8. This might, however, be subject to differentiation depending upon whether it is cellular samples, profiles or fingerprints that are being retained, again, where the regime is not so blanket as in the present case. Ultimately, in deciding whether a state has struck an inappropriate balance between public and private interests, the individual factors in each case are of crucial importance.

One further aspect of this case that is worth noting is the way in which the Court determined the balance of proportionality. As is clear from paragraph 108 of the judgment, the Court reasoned by means of comparison with the other contracting states in the Council of Europe. In effect, the Court took a stand not on some abstract principle of privacy but on the fact that the UK government has run ahead of the pack and thus finds itself outside the current consensus (as determined by the Court) on what is an acceptable balance between the legitimate aim of crime detection and prevention and the rights of the individual.[28] Given the weight that the Court accords to the European consensus, we might think that, if the consensus were to shift in favour of the public interest – in other words, were the majority of the Convention's members to follow the UK (Scotland excepted) down the route of a more indiscriminate collection and storage of DNA material – then the Court may well accord less weight to the protection of privacy in the future.[29] Suppose, though, that the herd instinct amongst members was not quite so strong; suppose that, while some members took their lead from the UK (Scotland excepted), others held their ground; suppose, in other words, that, after some movement of members' positions, the Court would declare that there was simply no consensus. In such circumstances, would the margin of appreciation be so broad that members, no matter what their regulatory position, could expect to survive a challenge under Articles 8 or 14?

---

[28] This method of reasoning is not unique to this case but is an established methodology of the Court. For more information on the so-called 'margin of appreciation doctrine' as it relates to Article 8, see D. J. Harris, M. O'Boyle, E. P. Bates and C. M. Buckley, *Harris, O'Boyle & Warbrick: Law of the European Convention on Human Rights* (2nd edn, Oxford: Oxford University Press, 2009), 349–59. For a strongly worded criticism of this method of reasoning by one of the UK's foremost human rights lawyers, see Lord Hoffmann's lecture to the Judicial Studies Board (19 March, 2009) entitled 'The universality of human rights'; available online at www.jsboard.co.uk/downloads/Hoffmann_2009_JSB_Annual_Lecture_Universality_of_Human_Rights.doc

[29] Compare Roger Brownsword, 'After *Marper*: Two Readings, Two Responses', *SCRIPTed*, 6(1) (2009), 1.

The case of *S. H. and Others* v. *Austria*[30] offers some clues. Here, on very different facts to *Marper*, a lower chamber of the Court found that members took up so many different regulatory positions with regard to access to IVF treatment that there was no guiding consensus. In some countries, the heterologous donation of gametes, sperm or ova, is prohibited; in others, it is just the donation of ova that is prohibited; and, in others, the donation of both sperm and ova is permitted. Given such a variety of regulatory positions, the Court recognised that members enjoyed a wide margin of appreciation. Nevertheless, the Court emphasised, it did not follow that 'any solution reached by a legislature [was] acceptable'.[31] Moreover, the Austrian legislation that was being challenged in the case (legislation that closely followed that of Germany by restricting IVF treatment to couples who supplied their own gametes) was held by the majority of the Court to be incompatible with the applicants' Convention rights.

If the Court could not refer to the governing consensus to test the acceptability of the Austrian position, how could it subject it to critical scrutiny? Seemingly, the majority applied a test of coherence and internal consistency. Thus, in response to the Austrian government's argument that there were serious concerns about couples being permitted to select their gametes, the Court said:

> The Court considers that concerns based on moral considerations or on social acceptability are not in themselves sufficient reasons for a complete ban on a specific artificial procreation technique such as ova donation. Such reasons may be particularly weighty at the stage of deciding whether or not to allow artificial procreation in general, and the Court would emphasise that there is no obligation on a State to enact legislation of the kind and to allow artificial procreation. However, once the decision has been taken to allow artificial procreation…the legal framework devised for this purpose must be shaped in a coherent manner which allows the different legitimate interests involved to be taken into account adequately and in accordance with the obligations deriving from the Convention.[32]

According to the Court, concerns about abusive selection could be handled less intrusively through the ethical rules of the medical profession (rather than a legal prohibition on ova donation); concerns about the possible exploitation of women do not relate distinctively to the practices prohibited by the Austrian law; and, similarly, concerns about the welfare of children who are brought up by social rather than biological parents are not distinctively prompted by the prohibited practices (compare the case of adoption). The majority also pointed out that the Austrian law seemed to be inconsistent in prohibiting the (heterologous) donation of sperm for IVF procedures when there was no such prohibition on the (heterologous) donation of sperm for in vivo fertilisation. By contrast, the two dissenting opinions (anticipating the reasoning of the Grand

---

[30] Application no. 57813/00 (1 April 2010). The Judgment of the Grand Chamber, reversing the lower Chamber, was given on 3 November 2011.

[31] *Ibid.*, at para. 69.   [32] *Ibid.*, at para. 74.

Chamber which, on appeal, ruled by a majority of 13 to 4 that Austria had not violated its Convention responsibilities under Article 8) highlighted the breadth of the margin of appreciation together with the fact that Austria is not the only member to have legislative prohibitions on gamete donation for IVF procedures.[33]

In the light of these two decisions to which the Court came, how might we begin to formulate the house rules for those States that are members of the Strasbourg human rights club? First, applying *Marper*, where the regulatory positions taken up by members display a broad similarity (or convergence) on a particular point of Convention law, any member with an outlying position is liable to be brought back into line. Second, a member can modify its regulatory position so long as, applying the majority reasoning of the lower Chamber in the Austrian case, the new position meets a test of coherence. Third, there can be a general change in members' positions so long as they hold a consensus. Fourth, where the regulatory positions taken up by members do *not* display a broad similarity (or convergence) on a particular point of Convention law, then members who are at the outlying positions of the range are not liable to be corrected by reference to the range.

Finally, to return to *Marper*, how should we view it in the larger scheme of things? For example, should we agree with Paul de Hert that it represents 'a breathtaking tribute' to Orwellian ideals?[34] Certainly, so far as it goes, it is a tribute to the ideals of a free society. However, it does not address the full set of questions to which the use of DNA evidence gives rise. First, it does not address questions such as the legitimacy of the police collecting samples of DNA from a glass touched by a suspect, or from a discarded cigarette butt; and *a fortiori* where the police have tricked the suspect into providing a sample as in *State of Washington* v. *Athan* where the police, presenting themselves as a law firm, tricked the suspect into licking and returning an envelope.[35] Second, it does not question the way that the use of DNA evidence reflects the embedded biases of a particular criminal justice regime – for example, biases against reopening cases where there has been a possible miscarriage of justice (and allowing DNA evidence to be used for exculpatory purposes), or biases against racial or ethnic minorities, and so on. Third, even though the Grand Chamber cited the practice of familial searching as a reason for privacy being engaged by the retention of DNA profiles, it did not question the practice itself. Arguably, however, the use of partial matches and familial searching merits a hard look. Fourth, in a comprehensive review of the use of DNA evidence, questions would be asked about the legitimacy of targeting groups in 'dragnet' searches. In other words, even if *Marper* succeeds in setting some limits on the retention of samples and

---

[33] Judge Jebens disagreed with the majority *in toto*; Judge Steiner delivered a partial dissent.
[34] Paul de Hert, *Citizens' Data and Technology: An Optimistic Perspective* (The Hague: Dutch Data Protection Authority, 2009), at 26.
[35] Discussed in Krimsky and Simoncelli, *Genetic Justice*, at 109–16.

profiles, there are other aspects of the burgeoning use of DNA evidence that might trouble a community with human rights commitments.[36]

6 Summary

Mark Rothstein and Meghan Talbott[37] have cautioned that, whenever the State adopts a particular new technological instrument, we need to keep an eye on the larger regulatory environment. Hence:

> The prospect of expanded use of DNA forensics needs to be placed in context. In a world in which personal privacy is difficult to maintain against an onslaught of computer file sharing, surveillance cameras, biometric imaging, thermal imaging, and other technological 'advances', for many people, the last 'off limit' area for access to personal information is law enforcement...
>
> Assume that a hypothetical country routinely required all of its residents to submit the following items to the police: a DNA sample, a yearly photograph, handwriting exemplar, voiceprint, fingerprints, hair samples, retinal scans, bank statements, credit card information, health records, and other details of their personal life. Obviously, ready access to this information by police would help solve crimes. Nevertheless, such comprehensive information submission to law enforcement would be widely viewed as hallmarks of a repressive, totalitarian state.

Where regulators turn to technology, where surveillance is intensified, where control is tightened, where the technology takes over, a number of dystopian images – whether drawn from Orwell, Kafka or Huxley – spring to mind. If such dystopias are to be kept at bay, it will take more than a single court judgment; it will take a regulatory environment that pervasively reflects this commitment to respect for human rights and human dignity.[38] If we are to optimise the benefits of the technologies of the twenty-first century, we need a legal framework that is effective in managing both the risks and the regulatory temptations that they present.

[36] See further, e.g., Richard Hindmarsh and Barbara Prainsack (eds.), *Genetic Suspects* (Cambridge: Cambridge University Press, 2010).
[37] Mark A. Rothstein and Meghan K. Talbott, 'The Expanding Use of DNA in Law Enforcement: What Role for Privacy?', *Journal of Law, Medicine and Ethics*, 34 (2006), 153, at 160–1.
[38] Compare the conspectus of technologies now employed in criminal justice systems together with questions as to their legitimacy in Ben Bowling, Amber Marks and Cian C. Murphy, 'Crime Control Technologies', in Brownsword and Yeung, *Regulating Technologies*, 51.

Part II
Regulatory prudence and precaution

5

Regulatory prudence I: health, safety and environment: GM crops, nanoparticles and sound science

1 Introduction

In our opening chapter, we said that one of the first concerns for any community will be whether a novel technology is safe, whether it presents any risk to human health or safety, or to the environment (the integrity of which is, of course, essential for human health and well-being). There is nothing noble about such concerns; they are entirely self-serving prudential concerns; but, because these are concerns that are common to all humans with the instinct for survival, they are not controversial in themselves. To some extent, individuals can take their own protective measures – for example, an individual who is worried about the safety of washing machines or tumble-dryers might simply hand-wash and hang clothes out to dry in the traditional way; or, a consumer might check the labelling on foods to avoid any GM products – but there are limits to how far such protective steps can be taken. Where individuals are employed in workplaces that are equipped with machines, where getting from A to B involves an encounter with road traffic, and so on, it is not reasonably practicable to conduct one's life in a way that maintains a safe distance from industrial and transport technologies. Accordingly, it falls to regulators to protect the public against technologies that give rise to safety concerns; and the challenge of regulatory prudence is essentially one of reducing risk to an acceptable level.

Reviewing the regulatory response to a range of technologies that were developed in the previous two centuries, Susan Brenner has suggested that regulators have tended to focus on two forms of harmful use: defective implementation and (intentional) misuse.[1] Consider, for example, the case of the motor car. The cars that come off the production lines today bear some resemblance to the cars that were first manufactured by Henry Ford. Functionally, the cars of Henry Ford's time, like the cars of today, facilitate travel. More importantly, from a regulatory perspective, in the wrong hands, the cars of both periods are extremely dangerous, being capable of causing death, personal injury, and

---

[1] Susan W. Brenner, *Law in an Era of 'Smart' Technology* (New York: Oxford University Press, 2007).

damage to property. Dealing with intentional misuse (dealing with those drivers who are minded to cause harm to others) is rightly a regulatory priority. When it comes to the safety and design of motor cars, however, the differences between the early cars and today's smart cars are more obvious. Careless driving can still cause harm to others but regulators have taken steps to minimise the risk that defective implementation can present to drivers and their passengers.

Cars are not the only potential hazard on the roads. When a peloton of bicycles races out of Trinity Street onto Queen's Parade in the centre of Cambridge, pedestrians need to watch their step. What, though, was the initial response of regulators when bicycles first appeared in the nineteenth century? According to Brenner:

> Legislators at first simply banned bicycles from major thoroughfares, including sidewalks. These early enactments were at least ostensibly based on public safety considerations. As the North Carolina Supreme Court explained in 1887, regulations prohibiting the use of bicycles on public roads were a valid exercise of the police power of the state because the evidence before the court showed 'that the use of the bicycle on the road materially interfered with the exercise of the rights and safety of others in the lawful use of their carriages and horses in passing over the road'.[2]

Over time, though, the regulatory response to bicycles mellowed so that, by the end of the nineteenth century, bicycle users were being treated on much the same footing as other road users. This meant that there needed to be some rules of the road – for example, in 1897, New York's traffic code 'established a speed limit of eight miles per hour and required cyclists to give pedestrians the right of way'; it also 'forbade cyclists from coasting on city streets', although at that time opposition from cyclists blocked moves to require the fixing of brakes on bicycles.[3] With modern technology, brakes are as much a part of the design of the bicycle as are the pedals, and '[m]odern statutes regulate various aspects of cycling, such as limiting how many people can ride a bicycle at one time, specifying how bicycles are to be operated, and requiring helmets for operators and lamps for cycles being operated after dark'.[4] Indeed, one might see in modern regulatory measures, a concern not only for the safety of pedestrians and other road users but also a (paternalistic) concern for the safety of the cyclist.

While machines and modes of transport might elicit rather obvious concerns about the safety of both users and those who are close enough to be killed or injured, does the same apply to communication technologies? What kind of safety concerns might have moved regulators faced with, say, early printing technology? Having noted that regulators 'were not concerned with physical "harms" – such as injured printers or readers poisoned by toxic inks – resulting from inept use of the technology',[5] Brenner continues:

---

[2] *Ibid.*, at 36–7.   [3] *Ibid.*, at 39.   [4] *Ibid.*   [5] *Ibid.*, at 55.

> Instead, they targeted a somewhat culturally sensitive conception of improper implementation or misuse ... [criminal liability being used] to inhibit the application of printing technology to disseminate material inflicting what are *generally* recognized as uniquely egregious 'harms'.[6]

In some places, what this amounted to was the application of the law to criminalise the use of the technology to disseminate ideas that were not conducive to peace and good order. That is to say, even if printing machines were not dangerous either to those who used them or who were in the immediate vicinity, there nevertheless was a concern that the technology might be applied in ways that, intentionally or otherwise, created a more remote risk of injury.

In this light, what are the prudential concerns that are generated by today's technologies? Some of these technologies, like their predecessors, give rise to straightforward safety concerns but, with others, the concerns relate much more to the health of persons and the protection of the environment. In part, this might be because, in the twenty-first century, following BSE, thalidomide, contaminated blood products, Chernobyl and a host of similar cause célèbres, there is a much greater sensitivity to the ways in which our health is affected by the food, drugs, and technologies of our time as well as an awareness of the way in which the cumulative use of technologies can be environmentally damaging.[7] Having said that, some technologies – for example, agricultural biotechnologies and nanotechnologies – seem to elicit very direct concerns about their impact on our health and our environment.

In one respect, however, we might think that the safety concerns relating to the technologies of the twenty-first century are rather different to earlier regulatory experiences. Today, there are often major question marks about how dangerous some technologies are – for example, there is uncertainty about the impact of GMOs on the environment; there is uncertainty about the properties of nanomaterials; there is uncertainty about whether unfixed nanoparticles might be the new asbestos; and there is uncertainty about whether synthetic biology might be species endangering, and so on. Equally, there are question marks about the practical benefits of some technologies – for example, the likelihood of stem cell technologies delivering clinical benefits remains highly contentious. In sum, the following three factors are at work:

1 citizens are eager to embrace the benefits of new technologies (they are largely technophiles);
2 at the same time, however, citizens are highly risk averse; and
3 there is a great deal of uncertainty surrounding both the benefits and, particularly, the risks of new technologies.

The interaction between these factors sets up a number of tensions and regulatory dilemmas. For example, how are the risks to be balanced against the

---

[6] *Ibid.*

[7] See, e.g., Gavin Little, 'BSE and the Regulation of Risk', *Modern Law Review*, 64 (2001), 730.

benefits? And, when scientists are unable to assure citizens as to the safety of particular technologies, how should regulators proceed? For regulators, zero risk is rarely an option; rather, the challenge of prudence is one of finding the level at which risk is judged to be acceptable; but how is acceptability to be judged when both risks and benefits are calculated in ways that are personal to each individual and where the background data are uncertain?

So, for example, in the ministerial foreword to a recent UK strategy document, we read that the government is determined 'to develop the nanotechnologies industry while protecting the health of consumers and employees and avoiding damage to the environment'.[8] With a spectacular predicted growth in the global revenue of nanotechnologies, especially in the field of ICT,[9] the government has strong commercial reasons for wanting to see the UK positioned 'at the forefront of nanotechnologies development ... maintain[ing] momentum and keep[ing] pace with the biggest players on the international stage'.[10] The document presents four illustrative case studies: one concerning the development of nanofluids that can be used, with energy-saving effects, in motor car cooling systems; a second concerning the use of a handheld nanosensing device that will help asthma sufferers to monitor their condition; a third concerning the application of nanoscience to reduce the fat content in ice cream; and the fourth concerning the use of titanium dioxide nanoparticles in third-generation solar cells. If nanotechnologies are applied in ways that are environmentally friendly as well as facilitating healthier lives, all seems well and good; but, of course, until the underlying science is better understood, we cannot reasonably expect to enjoy the best of all nanoworlds.

Although prudential assessment of the respective risks and benefits seems an appropriate approach to modern technologies, regulators need to be careful that, by framing the issues in terms of a calculation of risks and benefits, they do not ignore or downgrade those concerns that lie beyond the risk paradigm (narrowly conceived).[11] As Maria Lee[12] has observed:

> The proper regulation of controversial technologies ... is complex and contested. Difficult questions about the safety of these technologies, for the environment and for human health, resonate at the highest political level. There is also however *another* politics of regulation: whilst environmental and human safety are important, complex and political, so may be, for example, the way a technology distributes risk and benefit; the social and political arrangements a technology might favour; and the real purposes of the technology.[13]

---

[8] *UK Nanotechnologies Strategy: Small Technologies, Great Opportunities*, London, March 2010, at 2.

[9] *Ibid.*, at 12.   [10] *Ibid.*, at 2.

[11] See Roger Brownsword, 'Human Dignity and Nanotechnologies: Two Frames, Many Ethics', *Jahrbuch für Recht und Ethik*, 19 (2011), 429–39.

[12] Maria Lee, 'Beyond Safety? The Broadening Scope of Risk Regulation', *Current Legal Problems*, 62 (2009), 242.

[13] *Ibid.*, at 243.

Beyond the politics of risk regulation, there are indeed difficult questions of equity and ethics that take us into questions of regulatory legitimacy that we will discuss in Part III.

In this chapter, we will stick to prudential concerns, starting by sketching the form of such a calculation where the relevant body of scientific and technical knowledge is both settled and clear. This leads us to two sets of questions. The first set centres on the problem of prudential pluralism, that is to say, on the problem that arises from different persons, and different constituencies, making their own prudential calculations in their own way and arriving at competing judgements as to the balance between benefit and risk. As we saw in Chapter 1, the *Biotech Products*[14] dispute at the WTO (concerning the safety of GM crops) is a multifaceted regulatory landmark; however, it can be seen, *inter alia*, as an illustration of this particular regulatory problem. The second set of questions focuses on the problem of scientific uncertainty and controversy. Where the relevant body of scientific and technical knowledge is not clear and settled, how are regulators to proceed? In cases of this kind – and we will use the safety of nanoparticles as an example – we seem to reach the limits of 'evidence-based' decision-making where regulators can rely on the judgements of 'sound science'. Arguably, this is where regulators should turn to a precautionary approach, responding to scientific uncertainty by prioritising safety concerns, particularly where there is any suggestion that the technology might cause serious and irreversible damage to human health or to the environment. Although we will address the question of sound science in this chapter, we defer our discussion of the much-debated precautionary principle to the next chapter.

2 Prudential calculation: assessing the risks and benefits

In principle, we might carry out a risk–benefit assessment for any new product or procedure that is not only personal – in the sense that it reflects our own personal judgement on the respective risks and benefits – but also is strictly prudential, in the sense that the judgement is confined to risks and benefits that impact only on our own interests. Consider, for example, the case of mobile phones.[15] On the risk side, we will make a judgement about the possible health risks associated with various forms and frequencies of use; and, on the other side, we will assess the benefits. On both sides of the calculation, it is purely a matter of assessing whether we think that it is for or against our own personal interests to use a mobile phone. If one person judges the benefits as outweighing any risks, and if another person judges that the risks outweigh the benefits, there is no problem; the former will use a mobile phone and the latter will not.

---

[14] WT/DS291/23 (United States), WT/DS292/17 (Canada) and WT/DS293/17 (Argentina), 8 August 2003.

[15] Compare Adam Burgess, *Cellular Phones, Public Fears, and a Culture of Precaution* (Cambridge: Cambridge University Press, 2004).

Over time, each person will find out whether their initial prudential judgement was in line with their interests. If the former suffers brain damage as a result of using a mobile phone or becomes addicted to use (becomes a so-called 'CrackBerry'), or if the latter finds that friends no longer get in touch, they might come to regret their choices and, where possible, they might reassess their position. However, neither party has any reason to be troubled by the (opposite) choice made by the other – as Mill might have said, over the health and safety of his/her own body and mind, over his/her own prudential choices, each person is sovereign.

This simple form of prudential pluralism presents regulators with no serious difficulty. Where the effect of prudential judgements is purely self-regarding, it matters not that individuals make different assessments of the balance of benefits and risks (relative to their own individual interests). Accordingly, where judgements of this kind need to be made, the obvious strategy for regulators is to facilitate the making of individual prudential calculations. Provided that regulators have done their best to ensure that each individual assessor is adequately informed, there is nothing more to be done.[16]

In complex modern societies, where there is a great deal of interdependence, we might wonder just how many purely self-regarding choices there are. In the case of mobile phones, the choice that one makes is likely to impact, at minimum, on the communication options available to others and, of course, there might be calls on publicly funded health care if phone usage does prove to be damaging to the user's health. Moreover, there is also the possibility that the masts that transmit the signals might be a hazard to health or the environment, in which case we cannot treat the impact of the individual's choice as limited to that person's own interests. In the light of this, if individuals are invited to calculate their prudential interests, but now in the knowledge that there might be less obvious consequential or indirect costs (relating to the individual's own interests), we are again likely to find many different assessments of the balance of benefits and risks. How are regulators to deal with this kind of prudential pluralism?

Before we address this question, however, we need to be a bit clearer about the form of personal prudential assessment – and, concomitantly, how we might then interpret remarks to the effect that a technology is 'high risk', 'low risk' or

---

[16] Compare Roger Brownsword and Jonothan Earnshaw, 'The Ethics of Screening for Abdominal Aortic Aneurysm', *Journal of Medical Ethics* 36 (2010), 827. However, it is important that background regulation is sensitive to the varying prudential judgements that will be made by differently situated individuals. See, the Academy of Medical Sciences, *A New Pathway for the Regulation and Governance of Health Research* (London, January 2011): '[T]he potential benefits of research will also vary and although a favourable benefit–harm balance is fundamental, the acceptable balance between benefits and risks varies. For example, a healthy individual would expect there to be minimal harm from volunteering to help study a new diagnostic test. In contrast, a patient with a life-threatening disease may be willing to accept some uncertainty to take part in a higher risk, first-in-man, trial of a potential new medicine. It is important that the regulation and governance pathway recognises these differences and that, rather than focus simply on process, it is proportionate' (*ibid.*, at 19).

even 'safe'. Let us suppose that we are trying to assess, in a purely personal prudential way, the risks and benefits that are attached to the use of a product such as a mobile phone, or a procedure such as pre-implantation genetic diagnosis of a human embryo (PGD), or a cognition-enhancing drug such as methylphenidate (Ritalin), donepezil (Aricept), or modafinil, and the like.[17] Moreover, let us suppose that our assessment is made under the following conditions:

1 There is a clear and settled 'expert' understanding of the risks and benefits associated with the practice, product or procedure.
2 The assessment takes no account either of any protective steps that might be taken to 'manage' the risks or of any proactive measures that might be taken to enhance the benefits.
3 The assessment takes no account of any human intervention or application that is intended to be harmful to one's interests.

These are major limiting and simplifying conditions. First, we do not have to factor in any scientific doubt, controversy or uncertainty; second, we have a clear line between the stage of risk assessment and that of risk management (before reassessment); and, third, we do not need to worry about potentially malign uses or applications.[18] Nevertheless, to see prudential assessment at its simplest, we need these limiting conditions.

Presupposing these conditions, the assessment will work on two axes, one concerning the importance of the interests that are impacted and the other the likelihood of there being an impact. For risk assessment, we would plot in the space represented by Figure 5.1; and for benefit, we would plot in the space represented by Figure 5.2.

We need to be very careful here with the terminology of 'high' and 'low' risk, for there is some difference between lay usage of these terms and that employed by professional risk assessors. In most non-expert circles, with the kind of damage in the foreground, nuclear technology seems pretty high risk. Yet, professional risk assessors will say that 'technically', nuclear technology is low risk,[19] meaning that '[n]uclear power is characterized by high damage potential with relatively low probability'.[20] At all events, whether high or low risk, the overall *acceptability* of the risk depends on our calculation of the offsetting benefit.

---

[17] See the BMA discussion paper, *Boosting Your Brainpower: Ethical Aspects of Cognitive Enhancements* (London, November 2007).

[18] Compare Ruth Sheldon, Nicola Cleghorn, Clarissa Penfold, Ashley Brown and Thomas Newmark, *Exploring Attitudes to GM Food* (London: Social Science Research Unit, Food Standards Agency, 24 November 2009), at 21 where it is reported that some of the participants who were undecided about GM foods 'argued that it is not predetermined whether the technology will be used for good or bad purposes and judgement should be withheld until it is possible to see what happens in practice'.

[19] See Martin Bauer, 'Resistance to New Technology and its Effects on Nuclear Power, Information Technology and Biotechnology', in Martin Bauer (ed.), *Resistance to New Technology* (Cambridge: Cambridge University Press, 1995) 1, at 8.

[20] *Ibid.*, at 19.

118 Law and the technologies of the twenty-first century

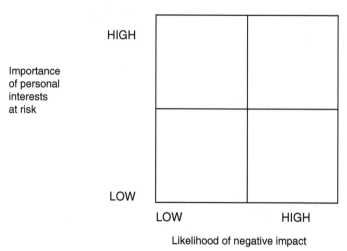

Figure 5.1 Risk profile

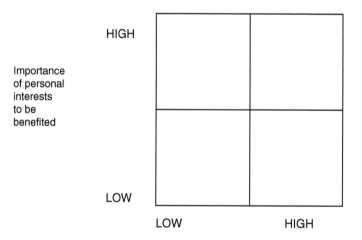

Figure 5.2 Benefit profile

Once we have filled in the spaces in these two fields, we will be in a position to make an initial assessment. Depending upon how the risks and benefits stand, our initial prudential attitude will fall somewhere on a spectrum between positive and negative. To the extent that there are risks, we will say whether (bearing in mind the projected benefits) we find the risk acceptable.

For those who are risk averse, while an entry in the right-hand upper quartile (of Figure 5.1) will trigger a negative response, an entry in the left-hand lower quartile will be reassuring. At this stage, this is as close as we can get to 'safe'; and, possibly, after some measures of risk reduction, we can get close to 'zero-risk'.

For those who are more focused on benefits than risks, an entry in the right-hand upper quartile (of Figure 5.2) will trigger a positive response, an entry in the left-hand lower quartile will be disappointing.

With a variety of natural predispositions, and many permutations of risk and benefit, there is unlikely to be a uniformity of prudential response. Even in these most favourable of conditions, prudential assessments are likely to vary from one person to another. There will be a prudential plurality with regard to the acceptability of whatever risk is presented.

Once we relax these simplifying conditions, prudential calculation becomes more complex. Each week, the latest research paper purports to find some correlation between a particular kind of diet and a state of good or bad health. However, where the correlations are weak and where the risk is of a speculative kind, how should prudential calculators proceed? In one study, looking at consumer perceptions of genetic modification technologies, three categories of risk were identified.[21] Thus:

> The first category, probabilistic risks, is defined as those that involve theoretically grounded and empirically demonstrated risks related to the product or its technology. For example, the EPA advisory panel that rejected StarLink maize found troubling aspects of the protein (for example, resistance to digestion) that led to a precautionary decision based on the probability of allergenicity. The methods and much of the evidence about probabilistic risks is available in peer-reviewed journals or public records. The second category, hypothetical risks, involves those possibilities grounded in accepted theory but lacking in empirical experience or evidence that can establish probabilities. A good example of this would be the question of whether antibiotic resistant DNA or other viral proteins from biotech crops could ever merge with gut bacteria (making pathogens resistant to antibiotics) … [This hypothetical risk is] undergoing extensive testing …
>
> The third category, speculative risks, has neither a credible hypothesis nor empirical experience to indicate the actual existence of these risks. When using the precautionary approach to [assess] biotech crop risks, theories range from Bt-pollen impacting bees … the 'Canola Myth', and semi-spiritual ideas about 'biodynamic' agriculture that are very hard to explain as scientific hypotheses … These thought exercises illustrate that almost any correlation can be made to show the potential for risk, irrespective of whether there is any qualified theoretical basis for the speculative possibility.[22]

At all events, speculative or not, having carried out the risk assessment, without taking into account any possible measures of risk management, the prudential calculation is not yet complete. Quite possibly, there are protective measures that reduce the severity or the likelihood of a negative impact. For example, in a recent survey of public attitudes to GM food,[23] one perspective was that 'there are always risks in relation to food and that as long as GM food is developed with sufficient regulation to ensure that these risks are managed, the benefits

---

[21] Wolfgang van den Daele, Alfred Pühler, and Herbert Sukopp, *Biotech Herbicide-Resistant Crops: A Participatory Technology Assessment* (Berlin: Federal Republic of Germany Ministry for Research and Technology, 1997), reported in Stuart J. Smyth, A. Bryan Endres, Thomas P. Redick and Drew L. Kershen, *Innovation and Liability in Biotechnology* (Cheltenham: Edward Elgar, 2010), at 82–3.

[22] *Ibid.*

[23] See Sheldon *et al.*, *Exploring Attitudes.*

are likely to outweigh the risks'.[24] Hence, even a risk-averse assessor might be persuaded to employ a technology if there are risk management measures that can move the entry in the right-hand upper quartile (of Figure 5.1) to an entry in the left-hand lower quartile. These further possible adjustments to prudential assessments, however, are unlikely to remove the variations in the calculations. From a regulatory perspective, there are likely to remain significant differences in the prudential preferences of regulatees; and the challenge for regulators is finding a strategy for responding to this prudential plurality.

In a democratic polity, regulators should not shirk their responsibility for assessing the breadth and depth of the preferences of their regulatees. Discharging this responsibility, however, is no straightforward matter. How are regulators to engage the public on questions concerning emerging technologies?[25] For example, how are researchers to cope with what can be extremely variable levels of public understanding of the technology; how are they to distil attitudes towards a particular technology from a medley of predispositions (to science, technology, commerce, and so on); and how are they to overcome the public's suspicion of stakeholders in the technology?[26] Reflecting on the public debate on GM foods in the UK, Sheila Jasanoff identifies a number of difficulties and dilemmas:

> It was conducted, to start with, under severe resource and time constraints by the government's dubiously legitimate and competent public relations unit, the Central Office of Information. As a result, many regional meetings drew those already knowledgeable about the issues, who were least likely to contribute fresh perspectives to the exchanges. Coordination with the other two strands of the process [the first strand was a cost–benefit study undertaken by the Strategy Unit, and the second was a Science Review led by the government's chief scientific adviser] proved difficult. Even the website, organized around bland questions and oversimplified answers, seemed ill suited to arousing the interest of persons not already involved in the debate. In sum, the effort underscored a dilemma confronting state efforts to democratise the politics of new and emerging technologies: on the one hand, interacting only with identifiable stakeholders may simply strengthen the traditionally cozy relations between business and government; on the other hand, the public that needs to be engaged in broader debates about the pros and cons of technology is elusive and, in the absence of reliable precedents, hard to engage in deliberations whose very authenticity and purpose are widely questioned.[27]

---

[24] *Ibid.*, at 20.

[25] Compare, e.g., International Risk Governance Council, *Risk Governance of Synthetic Biology* (Geneva, 2009); and Sarah Davies, Phil Macnaghten and Matthew Kearnes (eds.), *Reconfiguring Responsibility: Lessons for Public Policy (Part 1 of the Report on Deepening Debate on Nanotechnology)* (Durham: Durham University, 2009). See, too, Lee, 'Beyond Safety?', at 253–60, for a critical case study on the UK's public consultation on nuclear energy

[26] See Sheldon *et al.*, *Exploring Attitudes*. And, see text at pp. 133–5 below.

[27] Sheila Jasanoff, *Designs on Nature* (Princeton: Princeton University Press, 2005), 129.

How might these obstacles be overcome? In the influential report by the Royal Society and the Royal Academy of Engineering, *Nanoscience and Nanotechnologies: Opportunities and Uncertainties*,[28] it is recommended that:

- dialogue and engagement should occur early, and before critical decisions about the technology become irreversible or 'locked in';
- dialogue should be designed around clear and specific objectives;
- the sponsors should publicly commit to taking account of the outcome of the engagement process;
- dialogue should be properly integrated with other related processes of technology assessment; and
- resourcing for the dialogue should be adequate.[29]

Even with attention to these matters, however, there might be doubts about how fully the public is engaged; and, of course, it is difficult to immunise a citizens' jury against the influence of the media.

Assuming, though, that the public can be adequately engaged, their prudential calculations are likely to be varied and, concomitantly, their preferred regulatory responses will be at different points of the spectrum from outright prohibition to simple permission or even promotion. Let us suppose that a public consultation on the developments and use of mobile phones (accurately) discloses the following four kinds of judgements:

1 A small number of people forming the first group believe that the masts that transmit the signals are a serious health hazard, that the benefits to be obtained from the use of mobile phones are trivial, and that, in consequence, there should be an outright prohibition on the building of masts and the use of mobiles.
2 A second group, also small in numbers, believes that both the masts and the phones might represent serious health hazards but judges that the benefits of mobile phones could be significant; accordingly, its position is that there should be strict controls over the building of masts and that phones should be designed so that they can only be used at a safe distance from the head.
3 The majority of consultees fall in a third group. Here, it is believed that the likelihood of the masts or phones causing any harm to health or the environment is low; and that the regulators should treat the technology in the same (permissive) way that it treats traditional land-line telephone technology. However, it also favours some ongoing monitoring of the impact of masts and mobile-phone usage, with a view to taking appropriate action if and when significant risks are detected.
4 The fourth group, also small in numbers, believes that there has been unwarranted scaremongering; that masts and mobiles present no risk at all; and that there should be no regulatory restriction on their location or use.

---

[28] RS Policy document 19/04 (London, July 2004).   [29] *Ibid.*, at para. 38.

If regulators are to satisfy the weight of prudential preferences, they should be guided by the views of the third group. However, if regulators take this course, those who follow the views of the first two groups will complain that insufficient precaution is being exercised; and, of course, those who are in the fourth group will think that regulators are being overcautious. Still, it is arguable that regulators have done as much as they can; they cannot satisfy everyone; and the judgement is not one of deep principle, merely a prudential calculation that reflects the balance of personal preferences. Provided that the process of consultation and deliberation is inclusive and transparent, regulators might think that this is good enough.

What, though, if the majority view is that of the fourth group and that this view is opposed by the expert advisers upon whom the regulators normally rely (and, it is worth emphasising that, in Europe, as in many other parts of the world, regulators rely extensively on their expert scientific committees); or what if, while the expert advisers take the third or the fourth view, the vast majority of the public takes the first view – what then? Should regulators allow themselves a discretion to override the lay prudential judgement in order to prioritise expert assessments of safety or expert advice on the need for precaution? In the first of the test cases that follows, we will see the makings of just such a tension.

3 GM crops

Anticipating a report from the Royal Society on GM crops, a government spokesperson said:

> We have not yet seen the report ... [but] our top priority is to safeguard human health and the environment and always follow the science. We recognise that GM crops could offer a range of potential benefits over the longer term.[30]

This sounds reassuring; but once we examine the small print, the difficulties of implementing such a prudential approach become apparent. Where the science is clear and uncontroversial, it is fine to say that regulators will 'follow the science' to prioritise the safeguarding of human health and the environment. But, where the science is not clear, where the evidence is uncertain or controversial, what then? How is the paramount concern for human health and the environment to be translated into regulatory policy? Does this imply a precautionary approach, an approach that advocates protective measures where there is reason to think that a harmful impact in relation to human health and the environment is not wholly speculative? Possibly, but the immediate recognition of the potential benefits of GM crops implies some adjustment of position. The nature of the regulatory challenge is to capture the benefits of GM crops, to

---

[30] Felicity Lawrence, 'It is too late to shut the door on GM foods', *The Guardian*, 17 October 2009, 27.

Regulatory prudence I

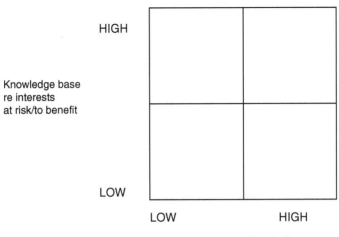

Figure 5.3 Knowledge profile

safeguard human health and the environment, and to do both things in a context of uncertainty and a lack of scientific consensus.[31]

How should we map the nature and extent of scientific uncertainty? If we focus on the extent of scientific knowledge in relation to a particular technology, we will plot it as in Figure 5.3 (with knowledge as to the *interests* that are likely to be impacted on one axis and knowledge as to the *likelihood* of the impact on the other); and if we focus on the extent of the expert consensus, we will plot the position as in Figure 5.4. When we discussed simple risk assessment in the most favourable conditions, our assumption amounted to plotting the relevant scientific knowledge and consensus as falling in the upper right-hand quartile of Figures 5.3 and 5.4. However, under so-called conditions of scientific uncertainty,[32] the appropriate plotting will be rather different. Most worryingly, the plotting will lie in the lower left-hand quartile of these figures, signifying that the experts do not know which interests are likely to be impacted, that they do not know how likely it is that there will be an impact on relevant interests, and that there is little consensus about any aspect of these

---

[31] Compare, David Winickoff, Sheila Jasanoff, Lawrence Busch, Robin Grove-White and Brian Wynne, 'Adjudicating the GM Food Wars: Science, Risk, and Democracy in World Trade Law', *Yale Journal of International Law*, 30 (2005), 81, 104–6.

[32] For a helpful analysis, see Fritz Allhoff, Patrick Lin and Daniel Moore, *What Is Nanotechnology and Why Does It Matter?* (Chichester: John Wiley & Sons, 2010), ch. 5. The following four scenarios are specified: 1. decision-making with full knowledge of outcomes and probabilities; 2. decision-making with full knowledge of outcomes and some, though not all, knowledge of probabilities; 3. decision-making with full knowledge of outcomes and no knowledge of probabilities at all; and 4. decision-making with incomplete knowledge of outcomes (as well as their associative probabilities) (*ibid.*, at 77). Whereas 1 is the straightforward case, scenario 2 involves some uncertainty (as to the probability of a known outcome eventuating), and scenarios 3 and 4 involve ignorance of one relevant kind or another.

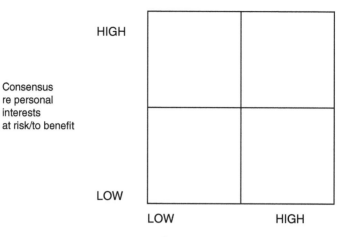

Figure 5.4 Expert consensus profile

matters. Clearly, in such conditions, it would be disingenuous for regulators either to 'average' the different views taken in the scientific community, or to suppress the differences.[33]

We can earth some of these difficulties by considering the long-running dispute between the US and the European Union concerning the safety of GM crops. While the former asserted the safety of GM products and argued that it should have access to the European marketplace for GM products, the latter operated with a de facto moratorium against the approval of GM crops. Finally, matters came to a head at the WTO in the *Biotech Products* case, where the legality of the EU's policy was challenged by the US, Canada and Argentina.[34]

Where, as in *Biotech Products*, the science relating to the safety of GM crops is contested, how is the matter to be resolved? An innocent response is that the question should be determined by reference to the view supported by 'sound science', this being taken to be a neutral and reliable arbiter. However, for many commentators on the practice and politics of science, this is a naïve view.[35] Science is just not like that. Scientists reasonably disagree with one another, not just about the bottom-line questions, but about matters of methodology, relevance and focus, and so on. Science is never going to be theory neutral (that is the whole point of the enterprise) but some deny, too, that it is 'value neutral'.

For those who are sceptical about the possibility of neutral science, the case of GM crops is almost a textbook example. Thus:

> The 'products approach' to regulating GMOs assumes that no untoward risk occurs merely from applying this technology to agricultural production. GMOs

---

[33] Compare Andy Stirling, '"Opening Up" and "Closing Down": Power, Participation, and Pluralism in the Social Appraisal of Technology', *Science, Technology, and Human Values*, 33 (2008), 262.

[34] Note 14 above.   [35] See, e.g., Winickoff *et al.*, 'Adjudicating the GM Food Wars', 81.

are subjected to strict rules only when the end products are not substantially equivalent to their conventional counterparts. In contrast, the 'process approach' rests on the idea that genetic engineering itself may entail novel and unique risks to human health or the environment. Whereas the United States has embraced the products approach to GM agriculture, the European Union and its member states have tended to adopt the more precautionary process approach.[36]

So, if scientists on one side of the Atlantic make safety judgements by reference to the end product while scientists on the other side of the Atlantic make (different) safety judgements by reference to the process used, and if both practices are regarded in their own territories as sound science, then 'sound science' simply cannot serve as a neutral court of appeal.

In the event, the WTO Disputes Panel in *Biotech Products* made no attempt to settle the question of whether GM crops are safe. The question was not whether the EU position was scientifically vindicated, nor even whether it was a reasonable position as judged by common opinion. Rather, the question was the narrower and more specific one of whether the EU position was consistent with Member States' obligations under the Sanitary and Phytosanitary (SPS) Agreement.

According to Article 2 of the Agreement:

1. Members have the right to take sanitary and phytosanitary measures necessary for the protection of human, animal or plant life or health, provided that such measures are not inconsistent with the provisions of this Agreement.
2. Members shall ensure that any sanitary or phytosanitary measure is applied only to the extent necessary to protect human, animal or plant life or health, is based on scientific principles and is not maintained without sufficient scientific evidence, except as provided for in paragraph 7 of Article 5.
3. Members shall ensure that their sanitary and phytosanitary measures do not arbitrarily or unjustifiably discriminate between Members where identical or similar conditions prevail, including between their own territory and that of other Members. Sanitary and phytosanitary measures shall not be applied in a manner which would constitute a disguised restriction on international trade.
4. Sanitary or phytosanitary measures which conform to the relevant provisions of this Agreement shall be presumed to be in accordance with the obligations of the Members under the provisions of GATT 1994 which relate to the use of sanitary or phytosanitary measures, in particular the provisions of Article XX(b).

However, the right in Article 2.1 has to be read in the light of the provisions in Article 5; and it is worth noting in advance that the general obligation to apply an SPS measure only where there is sufficient scientific evidence is qualified by Article 5.7. Article 5 provides:

---

[36] *Ibid.*, at 87.

1. Members shall ensure that their sanitary or phytosanitary measures are based on an assessment, as appropriate to the circumstances, of the risks to human, animal or plant life or health, taking into account risk assessment techniques developed by the relevant international organizations.

2. In the assessment of risks, Members shall take into account available scientific evidence; relevant processes and production methods; relevant inspection, sampling and testing methods; prevalence of specific diseases or pests; existence of pest – or disease – free areas; relevant ecological and environmental conditions; and quarantine or other treatment.

3. In assessing the risk to animal or plant life or health and determining the measure to be applied for achieving the appropriate level of sanitary or phytosanitary protection from such risk, Members shall take into account as relevant economic factors: the potential damage in terms of loss of production or sales in the event of the entry, establishment or spread of a pest or disease; the costs of control or eradication in the territory of the importing Member; and the relative cost-effectiveness of alternative approaches to limiting risks.

4. Members should, when determining the appropriate level of sanitary or phytosanitary protection, take into account the objective of minimizing negative trade effects.

5. With the objective of achieving consistency in the application of the concept of appropriate level of sanitary or phytosanitary protection against risks to human life or health, or to animal and plant life or health, each Member shall avoid arbitrary or unjustifiable distinctions in the levels it considers to be appropriate in different situations, if such distinctions result in discrimination or a disguised restriction on international trade. Members shall cooperate in the Committee, in accordance with paragraphs 1, 2 and 3 of Article 12, to develop guidelines to further the practical implementation of this provision. In developing the guidelines, the Committee shall take into account all relevant factors, including the exceptional character of human health risks to which people voluntarily expose themselves.

6. Without prejudice to paragraph 2 of Article 3, when establishing or maintaining sanitary or phytosanitary measures to achieve the appropriate level of sanitary or phytosanitary protection, Members shall ensure that such measures are not more trade-restrictive than required to achieve their appropriate level of sanitary or phytosanitary protection, taking into account technical and economic feasibility.

7. In cases where relevant scientific evidence is insufficient, a Member may provisionally adopt sanitary or phytosanitary measures on the basis of available pertinent information, including that from the relevant international organizations as well as from sanitary or phytosanitary measures applied by other Members. In such circumstances, Members shall seek to obtain the additional information necessary for a more objective assessment of risk and review the sanitary or phytosanitary measure accordingly within a reasonable period of time.

8. When a Member has reason to believe that a specific sanitary or phytosanitary measure introduced or maintained by another Member is

constraining, or has the potential to constrain, its exports and the measure is not based on the relevant international standards, guidelines or recommendations, or such standards, guidelines or recommendations do not exist, an explanation of the reasons for such sanitary or phytosanitary measure may be requested and shall be provided by the Member maintaining the measure.

The key distinction, therefore, is between those cases where the scientific evidence is sufficient to justify adopting an SPS measure and those cases where it is not. If the disputants were not parties to a trade agreement, the idea of scientific sufficiency would not be fundamental, or, at any rate, not determinative; each party would simply make its own prudential calculation in its own unconstrained way. However, as parties to a trade agreement, prudence is constrained. It is not open to the parties to plead that they give a low weighting to the benefits; and, to this extent, the scope for prudential pluralism is reduced. So, the focus is entirely on the risks that are recognised in the SPS agreement and it is open to the parties to plead those risks only where the scientific evidence is sufficiently supportive (whatever this might mean).

What, though, about cases where scientific opinion is divided? In such circumstances, Article 5.7 permits the provisional adoption of SPS measures; and in the *Biotech Products* case, this was central to the EU's defence. In other words, the EU argued that, where there were different views in the scientific community as to the negative impact of GM crops on human health and the environment, it was open to a party to take protective measures pending the formation of a clearly better view. What did the Disputes Panel make of this?

In favour of the EU, it was decided that the de facto moratorium on the approval of biotech products was a legitimate response to the uncertain state of the scientific evidence – in other words, the moratorium was a legitimate provisional and precautionary measure as contemplated by Article 5.7 of the SPS Agreement. However, in favour of the complainants, it was found that the EU was in breach of its obligations by failing to progress individual approval procedures without undue delay and that it was vicariously in breach of its obligations in respect of the safeguard measures taken by the six member states that represent the strongest opposition to GM crops in Europe.[37] Bearing in mind that the Commission had itself defended its own internal market principles by refusing to permit Austria (one of the group of six) to establish a 'GMO-free area', one imagines that, at least in some quarters of Brussels, the latter part of the WTO ruling was neither unexpected nor altogether unwelcome.[38]

---

[37] Annex C1(a) of the SPS Agreement requires Members to undertake and complete 'without undue delay' procedures for checking and ensuring the fulfilment of sanitary or phytosanitary measures.

[38] Compare Sara Poli, 'Restrictions on the Cultivation of Genetically Modified Organisms: Issues of EC Law', in Han Somsen (ed.), *The Regulatory Challenge of Biotechnology* (Cheltenham: Edward Elgar, 2007), 156.

This, however, is hardly the full story. There are at least three reasons that Europeans might give for resisting GM crops:

1 That there is some risk that GM will cause damage to human health and the environment; that the benefits do not compensate for the risk; so that, all things considered, the risk is unacceptable.
2 That there is a high likelihood that GM will cause damage to human health and the environment.
3 That, irrespective of risk and benefit, the manipulation of crops in this way is unethical (for example, by offending against the dignity of nature).

The first two of these reasons are prudential; the third is ethical. Although the first kind of reason is available to individual Europeans, who (given regional labelling requirements) can make every effort to avoid GM products, it is not available to the EU as a signatory to a trade agreement that excludes such reasoning. The second reason is also prudential; and it is again available to individual Europeans. However, it is available to the EU only to the extent that the Articles of the SPS Agreement permit; and, in a context of scientific uncertainty, it is unclear how much latitude the terms of trade permit. Finally, the third reason, while available to individual Europeans, is not factored into the SPS Agreement and it is moot how far the terms of trade permit reliance on such reasons.

Given that European resistance to GM crops was not (and is not) straightforwardly scientific and precautionary but also was (and is) fuelled by moral concerns,[39] if we do not remit disputes such as *Biotech Products* to the court of 'sound science', are we writing a blank cheque for ethical exceptionalism? This is certainly not the lesson that we should draw from *Biotech Products*. On the one hand, the Panel recognises that, where there is a level of scientific uncertainty that leaves room for legitimate disagreement, those states that prefer to take a risk-averse approach are allowed, at least provisionally, to do so; on the other hand, where there is little room for scientific doubt, members are not to be encouraged to dress up their moral objections as if they are concerns about safety.

We can infer, too, that this is not the position taken by those who problematise the relationship between science, culture, and value. Everyone recognises that exceptions against free trade are open to opportunism and abuse. It is important, therefore, that any allowance made for local scientific or ethical judgements is not open to being exploited as a pretext for trade protectionism. Accordingly, it is suggested that arguments are presented transparently;[40] and that decision-makers should take a hard look at arguments, such as those presented by the EU in *Biotech Products*; and if, and only if, those arguments

---

[39] See Robert Lee, 'GM Resistant: Europe and the WTO Panel Dispute on Biotech Products', in Jennifer Gunning and Søren Hom (eds.), *Ethics, Law and Society* (Aldershot: Ashgate, 2005), vol. 1, 131.
[40] The need for transparency (and the encouragement of deliberative democracy) is strongly supported by Robert Howse, 'Democracy, Science, and Free Trade: Risk Regulation on Trial

survive such a level of strict scrutiny, should they be accepted as sufficient reason for denying market access.[41]

4 Nanoparticles

Where technologies are in an emergent state, the knowledge base will tend to be low; in particular, without any experience of use, the longer-term consequences will be unknown. Moreover, where technologies, such as nanotechnologies and synthetic biology, are characterised by their novel properties, uncertainty is almost an immanent virtue. In these circumstances, there will be a lack of scientific consensus to guide regulators. How should regulators proceed in such conditions of low knowledge and low consensus?

The obvious first step is to establish precisely what is and what is not known. And, indeed, the UK government did just this in June 2003 when it commissioned the Royal Society and the Royal Academy of Engineering to carry out an independent study into the current and future developments in nanoscience and nanotechnologies and their impacts. A year later, the report, *Nanoscience and Nanotechnologies: Opportunities and Uncertainties*, was published.[42] At the core of the report is the (not unexpected) finding that there is a lack of evidence about the health and environmental risks presented by manufactured nanoparticles and nanotubes, leading to a considerable uncertainty. Thus:

> Many nanotechnologies pose no new risks to health and almost all the concerns relate to the potential impacts of deliberately manufactured nanoparticles and nanotubes that are free rather than fixed to or within a material.[43]

The report flags up a range of such concerns, including the possibility that carbon nanotubes might have 'toxic properties similar to those of asbestos fibres'[44] and that nanoparticles used in sunscreens and cosmetics might penetrate the skin.[45] As for the possibility of environmental harm, we read:

> There is virtually no information available about the effect of nanoparticles on species other than humans or about how they behave in the air, water or soil, or about their ability to accumulate in food chains.[46]

at the World Trade Organization', *Michigan Law Review*, 98 (2000), 2329. Concluding, Howse argues: 'Where there is a concern that domestic regulations may constitute protectionist cheating on negotiated trade concessions, an alternative to harmonization may well be to enhance confidence in the ability to distinguish legitimate domestic regulations from protectionist cheating. Requiring that regulations be defensible in a rational, deliberative public process of justification may well enhance such confidence, while at the very same time serving, not frustrating, democracy' (*ibid.*, at 2357).

[41] Winickoff *et al.*, 'Adjudicating the GM Food Wars', at 108–11. As Lee puts it: 'The key question is no longer whether technologies are socially embedded or whether political and social and ethical commitments are relevant in risk regulation. They are. The question is how to fix that recognition within regulatory decision-making' ('Beyond Safety?', at 280).

[42] RS Policy document 19/04 (London, July 2004).

[43] *Ibid.*, at para. 19. [44] *Ibid.*, at para. 21.

[45] *Ibid.*, at para. 22. [46] *Ibid.*, at para. 24.

Faced with this lack of information, the report advises that, until more is known about their environmental impact, the release of nanoparticles and nanotubes should be avoided as far as possible. And, broadly speaking, this typifies the report's dual-track approach which is to urge that there should be more investment in establishing the facts while adopting precautionary measures until it is clear that the potential benefits outweigh the risks.

Despite these reservations, nanoproducts are rapidly finding their way into the marketplace. Titanium dioxide nanoparticles are used in sunscreens, nanosilver particles are used in odour-free sportswear, carbon nanofibres are added to car tyres and to body panels in order to strengthen them, and so on. Four years on from the Royal Society's seminal report, the Royal Commission on Environmental Pollution reviewed the position. In this more recent report, *Novel Materials in the Environment: The Case of Nanotechnology*,[47] the focus is particularly on nanoparticles (that is, nanoscale materials that are in three dimensions). The novel features of nanoparticles include changes in surface reactivity and charge, and modified electronic characteristics. While some of these properties are predictable, many are not. Addressing the question of whether this is a cause for concern, the Commission writes:

> It is a matter of concern that we were repeatedly told by competent organisations and individuals that there is currently insufficient information to form a definitive judgement about the safety of many types of nanomaterials. In some cases, the methods and data needed to understand the toxicology and exposure routes of nanomaterials are insufficiently standardised or even absent. There appears to be no clear consensus among scientists about how to address the deficit.
>
> [W]ith novel materials and particularly nanomaterials, there are virtually no data on chronic long-term effects on people, other organisms or the wider environment …
>
> Difficulties also arise because the form in which materials make their way into the environment might not be the same as that encountered during manufacture. Many free nanoparticles agglomerate and aggregate in the natural environment, forming larger structures that may have different toxicological properties to those exhibited in the original nanoform.
>
> Most nanomaterials are incorporated into products whose specific behaviour and properties are often well understood, but our inquiries suggest that very little thought has been given to their environmental impact as they become detached from products in use or at the point of final disposal … Laboratory assessments of toxicity suggest that some nanomaterials could give rise to biological damage. But to date, adverse effects on populations or communities of organisms *in situ* have not been investigated and potential effects on ecosystem structure and processes have not been addressed. Ignorance of these matters brings into question the level of confidence that can be placed in current regulatory arrangements.[48]

---

[47] London, November 2008 (summary).   [48] *Ibid.*, at 9–10.

Given such a lack of information, it is no surprise that the evidence presented to the Commission was often contradictory. Thus:

> On the one hand, some environmental scientists and policy-makers feel strongly that the threat posed by most nanomaterials is small, whereas others are clearly worried about the possible toxicity of some nanomaterials, both to the wider environment and to human health. For example, concern was expressed about an increased risk of lung and cardiovascular damage from carbon nanotubes and C60 in humans, and the effects of nanosilver particles on microbial communities and sediment-feeding organisms.[49]

Once again, the sobering conclusion is that, in our current state of ignorance, 'it is extremely difficult to evaluate how safe or how dangerous some nanomaterials are'.[50]

In such conditions, ranging 'from high uncertainty to profound ignorance',[51] how should regulators respond? The Commission identified three approaches that had been put to it as follows:

1 No regulatory steps should be taken unless and until there are clear indications that harm is being caused.
2 Regulators should take a 'risk-based' approach, meaning that 'the technology should be controlled only to the extent that there are clearly articulated scientific reasons for concern, and only then where the cost of risk reduction is deemed proportionate to the probability and extent of danger'.[52]
3 There should be a regulatory prohibition until nanomaterials have been shown beyond any reasonable doubt to be safe.

The Commission rejected each of these approaches: the first, as the historical record shows, is simply reckless;[53] the second credits science with more detecting and directing power than it has; and the third fails to take into account the potential benefits that are foregone by such a precautionary prohibition.[54]

Instead, the Commission sees the need to look beyond traditional regulatory forms to find more imaginative solutions. If regulation is to be *effective*, there is the need for 'an adaptive governance regime capable of monitoring technologies and materials as they are developed and incorporated into processes and products'.[55] Such a regime will need to develop the capacity to 'intervene selectively in areas where it deems that a material represents a danger to the environment or human health'.[56] Normally, a moratorium would not be appropriate, but 'there may well be specific cases where it is necessary to slow or even hold up the

---

[49] *Ibid.*, at 12.   [50] *Ibid.*   [51] *Ibid.*, at 14.   [52] *Ibid.*

[53] However, in the context of information technology, there is significant support for the so-called 'procrastination principle', favouring *ex post* intervention if and when harms, excesses and abuses occur, rather than *ex ante* interventions that are anticipatory and preventive in their intent: see, e.g., Jonathan Zittrain, *The Future of the Internet* (London: Penguin, 2008), 119.

[54] Cf. Cass Sunstein, *Laws of Fear* (Cambridge: Cambridge University Press, 2005).

[55] Royal Commission on Environmental Pollution, *Novel Materials*, at 15.

[56] *Ibid.*

development while concerns are investigated'.[57] At the same time, if regulation is to be responsive and *legitimate*, it is necessary 'to find the means through which civil society can engage with the social, political, and ethical dimensions of science-based technologies and democratise their "licence to operate"'.[58] In sum:

> We have argued that a system of adaptive governance for novel materials would in part be served by modifying and extending the existing regulatory framework as a matter of urgency, and by developing an early warning system, which must include robust arrangements for environmental monitoring. But, as in other fields characterised by ignorance, uncertainty and ubiquity, regulation must be complemented and informed by the full range of perspectives on innovation.[59]

Moreover, in the context of emergent technologies, where the Collingridge dilemma[60] applies – that is, where regulators find themselves in a position such that either they do not know enough about the (immature) technology to make an appropriate intervention or they know what regulatory intervention is appropriate but they are no longer able to turn back the (now mature) technology – the Commission sees its advocacy of an adaptive approach having a more general application.[61]

5 Sound science

Prudential judgements made in relation to emerging technologies rely heavily on expert assessment of risk. Even if it is naïve to suppose that 'sound science' can unfailingly deliver clear, consensual, knowledge-based guidance, what can we minimally expect from the community of experts? At a time when there is something of a crisis of confidence in science, what are the preconditions for trust? Who should we trust and why?

As an illustrative indication of the scope and depth of public trust and mistrust, consider the following finding of a team researching attitudes to GM food:[62]

---

[57] *Ibid.*   [58] *Ibid.*, at 21.   [59] *Ibid.*, at 22.

[60] See David Collingridge, *The Social Control of Technology* (New York: Francis Pinter, 1980).

[61] Compare the Presidential Commission for the Study of Bioethical Issues, *New Directions: The Ethics of Synthetic Biology and Emerging Technologies* (Washington, DC, December 2010). Having identified, five key principles (namely, public beneficence, responsible stewardship, intellectual freedom and responsibility, democratic deliberation, and justice and fairness), the Commission states that the 'principle of responsible stewardship rejects two extreme approaches: an extreme action-oriented [proactionary] approach that pursues technological progress without limits or due regard for public or environmental safety, and an extreme precautionary approach that blocks technological progress until all possible risks are known and neutralized' (*ibid.*, at 26). Instead, as a middle way between proaction and precaution, the Commission advocates 'the development of agile, measured oversight mechanisms' (*ibid.*). In other words, '[r]esponsible stewardship calls for *prudent vigilance*, establishing processes for assessing likely benefits along with safety and security risks both before and after projects are undertaken' (*ibid.*, 27). For further elaboration of prudent vigilance as an articulation of responsible stewardship, eschewing both extreme proaction and precaution, see *ibid.*, at 123–4.

[62] Sheldon *et al.*, *Exploring Attitudes*, at 36.

Participants said that they were less convinced by arguments from those sources that were perceived to have a vested political or economic interest in GM food. Two types of organisations were judged to have strong interests in the subject; third sector organisations with political interests and businesses with economic interests. There was a perception that statements made by such organisations were likely to be based on rhetoric as opposed to science or research. They also felt that organisations might use extreme tactics in order to get the issue on the agenda. More generally, questions were raised about who funds research conducted by third sector organisations. Industry and business sources, such as [a biotechnology company] were also perceived to have clear economic interests in the issue. Participants suggested that their arguments would focus on the benefits of GM food because they were motivated by making profits from the development of GM food.

In comparing the different information sources, participants felt that particular sources were more trustworthy. One perspective was that charities were less biased than business, while another viewpoint expressed was greater trust in academics as opposed to campaigning organisations. Participants said that they would disregard any argument made by a politician, not because politicians were perceived to hold a particular position on GM food but because they were generally untrustworthy. However, it was also suggested that the government should be a key source of independent information on the subject. Finally, there was a view that *all* the arguments provided in the exercise reflected vested interests. Participants holding this view emphasised that they would like information from an independent source, which they could take at face value, although there was no consensus on what type of source could play this role.

Clearly, with such attitudes in play, there will be a good deal of guesswork, or fatalism, in the production of prudential judgements.

We can pursue this theme by drawing on Onora O'Neill's important analysis of the apparent breakdown of trust in modern risk societies.[63] Given a litany of widely publicised failures – such as the UK government's various failures to be open with the public during the BSE crisis, the one-sidedness of Monsanto's advocacy of GM crops, and the concealment of contaminated blood supplies[64] – the provocation of distrust is not surprising. Moreover:

There are cases of outright fraud that go beyond disingenuous communication and evasion: scientists, biotech companies and journalists all sometimes misreport and exaggerate the significance of new discoveries; scientific misconduct and fraud sometimes arises from competition for grants, results and glory; peddlers of untried and untested remedies sometimes prey on desperate people. Sporadic deception can be found almost anywhere: among scientists tempted to falsify experimental data; among government agencies tempted to keep worrying medical or scientific facts confidential; among journalists tempted to exaggerate

---

[63] *Autonomy and Trust in Bioethics* (Cambridge: Cambridge University Press, 2002).
[64] For a comprehensive discussion, see Anne-Maree Farrell, *The Politics of Blood: Ethics, Innovation and the Regulation of Risk* (Cambridge: Cambridge University Press) (forthcoming).

and sensationalise biomedical 'stories'; among campaigning groups eager to persuade the public of their views.[65]

Whether we are relying on expert views in the public or the private sector, whether focusing on risks or benefits, there seems to be good reason to withdraw trust. Yet, how practical is this? Sadly, for most of us, this is not an option. Thus:

> [T]his seemingly sensible advice is neither feasible nor coherent. It is not feasible because our lives depend in a myriad ways on medicine, science and biotechnology. We cannot avoid using them except by withdrawing from the modern world … [but] for most people there is no chance whatsoever of withdrawing into self-sufficiency.
>
> And the problem is not merely practical. The deeper difficulty is that *wholesale* mistrust is intrinsically incoherent. Those who claim to mistrust high-tech medicine, science and biotechnology *wholesale* have in practice to put their trust in something else. Some may place selective trust in alternative medicine or spiritual healing, others in the claims of 'green' campaigners or in traditional technologies. Others may place trust in religious teachings, or current fashion, or local gossip, or the suggestions of friends. Or they may place their trust in an eclectic mix of therapies, theories and technologies.[66]

If we are to be assisted in making reliably informed prudential judgements, we need more than open information flows; we need a regulatory environment for scientific inquiry that is conducive to the production of expert opinions that can be trusted. This is not the same as a regulatory environment that channels scientists towards an agreed view; but at least it conduces towards integrity and independence, as well as professional competence. How is such an environment to be created?

A variety of regulatory mechanisms might contribute to such an environment. For example, professional codes of conduct might encourage honesty and the need for some distance between the funders of research and those who carry out the research; the training of scientists should be able to control for competence; and the peer-reviewing of outputs should also push towards reliability.

Still, in a world of second-generation science, where results are what really matter, this might seem unrealistic. In such a world, the pressures on individual researchers to falsify and fabricate their results are intensified. In this light, we should note the long list of contributory factors that were identified at an OECD Global Science Forum workshop that was held in Tokyo in 2007.

First, the report lists those factors that relate 'primarily to individual researchers and their careers'.[67] These are:

---

[65] O'Neill, *Autonomy*, at 120.

[66] *Ibid.*, at 121.

[67] OECD Global Science Forum, *Best Practices for Ensuring Scientific Integrity and Preventing Misconduct* (2007), 12.

- Pressure of severe competition for funds.
- Requirements to achieve significant positive results (and to publish extensively) in order to obtain and secure a staff position in a research institution, or to receive favourable consideration for future funding of research.
- Lack of knowledge/preparation about the realities and stresses of a scientific career.
- Pressure to achieve a desired result in the case of sponsored applied research.
- Assorted personal failings (e.g., a craving for fame, a desire to hurt colleagues, a general lack of moral rectitude).

Second, there are a number of factors that relate 'primarily to the evolving nature of science and of the research enterprise'.[68] These are:

- The negative aspects of fragmentation, isolation and specialisation. In some scientific domains, researchers work for long periods without adequate contact or interaction with colleagues who would be in a position to scrutinise and review their results …
- The proliferation of highly specialised, custom-built scientific instruments that can only be meaningfully operated by one researcher, thus making it difficult to independently verify that measurements are untainted or, in the event of controversy, to reproduce questionable measurements.
- The ready availability of complex, opaque software for statistical analysis or other manipulations (notably, image processing) that make it easier to commit and conceal falsification and fabrication.
- Lack of awareness of the rules and standards of proper scientific conduct …
- Misapplication of the mission-oriented research paradigm (where concrete, usable results are expected in the relatively short term) to the traditional curiosity-driven research process.
- Expectations and pressure from supervisors, sponsors or publishers for positive, unambiguous and significant results. In general, the prevalence of misconduct can be aggravated by an unsupportive or indifferent environment where integrity is ignored or downplayed.

As this last point underlines, the key is putting in place the right kind of regulatory environment, one that attends to preventive design as well as deterrent signals.[69] Moreover, as O'Neill has highlighted, this needs to be done in a way that does not aggravate the public perception that scientists cannot be trusted.[70]

---

[68] *Ibid.*

[69] For a cautionary tale, see J. William Hirzy, 'Scientific Integrity in a Regulatory Context – An Elusive Ideal at EPA', available online at www.slweb.org/hirzy-commentary1.html (last accessed 10 December 2009).

[70] O'Neill, *Autonomy.*

6 Conclusion

Frequently, emerging technologies are presented as promising various benefits; but they also come with a risk profile. If our expectation is that regulators will take the lead responsibility for setting a level of 'acceptable risk', how is this to be done? And, how is it to be done when the background information relating to risk and benefit is itself contested in expert communities?

In some cases, it is arguable that regulators can discharge their prudential responsibilities by ensuring that their publics are properly informed, leaving it to each individual to make their own risk–benefit assessment relative to their own perception of self-interest. For example, in the case of new screening or scanning technologies, each individual can be left to make a free and informed decision about the balance of medical risks and benefits. However, where the background information is unclear or contested, there is no easy way of ensuring that the public is in a position to make a properly informed choice; and where individual prudential choices impact on others, regulators cannot avoid making a decision for the community.

Where regulators are expected to act as prudential proxies for their publics, how can they do this? Clearly, before regulators act, they need to have engaged the public. They need to inform the public about the technology (so far as this is possible) and, in turn, they need to get a feel for public preferences. On both sides, this is a considerable challenge – and, for regulators, there is also the challenge of creating an environment that militates against scientific fabrication and falsification and that has the confidence of the public. Moreover, whatever judgements are made about acceptable risk, they need to be provisional; there needs to be a flexibility in the regulatory oversight that allows for adjustment of the regulatory environment as more is known about the technology and as the prudential attitudes of the public evolve.

Into this mix of plurality, uncertainty and pressure on scientific integrity, some insist that regulators should take a precautionary approach – and, as we have seen, even though international trade agreements may confine parties to one-sided risk restrictions, they may allow for some provisional measures of precaution. However, precaution has a potential application that reaches well beyond questions of market access, and it is to this idea that we turn in the next chapter.

6

Regulatory prudence II: precaution

1 Introduction

According to Elizabeth Fisher, Judith Jones and René von Schomberg:[1]

> At its most basic, the precautionary principle is a principle of public decision making that requires decision makers in cases where there are 'threats' of environmental or health harm not to use 'lack of full scientific certainty' as a reason for not taking measures to prevent such harm.[2]

Significantly, the principle can be viewed as representing 'a departure from the previous state of affairs where political actors could use or abuse a persistent dissent among scientists as a reason (or excuse) for not taking action at all'.[3]

In line with this principle, and possibly as its most celebrated articulation, Principle 15 of the Rio Declaration in 1992 enjoins states to take measures to prevent serious and irreversible damage to the environment even if there is a 'lack of full scientific certainty'. In other words, even if there is some doubt about whether, say, carbon emissions cause serious and irreversible climate change, at the very least, lack of clinching evidence should not stand in the way of preventive measures and, at strongest, preventive measures should be taken. Similarly, in a health care context, it might be urged that, even if there is some doubt about whether smoking tobacco causes lung cancer and heart disease, this should not bar the taking of preventive measures. As the Appellate Body at the WTO remarked in the *Hormones* dispute, 'responsible, representative governments commonly act from perspectives of prudence and precaution where risks of irreversible, e.g., life-terminating, damage to human health are concerned'.[4] Although the Rio Declaration qualifies the protective obligation by limiting it to the capabilities of particular states, and even though the

---

[1] 'Implementing the Precautionary Principle: Perspectives and Prospects', in Elizabeth Fisher, Judith Jones and René von Schomberg (eds.), *Implementing the Precautionary Principle: Perspectives and Prospects* (Cheltenham: Edward Elgar, 2006).

[2] At 2.

[3] René von Schomberg, 'The Precautionary Principle and its Normative Challenges', in Fisher *et al.*, *Implementing the Precautionary Principle*, at 23.

[4] EC Measures Concerning Meat and Meat Products (Hormones), Report of the Appellate Body WT/DS26/AB/R, WT/DS48/AB/R, 16 January, 1998, at para. 124.

nature of the measures to be taken is unspecified, the precautionary principle has attracted a huge amount of criticism.

In practice, the precautionary principle is formulated in many different ways[5] – indeed, as its critics would have it, in far too many different ways. If, as Neil Manson has suggested, all versions of the principle specify a particular 'damage' condition, a particular 'knowledge' condition, and a particular 'remedial' condition,[6] each of which can be specified in many different ways, then there are (at least) dozens of possible formulations of the principle. Moreover, while the principle certainly challenges the absence of 'full scientific certainty' as a sufficient reason for regulatory *inaction*, it is not clear whether the residual regulatory tilt[7] is for or against intervention, or neither for it nor against it. Whereas the Rio Declaration reads as though it is pushing for action, some articulations – particularly those that focus on specifying the threshold conditions for intervention – imply some resistance to action;[8] and yet others present the principle as being broadly enabling but without disclosing any obvious bias either towards or against intervention.[9] It is hardly surprising then that some have condemned the principle as being unfit for regulatory purpose[10] – or, to be blunt, as being 'an overly-simplistic and under-defined concept that seeks to circumvent the hard choices that must be faced in making any risk management decision'.[11]

Despite these criticisms, the principle has a foothold in many regulatory regimes, as highlighted by Annex II of the European Commission's

[5] See, e.g., Robert Lee and Elen Stokes, 'Ecological Modernisation and the Precautionary Principle', in Jennifer Gunning and Søren Hom (eds.), *Ethics, Law and Society* (Aldershot: Ashgate, 2005), vol. 1, 103. For helpful overviews of the EC jurisprudence, see Veerle Heyvaert, 'Guidance without Constraint: Assessing the Impact of the Precautionary Principle on the European Community's Chemicals Policy', *Yearbook of European Environmental Law*, 6 (2006), 27, esp. 29–37, and 'Facing the Consequences of the Precautionary Principle in European Community Law', *European Law Review*, 31 (2006), 185.

[6] Neil Manson, 'Formulating the Precautionary Principle', *Environmental Ethics*, 24 (2002), 263.

[7] For the concept of a 'regulatory tilt', see Roger Brownsword, *Rights, Regulation and the Technological Revolution* (Oxford: Oxford University Press, 2008).

[8] See, e.g., *Pfizer* [2002] ECR II-3305, at para. 143: 'a preventive measure cannot properly be based on a purely hypothetical approach to risk, founded on mere conjecture which has not been scientifically verified'. So, mere conjecture and hypothesis will not suffice. Moreover, the underlying science must be consistent with principles of 'excellence, transparency and independence' (*ibid.*, at para. 172).

[9] Compare, e.g., the Nuffield Council on Bioethics, *Genetically Modified Crops: The Ethical and Social Issues* (London, 1999), at 162 where the principle is expressed as permitting the imposition of restrictions 'on otherwise legitimate commercial activities, if there is a risk, even if not yet a scientifically demonstrated risk, of environmental damage'.

[10] Gary E. Marchant and Douglas J. Sylvester, 'Transnational Models for Regulation of Nanotechnology', *Journal of Law, Medicine and Ethics*, 34 (2006), 714.

[11] *Ibid.*, at 722. In this remark, there are echoes of Marcia Angell's distinction between precautionary cynicism (which avoids distinguishing between reliable and unreliable evidence, between the likely and the unlikely, between the large danger and the small one, and so on) and engaged scepticism which tries to draw such distinctions: see Marcia Angell, *Science on Trial: The Clash of Medical Evidence and the Law in the Breast Implant Case* (New York: W. W. Norton, 1997), esp. at 158.

Communication on the precautionary principle,[12] in which the leading occurrences of the principle in international law are listed.

THE PRECAUTIONARY PRINCIPLE IN INTERNATIONAL LAW

The environment

Although applied more broadly, the precautionary principle has been developed primarily in the context of environmental policy.

Hence, the Ministerial Declaration of the Second International Conference on the Protection of the North Sea (1987) states that 'in order to protect the North Sea from possibly damaging effects of the most dangerous substances, a precautionary approach is necessary which may require action to control inputs of such substances even before a causal link has been established by absolutely clear scientific evidence'. A new Ministerial Declaration was delivered at the Third International Conference on the Protection of the North Sea (1990). It fleshes out the earlier declaration, stating that 'the participants ... will continue to apply the precautionary principle, that is to take action to avoid potentially damaging impacts of substances that are persistent, toxic and liable to bioaccumulate even where there is no scientific evidence to prove a causal link between emissions and effects'.

The Precautionary Principle was explicitly recognised during the UN Conference on Environment and Development (UNCED) in Rio de Janeiro 1992 and included in the so-called Rio Declaration. Since then the Precautionary Principle has been implemented in various environmental instruments, and in particular in global climate change, ozone-depleting substances and biodiversity conservation.

The precautionary Principle is listed as Principle 15 of the Rio Declaration among the principles of general rights and obligations of national authorities:

> In order to protect the environment, the precautionary approach should be widely applied by States according to their capabilities. Where there are threats of serious or irreversible damage, lack of full scientific certainty shall not be used as a reason for postponing cost-effective measures to prevent environmental degradation.

Principle 15 is reproduced in similar wording in:

1 The preamble of the Convention of Biological Diversity (1992):
Noting also that where there is a threat of significant reduction or loss of biological diversity, lack of full scientific certainty should not be used as a reason for postponing measures to avoid or minimise such a threat ...

2 In Article 3 (Principles) of the Convention of Climate Change (1992):
The Parties should take precautionary measures to anticipate, prevent or minimise the causes of climate change and mitigate its adverse effects. Where there are threats of serious or irreversible damage, lack of full scientific certainty should not be used as a reason for postponing such measures, taking into account that policies and measures to deal with climate

---

[12] COM(2000) 1, Brussels 02.02.2000.

change should be cost-effective so as to ensure global benefits at the lowest possible cost. To achieve this, such policies and measures should take into account different socio-economic contexts, be comprehensive, cover all relevant sources, sinks and reservoirs of greenhouse gases and adaptation, and comprise all economic sectors. Efforts to address climate change may be carried out cooperatively by interested Parties.

In the Paris Convention for the protection of the marine environment of the north-east Atlantic (September 1992), the precautionary principle is defined as the principle 'by virtue of which preventive measures are to be taken when there are reasonable grounds for concern that substances or energy introduced, directly or indirectly, into the marine environment may bring about hazards to human health, harm living resources and marine ecosystems, damage amenities or interfere with other legitimate uses of the sea, even when there is no conclusive evidence of a causal relationship between the inputs and the effects'.

Recently, on 28 January 2000, at the Conference of the Parties to the Convention on Biological diversity, the Protocol on Biosafety concerning the safe transfer, handling and use of living modified organisms resulting from modern biotechnology confirmed the key function of the Precautionary Principle. In fact, article 10, paragraph 6 states: 'Lack of scientific certainty due to insufficient relevant scientific information and knowledge regarding the extent of the potential adverse effects of a living modified organism on the conservation and sustainable use of biological diversity in the Party of import, taking also into account risks to human health, shall not prevent that Party from taking a decision, as appropriate, with regard to the import of living modified organism in question as referred to in paragraph 3 above, in order to avoid or minimize such potential adverse effects.'

Besides, the preamble to the WTO Agreement highlights the ever closer links between international trade and environmental protection.

The WTO SPS Agreement

Although the term "Precautionary Principle" is not explicitly used in the WTO Agreement on the Application of Sanitary and Phytosanitary Measures (SPS), the Appellate Body on EC measures concerning meat and meat products (Hormones) (AB-1997-4, paragraph 124) states that it finds reflection in Article 5.7 of this Agreement. Article 5.7 reads:

> In cases where relevant scientific evidence is insufficient, a Member may provisionally adopt sanitary or phytosanitary measures on the basis of available scientific information, including that from the relevant international organizations as well as from sanitary and phytosanitary measures applied by other Members. In such circumstances, Members shall seek to obtain the additional information necessary for a more objective assessment of risk and review the sanitary or phytosanitary measure accordingly within a reasonable period of time.

The Appellate Body on Hormones (Paragraph 124) recognises, 'that there is no need to assume that Article 5.7 exhausts the relevance of a precautionary principle'. Moreover, Members have the 'right to establish their own level of sanitary protection, which level may be higher (i.e. more cautious) than that implied in existing international standards, guidelines and recommendations'. Furthermore, it accepts that 'responsible, representative governments commonly act from perspectives of prudence and precaution where risks of irreversible, e.g. life-terminating, damage to human health are concerned'. The Appellate Body on Japan – Measures affecting agricultural products (AB-1998-8, paragraph 89) clarifies the four requirements which must be met in order to adopt and maintain provisional SPS measures. A Member may provisionally adopt an SPS measure if this measure is:

1) imposed in respect of a situation where 'relevant scientific information is insufficient'; and
2) adopted 'on the basis of available pertinent information'.

Such a provisional measure may not be maintained unless the Member which adopted the measure:

1) 'seek(s) to obtain the additional information necessary for a more objective risk assessment'; and
2) 'review(s) the ... measure accordingly within a reasonable period of time'.

These four requirements are clearly cumulative and are equally important for the purpose of determining consistency with the provision of Article 5.7. Whenever one of these four requirements is not met, the measure at issue is inconsistent with Article 5.7. As to what constitutes a 'reasonable period of time' to review the measure, the Appellate Body points out (para. 93), that this has to be established on a case-by-case basis and depends on the specific circumstances of each case, including the difficulty of obtaining the additional information necessary for the review and the characteristics of the provisional SPS measure.

In this chapter, we can start by considering the Commission's guidance on the appropriate use of the principle and, in particular, Elizabeth Fisher's reading of the Communication as a push back towards what she terms a 'rational–instrumental' style of regulation;[13] then we can review attempts to apply the principle to questions of health and safety rather than environmental damage (where Han Somsen has warned that it might operate as a Trojan Horse);[14] and, finally, we can seek out the most coherent version of the principle.

---

[13] Elizabeth Fisher, *Risk Regulation and Administrative Constitutionalism* (Oxford: Hart, 2007).
[14] Han Somsen, 'Cloning Trojan Horses: Precautionary Regulation of Reproductive Technologies', in Roger Brownsword and Karen Yeung (eds.), *Regulating Technologies* (Oxford: Hart, 2008), 221.

2 The European Commission's guidance

In 2000, following concern about the way in which the precautionary principle might be pleaded rather too freely and inconsistently as a justification for limiting the standard market freedoms, the European Commission issued a benchmark note of general guidance. The Commission's declared intention was to establish a common understanding of the principle and to offer guidance for its reasoned and coherent application.

1. Introduction

A number of recent events has shown that public opinion is becoming increasingly aware of the potential risks to which the population or their environment are potentially exposed.

Enormous advances in communications technology have fostered this growing sensitivity to the emergence of new risks, before scientific research has been able to fully illuminate the problems. Decision-makers have to take account of the fears generated by these perceptions and to put in place preventive measures to eliminate the risk or at least reduce it to the minimum acceptable level. On 13 April 1999 the Council adopted a resolution urging the Commission inter alia 'to be in the future even more determined to be guided by the precautionary principle in preparing proposals for legislation and in its other consumer-related activities and develop as priority clear and effective guidelines for the application of this principle'. This Communication is part of the Commission's response.

The dimension of the precautionary principle goes beyond the problems associated with a short or medium-term approach to risks. It also concerns the longer run and the well-being of future generations.

A decision to take measures without waiting until all the necessary scientific knowledge is available is clearly a precaution-based approach.

Decision-makers are constantly faced with the dilemma of balancing the freedoms and rights of individuals, industry and organisations with the need to reduce or eliminate the risk of adverse effects to the environment or to health.

Finding the correct balance so that proportionate, non-discriminatory, transparent and coherent decisions can be arrived at, which at the same time provide the chosen level of protection, requires a structured decision making process with detailed scientific and other objective information.

This structure is provided by the three elements of risk analysis: the assessment of risk, the choice of risk management strategy and the communication of the risk.

Any assessment of risk that is made should be based on the existing body of scientific and statistical data. Most decisions are taken where there is sufficient information available for appropriate preventive measures to be taken but in other circumstances, these data may be wanting in some respects.

Whether or not to invoke the Precautionary Principle is a decision exercised where scientific information is insufficient, inconclusive, or uncertain and where there are indications that the possible effects on the environment, or human, animal or plant health may be potentially dangerous and inconsistent with the chosen level of protection.

The Communication then expresses its goals before summarising the recognition of the precautionary principle in both EU law and international law. It continues:

5. The constituent parts of the precautionary principle

An analysis of the precautionary principle reveals two quite distinct aspects: (i) the political decision to act or not to act as such, which is linked to the factors triggering recourse to the precautionary principle; (ii) in the affirmative, how to act, i.e. the measures resulting from application of the precautionary principle.

There is a controversy as to the role of scientific uncertainty in risk analysis, and notably as to whether it belongs under risk assessment or risk management. This controversy springs from a confusion between a prudential approach and application of the precautionary principle. These two aspects are complementary but should not be confounded.

The prudential approach is part of risk assessment policy which is determined before any risk assessment takes place and which is based on the elements described in 5.1.3; it is therefore an integral part of the scientific opinion delivered by the risk evaluators.

On the other hand, application of the precautionary principle is part of risk management, when scientific uncertainty precludes a full assessment of the risk and when decision-makers consider that the chosen level of environmental protection or of human, animal and plant health may be in jeopardy.

The Commission considers that measures applying the precautionary principle belong in the general framework of risk analysis, and in particular risk management.

5.1. Factors triggering recourse to the precautionary principle

The precautionary principle is relevant only in the event of a potential risk, even if this risk cannot be fully demonstrated or quantified or its effects determined because of the insufficiency or inclusive [*sic*: inconclusive?] nature of the scientific data.

It should however be noted that the precautionary principle can under no circumstances be used to justify the adoption of arbitrary decisions.

5.1.1. Identification of potentially negative effects

Before the precautionary principle is invoked, the scientific data relevant to the risks must first be evaluated. However, one factor logically and chronologically precedes the decision to act, namely identification of the potentially negative effects of a phenomenon. To understand these effects more thoroughly it is necessary to conduct a scientific examination. The decision to conduct this examination without awaiting additional information is bound up with a less theoretical and more concrete perception of the risk.

5.1.2. Scientific evaluation

A scientific evaluation of the potential adverse effects should be undertaken based on the available data when considering whether measures are necessary to protect the environment, the human, animal or plant health. An assessment of risk should be considered where feasible when deciding whether or not to invoke the precautionary principle. This requires reliable scientific data and logical reasoning, leading to a conclusion which expresses the possibility of occurrence and the severity of a hazard's impact on the environment, or health of a given population including the extent of possible damage, persistency, reversibility and delayed effect. However it is not possible in all cases to complete a comprehensive assessment of risk, but all effort should be made to evaluate the available scientific information.

Where possible, a report should be made which indicates the assessment of the existing knowledge and the available information, providing the views of the scientists on the reliability of the assessment as well as on the remaining uncertainties. If necessary, it should also contain the identification of topics for further scientific research.

Risk assessment consists of four components – namely hazard identification, hazard characterisation, appraisal of exposure and risk characterisation (Annex III). The limits of scientific knowledge may affect each of these components, influencing the overall level of attendant uncertainty and ultimately affecting the foundation for protective or preventive action. An attempt to complete these four steps should be performed before decision to act is taken.

5.1.3. Scientific uncertainty

Scientific uncertainty results usually from five characteristics of the scientific method: the variable chosen, the measurements made, the samples drawn, the models used and the causal relationship employed. Scientific uncertainty may also arise from a controversy on existing data or lack of some relevant data. Uncertainty may relate to qualitative or quantitative elements of the analysis.

A more abstract and generalised approach preferred by some scientists is to separate all uncertainties into three categories of – Bias, Randomness and True Variability. Some other experts categorise uncertainty in terms of estimation of confidence interval of the probability of occurrence and of the severity of the hazard's impact.

This issue is very complex and the Commission launched a project 'Technological Risk and the Management of Uncertainty' conducted under the auspices of the European Scientific Technology Observatory. The four ESTO reports will be published shortly and will give a comprehensive description of scientific uncertainty.

Risk evaluators accommodate these uncertainty factors by incorporating prudential aspects such as:

- relying on animal models to establish potential effects in man;
- using body weight ranges to make inter-species comparisons;

- adopting a safety factor in evaluating an acceptable daily intake to account for intra- and inter-species variability; the magnitude of this factor depends on the degree of uncertainty of the available data;
- not adopting an acceptable daily intake for substances recognised as genotoxic or carcinogenic;
- adopting the 'ALARA' (as low as reasonably achievable) level as a basis for certain toxic contaminants.

Risk managers should be fully aware of these uncertainty factors when they adopt measures based on the scientific opinion delivered by the evaluators.

However, in some situations the scientific data are not sufficient to allow one to apply these prudential aspects in practice, i.e. in cases in which extrapolations cannot be made because of the absence of parameter modelling and where cause–effect relationships are suspected but have not been demonstrated. It is in situations like these that decision-makers face the dilemma of having to act or not to act.

Recourse to the precautionary principle presupposes:

- identification of potentially negative effects resulting from a phenomenon, product or procedure;
- a scientific evaluation of the risk which because of the insufficiency of the data, their inconclusive or imprecise nature, makes it impossible to determine with sufficient certainty the risk in question.

5.2. Measures resulting from reliance on the precautionary principle

5.2.1. The decision whether or not to act

In the kind of situation described above – sometimes under varying degrees of pressure from public opinion – decision-makers have to respond. However, responding does not necessarily mean that measures always have to be adopted. The decision to do nothing may be a response in its own right.

The appropriate response in a given situation is thus the result of an eminently political decision, a function of the risk level that is 'acceptable' to the society on which the risk is imposed.

5.2.2. Nature of the action ultimately taken

The nature of the decision influences the type of control that can be carried out. Recourse to the precautionary principle does not necessarily mean adopting final instruments designed to produce legal effects that are open to judicial review. There is a whole range of actions available to decision-makers under the head of the precautionary principle. The decision to fund a research programme or even the decision to inform the public about the possible adverse effects of a product or procedure may themselves be inspired by the precautionary principle.

It is for the Court of Justice to pronounce on the legality of any measures taken by the Community institutions. The Court has consistently held that when the

Commission or any other Community institution has broad discretionary powers, notably as regards the nature and scope of the measures it adopts, review by the Court must be limited to examining whether the institution committed a manifest error or misuse of power or manifestly exceed the limits of its powers of appraisal.

Hence the measures may not be of an arbitrary nature.

Recourse to the precautionary principle does not necessarily mean adopting final instruments designed to produce legal effects, which are subject to judicial review.

6. Guidelines for applying the precautionary principle.

6.1. Implementation

When decision-makers become aware of a risk to the environment or human, animal or plant health that in the event of non-action may have serious consequences, the question of appropriate protective measures arise. Decision-makers have to obtain, through a structured approach, a scientific evaluation, as complete as possible, of the risk to the environment, or health, in order to select the most appropriate course of action.

The determination of appropriate action including measures based on the precautionary principle should start with a scientific evaluation and, if necessary, the decision to commission scientists to perform an as objective and complete as possible scientific evaluation. It will cast light on the existing objective evidence, the gaps in knowledge and the scientific uncertainties.

The implementation of an approach based on the precautionary principle should start with a scientific evaluation, as complete as possible, and where possible, identifying at each stage the degree of scientific uncertainty.

6.2. The triggering factor

Once the scientific evaluation has been performed as best as possible, it may provide a basis for triggering a decision to invoke the precautionary principle. The conclusions of this evaluation should show that the desired level of protection for the environment or a population group could be jeopardised. The conclusions should also include an assessment of the scientific uncertainties and a description of the hypotheses used to compensate for the lack of the scientific or statistical data. An assessment of the potential consequences of inaction should be considered and may be used as a trigger by the decision-makers. The decision to wait or not to wait for new scientific data before considering possible measures should be taken by the decision-makers with a maximum of transparency. The absence of scientific proof of the existence of a cause–effect relationship, a quantifiable dose/response relationship or a quantitative evaluation of the probability of the emergence of adverse effects following exposure should not be used to justify inaction. Even if scientific advice is supported only by a minority fraction of the scientific community, due account should be taken of their views, provided the credibility and reputation of this fraction are recognised. [2]

[2] cf. The WTO Appellate Body report on hormones, paragraph 124: 'In some cases, the very existence of divergent views presented by qualified scientists who have investigated the particular issue at hand, may indicate a state of scientific uncertainty.'

The Commission has confirmed its wish to rely on procedures as transparent as possible and to involve all interested parties at the earliest possible stage [3]. This will assist decision makers in taking legitimate measures which are likely to achieve the society's chosen level of health or environmental protection.

[3] A considerable effort has already been made notably as regards public health and the environment. As regards the latter, the Community and the Member States have demonstrated the importance they attach to access to information and justice by signing the Aarhus Convention of June 1998.

An assessment of the potential consequences of inaction and of the uncertainties of the scientific evaluation should be considered by decision-makers when determining whether to trigger action based on the precautionary principle.

All interested parties should be involved to the fullest extent possible in the study of various risk management options that may be envisaged once the results of the scientific evaluation and/or risk assessment are available and the procedure be as transparent as possible.

6.3. The general principles of application

The general principles are not limited to application of the precautionary principle. They apply to all risk management measures. An approach inspired by the precautionary principle does not exempt one from applying wherever possible these criteria, which are generally used when a complete risk assessment is at hand.

Thus reliance on the precautionary principle is no excuse for derogating from the general principles of risk management.

These general principles include:

- proportionality,
- non-discrimination,
- consistency,
- examination of the benefits and costs of action or lack of action
- examination of scientific developments.

6.3.1. Proportionality

The measures envisaged must make it possible to achieve the appropriate level of protection. Measures based on the precautionary principle must not be disproportionate to the desired level of protection and must not aim at zero risk, something which rarely exists. However, in certain cases, an incomplete assessment of the risk may considerably limit the number of options available to the risk managers.

In some cases a total ban may not be a proportional response to a potential risk. In other cases, it may be the sole possible response to a potential risk.

Risk reduction measures should include less restrictive alternatives which make it possible to achieve an equivalent level of protection, such as appropriate treatment, reduction of exposure, tightening of controls, adoption of provisional limits, recommendations for populations at risk, etc. One should also consider replacing the products or procedures concerned by safer products or procedures.

The risk reduction measure should not be limited to immediate risks where the proportionality of the action is easier to assess. It is in situations in which the adverse effects do not emerge until long after exposure that the cause–effect relationships are more difficult to prove scientifically and that – for this reason – the precautionary principle often has to be invoked. In this case the potential long-term effects must be taken into account in evaluating the proportionality of measures in the form of rapid action to limit or eliminate a risk whose effects will not surface until ten or twenty years later or will affect future generations. This applies in particular to effects on the eco-system. Risks that are carried forward into the future cannot be eliminated or reduced except at the time of exposure, that is to say immediately.

Measures should be proportional to the desired level of protection.

6.3.2. Non-discrimination

The principle of non-discrimination means that comparable situations should not be treated differently and that different situations should not be treated in the same way, unless there are objective grounds for doing so.

Measures taken under the precautionary principle should be designed to achieve an equivalent level of protection without invoking the geographical origin or the nature of the production process to apply different treatments in an arbitrary manner.

Measures should not be discriminatory in their application.

6.3.3. Consistency

Measures should be consistent with the measures already adopted in similar circumstances or using similar approaches. Risk evaluations include a series of factors to be taken into account to ensure that they are as thorough as possible. The goal here is to identify and characterise the hazards, notably by establishing a relationship between the dose and the effect and assessing the exposure of the target population or the environment. If the absence of certain scientific data makes it impossible to characterise the risk, taking into account the uncertainties inherent to the evaluation, the measures taken under the precautionary principle should be comparable in nature and scope with measures already taken in equivalent areas in which all the scientific data are available.

Measures should be consistent with the measures already adopted in similar circumstances or using similar approaches.

6.3.4. Examination of the benefits and costs of action and lack of action

A comparison must be made between the most likely positive or negative consequences of the envisaged action and those of inaction in terms of the overall cost to the Community, both in the long- and short-term. The measures envisaged must produce an overall advantage as regards reducing risks to an acceptable level.

Examination of the pros and cons cannot be reduced to an economic cost-benefit analysis. It is wider in scope and includes non-economic considerations.

However, examination of the pros and cons should include an economic cost-benefit analysis where this is appropriate and possible.

Besides, other analysis methods, such as those concerning the efficacy of possible options and their acceptability to the public may also have to be taken into account. A society may be willing to pay a higher cost to protect an interest, such as the environment or health, to which it attaches priority.

The Commission affirms, in accordance with the case law of the Court that requirements linked to the protection of public health should undoubtedly be given greater weight that [*sic*: than?] economic considerations.

The measures adopted presuppose examination of the benefits and costs of action and lack of action. This examination should include an economic cost-benefit analysis when this is appropriate and feasible. However, other analysis methods, such as those concerning efficacy and the socio-economic impact of the various options, may also be relevant. Besides the decision-maker may, in certain circumstances, by guided by non-economic considerations such as the protection of health.

6.3.5. Examination of scientific developments

The measures should be maintained as long as the scientific data are inadequate, imprecise or inconclusive and as long as the risk is considered too high to be imposed on society. The measures may have to be modified or abolished by a particular deadline, in the light of new scientific findings. However, this is not always linked to the time factor, but to the development of scientific knowledge.

Besides, scientific research should be carried out with a view to obtaining a more advanced or more complete scientific assessment. In this context, the measures should be subjected to regular scientific monitoring, so that they can be reevaluated in the light of new scientific information.

The Agreement on Sanitary and Phytosanitary Measures (SPS) provides that measures adopted in the context of inadequate scientific evidence must respect certain conditions. Hence these conditions concern only the scope of the SPS Agreement, but the specific nature of certain sectors, such as the environment, may mean that somewhat different principles have to be applied.

Article 5(7) of the SPS agreement includes certain specific rules:

- The measures must be of a provisional nature pending the availability of more reliable scientific data. However this provisional nature is linked to the development of scientific knowledge rather than to a time factor.

- Research must be carried out to elicit the additional scientific data required for a more objective assessment of the risk.
- The measures must be periodically reviewed to take account of new scientific data. The results of scientific research should make it possible to complete the risk evaluation and if necessary to review the measures on the basis of the conclusions.
- Hence the reasonable period envisaged in the SPS Agreement includes the time needed for completion of the necessary scientific work and, besides, the time needed for performance of a risk evaluation based on the conclusions of this scientific work. It should not be possible to invoke budgetary constraints or political priorities to justify excessive delays in obtaining results, re-evaluating the risk or amending the provisional measures.

Research could also be conducted for the improvement of the methodologies and instruments for assessing risk, including greater integration of all pertinent factors (e.g. socio-economic information, technological perspectives).

The measures, although provisional, shall be maintained as long as the scientific data remain incomplete, imprecise or inconclusive and as long as the risk is considered too high to be imposed on society.

Maintenance of the measures depends on the development of scientific knowledge, in the light of which they should be reevaluated. This means that scientific research shall be continued with a view to obtaining more complete data.

Measures based on the precautionary principle shall be reexamined and if necessary modified depending on the results of the scientific research and the follow up of their impact.

6.4. The burden of proof

- Community rules and those of many third countries enshrine the principle of prior approval (positive list) before the placing on the market of certain products, such as drugs, pesticides or food additives. This is one way of applying the precautionary principle, by shifting responsibility for producing scientific evidence. This applies in particular to substances deemed 'a priori' hazardous or which are potentially hazardous at a certain level of absorption. In this case the legislator, by way of precaution, has clearly reversed the burden of proof by requiring that the substances be deemed hazardous until proven otherwise. Hence it is up to the business community to carry out the scientific work needed to evaluate the risk. As long as the human health risk cannot be evaluated with sufficient certainty, the legislator is not legally entitled to authorise use of the substance, unless exceptionally for test purposes.
- In other cases, where such a prior approval procedure does not exist, it may be for the user, a private individual, a consumer association, citizens or the public authorities to demonstrate the nature of a danger and the level of risk posed by a product or process. Action taken under the head of the precautionary principle

must in certain cases include a clause reversing the burden of proof and placing it on the producer, manufacturer or importer, but such an obligation cannot be systematically entertained as a general principle. This possibility should be examined on a case-by-case basis when a measure is adopted under the precautionary principle, pending supplementary scientific data, so as to give professionals who have an economic interest in the production and/or marketing of the procedure or product in question the opportunity to finance the necessary research on a voluntary basis.

Measures based on the precautionary principle may assign responsibility for producing the scientific evidence necessary for a comprehensive risk evaluation.

7. CONCLUSION

This Communication of a general scope sets out the Commission's position as regards recourse to the precautionary principle. The Communication reflects the Commission's desire for transparency and dialogue with all stakeholders. At the same it is provides concrete guidance for applying the precautionary principle.

The Commission wishes to reaffirm the crucial importance it attaches to the distinction between the decision to act or not to act, which is of an eminently political nature, and the measures resulting from recourse to the precautionary principle, which must comply with the general principles applicable to all risk management measures. The Commission also considers that every decision must be preceded by an examination of all the available scientific data and, if possible, a risk evaluation that is as objective and comprehensive as possible. A decision to invoke the precautionary principle does not mean that the measures will be adopted on an arbitrary or discriminatory basis.

This Communication should also contribute to reaffirming the Community's position at international level, where the precautionary principle is receiving increasing attention. However the Commission wishes to stress that this Communication is not meant to be the last word; rather, it should be seen as the point of departure for a broader study of the conditions in which risks should be assessed, appraised, managed and communicated.

What should we make of this Communication? According to Elizabeth Fisher, we should interpret the Commission's guidance through the lens of administrative constitutionalism; in which case, we will read it as in line with what she terms the ideal-type of 'rational-instrumentalism' rather than a rival 'deliberative–constitutive' model.[15] This takes some unpacking.

First, Fisher argues that it is unhelpful to suppose that, for the purposes of regulating risk, we must choose between following the science or throwing the question open for democratic decision. Science and democracy each have their part to play in the decision-making process. Nevertheless, there is a choice to

---

[15] Elizabeth Fisher, *Risk Regulation and Administrative Constitutionalism* (Oxford: Hart, 2007).

be made; and it is a choice between two paradigms, one rational–instrumental (RI), the other deliberative–constitutive (DC) in nature.

Second, if we adopt an RI approach, we will want to set out a staged and structured framework for decision-making. The facts, whether concerning the science or public attitudes, will need to be established (such facts being understood to be relatively hard and objective); there will be thresholds for, and burdens of, proof; there will be little room for discretion; the process will be transparent; and decision-makers can be straightforwardly held to account. By contrast, the DC approach contemplates a much more fluid and flexible framework; the facts are understood as being more complex; decision-makers need discretion; and so the benchmarks for accountability are less sharply defined. If RI tries to disaggregate the regulation of risk into a series of discrete phases, DC presupposes a more holistic approach.

Third, suppose that we now set the rival readings of the precautionary principle against these two paradigms. What we will see is that, while a broad facilitative reading of the principle (allowing for the possibility of regulatory intervention, lack of full scientific certainty notwithstanding) is in line with the DC approach, a less facilitative reading (with a regulatory tilt that is against intervention) is more in line with the RI approach. As Fisher spells this out in relation to the DC model:

> From a DC perspective, the precautionary principle can be understood as a natural outgrowth of the DC paradigm. If public administration is constituted to address complex and uncertain technological problems in an ongoing and flexible fashion then the need for decision-makers not to be constrained by a requirement of 'full scientific uncertainty' before they can take action is obvious. In such circumstances the principle is not a 'prescribed formula' but a flexible principle that ensures that decision-makers are not ignoring problems of scientific uncertainty. Both 'information' and 'scientific uncertainty' are interpreted broadly and it is a principle that applies to all aspects of the decision-making … [The] context is a dynamic and polycentric one in which a decision-maker needs to be engaging in an ongoing process of analysis and deliberation.[16]

Where the DC paradigm holds, the expectation is that decision-makers will apply the precautionary principle in good faith and in a way that is sensitive to the complexities of the matter; and, it is on this basis that regulators will be held to account.

Turning to the RI paradigm and its relationship with the precautionary principle, Fisher says:

> From this [RI] perspective, the principle is allowing decision-makers to deviate from the normal definition of reasonable action – that decision-makers should act on the basis of proof – but only in limited circumstances. On this basis, the principle is interpreted far more narrowly. The principle is primarily understood

---

[16] *Ibid.*, at 43 (footnotes omitted).

as applying to the decision to act after there has been the assessment of information if that assessment has identified a threat. In such circumstances, the principle gives a margin of discretion to decision-makers but it is not an enabling principle in the way that it is under the DC paradigm. In particular, the principle is only applying to how information is used in risk evaluation and, in so doing, it is not altering the fact that the starting point for judging the reasonableness of decision-making is proof.[17]

Fourth, how does the Commission's Communication look in this light? As we have said, Fisher reads the Communication as a reaction against a DC tendency and as an assertion of the RI paradigm. Thus:

> Throughout the Communication, the Commission stresses that one of the explicit aims of the Communication is to 'avoid unwarranted recourse to the precautionary principle, as a disguised form of protectionism' and that the precautionary principle should never be used as a justification for arbitrary decision-making. The important point is that the concept of arbitrariness is being defined in RI terms. In the Communication, decision-makers are understood to be carrying out a series of discrete tasks, and environmental and public health decision-making is characterised as a three step process: a scientific process of risk assessment; a political process of risk management; and a process of risk communication.[18]

Although there are mixed signals in the Communication, the thrust seems to be against interventions that are not evidence based. There needs, at least, to be support from a responsible body of scientific opinion (whatever this might mean or however the credibility and reputation of such a group might be assessed). Summing up, Fisher says:

> The Communication is thus creating a rigid RI framework for decision-makers to follow if they wish to apply the precautionary principle. Decision-makers are being assigned two specific tasks of assessing and managing risks, and in regard to each are constrained by methodologies such as risk assessment and regulatory impact assessment. Not only must a decision-maker use those methodologies in making those decisions but a decision made pursuant to those methodologies is held to be valid ... Moreover, the overall legitimacy of the decision is judged by the factual basis. Decision-making pursuant to the principle should start with 'a scientific evaluation', must be based on 'a scientific evaluation, as complete as possible', and will probably involve commissioning scientists to perform 'as objective and complete as possible scientific evaluation'. In other words, scientific evaluation, according to the document, is the central activity in the application of the precautionary principle.[19]

Following the Communication, Fisher detects in the Community case law a shift toward the RI approach, the focus being 'less upon deliberative problem-solving than upon accurate analysis and the application of methodology', the

---

[17] *Ibid.* (footnotes omitted).   [18] *Ibid.*, at 226 (footnotes omitted).
[19] *Ibid.*, at 228 (footnotes omitted).

courts going 'from understanding precautionary reasoning as broad ranging and deliberative to understanding it as an exception that operates in specific circumstances'.[20]

Even if the Commission is able to contain reliance on the precautionary principle in areas where the Community has competence, there are many opportunities for precautionary reasoning to operate in accordance with local rules; and in contexts other than environmental protection.

3 Beyond environmental protection

In principle, we might apply precautionary reasoning in any context where we have prudential concerns for our health and safety, or the environmental conditions for our well-being. However, the broader the range of the principle, the more likely it is that it will be applied either opportunistically or in quite deviant ways. One recalls, for example, the notorious House of Commons Science and Technology Committee report entitled *Human Reproductive Technologies and the Law*,[21] where it was said that the regulation of human reproductive technologies should adopt a precautionary principle [*sic*] such that we proceed cautiously so long as 'there is no evidence of sufficiently serious harm or potential harm to outweigh benefit or potential benefit'.[22] Bizarrely, the Committee uses the principle to support a libertarian approach, treating it as a licence to proceed; but, it can be misapplied in quite the opposite way when it is pleaded as a pretext for conservative moral protectionism. Concerns about the latter kind of misapplication are taken up by Han Somsen (see the extract below).

Having highlighted the enabling nature of the precautionary principle, Somsen declares his support for such an approach in the special circumstances of grave environmental risk. However, even if precaution is appropriate in relation to certain types of green biotechnology, it does not follow that this is the case with red biotechnology. Here, the danger is that the principle can be invoked by ideologically opposed interests, as has happened recently in the Netherlands in the course of debates concerning the regulation of technologies such as PGD.

---

[20] *Ibid.*, at 239. But, compare, von Schomberg, 'Precautionary Principle', who interprets the European approach as essentially deliberative. In particular, at 31, von Schomberg argues that: 'the qualifier "reasonable grounds for concern" as employed by the EC guidelines makes ... no statement about the degree of likelihood, but this qualifier relates in fact to a judgement on the quality of the available information'. According to von Schomberg, the key difference between standard risk-based regulation and precautionary deliberation is that there is 'a shift in science-centred debates on the probability of risk towards a science-informed debate on uncertainties and plausible adverse effects' (*ibid.*, at 34).

[21] HC 7–1, Science and Technology Committee, *Human Reproductive Technologies and the Law* (Fifth Report of Session 2004–5) (London: TSO, 24 March 2005).

[22] Para. 47.

Somsen, 'Cloning Trojan Horses', 224–31 (footnotes omitted)

II. Origins and rise of the precautionary state

A. CONTEXT SPECIFIC JUSTIFICATIONS FOR ENVIRONMENTAL PRECAUTION

Although we should avoid waxing dogmatically on the proper interpretation of the precautionary principle, some illumination of its core is inescapable if we are to understand its development from a uniquely environmental regulatory tool into a principle that is increasingly invoked in many different contexts of uncertainty, which most definitely includes reproductive technologies.

Numerous articulations of the precautionary principle are in simultaneous circulation, but Principle 15 of the Rio Declaration is generally deemed to offer an important and fairly representative example of its original meaning …

Provided that … judicial checks and balances in place, there are numerous persuasive reasons for embracing precautionary environmental regulation. This is because, despite its obvious imperfections, as long as precaution is used for *environmental* regulation the principle helps redress some very clear and serious imbalances that ultimately undermine mankind's chances of survival.

First, there exists a worrisome imbalance between what we can *do* and what at present we can *understand*. Environmental precaution is a principle appropriate for a civilization in which technological and economic capabilities are out of sync with its scientific grasp of the ecological impacts of those activities. Crucial amongst the known unknowns that justify environmental precaution is the nature of ecological thresholds that trigger sudden global environmental catastrophes, e.g. the increasingly rapid disappearance of polar ice that in turn may reverse the gulf stream, etc.

Second, we must acknowledge the disequilibria between those having a legal interest and voice in pursuing some industrial activity, and the environment, which does not possess legal personality and is not easily represented in the law, even if the law provides for access to justice for environmental Non Governmental Organizations (NGOs).

Third, there are obvious conflicts of interest between present and future generations. The costs of irreversible harm to the environment by definition are borne by future generations who are not represented in political and legal process. Precaution gives future generations a voice in legal and political processes.

Some, but not all of the above imbalances exist in other policy fields where precaution is now surfacing. For human genetics, the first imbalance between human capabilities to act and to understand clearly applies, but it is not self-evident that critical thresholds exist in the way exemplified above. Neither, in the main, is the survival of future generations at stake. As for the protection of future generations: parents routinely unilaterally decide what is good for their children, often before birth, and there is no obvious reason to impose additional constraints on that parental prerogative when it comes to the use of modern reproductive technologies. Finally, informed consent serves to redress any imbalance between those having a legal interest in pursuing the activity (doctors, researchers, patent applicants, etc.) and the target of those activities (patients and research subjects).

For all these reasons, calls for precautionary constraints on genetic technologies are much less persuasive and the consequences of inevitable, even if only occasional, arbitrariness much harder to justify.

In view of these reservations against precautionary creep to more and more policy fields besides environmental policy, it becomes important to understand the rise of the precautionary state. Because risk is a sociological and psychological construct, and hence can be easily manipulated, explanations may range from the sociological, the psychological, the cultural, to the political. This is a fact well understood by van den Daele [see W. van den Daele, 'Legal Framework and Political Strategy in Dealing with the Risks of New Technology: The Two Faces of the Precautionary Principle', in Han Somsen (ed.), *The Regulatory Challenge of Biotechnology* (Edward Elgar, 2007), 118–38]. The precautionary principle, he compellingly argues, is not a *legal* principle aimed at risk prevention, but has become a *political* tool allowing states to exercise control over the direction of technological innovation. There is an abundance of empirical evidence to support this thesis, including the regulatory history of Novartis' Bt-176 maize and the EU moratorium on genetically modified organisms (gmo's) more generally. Scientific evidence regarding risks of gmo's resulting in proposals to allow the cultivation of gm crops or the marketing of gm produce has been routinely flouted by the executive, clearly for reasons that have little to do with risk and all the more with (manipulated) public opinion. Precaution in those cases serves as an alibi to duck otherwise manifest and inescapable charges of breaches of constitutional law.

Indeed, whereas globalization irreversibly eats away at states' regulatory powers, *risk* regulation invariably requires strong state involvement. By emphasizing risk and embracing precaution, states have hence mobilized forces that partly offset those losses of regulatory control. After all, the essence of precaution is to enable government to take action where it otherwise could not. It makes sense, therefore, that the principle should have become an attractive proposition for legislators that would otherwise lack justification to exercise their regulatory powers. This applies to the European Commission, for which the precautionary principle has been a vehicle allowing it gradually to occupy a number of new key policy fields, but also to national regulatory agencies that traditionally have been excluded from clinical arena's in which they might have a (political, religious, or ethical) interest.

This takes us to the next part of this paper, which distinguishes ways in which the precautionary principle can conceivably operate in the arena of human genetics, and human reproductive technologies in particular.

B. FACT-FINDING PRECAUTION

Conventionally, precaution is predominantly associated with risk management in cases where preceding risk assessments have to be conducted under circumstances of scientific uncertainty. In such cases, where 'science' alone cannot give conclusive evidence as to the risks that should be associated with any given technology, there are no good reasons to exclude other sources of discourse, e.g. ethics, religion, etc.

There are some increasingly strong voices, however, that advocate extending precaution to the risk assessment phase of risk analysis which, as is evidenced by legal articulations of risk assessment procedures, traditionally has been the preserve of the science designed to expose the facts about adverse effects, their likelihood, and impacts. Yet, to say that precaution rationally stimulates deliberation in risk *management* under circumstances of scientific uncertainty is evidently quite different from implying that precaution in risk *assessment* results in *more accurate* decisions (i.e. less uncertainty, for example, in respect of the question whether 'saviour siblings' in later life will more often be lacking in self respect than naturally conceived donors). When it comes to arriving at accurate decisions (finding the factual basis of risk, or of anything else for that matter), which is what risk assessments are about, the pedigree of deliberation is rather less compelling. In fact, as Sunstein argues, not only is there no evidence that deliberation between opposing perspectives more often than not results in establishing the truth, it often does not even lead to accurate use of the available information, nor even can it be shown to result in establishing truth *more often* than do non-deliberative models of decision-making [see Cass R. Sunstein, *Infotopia* (Oxford University Press, 2006)].

This means that precautionary deliberation to reveal truths, what I will term 'fact-finding precaution', is a risky idea. In line with European and international case law, I therefore feel that precaution should not be employed as a tool to ascertain scientific truth, and for that reason also should play no role in the risk assessment phase of risk regulation.

C. DELIBERATIVE PRECAUTION

Decisions about the acceptability of particular applications of biotechnology, Julia Black argues, are often informed by a single predominant paradigm [Julia Black, 'Regulation as Facilitation: Negotiating the Genetic Revolution', *MLR*, 61 (1998), 621]. Indeed, it is true that decisions about, for instance, genetically modified organisms (gmo's) to a large degree continue to be outcomes of quantitative risk assessments, with mere lip service being paid to qualitative considerations such as ethics, the esthetics of the country-side, socio-agricultural impacts of gmo's, etc. Similarly, decisions about the introduction of new reproductive technologies, such as pgd, are usually framed in terms of ethics.

Black, in the company of many eminent scholars, is of the opinion that predominance of any given paradigm that unduly discriminates against relevant societal actors hinders the articulation of regulatory goals that enjoy broad support, and ultimately undermines effective regulation of the biotechnologies more generally. Presuming that this is true, then there surely is something to be said for the proposition that biotechnology regulation should stimulate dissemination of important insights that representatives of different paradigms may offer on one and the same problem in circumstances where uncertainty prevails.

Precaution serves this role and as such accords with our notion of common sense (although it is prudent to presume that common sense may not be very common). The precautionary principle requires deliberation at the interface between science and policy in circumstances where science is unable to speak with a single and unequivocal voice. Schomberg therefore believes that the precautionary principle is first and foremost a deliberative principle [R. von Schomberg, 'The Precautionary Principle and its Normative Challenges', in E. Fisher, J. Jones and R. von Schomberg (eds.), *Implementing the Precautionary*

Principle (Edward Elgar, 2006), ch. 2]. This implies that the precautionary principle is not so much a principle that urges regulators to stray on the side of caution (informing us *what* to choose), as a procedural principle that instructs to take account of all relevant knowledge in circumstances of scientific uncertainty and ignorance (directing us *how* to choose).

Because risk management, as opposed to risk assessment, is in any event a political process, deliberative precaution can be plausibly accommodated in that part of risk regulation, and indeed has been widely employed in that way in environmental risk regulation in Europe since the early 1990s. In this guise, the value of precaution resides simply in the fact that it stimulates deliberation as a response to situations of scientific uncertainty. Precaution in those circumstances in is attractive for the *same reasons* as we pursue deliberation in liberal democracies generally. Scientific uncertainty exists in respect of, for example, clinical risks of xeno-transplantation, germ-line therapy or reproductive cloning, and there is much to be said for deliberative precaution in such instances.

In European institutional practice and case law there exists a (slim) majority opinion that, even though precaution operates in the twilight of science and policy, the role of precaution ought to be confined to the risk management phase of risk regulation. The European Commission Communication of February 2000 presents the precautionary principle as a risk management tool, and in the process emphasizes the importance of keeping it out of risk assessment:

> The precautionary principle is particularly relevant to the *management* of risk. The principle, which is essentially used by decision-makers in the management of risks should not be confused with the element of caution that scientists apply in their assessment of scientific data.

The precautionary principle is likewise perceived by the European Court of Justice (ECJ) as constituting 'an integral part of the decision-making processes leading the adoption of any measure for the protection of human health' [Case C-236/01, *Monsanto* ECR 2003 I-08105, para. 133].

The difference between 'deliberative precaution', in favour of which all the usual justifications of political deliberation speak, and 'fact-finding precaution', for which there exists no such obvious justification, is important for another self-evident reason. In liberal democracies that foster autonomy and equality, the distinction implies that when we need to decide about technologies that interfere in the public sphere, as is the case with for example nuclear power or gmo's that are released into the environment, there is in any event a good case for deliberation and hence deliberative precaution which, as I suggested, can and probably should take place in the risk management phase.

When impacts of those technological interventions remain in the private sphere, however, and where the only interest can possibly be to establish truths that direct autonomous individuals in the pursuit of the good life (e.g. about clinical risks associated with pgd) there is no obvious role for deliberative precaution, unless the sum total of those individual choices will give rise to interferences in the public sphere that are manifestly undesirable.

D. ENABLING PRECAUTION

Typically, at least in the all important political arena, the precautionary principle is advocated mainly as a *enabling principle*. As an enabling principle, precaution differs from both deliberative precaution and fact-finding precaution, in that its effect is not to stimulate and structure deliberation in the risk management phase, nor to establish scientific facts in the risk assessment phase. Rather, 'enabling precaution' directs regulators in their decisions if due to scientific uncertainty no risk assessment is possible, or if notwithstanding a risk assessment a state of uncertainty remains. When under such circumstances uncertainty about the impact of a technology persists, enabling precaution posits that regulators should temporarily prohibit or constrain that technology until there is new evidence suggesting no risk or acceptable risk.

The underlying sentiment that appears to inform enabling precaution is that the road to hell is paved with dangerous precedent for change. It is also often implicit that precaution should apply to proposed change, but not to the *status quo*. However, as I observed elsewhere [in an inaugural lecture] the presumption that the value of maintaining the *status quo* is worthy of priority over conscious change is without empirical foundation (we have as little notion of how dangerous a future without change will be, as we understand risks of introducing new technologies), and against the background of the unstoppable evolution of life even illogical.

We would also do well to remember that the impact of overly liberal use of *environmental* precaution comes in the shape of lost commercial product development that could have answered real societal needs. This is a problem serious enough to justify some strong reservations about precaution. Importantly however, in other cases benefits often *do* accrue to an environment that structurally receives a rough deal from both society and the law. Occasional misuse of precaution thereby becomes somewhat easier to swallow, although thereby not acceptable. Also, within the sphere of environmental regulation, the impact of precaution on regulatory tilt is crystal clear: where precaution kicks in, activities with environmental impacts will be prohibited, or in some way made subject to restraint. Finally and probably most importantly, precautionary regulation is *always* temporary, i.e. for as long as scientific uncertainty prevails, and implies an obligation actively to engage in research to end that uncertainty.

Contrast this with use of precaution in the sphere of reproductive cloning. Here the effect of precaution is to justify a permanent erosion of rights of present right-holders, whilst benefits exist only in the realm of our imagination. After all, as I will explore in more detail below, it is uncertainty about the rights of, for instance, *future* clones that triggers precautionary bans on reproductive cloning, so that those future right holders (clones) will remain imaginary and impacts on their rights forever uncertain. Precautionary regulatory powers thereby become self perpetuating. Put differently, unlike scientific uncertainty, uncertainty about for instance the impact of reproductive cloning on individual autonomy will be eternal, presuming at least that bans on reproductive cloning prove effective. What we should acknowledge too is that, as subsequent examples will show, for the sake of 'potential rights' and 'potential rights holder', this kind of reproductive precaution has an all too real potential to result in unnecessary *actual* death and *actual* appalling illness of present and real right holders (children and adults).

In short, the case for enabling precaution in the sphere of reproductive technologies is weak on many counts. *If* we wish to invoke enabling precaution (e.g. in respect of reproductive cloning), it ought to be accompanied by some guarantees so as to ensure that precautionary restrictions do not become *de facto* self-perpetuating. For gmo's, such guarantees have taken the form of a step-by-step approach in respect of field trials. This requires small-scale experience to be gained with risks concerning, for example, cross-pollination, before a gradual increase in the acreage of gm crops is sanctioned. I see no reason why such a step-by-step approach could not also allow small scale reproductive cloning.

III. 'Enabling precaution' in reproductive technologies

In the previous sections, after having identified the precautionary principle as a principle enabling public regulatory intervention, I argued that precaution fulfils different roles that should be clearly distinguished.

'Fact-finding precaution' would be justified only if that mode of deliberative fact finding could be shown to be more reliable than competing methods, in particular the kind of specialist independent scientific expertise that currently forms the basis of risk assessments. Couples could then use that more accurate information to arrive at the best possible informed autonomous decision about whether or not to avail themselves of a reproductive technology. In reality, however, there is no evidence that fact finding precaution yields more accurate information than independent scientific expertise, which is of course why international and domestic courts insist that the role of precaution should be confined to deliberation in the political risk management phase of risk analyses.

'Deliberative precaution' may serve useful purposes in all those cases in which deliberation traditionally features, or should feature which, in liberal democracies like our own, may include risk management. However, in as far as we do not normally deliberate about the reproductive rights of couples, there is also no compelling case for introducing deliberative precaution in respect of new reproductive technologies.

'Enabling precaution', finally, often is based on the flawed assumption that it should only apply to change, and not equally to the *status quo*, and in any event requires rigorous judicial control to address the real prospect of unbridled state power.

In sum, there are few arguments that direct us to embrace any of the manifestations of precaution that could empower public authorities to hinder individuals in the pursuit of their uniquely individual visions of the good life. At best, a difficult argument may be construed that some technologies impact on the common heritage of mankind in manners that are reminiscent to those we are now witnessing in the shape of environmental decline. Indeed, UNESCO's International Bioethics Committee has taken the first vital step that is necessary for the construction of such an argument by arguing that 'the human genome must be preserved as the common heritage of mankind'. How the IBC thinks the human genome can be preserved without artificially intervening in the continuous process of natural evolution must by necessity forever remain a mystery. This being as it may, such an argument, if indeed it could be construed, would at best justify recourse to deliberative precaution in a very limited number of cases, e.g. to decide about reproductive macro cloning. Enabling precaution would have to be made subject to some regulatory device, such a step-by-step approach, that is aimed to ending states of scientific uncertainty in the future.

To relate this critique back to Fisher's analysis, we might say that Somsen feels more comfortable with the precautionary principle where the circumstances for its legitimate employment are fairly carefully defined and susceptible to meaningful review; if not quite an RI view, it pushes in that direction. If we relax these requirements, we are at the mercy of regulators who might deploy the principle illicitly for the purposes of trade protectionism as much as for the defence of dignitarian values.

4 Precaution as a coherent regulatory response

Where the precautionary principle is invoked to open up a regulatory debate that otherwise is blocked by an absence of scientific consensus, this seems to be a mature response to a state of expert difference of opinion – difference that, for the most part, might well be genuine but which, in part, might involve special pleading and bad faith. Advocates of precaution will rightly argue that we should not make it so easy for those whose interests favour inaction. However, where the precautionary principle is pleaded as the reason for preventive regulatory action, scientific uncertainty notwithstanding, the stakes are higher. Here, the principle asserts that, where there are concerns that emerging technologies might cause serious and irreversible damage, then it is prudent to take preventive (or damage limiting) action even though those concerns are not supported by clear scientific evidence – in the sense that there is no scientific agreement other than that the probability of the damage eventuating is somewhere on the scale, inclusively, between 0.1 and 0.9. Even if this accords with the folk wisdom that it is better to be safe than sorry, how can this be a coherent response to scientific uncertainty?

If we were to express this principle for the guidance of regulators, we might start by saying that, *other things being equal*, prudence suggests that the more serious or irreversible the damage to which our concerns relate, the less demanding we should be in setting the threshold for (a) the likelihood of harm and (b) the confidence with which we make the judgement of likelihood. Indeed, the logic of this is that, where there are concerns that emerging technologies might occasion serious and irreversible harm, and where precautionary measures are costless (relative to whatever interests are material), then such measures should be taken regardless of uncertainty concerning the likelihood of harm.[23] In other words, if taking steps to be safe rather than sorry is costless, this is always the prudent course no matter how uncertain the threat. As many critics of the precautionary principle have pointed out, however, the problem is that precaution is rarely costless.[24] The more difficult question, therefore, is whether we can give the precautionary principle a coherent prudential interpretation where the 'other things being equal' proviso does not apply.

Where regulators are acting as proxies for the purely private prudential calculations of their stakeholders, there seems no reason to privilege the preferences of the more risk averse; and this is not affected, as such, by the extent of the knowledge or scientific consensus backing the information on which the risk and benefit assessments are made. However, if regulators have reason to believe that there might be more at risk than the health and safety of those individuals who opt to make use of the technology, then we might find a place for the precautionary principle. What else might be at risk?

First, let us suppose that regulators have reason to believe that an emerging technology might be damaging to the conditions that are essential for the basic well-being of their stakeholders, whoever those stakeholders are and whatever their projects. For example, let us suppose that the concern relates to the sustainability of the natural environment or to the conditions for public health. Even if there is a lack of full scientific uncertainty about the link between the technology and this mooted damage, or about the likelihood of its occurrence, regulators might think that the precautionary principle points them in the prudent direction. What this means is that, where there are contested but not crazy concerns about a threat to the essential conditions for human existence, these concerns outrank the prudential calculations of individuals who judge that the benefit outweighs the risk to them (unless, of course, the benefit is also directly related to the essential conditions).[25]

Before we move on to the second kind of feared harm (harm to morally protected interests), we can pause to think about the relationship between the regulatory environment, infrastructures, and precautionary reasoning.

As we have explained in Chapter 2, our idea of the regulatory environment is one of signals and steering mechanisms that are intended to direct the actions, transactions, and interactions of regulatees. However, this already presupposes

---

[23] Compare Deryck Beyleveld and Roger Brownsword, 'Complex Technology, Complex Calculations: Uses and Abuses of Precautionary Reasoning in Law', in Marcus Duwell and Paul Sollie (eds.), *Evaluating New Technologies: Methodological Problems for the Ethical Assessment of Technological Developments* (Dordrecht: Springer, 2009), 175.

[24] Notably, see Cass R. Sunstein, *Laws of Fear* (Cambridge: Cambridge University Press, 2005); but note, too, the constructive approach in *Worst-Case Scenarios* (Cambridge, MA: Harvard University Press, 2007), esp. ch. 3.

[25] Compare Wolfgang van den Daele, Alfred Pühler and Herbert Sukopp, *Biotech Herbicide-Resistant Crops: A Participatory Technology Assessment* (Berlin: Federal Republic of Germany Ministry for Research and Technology, 1997), reported in Stuart J. Smyth, A. Bryan Endres, Thomas P. Redick and Drew L. Kershen, *Innovation and Liability in Biotechnology* (Cheltenham: Edward Elgar, 2010), at 82–3.

a space in which such activities are viable; it presupposes an infrastructure. The general idea of an infrastructure as the underlying foundation for a system is reasonably settled; and the conventional wisdom is that infrastructures in this sense are found in transportation and communication systems, as well as being constituted by basic public services such as sewers, water and energy.

Now, we can draw a distinction between those infrastructural features that are generic and, thus, essential for any human activity and those that are specific to particular activities. While a particular infrastructure is necessary for, say, a railway transport system, it is not generic. It is not even generic in the context of transport systems because road traffic, for example, can function perfectly well in the absence of a railway infrastructure; and it is certainly not generic in the broader sense of being essential for any kind of activity to be viable. What, then, might be candidates for the generic infrastructure in this broader and most fundamental sense?

One thing that humans must have before they are capable of acting, transacting or interacting in the purposive (goal-directed) way that we associate with agency is a minimal level of health and well-being. For humans whose basic health and well-being is under threat, there is little prospect of actualising their agency – it is akin to the train system being paralysed by threats to the tracks. Immediately, this gives rise to two difficult questions. First, what are the elements that are relevant to an agent's basic health and well-being? And, second, where do we draw the line between the generic infrastructure, specific infrastructures and activities on these infrastructures?

With regard to the first question, let us suppose that we have a rough sense of what it means to say that a human enjoys basic health and well-being. Rather than asking what factors are conducive to such a condition, we can readily identify the kind of factors that are antithetical to such a condition. For example, we can point to problems with food security and clean water, to environmental pollution, and to the prevalence of disease. Sadly, chronic conditions of this kind can be found in many parts of the world and, following a natural disaster, we will often see some of these conditions in an acute form. In these cases, we can say that the infrastructure is deficient or, in the case of an emergency, that it has collapsed.

This leads to the second question. How do we draw the line between the generic infrastructure, specific infrastructures, and activities on these infrastructures? In the light of what we have already said, it is not too difficult to distinguish between generic and specific infrastructures. To return to railway systems, their specific infrastructures are important and valued; they enhance agency but they are not essential to it. Human agency does not presuppose railway tracks, roads, or any other kind of transport infrastructure. These are not part of the *generic* infrastructure. We might say much the same about the infrastructural elements of a modern information technology system. Cybercrime is particularly serious when it strikes at these infrastructural elements; and, for those communities that increasingly transact and interact online, this (as we have already observed in an earlier chapter) is an extremely serious matter. Nevertheless, this is not part of the *generic* infrastructure. Having said that, it is much less clear how we should distinguish between infrastructures and activities that take place on those infrastructures. An agent's basic health and well-being can be damaged by the act of another human just as much as by deficient living conditions. What makes a feature generically infrastructural is that it strikes at the general possibility of agency, irrespective of the agent and of an agent's particular purposes, rather than the particular occurrent prospects of the agent. Or, to put this another way, there first has to be infrastructure and then there can be activity: while there can be infrastructure without activity, there can be no activity without infrastructure.

If we think about the regulatory environment in this kind of way, we can distinguish between those parts of the environment that are designed to secure the infrastructural conditions and those parts that are intended to direct the conduct of regulatees as they act, transact and interact on the infrastructure. Arguably, a number of major regulatory implications follow from this, one of which is precisely that regulators should have a special precautionary competence (jurisdiction) to take steps to protect the generic infrastructural conditions.

Now, to return to matters of moral harm, let us suppose that there is a concern that acceptance and use of the technology will impact negatively on the morally protected interests of some individuals. Here, the prudential preferences of some (possibly the majority) are in tension with an uncertain and contested threat to moral interests. If a community's morality is based on (preference) utilitarian standards, it is unlikely to experience this problem – because the summing of preferences will coincide with the maximising of utility; but, if the relevant moral standards are those of respect for human rights and human dignity, the problem might arise. If so, the thrust of the precautionary principle might once again be that regulators should privilege whatever moral interests are engaged (even though the matter is contested) rather than the prudential preferences of the public.

Gathering this up, we can perhaps identify three versions of the precautionary principle, where it is appropriate for regulators to take preventive or protective measures, expert uncertainty notwithstanding.[26] The three versions are as follows:

1 Common-sense precaution: where V is valued, and where there is a concern that T might cause damage to V, and where not-T involves no loss of value, then precaution dictates not-T, even though there might be some uncertainty about whether T actually will cause damage to V.

2 Pure prudential precaution: where V is valued as an essential infra-structural condition for T (and T-related activities), and where there is a concern that T

---

[26] See further, Roger Brownsword, 'Responsible Regulation: Prudence, Precaution and Stewardship', *Northern Ireland Legal Quarterly*, 62 (2011), 573–7.

might cause damage to V, then precaution dictates not-T so long as the probability of the damage eventuating is somewhere on the scale between 0.1 and 0.9 but irrespective of uncertainty as to the degree of probability. In other words, pure prudential precautionary reasoning arises in a context in which, exceptionally, it becomes irrelevant to try to calculate the precise probability of T causing damage to V.[27]

3 Moral precaution: where V is morally valued, and where there is a concern that T might cause damage to V, then precaution dictates not-T even though the relationship between T and V is contested (uncertain) and provided that the only counter-interests are of a non-moral prudential kind.[28]

In all these cases, it is characteristic of precautionary reasoning that the debates about the likelihood of the harm eventuating are superseded; and, to this extent, this is a form of reasoning that, perhaps exceptionally, departs from standard risk–benefit calculation. Finally, it should be noted that one form of 'precautionary' reasoning that does not qualify as appropriate is that in which regulators simply privilege the prudential preferences of the more risk-averse members of their community. There might be good reasons for adopting a risk-averse approach but it cannot be simply because this is the preference of some regulatees.

5 Conclusion

In the last two chapters, we have discussed the challenge of regulatory prudence. Stated simply, the challenge is for regulators to put in place an environment within which risk is held at an acceptable level – that challenge, in short, is one of acceptable risk regulation. However, as we have seen, the challenge is neither simple nor short.

Even if the prudential challenge is limited to reflecting public preferences and then managing risk accordingly, regulators might lack adequate information as to the risk as well as reliable indicators of public attitudes. Sadly, the precautionary principle, although designed as a response to scientific uncertainty, is no quick fix; for, like the scientific evidence, it, too, is open to interpretation and opportunistic use.

---

[27] Compare Fritz Allhoff, Patrick Lin and Daniel Moore, *What is Nanotechnology and Why Does It Matter?* (Chichester: John Wiley & Sons, 2010), 89ff., where a 'catastrophic' version of the precautionary principle (i.e., if there is a possibility of some activity causing a catastrophic event, it should be banned) is critically evaluated. Allhoff *et al.* conclude that the precautionary principle is neither the same as traditional cost–benefit analysis, nor something quite different; rather, they argue that 'precaution *supplements* cost–benefit analysis *given uncertainty*' (*ibid.*, at 94ff.). On this account, precaution is simply 'a risk-averse strategy for dealing with uncertainty' (*ibid.*, at 95).

[28] See, further, Roger Brownsword, 'Nanoethics: Old Wine, New Bottles?', *Journal of Consumer Policy*, 32 (2009), 355, 366–7 (on precautionary and, so to speak, 'procautionary' reasoning in a community of rights).

Nevertheless, there is a core of good sense in the precautionary idea that our interests are not always best served by waiting until the evidence of serious and irreversible damage is overwhelming. Moreover, this idea makes sense whether we are relating risk to our personal interests, to our moral interests, or to the interests that the community has collectively in protecting its infrastructural conditions. Indeed, there is some artificiality in trying to keep a clear distance between our purely prudential judgements (thinking only about our own interests) and our moral judgements (where we also take into account the legitimate interests of others); in the case of the environment or public health, for example, we have a prudential interest in such matters but moral interests are also implicated. It is high time, then, to put prudence to one side and focus instead on those questions of morality, of respect for human rights and human dignity, that lie at the heart of the challenge of regulatory legitimacy.

Part III
Regulatory legitimacy

7

The legitimacy of the regulatory environment: basic ideas

1 Introduction

In 1990, the European Union established a regulatory regime in response to applications for the licensing and commercial marketing of genetically modified organisms (GMOs). Although Member States retained considerable regulatory powers over the licensing of GMOs, the responsibility for risk assessment and authorisation for products being released throughout the European Union area were shared between the Member States and Community institutions. Under the regime established by Directive 90/220/EC, eighteen genetically modified crops were licensed for sale within the European Union and thousands of field trials were approved.[1]

However, by the late 1990s, faced with strong public protest against GMOs, Member States were refusing to license new products, and even where products had been authorised by the Council of Ministers, individual Member States were invoking the safeguard clause in the Directive to prevent licensing of these products in their own countries. Such was the collapse in confidence of the European regulatory regime for GMOs that by 1999 all new approvals of GMOs for commercial application were stopped. The regulatory framework had failed, but why?

According to an analysis of the regime by Grace Skogstad:

> Both the input and output legitimacy of the 1990 regulatory framework were under attack by the time the moratorium was invoked in 1999. On input legitimacy grounds, the procedures by which GMOs and their products were being regulated were chastised as undemocratic. The deliberations of the Commission and national officials over whether to authorize the marketing of GMO and GMO-derived products were confidential, officials gave 'only perfunctory explanations' for their decisions, and interest groups were denied the possibility of judicial review of officials' *in camera* decisions. The system was accused of being opaque and poor in terms of accountability. On output-legitimation grounds, proponents and opponents of GMOs alike faulted Directive 90/220/EC for failing to deliver desirable policy outcomes. On the one hand, the biotechnology industry

---

[1] Council Directive of 23 April 1990 on the deliberate release into the environment of genetically modified organisms (90/220/EC), OJ L 117/15.

and various services within the Commission (Research, Trade, Internal Market) blamed the lack of harmony across member states in their risk assessment procedures, and the two level (national and EU) approval process for impeding the licensing of GMOs and causing the EU biotechnology sector to become uncompetitive ... In their view, jobs, markets and economic growth were being lost to the US, even as the GMO regulatory framework created trade tensions with the US. They argued for more efficient and scientifically based regulatory procedures that would not stigmatize and discriminate against genetic engineering ... On the other hand, consumers and environmentalists faulted the regulatory regime as incomplete and insufficiently rigorous in protecting the environment and citizens from the risk posed by GMOs and their products. Existing regulatory approval procedures and labelling requirements exempted certain GMO products and there were no provisions to trace GMO products through the food chain should they need to be recalled for reasons of environmental or human and animal health protection.[2]

Although there is now a functioning GMO regime operating at the EU level, the first attempt at establishing a European regulatory framework failed because of a widely perceived lack of legitimacy.

As the extract from Skogstad suggests, we can conceive of legitimacy in different ways. In her analysis of the crisis in this particular regulatory regime, she focuses on legitimacy as determined by procedure and legitimacy as determined by results – in her terminology, input and output. Skogstad suggests a very practical approach to whether a regime produces the right results: whether it allows regulatees to be competitive internationally or whether it ensures the safety and well-being of regulatees and consumers. She suggests, therefore, that the legitimacy of this regulatory regime was judged by its efficiency and the process by which it was created. Not considered in the account presented above are any ethical concerns surrounding the decision to press ahead with GMOs; concerns, as we saw in Chapter 1, that Mary Warnock defined as raising questions about justice, rights or human decency. While one can present human and animal welfare or concerns about the environment as practical issues, such framing is nonetheless underpinned by certain normative understandings about, for example, why we should care about the safety of each individual human life, why we should seek to minimise animal suffering or why the environment is deserving of protection. Our ethical or normative outlook determines the way in which we frame the concerns raised by technology and how we determine what those concerns are. It is the ethical questions about regulatory regimes and the normative frameworks that guide them that are the focus of the following four chapters.

The rapid pace and fundamental nature of technological developments are pushing the boundaries of our common ethical and moral frameworks further and faster than any other area of human activity. The far-reaching developments

---

[2] Grace Skogstad, 'Legitimacy and/ or Policy Effectiveness?: Network Governance and GMO Regulation in the European Union', *Journal of European Public Policy*, 10 (2001), 321, 328–9.

within biotechnology, for example, are forcing us to reassess our answers to profound questions about what it is to be human; about our relationship to the world around us and to each other; about the nature of obligation between parent and child; and about the purpose of human existence itself. As the philosopher Michael Sandel has noted in the context of his essay on the moral quandaries of genetic engineering, the ethical implications of these new technologies require us 'to confront questions largely lost from view in the modern world – questions about the moral status of nature, and about the proper stance of human beings toward the given world'.[3]

The fundamental importance of the questions at stake in technological regulation have been sketched by another American philosopher, Ronald Dworkin, also writing of the possibility of genetic engineering:

> even the bare possibility of achieving dramatic control over our children's genetic structure undermines our most basic assumptions about the boundary between what we are responsible for choosing and what, for better or worse, lies beyond our control because it is fixed by chance or nature or the Gods ... Once we understand that it is up to us, at least collectively, whether we allow and encourage our scientists to pursue such technological possibilities and whether we exploit whatever technology they develop, then it is too late to wish the old boundary back in place, because a decision to turn away from what science may provide is itself a choice we might have made differently. For better or worse, when even the possibility of genetic engineering has been impressed upon us, a basic assumption of much of our conventional morality and attitude has been challenged, and we stand in a state of what I called a state of moral free-fall.[4]

Such moral questions matter in the context of regulation because they determine whether or not we perceive a particular regulatory act or a regulatory regime as legitimate. For some, depending upon how they determine the validity of law, moral legitimacy goes to the heart of whether or not we have an obligation to obey rules that we hold to be illegitimate. From the perspective of a certain kind of legal positivism, where a piece of legislation is legitimate – where it has been created in accordance with the rules of the system – we should obey it, even where we fundamentally disagree with what it requires of us. According to this way of thinking, we may not like speed restrictions on highways limiting us to 120 km/h, and we may even think that driving 130 km/h will not have a negative impact on the aims that speed restrictions are in place to achieve, but we accept that we have an obligation to obey these limits anyway and we expect to be punished when we do not.[5] For non-positivists, legitimacy is not simply

---

[3] Michael J. Sandel, *The Case Against Perfection* (Cambridge, MA: Harvard University Press, 2007), 9.

[4] Ronald Dworkin, 'Playing God: Genes, Clones and Luck', in *Sovereign Virtue* (Cambridge, MA: Harvard University Press, 2000), 447–8.

[5] See H. L. A. Hart, *The Concept of Law* (1961) (2nd edn, Oxford: Clarendon Press, 1994, ed. P. Bulloch and J. Raz). Also, H. L. A. Hart, 'Positivism and the Separation of Law and Morals', *Harvard Law Review*, 71 (1957–8), 593–629.

concerned with how rules are made but also with what they do. There are limits, for example, to the substance of rules that we can enact.[6] Those who argue that the concept of human dignity prevents any rules permitting the use of human embryos in research do so on the basis of an appeal to something beyond legal norms, such as the fundamental dignity we all allegedly possess, our relationship to a God or to natural rights – the notion, classically understood, that universal moral rules can be deduced on the basis of human nature that are binding for all time. Even where one supports a classic legal positivist perspective perceptions of the moral legitimacy of regulation are not irrelevant. As we saw with the GMO controversy within Europe, the widespread belief that regulation is illegitimate will undermine the functioning of a regulatory regime and, where strongly held views are consistently ignored, such deep disagreement is likely to have far-reaching political and social consequences. Perceptions of the moral legitimacy of regulatory instruments and regimes go therefore not only to the efficiency of the instruments themselves but to matters of social and political cohesion, and ultimately to the (self-)identity of the community itself.

As we suggested in the introductory chapters, the legitimacy challenge for regulatory efforts presented by contemporary technological developments is three-pronged. The first relates to the particular challenge that technology regulation poses for our understanding of procedural legitimacy. Although procedures dominate contemporary understandings of social justice, the demands of procedural legitimacy are especially acute in the governance of science and technology. This is reflected, for example, in the move towards direct public participation at all levels of technology policy-making.[7] This is the subject of Chapter 10. Below, we consider the general implications of questions of legitimacy of the shift from government to governance and of the changing locations and identities of regulatory actors.

The second prong concerns the way in which existing moral concepts, understandings and agreements are being stretched in order to continue to provide a frame for these new areas of human knowledge, particularly where that knowledge touches upon the essence of life itself. One example of this is the way in which we apply concepts such as autonomy or consent when dealing with our ability to manipulate genetic material in plants, animals and in ourselves. What happens, for example, as has been highlighted in a popular novel by Jodi Picoult, and in the more recent film of the book,[8] to notions of human autonomy when a so-called 'saviour sibling' is created in order to provide bodily

---

[6] For the classic response to Hart's position from a natural law perspective, see Lon L. Fuller, 'Positivism and Fidelity to Law – A Reply to Professor Hart', *Harvard Law Review*, 71 (1957–8), 630–72; more fully, Lon L. Fuller, *The Morality of Law* (New Haven: Yale University Press, 1969).

[7] See, for example, House of Lords Select Committee on Science and Technology, *Science and Society* (2000); available online at: www.publications.parliament.uk/pa/ld/ldsctech.htm (last accessed 24 January 2012).

[8] Jodi Picoult, *My Sister's Keeper* (London: Hodder & Stoughton, 2004). The film, *My Sister's Keeper*, was released in 2009, made by Curmudgeon Films and was directed by Nick Cassavetes.

materials that may save a sick sibling's life? Does it still make sense to talk of consent as an expression of human autonomy in a situation in which a child has been created – chosen from all the other alternative embryos – specifically for the purpose of 'servicing' another? The question of legitimacy will be approached from the angle of limits to legitimacy. Chapter 8 will introduce the idea of 'boundary-marking concepts' as a means of making sense of the way in which participants in discussions about technology express their deep-seated moral beliefs and thus the boundary of ethical legitimacy for them. By focusing on boundary-marking concepts, we will attempt to structure the ways in which an ethical concept or right such as nature or the right to property is wielded by stakeholders across the various areas of technological development.[9] Chapter 9 is dedicated to consideration of how human rights function as boundary markers and how they structure our understanding of the challenges that new technologies pose.

The third prong of the challenge to ethical frameworks posed by technology concerns the use of technology *as* regulation, whereby technology is used as a 'fix' to control and determine human behaviour. This ability to limit and determine human behaviour raises profound ethical concerns in relation to human autonomy, as well as perhaps to the continuation of shared ethical frameworks themselves. The use of technology as a means of regulation is discussed in detail in the final chapter of the book and thus is not a central subject of this section.

We begin, however, in this chapter by considering how legitimacy is understood and used as a political concept, framing the application of legitimacy to technology regulation in terms of limits to legitimacy.

2 Political legitimacy

Legitimacy is one of the oldest concepts in political theory. It concerns questions of justification of the exercise of power by those over whom that power is exercised. Political legitimacy can be classified into two dimensions. The first concerns the source of authority, or how a government has come to be in power. For example, we no longer accept as legitimate a government that has come to power by deposing a democratically elected government in a military coup. Similarly, we do not accept a government as legitimate where it is imposed by a foreign occupying power. Rather, we generally hold that the source of authority for a government is the will of the people, its self-determination, however that might be expressed or measured. Where the source of power is illegitimate, the exercise of power or what the (illegitimate) government then does once in power is also deemed illegitimate, even were it to be generally perceived as acting for the social good.

---

[9] The suggestion that concepts are 'boundary-marking' is thus a means of understanding and structuring how we use certain concepts and not a deeper philosophical claim about concepts in general or about the concepts highlighted here.

(a) Source legitimacy

While in most cases we can assume that the source of authority to regulate, particularly where this occurs at the national level, is uncontroversial, this aspect of legitimacy is not irrelevant to questions about the legitimacy of technology regulation. For example, a multicultural society may include groups that seek to impose a different understanding of the source of political power to that of the will of the people; such a group may wish to replace this source with the will of God, for example. Where this is the case, legislation issued by a government chosen in free and fair elections may be seen as illegitimate, particularly where it seeks to regulate issues that go to the heart of the nature and purpose of our existence or permits experiments that are seen as appropriating a creating power that belongs to God alone. Even where groups within society agree on the basic organisation of governance, inequality in participation between groups can also call the legitimacy of rule-making into question – a point we pick up again briefly in Chapter 10.

Moreover, technology is not simply a matter for regulators at the national level. The extent to which national states are embedded in systems and networks of governance beyond the state, coupled with the ability of technological and scientific knowledge to flow unimpeded across national borders, entails that much of the regulation of technological developments no longer takes place at the national level. Instead, regulation is likely to occur at the regional level, such as the European Union – as with the GMO regime considered above – or at the international level, for example, within the framework of the World Trade Organization (WTO). This raises questions of legitimacy in relation to the source of authority to regulate, questions heightened and made more controversial by the challenge such developments pose to our ethical and moral frameworks.

If we look, for example, at the data protection regime within Europe, the 1995 European Union Data Protection Directive lays down norms and standards for all Member States of the European Union on questions of the collection, storage and movement of personal data.[10] At the heart of the protection of personal data are questions concerning privacy and why privacy is something that we have reason to value. While it may make practical sense to regulate the issue of data protection at the European level, given the extraordinary ease with which it is possible to transfer data across national boundaries, the decision to regulate beyond the national level inevitably provokes questions concerning the normative or moral standards encapsulated in the legislation. Does the Directive, for example, reflect a shared European understanding of what privacy consists in and of where the boundaries of privacy lay? Can we assume that

---

[10] Council and European Parliament Directive 95/46/EC on the Protection of Individuals with Regard to the Processing of Personal Data and the Free Movement of Such Data [1995] OJ L281/31.

such a common understanding exists between the many Member States of the European Union?

The difficulty of agreeing privacy standards within the European space has been highlighted by the *Caroline of Monaco* case.[11] Considering the question of the right to privacy through the lens of constitutional patriotism, Francesca Bignami has compared *Von Hannover* v. *Germany* as it made its way through the German courts, up to the European Court of Human Rights.[12] She summarises the twists and turns as follows:

> The first series of photographs captured the Princess in a variety of situations. She was shown with Vincent Lindon, the French actor and her boyfriend at the time, in a secluded restaurant courtyard. She appeared together with her children in various public places, such as the market. And she was shown alone, horseback riding and shopping. Both the German court of first instance and the German court of appeals took the conventional view of privacy and held against the Princess. They found that as an 'absolute figure of contemporary history' the Princess could not protest the publication of her photographs. Because of their importance to contemporary debate, such figures could only claim a right to privacy when in the home, and not in public spaces. The highest court – the Federal Court of Justice – was more sympathetic to the Princess. It found that a concept of privacy limited to the home, even in the case of public figures like the Princess, was too narrow. In the Court's view, the restaurant courtyard in which the Princess was photographed eating with Vincent Lindon was precisely such a space of 'seclusion'. The Court, therefore, enjoined the publication of the restaurant photographs but permitted publication of the remaining photographs since they involved entirely public places.
>
> That, however, was not the end of the matter. The Princess of Monaco filed a constitutional complaint with the Federal Constitutional Court. In one respect, the Constitutional Court expanded her right to privacy. It found that children's privacy should receive special constitutional protection ... Unless a public figure like the Princess of Monaco intentionally took centre stage at a public event with her children, the interest of the press and the public in knowing about the children must give way to the children's privacy. The Constitutional Court therefore enjoined the publication of all those photographs in which the Princess's children appeared. Remaining in the public eye were only those photos in which she appeared horseback riding and shopping.
>
> ...
>
> The Princess had better luck before the European Court of Human Rights. The Court found that the publication of all the photographs at issue in the three German proceedings violated the Princess's right to private life.

---

[11] *Von Hannover* v. *Germany*, Judgment of the European Court of Human Rights of 24 June 2004, application no. 59320/00.

[12] Francesca Bignami, 'Constitutional Patriotism and the Right to Privacy: A Comparison of the European Court of Justice and the European Court of Human Rights', in T. Murphy, *New Technologies and Human Rights* (Oxford: Oxford University Press, 2009), 152–3.

Given the very real difficulty in determining a European standard of privacy in relation to press freedom,[13] is it then reasonable to expect that standards of privacy protection in relation to data protection can be so easily harmonised? If the answer to this question is no, it may diminish the legitimacy of the regulatory effort.

(b) Substantive legitimacy

The second dimension of political legitimacy concerns how a government exercises its power. This form of legitimacy is sometimes known alternatively as substantive or outcome-based legitimacy. It is derived from what is done with power, not from the source of it. There are two ways of viewing outcome-based legitimacy: the intention of those in power and outcome *stricto sensu*. These approaches are not rigidly distinct and both are important in determining whether the actions of a governing entity are viewed as legitimate. However, one reason for attempting to make such a distinction is because governments or other regulatory authorities can never achieve perfection: despite the best efforts in the world, regulation will never be able to ensure that no one is harmed by a technology or ensure fully equal access to a beneficial new technology. But does the inability to ensure the full realisation of a regulator's aims entail that a regulator's actions or the regulator itself are illegitimate? Ronald Dworkin in his latest book has suggested that legitimacy must necessarily concern a government's intention rather than the results:

> Legitimacy is a different matter from justice. Governments have a sovereign responsibility to treat each person with equal concern and respect. They achieve justice to the extent they succeed ... Governments may be legitimate, however – their citizens may have, in principle, an obligation to obey their laws – even though they are not fully, or even largely, just. They can be legitimate if their laws and policies can nevertheless reasonably be interpreted as recognizing that the fate of each citizen is of equal importance and each has a responsibility to create his own life. A government can be legitimate, that is, if it strives for its citizens' full dignity so understood even if it follows a defective concept of what that requires.[14]

While justice is clearly not irrelevant for Dworkin, his version of liberalism makes a distinction between the concepts of legitimacy and justice in order to suggest that the simple fact of inequality in society, where some have greater access to the resources of society that enable us to make choices about the way in which to live our lives, does not render that system illegitimate. For Dworkin, then, declaring a government illegitimate and thus releasing its citizens from the obligation to obey the law requires such a serious, widespread

---

[13] We return to this topic in Chapter 9.
[14] Ronald Dworkin, *Justice for Hedgehogs* (Cambridge, MA: Harvard University Press, 2011), 321–2.

and systematic breach of the obligation to protect and promote the dignity of all that the intention to fulfil that obligation can no longer be accepted.[15] What Dworkin is highlighting is that legitimacy is a question of degree, rather than something that can be understood as an all-or-nothing concept. The fact that the perfectly just society – no matter how one defines the just society – does not exist cannot be used to declare a government illegitimate. Instead, some governments are more legitimate than others because they take the obligation to treat all with equal concern more seriously; of course, the likely outcome is a more just society.

Yet, the outcome still matters a great deal. One of the most infamous medical scandals in recent western history concerned the drug Thalidomide. In the 1970s, Thalidomide was prescribed to pregnant women to mitigate the symptoms of morning sickness. However, unknown to the drug manufacturer, the regulators and the health professionals prescribing it was that Thalidomide caused grotesque foetal deformations. Once the connection between the drug and the tragedy of so many dead and deformed babies was made, Thalidomide was banned. However, the harm done to the many human lives affected was irreversible. While the intention of the regulator in allowing the drug was benign and there is no suggestion that the regulator was cavalier about the risk to human well-being, the outcome in such a situation is also clearly relevant. Yet, most of us would not conclude that the legitimacy of the regulatory action that allowed Thalidomide on to the market was called into question simply because it had such tragic consequences. We would not suggest, for example, that what happened to these babies and their families constituted a violation of the right to life, albeit that we can talk of regulatory failure in this situation. Although a regulatory action may cause harm, the fact that it does so does not automatically render it illegitimate.

But what does the obligation to treat all with equal concern to the end of protecting the dignity of each citizen look like? There are almost as many answers to this question as there are people to answer it. However, most agree – at least in western societies – that for the exercise of power to be legitimate, it must respect certain basic rights of the individual and all, including those in power, must be equally subject to the law.[16] Where, for example, a system of government regularly disregarded the substantive rights of individuals, perhaps through systemic surveillance, such as that famously described in Orwell's *Nineteen Eighty-Four*,[17] we would perhaps conclude that the exercise of power

---

[15] 'particular policies may stain the state's legitimacy without destroying it altogether' (*ibid.*). See also *Sovereign Virtue*.

[16] For an excellent charting of the historical development of notions of the rule of law, see Brian Tamanaha, *On the Rule of Law* (Cambridge: Cambridge University Press, 2004).

[17] Of the telescreens established in all rooms in Oceania, Orwell wrote: 'Any sound that Winston made, above the level of a low whisper, would be picked up by it; moreover, so long as he remained within its field of vision which the metal plaque commanded, he could be seen as well as heard. There was of course no way of knowing whether you were being watched at any given moment. How often, or on what system, the Thought Police plugged in on any individual wire

is illegitimate. Similarly, where the exercise of power systematically discriminates between various groups in society, whether on the ground of gender or ethnicity or on an arbitrary physical characteristic, such as eye colour, we often consider the government to be illegitimate as a consequence. The case of South Africa under apartheid is a good example of a regime that was widely held to be illegitimate because of the blatant denial of equality before the law to one group within society on the basis of the colour of their skin.[18]

We determine what form such a minimum set of standards will take – what basic rights shall be respected and how solid a boundary they form, i.e. what concepts we use to mark the boundary of legitimacy and where we locate those boundaries – by reference to the normative framework to which we subscribe. While we may agree on the fundamental importance of basic rights and equality before the law, we are unlikely to agree on what it means to treat citizens with 'full dignity' in a given situation unless we share the same normative perspective, and, even then, we are likely to give slightly different emphasis to different markers and locate them slightly differently as well. There is thus unlikely to be a shared understanding in any society on how we should judge the legitimacy of regulatory purposes and standards.

This lack of shared understanding is exacerbated in relation to technology regulation. While regulation in the field of technology must meet a certain minimum threshold of safeguarding individual rights and demonstrating equal concern in order to be perceived as legitimate, as new developments, particularly in the area of biotechnology but also in the field of robotics[19] for example, challenge our most fundamental assumptions about human nature and the purpose of human existence, regulation of those developments is judged by more exacting ethical standards. As we move further away from a minimum threshold, disagreement about the standards and norms to apply becomes more intense.

Moreover, we are likely to apply different standards of legitimacy at the different regulatory levels (national, European or global). For example, what we deem 'fair' at the national level when weighing up costs against benefits or examining the extent to which regulation should take into account questions of equality of access or issues of distribution are likely to differ when the 'Other' whose needs

---

was guesswork … You had to live – did live, from habit that became instinct – in the assumption that every sound you made was overheard and, except in darkness, every movement scrutinised' (George Orwell, *Nineteen Eighty-Four* ((1949), London: Penguin Books, 1990 repr.), 4–5).

[18] See, for example, the series of Security Council resolutions condemning apartheid and implementing an arms embargo against South Africa: SC Resolution 421 (1977); SC Resolution 473 (1980); SC Resolution 558 (1984); and SC Resolution 591 (1986).

[19] See Sherry Turkle, *Alone Together. Why We Expect More from Technology and Less from Each Other* (New York: Basic Books, 2011), for the suggestion that the intensity of interaction with new social robots entails a process of mutual shaping: as we train them to be better companions, their programmed demands are changing us, allowing us (but especially children exposed to the robots) to bother less about working at relationships with human others, in all their complexity (*ibid.*, esp. 55–6).

we should take into account is our fellow citizen. At the global level, where common bonds are non-existent or weaker we may set the balance differently and, in so doing, locate the legitimacy standard differently. A good example of this is the balance we strike between the protection of western technological superiority by strict intellectual property law and notions of fairness related to open access to knowledge and the needs of developing nations. It seems likely that we would be less willing to accept such restrictions as legitimate where they impacted so negatively upon our fellow citizens. It is in recognition of the different standards of legitimacy that we apply, particularly at the global level, that there have been calls for technical knowledge to be considered as the 'common heritage of mankind' and thus made freely available to all.[20]

(c) Procedural legitimacy

Procedural legitimacy concerns the processes and procedures of the exercise of power in contrast to the standards and intentions contained in the content of regulation. This is what Skogstad in the opening extract referred to as 'input legitimacy'. Procedural or input legitimacy relates to whether decision-making concerning the design, enactment and enforcement of regulation is legitimate. In contemporary political thinking, procedural legitimacy manifests itself in concepts such as transparency, freedom of information and accountability, enabling citizens to participate in debates concerning the content of regulation by allowing access to both the process and the information necessary to make sense of it, and in holding government to account for the implementation and enforcement of that regulation. How we define procedural legitimacy – the processes by which power is exercised – depends very much upon the source of legitimacy: where the source of authority is the representation of the divine, a ruler cannot be held accountable in principle and thus rights of access to the information necessary to be able to make an informed judgement about the exercise of power is outside such a frame of political thought. Where, however, we determine the source of legitimacy to be the consent of the governed, then access to information, participation in decision-making and holding those in power to account all form crucial elements in legitimising the exercise of power. Just as we do not accept as legitimate a dictator, even when benign, where the outcome of the exercise of power is perceived as in the best interests of society, where we are kept in the dark about the exercising of power, we do not accept it as legitimate.

Despite the distinction normally drawn between substantive and procedural legitimacy, there is necessarily overlap between the two. For a government to be held accountable and for citizens to be able to participate in decision-making,

---

[20] See, for example, the call by Hailemichael T. Demissie for nanotechnology to be considered part of the common heritage of humankind and the fruits of research to be shared with all. Demissie, 'Taming Matter for the Welfare of Humanity: Regulating Nanotechnology', in Roger Brownsword and Karen Yeung (eds.), *Regulating Technologies* (Oxford: Hart, 2008), 352.

certain rights are indispensable. These rights include freedom of speech and freedom of association, among others. Moreover, where the process of the exercise of power is illegitimate, it is more likely that the outcome will be illegitimate, i.e. fail to show equal concern. Certain theories of political legitimacy (notably modern republican theories) take the right to question power further and make the procedure of the exercise of power the central element of their understanding of legitimacy. For a civic republican such as Phillip Pettit, power can only be legitimate where citizens have the ability to participate actively in the exercise of power; in this way of thinking, citizenship is an activity rather than a status, something that one does rather than is.[21]

However, active public or citizen participation in the regulation of technology is not straightforward. As we shall examine in Chapter 10, public participation in decision-making processes concerning risk assessment or in the regulation of any complex scientific issue is highly problematic. As the regulation of GMOs in Europe has shown, the public interprets 'risk' differently to the experts and gives far less weight to scientific evidence than to their instinctive feeling that, in this case, GMOs are simply 'unnatural' and therefore high risk. While one may share the European public's unease about GMOs, we would not perhaps conclude that policy-making with regards to, for example, nanotechnology should follow a similar zero-risk approach that many would like.

Ultimately, whether or not we choose to subscribe to the republican conception of citizenship as action, we view a government nowadays as legitimate because it is accepted as such by the people over whom it governs. We can sketch the standards and norms that communities at the beginning of the twenty-first century are likely to use as the basis by which they determine whether the authority that commands them is legitimate. Yet, the means by which we judge whether or not a regime can be said to be legitimate will depend upon the specific norms of a given community as well as the particular understanding of what is desirable or of how to achieve that common good. Legitimacy can take shape in many different ways and combinations of forms.[22] Citing human rights or the rule of law as the definition of legitimacy is not only problematic outside a liberal constitutional framework but also, as we shall consider further in Chapter 9, only takes us so far in coming to agreed standards of ethical legitimacy.

Our consideration of political legitimacy has thus far laid out a rather traditional account of how we determine whether or not those in power and what they do with it is legitimate. But the last decades of the twentieth century witnessed a radical change in the location of power and in the identity of those

---

[21] See, from his body of work, Phillip Pettit, *Republicanism: A Theory of Freedom and Government* (Oxford: Clarendon Press, 1997).

[22] Although some argue that legitimacy must take a specific form and have made the case for a 'right to democratic governance'. The article that started the debate is Thomas Franck, 'The Emerging Right to Democratic Governance', *American Journal of International Law*, 86 (1992), 46; more recently, Susan Marks, 'What Has Become of the Emerging Right to Democratic Governance?', *European Journal of International Law*, 22 (2011), 507–24.

The legitimacy of the regulatory environment

actors that set regulatory standards. These far-reaching changes to the way in which we are governed affect the way in which we understand legitimacy.

3 From government to governance

One of the most important shifts in the study of law and regulation in the last thirty years concerns the move away from an exclusive or predominating focus on the state as the source of regulation.[23] In an essay reflecting back on nearly forty years of the journal *Law and Policy*, Fiona Haines, Nancy Reichman and Colin Scott[24] note this trend as follows:

> Given our understanding of the importance of informal governance within public and private bureaucracies, and within societies more generally, what counts as 'public' in some sense is no longer, if it ever was, the exclusive monopoly of state bodies … Authority to make rules for social and economic behaviour is located not only within central state institutions, but also within supranational and transnational governmental bodies and within nongovernmental organizations at both the national and supranational level.

This shift has been characterised as a movement from government to governance,[25] where 'government' here refers to the traditional authority of the sovereign state under international law. In its place, we have entered a realm of 'governance' – a term used to capture the collective outcome of a vast array of actors and mechanisms that act to set, implement or enforce norms at or across various national or transnational sites of authority. The distinction between 'government' and 'governance' has been described by James Rosenau in the following way:

> Both governance and government consist of rule systems, of steering mechanisms through which authority is exercised in order to … move towards desired goals. While the rule systems of governments can be thought of as structures, those of governance are social functions or processes that can be performed or implemented in a variety of ways at different times and places (or even at the same time) by a wide variety of organizations.[26]

The change in our understanding of the exercise of authority has been described by Saskia Sassen as 'a new geography of power'.[27] However, this shift from

---

[23] It is important to note that alternative sources of law have always existed; what is recent is the widespread recognition of alternative sources of law within the legal discipline or as objects of legal study. See *inter alia* Sally Engle Merry, 'Legal Pluralism', *Law and Society Review*, 22(5) (1988), 869–96; Philip Jessup, *Transnational Law* (New Haven: Yale University Press, 1956); Gunther Teubner, 'Global Bukowina: Legal Pluralism in the World Society', in Teubner (ed.), *Global Law without a State* (Aldershot: Dartmouth Gower, 1997), 3–28.

[24] 'Problematizing Authority and Legitimacy in Law and Policy', *Law and Policy*, 30(1) (2008), 1.

[25] See, for example, the collection of essays in Karl-Heinz Ladeur (ed.), *Public Governance in the Age of Globalization* (Aldershot: Ashgate, 2004).

[26] James N. Rosenau, 'Governance in a New Global Order', in David Held and Anthony McGrew, *Governing Globalization: Power, Authority and Global Governance* (Cambridge: Polity, 2002), 70.

[27] Saskia Sassen, 'De-nationalized State Agendas and Privatized Norm-Making', in Ladeur, *Public Governance*, 51.

government to governance is not only one that we can witness at the regional or international level, where it is most obvious that a state cannot alone hope to regulate cross-border data movements, for example; but is one that affects the internal balance within a state as well. As Colin Scott has noted:

> We are said to be living in the age of the regulatory state. This refers to a style of governance away from the direct provision of public services, associated with the welfare state, and towards oversight of provision of public services by others.[28]

This diffusion of public or state authority raises a normative question about the source of legitimacy. From where do these non-state actors acquire their authority to regulate our behaviour?

As was suggested by Skogstad's account of European efforts to regulate GMOs, the question of where non-state actors gain their legitimacy to regulate our behaviour is generally answered in two ways. The first answer concerns output legitimacy. Regulation in the era of global governance has become so extraordinarily complex that no single actor, including states, can hope to manage effectively the processes of modern life. Part of the answer to the legitimacy question, therefore, is that it is more efficient and the outcomes more likely to be conducive to the common good if non-state actors take over certain regulatory tasks from government. In considering the legitimacy of regulation in the modern era, the outcome is salient to a degree that is unfamiliar in traditional questions of political legitimacy.

One of the most commented upon delegations of public authority to set standards or norms of regulation concerns the Codex Alimentarius. The Codex is a collection of texts that lay down standards, guidelines and codes of practice for food safety. It is overseen by the Codex Alimentarius Commission, a body established jointly by the UN Food and Agricultural Organization (FAO) and the World Health Organization (WHO) to protect consumers and promote fair trade practices. As the explanatory document drawn up by the FAO and WHO proclaims:

> The Codex Alimentarius, or the food code, has become the global reference point for consumers, food producers and processors, national food control agencies and the international food trade.[29]

However, the Codex has become more than simply a global reference point. As the same document goes on to detail, the Codex has become the standard by which the WTO determines whether parties to the Agreement on the Application of Sanitary and Photosanitary Measures (SPS) can restrict trade in order to protect the health of consumers. Article 2(2) of the SPS Agreement provides:

> Members shall ensure that any sanitary and photosanitary measure is applied only to the extent necessary to protect human, animal or plant life or health,

---

[28] Colin Scott, 'Accountability in the Regulatory State', *Journal of Law and Society*, 27(2) (2000), 38–60.

[29] FAO/WHO, *Understanding the Codex Alimentarius* (3rd edn Rome, 2006) (available online at: ftp://ftp.fao.org/codex/Publications/understanding/Understanding_en.pdf).

is based on scientific principles and is not maintained without sufficient scientific evidence.

It is thus the Codex Commission that determines the scientific standard that will be applied in interpreting whether or not a technological development is harmful to human, animal or plant life or to human health.

The Codex therefore plays a crucial role in regulating the use of biotechnology in agriculture. For example, it is the Codex Commission that determines whether the trade in GM crops or organisms or of meat from cattle raised on antibiotics can be restricted as unsafe for human consumption, and not national governments. The reason for the delegation of the authority to regulate biotechnology in the food industry to an unelected body based in Geneva is that the regulation of global trade is most efficiently achieved not at the national level but with states acting collectively to establish bodies that produce rules that then bind all parties to an agreement. What of the case, though, where consumers in a particular country do not wish to consume GM organisms?[30]

The second part of the answer to the legitimacy question concerns the process of regulation, what we considered as procedural legitimacy in the previous section. One of the complaints concerning the regulatory framework for GMOs, as Skogstad suggested, concerned the opaqueness of the procedure for authorisation and the lack of accountability for the decisions taken. The understanding of how the process contributes to a sense of ethical legitimacy will be explored further in Chapter 10.

To note how the question about the legitimacy of non-state actors acting as regulators is usually answered is not to suggest that source legitimacy – the first of the types of legitimacy that we considered – has no place in discussions over the legitimacy of technology regulation. One of the most common charges levied against the European Union, for example, is that it suffers from a 'democratic deficit'.[31] This complaint challenges not the outcome or procedure of the actual exercise of power at the European level but the legitimacy of making a decision at the European level at all. These concerns are visible not just in Europe – expressed in the 2004 refusal by the French and the Dutch to ratify the Constitutional Treaty and the rise of political parties across the European Member States that give voice to voter dissatisfaction with the extent of European influence at the national level – but are expressed by frustrated people around the world who see decisions affecting their lives being taken by unelected and unaccountable bodies. In a different context, the Seattle riots of

---

[30] See Robert Howse, 'Democracy, Science and Free Trade: Risk Regulation on Trial at the World Trade Organization', *Michigan Law Review*, 98 (1999–2000), 2329.

[31] See, among the large amount of literature on the subject, Andrew Moravcsik, 'In Defense of the "Democratic Deficit": Reassessing the Legitimacy of the European Union', *Journal of Common Market Studies*, 40(4) (2002), 603–34.

1999 are one example of how frustration against the power of the WTO spilled over into violent unrest.[32]

What makes regulation in general ethically legitimate in the era of governance? How one answers this question will in part depend upon the identity of the regulator: where the regulator is an elected legislature and the regulatory act a duly enacted legislative act, then our approach to the question may raise different issues to a situation in which the authority of government has been delegated to or simply assumed by a non-elected entity or where our behaviour is being regulated by individual market actors. Ultimately, however, as the doctrine of positive obligations and the fallout of the 2008 financial collapse both suggest, we continue to hold governments responsible for the actions of non-state actors. It is the state to which we turn to ensure that our basic rights are protected and fulfilled and the state that we hold accountable for constructing the forum in which we debate technological developments. While it is important to keep in mind the changing nature of the exercise of power, these changes take a back seat in the remainder of our examination of legitimacy.

4 The legitimacy of technology regulation: framing the limits

In the most influential effort at designing a basic frame through which we can understand how we talk about regulation, Roger Brownsword has put forward the notion of a three-cornered matrix that dictates the form in which ethical reasoning about technology takes place. This is best illustrated by his bioethical triangle as an explanation of the collapse of regulatory consensus in the area of biotechnology. Brownsword explains the matrix underlying the triangle:

> To avoid any misunderstanding about the nature of the bioethical triangle, it is important to be clear about its relationship with what I see as the basic matrix that sets the form, rather than the substance, of ethical reasoning. I take it that the basic matrix – the matrix that sets the mould for ethical debates – involves three essential *forms*: namely, goal-orientated (consequentialism), rights-based, and duty-based forms. Each of these forms is open to a variety of *substantive* articulations, with various goals, various rights and various duties being advocated. The bioethical triangle fully expresses the *form* of the matrix because it is constituted by a particular goal-orientated ethic, a particular rights-based ethic and a particular duty-based ethic.[33]

What Brownsword's matrix articulates is that how we choose to frame the limits of regulation – whether as individuals or as a society – matters greatly. Despite

---

[32] Jackie Smith, 'Globalizing Resistance: The Battle of Seattle and the Future of Social Movements', *Mobilization*, 6 (2001), 1–19. Also interesting in looking beyond the landmark 'moment' that the Seattle riots have become in the story of globalization – see David Morse, 'Beyond the Myths of Seattle', *Dissent* (summer 2001); available online at: www.dissentmagazine.org/article/?article=1080 (last accessed 15 August 2011).

[33] Roger Brownsword, *Rights, Regulation and the Technological Revolution* (Oxford: Oxford University Press, 2008), 32.

ostensible agreement on the broad conditions that must exist for a regulatory action to be viewed as ethically legitimate, the devil remains in the detail. We may agree on the importance of the respect of basic individual rights for both the process and substance of regulation to be viewed as legitimate, yet our reasons for arguing in favour of individual human rights will differ. The fact that we have different reasons for making an argument – different underlying conceptions of the purpose of human existence, of the demands of human autonomy and of the relationship between the individual and the wider community – will impact upon how fundamental we believe such rights to be. That in turn will determine where we place the boundary of these concepts; and it is where we locate the boundary that determines which technological developments we deem to be acceptable or legitimate, and which are not; which require regulation, which we should welcome and which we must simply prohibit. Although we have chosen here to represent the way in which legitimacy questions about technology regulation are articulated as boundary markers, the basic underlying ethical matrix remains the same.

Corresponding with the ethical matrix identified by Brownsword, we would suggest that the main normative frameworks at play in technology regulation are utilitarianism (goal oriented), deontology (duty based) and liberalism (rights based). This is not to suggest that there are not other frameworks that play a role in motivating particular arguments about how we perceive technology and attempts to regulate its development: for example, communitarianism – the school of thought that lays emphasis on the need to balance the rights of individuals against the needs of the community as a whole and holds that individuals are inescapably shaped by the cultural and social norms of their community – plays an influential role in expression of all three of the main frameworks identified here.[34] Moreover, as we will see in the examination of 'nature' as a boundary-marking concept, a number of Japanese authors reject the western reliance on utilitarianism as a frame for deliberations on human enhancement and suggest instead a Japanese approach that does not fall within any of those outlined here.[35] However, while we will consider arguments motivated by alternative moral frameworks, the majority of arguments stem, at least in the western world, from the three frameworks identified above. An account of these frameworks is given in the textboxes below. It is important to note, however, that these different frameworks are not sealed off from external influence or internally consistent; arguments based on one framework do not

[34] See, e.g., Joseph Rees, 'Development of Communitarian Regulation in the Chemical Industry', *Law & Policy*, 19(4) (1997), 477–528. One could also argue that some of the arguments that focus on issues of equality raised by technological developments, notably in the area of biotechnology and human genetic enhancement, stem from communitarian concerns rather than simply the liberal need to balance equality and liberty.

[35] See, notably, Ryuichi Ida, 'Should We Improve Human Nature? An Interrogation from an Asian Perspective', in Julian Savulescu and Nick Bostrom (eds.), *Human Enhancement* (Oxford: Oxford University Press, 2009).

preclude the same individual or organisation from making arguments based upon another. Yet they are distinct frameworks, the adherents of which will be led to identify different boundary-marking concepts and to use them in different ways. It is to the identity of the key boundary-marking concepts that we now turn.

A utilitarian framework: Utilitarianism – an approach to morality that views the morality of human actions as determined solely by their consequences for human well-being – has its origins in seventeenth-century Britain and the work of Jeremy Bentham and John Stuart Mill, among others. The focus on consequences of actions, as opposed to the inherent character or motives of acting, means that this way of thinking is often also referred to as consequentialism. A consequentialist approach requires a weighing up of improvements to human well-being with the costs of achieving those benefits. Where the gains outweigh the costs, the action is legitimate from a utilitarian standpoint. While there is much that is intuitive or common sense about a cost–benefit analysis as a way of approaching complicated questions of regulation, measuring benefit (or 'utility') requires an instrumental way of thinking about human beings; instead of each individual being valued and respected in their own right, in utilitarianism they become a means to the realisation of greater well-being for all. In this approach, the rights or dignity of some can be traded for the greater good of the many. It is this framework that is the dominant approach to technology regulation in the western world, whereby regulators attempt to permit and even encourage the benefits offered to human well-being by technology for the greatest number whilst keeping the risk of harm to a minimum.

A deontological approach: Whereas utilitarianism focuses on the outcome or consequences of action, a deontological approach locates the morality of action in the acts themselves. An act, such as breaking a promise, is wrong simply because it is wrong, not because of any consequences that the act of breaking the promise may have. The most influential of deontological proponents is the eighteenth-century German philosopher, Immanuel Kant. Kant famously argued that it can never be right to treat each other purely as a means to an end, but that we must treat our fellow human beings always as ends in themselves. This ethical approach can be grounded both in religious belief that sees humankind as made in the image of God and hence as 'sacred' and in a secular humanist approach that locates the individual's sacredness in reason. A deontological framework explicitly rules out the utilitarian notion of sacrificing the needs of some for an increase in the greater overall well-being. In the context of technology regulation, a deontological approach manifests itself most typically in appeals to human dignity.

Liberalism: Liberalism is not opposed to either a utilitarian or deontological perspective; it is instead a political ideology rather than a philosophical school and it is possible to be both a liberal deontologist and a utilitarian liberal. However, despite its apparent flexibility, it is worth examining liberalism for the way in which it structures the background conditions under which debates about technology regulation take place in the west. Liberalism focuses on the individual and views society and the state as a means of providing a framework in which the individual can make meaningful choices about the life they wish to lead. As such, liberalism attaches great importance to individual rights, such as freedom of thought and conscience and freedom of speech, and thus provides what others have labelled a 'human rights perspective' on technology regulation. Human rights can be used as a guide to the content and process of regulation, weighing up needs and limits in a manner reminiscent of utilitarians; or human rights can be wielded as uncompromising trump cards. Liberalism, however, is not simply concerned with the freedom of the individual and attempts to balance freedom with equality; the extent to which one is willing to limit individual freedom with the demands of equality will depend upon the wing of the liberal church in which one sits.

8

Key boundary-marking concepts

1 Introduction

In 2010, the Nobel Prize Committee awarded the prize for medicine to Robert Edwards, the British pioneer of in vitro fertilisation (IVF) treatment. The Vatican reaction was swift. The head of the Pontifical Academy for Life, Ignacio Carrasco de Paula, described the award as 'completely out of order', as without the work of Dr Edwards 'there would not be a large number of freezers filled with embryos in the world'.[1] In making his comment on the decision to honour Dr Edwards, Bishop Carrasco de Paula is using the concept of the sanctity of life, or what we shall term below as 'human dignity', to determine the boundary of what he finds morally acceptable or legitimate. The concepts that we use in discussions about technology regulation to mark the boundary of legitimacy are the subject of this chapter.

Such moral concepts help us to determine what technology can be licensed, what cannot be entertained, and how far we can go. They determine the boundary of what can be permitted: although a technology may be allowed, there may be limitations to its use or development; or attempts made in regulation to mitigate certain unhappy or unhealthy consequences. We determine these limits by reference to what we term here as our 'boundary-marking concepts', i.e. those concepts that are most commonly used by participants in debates about the legitimacy of technological developments to mark the outer limit of moral acceptability. These concepts are used by participants because they give expression to beliefs or understandings that we find intrinsically valuable, that have, in the language of Ronald Dworkin, a touch of sacredness about them for the role they play in human life.[2]

The concepts that we use to mark our boundaries are therefore more than simply social norms; they speak to something deeper about how we understand the purpose of human existence. We may find, for example, the surgical

---

[1] BBC Online News Report, 'Vatican official criticises Nobel win for IVF pioneer', 4 October 2010; available online at: www.bbc.co.uk/news/health-11472753?print=true (last accessed 5 October 2010).

[2] Ronald Dworkin, *Life's Dominion. An Argument about Abortion, Euthanasia, and Individual Freedom* (London: Vintage Books, 1994), 73–4.

manipulation of our bodies for fashion purposes distasteful or we may hold it to be an expression of individual autonomy, but it is unlikely that we will feel as strongly about even radical cosmetic surgery as we do about a trade in human organs, GMOs or the creation and destruction of embryos for the purpose of scientific research. We respond to the moral challenges and risks posed by technological advances by applying our most fundamental assumptions about human existence. It is these assumptions that we identify as 'boundary-marking concepts'.

In choosing to frame the question of legitimacy as it applies to technology regulation in this way, we are not suggesting that concepts used in this way, i.e. to mark the moral boundary, are solely concerned with prohibition. Instead, they provide us with a frame within which to make decisions about technology. Indeed, out-and-out prohibition is rare. Rather, as Brownsword has argued, regulation has a 'range':

> Where traditional law-like regulation is employed, in its crudest form negative channelling presupposes a legislated rule that prohibits x; positive channelling a rule that requires x; and neutral channelling a rule that permits x. For example, in relation to the regulation of human genetics, legislation might prohibit reproductive cloning, permit therapeutic cloning and require (hypothetically) all citizens to contribute samples for a national genetic database ... [T]here is a lot more to the regulatory range than simple red light prohibitions and green light permissions.[3]

Identifying certain concepts as boundary-marking helps us therefore to understand how we and others construct arguments in the decision-making process over whether something should be prohibited, positively required or permitted under certain conditions.

However, while describing concepts as 'boundary-marking' does not automatically suggest prohibition, certain of these concepts contain within themselves suggestions for an outer limit. Notions of how far we can go are, to a certain extent, inherent to some of the concepts themselves. For example, in the case of the Vatican reaction to the decision to award the Nobel Prize to Robert Edwards, the understanding of life as an expression of divinity parcelled in the notion of human dignity determines the outer limit of technological progress for the Catholic leadership. In such a context, the appeal to human dignity is intended to be a 'conversation-stopper';[4] it is not an invitation to discuss where the boundary should lie. In contrast, the concept of equality, which we also identify below as a boundary-marking concept, is rarely used in such absolute ways. Instead, concern about the impact of a given technology on equality in

---

[3] Roger Brownsword, 'Red Lights and Rogues: Regulating Human Genetics', in Han Somsen (ed.), *The Regulatory Challenge of Biotechnology. Human Genetics, Food and Patents* (Cheltenham: Edward Elgar, 2007), 44.

[4] Roger Brownsword, *Rights, Regulation and the Technological Revolution* (Oxford: Oxford University Press, 2008), 39.

society is more likely to lead to discussion about how best to use regulation or policy design so as to mitigate the worst effects of inequality likely to be created by technological developments.

Boundary-marking concepts are not 'free-floating'. The particular mix of boundary-marking concepts that we as individuals, communities or societies consider relevant are determined by our normative frameworks. It is our guiding meta-narrative, what we understand the human story to consist in, that will determine the choice of concepts that act as boundary markers for us. The belief in a divine power as the source and purpose of human existence, for example, will entail that certain markers are viewed as more relevant than others, and will also suggest the location of the boundary. It is important to realise, however, that a society is made up of a variety of different normative outlooks, some of which are irreconcilable with one another. The perspective that sees IVF treatment as worthy of a Noble Prize for its huge contribution to medical science, and thus to human life, cannot be reconciled with a standpoint that sees any interference with the reproductive process as 'playing God'.[5] Where we begin from a liberal framework, how we understand freedom and equality (and how we understand the relationship between the two) will determine what we mean by human dignity or human nature. Where we place a deity at the centre of human existence, He will be our reference point for defining what it is to lead a human life. Yet again, where we view the purpose of life to be that of maximising happiness for the greatest number of people, human dignity may not be a boundary-marking concept at all. However, the normative frameworks we use to orient our lives are rarely internally consistent or constant; contemporary liberal societies, for example, arguably place more emphasis on freedom than equality than was perhaps the case some thirty years ago. This stress on the freedom to make individual choices over concern with societal equality will tilt the liberal normative framework in a libertarian direction and change both how we use our boundary-marking concepts and where we place the outer limits of acceptability. Where different frames locate the boundary now at the beginning of the century is unlikely to be the same at this century's close.

Finally, by highlighting concepts that are boundary-marking from a particular normative perspective, we do not wish to suggest that these concepts are not relevant for other groups. Thus, while human dignity is not a boundary marker for those who espouse a utilitarian perspective, it is nonetheless a vital element of the utilitarian calculus. To be able to weigh human suffering, it is necessary to conceive of a human being as an individual unit and to assign value to them. However, the notion of dignity that determines the assignment of value to an individual is not a key boundary marker for utilitarians. Instead,

---

[5] See the Vatican's Congregation for the Doctrine of the Faith, *Instruction* Dignitas Personae *on Certain Bioethical Questions* (2008); available online at www.vatican.va/roman_curia/congregations/cfaith/documents/rc_con_cfaith_doc_20081208_dignitas-personae_en.html (last accessed 26 August 2011).

we shall suggest that it is the concept of harm that marks the main utilitarian boundary. In the same way, while harm is not a key boundary-marking concept for those who subscribe to a liberal framework that is rooted in deontological thinking, the element of the utilitarian calculus that relates to understanding risk may well also play an important role in determining the outer boundary limit of individual rights, where rights may be limited to ensure respect for the rights of others.

What we will do in this chapter is attempt to identify the main boundary-marking concepts that are used to determine whether or not the normative position taken in regard to the regulation of technology is legitimate. We do not claim that these are the only concepts used to mark moral boundaries, but only that these are the ones that feature most strongly in such discussions. At the same time, we will tease out the different ways in which these key concepts are used and where different standpoints place the boundary. Yet, as we use concepts to construct arguments about ethical boundaries, we participate in a process of constructing those boundaries within our communities but also in constructing the concepts themselves.[6] There is of course no fixed notion of property; no objective idea of what human dignity requires. What we mean by 'privacy' as this century begins is unlikely to be the same at its close. The role that human rights play as boundary markers, although considered briefly below, is properly the subject of Chapter 9.

2 Human dignity

Human dignity is the first key boundary-marking concept we will consider. Reference to human dignity is ubiquitous in debates about technological regulation, particularly where the application of scientific knowledge touches upon the foundations of life, and, in particular, human life.[7] In many ways, it is the ultimate boundary marker – the one line that cannot be crossed; to do so, to step across the line, places both the action and the actor outside the bounds of humanity itself, which is a very dangerous place to be.[8] In this way, human dignity can act as a trump card. Moreover, in the way that it functions as a conversation stopper, appeals to human dignity are found at the root of many other claims concerning the moral legitimacy of technological advances. For example, below we identify equality as a boundary marker; however, arguments about whether certain developments impact negatively, positively or neutrally

---

[6] John R. Searle, *The Construction of Social Reality* (London: Penguin, 1995).

[7] See, for example, the 2005 UNESCO Universal Declaration on Bioethics and Human Rights, provided in Chapter 3, pp. 52–8.

[8] The way in which this narrative operates is clear from the abortion debate in the United States, where certain groups view the murder of doctors willing to perform abortions as divine intervention. The threat that these doctors are seen as posing to human dignity sets them outside the prohibition on the taking of human life for members of such anti-abortion groups. See, further, Carl Schmitt, *The Concept of the Political*, trans. George Schwab (Chicago: University of Chicago Press, 2007), ch. 3.

upon our equality as individuals in relation to each other presupposes a belief in the intrinsic worth of every human being and thus is ultimately a claim that is rooted in a certain understanding of human dignity. Likewise, the suggestion that transparency marks the boundary of legitimacy for some actors. We prize openness and participation in the exercise of power so highly because it pertains to our existence as individual autonomous beings – one interpretation of human dignity. Some views of what makes humans special thus underpins all efforts at facilitating or safeguarding individual human flourishing, and thus the main normative frameworks considered here. To a certain extent, then, human dignity is a catch-all phrase to capture why we believe there is anything valuable about human existence and therefore a reason why we care about the legitimacy of regulation; the concept of legitimacy thus presupposes a belief in human dignity, however we might choose to ground it. However, human dignity as a boundary marker is used in a particular way in debates about technology, and the fact that participants in societal debates choose not to articulate their concerns as human dignity but as openness, equality or harm necessitates viewing these concepts separately here. Thus, while human dignity is a common thread across all the boundary-marking concepts, to greater or lesser degrees, what we consider here is how human dignity is explicitly used in these debates.

The concept of dignity has a complex history within the western philosophical tradition.[9] *Dignitas hominis* in classical Roman thought generally referred to 'status' rather than to any idea of intrinsic human worth, and could therefore be lost as one's status in society waned. This idea of dignity has generally fallen out of favour. Contemporary use of the concept instead assumes that dignity attaches to all human beings by virtue either of their being human or, more particularly, because of certain human qualities, such as reason or freedom or God-likeness. This understanding of human dignity is primarily used in three ways in debates on technology regulation: the first we have chosen to call 'dignity as autonomy'; the second use of dignity is religious in origin and stems from the belief that man is made in the image of God; the third way in which dignity appears in the discussions is human dignity as manifest in a human nature or human essence. Before we examine in turn each of these approaches to human dignity, it is worth considering the function that appealing to human dignity is intended to have.

Human dignity, whatever the source or grounding of the appeal, performs two main functions as a boundary-marking concept: it is both empowering and constraining.[10] The way in which the same understanding of dignity can both empower and constrain is visible in the eighteenth-century writings of Immanuel Kant, responsible for bringing human dignity to the fore of western thought. This famous passage from *The Metaphysic of Morals* that is one of the

---

[9] For a helpful overview of dignity in the history of ideas, see Christopher McCrudden, 'Human Dignity and Judicial Interpretation of Human Rights', *European Journal of International Law*, 19 (2008), 655.

[10] See, further, Deryck Beyleveld and Roger Brownsword, *Human Dignity in Bioethics and Biolaw* (Oxford: Oxford University Press, 2001).

prime references for deontological thinking is helpful here because it shows Kant attempting to ground his understanding of the moral development of human persons both in the idea of duties that we have to others and duties that we have to ourselves:

> Every human being has a legitimate claim to respect from his fellow human beings and is in turn bound to respect every other. Humanity itself is a dignity; for a human being cannot be used merely as a means by any human being ... but must always be used at the same time as an end. It is just in this that his dignity (personality) consists, by which he raises himself above all other beings in the world that are not human beings and yet can be used, and so over all things. But just as he cannot give himself away for any price (this would conflict with his duty of self-esteem), so neither can he act contrary to the equally necessary self-esteem of others, as human beings, that is, he is under obligation to acknowledge, in a practical way, the dignity of humanity in every other human being.[11]

Humans have an incomparable worth by virtue of being moral agents capable of taking responsibility for our choices in life. In claiming human dignity in debates, we are often making reference to this ability that humans possess to determine preferences and assign value to them, and, as such, we are viewing human dignity as supportive of human autonomy, as something that empowers human beings to make decisions about their lives. However, as Kant makes equally clear, our duty to respect others as a consequence of their dignity can also constrain our autonomy, limiting our freedom of action in regard to our relations with others.

The source of the appeal to human dignity does not guide whether dignity is empowering or constraining. Moreover, the appeal to human dignity can be used both in an empowering or constraining way in the same discussion, as the nature of the abortion debate suggests. If one views human dignity as empowering women to make choices about their bodies, then one is likely to look favourably upon legalised abortion; if one instead interprets human dignity as constraining an action that leads to the destruction of a human life, one goes in the other direction, that of rejecting the legalisation of what anti-abortionists view as the murder of innocents. Further, simply because one uses a constraining argument in one context does not entail that one will use dignity similarly in another situation. It is possible to imagine, for example, that those who use dignity as constraining in the US abortion debate would view personal property rights from a 'dignity as empowerment' perspective. Yet, as the abortion example shows, there is a fundamental incompatibility between appeals to dignity as empowerment and demands for dignity as constraint in a single instance.[12] It is not possible to satisfy both the human dignity of women by acknowledging their

---

[11] Immanuel Kant, *The Metaphysics of Morals*, trans. and ed. Mary Gregor (Cambridge University Press, 1996), 209.

[12] Roger Brownsword, 'What the World Needs Now: Techno-Regulation, Human Rights and Human Dignity', in Brownsword (ed.), *Human Rights* (Oxford: Hart, 2004), 206.

autonomy as expressed by rights over their own bodies and the human dignity of the foetus understood as autonomy through the right to life itself.

Of course, the fact that dignity performs two functions in our debates about the regulation of technology tells us little about why it is used in either way. What determines whether one uses dignity as an argument for empowerment or constraint will depend both on the given topic and upon one's underlying normative frame of reference. The danger of the incompatibility of empowering and constraining approaches is, as Brownsword has suggested elsewhere, that we talk past one another,[13] which makes it all the more important that we have a clear idea of what we are talking about when we talk about dignity.

(a) Dignity as autonomy

An understanding of 'dignity as autonomy' stems from the idea that the central quality intrinsic to human beings – a quality that marks us off from other animals and demands special recognition and protection – is our ability to reason. Thus, what makes human beings special is our capacity to decide for ourselves what our priorities are and to rank those preferences. From this perspective, human beings have dignity because we are able to determine for ourselves what is important to us; from this capacity to reason emerges the belief that human beings are fundamentally free. An understanding of dignity as stemming from some intrinsic quality of human beings, rather than solely as an attribute of office, can also be dated back to the classical period. Cicero, for example, argued that man was superior to all other living creatures because we can rise above pure bodily needs, reflect and improve our minds.[14] For Kant, too, dignity attaches to human beings by virtue of our being free.[15] It is this understanding of the foundation of human dignity that we are calling 'dignity as autonomy'.[16]

The capacity to reason is, from this perspective, declared to be an innate characteristic of human beings; some individuals may be better at logic, smarter in some other way or better educated, but we are nonetheless all born with the capacity – the freedom – to think for ourselves and choose, albeit in relationship with our significant others, what our life should be for us. Dignity as autonomy is the basis of the harm principle explored in the next section and has been used to argue in favour of as wide an access to technology as possible.[17] Robert Nozick, for example, has famously argued for a 'genetic supermarket' in which

---

[13] *Ibid.*

[14] Marcus Tullius Cicero, *De Officiis*, I, 30; E. M. Atkins and M. T. Griffin (eds.), *Cicero: On Duties* (Cambridge: Cambridge University Press, 1991).

[15] Oliver Sensen, 'Kant's Conception of Human Dignity', *Kant-Studien 100. Jarg.* (2009), S.309–31.

[16] This is a considerable simplification of the complexity of these discussions but suffices for the points we wish to make in these chapters.

[17] It is also used as an argument for empowerment against overcautious risk regimes; see Wolfgang van den Daele, 'Access to New Technology: In Defense of the Liberal Regime of Innovation', in M. Goodwin et al., *Dimensions of Technology Regulation* (Nijmegen: Wolf Publishing, 2010).

parents can design children to order.[18] Here Nozick's libertarian approach to what constitutes an appropriate relationship between the state and the individual locates the boundary marker of dignity as autonomy at an extreme end of the permissive spectrum. Dignity is thus used as an argument by both progressives and conservatives.

The belief that our lives are uniquely valuable is the foundation of human rights. Article 1 of the Universal Declaration of Human Rights declares that: 'Human beings are born free and equal in dignity and rights'. The idea that individuals possess rights flows from the belief in our innate freedom. At the same time, those rights are considered necessary to protect that freedom from encroachment by others, notably the state. Human rights are thus intimately bound up with the notion of human dignity as autonomy. This idea of human dignity as autonomy thus appears most frequently in the context of technology regulation alongside human rights; for example, in UNESCO's preliminary draft for the Universal Declaration on Bioethics and Human Rights, which concerns technological developments in medicine and the life sciences. The explanatory memorandum to an early draft of the text elaborated on the purpose of the Declaration, which was to ensure:

> that such development occurs within the framework of ethical principles that respect human dignity and protect human rights and fundamental freedoms, and ... prevent practices contrary to human dignity.[19]

Similarly, the preamble to the 1997 Universal Declaration on the Human Genome and Human Rights notes that it is 'imperative' that research in this field 'fully respect human dignity, freedom and human rights'.[20]

Yet, the fact that human dignity appears alongside human rights – suggesting simultaneously closeness and difference – intimates that the relationship between human dignity and human rights is not as straightforward as simply the former being the foundation of the latter.[21] Were this the case, it would not be necessary to mention human rights at all in the contexts above. In part, the

---

[18] Robert Nozick, *Anarchy, State and Utopia* (New York: Basic Books, 1974), 315. Tom Campbell and Laura Cabrera have made a similar case for presumptive parental freedom, although not as extreme. They argue that although moral considerations may well influence parental decision-making about what is best for their child, they should not be the basis of restrictive regulation. Tom Campbell and Laura Cabrera, 'The Weak Moral Basis for Restrictive Regulation of Preimplantation Genetic Diagnosis', in Sheila A. M. McLean and Sarah Elliston (eds.), *Regulating Pre-implantation Genetic Diagnosis: A Comparative and Theoretical Analysis* (Abingdon: Routledge, forthcoming 2012).

[19] Explanation to Article 2 of *Elaboration of the Declaration on Universal Norms on Bioethics: Third Outline of a Text* (Paris, 27 August 2004); cited in Brownsword, *Rights*, 33.

[20] *Universal Declaration on the Human Genome and Human Rights*, UNESCO Declaration, adopted at 29th session, 11 November 1997; the Declaration was endorsed by the UN General Assembly in its 53rd session on 9 December 1998, (AIRES/53/152).

[21] For a helpful discussion of the complexity of the relationship between dignity and human rights, see McCrudden, 'Human Dignity'. See also George Kateb's claim in a recent essay that human dignity is an existential claim whereas human rights are primarily concerned with the

reference to human dignity alongside human rights is as a catch-all concept to which everyone can subscribe; whereas human rights remain contentious for many, human dignity can be read in a variety of ways, to which the three approaches teased out here attest. Moreover, the boundary between human dignity as autonomy and human rights is particularly susceptible to blurring, given that this manifestation of dignity is generally used in an empowering fashion.

In contrast to human rights, however, human dignity, as an existential claim about the value of human beings, is not capable of compromise. If we follow Kant in deciding that the duty to treat others always as an end in themselves is a categorical imperative, it follows that the idea of human dignity upon which Kant bases his imperative is of an absolute nature; it allows for no derogation. Human dignity, in whatever manifestation, has absoluteness at its core. Human rights, on the other hand, are rarely possessed of an absolute nature.[22] The tension between human dignity and human rights becomes particularly visible over questions such as consent. The existential foundation of human dignity limits the absolute autonomy of each individual; in other words, human dignity, even where it is based upon our innate autonomy, is a collective concept: we are responsible in our actions for upholding the collective dignity of others as well as satisfying our own desires. As the German Constitutional Court has held, 'human dignity means not only the individual dignity of the person but the dignity of man as a species. Dignity is therefore not at the disposal of the individual.'[23] It is human dignity that therefore forms the basis of rules preventing an individual from choosing to sell an organ; that famously stops a dwarf from being allowed to consent to participation in a circus act,[24] or adults from seeking pleasure in hard-core physical pain;[25] and it is human dignity that forms the basis of our concern about those no longer capable of caring about the exercise of their autonomy.[26] Dignity cannot therefore be waived.

The absolute nature of human dignity comes more clearly to the fore in the manifestation to which we now turn.

(b) Faith-based dignity

A second central understanding of dignity in contemporary discussions concerns the relationship of man with a Creator. The foundation of human dignity

---

moral question of reducing suffering; George Kateb, *Human Dignity* (Cambridge, MA: Harvard University Press, 2011), 10–24.

[22] This point is picked up in Chapter 9.

[23] BVerfGE 45, 187, 229 (1977). Cited in McCrudden, 'Human Dignity', 705.

[24] The French prohibition on dwarf throwing for commercial purposes was upheld by the Conseil d'État and, subsequently, the Human Rights Committee. Conseil d'État, 27 October 1995, req. Nos. 136–720 (Commune de Morsang-Orge) and Nos. 143–578 (Ville d'Aix-en-Provence); *Wackenheim* v. *France*, CCPR/C/75/D/854/1999, 26 July 2000.

[25] *Laskey, Jaggard and Brown* v. *The UK* (1997) 24 EHRR 39; otherwise known as the Spanner case.

[26] See, for example, Articles 6 and 17 of the Oviedo Convention on Human Rights and Biomedicine protecting the dignity of those unable to give consent. Council of Europe Convention on Human Rights and Biomedicine, ETS no. 164, Oviedo, 4 April 1997.

on the relationship of human beings with an all-powerful deity, whether God, Yahweh or Allah, is used both by subscribers to a rights-based and to a duty-based normative perspective.

The first element of this approach is the idea that man has dignity because he is made in the image and likeness of God, alone of all the species.[27] Human dignity is intrinsic in this conception. This belief in a unique relationship with a Creator is clearly visible in the Catechism of the Catholic Church, and forms much of the basis of the Vatican's intervention in debates about technological regulation, in particular the biotech revolution. The Catechism provides:

> Of all visible creatures only man is 'able to know and love his creator'. He is 'the only creature on earth that God has willed for its own sake', and he alone is called to share, by knowledge and love, in God's own life. It was for this end that he was created, and this is the fundamental reason for his dignity … Being in the image of God the human individual possesses the dignity of a person, who is not just something, but someone. He is capable of self-knowledge, of self-possession and of freely giving of himself and entering into communion with other persons. And he is called by grace to a covenant with his Creator … [28]

To believe that man is made in the image of God is to view each individual human being not simply as a product of the Creator's benevolence but as a representation of the divine. One consequence of basing human dignity on the belief that we are made in the image of God is that it extends the protection of the boundary marker of human dignity to entities unable to reason, notably embryos. The influence of arguments of this type was clearly visible in US federal policy prior to 2009 towards stem cell research. Under former US President George W. Bush, a devout Christian, embryonic stem cells could not be derived from aborted foetuses, thus limiting research to existing stem cell lines. The policy provided:

> Section 1.
> The Secretary of Health and Human Services (Secretary) shall conduct and support research on the isolation, derivation, production and testing of stem cells that are capable of producing all or almost all of the cell types of the developing body and may result in improved understanding of our treatments for diseases and other adverse health conditions, but are derived without creating a human embryo for research purposes or destroying, discarding or subjecting to harm a human embryo or fetus.

This restriction on research activities was motivated by concerns for human dignity that extend to the unborn:

---

[27] See Arieli, 'On the Necessary and Sufficient Conditions for the Emergence of the Dignity of Man and His Rights', cited in McCrudden, 'Human Dignity', 658.

[28] *The Catechism of the Catholic Church*, pt. 1: The Profession of the Faith, Section 2: The Profession of the Christian Faith, ch. 1, Article 1, paras. 6, 356–7; available online at www.vatican.va/archive/catechism/p1s2c1p6.htm

(c) the destruction of nascent life for research violates the principle that no life should be used as a mere means for achieving the medical benefit of another;

(d) human embryos and foetuses, as living members of the human species, are not raw materials to be exploited or commodities to be bought or sold;[29]

Of course, it is not only Christians that locate human dignity in a likeness with a Creator. It is an understanding shared with the other main theistic religions, notably Judaism and Islam. According to the Holy Qur'an, God created man not in his image but gave him honour and dignity by endowing him with His spirit: 'I breathed into him my spirit' (15:29; 38:72). Such dignity ennobles us in our interaction with one another. Moreover, it is this dignity of every individual because he or she is infused with God's spirit that forms the foundation of human rights in the Muslim world. The Cairo Declaration of Human Rights in Islam, issued by the Islamic Conference of Foreign Ministers in Egypt in 1990, clearly locates the source of human rights in the will of Allah. Article 2 of the Declaration, for example, provides: 'Life is a God-given gift and the right to life is guaranteed to every human being.' The rights in the Cairo Declaration are rooted in the kinship of man to God and make not only the fact of life but also make sacred the freedom to live our own life of faith.

Yet, an understanding of dignity based upon faith also places obligations on us towards others, notably to prevent and to relieve suffering and can therefore be interpreted as a duty to protect and preserve life. As a Jewish scholar has noted in support of embryonic stem cell research:

Our bodies belong to God; we have them on loan during our lease on life. God, as owner of our bodies, can and does impose conditions on our use of our bodies. Among these conditions is the requirement that we seek to preserve our lives and our health.[30]

Being made in the likeness of God can thus also be used as an argument in support of technological advancement; human endeavour for scientific advancement is from this perspective a form of worship – a perspective endorsed by numerous Islamic scholars.[31] A religious foundation for human dignity is by no means always a constraining voice in technology debates.

---

[29] Executive Order 13435 – Expanding Approved Stem Cell Lines in Ethically Responsible Ways, 22 June 2007; available online at http://stemcells.nih.gov/policy/defaultpage.asp The restrictions were lifted by President Obama upon taking office in 2008.

[30] Testimony of Rabbi Elliot N. Dorff, *Ethical Issues in Human Stem Cell Research*, Commissioned Papers, vol. 3: Religious Perspectives, 2000; available online at www.bioethics.gov/reports/past_commissions/nbac_stemcell3.pdf

[31] Ahmed Dallal, *Islam, Science and the Challenge of History* (New Haven: Yale University Press, 2010); Bagher Larijani and F. Zahedi, 'Islamic Perspective on Human Research and Stem Cell Research', *Transplantation Proceedings*, 36(10) (2004), 3188–9. See also 'Iran: stem cell research is halal', *Muslim Observer*, 29 August 2011.

Yet while the belief in human beings as both a representation of the divine and a product of His love can be used as an argument for pushing forward with scientific advancement, the relationship between man and His Creator is not an equal one. Rather, the role of man is to glorify and praise the Lord.[32] The exalted status of the Creator and the need for humility in the face of the results of God's Creation presents itself in regulatory debates as an Icarus-type concern about 'playing God'. Such fears about divine punishment as retribution for exuberance in success have been a mainstay of western culture since the classical period. Writing in the sixteenth century, the English playwright Christopher Marlowe beautifully captured the relationship between hubris and divine wrath: 'Till swol'n with cunning of a self-conceit/ His waxen wings did mount about his reach/ And melting, heaven conspired his overthrow'.[33] It is this fear that is visible in the Vatican Instruction concerning the morality of embryo selection:

> in the attempt to create a new type of human being one can recognize an ideological element in which man tries to take the place of his Creator.[34]

This is religiously grounded human dignity used in a constraining fashion. These two elements – humankind made in the image of God and yet subordinate to the magnificence of the Creator – form the basis of religiously grounded human dignity claims.[35]

(c) Human dignity as human nature

The third way in which human dignity is used as a boundary marker in discussions over technology regulation is the appeal to a species identity – the idea that we share a human nature that is more important than individual autonomy. There is of course some clear overlap with concepts of human dignity as autonomy – human nature can consist in our ability to reason. Yet, conceptualising human dignity as human nature places emphasis on identity rather than autonomy. Moreover, as we will see, the human nature argument sees dignity not as innate but as relational.

The fear that technological developments threaten our very identity as a species is often expressed as the belief that something is 'unnatural', by which the speaker believes that this or that development is unnatural for us as human

---

[32] Isaiah, 2:17 (*New Jerusalem Bible*).

[33] Christopher Marlowe, *Faustus*, Chorus, ll. 20–2, intro. J. B. Sloane, *The Complete Plays* (London: Penguin, 1969).

[34] Congregation for the Doctrine of the Faith, *Instruction* Dignitas Personae *on Certain Bioethical Questions* (2008), ch. 27, n. 5.

[35] Another element of religiously based human dignity is suggested by Pico della Mirandola's famous oration *On the Dignity of Man*, in which it is God that has granted man reason and the freedom to choose; however, this strand of thought does not feature in regulatory debates over technology. See Pico della Mirandola, *On the Dignity of Man*, trans. C. Glenn Wallis (Indianapolis: Hackett, 1965).

beings.[36] This idea was expressed by Heidegger in his famous 1954 essay entitled 'The Question concerning Technology', in which he argued that the danger of technology is that it prevents man from realising the possibility of Being in the world. Despite writing in a post-Second World War world in which the power of technology to destroy both our species and the planet had been revealed in the nuclear attack on Japan, Heidegger wrote:

> The threat to man does not come in the first instance from the potentially lethal machines and apparatus of technology. The actual threat has always afflicted man in his essence.[37]

A similar type of concern appears to underlie the European Court of Human Rights' recent decision to accept Austria's restrictive approach to regulating methods of non-natural conception.[38] It is this capacity for technology to alter the essence of what it is to be human that was the subject of Aldous Huxley's visionary dystopia, *Brave New World*.[39] In the New World sketched in the novel, humans are compelled to live in an orderly society not by force but by the use of subliminal messages and drugs to make everyone happy. Huxley envisioned a world in which there is no disease, no crime, no social disorder of any kind and in which everyone's desires are fulfilled. And yet as Fukuyama notes (paraphrasing a typical student essay on the book):

> the people in *Brave New World* may be happy, but they have ceased to be *human beings*. They no longer struggle, aspire, love, feel pain, make difficult moral choices, have families, or do any of the things that we traditionally associate with being human. They no longer have the characteristics that give us human dignity … Their world has become unnatural in the most profound sense imaginable, because *human nature* has been altered.[40]

Huxley's vision centred on pharmaceuticals and psychological manipulation. The concern for Habermas in *The Future of Human Nature* is the possibility of alteration of the human genome:

> What is so unsettling is the fact that the dividing line between the nature we *are* and the organic equipment we *give* ourselves is being blurred … Gene manipulation is bound up with issues touching upon the identity of the species.[41]

---

[36] See, for a helpful attempt to categorise 'unnatural'-type arguments, Phillip Karpowicz, Cynthia B. Cohen and Derek van der Kooy, 'Developing Human–Nonhuman Chimeras in Human Stem Cell Research: Ethical Issues and Boundaries', *Kennedy Institute of Ethics Journal*, 15 (2005), 107–34.

[37] Martin Heidegger, 'The Question concerning Technology' (1954), in David Farrell Krell (ed.), *Basic Writings* (London: Routledge & Kegan Paul, 1978), 309.

[38] *S. H. and Others* v. *Austria*, Judgment of the Grand Chamber of 3 November 2011, application no. 57813/00.

[39] Aldous Huxley, *Brave New World* (1932) (London: Flamingo, 1994).

[40] Francis Fukuyama, *Our Posthuman Future. Consequences of the Biotechnology Revolution* (New York: Farrar, Straus and Giroux, 2002), 6 (italics his).

[41] Jürgen Habermas, *The Future of Human Nature* (Cambridge: Polity, 2003), 22–3 (italics his).

The argument that (certain) technological development(s) threaten our very identity as a species presumes that we can identify what it is that constitutes that identity – what it is that makes us human and that we all share. While many people would probably agree that there is something that constitutes a human nature of sorts, it is difficult to put our finger on what it is. Fukuyama, in the extract above, gives a list of things that humans do. But are we to prohibit all technologies that limit our opportunity to make difficult moral choices, or can we do away with some hard choices on the basis that others remain? As Karpowicz *et al.* have put it:

> The basic difficulty with the 'unnaturalness' argument is that it does not explain when an intervention into nature is ethically acceptable and when it is not, why certain natural features always bear a certain moral import and therefore should not be changed. That organisms normally function in certain ways in the natural world does not indicate that it is wrong to intervene into these functions or to keep them from reaching their biological ends.[42]

Habermas's use of human nature as a defence against the unacceptable is based upon the belief that a vital characteristic of what it is to be human is that our beginning – each individual beginning – is not at the disposal of another. While this seems on the surface very similar to dignity as autonomy in its relation to freedom, the following passage suggests that Habermas has something rather different in mind:

> Irrespective of how far genetic programming could actually go in fixing properties, dispositions, and skills, as well as in determining behaviour of the future person, *post factum* knowledge of this circumstance may intervene in the self-relation of the person, the relation to her bodily or mental existence … [A]s a consequence of a genetic intervention carried out before we were born, the subjective nature we experience as being something we cannot dispose over is actually the result of an instrumentalization of a part of our nature. The realization that our hereditary factors were, in a past before our past, subjected to programming, confronts us on an existential level, so to speak, with the expectation that we subordinate our being a body to our having a body … We experience our own freedom with reference to something which, by its very nature, is not at our disposal. The person, irrespective of her finiteness, knows herself to be the irreducible origin of her own actions and aspirations. But in order to know this, is it really necessary for this person to be able to ascribe her own origin to a beginning which eludes human disposal, to a beginning, that is, which is sure not to prejudge her freedom only if it may be seen as something – like God or nature – that is not at the disposal of some *other* person?[43]

In answering the question in the positive, Habermas draws out that the origin of what it is that makes human beings special – our dignity[44] – concerns not some

---

[42] Karpowicz *et al.*, 'Developing Human–Nonhuman Chimeras', at 115.
[43] Habermas, *Future of Human Nature*, at 53–4, 58.
[44] Habermas distinguishes between human dignity, which for him is an ethical question (for example, whether a ball of human stem cells is viewed as a human life or not is a matter of

innate ability of human beings – something that we both possess and need in order to live a fulfilling life – but relates instead to our relationship to ourselves and to how we understand what makes us who we are. Habermas expresses this in the language of 'being the author of our own life histories'.[45] The ability of a third party to determine in advance of our existence some element of who we will be by manipulating our genetic make-up constitutes a gross infringement of our authorial rights over our own lives. Instead of being born free, we are born into a story that has already begun.

The understanding that an essential element of a life well lived is that we are the authors of our own life stories is an idea associated with the German thinker, Hannah Arendt. For Arendt, the dignity of humans is rooted in her concept of 'natality'. In her understanding of the human condition, the freedom that is necessary for us to achieve our unique potential is located not in the freedom to choose between alternatives (the autonomy of liberals), but in the freedom to begin anew, to be reborn, in the plurality of the potentiality of human existence. As Arendt writes:

> the new beginning inherent in birth can make itself felt in the world only because the newcomer possesses the capacity of beginning something anew ... In this sense of initiative, an element of action, and therefore of natality, is inherent in all human activities.[46]
>
> It is in the nature of beginning that something new is started which cannot be expected from whatever may have happened before. This character of *startling unexpectedness* is inherent in all beginnings and in all origins.[47]

It is the startling unexpectedness of natality, of human existence, that allows us to be the authors of our own life stories. It is only by reference to beginnings 'not at our disposal', as Habermas would put it, that allows the individual to understand herself as the initiator of her own actions and desires.

The irreversible nature of genetic engineering limits the individual's potential for new beginnings, and reins in the 'boundlessness' of their existence;[48] it is this boundlessness that is miraculous about human existence.

> It is, in other words, the birth of new men and the new beginning, the action they are capable of by virtue of being born. Only the full experience of this capacity can bestow upon human affairs faith and hope, those two essential characteristics of human existence.[49]

---

culturally specific ethics), and our identity as a species, which speaks to universisable morals. While making this distinction is important for Habermas's broader work, his idea that there is something special about human beings that makes each life uniquely valuable falls under the conception of dignity being used here. For more on this human dignity–human nature distinction, see *ibid.*, at 31, 39.

[45] *Ibid.*, at 25.
[46] Hannah Arendt, *The Human Condition* (1958) (New York: Doubleday Books, 1959 edn), 10–11.
[47] *Ibid.*, at 157 (emphasis ours).   [48] *Ibid.*, at 169–71.
[49] *Ibid.*, at 222.

Key boundary-marking concepts

This for Habermas is a line in the sand – the moment at which 'modernity … realizes its own limits'[50]

A similar idea has been expressed by another philosopher, Michael Sandel. In a long essay, Sandel makes a case against parents designing their offspring, opting for ever brainier, taller, more athletic children. In his plea against perfectionism, he presents the concept of 'giftedness' to explain what it is that so unsettles us in the thought of widespread genetic manipulation by choice. He bases his argument on the dangers of the drive to mastery. In a secular version of the 'playing God' type arguments that we considered above, Sandel introduces another Greek legend, that of Prometheus:

> I do not think that the main problem with enhancement and genetic engineering is that they undermine effort and erode human agency. The deeper danger is that they represent a kind of hyper-agency, a Promethean aspiration to remake nature, including human nature, to serve our purposes and satisfy our desires. The problem is not the drift to mechanism but the drive to mastery. And what the drive to mastery misses, and may even destroy, is an appreciation of the gifted character of human powers and achievements.
>
> To acknowledge the giftedness of life is to recognize that our talents and powers are not wholly our own doing, nor even fully ours, despite the efforts we expend to develop and to exercise them. It is able to recognize that not everything in the world is open to any use we may desire or devise. An appreciation of the giftedness of life constrains the Promethean project and conduces to a certain humility.[51]

Where Habermas focuses on our nature as being something that others may not begin to write for us, Sandel instead identifies the consequences of the requirement to make the most of the lottery-like nature of our genetic inheritance – humility, responsibility and solidarity[52] – as the fundamental aspect of human nature that he would not want to see lost:

> To appreciate children as gifts is to accept them as they come, not as objects of our design, or products of our will, or instruments of our ambition.[53]

Here the boundary of human nature is located at what Dworkin has pithily phrased the 'choice/chance' point.[54] It is this distinction between chance, and our response to the vagaries of fate as a species – Shakespeare's slings and arrows of outrageous fortune – and choice that forms the focus of both these appeals to human nature as a boundary marker.

Dworkin, however, does not buy the argument that chance or fate is an essential feature of human nature. In his own essay on genes and luck, he instead

---

[50] Habermas, *Future of Human Nature*, 27.
[51] Michael Sandel, *The Case Against Perfectionism* (Cambridge, MA: Harvard University Press, 2007), 26–7.
[52] *Ibid.*, at 86.   [53] *Ibid.*, at 45.
[54] Dworkin, 'Playing God: Genes, Clones and Luck', in *Sovereign Virtue* (Cambridge, MA: Harvard University Press, 2000), 446.

argues that human nature is not to be found in humility, as Sandel suggests, but in precisely the opposite; that it is our willingness to challenge our limitations that defines us as a species:

> Playing God is indeed playing with fire. But that is what we mortals have done since Prometheus, the patron saint of dangerous discovery. We play with fire and take the consequences, because the alternative is cowardice in the face of the unknown.[55]

For Dworkin, then, human dignity as human nature is not a constraint to technological advancement but an encouragement. This is an understanding of human nature shared by many transhumanists – a movement that seeks to overcome the limitations of the human condition and transform humans into 'post-humans'. As one transhumant enthusiast puts it, what makes humans special is that we 'are creatures that can imagine themselves to be other than they are'.[56]

Whether human nature is used as a constraining or empowering marker, it has been confined largely to debates concerning the biotech revolution that will continue to unfold throughout this century. However, as Francis Fukuyama stresses:

> In speaking about the biotech revolution, it is important to remember that we are talking about something much broader than genetic engineering. What we are living through today is not simply a technological revolution in our ability to decode and manipulate DNA, but a revolution in the underlying science of biology. This scientific revolution draws on findings and advances in a number of related fields besides molecular biology, including cognitive neuroscience, population genetics, behaviour genetics, psychology, anthropology, evolutionary biology, and neuropharmacology. All of these areas of scientific advance have potential political implications, because they enhance our knowledge of, and hence our ability to manipulate, the source of all human behaviour, the brain.[57]

The fields of science, then, involved in this biotech revolution are many. Moreover, as the century advances, developments both in nanotechnology, particularly in relation to medical science, and in robotics are equally likely to challenge our understanding of what it is to be human.[58] The internet, too, is raising concerns about altering our human functioning, if not our nature.[59]

Ultimately, whatever foundation one chooses, an appeal to human dignity is based upon the idea that there is something that all humans share by virtue

---

[55] *Ibid.*

[56] Patrick D. Hopkins, 'A Moral Vision of Transhumanism', *Journal of Evolution and Technology*, 19(1) (2008), 3, 3

[57] Fukuyama, *Our Posthuman Future*, 19.

[58] See as one example of the impact of robots on human nature, Sherry Turkle, *Alone Together: Why We Expect More from Technology and Less from Each Other* (New York: Basic Books, 2011).

[59] See, for example, Nicholas Carr, *The Shallows: How the Internet Is Changing the Way We Read, Think and Remember* (London: Atlantic Books, 2010).

of being human, some species-typical characteristics that are threatened by technological developments. For those who argue from the first position we considered – dignity as autonomy – those characteristics relate simply to our ability to make decisions about our lives for ourselves; for those who believe in a deity, that shared characteristic is that we are all made in the image of God; for those who appeal to human nature as a boundary, what human beings share is an identity that is predicated upon an understanding that entails that we are not the product of a third party intervention but are open to the boundlessness of the human condition. For Dworkin the characteristic that we share, that defines our dignity, is a 'sacred-ness' that combines the natural and the human:

> The idea that each individual human life is inviolable is ... rooted ... in two combined and intersecting bases of the sacred: natural *and* human creation. Any human creature, even the most immature embryo, is a triumph of divine or evolutionary creation, which produces a complex, reasoning being from, as it were, nothing.[60]

Whether one views the 'natural' as secular or divine, or whether one takes a romantic or conservative view of human existence, and where one locates the balance between them will determine what one means by the appeal to 'human dignity' as a boundary of ethical legitimacy.

3 The harm calculus

In the UK House of Commons Science and Technology Committee's 2005 report on the regulation of human reproductive technologies, the Committee stated:

> Many of the decisions about what to regulate or to legislate depend on the approach taken with regard to the balance of harm and benefit or potential harm and potential benefit. It has become fashionable to specify that authorities (whether that be Governments, agencies, industry, watchdogs etc) should take a 'precautionary approach' or adopt the 'precautionary principle'. This means different things to different pressure groups, and to different sides of the argument. In respect of medical advances it has never meant 'proceed only where there is evidence of no harm'. If it did many of the advances would never be made. In medical research practice it means proceeding through carefully regulated and tightly overseen research stages, requiring – among other things – vigilance and peer review. In clinical practice it means proceed cautiously and in a manner amenable to ethical oversight and clinical audit while there is no evidence of sufficiently serious harm or potential harm to outweigh benefit or potential benefit, while being vigilant in looking for unintended and otherwise adverse outcomes.[61]

---

[60] Dworkin, *Life's Dominion*, 83.

[61] House of Commons Science and Technology Committee, *Human Reproductive Technologies and the Law*, Fifth Report of Session 2004–5, vol. 1, 22, para. 47.

The approach articulated by the Committee is one in which it is the balance between harm and benefit – the classic utilitarian calculus[62] – that not only determines the purpose of regulation but also therefore marks the legitimacy boundary. Although the Committee's report is controversial for the way in which it formulated and applied the precautionary principle (see Chapter 6), the harm calculus is found at the heart of many other attempts at articulating the aim of technology regulation, whether in bioscience or in the emerging field of nanotechnology. The 2000 Cartagena Protocol on Biosafety – part of the Convention on Biological Diversity concerned with the safe handling and transport of living modified organisms (LMOs) across international borders – espouses an almost identical understanding of the underlying purpose of the agreement as being one of balancing harm against benefit.[63] The preamble stresses as motivation for the Convention that the state parties are:

> *Aware* of the rapid expansion of modern biotechnology and the growing public concern over its potential adverse effects on biological diversity, taking also into account risks to human health,
> *Recognizing* that modern biotechnology has great potential for human well-being if developed and used with adequate safety measures for the environment and human health.

For those for whom utilitarianism forms their main normative framework, therefore, while questions of human dignity determine that the happiness of each individual human is of value, the legitimacy of regulation is judged solely on the basis of whether it contributes to the maximisation of human well-being. In setting out his case for human enhancement as a moral obligation, John Harris dismisses both attempts to distinguish between enhancement and therapy, as well as alternative efforts to ground arguments for human enhancement:

> The moral question is and remains: how beneficial will be the proposed enhancements and whether or not the risks of achieving them are worth running for individuals or societies? The moral imperative is the safety of the people and the duty to compare risks with benefits, not on the basis of the normality of the risks nor of the benefits, nor on the basis of the contribution to equality of opportunity, but on the basis of the magnitude and probability, on whether they will save life, or what is the same thing, postpone death and on how much harm and suffering may be prevented or avoided by the enhancements in question.[64]

---

[62] J. S. Mill, *Utilitarianism, On Liberty and Considerations on Representative Government* (London: Dent, 1993), ch. 1, para. 9. For a helpful introduction and analysis of Mill's statement, see John Stanton-Ife, 'The Limits of Law', in Edward N. Zalta (ed.), *Stanford Encyclopaedia of Philosophy* (winter 2008 edn); available online at: http://plato.stanford.edu/archives/win2008/entries/law-limits (last accessed 30 June 2011).

[63] The Cartagena Protocol on Biosafety to the Convention on Biological Diversity, Montreal, 29 January 2000, 2226 UNTS 208.

[64] John Harris, 'Enhancements Are a Moral Obligation', in J. Savulescu and N. Bostrom (eds.), *Human Enhancement* (Oxford: Oxford University Press, 2009), 151.

Key boundary-marking concepts

As Harris makes clear, from such a perspective the weighing up of harm against benefit – the harm calculus – will function as the primary boundary marker.

What this might mean in the area of the creation of embryos for use in stem cell research has been considered by Brownsword:

> First, utilitarians would surely accept efficiency arguments in favour of prioritizing the use of embryos that are surplus to requirement in IVF programmes and that will have to be destroyed anyway. Not only would it seem wasteful not to use such supernumerary embryos before turning to other sources, it might also chime in with public preferences and sentiment. Against such utilities, there might be deficits if the embryos that are available to be sourced from IVF programmes are lower grade and not optimal for stem cell research ...
>
> Secondly, if the regulatory position prohibits the creation of embryos specifically for research, this might prove a serious obstacle to stem cell research which relies on specially designed embryos as its research tools. To be sure, stem cell research would not grind to a standstill: therapies might be developed using adult stem cells (or even foetal stem cells); stem cell lines might be imported; and there would still be supernumerary embryos available for research. Nevertheless, if the prohibition seriously interferes with research, utilitarians would need some convincing that it makes sense ...
>
> Thirdly, what would utilitarians make of the twin constraints of *necessity* (meaning that the research cannot be carried out without using human embryos – in particular, that it cannot be conducted using non-human animals) and *proportionality* (meaning that human embryos should not be used for 'trivial' research purposes, such as, to take the standard example, research into baldness)? On the face of it, neither restriction would make immediate sense. If research on human embryos causes no distress [eds.: at least not to the embryo], while research on animals causes distress ... utilitarians surely would be quick to point out that the argument of necessity cuts in the wrong direction. They would also resist the intuition that so-called 'trivial' research purposes should be excluded. If undertaking such research generates more utility than not doing so, the argument of proportionality tries to rewrite the basic arithmetic of utilitarian calculation.[65]

However, the weighing up of harm and happiness (or benefit) is not only a boundary marker for those who make utilitarianism their main normative perspective. Despite their strong insistence on support for what van den Daele has called a liberal regime of innovation,[66] the House of Commons Committee is not suggesting that it is *only* the benefit–harm balance that forms the decisive marker of legitimacy: in the extract presented above, the Committee also refers to 'ethical oversight', suggesting that a normative perspective other than the pragmatic utilitarianism that dominates the report forms an additional part of the legitimacy test for regulation in this area. It is important to ensure that harm

---

[65] Brownsword, *Rights*, 52–3.
[66] Wolfgang van den Daele, 'Access to New Technology: In Defense of the Liberal Regime of Innovation', in Goodwin *et al.*, *Dimensions*.

is minimised and benefit maximised, the Committee is saying, but in an overall context in which other ethical perspectives set the normative framework.

Yet while there is agreement across normative frameworks on the importance of minimising harm, differences arise in determining what it means to say that someone has been harmed. Utilitarians are likely to interpret harm in a minimalistic manner; deontologists in an expansive fashion, for example, so as to include the harm done to human dignity. While the definition of harm is a central question of moral and political philosophy, in the context of technology regulation the harm calculus is most frequently defined as a balance of more or less suffering. Where the suffering to, for example, an embryo is limited, and where the possibilities that stem cell research offer to reduce suffering are weighed together, the harm calculus comes down in favour of stem cell research. Defined in such a way, harm will include, as discussed in Chapter 6 in the context of precautionary prudence, injury to the essential conditions of human existence, such as access to food, or the sustainability of the natural environment. It can also thus include a future element and thus requires the weighing up of short-term benefits over (possible) long-term consequences. Harm is also likely to include, for some, violations of individual human rights. In the context of technology regulation, then, definitions of harm will include not only the unintended consequences of technological developments but also situations in which the failure to develop technological options – such as genetically modified food in the context of a world in which one billion people are severely malnourished – impacts negatively on vital human needs. However, as Brownsword reminds us, there is also an additional category of harm that is arguably specific to the far-reaching consequences of technology, in particular biotechnology: the intended consequences. Interpreting Fukuyama's fears about the biotech revolution, Brownsword writes:

> Paradoxically ... the hidden danger of biotechnology is not so much an accident waiting to happen when the technology goes wrong but a contextual catastrophe that happens when the technology works – that is, when the scientific assessment is that the technology is 'safe' and 'reliable', we are most at risk.[67]

Moreover, our understanding of what constitutes harm in the technology context also requires us to address questions of whether non-existent persons can suffer harm.[68]

The question of what can be thrown into the harm calculus remains a non-exhaustive and uneasy one. The filtering techniques used by a UK-based telecoms company, BT, to prevent its users accessing child pornography websites is likely to be a relatively uncontroversial restriction on individual autonomy for

---

[67] Roger Brownsword, 'Biotechnology and Rights: Where Are We Coming from and Where Are We Going?', in Mathias Klang and Andrew Murray (eds.), *Human Rights in the Digital Age* (Abingdon: Routledge-Cavendish, 2005), 220.

[68] For more on the non-identity problem, see Derek Parfitt, *Reasons and Persons* (Oxford: Clarendon Press, 1987).

the sake of preventing harm to others, particularly given that those others are children.[69] The Chinese government uses the same balancing technique to justify its decision to block access to certain searches such as 'Tiananmen Square', on Google's Chinese-language site by adding the welfare of the Chinese people in the onward march of economic progress to the scales. Against such a measure, the autonomy of individuals to explore China's recent past is drowned out. Harm also does not include the societal costs of innovation. The liberal capitalist framework of western societies views the loss of thousands of jobs as a consequence of technological progress that brings greater levels of efficiency in industry as a permissible, even desirable, cost to those individuals, their families and communities. As such, the damage done in this way by technological developments is not viewed by the mainstream as harm within the concept of the boundary-marking harm calculus. Yet, the interests taken into account in the harm calculus may be more than simply human interests. As we saw in Chapter 1 with the example of the Harvard Onco-mouse, the possible distress to the mouse was an important element in the harm calculus undertaken by the patent officer. Harm to the mouse was thus influential in determining the limits of patent regulation.[70] At the same time, however, western societies are becoming increasingly conservative about the level of risk they are willing to tolerate.[71] The fluctuating trends of contemporary society – towards globalisation; against risk – will thus affect what weighs in the harm balance and in which direction the scales tilt.

Moreover, what constitutes suffering, and how we thus view 'benefit', are likely to be viewed differently beyond western normative frames. Ryuichi Ida, a Japanese scholar, has argued that what may be intuitive for western culture, such as ethical welfare arguments for the use of technology for human improvement, is alien to non-western cultures.[72] Ida's description of the approach to human enhancement from the perspective of Japanese culture highlights the culturally specific nature of definitions of what constitutes benefit or harm:

> A human being may be improved in two ways, extrinsic and intrinsic. The first is by way of scientific or technological means. This improvement is extrinsic and artificial. The body of the human being is just an object of change. Such improvement, if this counts as improvement, generates a materialistic attitude to human beings, because here the body is granted only instrumental value. A dualism of body and soul is assumed, with the soul seen as the core of the value of human existence, and the body as merely a kind of material.

---

[69] Examples taken from T. J. Mcintyre and Colin Scott, 'Internet Filtering: Rhetoric, Legitimacy, Accountability and Responsibility', in Roger Brownsword and Karen Yeung (eds.), *Regulating Technologies* (Oxford: Hart, 2008), 109. See also Ronald J. Deibert and Nart Villeneuve, 'Firewalls and Power: An Overview of Global State Censorship of the Internet', in Klang and Murray, *Human Rights*, 111–26.

[70] See Chapter 1, 6–12; also Brownsword, *Rights*, ch. 7, for further discussion.

[71] See Antony Giddens, 'Risk and Responsibility', *Modern Law Review*, 62 (1999), 1–10.

[72] Ryuichi Ida, 'Should We Improve Human Nature? An Interrogation from an Asian Perspective', in Savulescu and Boston, *Human Enhancement*, 59–70.

Another way of improvement is improvement through daily effort and training. This improvement is intrinsic. Here the body and the soul are integrated in the existence of the human person. The body is trained by the will to improve in the case of physical improvement, and in the case of intellectual improvement, the will itself is the most important factor. There is no intervention from outside.

Needless, to say, the former conception of improvement is not easily accepted by the Japanese people and some other Asians. Japanese people and some Asian peoples have a long history of a lifestyle dominated by agriculture which is always conditioned by Nature. Climate, soil, water, and minding the plants, these elements are associated in their life. Crops are deemed as presents or grace from Nature. People believe that humans are *allowed* to live, and do not live only by themselves. From the standpoint of such a conception of life, it is hard to think that humans could change or improve nature.[73]

From this perspective, humans are harmed not helped by enhancement that takes them beyond their place in the natural world.

Ultimately, the harm calculus as a boundary marker cuts both ways: it requires the state to weigh up the interference with individual autonomy caused by regulation against positive obligations upon the state to minimise suffering. The harm calculus thus functions in a way similar to human rights, a point we pick up again in Chapter 9.

4 Enacting equal concern: fairness, non-discrimination and equal access

In making the case for the continuing relevance of equality as a political ideal, Ronald Dworkin has argued that 'No government is legitimate that does not show equal concern for the fate of all those citizens over whom it claims dominion and from whom it claims allegiance.'[74] It is this idea of equal concern that forms our third boundary marker. In the ground-breaking 2000 book by Allen Buchanan *et al.*, the authors argue that genetic engineering is not objectionable and may even be morally required *provided* that the benefits and burdens are fairly distributed. Buchanan enumerates the challenges to equality posed by genetic engineering:

> The genetic revolution in molecular biology will not benefit all equally, and some may in fact be greatly disadvantaged by particular applications of genetic science … Many of the distributive issues are near-term and quite tangible. They include:
>
> - Whether it is just to exclude individuals from employment or from health, life or disability insurance if they are known to have genetic diseases or genetic factors that predispose them to diseases
> - Whether it is just for only those who can afford genetic services to have access to them, especially since much of the initial research that led to these services was publicly funded

---

[73] *Ibid.*, at 64.   [74] Dworkin, *Sovereign Virtue*, 1.

- Whether the right to health care includes entitlements to genetic enhancements as well as treatment and prevention of diseases
- Whether international distributive justice requires that the fruits of genetic science (in medicine and agriculture in particular) be shared with those in poorer countries ...
- Whether the direction of genetic research and development should be shaped by expected market demands, as opposed to having ethical principles determine priorities (e.g. channelling funds to cure devastating diseases that afflict large numbers of people rather than to the enhancement of normal traits for the rich ... such as baldness ...)[75]

However, Buchanan's main focus is not on the challenges posed to our present understanding of equality or of justice by the genetic revolution but the potential for large-scale genetic interventions to expand radically our conceptions of what justice requires. These technologies may demand that natural as well as social assets be included among the goods that are to be distributed across society. In exploring this theme, Buchanan calls for a 'genetic decent minimum' to be ensured to all:

the fact of value pluralism and the fact that the value of traits is relevant to social conditions call for caution about any commitment to genetic equality – and perhaps point towards a more modest goal. At least for the foreseeable future (if not forever), the appropriate objective, from the standpoint of both the brute luck conception of equal opportunity and resource egalitarianism, may be something more like the attainment of a 'genetic decent minimum' – to the extent that this can be identified with a reasonable degree of consensus – than the elimination of all inequalities in natural assets.

In practice, this would mean a strong societal commitment to use advances in genetic intervention to prevent or ameliorate the most serious disabilities that limit individuals' opportunities.[76]

Thus the moral restriction on genetic engineering for the authors is not one of human dignity, nor of harm versus benefit, but one of equal access. Whether the regulation of genetic engineering is legitimate will therefore depend upon whether the government discharges its duty of equal concern by ensuring that the costs and benefits are distributed equally across society.

A similar concern motivates Dworkin's consideration of how best to regulate the issue of genetic testing for inherited diseases:

Critics of genetic testing have cited various kinds of harm that might result from dissemination of test results. If it is widely known that someone will die early or is particularly vulnerable to a particular disease, others will treat that person differently in consequence. They will regard marriage, and may even regard friendship, with such a person as less attractive, for example. At the opposite extreme,

---

[75] Allen Buchanan, Dan W. Brock, Norman Daniels and Daniel Wikler, *From Chance to Choice. Genetics and Justice* (Cambridge: Cambridge University Press, 2000), 61–2.

[76] *Ibid.*, at 81–2.

people may be overly solicitous or attentive, and this behaviour might be equally undesirable. In some cases, particularly in those of employers and insurers, the consequences might be financial and devastating: someone might be unemployable, at any rate in a preferred occupation, or uninsurable, except perhaps at discriminating and prohibitive rates, in consequence of what others know about his genes. How far are these devastating consequences fair?

We should begin by recognizing that the unfairness, if any, is already part of our lives. People who are visibly disabled suffer social and emotional harm in consequence, and employers and insurance companies have a right to ask for, and act on the basis of, much information about medical history. Nevertheless access to a complete genetic profile or even selective information about genetic disposition to cancer, heart disease, aggressive behaviour or, so long as the AIDS epidemic continues, sexual orientation would measurably increase many people's vulnerability to different forms of discrimination.[77]

For this reason, then, while Dworkin argues that we should allow individuals to choose for themselves whether they have themselves or their children tested for genetic illnesses, he calls for appropriate regulation to protect against the dissemination of that information and the discrimination that would likely result. The aim is not only to ensure that vulnerability to discrimination is minimised but that the costs of the misfortune of inheriting a genetic disease or condition are spread across society rather than borne solely by the individual concerned.

Concerns about non-discrimination make an appearance, too, in the context of embryo selection and genetic manipulation, where the charge is one of eugenical engineering. In its 'Instruction *Dignitas Personae* on Certain Bioethical Questions', the Catholic Church voices its objection to pre-implantation diagnosis in part because of the discriminatory consequences of embryo selection:

> Preimplantation diagnosis is … the expression of a eugenic mentality that 'accepts selective abortion in order to prevent the birth of children affected by various types of anomalies. Such an attitude is shameful and utterly reprehensible, since it presumes to measure the value of a human life only within the parameters of "normality" and physical well-being, thus opening the way to legitimizing infanticide and euthanasia as well.'[78]

Similar concerns have been voiced by Japanese scholars. In a fascinating contribution on Japanese scholarship on prenatal screening for Down's syndrome, Susumu Shimazono notes the calls for prudence in instituting wide-scale screening. The survey suggests support for the idea that wide-scale screening creates a eugenic attitude in which children with Down's syndrome are seen as less worthy

---

[77] Dworkin, 'Playing God', 433–4. See also, Janneke H. Gerards, Aalt-Willem Heringa and Heleen L. Jannsen, *Genetic Discrimination and Genetic Privacy in a Comparative Perspective* (Antwerp and London: Intersentia, 2005).

[78] Congregation for the Doctrine of the Faith, *Instruction*, ch. 22. The citation within this extract from the *Instruction* is from John Paul II, Encyclical Letter Evangelium vitae, 63: AAS 87 (1995), 473.

of life, thereby 'enshrining a discriminatory judgement in law as a universal fact'. In Japan, where prenatal screening is not encouraged, there is a much lower rate of selective induced abortion of affected children and no evidence that families containing a Down's syndrome child are less happy. Shimazono notes, highlighting the consequences for individuals of the social harm calculus:

> many disabled people lead happy lives. Few of them deplore their own birth. Why is it considered natural to prevent disabled people from being born? It is because society has created the idea that disabled people should be excluded. This idea is based on a eugenic thought ... Eugenic selection is based on the concept that it is appropriate to exclude the weak artificially from the standpoint of social loss and gain calculation.[79]

This fear has, for some, been realised in the Human Fertilisation and Embryology Act 2008. This updating of the UK legislation concerning human-assisted reproduction inserted the provision that embryos known to have a significant risk of 'serious physical or mental disability' or 'serious illness ... must not be preferred to those that are not known to have such an abnormality'. Section 14(4)(9) thus positively prohibits parental selection for an embryo with a disability. This insertion, in combination with the Explanatory Notes that accompanied an earlier version of the Bill, caused outrage among disability advocacy groups, not least among the Deaf community.[80] The Notes made explicit that deafness was to be included in the definition of a serious physical disability, preventing Deaf parents from selecting a child that would share their deafness. However, as Gavaghan suggests, deafness is not 'unambiguously a disability at all', let alone a serious disability.[81] Indeed, many Deaf people view deafness as a minority linguistic culture. The resulting backlash forced the reference to be removed from the Explanatory Notes to the Act, although the provision remained.

While the 2008 Act requires discrimination on the grounds of disability,[82] it elevates the working practice of the Human Fertilisation and Embryology Authority (HFEA) of excluding social gender selection to a legal prohibition. Dworkin explains why it is that we accept the destruction of would-be babies in the normal course of an IVF procedure – because we must choose – but why there is something unsettling about a decision to terminate a pregnancy based upon the gender of the foetus:

> We accept in vitro fertilization as a reproductive technique because we do not believe that it shows disrespect for the human life embodied in one zygote to

---

[79] Susumu Shimazono, 'Reasons Against the Selection of Life: From Japan's Experience of Prenatal Genetic Diagnosis', in Savulescu and Bostrom, *Human Enhancement*, 298. See also, Parfitt, *Reason and Persons*.

[80] For fuller consideration of the impact of Section 14(4)(9), see Colin Gavaghan, 'Regulating after Parfit: Welfare, Identity and the UK Embryology Law', in Goodwin *et al.*, *Dimensions*.

[81] *Ibid.*, at 151.

[82] For the argument in favour of a duty of 'procreative beneficence', see Julian Savulescu, 'Procreative Beneficence: Why We Should Select the Best Children', *Bioethics*, 15 (2001), 413.

allow it to perish when the process that both created and doomed it also produces a flourishing human life that would not otherwise have existed. When one zygote has already been implanted, a decision to terminate its life because it is female shows a disdain for its life, because the question is then whether a single, isolated human life will continue or cease.[83]

The inclusion of social gender selection in the 2008 Act brought it into line with other jurisdictions, which permit the selection of zygotes on grounds of gender where there is a risk of a serious gender-specific illness, but do not permit either embryo selection or pregnancy terminations on gender grounds alone. The Oviedo Convention on Human Rights and Biomedicine[84] contains such a prohibition, as does the 1994 Indian Pre-natal Diagnostic Techniques (Regulation and Prevention of Misuse) Act (PNDT), as amended in 2002. According to its preamble, the main purpose of the Indian Act is:

> to provide for the prohibition of sex selection, before or after conception, and for regulation of pre-natal diagnostic techniques for the purposes of detecting genetic abnormalities or metabolic disorders or chromosomal abnormalities or certain congenital malformations or sex-linked disorders and for the prevention of their misuse for sex determination leading to female feticide.

However, discrimination concerns arise not only in the context of biotech developments. Similar worries have been articulated in the area of data profiling. The unprecedented level of information that is collected and stored about us as data is increasingly used to generate profiles that can be exploited both by public authorities and private actors to determine not only our shopping preferences but also our risk factors across a whole range of areas. These profiles can also be used to differentiate the services offered to individuals, all of which may have the effect of discriminating against us.[85]

Yet, while gender constitutes a protected ground and thus discrimination on gender grounds forms a boundary marker in the UK and India, as in many other jurisdictions, in the context of embryo selection, the same is not the case for disability. Non-discrimination is thus not a boundary marker across all grounds usually protected in all circumstances.[86] Nonetheless, it can, for example in access to life-saving medical techniques, mark a formidable legitimacy boundary; we may accept that access to expensive new techniques may need to be rationed, but we would not accept decisions concerning rationing

---

[83] Dworkin, 'Playing God', 433.

[84] Council of Europe Convention on Human Rights and Biomedicine, ETS no. 164, Oviedo, 4 April 1997.

[85] These issues are discussed in Bart Custers, *The Power of Knowledge: Ethical, Legal, and Technological Aspects of Data Mining* (Nijmegen: Wolf Publishing, 2004); Mireille Hildebrandt and Bert-Jaap Koops, 'The Challenges of Ambient Law and Legal Protection in the Profiling Era', *Modern Law Review*, 73(3) (2010), 428–60.

[86] Those grounds, under European Union law, are sex, racial or ethnic origin, religion or belief, disability, age or sexual orientation (Article 19 Treaty on the Functioning of the European Union).

to be made on grounds of religion, racial or ethnic origin, sexual orientation or gender.

However, equal concern is used as a boundary marker beyond the relatively simple question of discrimination. As Buchanan has suggested, new developments expand our sense of what goods form an indispensable element of distributive justice. To what extent does the requirement of equal concern constitute a positive obligation upon regulators to ensure equal access as a price of legitimacy? The 1992 Convention on Biological Diversity, for example, has as one of its central motivations concerns about equal access. Article 1 provides:

> Article 1. Objectives
> The objectives of this Convention ... are the conservation of biological diversity, the sustainable use of its components and the fair and equitable sharing of the benefits arising out of the utilization of genetic resources, including by appropriate access to genetic resources and by appropriate transfer of relevant technologies.[87]

What we see in practice, however, is that it is once technology has reached a sufficient degree of societal uptake or normality that questions of equal access arise. This is visible in debates about internet access expressed as concern about the digital divide. A 2009 decision by the French Constitutional Council struck down a law that would allow access to the internet to be switched off to those who repeatedly indulged in illegal downloading.[88] Although the decision was largely motivated by concerns about freedom of speech and presumption of innocence,[89] access to the internet is increasingly viewed as an essential human need. Where access to a technology comes to be viewed as normal, equal access will arise as a boundary-marking consideration. This is what we see expressed as concerns about the 'digital divide'.[90] However, even where a technology has not yet established itself as a part of everyday life, concern about equal access was shown to be a key consideration of legitimacy for public consultation exercises carried out for the UK government in relation to

---

[87] Convention on Biological Diversity, Rio de Janeiro, 1992; 1760 UNTS 79.

[88] Conseil Constitutionnel, Decision no. 2009–580 of 10 June 2009. Access to the internet is already considered a fundamental right in Estonia, Costa Rica, Finland, Greece and Spain. The UN Special Rapporteur on the promotion and protection of the right to freedom of opinion and expression Frank La Rue recently noted that internet access is 'an essential part' of realising basic human rights and stressed the urgency of wealthy states fulfilling their commitment to close the global digital divide. Report of the Special Rapporteur on the promotion and protection of the right to freedom of opinion and expression, Frank La Rue, Human Rights Council Seventeenth session, A/HRC/17/27, 16 May 2011.

[89] A revised version of the French bill requiring court approval for denial of access was accepted by the Conseil Constitutionnel in October 2009.

[90] See Report of the Special Rapporteur on the promotion and protection of the right to freedom of opinion and expression. Also, P. DiMaggio and E. Hargittai, 'From the "Digital Divide" to "Digital Inequality"', Working Paper No. 15, Princeton University Center for Arts and Cultural Policy Studies, 2001. R. Mansell, 'Digital Opportunities and the Missing Link for Developing Countries', Oxford Review of Economic Policy, 17(2) (2001), 282.

the development of nanotechnology. The report on the findings of these consultations notes:

> Public participants ... expressed concern that the development of nanotechnologies in the UK would benefit only the manufacturing industries and professionals not the poor or unemployed. There were also concerns that any potential risks associated with nanotechnologies would disproportionately affect poor and marginalised people in the UK or abroad.[91]

Equal concern thus was applied not only to the poor and marginalised at home but also beyond the borders of the national political community.

5 Nature

The use of nature as a moral boundary marker against technological developments expresses a number of interconnected ideas. It can relate to concern about harm to the environment, thus an inclusion of environmental issues such as sustainability and the possibility of a human future on earth in the weighing of the harm calculus. It can also reflect an expression of human dignity, part of an understanding of human nature as one in which we seek to understand our place as a species in the world.[92] The concept of nature can also express a duty-based approach, both secular and religious, in which human action is limited by the duties we bear as stewards of the earth.[93] However, it can also – in an approach that less obviously places us at the centre of the world – reflect the desire to live in harmony with our environment. It is this latter use of nature – in which nature is valued for its own sake and not simply for the role it plays in sustaining human life or species status – that warrants its inclusion in a list of key boundary markers.

This idea of nature has been articulated by Ronald Dworkin in his exploration of the sacred:

> we tend to treat distinct animal species (though not individual animals) as sacred. We think it very important, and worth considerable economic expense, to protect endangered species from destruction at human hands or by a human enterprise – a market in rhinoceros tusks, valued for their supposed aphrodisiac power; dams that threaten the only habitat of a certain species of fish; or timbering practices that will destroy the last horned owls. We are upset – it would be terrible if the rhinoceros ceased to exist ... Someone might say: we protect endangered species because we want the pleasure of continuing to see animals of each species, or because we want the useful information we might gain by studying them, or

---

[91] Involve, *Democratic Technologies? The Final Report of the Nanotechnology Engagement Group (NEG)* (2007), prepared on behalf of the UK government, ch. 3.2.2, 40; available online at www.involve.org.uk/wp-content/uploads/2011/03/Democratic-Technologies.pdf

[92] See, for example, the reflection on Asian perspectives on nature and human beings in the context of human enhancement, Ida, 'Should We Improve Human Nature?', 63–7.

[93] For example, Donald Bruce and Ann Bruce (eds.), *Engineering Genesis: Ethics and the GM Revolution* (2nd edn, London: Earthscan, 2003). Also, Kateb, *Human Dignity*.

because it is more interesting for us that there be more rather than fewer species. But none of these arguments rings true. Many – perhaps most – of the people who consider endangered species important are unlikely to ever encounter any of the animals they want to protect. I doubt that many who have labored to protect the horned owl have any plans to visit the habitat of those birds or to look them up in zoos, nor do I think they believe that in keeping horned owls alive we will learn enough useful information to justify the expense. These people struggle to protect the species simply because they think it would be a shame if human acts and decisions caused it to disappear ... this is another example of something many of us take to be of intrinsic rather than instrumental value. It is also an example of sacred rather than incremental value: few people think that the world would be worse if there had been fewer species of birds, and few would think it important to engineer new bird species if that were possible. What we believe important is not that there be any particular number of species but that a species that now exists not be extinguished by us. We consider it a kind of cosmic shame when a species that nature has developed ceases, through human actions, to exist.[94]

This notion of the sacred as attaching to the natural world can be seen in discussions on the regulation of technological advances in the fields of nanotechnology but is most visible in the area of bioscience. Here, nature acts as a powerful boundary marker for environmentalists and green sympathisers in particular; but it is also an important element in mainstream discussions. It has become commonplace, for example, to view the indigenous way of life as inherently superior to industrial and post-industrial societies because they are believed to live in harmony with nature.[95]

A further example is provided by a remarkable series of reports by the Swiss Federal Committee on Non-Human Biotechnology (ECNH), created in 1998 to advise federal and cantonal authorities on the ethics of regulation with regard to non-human biotechnology. The Committee's 2008 report, *The Dignity of Living Beings with Regard to Plants*,[96] concluded the following points in relation to the handling of plants:

1. Arbitrariness:
   The Committee members **unanimously** consider an arbitrary harm caused to plants to be morally impermissible. This kind of treatment would include, e.g. decapitation of wild flowers at the roadside without rational reason.
2. Instrumenalisation:
   For the **majority** the complete instrumentalisation of plants – as a collective, as a species, or as individuals – requires moral justification.

---

[94] Dworkin, *Life's Dominion*, 75.
[95] Graham Dutfield, 'Should We Regulate Biotechnology through the Patent System? The Case of Terminator Technology', in Han Somsen (ed.), *The Regulatory Challenge of Biotechnology* (Cheltenham: Edward Elgar, 2007), 203. Also, R. Lawrence Barsh, 'Indigenous Peoples: An Emerging Object of International Law', *American Journal of International Law*, 80 (1986), 369.
[96] Federal Ethics Committee on Non-Human Biotechnology, *The Dignity of Living Beings with Regard to Plants: Moral Consideration of Plants for Their Own Sake* (2008); available online at www.ekah. admin.ch/en/topics/dignity-of-livingbeings/index.html (last accessed 22 August 2011).

3. Ownership of plants:

For the **majority** here too, plants – as a collective, as a species, or as individuals – are excluded for moral reasons from absolute ownership. By this interpretation no one may handle plants entirely according to his/her own desires. A **minority** concludes that no limits apply to handling plants insofar as they are property.

4. Genetic modification:

According to the **majority** position, there is nothing to contradict the idea of dignity of living beings in the genetic modification of plants, as long as their independence, i.e. reproductive ability and adaptive ability are ensured. Social–ethical limits on genetic modification of plants may exist, but are not the subject of this discussion.

5. Patenting:

For the **majority** the ethical justification of patenting plants is a question of social ethics. It is not one involving the consideration of plants *for their own sake* and therefore not the object of this discussion either. For a **minority** the patenting of plants as such is morally impermissible and contradicts the dignity of living beings with regard to plants.

6. Diversity:

Genetic modification of plants should, in the **majority** opinion, always involve consideration of conserving and safeguarding the natural, i.e. not man-made, network of relationships.

7. Proportionality:

A **majority** considers any action with or towards plants that serves the self-preservation of humans to be morally justified, as long as it is appropriate and follows the principle of precaution.

The Committee's conclusions, concerned with ensuring the dignity of plants and their ability to continue an independent existence, shows how the idea of nature can form a strong boundary marker in the field of biotechnology.

A more visible way in which nature is also used as a boundary marker is where technological developments are labelled, and thus condemned, as 'unnatural'. Here, nature as a whole, as opposed to individual animal species or humankind's species identity, is treated as sacred and such arguments can function in a similar way to human dignity-based assertions, i.e. as conversation stoppers. A Europe-wide research project examining public attitudes to agricultural biotechnology at the beginning of this century found that the many publics of the European Union generally viewed GMOs as 'unnatural' and thus undesirable:

GMOs were indeed frequently characterised as 'unnatural' by focus group participants. They expressed the feeling that directly modifying the genome was qualitatively different from any previously used technique. A common viewpoint was that we have previously only been crossing already existing organisms, while we are now also creating novel life-forms that would not have existed otherwise.

Thus, genetic engineering techniques were described as 'pushing Nature beyond its limits', and were thought to 'upset the equilibrium of Nature'. This was related to the idea that scientists do not know or understand the full extent of their work, and cannot anticipate the long-term consequences of their actions on ecosystems, human health and social relations. It was in this sense that participants spoke of 'playing God', describing those involved in the creation and management of GMOs as 'sorcerers' apprentices'.[97]

However, research by the CESC into public attitudes towards GMOs in the UK found that, while participants were indeed likely to reject the use of GMOs in food or agriculture as unnatural, they were less likely to hold that view where GMOs were used in the development of new medical products.[98] This difference in approach depending upon whether the use was in food production or healthcare suggests that the majority of the public use the concept of nature as a boundary marker but in a way that is more pragmatic than the dramatic nature of much discourse about GMOs suggests.

6 Property

In his *Two Treatise of Government*, Locke argued that man possesses certain rights that are independent of the laws governing any particular society. These natural rights were life, liberty and property.[99] Property is increasingly used alongside or in place of privacy to determine the frame within which activities in relation to our personal data are legitimate, for example.[100] As Julie Cohen has suggested, 'property talk' is one of the key ways in which we express matters of great importance to us.[101] Similarly, property – in the form of intellectual property – constitutes a powerful boundary marker in our present global political constellation in our ideas about what we can do with technology.[102] The belief that ideas and inventions are the exclusive property of the inventor is used to place strict limits on the free exchange of technology and technological blueprints. So powerful is the notion of ownership in the form of intellectual property that we accept the prioritising of

---

[97] Claire Marris, 'Public Views on GMOs: Deconstructing the Myths', *EMBO Rep.*, 2(7) (2001), 545–8, 546. For the full findings, see CSEC, 'Public Attitudes to Agricultural Biotechnologies in Europe: Final Report of PABE Project' (CSEC, Lancaster University, 2001).

[98] ESRC, *The Politics of GM Food. Risk, Science and Public Trust*, Special Briefing No. 5, October 1999, 9. See also CSEC, 'Public Attitudes'.

[99] John Locke, *Two Treatise of Government*, ed. P. Laslett (Cambridge: Cambridge University Press, 1988).

[100] Lawrence Lessig, 'Privacy as Property', *Social Research*, 69 (2002), 255. Also, Nadezhda Purtova, 'Property rights in personal data: a European perspective' (Uitgeverij BOXPress); thesis defended Tilburg University 2011.

[101] Julie Cohen, 'Examined Lives: Informational Privacy and the Subject as Object', *Stanford Law Review*, 52 (2000), 1378.

[102] See the collection by Keith E. Maskus and Jerome H. Reichman (eds.), *International Public Goods and Transfer of Technology Under a Globalized Intellectual Property Regime* (Cambridge: Cambridge University Press, 2005).

these rights over the basic needs of other human beings, such as access to food and to medicine.

The use of property as a boundary marker is also increasingly coming to the fore in biotechnology and, as it does so, it pushes back the boundary of where we have traditionally located human dignity. Ideas of human dignity have in the past prevented consideration of the human body in terms of property. A human body, and the tissues that make it up, lies at the boundary of a person – that cannot be owned[103] – and a thing – that can. However, biotechnological developments are blurring the distinction between human being and object, and property rights are being increasingly employed to determine the boundary of what is acceptable in relation to how we perceive our own bodies and those of others.[104]

A recent case before the Supreme Court of New South Wales, for example, established the right of a widow to possession of her dead husband's sperm.[105] Although legislation in New South Wales prevents Ms Edwards from using the sperm for the purposes of conceiving a child via in vitro fertilisation – because of the lack of written consent on the part of Mr Edwards prior to his death – the Court held that sperm could be conceived of as property and that Ms Edwards was entitled to take possession of it. The Court might have been expected to follow the classic common law precedent laid down in *Williams* v. *Williams* [1882], in which it was established that a man's executors have no property rights over his dead body. Instead of using human dignity as a way of determining the boundary of acceptability, the Court in New South Wales chose property.

Property is a rich and complex legal concept; it includes the right to use or dispose of something, and to prevent others from interfering with it.[106] It is thus more than simply the possession of something but entails a variety, or bundle, of rights that may or not apply in different circumstances according to the various relationships concerned. Ownership and possession are thus different concepts under property law; although one may have possession of something, one does not necessarily own it and is therefore bound by the rights of the owners in one's enjoyment of possession. This will limit, for example, one's rights to transfer or sell the object of the right. In the case of Ms Edwards, her successful claim to possession did not entail ownership of her husband's sperm; as a consequence she still required his consent in order to use it for the purpose of conceiving a child (at least, under New South Wales state law).

Who then can claim property rights in this common law example? In *Edwards*, the Court ruled out the notion that Mr Edwards owned his own sperm that could be bequeathed as part of his estate; it also decided that although it

---

[103] See Article 4, Universal Declaration on Human Rights (1948).

[104] See Remigius N. Nwabueze, 'Biotechnology and the Challenge of Property' in Sheila McLean (ed.), *Medical Law and Ethics* (Aldershot: Ashgate, 2007).

[105] *Jocelyn Edwards; Re the estate of the late Mark Edwards* [2011] NSWSC 478.

[106] James Gordley, *Foundations of Private Law: Property, Tort, Contract, Unjust Enrichment* (Oxford: Oxford University Press, 2006).

was possible for the doctors and technicians that removed and stored Mr Edwards' sperm to claim possession, the fact that they acted as agents of Ms Edwards in performing their actions – and thus applying their skill – meant that they did not acquire any proprietary rights themselves.[107] As his widow and as the only person interested in acquiring possession of his sperm, the Court found that Ms Edwards was entitled to its possession. This ruling thus appears to leave open the possibility that where someone other than the deceased's next of kin has an interest in acquiring possession, the Courts will look favourably upon it.[108]

The *Edwards* case concerned ownership over the body tissue of another. As with property rights over another's body, human dignity concerns have similarly limited support for perceiving of our own body in property terms. For example, it is widely recognised that the right to physical integrity does not entail that we have ownership of our own bodies for exploitation for financial gain beyond simple labour. There are few jurisdictions, if any, that allow for the sale of human organs or other body parts.[109] Indeed Article 21 of the Convention on Human Rights and Biomedicine states categorically that 'The human body and its parts shall not, as such, give rise to financial gain.'[110] Here, too, new developments in biomedicine and biotechnology are seeing property come to the fore, pushing aside human dignity as the prime conceptual frame of ethical reasoning.

In *Yearworth*, a 2009 case from England and Wales, the Court of Appeal found unanimously that sperm could be property for the purpose of a negligence claim.[111] This case concerned a negligence suit brought by a group of men against the local health authority for failure to store at the correct temperature sperm that they had donated, causing irreparable damage to the sperm. The

---

[107] *Doodeward* v. *Spence* [1908] HCA 45; (1908) 6 CLR 406. This case created the principle that the lawful exercise of skill upon a human body or body part can entail the creation of possession rights. It has subsequently been applied to grant doctors rights over human tissue extracted during surgery and to sperm that has been extracted and stored. Under *Doodeward*, therefore, property rights can be asserted over human body parts as long as they are not one's own.

[108] This has in fact already happened in another recent Australian case, this time from the Supreme Court of Western Australia. In *Roche* v. *Douglas*, the applicant seeking property rights over the deceased's gametes was unknown to the deceased but sought possession – successfully – in order to be able to determine whether or not she was the dead man's daughter and thus entitled to a claim upon his estate. *Roche* v. *Douglas* [2000] WASC 146.

[109] Stephen Wilkinson, *Bodies For Sale: Ethics and Exploitation in the Human Body Trade* (Abingdon: Routledge, 2003).

[110] Convention for the Protection of Human Rights and Dignity of the Human Being with regard to the Application of Biology and Medicine: Convention on Human Rights and Biomedicine, Oviedo, 1997, ETS no. 164. See also Deryck Beyleveld and Roger Brownsword, 'Articles 21 and 22 of the Convention on Human Rights and Biomedicine: Property and Consent, Commerce and Dignity', in Peter Kemp (ed.), *Research on Basic Ethical Principles in Bioethics and Biolaw* (Copenhagen and Barcelona: Centre for Ethics and Law, 1998).

[111] *Yearworth and Others* v. *North Bristol NHS Trust* [2009] EWCA Civ. 37; [2010] QB 1. However, the origins of the sperm in this case were the applicants themselves, i.e. they were claiming property rights over their own body tissue.

men had donated the sperm prior to cancer treatment, which was likely to leave them infertile. Thus the case concerned property rights over their own body tissue. Acknowledging the problems that such technological developments are creating for the law in this area, the Court noted:

(a) In this jurisdiction developments in medical science require a re-analysis of the common law's treatment of and approach to the issue of ownership of parts or products of a living human being, whether for present purposes (viz an action in negligence) or otherwise.

...

(c) For us the easiest course would be to uphold the claims of the men to have had ownership of the sperm for present purposes by reference to the principle first identified in *Doodeward*'s case (1908) 6 CLR 406. We would have no difficulty in concluding that the unit's storage of the sperm in liquid nitrogen at minus 196 C was an application to the sperm of work and skill which conferred on it a substantially different attribute, namely the arrest of its swift perishability.

(d) However ... we are not content to see the common law in this area founded upon the principle in *Doodeward*'s case, which was advised as an exception to the principle, itself of exceptional character, relating to the ownership of a human corpse. Such ancestry does not commend it as a solid foundation. Moreover a distinction between the capacity to own body parts of products which have, and which have not, been subject to the exercise of work or skill is not entirely logical. Why, for example, should the surgeon presented with a part of the body, for example, a finger which has been amputated in a factory accident, with a view to re-attaching it to the injured hand, but who carelessly damages it before starting the necessary medical procedures, be able to escape liability on the footing that the body part had not been subject to the exercise of work or skill ... ?

As these cases, in line with the much earlier case of *Moore*,[112] suggest, questions of proprietary rights over human tissue concern not only deeply emotional issues but also ones of great commercial consequence. New techniques concerning, for example stem cell storage, as well as the existence of millions of embryos created and stored globally,[113] are likely to increase the weight of assertions of property as the main frame for these questions of ethical legitimacy. Moreover, these cases also suggest that the courts themselves are increasingly willing to acknowledge property rights claims as a boundary marker of acceptability– in interpreting the law relating to the value – both commercial and otherwise – that is contained within our body parts, even for so intimate a body tissue as gametes and where the applicant was unknown to the person whose gametes they are. Given these developments, it seems reasonable to suggest that property will become one of the key markers of this century, at least in common law jurisdictions, as property

[112] *Moore* v. *Regents of the University of California* (1988) 249 Cal Rptr; (1990) 271 Cal Rptr 146, (1990) 793 P2d 479; cert denied (1991) 111 SCt 1388. The Supreme Court of California ruled in this case that Moore could not claim a share of the profits from a highly lucrative cell line developed by his physician from tissue removed as part of his treatment of cancer.

[113] See, for the argument that property rights have an important place in determining the status of embryos, Jessica Berg, 'Owning Persons: The Application of Property Theory to Embryos and Fetuses', *Wake Forest Law Review*, 40 (2005), 159–219.

pushes back previously accepted understandings about the limitations imposed on accepted understandings of what it is possible to own or possess by human dignity concerns.

7 Privacy

Our sixth and final boundary-marking concept is privacy. Privacy remains a central element of ethical reasoning about technology, despite the increasing shift to property talk. Rapid developments in information and communication technologies allow for the collection and storage of vast quantities of information about us and the minutiae of our lives; we increasingly live in surveillance societies, where that surveillance is conducted by both public and private actors, and in which the threat to our privacy comes at us from all angles. It is no surprise then that privacy is one of the most discussed aspects of technology – from the information that we post about ourselves on social-networking sites to seemingly innocuous (and helpful) developments such as satellite navigation technology in our cars and on our phones.[114]

A good example of the way in which privacy is used as a boundary marker of acceptability is the public debate in the Netherlands about the introduction of smart meters. In a study commissioned by the Dutch Consumer Association, Colette Cuijpers and Bert-Jaap Koops assessed the proposed legislation regulating the introduction of compulsory smart meters against the standard of privacy contained in Article 8 of the European Convention on Human Rights, and found the Bill wanting.[115] In order to work efficiently, smart meters need to make information about their energy consumption available to consumers. The problem for Cuijpers and Koops was that the model proposed would have seen information on, for example, lifestyle patterns, relationships, type of electrical products in a given home, etc. being made available to energy network operators and providers. The possible invasions of privacy enabled by such data were wittily captured in a poster campaign by the civil society group, Loesje: one poster carried the slogan 'My little brother is going to shower for longer in the hope that the controllers think he has a girlfriend'.[116] The result of these privacy-based objections and the campaign of civil society organisations was that the

---

[114] See, from the wealth of literature, Daniel J. Solove, *The Digital Person: Technology and Privacy in the Information Age* (New York: New York University Press, 2004); Helen F. Nissenbaum, *Privacy in Context: Technology, Policy and the Integrity of Social Life* (Stanford: Stanford University Press, 2009); Viktor Mayer-Schönberger, *Delete: The Virtues of Forgetting in the Digital Age* (Princeton: Princeton University Press, 2011).

[115] The study is available in English: Colette Cuijpers and Bert-Jaap Koops, 'The "Smart Meters" Bill: A Privacy Test Based on Article 8 of the ECHR', on file with the authors. See by the same authors, 'Begluren en besturen door slimme energiemeters: een ongerechtvaardige inbreuk op onze privacy', *Privacy en informative*, 1 (2009), 2–8.

[116] 'Mijn broertje gaat langer douchen in de hoop dat de controleurs denken dat hij een vriendinnetje heeft', Loesje poster, March 2009; available online at www.loesje.nl (our translation).

legislation was amended to give households the choice of whether to switch to a smart meter and a choice about the degree of information that is made available to energy providers.[117] In this case, privacy was (more or less) successfully asserted as a boundary marker by the civil society groups and other actors that campaigned against the compulsory introduction of smart meters.

Such is the scale of the challenge to traditional notions of privacy that it is regularly declared to be deceased.[118] Other scholars and commentators put forward the more nuanced claim that how we conceptualise privacy is changing.[119] John Palfrey and Urs Gasser have suggested that the way in which so-called digital natives view what is meant by privacy is fundamentally different from what their parents and grandparents consider to be infringements of privacy. They write:

> The digital age has brought about new incentive [*sic*] to reveal information about oneself (social norms suggest that the more information you reveal, the more friends you will attract) while reducing checks on imprudent behaviour ... In this fast-changing environment, expectations of privacy among young people are shifting.[120]

However, while expectations of privacy appear to be shifting in the younger generation and although we are increasingly turning to property to express the idea that 'something is important', privacy nonetheless remains – at least at present – an important marker for determining questions of legitimacy. We build on this cursory consideration of privacy in the following chapter through the frame of the right to a private life.

It is to the role that human rights play as boundary markers of ethical legitimacy that we now turn.

---

[117] See Colette Cuijpers, 'Slim kiezen bij slimme meters', *Privacy en informatie*, 95 (2011), 131–41.

[118] See, for example, Kieron O'Hara, *The Spy in the Coffee Machine: The End of Privacy as We Know It* (Oxford: Oneworld Publications, 2008); and Simson Garfinkel, *Database Nation: The Death of Privacy in the 21st Century* (Sebastopol, CA: O'Reilly Media, 2000).

[119] See, for example, Debbie V. S. Kasper, 'The Evolution (or Devolution) of Privacy', *Sociological Forum*, 20 (2005), 69–92; also Helen F. Nissenbaum, 'Privacy as Contextual Integrity', *Washington Law Review*, 79 (2004), 119–58.

[120] John Palfrey and Urs Gasser, *Born Digital. Understanding the First Generation of Digital Natives* (New York: Basic Books, 2008), 54.

9

Human rights as boundary markers

1 Introduction

Human rights are increasingly seen as a relevant point of departure in considering the legitimacy of the content and consequences of technology regulation. This is visible not only from the expanding scholarly literature emphasising the human rights perspective on technology but also from the growing number of international documents laying down principles to guide and regulate technological development that are openly based upon human rights norms.

The Universal Declaration on the Human Genome and Human Rights was drawn up in 1997, followed by the International Declaration on Human Genetic Data in 2003 and the Universal Declaration on Bioethics and Human Rights in 2005, for example. Beyond the field of biotechnology, the World Summit on the Information Society, organised under the auspices of the United Nations in 2003, acknowledged the importance of the human rights to freedom of opinion and freedom of expression in ensuring that the benefits of information and communication technologies are equitably shared as well as in protecting against the dangers posed by these technologies. The Summit's Declaration of Principles, articulating a vision of the information society, provide:

> 1 We reaffirm, as an essential foundation of the Information Society, and as outlined in Article 19 of the Universal Declaration of Human Rights, that everyone has the right to freedom of opinion and expression; that this right includes freedom to hold opinions without interference and to seek, receive and impart information and ideas through any media and regardless of frontiers. Communication is a fundamental social process, a basic human need and the foundation of all social organisation. It is central to the information society. Everyone, everywhere should have the opportunity to participate and no one should be excluded from the benefits the Information Society offers.[1]

In addition to these technology specific declarations, concern about the impact of technology regulation or a lack of appropriate regulation has also begun to

---

[1] World Summit on the Information Society Declaration of Principles, 12 December 2003, WSIS-03/GENEVA/DOC/4-E, available online at www.itu.int/wsis/docs/geneva/official/dop. html (last accessed 11 May 2011).

creep into traditional human rights fora. A prohibition on human cloning was included in the European Union Charter of Fundamental Rights and Freedoms, proclaimed in Nice in 2000.[2] Similarly, the challenges and potential opportunities offered by technological developments are increasingly making an impact on the case law of human rights bodies, notably the European Court of Human Rights.[3] At the same time, technology and human rights are increasingly coming together in an explosive way before national courts.

This increasing recourse to human rights law and norms to evaluate and frame technological developments should come as no surprise. As Joseph Raz has remarked, human rights has become our contemporary moral lingua franca.[4] Whether we welcome this development or not – and there are reasons to be hesitant about the related decline in other ways of thinking about legitimacy[5] – human rights exercise a powerful hold on our way of imagining our relations with each other and with authority. Moreover, the importance of a normative language with which we can communicate across borders is unlikely to diminish as this century progresses.

However the connection between human rights and technology regulation is not as straightforward or as uncontroversial as one might expect given the contemporary dominance of the human rights narrative. Introducing an edited collection examining the interaction between human rights and new technologies, Thérèse Murphy has identified the hesitation that many scholars within the field of technology regulation feel about the growing dominance of the human rights voice:

> And. It's such a little word but, in international legal circles where linkage is *de rigueur*, it is almost ridiculously popular. The 'trade and' (or 'trade linkage') literature is possibly the premier example of this, but it does not stand alone. There is also, for instance, a growing literature on regulation and rights, health and rights, security and rights, and risk and rights. Is it the case, then, that 'new technologies and human rights' … is merely an attempt to tag along or be in fashion by invoking the apparent power of that one little word, 'and'?[6]

---

[2] [2000] OJ C364/1. Since the entry into force of the Lisbon Treaty on 1 December 2009, the Charter constitutes a primary source of European Union law.

[3] See for an attempt to map the extent to which technology features in cases before the European Court, Thérèse Murphy and Gearóid Ó Cuinn, 'Works in Progress: New Technologies and the European Court of Human Rights', *Human Rights Law Review*, 10 (2011), 601.

[4] Joseph Raz, 'Human Rights without Foundations', in Samantha Besson and John Tasioulas (eds.), *The Philosophy of International Law* (Oxford: Oxford University Press, 2010), 321.

[5] See, for example, the critique by Carl Schneider of the dominance of the rights perspective in the Universal Declaration on Bioethics and Human Rights, 'Bioethics in the Language of the Law', *Hastings Center Report*, 24 (1994), 16–22. Schneider argues that the overwhelming focus on rights appears to privilege autonomy above all competing values, thereby losing sight of issues of mutual dependency and human vulnerability. Instead, people are abandoned to their rights at a time when they are at their most vulnerable.

[6] Thérèse Murphy, 'Repetition, Revolution and Resonance', in Murphy (ed.), *New Technologies and Human Rights* (Oxford: Oxford University Press, 2009), 1 (all footnotes removed).

Put in other words, what does the human rights discourse offer the field of technology regulation?

In the extract above, Murphy highlights the relatively late turn to 'technology and human rights' in legal scholarship. This tardiness in the creation of a sub-genre of 'technology and human rights' is arguably the result of two separate factors: the first is that human rights scholars were slow to appreciate the challenges posed by technology; this was not aided by the fact that the main human rights treaties were drawn up in the 1960s, in an era before personal computers, mobile phones, satellite technology, the internet; before DNA fingerprinting, the mapping of the human genome, and the possibility of genetic manipulation of plant, animal and human life – to name only a few of the developments that together constitute a revolution in the way in which we as individuals relate to and interact with each other and with the state. Thus documents containing binding human rights obligations and their established interpretation in case law are often ill-equipped to deal with the challenges posed by modern technology – a phenomenon we shall consider below in the context of the assertion of the right to be a genetic parent before the European Court of Human Rights.

The second factor explaining the relatively late linking of 'technology and human rights' is that scholars in the area of technology regulation had alternatives to hand. Although they have long been aware of the relevance of human rights to their field,[7] they have not viewed human rights as the sole or even primary narrative for understanding the legitimacy of technology regulation.[8] Medical ethics or bioethics, for example, provided a solid point of departure for understanding the challenges posed by developments in the field of biotechnology in the context of medicine or medical treatment. Yet this alternative framework of norms, institutions and practices for determining the legitimacy of developments in the life sciences now finds itself challenged by the turn towards human rights.[9] Despite the lack of a legally binding text specifically regulating the interaction of technology and rights at the global level, human rights is, as in other areas of legal study, establishing itself as the dominant narrative.

---

[7] See for example the 1997 Council of Europe's Oviedo Convention for the Protection of Human Rights and Dignity of the Human Being with Regard to the Application of Biology and Medicine, ETS No. 164. The Oviedo Convention is legally binding.

[8] For example, Brownsword's well-known bioethical triangle, in which human rights constitute one point of departure for assessing the legitimacy of biotechnological developments. See Brownsword, *Rights, Regulation and the Technological Revolution* (Oxford: Oxford University Press, 2008), 35–41. For an early consideration of human rights in the biomedical context, see Eugene B. Brody, *Biomedical Technology and Human Rights* (Sudbury, MA: Dartmouth, 1993).

[9] See Thomas Faunce, 'Will International Human Rights Subsume Medical Ethics? Intersections in the UNESCO Universal Bioethics Declaration', *Journal of Medical Ethics*, 31 (2004), 173; also Roberto Adorno, 'Human Dignity and Human Rights as a Common Ground for a Global Bioethics', *Journal of Medicine and Philosophy*, 34 (2009), 223; for a response to these claims, see Richard E. Ashcroft, 'Could Human Rights Supersede Bioethics?', *Human Rights Law Review*, 10 (2011), 639.

The aim of this chapter, then, is to explore how human rights are used and claimed in the context of the challenges posed by technology and efforts to regulate it; how human rights presently function as boundary markers; and how the position of human rights is likely to develop in the future.

2 Human rights as boundary markers

We have suggested above that the growing dominance of human rights in the field of technology regulation is a relatively new phenomenon; yet human rights themselves are of course not recent inventions. They are most commonly seen as emerging in a recognisable form at the end of the eighteenth century, although the use of the language of rights to challenge authority and to make claims to certain universal standards of behaviour date much further back in history.[10] What this long history of rights suggests is that human rights, despite their source in conceptions of human dignity,[11] have their own conceptual history and their own internal dynamics as a discourse. This is not to suggest that the manner in which human rights function is set in stone; but in order to understand how human rights function as boundary markers in the context of technology regulation at the beginning of this century, it is first necessary to consider briefly what human rights are and what they do independently of the 'and technology' linkage.

In a well-known attempt at defining human rights, James Nickel concluded that they should be understood as:

> basic moral guarantees that people in all countries and cultures allegedly have simply because they are people. Calling these guarantees 'rights' suggests that they attach to particular individuals who can invoke them, that they are of high priority, and that compliance with them is mandatory rather than discretionary. Human rights are frequently held to be universal in the sense that all people have and should enjoy them, and to be independent in the sense that they exist and are available as standards of justification and criticism whether or not they are recognized and implemented by the legal system or officials of a country.[12]

Nickel's definition is helpful because it picks out what we may call the core elements of human rights. The first of these is that human rights are necessarily universal; that is, they presuppose a moral universalism that rests upon rationally

[10] Of course, paradoxically, what is defined as universal will vary across time and place. For a very useful account of the genealogy of human rights, see Michael Freeman, *Human Rights* (Cambridge: Polity, 2002), esp. ch. 2; also, Costas Douzinas, *The End of Human Rights* (Oxford: Hart, 2000).

[11] '[H]uman dignity constitutes the intellectual centre of the entire culture of human rights' (Christian Tomuschat, *Human Rights: Between Idealism and Realism* (2nd edn, Oxford: Oxford University Press, 2008), 3).

[12] James Nickel, *Making Sense of Human Rights: Philosophical Reflections on the Universal Declaration of Human Rights* (Berkeley, CA: University of California Press, 1987); cited in Andrew Fagen, 'Human Rights', *Internet Encyclopaedia of Philosophy*; available online at www.iep.utm.edu/hum-rts (last accessed 8 June 2011).

identifiable a-cultural and a-historical truths.[13] In other words, if human rights are to claim the *epithet* 'human', they need to claim a moral truth across time and culture.[14] One reason, then, for the success of the human rights narrative is that they provide a means of talking about legitimacy beyond a single community – an increasingly important attribute given the huge rise in regulation beyond the state.[15]

The second core element that Nickel identifies is the sense in which respect for human rights is mandatory because what we express as rights are moral guarantees that are necessary for even a minimal functioning of a good life. In this way, human rights express the basic 'things' that we need to exist *as* human beings, from the material requirements of food, water and shelter to freedom from pain and humiliation, as well as such spiritual requirements as freedom of thought, expression or association with others. This idea is more frequently expressed in the language of rights as 'trump' cards.[16] The aim in characterising human rights in this way is to suggest, in Dworkin's own words, that 'rights are best understood as trumps over some background justification for political decisions that states a goal for the community as a whole'.[17] Thus rights, and particularly human rights because of the special nature of their moral claim, should override policy considerations. This image of rights as trumps presents human rights as a claim that must be fulfilled, and in doing so brings human rights very close to claims of human dignity. Yet the distinct difference between an appeal to human dignity as a boundary marker and the way in which human rights function is that human dignity is a claim made on behalf of a community – human beings as a whole – whereas human rights are primarily claimed by an individual against a community.[18] The notion of rights as trumps in the political decision-making of a community also highlights that it is the embodiment of that community against which rights are claimed, i.e. the state. This understanding arises from the origins of human rights as rights to limit state power and to provide guarantees to individuals against encroachment on their liberty, whether by public or private actors. Human rights are thus capable of

---

[13] For more on the historical development of the moral origins of human rights, see Fagen, 'Human Rights'.

[14] Richard Rorty, 'Human Rights, Rationality and Sentimentality', in Stephen Shute and Susan Hurley (eds.), *On Human Rights. The Oxford Amnesty Lectures* (Oxford: Oxford University Press, 1993). See also Moyn's thesis concerning the success of human rights as a utopian narrative, Samuel Moyn, *The Last Utopia: Human Rights in History* (Cambridge, MA: Harvard University Press, 2010).

[15] See Brownsword, *Rights*, ch. 7.

[16] Ronald Dworkin, 'Rights as Trumps', in Jeremy Waldron (ed.), *Theories of Rights* (Oxford: Oxford University Press, 1984).

[17] Ronald Dworkin, *Taking Rights Seriously* (London: Duckworth, 1977), 153.

[18] There are also of course group-based human rights, such as self-determination or minority rights; however, these rights operate in the same way, i.e. empowering an entity acting as a singular unity against a larger collective (if a group has the power to assert its claim to self-determination, it does not need a right to it). See Chapter 8, section 2, for comparison of human dignity and human rights.

having meaning – the notion of trumps implies – in a bounded political community of which the claimant is a member. This is notwithstanding recent efforts to expand the human rights discourse to incorporate rights against non-state actors, such as transnational corporations or international bodies such as the World Trade Organization.[19] That such claims resonate and have traction in contemporary global political discourse, however, has everything to do with the third and final fundamental characteristic that Nickel captures.

This third aspect is the dualism of human rights; that human rights are both at the same time moral claims that exist outside of, and prior to, a positive legal order, and at the same time legal rights enshrined in positive law. This dualism, in which human rights are simultaneously legal entitlements and moral claims, means that human rights are more than simply the rights laid down in the various human rights catalogues at the national, regional or international level. It is what gives the human rights narrative its power and revolutionary potential; or, in the words of Sundhya Pahuja, their 'symbolic valence'.[20] According to Pahuja:

> This symbolic valence is crucial to the emancipatory, or what I call 'political', aspect of human rights. This 'political' aspect arises in concrete terms in the gap between the body of human rights norms in international law at a given time, and the imaginative appeal of human rights which will never be coincident with the rights 'on the books'. In other words, at any given moment, there is both a set of positive legal rules laid down in treaties or found in customary international law, and a whole range of people making claims in the name of human rights – either in terms of rights which are yet to be 'recognized' as law, or with respect to the identities which are excluded from the terms of a particular existing right.

The importance of the symbolic or political aspect of rights as Pahuja describes it is that the potential of human rights necessarily outruns human rights as laid down and enforced in legislation or international documents and as enforced by courts and other tribunal-type bodies. This ability of human rights to outrun established definitions – the way in which human rights 'contain the seeds of their own excess' – is what enables human rights to continue to adapt to new social, political and economic situations and thus prevent an established definition of a particular right from becoming itself a source of injustice.[21] This political aspect – this almost limitless possibility – allows human rights to appear as if they have the potential to be all things to all people.

---

[19] From the wealth of literature on this subject, see Menno Kamminga and S. Zia-Zarifi (eds.), *Liability of Multinational Corporations under International Law* (The Hague: Kluwer Law International, 2000); Erika de Wet, 'The Emergence of International and Regional Value Systems as a Manifestation of the Emerging International Constitutional Order', *Leiden Journal of International Law*, 19 (2006), 611–32; Ernst-Ulrich Petersmann, 'Human Rights, Constitutionalism and the World Trade Organization: Challenges for World Trade Organization Jurisprudence and Civil Society', *Leiden Journal of International Law*, 19 (2006), 633–67.

[20] Sundhya Pahuja, 'Rights as Regulation: The Integration of Development and Human Rights', in Bronwen Morgan (ed.), *The Intersection of Rights and Regulation* (Aldershot: Ashgate, 2007), 168.

[21] Wendy Brown, 'Suffering Rights as Paradoxes', *Constellations*, 7 (2000), 230–41.

Costas Douzinas has drolly captured this aspect of their nature in the opening to his genealogical account of human rights:

> A new ideal has trumped in the global world stage: human rights. It unites left and right, the pulpit and the state, the minister and the rebel, the developing world and the liberals of Hampstead and Manhattan. Human rights have become the principle of liberation from oppression and domination, the rallying cry of the homeless and the dispossessed, the political programme of revolutionaries and dissidents. But their appeal is not confined to the wretched of the earth. Alternative lifestyles, greedy consumers of goods and culture, the pleasure-seekers and playboys of the Western world, the owner of Harrods, the former managing director of Guinness Plc as well as the King of Greece have all glossed their claims in the language of human rights.[22]

The broad appeal of human rights due to their apparent infinite flexibility is a consequence of their indeterminateness in the abstract. As James Griffin has noted in his recent examination of the philosophical foundation of human rights, 'the term "human right" is nearly criterionless'.[23] Human rights, then, can be characterised as an empty vessel that takes concrete shape in their practical application at the moment that they are applied as a legal right that imposes obligations on the state. While we might all be able to agree that human beings possess certain moral guarantees by virtue of their being human, and that these guarantees are important enough to label 'rights' whether or not they form part of positive law in a given community, such agreement only takes us so far. It is one thing to agree that the state should not arbitrarily deprive us of our lives; quite another to determine what that might mean in a concrete situation, i.e. the questions of to whom and how that right applies – for example, whether it includes the use of deadly force to restore public order in the situation of a riot, the death penalty, or the destruction of embryos for stem cell research.

How, then, should we understand human rights as boundary markers? In the previous chapter, we identified boundary markers as concepts that are used by individuals and societies to indicate the boundary beyond which a technology or the consequences of a given technology are incompatible with their moral code; and suggested that the identity and location of these markers speak to our most fundamental assumptions about the purpose of human existence. What, then, should we draw from the analysis of the internal logic of human rights for the purpose of technology regulation?

First, the universality of moral truth that human rights must necessarily aspire to can be, and frequently is, challenged; and this challenge is often staked in the language of human rights. Human rights are thus not a fact, something tangible that can be empirically verified, but are a claim to moral truth; that truth is contested on a number of levels. Respect for human rights is not therefore a source

---

[22] Douzinas, *End of Human Rights*, 1 (footnotes omitted).
[23] James Griffin, *On Human Rights* (Oxford: Oxford University Press, 2008), 14–18.

of legitimacy to which all will subscribe.[24] Human rights thus cannot be a solution to the incommensurability problems of normative frameworks; instead they represent an alternative means of moral reasoning. Second, where human rights function as legal entitlements they do so primarily as individual claims in the context of a bounded political community; they constitute claims against the state, whether as a negative claim to protection, or a positive claim to fulfilment.[25] Human rights quickly become legally irrelevant, therefore, where the claim is either transnational in nature or it touches upon the life of the state.[26] Third, the dualistic nature of human rights entails that legal rights retain a revolutionary potential despite enshrinement in legal rules and are thus a highly flexible tool for phrasing demands; however, these demands have no legal standing. A starving Ethiopian citizen does not have a legal right to food against the Netherlands, for example. An individual may claim that their right to food is being violated by the unfair nature of the global trading system or by international intellectual property rules that prevent farmers in the region of Horn of Africa from accessing crops enhanced by biotechnology that would increase yields, but it is a moral statement. By putting a need in the language of human rights, we highlight that others have a moral duty to take the claim seriously, perhaps even a moral duty to act to address the problem, but the duty is not a legal one.[27] Finally, human rights are also an empty vessel and this entails that, prior to application and a decision about how human rights apply in a given situation, human rights may tell us very little about whose rights should prevail, or about standards of legitimacy of regulation. Thus, despite the popular perception of human rights as trump cards, their central characteristic as boundary markers is their porosity. Although human rights appeals assert a wall-like claim similar to human dignity in the abstract,[28] human rights are essentially limited in the practicality of their application as legal entitlements in relation to the needs of the broader community and in relation to the individual claims of others. Human rights frequently clash not only with policy concerns but also with each other.

---

[24] Rorty, 'Human Rights'. See also William Twining (ed.), *Human Rights, Southern Voices* (Cambridge: Cambridge University Press, 2009).

[25] The three essential characteristics of positive human rights, or human rights as law, according to Tomuschat, are that they are catalogued, binding and enforceable (*Human Rights*).

[26] For example, the ICJ Advisory Opinion on the Legality of Nuclear Weapons found in effect that human rights and humanitarian life could not constrain the actions of a state when its very existence was threatened. *Legality of the Threat of the Use of Nuclear Weapons*, Advisory Opinion, ICJ Reports 1996, 226. However, see claims under the US Alien Tort Act, which allows victims of crimes that violate the laws of nations to sue the perpetrator in US courts no matter where the crime took place.

[27] See, famously, Peter Singer, 'Famine, Affluence and Morality', *Philosophy and Public Affairs*, 1 (1972), 229–43; also Thomas Pogge, '"Assisting" the Global Poor', in Deen K. Chatterjee (ed.), *The Ethics of Assistance: Morality and the Distant Needy* (Cambridge: Cambridge University Press, 2004), 260–88.

[28] We are not suggesting that appeals to human dignity are successful in erecting walls, only that that is the nature of such appeals – that an essential feature of such claims is their assertion of unwillingness to compromise.

The following two sections focus on two concrete examples of the attempt to assert human rights as boundary markers: the right to freedom of speech and the right to privacy in the context of communication technology; and the right to private life in the context of the regulation of IVF treatment.

3 Privacy, freedom of speech and human rights: technology 'out of control'?

P. J. O'Rourke, the American satirist, famously quipped: 'You can't shame or humiliate modern celebrities. What used to be called shame and humiliation is now called publicity.'[29] Control over such publicity is an ongoing battle between the UK press and modern UK celebrities; and the tools the protagonists increasingly wield are human rights.

On 20 May 2011 at a press conference to launch the publication of a report by the judiciary examining the phenomenon of 'super-injunctions', the Lord Chief Justice of England and Wales, Lord Judge, made the unscripted remark that 'Modern technology is totally out of control.'[30] His fear about the uses to which technology were being put related to the use of modern technologies of communication to evade court orders prohibiting the publication of certain information. The Lord Chief Justice was referring to social-networking instruments such as Facebook and Twitter, and his comments came in the middle of a media storm concerning the use of so-called super-injunctions to prevent the publication of stories about the private lives of well-known figures in UK public life, notably footballers, but also including disgraced bankers and BBC journalists.[31]

Only a week earlier, *The Guardian* had led with the headline, 'Twitter and Facebook publication banned for first time in injunction.'[32] The story continued:

> A high court judge has issued an injunction which for the first time explicitly bans publication of information on Twitter and Facebook. The order, made by Mr Justice Baker in the court of protection – linked to the family division of the high court – places a specific ban on publishing information on any 'social network or media including Twitter or Facebook', as well as in other media. The normal orders issued by the family division judges to prevent identification of

---

[29] P. J. O'Rourke, *The Enemies List* (New York: Atlantic Monthly Press, 1996).

[30] Lord Judge's comments were reported by Joshua Rozenberg, 'Lord Chief Justice allowed himself to be labelled "enemy of free speech"', *Law Society Gazette*, 26 May 2011; available online at www.lawgazette.co.uk/opinion/joshua-rozenberg/lord-chief-justice-allowed-himself-be-labelled-039enemy-free-speech039 (last accessed 6 June 2011).

[31] A super-injunction is an injunction that not only prevents publication of the original story but prevents any reporting of the fact that an injunction has been granted. See Master of Rolls report, 'Report of the Committee on Super-Injunctions: Super-Injunctions, Anonymised Injunctions and Open Justice', iv; published online and available at www.judiciary.gov.uk/media/media-releases/2011/committee-reports-findings-super-injunctions-20052011. The term 'super-injunction' was coined by Alan Rusbridger, *The Guardian* editor.

[32] 'Twitter and Facebook publication banned for first time in injunction', *The Guardian*, 13 May 2011; available online at www.guardian.co.uk/media/2011/may/13/twitter-and-facebook-publicationbanned-injunction (last accessed 19 May 2011).

children and others involved in cases simply ban publication of specified information in 'any newspaper, magazine, public computer network, internet website, sound or television broadcast or cable or satellite programme'. The decision follows the publication on Twitter over the weekend of a number of tweets purporting to reveal the identities of celebrities involved in 'superinjunctions'.

Millions of people logged into the Twitter account of the anonymous poster in the days following to satisfy their curiosity, although reports suggest that a number of the names mentioned as involved in indiscretions were inaccurate.

The backdrop to this media drama – a drama still unfolding as this book was written – is the incorporation of a right to privacy into UK law with the transposition into domestic law of the European Convention on Human Rights as the 1998 Human Rights Act. This introduction into the domestic legal system of a right to privacy, which includes the obligation upon national courts to follow the Strasbourg Court's interpretation, has created a clash with freedom of expression as exercised by the UK's media. It is this substantive change that has led to the development in procedural law of new types of injunctions, such as the super-injunction.[33] They became necessary as certain media organisations viewed their right to freedom of expression as an absolute right and attempted to circumvent the balance established in individual cases by the courts between privacy and freedom of expression. By publishing their story exposing a celebrity's private life as anonymised information alongside an ostensibly unrelated story about the same celebrity, this time named, most readers were able to make the connection as to the identity of the celebrity concerned.[34] Yet, as the need for this new tool was created by the determination of certain media to assert freedom of information as an absolute right, the application for a super-injunction by a celebrity is also an attempt, in seeking to prevent any information at all being released – even the fact that an injunction has been sought – to view the right to privacy as an absolute. Super-injunctions came into being at the crosshairs of absolute assertions of the right of an individual to privacy and the right to freedom of expression of journalists, bloggers, Twitters and Facebook users to exchange information and gossip.

The idea that freedom of expression clashes with other rights and freedoms and thus requires balancing is not a new one. Restrictions have long been placed on the right to say whatever one wishes by demands of public safety – the famous restriction of shouting 'fire' in a crowded public space, for example – and by

---

[33] Master of the Rolls, 'Report of the Committee on Super-Injunctions', para. 1.10.

[34] This claim was made by Stephen Sedley, 'The Goodwin and Giggs Show', *London Review of Books*, 33(12) (2011). Sir Stephen Sedley was a member of the UK Court of Appeal until his retirement in 2011. However, super-injunctions have also been used to ensure silence over traditional reporting in the public interest, notably the Trafigura affair, in which *The Guardian*'s attempts to publish a story on the pollution of African coastline by this company were snuffed out by a super-injunction. See, 'Trafigura: anatomy of a super-injunction', *The Guardian*, 20 October 2009; available online at www.guardian.co.uk/media/2009/oct/20/trafigura-anatomy-super-injunction (last accessed 19 May 2011).

the need to protect the rights and freedoms of others.[35] Libel and slander laws thus protect the reputation of others against freedom of expression that is false or malicious; similarly, the exercise of justice limits the freedom of speech of some in order to help to ensure the right to a fair trial of another. The importance of recognising such limitations to freedom of expression has meant that they are built into the right itself, usually as a separate paragraph. Article 19 of the International Covenant on Civil and Political Rights is a typical example:

Article 19[36]

1. Everyone shall have the right to hold opinions without interference.
2. Everyone shall have the right to freedom of expression; this right shall include freedom to seek, receive and impart information and ideas of all kinds, regardless of frontiers, either orally, in writing or in print, in the form of art, or through any other media of his choice.
3. The exercise of the rights provided for in paragraph 2 of this article carries with it special duties and responsibilities. It may therefore be subject to certain restrictions, but these shall only be such as are provided by law and are necessary:
   (a) For respect of the rights or reputations of others;
   (b) For the protection of national security or of public order (ordre public), or of public health or morals.

Modern technology, however, gives the clash between freedom of expression and the right to privacy a new piquancy; yet this itself is not a new observation. In a classic article published in 1890 in the *Harvard Law Review*, Warren and Brandeis argued that new technologies had made it necessary to extend the traditional protection that common law afforded the individual's person and property to a right to privacy. Complaining of press intrusion into private lives in a way that remains familiar today, they wrote:

Recent interventions and business methods call attention to the next step which must be taken for the protection of the person, and for securing to the individual what Judge Cooley calls the right 'to be let alone'. Instantaneous photographs and newspaper enterprise have invaded the sacred precincts of private and domestic life; and numerous mechanical devices threaten to make good the prediction that 'what is whispered in the closet shall be proclaimed from the house-tops'.

Of the desirability – indeed of the necessity – of some such protection, there can, it is believed, be no doubt. The press is overstepping in every direction the obvious bounds of propriety and decency ... To satisfy a prurient taste the details of sexual relations are spread broadcast in the columns of daily papers.[37]

The potential of 'instantaneous photographs' to violate an individual's privacy was made abundantly clear several years after Warren and Brandeis's article in

---

[35] Wojciech Sadurski, *Freedom of Speech and Its Limits* (Dordrecht: Springer, 1999).
[36] International Covenant on Civil and Political Rights (1966), 999 UNTS 171.
[37] Samuel D. Warren and Louis D. Brandeis, 'The Right to Privacy', *Harvard Law Review*, 4(5) (1890), 193, 195.

a well-known German case. Otto van Bismarck, the man who unified Germany and a dominant figure in the world politics of the late nineteenth century, died in 1898; as he lay in state at his home, two men broke in and photographed his body. Wishing to prevent publication, and in the absence of a right to privacy, Bismarck's heirs successfully sued on the grounds that the two men should not be able to benefit from their illegal act of unlawfully entering the house; the court ordered that the photographs, any copies and the photographic plate should be destroyed.[38]

What has changed since such concerns were first raised is of course the arrival of handheld digital technology and a worldwide platform for truly instantaneous publication. The considerable time lag between the act of photographing Bismarck's body and the moment of public distribution was such that Bismarck's family were able to take legal action to prevent publication. In our age, the trespassers would be armed with smart phones and the pictures would likely have been uploaded to a social medium platform within seconds of being taken. The family could have sued for damages caused by the invasion of privacy, but they could not have stopped the invasion itself.[39] This, combined with the fact that the technology can be uploaded from anywhere and read globally, entails that such technology is fundamentally altering the ability of courts to enforce the balance between rights. Moreover, unlike with print media, as has often been observed, the story never dies: digital platforms ensure a permanent record, constantly available for perusal. As Daniel Solove has noted:

> For centuries – perhaps since the dawn of human society – people have spread rumours, gossiped about each other, and engaged in shaming for social transgressions. These social practices are now moving over to the Internet, where they are taking on new dimensions. Gossip used to travel in local circles. It rarely spread widely, and would be forgotten over time. On the Internet, however, gossip is no longer ephemeral. As with gossip, the Internet is having similar effects on the practice of shaming. Once localized and fleeting, shaming online creates a permanent record of people's past transgressions – a digital scarlet letter.[40]

The new tools of social media therefore not only significantly erode the ability of courts to enforce privacy decisions but also alter the speed, range and duration of privacy intrusions.

---

[38] RGZ 45, Judgment of 28 December 1899, Bismarck, 170, 173; discussed in Mathias Klang, 'Privacy, Surveillance and Identity', in Mathias Klang and Andrew Murray (eds.), *Human Rights in a Digital Age* (Abingdon: Routledge-Cavendish, 2005), 176.

[39] Note that the European Court of Human Rights ruled recently in *Mosley* v. *the UK* that the right to a private life does not include the requirement of prior notification of intention to publish a story likely to invade one's privacy; Judgment of 10 May 2011, application no. 48009/08 (this judgment is not yet final).

[40] Daniel Solove, 'Speech, Privacy, and Reputation on the Internet', in Saul Levmore and Martha C. Nussbaum (eds.), *The Offensive Internet* (Cambridge, MA: Harvard University Press, 2010), 16. See also Diane Rowland, 'Free Expression and Defamation', in Klang and Murray, *Human Rights*, 55–6.

The drama over super-injunctions arose because the participants attempted to assert their rights as trumps. The courts, however, viewed both rights as essentially limited by the needs of the community and by the rights of others. While the right to privacy is limited by the central importance that freedom of expression plays in creating the conditions for a flourishing democratic society, that freedom is itself limited by the rights of the individual. Yet the rights themselves contain no guidance as to their content or to the nature of the balance that must be undertaken. Instead it is left to the courts to interpret the interplay and hence the boundary of rights in a given instance, for example, whether a super-injunction is warranted, or whether a right to prior notification is contained within the right to privacy in the specific case before it, or whether an anonymised injunction is sufficient. In addition, the way in which the efforts of the courts to balance the competing rights were undone by an anonymous Twitter user posting – it is assumed – from outside the bounds of the High Court's jurisdiction reminds us that human rights are further limited by the identity of the duty-bearer. The UK has a responsibility to ensure respect for an individual's private life within its jurisdiction; but that obligation and the right it reflects are as good as meaningless if information protected by an injunction can be so easily flouted by an individual beyond the reach of the state's authority.

To assert a human right, then, is to make a claim about where the boundary should be; yet it is the courts that determine not only the location of the marker but given the indeterminateness of rights in the abstract (as, of course, with all concepts), the setting of the location also determines the substantive content of the marker. The meaning of freedom of expression is thereby determined by where one locates the boundary. Moreover, the use of human rights to determine regulatory boundaries for technology use and development is further complicated by the effects of technology itself.

4 To procreate or not to procreate: empowerment and consent in the right to privacy

In the previous section we considered the clash of human rights in the context of new social media technologies. The clash in this situation was set up by the appeal to one right as an attempt to constrain the behaviour of another; it represented an example of two legally enshrined entitlements colliding and their content and meaning being set in the details of individual cases. In this section we will use the example of technological advances in fertility treatment to examine the way in which human rights function and are used by individuals as tools of attempted empowerment. At the core of the human rights perspective is the belief that the rights of the individual cannot be sacrificed at the altar of the greater good of society; human rights are intended to provide a means to individuals of marking the boundary between their personal autonomy and competing (societal) claims. We begin by considering the case of *Evans* v. *the UK*.

Evans played out across national and European courts in the first decade of this century. The applicant was a young woman who was discovered to have ovarian cancer in the first phase of commencing fertility treatment with her then partner. As the treatment for her cancer would leave her infertile, Ms Evans had a number of eggs removed prior to treatment; from these eggs, embryos were created using her partner's sperm and then frozen. Ms Evans was advised to wait two years after the course of her treatment for cancer before seeking to have the embryos implanted. In that intervening period, the relationship with her partner broke down. The partner, J., contacted the fertility clinic to notify them of the withdrawal of his consent for the continued storage of the embryos and requested that they be destroyed. The destruction of the embryos would end any possibility of Ms Evans being able to have a child of her own. The case thus concerned the challenge of Ms Evans to the blanket rule in the relevant UK legislation that the consent of both would-be parents was the defining criterion for what should be done with embryos created in a relationship that no longer existed. According to Schedule 3 of the Human Fertilisation and Embryology Act 1990, in the absence of the continuing consent of either gamete donor, the embryos must be destroyed. Schedule 3 provides:

Consent

1. A consent under this schedule must be given in writing and, in this Schedule, 'effective consent' means a consent under this Schedule which has not been withdrawn.

…

Variation and withdrawal of consent

4. (1) The terms of any consent under this Schedule may from time to time be varied, and the consent may be withdrawn, by notice given by the person who gave the consent to the person keeping the gametes or embryo to which the consent is relevant.

(2) The terms of any consent to the use of any embryo cannot be varied, and such consent cannot be withdrawn, once the embryo has been used

(a) in providing treatment services, or

(b) for the purposes of any project of research.

…

In vitro fertilisation and subsequent use of embryo

6.(1) A person's gametes must not be used to bring about the creation of any embryo *in vitro* unless there is an effective consent by that person to any embryo the creation of which may be brought about with the use of those gametes being used for one of more of the purposes mentioned in paragraph 2(1) [not included in this excerpt]

(2) An embryo the creation of which was brought about *in vitro* must not be received by any person unless there is an effective consent by each person whose gametes were used to bring about the creation of the embryo …

…

8. (1) A person's gametes must not be kept in storage unless there is an effective consent by that person to their storage and they are stored in accordance with their consent.

(2) An embryo the creation of which was brought about *in vitro* must not be kept in storage unless there is an effective consent, by each person whose gametes were used to bring about the creation of the embryo, to the storage of the embryo and the embryo is stored in accordance with those consents.

The Act thus makes consent the key criterion for the creation, storage and use of gametes or embryos, and allows it to be withdrawn at any point by either of the involved parties for any reason up to the point of actual use, i.e. in the case of embryos, implantation in a uterus. Ms Evans's ex-partner was thus within his rights under UK law to request that the embryos be destroyed.

Against this, Ms Evans asserted her right to a private life under Article 8 of the Convention. Article 8 provides:

Right to respect for private and family life

1. Everyone has the right to respect for his private and family life, his home and his correspondence.
2. There shall be no interference by a public authority with the exercise of this right except such as is in accordance with the law and is necessary in a democratic society in the interests of national security, public safety or the economic well-being of the country, for the prevention of disorder or crime, for the protection of health or morals, or for the protection of the rights and freedoms of others.

In finding against the applicant by a margin of 13 to 4, the Court, sitting as the Grand Chamber, ruled that the UK had not exceeded its margin of appreciation by failing to provide for an exception in the legislation whereby the withdrawal of consent by one of the individuals concerned could be weighed against the rights of the other. Ms Evans lost her case and the embryos were destroyed.

The *Evans* case throws up a number of interesting elements both about the way in which human rights are asserted and the way they function as boundary markers. The applicant's primary claim[41] was that of the right to respect for her private life; the Court held, in keeping with its case law, that:

'private life', which is a broad term encompassing, *inter alia*, aspects of an individual's physical and social identity including the right to personal autonomy, personal development and to establish and develop relationships with other human beings and the outside world, incorporates the right to respect for both the decisions to become and not to become a parent.[42]

---

[41] The full claim concerned Article 2 (the right to life), Article 8 (the right to respect for private life), Article 8 (the right to respect for family life) and Article 14 in conjunction with Article 8 (non-discrimination on grounds of gender in the enjoyment of the right to respect for private life).

[42] *Evans v. the UK*, Judgment of the Grand Chamber, para. 71.

The right to respect for private life thus protects *both* the right to become a parent and the right not to, according to the Court; in contrast thus to the previous section in which two different rights collided, the *Evans* case concerns an internal conflict between two aspects of the same right.[43] What happens in such situations is that the case then turns on the issue of consent, as the legislation anticipated. Hence, the central question of the case was whether or not an exception to consent as the guiding principle in determining the moral boundary could be expected of the state under its positive obligations towards the applicant. Consent thus became a *default* boundary marker in such situations in which the substantive rights employed cannot themselves determine the outcome. In a similar ruling by the Supreme Court of Tennessee concerning custody of frozen embryos in divorce proceedings, the Court determined that embryos were neither property nor persons, and found:

> that disputes involving the disposition of preembryos produced by in vitro fertilization should be resolved, first, by looking to the preferences of the progenitors. If their wishes cannot be ascertained, or if there is dispute, then their prior agreement concerning disposition should be carried out. If no prior agreement exists, then the relative interests of the parties in using or not using the preembryos must be weighed. Ordinarily, the party wishing to avoid procreation should prevail, assuming that the other party has a reasonable possibility of achieving parenthood by means other than use of the preembryos in question. If no other reasonable alternatives exist, then the argument in favor of using the preembryos to achieve pregnancy should be considered. However, if the party seeking control of the preembryos intends merely to donate them to another couple, the objecting party obviously has the greater interest and should prevail.[44]

Although consent acted as the boundary marker in both cases, the Tennessee Court weighed up the different aspects of the right to private life and thus located the boundary differently to the Strasbourg Court, finding that where a party had no other option for becoming a genetic parent than the embryos in question, refusal of consent could be overridden. *Evans* suggests that where the boundary of consent is located for Europeans will depend upon a series of factors, such as whether or not the state concerned has thought carefully about the point of location – the Court made much of the carefully reasoned 1984 study conducted by a committee headed by the philosopher Mary Warnock into the ethical implications of IVF treatment, upon which the provisions of the 1990 Act were based[45] – as well as where most other European states place the boundary, i.e. whether a European consensus exists on where the boundary should be located.

---

[43] See, for critique of viewing rights as symmetrical, Daphne Barak-Erez and Ron Shapira, 'The Delusion of Symmetric Rights', *Oxford Journal of Legal Studies*, 19 (1999), 297.

[44] *Davis* v. *Davis* 842 SW2d 588, 597 (Tenn. 1992), para. 112.

[45] Department of Health and Social Security, *Report of the Committee of Inquiry into Human Fertilisation and Embryology* ('the Warnock Report'), July 1984 (Cmnd 9314); available online at www.hfea.gov.uk/docs/Warnock_Report_of_the_Committee_of_Inquiry_into_

What does this tell us about human rights as boundary markers? It suggests that how human rights interact with consent to form boundaries will depend not just on the location of consent as a boundary marker but on the physical location of the claimant. Thus, while the internal logic of human rights may be universal, the application is always local. Even within Europe, an overview survey conducted by the Court into the position of other European jurisdictions revealed that in Denmark, France, Greece, Switzerland, the Netherlands, Belgium, Germany, Iceland, Sweden and Turkey the male donor enjoys similar rights to withdraw his consent at any moment up until the point of implantation, either de jure or de facto. However, Hungarian rules concerning consent explicitly recognise that medically assisted reproduction places a much heavier burden upon the woman than the man and thus locate the boundary differently. In the absence of express written agreement to the contrary, the ability of a man to withdraw consent after the creation of the embryos is denied. Similarly, in Austria, Italy and Estonia, the point at which a man may withdraw his consent is limited to the period prior to fertilisation, beyond which the only consent that matters is that of the woman. Thus in the case of the latter four countries, consent is more strictly determined – the boundary is located nearer – and the right to become a genetic parent as seen through the lens of the right to respect for private life is used more permissively as a marker – the boundary is further away.

However, the indeterminateness of human rights goes deeper than simply the location of the claimant. In a dispute similar to *Evans*, Israeli courts disagreed among themselves about where to place the boundary. In *Nachmani* v. *Nachmani*, the Israeli District Court held that it was not possible for one of the gamete donors to withdraw their consent once the embryos have been created, following the logic that the ability to withdraw consent is not available to a man who fertilises his wife's ova through sexual intercourse. The Supreme Court, sitting as an appellate court, however reversed the decision of the lower court, holding that the right of the man not to be forced to be a parent could not be overridden. Finally, the Supreme Court reversed its first decision, finding in favour of Mrs Nachmani by a margin of 7 to 4. What this case so nicely highlights is that the indeterminateness of human rights claims requires a turn to a procedural marker – consent – as a means of resolving disputes that are framed as claims concerning private autonomy.[46]

Yet the fact that these cases are constructed as privacy issues tells us more about how human rights function as boundary markers. *Evans*, for example, fundamentally concerned the right to be a genetic parent. This right does not

Human_Fertilisation_and_Embryology_1984.pdf. The findings of this report were set out in a Green Paper, which was issued for public consultation – a point that the Court also stressed in determining whether the UK government had exceeded its margin of appreciation (*Evans* v. *the UK*, Judgment of the Grand Chamber, para. 87).

[46] See, *inter alia*, Roger Brownsword, 'The Cult of Consent: Fixation and Fallacy', *King's College Law Journal*, 15 (2004), 223.

appear in the human rights catalogue, however, and thus Ms Evans's claim concerning the existential question of procreation was therefore forced into another frame.[47] Notions of privacy cannot capture, for example, the existential agony of barrenness.[48] Yet even within the existing list of positive rights there were plausible alternatives to the construction of the claim as the right to a private life. The case could have been framed as a property claim – not so outrageous a suggestion given the development of case law assigning property rights to human tissue;[49] or it could have been viewed as falling under the right to family life, another element of Article 8. However, in the Court's interpretation of the Convention, the right to property is not relevant to disputes over embryos; similarly, the right to family life does not include a right to procreate but is restricted by the Court to the right to enjoyment of one's (existing) family. More fundamentally, the case could have been viewed from the perspective of the embryos. From such a perspective, the conflict was ultimately about whether or not the embryos that had been created were to be destroyed, and thus the case could have been heard as a right-to-life suit. Ms Evans did in fact assert a right-to-life claim on behalf of the embryos alongside her claim under Article 8. However, she did not make it the centre of her petition for the simple reason that it stood no possibility of success before either the national or European instances. Under English law an embryo does not have independent rights or interests and cannot claim a right to life. Similarly, in a series of cases, most recently *Vo* v. *France* and now *Evans*, the Strasbourg Court has ruled that in the absence of a European consensus on the point at which life begins, determination of that point falls within the margin of appreciation afforded to national jurisdictions.[50] Under the terms of human rights norms, therefore, embryos are not rights-holders.[51] In the regulation of biotechnology, a major limitation of the use of human rights as boundary markers for those that which to assert rights on behalf of embryos is that human rights are limited to legal persons. In asserting a right to be a genetic parent, Ms Evans was at the same time challenging the construction, or reduction, of her claim to one of private autonomy.

Evans represents a fascinating and ultimately tragic case of rights functioning as legal entitlements in a strictly regulatory way in contrast to the emancipatory claim that Ms Evans was making both for herself and the embryos against the

---

[47] See the later case of *Dickson* v. *the UK* for a similar claim; Judgment of the Grand Chamber of 4 December 2007, application no. 44362/04.

[48] Barak-Erez and Shapira, 'Delusion of Symmetric Rights', 302.

[49] See Chapter 8, section 6; see also Jessica Berg, 'Owning Persons: The Application of Property Theory to Embryos and Fetuses', *Wake Forest Law Review*, 40 (2005), 159–219, for discussion of US case law in this area.

[50] *Vo.* v. *France*, Judgment of the European Court of Human Rights, 8 July 2004; application no. 53924/00.

[51] See also, for example, the well-known statement by the US Supreme Court in *Roe* v. *Wade* that 'the unborn have never been recognized in the law as persons in the whole sense' (410 US 113 (1973), 162).

reduction of their claims to a balancing of personal autonomy that was determined by the location of consent as the boundary.

5 Human rights and technology

How should we understand human rights as boundary markers in the context of technology regulation and in the context of the other frames we have considered?

It is clear that human rights have a strong relationship to ideas about human dignity, particularly what we have called 'dignity as autonomy'. In Chapter 8 we suggested that human rights are a manifestation of the belief in human dignity, whether based on a secular rationality, our God-likeness or a romantic view of human nature. However, we also noted that there exists an irresolvable tension between claims of human dignity, that necessarily make a collective claim on behalf of the whole species, and how that dignity may be interpreted by each individual in the context of their own desires and conception of the good life. The needs and desires of individuals are not central to conceptions of human dignity as they are to human rights.

Human rights appear to sit most easily alongside a utilitarian perspective, at least on the surface. The emphasis in the harm principle on individual autonomy and the element of balancing inherent to both entails that they form twin elements of a pragmatic regime of technology regulation that dominates contemporary technology governance.[52] On such a reading, harm is interpreted by the needs and desires of the individual as represented by human rights. However, a human rights perspective and a consequentionalist outlook of course have fundamentally incompatible ideas about the centrality of the individual. The idea, for example, that the harm of one is compensated by benefit to another is thrown into sharp relief by a case such as *Evans*. Moreover, while it may have been possible to deduce that the harm and suffering caused to Ms Evans by destroying her possibility of becoming a genetic parent was greater than the harm that would have been done to her ex-partner by becoming a purely biological parent, the centrality of individual autonomy to the human rights perspective and the absence of substantive content to human rights meant that the case hinged on the question of consent. It is here in the use of consent as a means of locating the boundary between individual autonomy and the collective good, whether defined by human dignity or utilitarianism, that the inherent tension between human rights and other frames is most clearly visible.

Human rights thus constitute less a series of individual boundary markers than a normative framework in which the things we have reason to care about are (re)articulated. They are simultaneously tools of ethical reasoning about regulation, similar to the concepts that we considered in Chapter 8; and at the

---

[52] See Chapters 5 and 6.

same time they themselves are regulatory in their incarnation as legal entitlements. As we saw with *Evans*, human rights also exclude, closing down the emancipatory potential they appear to offer. What does this tell us about their interaction with technology?

Human rights currently interact in two ways in the context of technology regulation; and we wish to venture that a third is likely to open up in the course of this century. The first was illustrated by the role technology played in the century-long clash between freedom of speech and ideas about privacy. Here, technology, in the form of new social media, played an aggravating role, eroding the ability of courts to enforce decisions they have made about the appropriate balance between the two rights, at the same time as technology alters the speed, depth and durability of privacy intrusions. Yet, the essential nature of the clash is unaltered by the technological developments, at least for now.

The second type of interface is suggested by the *Evans* case, and the cases like it in other jurisdictions. Here the interaction is more complicated. The technological advancement itself is the cause of the dispute and we see the emancipatory potential promised by human rights outrunning the possibilities encased in the legal entitlement. In such a scenario, human rights themselves act as regulation, rewriting the claim into a language that is internally comprehensible but, in doing so, fundamentally altering and limiting the nature of the claim being made. The danger of reliance on a human rights framework in the context of technology regulation is thus that the rights that began as offering so much to disempowered individuals becomes a means of boxing them in.[53]

The third interaction we wish to suggest is one for the future: where human rights remain the dominant language for moral reasoning – and there is every reason to expect that they will – technological developments are likely to force the creation of new human rights. Buchanan suggested that the revolution in genetics may require us to alter our conception of justice; it is likely that this new understanding will be expressed in calls for additions to the human rights canon.[54] New rights that look to be on the horizon include the right to genetic privacy, the right to a unique identity,[55] and the right to internet access. Others, such as the right to forget, will no doubt be added to the list.

One of the elements of human rights that we have sought to highlight in this chapter is their necessary indeterminacy, both internally and externally. There is of course nothing original in such a suggestion, and indeterminancy is equally not solely a characteristic of human rights. However, it is worth

---

[53] For a study of the question of whether law more broadly can ever be emancipatory, see Boaventura de Sousa Santos, 'Chapter 9: Can Law Be Emancipatory?', *Towards a New Legal Common Sense* (London: Butterworths, 2002).

[54] See Chapter 8, section 4.

[55] See Hélène Boussard, 'Individual Human Rights in Genetic Research: Blurring the Line between Collective and Individual Interests', in Murphy, *New Technologies*, 252, 257. Also, slightly differently, Roger Brownsword, 'Friends, Romans and Countrymen: Is there a Universal Right to Identity?', *Law, Innovation and Technology*, 1(2) (2009), 223.

stressing because it reminds us of the incommensurability of ethical disputes that recourse to human rights cannot overcome. Human rights cannot settle disputes over boundaries but simply shifts the incommensurability to an alternative dynamic. We turn now from ideas about substantive legitimacy to procedural efforts to address questions of incommensurability between different ethical outlooks, in particular the idea of public participation.

10

A look at procedural legitimacy: the role of public participation in technology regulation

1 Introduction

At the site of the Soldiers' National Cemetery in Gettysburg, Pennsylvania, in 1863, in a ceremony commemorating the sacrifice of Union soldiers in the ongoing American Civil War, Abraham Lincoln delivered what has come to be known as the Gettysburg Address. In this powerful and eloquent statement, Lincoln sought to strengthen the resolve of those still alive to protect the achievements of the American Revolution, notably 'government of the people, by the people, for the people'.[1] As this famous phrase from one of the most well-known political speeches in history so succinctly captures, procedure lays at the heart of what we understand political legitimacy to be.

While boundary markers – such as respect for human rights, human dignity or the environment – function to set substantive limits on the acceptable outcomes of regulatory deliberations, the decision of regulators to stay within such boundaries is not itself sufficient to legitimise the regulatory outcome. Discussions about what markers are relevant and where they should be located take place in a broader process of decision-making, in which other standards or markers of legitimacy are relevant. If substantive legitimacy concerns itself with questions of 'what' – of what decisions can legitimately be made, procedural legitimacy focuses on the 'who' and the 'how'.[2] Not only, therefore, does the procedural frame need to be in place before issues of substance can be determined, we need to agree that the frame is legitimate. In other words, even if a regulatory decision cannot be criticised as illegitimate relative to one of the substantive boundary markers, it might still fail to pass muster relative to the requirements of procedural legitimacy. We focus in this chapter on the questions of 'who' and 'how', and suggest that public participation has become a key requirement of procedural legitimacy.

In the *Evans* case, which we examined in the preceding chapter, the European Court of Human Rights considered the compliance of UK legislation with obligations under Article 8 of the Convention. In coming to its decision,

---

[1] Gary Wills, *Lincoln at Gettysburg: The Words that Remade America* (New York: Simon & Schuster, 1992).

[2] See Nancy Fraser, 'Reframing Justice in a Globalizing World', *New Left Review*, 36 (2005), 69.

the Court placed considerable weight on the public consultations undertaken in regard to the content of the legislation. It held that the UK had not exceeded its margin of appreciation in determining that the continuing consent of both gamete donors was necessary for the created embryos to be stored and used, in part because:

> The subsequent Green Paper specifically asked interested members of the public what should happen where there was no agreement between a couple as to the use or disposal of an embryo and the 1987 White Paper noted that those respondents who agreed that storage should be permitted were broadly in favour of the [Warnock] Committee's recommendations [upon which the legislation was based].[3]

The act of public consultation and the subsequent broad support for the substantive content of the legislation was an important element for the Court in determining the legitimacy of this particular regulatory regime.

What the Court's reasoning suggests is that how a decision is taken – in particular, the level of public involvement in the design of regulation – is a crucial element in determining the legitimacy of regulatory efforts in an area of policy as sensitive as embryo storage. Put another way, the procedural aspects of decision-making constitute important elements of legitimacy, and nowhere more so than in the area of science and technology regulation.[4] This is reflected in renewed emphasis in past decades on the importance of public involvement at all levels of regulatory governance of science. The 1992 Convention on Biological Diversity, for example, provides for public participation in the design and monitoring of environmental impact assessments.[5] Similarly, within Europe, the 1997 Oviedo Convention on Human Rights and Biomedicine provides for public debate on the regulation of biotechnological developments. Article 28 of the Convention provides:

> Article 28 – Public debate
> Parties to this Convention shall see to it that the fundamental questions raised by the developments of biology and medicine are the subject of appropriate public discussion in the light, in particular, of relevant medical, social, economic, ethical and legal implications, and that their possible application is made the subject of appropriate consultation.[6]

As the House of Lords Science and Technology Committee recommended in its study on Science in Society, 'direct dialogue with the public should move from being an optional add-on to science-based policy-making and to the activities of research organisations and learned institutions, and should become a normal

---

[3] *Evans* v. *the UK*, Judgment of the Grand Chamber of the European Court of Human Rights, 10 April 2007, para. 87.

[4] See Ulrich Beck, 'The Reinvention of Politics: Towards a Theory of Reflexive Modernization', in U. Beck, A. Giddens and S. Lash (eds.), *Reflexive Modernization: Politics, Tradition and Aesthetics in the Modern Social Order* (Cambridge: Polity, 1994).

[5] Convention on Biological Diversity, Rio de Janeiro, 5 June 1992, 1760 UNTS 79, Article 14(1)(a).

[6] Council of Europe Convention on Human Rights and Biomedicine, ETS no. 164, Oviedo, 4 April 1997.

248   Law and the technologies of the twenty-first century

and integral part of the process'.[7] What we will suggest in this chapter is that direct dialogue with the public has become a key aspect of procedural legitimacy in technology regulation.

2 Why public participation matters

As Lincoln suggests, contemporary thinking about legitimate government requires that we govern ourselves – both in the sense that decisions are taken free from outside interference (of the people) as well as that the internal process is representative (by the people) – and that the process of government represent the wishes or be in the best interests of the people (for the people). This idea that consent to be governed forms the basis of how we conceptualise legitimacy has dominated political theory since Locke's rewriting of social contract theory.[8] Indeed, the principle of and right to self-determination has enshrined the belief in the consent of the governed as the basis of legitimate government as one of the central tenets of modern international law.[9] Yet the real differences lay in how we understand what this means in practice.

Locke understood the consent of the people to be tacit: it is given at the moment in which the *pouvoir constituant* becomes the *pouvoir constitué* – the mythical point at which a group of individuals constitute themselves as a people under a new social order. For Rousseau, however, this is not sufficient. Participation in government must run deeper than fictional consent. Instead, the general will is formed by the active participation of each particular will. Writing in *The Social Contract*, Rousseau, departing from Lockean theory, stated that 'the general will, to be really such, must be general in its object as well as its essence; that it must both come from all and apply to all'.[10] What Rousseau was arguing for was not simply the participation of all because forming the general will in this way is the best means of ensuring the best outcome; rather he understood legitimacy as consisting in the act of participation itself. It is this idea that was laid down in the previous century as a right to democratic government in the 1948 Universal Declaration of Human Rights. This right was developed into a right to participate in public affairs in the 1966 International

---

[7] House of Lords Select Committee on Science and Technology, *Science and Society*, 3rd Report, 1999–2000, HL Paper 38, para. 5.48.

[8] John Locke, *Two Treatises of Government*, intro. W. S. Carpenter (London: Everyman's Library, 1924), second treatise, ch. 9. Of course, there are a number of theories about how we should envisage the form that consent should take; see Joseph Raz, *Ethics in the Public Domain: Essays in the Morality of Law and Politics* (Oxford: Clarendon Press, 1995), 356.

[9] See GA Res. 1514 (XV), GAOR, 15th Session, Suppl. 16, 66 (1960). The provisions of the 1960 Declaration were declared to be customary international law by the ICJ in its Western Sahara Advisory Opinion. See *Western Sahara Case*, Advisory Opinion, ICJ Reports (1975), para. 56. Self-determination is also declared to be a right applicable to all as in Article 1 of the 1966 twin Covenants on Civil and Political Rights and on Economic, Cultural and Social Rights.

[10] Jean-Jacques Rousseau, *The Social Contract*, ed. Victor Gourevitch (Cambridge: Cambridge University Press), Book 2, 4.

Covenant on Civil and Political Rights (ICCPR). General Comment No. 25 from the UN Human Rights Committee on the Right to Participate in Public Affairs (Article 25 of the ICCPR) provides the following explanation of what participation in governance entails:[11]

> 5. The conduct of public affairs ... is a broad concept which relates to the exercise of political power, in particular the exercise of legislative, executive and administrative powers. It covers all aspects of public administration, and the formulation and implementation of policy at international, national, regional and local levels. The allocation of powers and the means by which individual citizens exercise the right to participate in the conduct of public affairs protected by article 25 should be established by the constitution and other laws.
>
> 6. Citizens participate directly in the conduct of public affairs when they exercise power as members of legislative bodies or by holding executive office ... Citizens also participate directly in the conduct of public affairs when they choose or change their constitution or decide public issues through a referendum or other electoral process ... Citizens may participate directly by taking part in popular assemblies which have the power to make decisions about local issues or about the affairs of a particular community and in bodies established to represent citizens in consultation with government ...
>
> 7. Where citizens participate in the conduct of public affairs through freely chosen representatives, it is implicit in article 25 that those representatives do in fact exercise governmental power and that they are accountable through the electoral process for their exercise of that power. It is also implicit that the representatives exercise only those powers which are allocated to them in accordance with constitutional provisions. Participation through freely chosen representatives is exercised through voting processes which must be established by laws that are in accordance with paragraph (b).
>
> 8. Citizens also take part in the conduct of public affairs by exerting influence through public debate and dialogue with their representatives or through their capacity to organize themselves. This participation is supported by ensuring freedom of expression, assembly and association.

Thus democratic governance is the basis for legitimate government according to the ICCPR;[12] the right to participate in the conduct of public affairs goes beyond periodic elections and the right to stand for office. It also includes the right to participate in public debates.

However, contrary to Rousseau, for John Stuart Mill participation is instrumental, i.e. it is less a good in itself than it is a means to an end. In *On Liberty and Considerations on Representative Government* Mill argues that both

---

[11] Human Rights Committee General Comment No. 25: The right to participate in public affairs, voting rights and the right of equal access to public service (Art. 25): 12 July 1996; CCPR/C/21/Rev.1/Add.7.

[12] The ICCPR has been signed and ratified by 167 states; the General Comments of the Human Rights Committee are an influential but not authoritative interpretation of the treaty.

individual freedom and the right to participate in politics are essential for the self-development of individuals.[13] Mill's instrumentalism – and his argument for the necessity of deliberative government – is based upon his belief in the power of ideas and the need for decision-makers to be well informed. To crudely paraphrase Mill, the more people that participate, the more likely that good ideas will be aired and thus better decisions made. Moreover, government by means of the active deliberation of all citizens would prevent the formation of sectoral interests that could threaten the happiness of the whole.[14]

In a contemporary attempt at summarising why public participation matters, Denis Galligan has suggested in the context of examining decision-making in the realm of biotechnology, that:

> The ideal for any society is that laws and policies should be for the common good. Since we do not trust claims that there is an objective way of determining the common good on any matter, some mechanism has to be deployed for doing so. In democratic societies, the guiding principle is that the common good is forged from considering and accommodating the different interests and viewpoints within the society. The usual mechanism for making that determination consists in electing representatives and empowering them to decide matters. Legitimacy is gained, not so much by the content of the outcomes, but from the fact that those who decide are elected by the people.
>
> But while this is a fundamental feature of democratic societies, normally it is not enough. In the first place, elected representatives are prone to making foolish or unwise decisions; there is also no guarantee that different viewpoints genuinely will be taken into account; and there is a risk that more powerful interests will exert excessive influence. Moreover, decisions are often delegated, as much by necessity as by choice, to officials, agencies and regulatory bodies who are neither elected nor directly accountable to the democratic process. The democratic principle plainly needs to be supplemented by other mechanisms that draw on and reinterpret it in terms of participation in administrative processes. This also has the effect of educating and informing officials with a view to better quality decision-making. Mechanisms can be devised to inform and educate decision-makers, to make them aware of the various aspects of an issue and the different viewpoints with respect to it. The British public inquiry is one mechanism, the American notice-and-comment procedure another; while several Australian states have adopted quite complex and exhaustive approaches. The range of fact-finding and consultative approaches available is extensive. The common factor, despite the differences, is the concern to provide decision-makers with information, analysis and a plurality of views. This can be linked to the common good

---

[13] John Stuart Mill, *Utilitarianism, On Liberty and Considerations on Representative Government* (London: Dent, 1993). See also David Brink, 'Mill's Deliberative Utilitarianism', *Philosophy and Public Affairs*, 21(6) (1992), 67–103. For a very useful brief account about the sources of legitimacy, see Fabienne Peter, 'Political Legitimacy', in Edward N. Zalta (ed.), *Stanford Encyclopaedia of Philosophy* (summer 2010 edn); available online at http://plato.stanford.edu/archives/sum2010/entries/legitimacy

[14] John Stuart Mill, *Collected Works*, ed. John M. Robson (London: Routledge & Kegan Paul, 1986), 19: 447.

and to the idea running through the liberal tradition represented by, for instance, John Stuart Mill, namely, that in order to make good decisions one needs to be well-informed, and that listening to the competing views in society is a good way of being informed.

This leads to a second consideration: in a democratic society it is important that all elements of civil society have their interests and views taken into account. This means ensuring that decisions of policy, at whatever level they are made, are responsive to the range of ideas and positions held within a society. We saw above how decisions are likely to be improved if individuals, groups and entities are able to insert their views into decision-making processes at various points. However, involvement is valued not just for its instrumental effect on outcomes; it is also important in the relationship between the state and the people. That relationship is mediated by rights of various kinds, where to have a right is to have an interest that has special protection. The rights we are concerned with here protect the interest each person has in being able to participate in the political process, but participation, while a basic element of the relationship, does not fully capture the range of interests at issue. It is not only to participate and to have one's interests represented, but also to have those interests considered and taken into account. This second aspect, which is often harder to achieve, I have described elsewhere as the right to consideration.[15]

In this extract, Galligan combines the two main perspectives as put forward by Rousseau and Mill on why public participation in governance matters: that participation is a good in itself – a part of the proper relationship between the governed and the governing – and the only means by which we can know the general will; and the instrumental – that the more views and ideas that are heard, the better the quality of the decision that will result.

This has been expressed in the Aarhus Convention on Access to Information, Public Participation in Decision-Making and Access to Justice in Environmental Matters – the reference text in the area of public participation in decision-making processes – as representing a right and a duty. The preamble to the Convention provides:

> *Recognizing also* that every person has the right to live in an environment adequate to his or her health and well-being, and the duty, both individually and in association with others, to protect and improve the environment for the benefit of present and future generations,
> *Considering* that, to be able to assert this right and observe this duty, citizens must have access to information, be entitled to participate in decision-making and have access to justice in environmental matters.[16]

---

[15] D. J. Galligan, 'Citizens' Rights and Participation in the Regulation of Biotechnology', in Francesco Francioni (ed.), *Biotechnologies and International Human Rights* (Oxford: Hart, 2007), 342–3 (italics and footnotes removed). See, for more on the right to consideration, D. J. Galligan, 'Rights, Discretion, and Procedure', in C. Sampford and D. J. Galligan (eds.), *Law, Rights, and the Welfare State* (London: Croom Helm, 1986).

[16] UNECE Aarhus Convention Access to Information, Public Participation in Decision-Making and Access to Justice in Environmental Matters (1998), 2161 UNTS 447.

It is thus on this combining of Rousseau and Mill that most contemporary thinking about procedural legitimacy in technology regulation is based.[17] However, as we shall see in this chapter, public participation in practice is most often structured along a liberal model, more in keeping with Mill than Rousseau. In this way, public participation is less concerned with giving expression to a collectively determined will, and more about guaranteeing rights to members of the public as individuals to be able to protect their private interests. Participation in this model is akin to what one expert giving evidence to the House of Lords Science and Technology Committee described as the 'social equivalent of informed consent'.[18]

The Human Rights Committee has laid out the different ways in which public participation must manifest itself. In this chapter, we focus on direct dialogue or engagement with the public. We do so because in the states that form the main examples in this book, we are fortunate enough that we can take periodic elections and the right to stand for office for granted; or put another way, without these expressions of procedural legitimacy, we are no longer able to talk about legitimacy at all. Moreover, the issue of direct public engagement has become central to perceptions of technology regulation in particular. This has happened for two main reasons. The first is that, as we suggested in the introductory chapter to this section, technological developments challenge our most fundamental assumptions about human identity – they pose ontological risks. The second is that the same developments pose potentially serious physical risks, both to us and our environment, and the public has become increasingly sceptical about the ability of decision-makers and scientists to manage those risks in a way that the public finds acceptable.[19]

Direct public participation, then, is an essential element of procedural legitimacy. But identifying public participation as the dominant feature of the legitimacy of technology regulation is only the beginning.

3 Identifying the elements of participation

If we accept that public participation is an essential element of the legitimacy of technology regulation – that deliberation between individuals and groups within society is essential not only in itself, i.e. input, but in reaching the best decision possible, i.e. output – a number of questions remain. These concern the identity of participants, the format of participation, the location of decision-making, and what background conditions, or prerequisites, are necessary for participation to

---

[17] See J. S. Dryzek, *Deliberative Democracy and Beyond: Liberals, Critics and Contestations* (Oxford: Oxford University Press, 2000).

[18] House of Lords Select Committee on Science and Technology, *Science and Society*, (2000), para. 5.2; the expert was Peter Healey, a sociologist of science and technology.

[19] See the excerpt from Han Somsen on precautionary deliberation in Chapter 6. Somsen, 'Cloning Trojan Horses: Precautionary Regulation of Reproductive Technologies', in Roger Brownsword and Karen Yeung (eds.), *Regulating Technologies* (Oxford: Hart, 2008).

be meaningful. We will examine these in turn in this section in order to provide contours to the requirement of public participation as a condition of legitimacy.

(a) The participants

We suggested that procedural legitimacy in the context of technology regulation is concerned with questions both of input and of output. These two overlapping but not identical goals contain the potential for tension in their realisation. To achieve the first aim – participation for its own sake – the identity of participants is clear: the 'all' of which Rousseau wrote is made up of individual citizens. It is they who come together to deliberate and who have, in Galligan's phrase, the 'right of consideration'.

However, as Galligan also notes, the right to consideration is unlikely to lead on its own to the second goal of deliberation – quality decision-making – as citizens themselves are unlikely to possess the requisite expert scientific knowledge to make the best decision. If the need to reach good outcomes is an essential element of procedural legitimacy, therefore, then the decision-making process needs to involve the elicitation and communication of scientific information. It is this that has led to a large role for experts in quantifying and communicating risks and likely benefits in the regulation of technology.[20] The importance of the role of experts in ensuring both that deliberations are meaningful and that decision-makers take quality decisions was recognised, for example, by citizens in a public consultation exercise undertaken on behalf of the UK government into attitudes towards nanotechnology. While those consulted stressed the importance of public participation, they did not feel that theirs was the only voice that should be heard or that it was the most important. The report collating the findings of these exercises concluded:

> It is notable that most public participants considered decision-making in relation to nanotechnology a complex process that requires a wide range of inputs:
>> I know there are experts out there who are concerned about nanotechnologies as well, and if our group adds to that sense of caution then that's a good thing. *But for us to want to take the decision ourselves would be a step too far.*
>
> Public participants' main concern has been that decision-making processes in science and technology are made more transparent and trustworthy, and that more effort is made to incorporate ethical and social considerations into the setting of research and funding priorities. Flexibility and openness have been stressed as important: *people are keen for as many voices as possible – including scientists, members of the public, NGOs, and industry – to be heard at the different stages of decision-making.*

---

[20] David Collingridge and Colin Reeve, *Science Speaks to Power: The Role of Experts in Policy-Making* (London: Pinter, 1986); Sheila Jasanoff, *The Fifth Branch: Science Advisors as Policy-Makers* (Cambridge, MA: Harvard University Press, 1990).

> In a survey done at a Citizen Science @ Bristol event [one of the consultation projects], 13% of respondents agreed with the suggestion that the public should be able to vote on funding allocation for nanotechnologies; 13% believed that nanoscientists are better equipped to do this task; 16% said that it is the government's job; and 52% agreed with the statement that 'it should be a three-way dialogue between the government, the public, and scientists'.[21]

What this extract suggests is that members of the public recognise their limitations in what they can contribute to a substantive contribute to discussions about technology; the same report remarked upon the generally low-level of scientific education among participants in the consultation sessions. The House of Lords Science and Technology Committee noted, in a recent report concerning the regulation of nanotechnology in relation to foodstuffs, the difficulty of engaging with the public over complex matters. The report suggested that the voice of the public is better heard when mediated through civil society organisations, such as consumer groups and NGOs:

> 7.28. There is general support for public engagement activity. But the concept of 'public' is a complex one. We recognise there are many different audiences within the public and that activities should be tailored to these different audiences … although people were in favour of information being placed in the public domain, in general they tended not to look at the information themselves but instead were reassured by the fact that someone else had access to the information and could perform a watchdog function … We acknowledge the importance of giving individual members of the public a voice. But we – and, it seems, members of the public – recognise also that this voice is often most effectively mediated by representative groups such as consumer groups, non-governmental organisations (NGOs) and individuals with a particular interest in the topic. Framing effective public engagement strategies needs to take into account these different audiences within the public.[22]

The mediating role of NGOs is not without controversy, however. While the majority of the public may be happy to delegate their role in safeguarding their own and the general interest to others, there is a danger that civil society actors cease to mediate and instead define the public interest. In the Dutch experience with public consultation over GM foods, a coalition of fifteen NGOs attempted not only to set the terms of the debate but also to determine the evidence that could be made available in the public debates in order to maximise the chance of the public expressing a view that accorded with the NGOs' own.[23]

---

[21] Involve, *Democratic Technologies? The Final Report of the Nanotechnology Engagement Group (NEG)* (2007), prepared on behalf of the UK government, ch. 3.2., 42 (emphases ours); available online at www.involve.org.uk/wp-content/uploads/2011/03/Democratic-Technologies.pdf

[22] House of Lords Select Committee on Science and Technology, 1st Report of Session 2009–10, *Nanotechnologies and Food*, vol. 1: Report, HL Paper 22-I, 8 January 2010, section 7.28; available online at www.publications.parliament.uk/pa/ld200910/ldselect/ldsctech/22/22i.pdf

[23] The story is recounted by Joel D'Silva and Geert van Calster, 'For Me to Know and You to Find Out? Participatory Mechanisms, the Aarhus Convention and New Technologies', *Studies in Ethics, Law, and Technology*, 4(2) (2010), article 3.

The idea – expressed by the House of Lords – that there are different audiences within the public suggests that certain actors warrant special consultation in decision-making procedures. This may be because they fulfil a mediating role on behalf of the public. However, it may also be because such actors are particularly affected by the question under consideration, perhaps because they live close to an industrial plant or research laboratory, or because they are patients and their families, or because the matter at hand speaks to the deeply held values of a defined group, such as a religious group, thus affecting its members more profoundly than non-members or non-believers. Another type of actor that merits special consultation is groups that have been traditionally marginalised within societies or are special for other reasons. For example, the rights of indigenous peoples to participate in decision-making that affects them have been recently and most comprehensively laid down in the UN Declaration on the Rights of Indigenous Peoples;[24] however, the right to be consulted is also explicitly included in documents regulating technology and the effects of technology. Article 7(j) of the Convention on Biological Diversity, requiring state parties to take special care of the needs and wishes of indigenous peoples, is a good example of this.

However, the public, in all its layers, is not the only type of audience consulted in decision-making processes. Like the idea that members of the public can be more affected by a regulatory question than others, the language of stakeholders suggests that some parties have more at stake in a procedure than others. A stakeholder therefore is consulted not because of the additional information that can be gained – although that might be a consequence of inclusion – but because they have an important personal interest at stake. Those with a commercial interest in the regulatory question at issue also therefore demand to be consulted. Within a stakeholder frame of reference, the public, as represented by civil society organisations, is therefore simply one interested party among others.[25] The danger for those who lay emphasis on the importance of participation for participation's sake is that the public becomes just one seat at the table, as suggested by the list of actors identified by van Asselt *et al.*, as the main players in EU decision-making in the licensing of three GMOs:

- Risk producers – those pursuing potentially hazardous activities or technologies: Monsanto
- Risk assessors – experts seeking to analyze risks: the GMO panel of the European Food Safety Authority (EFSA)
- Risk managers – decision-makers charged with regulating risks: the European Council and Commission, and the Member States
- Risk protestors – those objecting to new technologies or activities with reference to potential risks: Greenpeace and Friends of the Earth. These risk

---

[24] United Nations Declaration on the Rights of Indigenous Peoples, General Assembly Resolution 61/295, 13 September 2007, A/RES/61/295.

[25] See earlier consideration of public participation in the context of uncertainty in Chapter 5.

protestors do not have a formal role in this regulatory regime, but they aim to influence the regulation process through lobbying, protecting and critical reports.[26]

The identity of participants in a stakeholder model thus differs from the three-way model suggested by the public participants in Bristol, between the public, the government and scientists. Although there is only one extra additional chair at the table in stakeholder consultation, the model nonetheless differs fundamentally from the republican ideal of participation to form a common will. The aggregation of interests at the base of the stakeholder model demands that the identity of the participants be defined by the all-affected principle.[27] This principle requires that all those affected by a decision have the right to participate in deliberations concerning them. While the all-affected principle increasingly defines the identity of participants in regulatory discussions about technology, as the EU licensing procedure for GMO suggests, it has a major practical flaw in addition to the normative challenge already suggested. This is that, while intuitive, it is extremely difficult to delineate who is affected and who is not. If we consider the question of stem cell research, advances in medical science are generally to the benefit of humankind as a whole – if we ignore the grave disparity between the Global North and South in access to the benefits of medical knowledge: on this basis it would make sense for the whole world to have a say over whether those individual countries at the forefront of medical science prohibit, permit or actively encourage stem cell research. The same is true, of course, in relation to biotechnological developments in food. As technological development is driven largely by global forces, this entails that those interests – both public and private – affected by regulation in a single country stretch beyond national borders and thus beyond the dominant understanding of the modern era that the relevant entity for politics was the nation state. What are we to make of this challenge to decision-making at the national level?

(b) The location of decision-making

One of the most significant tests of the necessary conceit that we govern ourselves is the challenge to the state as the locus of decision-making. As we sought to suggest in Chapter 7, the context in which regulation concerning technology is designed and enforced is shifting away from the national setting: downwards to the sub-state or local level, upwards to the international and horizontally via private and other non-state actors to the transnational. This represents a serious

---

[26] Marjolein van Asselt, Ellen Vos and Tessa Fox, 'Regulating Technologies and the Uncertainty Paradox', in M. Goodwin *et al.*, *Dimensions of Technology Regulation* (Nijmegen: Wolf Publishing, 2010), 268–9.

[27] See Sofia Näsström, 'The Challenge of the All-Affected Principle', *Political Studies*, 59 (2011), 116–34.

challenge to the republican idea that we come together as citizens to form a collective will. The logistical difficulties of public engagement across borders entails that the public is represented in decision-making beyond the state primarily in two ways. The first is via our elected representatives, who negotiate international regulation on our behalf that is – in most systems – later ratified by the national legislature. The Universal Declaration on Bioethics and Human Rights is an outcome of this type of process.[28] The second sees the public interest represented by a wide variety of civil society organisations that mediate between political institutions and the wider public; such groups have gained increasing access rights to regulatory discussions within, for example, the WTO and the EU in recent years in order to fulfil this mediating role.[29] However, a number of fundamental questions remain about the effectiveness of delegating public participation in this way, of settling for indirect participation. The first is how representative civil society organisations really are of global public interest. To what extent can the Northern NGOs that dominate participation at the global level really represent Southern interests;[30] and to what extent do they represent Northern interests, in all their variety, either? The second concerns the limited opportunities at present for public participation in the transnational exercise of governance. The shift from government to governance and the correlating rise in private regimes of regulation risk denying the opportunity for the exercise of either the republican or liberal notions of citizenship,[31] reducing the citizen to little more than a consumer. Although by no means a new concern, nor one limited to questions of technology regulation, the issue of the legitimacy of decision-making beyond the state is likely to remain one of the most important political questions of this century, particularly but, not only, in the field of technology regulation.

(c) The format

In order for participation to meet the twin goals of ensuring both input and output legitimacy, we need to concern ourselves with the format of public

---

[28] See O. Carter Snead for an insider's description of the process, 'Bioethics and Self-Governance: The Lessons of the Universal Declaration on Bioethics and Human Rights', *Journal of Medicine and Philosophy*, 34 (2009), 204–22.

[29] Jens Steffek and Ulrike Ehling, 'Civil Society Participation at the Margins: The Case of the WTO', in Jens Steffek, Claudia Kissling and Patrizia Nanz (eds.), *Civil Society Participation in European and Global Governance. A Cure for the Democratic Deficit?* (Basingstoke: Palgrave Macmillan, 2008). Also, Jan Aart Scholte, 'Civil Society and Democracy in Global Governance', *Global Governance*, 8 (2002), 281–304.

[30] B. S. Chimni, 'Co-option and Resistance: Two Faces of Global Administrative Law', *New York Journal of International Law and Policy*, 37 (2004), 799. Jens Steffek and Kristina Hahn (eds.), *Evaluating Transnational NGOs. Legitimacy, Accountability, Representation* (Basingstoke: Palgrave Macmillan, 2010).

[31] See Robert Howse's consideration of the possibility of global deliberative politics in the context of the legitimacy of the SPS Agreement, 'Democracy, Science, and Free Trade: Risk Regulation on Trial at the World Trade Organization', *Michigan Law Review*, 98 (1999–2000), 2329.

participation; in other words, how participation is framed and modelled plays an important role in the public's perception of legitimacy. A model frame for public participation has been laid down in the Aarhus Convention Access to Information, Public Participation in Decision-Making and Access to Justice in Environmental Matters.[32] Article 8 of the Convention provides:

> Article 8
> Public Participation during the Preparation of Executive Regulations and/or generally applicable Legally Binding Normative Instruments
> Each party shall strive to promote effective public participation at an appropriate stage, and while options are still open, during the preparation by public authorities of executive regulations and other generally applicable legally binding rules that may have an significant effect on the environment. To this end, the following steps should be taken:
> a) Time-frames sufficient for effective participation should be fixed;
> b) Draft rules should be published or otherwise made publicly available; and
> c) The public should be given the opportunity to comment, directly or through representative consultative bodies.
> The result of the public participation shall be taken into account as far as possible.

Article 8 thus requires that public participation take place as early as possible; translated into the regulation of technology, the public needs to be consulted upstream in a technology's development, when all the options are still open, even where the science is uncertain and the applications unknown. One of the reasons cited for the public outcry against GM crops was that engagement with the public about the possible risks and benefits came at a point too late to influence the development of the technology. According to research into the public reaction in the UK, people were protesting not only about the reality of GMOs on farms and in the supermarket but also against the underlying assumptions, and the lack of consultation over them, that had allowed these products to be developed in the first place.[33] Moreover, in order for participation to be effective, Article 8 places the obligation upon state parties to ensure that sufficient time be planned for consultation; that the relevant information is made available and that comments on regulatory proposals may be submitted either directly, i.e. individually or indirectly, through representative civil society bodies, such as NGOs or consumer organisations.

However, the framing of Article 8 remains vague: note not only the vagueness of the terms (participation should take place 'at an appropriate stage' where

---

[32] UNECE Aarhus Convention Access to Information, Public Participation in Decision-Making and Access to Justice in Environmental Matters (1998), 2161 UNTS 447.

[33] J. Wilsdon and R. Willis, *See-Through Science: Why Public Engagement Needs to Move Upstream* (London: Demos, 2004). See also Joyce Tait, 'Upstream Engagement and the Governance of Science. The Shadow of the Genetically Modified Crops Experience in Europe', *EMBO Reports*, 10 (2009), S18–S22.

regulation 'may have a significant effect' and be taken into account 'as far as possible') but also the weakness of the normative language ('should' in place of 'shall'). The same Convention makes much more strict demands of state parties where members of the public are specifically affected by decisions. Article 6 provides:

> Article 6
> Public Participation in Decisions of Specific Activities
> …
> 2. The public concerned shall be informed, either by public notice or individually as appropriate, early in an environmental decision-making procedure, and in an adequate, timely and effective manner, *inter alia*, of:
> (a) The proposed activity and the application on which a decision will be taken;
> (b) The nature of possible decisions or the draft decision;
> (c) The public authority responsible for making the decision;
> (d) The envisaged procedure, including, as and when this information can be provided:
> (i) The commencement of the procedure;
> (ii) The opportunities for the public to participate;
> (iii) The time and venue of any envisaged public hearing;
> (iv) An indication of the public authority from which relevant information can be obtained and where the relevant information has been deposited for examination by the public;
> (v) An indication of the relevant public authority or any other official body to which comments or questions can be submitted and of the time schedule for transmittal of comments or questions; and
> (vi) An indication of what environmental information relevant to the proposed activity is available; and
> (e) The fact that the activity is subject to a national or transboundary environmental impact assessment procedure.
> 3. The public participation procedures shall include reasonable time-frames for the different phases, allowing sufficient time for informing the public in accordance with paragraph 2 above and for the public to prepare and participate effectively during the environmental decision-making.
> 4. Each party shall provide for early public participation, when all options are open and effective public participation can taken place.
> 5. Each Party should, where appropriate, encourage prospective applicants to identify the public concerned, to enter into discussions, and to provide information regarding the objectives of their application before applying for a permit.
> 6. Each Party shall require the competent public authorities to give the public concerned access for examination, upon request where so required under national law, free of charge and as soon as it becomes available, to all information relevant to the decision-making referred to in this article that is available at the time of the public participation procedure, without prejudice to the right of Parties to refuse to disclose certain information in

accordance with article 4, paragraphs 3 and 4 [where the public authority does not possess the information requested or is prevented from releasing it in order to protect community rights or the rights of others, such as national security or the confidentiality of commercial information]. The relevant information shall include at least, and without prejudice to the provisions of article 4:

(a) A description of the site and the physical and technical characteristics of the proposed activity, including an estimate of the expected residues and emissions;

(b) A description of the significant effects of the proposed activity on the environment;

(c) A description of the measures envisaged to prevent and/or reduce the effects, including emissions;

(d) A non-technical summary of the above;

(e) An outline of the main alternatives studied by the applicant; and

(f) In accordance with national legislation, the main reports and advice issued to the public authority at the time when the public concerned shall be informed in accordance with paragraph 2 above.

7. Procedures for public participation shall allow the public to submit, in writing or, as appropriate, at a public hearing or inquiry with the applicant, any comments, information, analyses or opinions that it considers relevant to the proposed activity.

8. Each Party shall ensure that in the decision due account is taken of the outcome of the public participation.

9. Each Party shall ensure that, when the decision has been taken by the public authority, the public is promptly informed of the decision in accordance with the appropriate procedures. Each Party shall make accessible to the public the text of the decision along with the reasons and considerations on which the decision is based.

10. Each Party shall ensure that, when a public authority reconsiders or updates the operating conditions for an activity referred to in paragraph 1, the provisions of paragraphs 2 to 9 of this article are applied *mutatis mutandis*, and where appropriate.

11. Each Party shall, within the framework of its national law, apply, to the extent feasible and appropriate, provisions of this article to decisions on whether to permit the deliberate release of genetically modified organisms into the environment.

As in Article 8, Article 6 requires that participation in decision-making take place as early as possible (paragraph 4); Article 6 also requires that all the necessary information be made available to facilitate public participation, and in a language and format that they can readily comprehend (paragraph 6). The public will be allowed to submit information themselves (paragraph 7) and the outcome of public participation is to be taken into account in the actual decision-making, i.e. public consultation cannot be an empty exercise (paragraph 8). Finally, the public must be informed about the decision and the reasoning motivating it (paragraph 9). These requirements of the Aarhus Convention represent benchmark standards for the framing of public participation. Yet, it is not solely the level of detail that separates Article 6 from Article 8. The terminology and language of Article 6 are tough and uncompromising: 'shall' in place of 'should' throughout the paragraphs, and requirements such as the need to inform the public promptly of decisions taken (paragraph 9).

What are we to make of the difference in language and tone between the two articles? The different approach reflects the Convention's liberal design. Emphasis – the stricter language of Article 6 – is laid not on the duty of participation for the sake of the collective – as guaranteed by Article 8 – but on the rights of individual members of the public to protect their own interests. The Aarhus Convention thus views public participation through a liberal lens, guaranteeing the projection of autonomy into the public realm and serving a guard-dog function of ensuring that the action of the collective, first, does not impinge unnecessarily upon the freedom of individuals and, second, that the decisions taken serve their interests. Here, public participation most resembles informed consent.

Beyond the type of public participation envisaged in the Aarhus Convention, other modes of participation involve bringing different stakeholders together, such as the public engagement exercises in the UK that brought scientists and members of the public together to talk through the issues involved in regulating nanotechnology. In their examination of science in society, the House of Lords Science and Technology Committee drew up a list of principal formats for engaging the public based upon experience in the UK and around the world. The list comprised:

- Consultations at national level
- Consultations at local level
- Deliberative polling
- Standing consultative panels
- Focus groups
- Citizens' juries
- Consensus conferences
- Stakeholder dialogues
- Internet dialogues
- The [UK] Government's Foresight programme[34]

In addition, public participation is not simply confined to exercises in public engagement but flows throughout the various stages of the regulatory process. An important aspect of this is the holding of decision-makers, whether from the public or private sector, to account for their actions or inactions. This

---

[34] House of Lords Select Committee on Science and Technology, *Science and Society* (2000), para. 5.3. The UK Government Foresight programme is designed to help government think systematically about the future in order to improve how we use science and technology within government and society. This information contributes both to the quality of public debate and to government decision-making. See www.bis.gov.uk/foresight/about-us (last accessed 24 July 2011).

requires access to justice for both individual members of the public and civil society organisations acting on behalf of individuals or groups in order to challenge the design of regulation, individual decisions affecting them or to assert liability when things go wrong. One of the three central pillars of the Aarhus Convention is therefore a guarantee of access to justice. However, in keeping with the liberal tilt of the Convention, the right of access to justice here, while containing a broad right to challenge the denial of a request for information, restricts a right of review to challenge the procedural or substantive legality of a decision to individuals with 'a sufficient interest' or whose rights have been impaired.

There is thus no one established format that is the norm in ensuring that participation meets its legitimacy goals; and most consultation exercises employ a combination of formats. The format or combination adopted will necessarily depend upon how legitimacy goals are defined and what the underlying normative framework is. For example, whether the focus is more on input legitimacy or whether output legitimacy is stressed will affect both the scale and format of participation. Moreover, as we attempted to show above, the normative tilt of the background politics will significantly affect understandings of whether the regulatory regime is successful in meeting demands for public participation.

(d) The background conditions for effective participation

Yet in order for participation to be meaningful or effective in terms of its stated goals, however they may be defined, certain prerequisites or background conditions need to be in place. For example, as the Human Rights Committee noted above in paragraph 8 of General Comment No. 25, freedom of expression, of assembly and of association constitute essential background conditions without which genuine public participation is not possible. In its most recent statement on freedom of expression, the Committee is more explicit about the role that this right in particular plays: 'Freedom of expression is a necessary condition for the realisation of the principles of transparency and accountability.'[35] Freedom of expression is so central to public participation not simply because it guarantees the freedom to voice one's opinion but also because it incorporates the freedom to seek and receive information – an essential part of communicating with others and of organising collectively to give one's opinion greater weight. Having access to a wide variety of sources of information is an important element of this. A report by the UK Food Standard Agency notes that the most trusted sources of information vary across location. For example, while in Asia the media is the preferred source of information; in the United States, regulators at the federal level inspire most confidence; and in Europe, information from consumer and activists groups was widely seen as the most

---

[35] Draft General Comment No. 34: Article 19 (upon first reading by the Human Rights Committee); 101st session, 2011; CCPR/C/GC/34/CPR.6.

trustworthy.[36] Citizen participation thus requires that citizens have access to a wide range of information of their choosing, as they decide themselves what they find trustworthy.

Related, but not identical, freedom of information constitutes a second background condition for effective participation. Freedom of information concerns the right of citizens to have access to official information and documents relating to the exercise of authority. Many countries in the world provide constitutional guarantees of freedom of information, matched by implementing laws.[37] The multiple roles that access to information plays in facilitating public participation in regulatory processes are stated in the preamble to the Aarhus Convention as follows:

> improved access to information and public participation in decision-making enhance the quality and the implementation of decisions, contribute to public awareness of environmental issues, give the public the opportunity to express its concerns and enable public authorities to take account of such concerns.[38]

The central importance of freedom of information to gaining public trust in regulation has been recognised by the House of Lords Science and Technology Committee in a recent report, which noted:

> For any new technology to succeed, the trust of consumers is vital. In the food sector, gaining that trust is a particular challenge – as recently demonstrated by the public reaction to the introduction of technologies such as genetic modification and irradiation. If the potential benefits of nanotechnologies are to be realised, consumers will need to feel confident that they are informed about the risks as well as the benefits and about the balance between them.[39]

The House of Lords Committee went on to note that consumer fear is often the result of a lack of official information. In studies provided to the Committee by the US-based Project on Emerging Nanotechnologies, based at the Woodrow Wilson International Center for Scholars, when focus groups were asked what was most important to reassuring them about the safety of nanotechnologies, they all responded with a single factor: 'transparency'.[40]

While the free flow of information – both official and unofficial – is an important element of transparency, which constitutes our third background condition or prerequisite for meaningful public participation, the two are not identical. Freedom of information is a claim on the part of citizens against public authorities for something concrete: data, files, intelligence, and so on.

---

[36] Brook Lyndhurst, *An Evidence Review of Public Attitudes to Emerging Food Technologies* (London: FSA, 2009), 10.

[37] See *Wikipedia*, 'Freedom of Information Legislation', for a global overview of such provisions; http://en.wikipedia.org/wiki/Freedom_of_information_legislation (last accessed 24 July 2011).

[38] Aarhus Convention, preamble.

[39] House of Lords Science and Technology Committee, 1st Report of Session 2009–2010, *Nanotechnologies and Food*, vol. 1, section 7.1.

[40] *Ibid.*, at section 7.15.

Transparency represents a broader concept, as a paper on internet filtering by Ronald Deibert and Nart Villeneuve illustrates. Deibert and Villeneuve note the harmful impact of internet filtering on freedom of information but, as the extract suggests, a lack of transparency constitutes a stand-alone harm:

> Internet control filtering is a term that refers to the techniques by which control is imposed on access to information on the Internet. Content filtering can be divided into two separate techniques. Blocking techniques refer to particular router configurations used to deny access to particular Internet Protocol (IP) addresses or blocking filter at the international gateway level that restricts access from within the country to websites that are deemed to be illegal, such as pornographic or human rights websites. Content analysis refers to techniques used to control access to information based on its content, such as in the inclusion of specific keywords. Because parsing mechanisms employ keywords to block access, they are often the source of mistaken or unintended blockages.
>
> ...
>
> Content analysis is a fast growing approach. Previously considered too restrictive and unreliable, content analysis technologies are taking advantage of the massive growth in computing power. Using this approach, content is filtered when keywords or phrases are found within the request for content or within the content itself. Content analysis techniques provide a potentially powerful way for states to parse out fine-grained bits of information contained within sites, as opposed to filtering entire sites altogether. The practice might be likened to censoring out individual sentences within books, as opposed to censoring entire books themselves.
>
> Content filtering technologies are prone to two inherent flaws: underblocking and overblocking ...
>
> Overblocking is a significant challenge to access to information on the Internet, for it can put control over access in the hands of private corporations and unaccountable government institutions. In addition, because filters can be proprietary there is no transparency in terms of the labelling and restricting of sites. The danger is most explicit when the corporations that produce content filtering technology work alongside undemocratic regimes in order to set up nationwide content filtering schemes.[41]

The harm that this extract describes lays not only in being denied access to certain sites or content but also in the fact that we do not know that access is being denied because the filtering takes place automatically. As we do not know that we are being refused access to certain content, we cannot challenge it. Transparency – including freedom of information – is essential therefore if we are not only to be able to hold government to account but also in order to be able to form a well-reasoned opinion, one based on all the facts.

A further background condition that has been put forward in the context of public participation in the regulation of technology is a reasonable level

---

[41] Ronald J. Deibert and Nart Villeneuve, 'Firewalls and Power: An Overview of Global State Censorship of the Internet', in Klang and Murray, *Human Rights*, 112–13.

of public education, i.e. that the public concerned are able to understand the information provided to them and form a reason-based decision. We noted above that a report on the outcome of public engagement exercises in the UK on nanotechnology remarked upon the challenge in such exercises posed by the low level of scientific education in the general population. However, the House of Lords took up this issue of public ignorance and emotionally driven risk aversion, noting research that suggests that common-sense provides a sufficiently solid basis for public participation:

> 2.55 It is widely assumed that one of the roots of public mistrust of science is ignorance, and in particular the public's apparent insistence on zero risk and absolute certainty. Many of our witnesses pointed to the tendency for opinion-formers to have an arts background and to regard science as difficult or at any rate different. 'Even among well-educated groups there is little stigma in United Kingdom society in claiming ignorance of science' (MRC p. 351) ...

> 2.56 However some current research suggests that the public in fact understands uncertainty and risk well, on the basis of everyday experience. People use common sense to interpret and evaluate what they hear about technological advances, and attempt to put it in its cultural, social and ethical context and to translate it into terms which are useful or at least relevant to themselves (Cons Assn Q 609; Nat Hist Mus p. 62). As illustrated by the survey data cited above, given proper information, people are often able to weigh risks against benefits, evaluate uncertainties, and reach sensible and even sophisticated judgements. On this view, one of the major factors engendering mistrust is the failure of institutional science at the frontiers of knowledge to admit publicly its own uncertainties and to provide accordingly.

> 2.57 So, for instance, there was no public outcry when genetically modified tomato paste went on sale in the United Kingdom in 1995, clearly labelled as such so as to allow consumers to choose to avoid it. What set the scene for the more recent uproar was the marketing of unsegregated mixtures of natural and GM soya and maize, implying not only, as noted above, that the only issue at stake was the science, but also that the science was sufficiently certain for consumers to be deprived of choice. Although it is highly likely that, in both cases, the natural and GM products are equally safe, it is possible that uncertainty over whether the cultivation of GM plants carried risks of affecting other plant species affected people's judgement about a wholly different type of risk, namely the possibility of toxicity to humans. It is notable that the US Food and Drug Administration (FDA) is reviewing its position on the issues of segregation and labelling of GM foods, in the light of events in Europe; the FDA held a series of public meetings on these issues in November and December 1999.

> 2.58 There is probably truth in both propositions. In areas where the risks are perceived to be imposed and regulated by others, such as public transport or food supply, people are understandably inclined to demand high

> and possibly unattainable levels of safety and certainty. In areas where people feel more control, such as smoking and driving, they tend to be more pragmatic and even reckless. It is hard to predict a priori what the public will regard as 'safe enough'; but it should cause little surprise if what the public find acceptable does not correspond with the objective risks as understood by science.[42]

Education is perhaps then less of a background condition than is a willingness to engage with the available information and with each other to form a reasoned opinion. For this to be effective, however, participants must be willing to listen to the evidence and also to change their minds. But what happens when participants in the discussion reason from a basis of incommensurable values?

4 Ethical plurality: the problem of incommensurability

The great Oxford historian of ideas, Isaiah Berlin, outlining his concept of value pluralism, wrote: 'there are many different ends that men may seek and still be fully rational, fully men, capable of understanding each other and sympathising and deriving light from each other'.[43] Many of the concepts that we identified as boundary markers in Chapter 8 not only sit uneasily alongside one another but are incompatible in a given moment. How, for example, are we to reconcile Nozick's advocacy of a genetic supermarket with the fundamental concerns about alterations to human species identity articulated by Habermas and Sandel? How should we attempt to combine a utilitarian position on artificial intelligence with a perspective that believes that humans are possessed of dignity because of our unique relationship with a deity? As Berlin suggests, to argue from such radically different normative standpoints does not make one unthinking, insane or less than fully human. Instead, such plurality is a fact of human existence.

It is because of this need to live with ethical plurality that deliberative politics has become such a dominant aspect of contemporary understandings of legitimacy. If we cannot agree on substantive questions, the idea is that we can at least agree on a procedure for how to decide on what to do in the face of competing conceptions of the good life. It is this idea that has motivated the theories of the most influential political philosophers of our time. John Rawls, for example, adopts what he terms a quasi-pure proceduralist theory of justice as a means of reconciling disagreement. Arguing from the position of an 'overlapping consensus', Rawls writes:

> if the law actually voted is, so far as one can ascertain, within the range of those that could reasonably be favoured by rational legislators conscientiously trying to follow the principles of justice, then the decision of the majority is practically

---

[42] House of Lords Select Committee on Science and Technology, *Science and Society* (2000).

[43] Isaiah Berlin, 'The Pursuit of the Ideal', in *The Crooked Timber of Humanity*, ed. Henry Hardy (London: Pimlico, 2003), 11.

authoritative, though not definitive ... We must rely on the actual course of discussion at the legislative stage to select a policy within the allowed bounds.[44]

Similarly, for Habermas, where the complex cultural mix of society inevitably means that citizens are unlikely to find consensus on values, they must find one in a legitimate process for the enactment of laws.[45] Diversity and differing conceptions of the good life thus remain distinct from the overarching political culture, which does not 'detract from the legal system's neutrality vis-à-vis communities that are ethically integrated at the subpolitical level.'[46]

However, proceduralism is not capable of overcoming radical disagreements over fundamental values. This is so in two ways. The first is that if boundary markers give expression in public discussions on technology to our most fundamental beliefs about what we understand the human story to consist in, we are unlikely to be able to compromise on them, even just a little bit. To leave our deeply rooted values at the door of the debating chamber is to betray them. For this reason, we are unlikely to be able to agree to disagree should we fail to persuade our fellow citizens or other interlocutors of our opinion; and any regulatory outcome that denies our most fundamental beliefs is unlikely to be legitimate in our eyes. We do not simply, as Habermas would have us do, leave our value systems at home as we enter the political realm. The private is political.

Where the first problem concerns the inability of pure proceduralism to overcome radical ethical disagreement, the second holds that proceduralism can never be pure or neutral in the first place. Instead, disagreement goes all the way down. The Canadian political philosopher James Tully has sought to capture the deep-seated nature of this difference. Tully has argued that the search for *uni*versality or a single common procedural frame is a dead-end alley; instead our societies are a multiverse and hence political dialogue must also be.[47] For example, what one perspective deems to be rational – as participants necessarily are in Rawls's original position – may not be rational from another; for most liberals and utilitarians, the legislator is irrational where it bases its decisions on the will of God. However, for believers, the will of God is the most important motivation of all and hence is entirely rational. In contrast to both Rawls and Habermas, Tully, and other advocates of agonism,[48] do not accept that there can be a neutral frame or language (such as public reason) in which deliberations can take place. Instead the rules of the game – *especially* the rules of the game – must themselves be capable of being challenged in the

---

[44] John Rawls, *A Theory of Justice* (1971) (rev. edn, Oxford: Oxford University Press, 1999), 318.
[45] Habermas, 'Equal Treatment of Cultures and the Limits of Postmodern Liberalism', *Journal of Political Philosophy*, 13 (2005) 1, 10.
[46] Habermas, 'Struggles for Recognition in the Democratic State', in *The Inclusion of the Other*, ed. C. Cronin and P. de Greiff (Cambridge, MA: MIT Press, 1996), 225.
[47] James Tully, *Strange Multiplicity* (Cambridge: Cambridge University Press, 1995), 131.
[48] See, for example, Chantal Mouffe, *The Democratic Paradox* (London: Verso, 2000); Also, Mouffe (ed.), *Dimensions of a Radical Democracy: Pluralism, Citizenship, Community* (London: Verso, 1992).

process of deliberation, as the procedure always already represents the dominant political language.

The failure of proceduralism to overcome radical disagreement is nicely demonstrated by the regulation of the commercialisation of biotechnology at the international level through WTO law.[49] It is not simply that allegedly ethically neutral trade rules fail to overcome ethical differences – as demonstrated by *European Communities – Measures Affecting the Approval and Marketing of Biotech Products* – but that trade rules are in themselves not neutral in the first place. Rather, they reflect the globally dominant language of liberal capitalism that sees scientific advancement as an unmitigated good. It is this failure that the House of Lords took explicit note of in its report entitled *Nanotechnologies and Food*; the Committee stated that public engagement activities 'will not settle ethical issues that can arise in the development and marketing of foods containing nanomaterials'.[50]

Yet, even where we acknowledge the devastating sharpness of the agonistic critique, the answer is not despair but to go on talking. We may not be able to achieve a consensus, and the rules governing the framing of decision-making processes may be subject to challenge, but this makes public deliberation all the more important, not less. We may, however, need to lower our expectations of what it can achieve.

5 Conclusion

In these four chapters, we have attempted to provide a frame for understanding how discussions about the ethical legitimacy of technology regulation – the purposes, standards and means of regulation – is constructed, debated and opposed. By suggesting that we view discussions about the ethical limits that communities set for themselves through the trope of boundary-marking concepts, we have attempted to provide an introduction to how we construct and use concepts to mark the ethical boundary and what background assumptions – or normative frameworks – motivate us to do so. Being clearer about how we do our ethical reasoning – what we do when we talk about human dignity, for example – is a crucial part of making our ethical deliberations both more effective and more open to the reasoning of others with whom we do not share the same basic moral assumptions, despite the ostensibly shared vocabulary. In this chapter we have sought to highlight how public participation is increasingly employed in technology policy-making in the context of radical disagreement over ethical boundaries and now constitutes a crucial marker of legitimacy itself. That we are unlikely to find agreement – whether at the national level or in the spaces beyond the state – should arguably not stop us from trying.

---

[49] For an examination of the problem of ethical plurality in the context of biotechnology at the WTO, see Thomas Cottier, 'Genetic Engineering, Trade and Human Rights', in F. Francioni, *Biotechnologies and International Human Rights Law* (Oxford: Hart, 2007).

[50] House of Lords, *Nanotechnologies and Food*, section 7.2.

Part IV
Regulatory effectiveness

11

Regulatory effectiveness I

1 Introduction

The regulatory environment will be defective if it does not assist in achieving the intended regulatory effects. Exceptionally, a regulatory intervention might be designed to have a purely symbolic effect, that is to say, its intention might be to make a moral statement rather than to actually change the conduct of regulatees. In such a case, regulatory effectiveness is, so to speak, intrinsically secured. Typically, however, regulatory interventions are designed to channel and to change conduct; the effectiveness of such interventions is not intrinsically secured; and the measure of effective regulation is whether the intervention impacts on the conduct of regulatees in the intended way. What, though, is the key (or what are the keys) to regulatory effectiveness? What is it about a regulatory environment that promises to make it fit for purpose?

Turning this question round, we might suppose that, in principle, there are three ways to account for a regulatory intervention that fails to be effective. First, there might be a failure with the regulators themselves; whether for reasons relating to a lack of regulatory integrity or intelligence or arising from a lack of resource, regulators simply do not go about their business in a way that serves the regulatory objectives. Second, there might be resistance on the part of regulatees; for whatever reason, regulatees do not comply. Third, the failure might be explained by the intervention of a third party, including a rival regulator, or by some circumstances that lie beyond the control of both regulators and regulatees. This being so, we can say that a particular regulatory environment will promise to be effective where regulators are competent and properly equipped for their task, where regulatees are disposed to comply, and where there are no disruptive externalities.

In principle, at each stage of the regulatory cycle – whether at the stage of standard-setting, monitoring compliance or correcting for non-compliance – these elements might be in play. So, for example, the incompetence of regulators or the lack of resources at their disposal might be problematic right from the start or it might only become problematic as attempts are made to implement and enforce the regulation (for example, where those who are responsible for standard-setting act with integrity but enforcers are corrupt). Similarly, regulatees who are not disposed to comply might be active at once, lobbying for loopholes or exemptions in the standards that are set, or they might only resist once the standard has been set; and the same applies to interference that stems from third parties or externalities.

Even if regulatory interventions are effective, some critics might still be less than fully satisfied, insisting that regulation should also be efficient and economical. Indeed, section 7 of the Human Fertilisation and Embryology Act 2008 requires the Human Fertilisation and Embryology Authority (the HFEA) to carry out its statutory functions 'effectively, efficiently and economically' and in such a way that it has 'regard to the principles of best regulatory practice (including the principles under which regulatory activities should be transparent, accountable, proportionate, consistent and targeted only at cases in which action is needed)'.[1]

In this chapter, we will introduce regulatory effectiveness in three stages. First, we will clarify the concept of regulatory effectiveness and how this relates to ideas of economy and efficiency. If the performance of the HFEA is subject to review on the grounds of effectiveness, efficiency and economy, we need to be clear about what is being required of the agency. Second, we will review a set of twenty regulatory guidelines that are proposed by Stuart Biegel at the conclusion of his study of the regulation of cyberspace.[2] So far as effectiveness is concerned, Biegel highlights the importance of regulators being smart and intelligent in their approach and of regulatees being supportive in their response. Where regulators are not smart in their selection of the appropriate regulatory instruments, any resulting ineffectiveness might be put down to regulatory incompetence; and, where there is a lack of consensus amongst regulatees that an intervention is appropriate, we can treat ineffectiveness as a consequence of regulatee resistance. Biegel also draws attention to the problem of interventions having unanticipated (and undesired) consequences. In the third part of this chapter, we will take this up by considering two cases – one concerning a restrictive approach to the use of genetic information by insurers and the other a permissive approach to the granting of patents on segments of the human genome – where regulatory interventions can be seen as having precisely such unwelcome consequences.

As we have said, where a regulatory intervention is ineffective, we might put this down to a failure on the part of the regulators, and/or to regulatee resistance, and/or to the disruptive effects brought about by third-party interference or externalities. In the three chapters that follow, we put the spotlight on each of these sources of regulatory ineffectiveness. Thus, in Chapter 12, our focus is on regulator failure; in Chapter 13, it is on regulatee resistance; and, in Chapter 14, we focus on third-party interferences, particularly those that have been facilitated by the development of the internet.

---

[1] Section 7 operates by inserting new sections 8ZA(1) and (2) into HFE Act 1990.
[2] Stuart Biegel, *Beyond Our Control?* (Cambridge, MA: MIT Press, 2003).

2 Effectiveness, economy and efficiency

In our introductory remarks, we noted that the Human Fertilisation and Embryology Act places the regulatory authority under a statutory obligation to discharge its functions 'effectively, efficiently, and economically'. Seemingly, it is not enough that the regulatory authority is effective in carrying out its supervisory, inspection and licensing functions; it must also apply its regulatory resources in ways that seek out economies and efficiencies.

This language – the language of the 3Es – derives from the regulatory thinking associated with so-called new public management (and, concomitantly, the philosophy of value-for-money governance). The UK Cabinet Office, giving some guidance as to these measures of performance, starts by differentiating between 'inputs', 'outputs' and 'outcomes'.[3] Thus:

> At the most basic level, three dimensions of a service may be measured:
> - the inputs – financial, human, material – that go into providing it (e.g. the cost of building a school)
> - the outputs achieved (e.g. the number of council houses available for let)
> - the outcomes achieved (for example, fewer deaths from heart disease).
>
> These measures may be applied to the service as a whole, or to the processes involved. Processes are likely to be simpler to measure, although clearly they will only present part of the picture.

The guidance then explains the 3Es relative to the three service dimensions as follows:

> In isolation, such measures are of limited value. However, expressed in relation to one another, they enable us to assess the economy, efficiency and effectiveness (the 3Es) of an organisation, and the overall value for money it achieves.
>
> Measures of **economy** reflect the cost of acquiring resources such as staff, premises or supplies. An organisation would have improved its economy if it acquired more units – for example, new computers – for less money.
>
> Measures of **efficiency** relate inputs to outputs, demonstrating how well the organisation makes use of its resources to achieve the desired end result. For example, how many detections were achieved per police officer? These may also be referred to as productivity measures. Improvements in efficiency occur when an organisation achieves more outputs without a commensurate increase in resource consumption (or a reduction in resource consumption for the same outputs).
>
> Measures of **effectiveness** relate outputs to outcomes, throwing light on the impact of the service provided. For example, what proportion of New Deal trainees were still in employment six months after they left the scheme?

What should we make of this? Although the guidance is helpful in drawing a broad distinction between inputs and outputs, arguably, it is less successful in

---

[3] See, Cabinet Office, 'Performance Measurement as a Tool for Modernising Government' (London: HMSO, 1999).

drawing a coherent distinction between outputs and outcomes. What precisely is the difference between action or intervention that produces a certain number of council houses for let and one that reduces the number of deaths caused by heart disease? Why is the former an example of an 'output' and the latter an example of an 'outcome'? This lack of clarity would be of no great import if it were not for the fact that 'efficiency' is expressed as relating inputs to 'outputs', and 'effectiveness' as relating 'outputs' to 'outcomes'; and this, again, would be of no great moment if regulatory agencies, such as the HFEA, were not liable to be called to account for the effectiveness, efficiency and economy of their performance.

While the HFEA and others might be subjected to the discipline of the 3Es, it is not so clear that all sections of government are held to account in quite the same way. For example, when the Nuffield Council on Bioethics examined the ethics of the rapidly growing National DNA Database, it was unable to establish how effective, efficient, and economical DNA profiling was in detecting crime.[4] On the face of it, the Council thought that the more modest Scottish database was at least as effective (and presumably more economical). Following the decision of the European Court of Human Rights in *Marper* (see Chapter 4), the government agreed to adopt the general features of the Scottish model; but this was because the database was judged to be incompatible with the UK's human rights commitments and not because there was any lack of confidence in its effectiveness. Indeed, as the following exchange between Tom Brake (for the House of Commons Home Affairs Select Committee) and Mr Alan Campbell MP (Parliamentary Under-Secretary of State at the Home Office, with a responsibility for crime reduction) indicates, government has an unshakeable (and unsubstantiated) belief in the technology.[5]

> **Q120 Tom Brake:** I would just, first of all, like to ask a question about the cost-effectiveness of the DNA Database. Earlier witnesses from the police have made it clear that there has been no assessment of whether maintaining a DNA Database is more cost-effective in tackling crime than any other policing approach. Does the Government carry out cost-effectiveness assessments of different crime-tackling approaches or not?
>
> *Mr Campbell:* We have not carried out an assessment in the way that you have described, but we do acknowledge – and I am sure I am sharing the view of the police – that we regard the DNA database as absolutely crucial in the fight against crime. To some extent, we are leading the way, both in the technology but, also, in the use of DNA and of the Database, and we regard it as of enormous importance and, therefore, of value when it comes to tackling crime.
>
> **Q121 Tom Brake:** However, you do not actually have any independent analysis of that which suggests that the DNA Database is more cost-effective at tackling crime than, say, investing in training officers to deal with rape cases, for instance?

---

[4] Nuffield Council on Bioethics, *The Forensic Use of Bioinformation: Ethical Issues* (London, September 2007).

[5] See House of Commons Home Affairs Committee, *The National DNA Database* (Eighth Report, Session 2009–10), evidence given on 5 January 2010.

Mr Campbell: I will go away and look to see whether any work has been done, but none to my knowledge. What I would say is that DNA is only one part of the fight against crime, but in our view it is a crucial part. There are a number of examples that I could give where DNA has been that vital piece of evidence which has led to detection and, ultimately, the conviction of some of the most serious criminals, not just to, as far as one can, put at rest the concerns of the families but, also, of course, to protect the wider public from what those people would have gone on to have done.

It is, actually, very difficult to measure the effectiveness of the DNA database. We can easily overestimate its effectiveness by assuming that 'matches' between profiles and crime-scene samples translate into convictions, or by assuming that without the match there would have been no conviction. When it comes to economy and efficiency, there is reason to think that, contrary to the belief that the larger the better, the marginal benefits decline rapidly as the profiles of petty criminals and the innocent are added to the database. Moreover, it is always important to remember that, on any calculation, DNA plays a role in only a tiny percentage of overall convictions – indeed, according to the calculations carried out by Sheldon Krimsky and Tania Simoncelli: 'DNA plays a role in only about 1 out of every 1,000 convictions.'[6]

For our purposes, the overriding priority is to clarify the concept of regulatory effectiveness. In our usage, the challenge of regulatory effectiveness focuses on (a) the impact of the intervention, whether the impact is expressed in terms of outputs or outcomes, and (b) the extent to which that impact is in line with the regulatory purposes (whether expressed as the regulatory targets, aims, or objectives). Once this key concept has been clarified, the less important notions of economy and efficiency can be given their own meaning.

(a) Regulatory effectiveness

Where should we start looking at, and for, regulatory effectiveness? Arguably, the criminal justice system is as good a place as any. Even if this regime is not an obvious benchmark or bellwether for regulatory effectiveness, it is a part of the regulatory environment that is under constant scrutiny for its effectiveness. Sadly, one of the facts of regulatory life seems to be that criminal justice systems fail to deter, fail to detect, and fail to correct a great deal of criminal activity.[7] Politicians, criminal lawyers, criminologists and penologists devote huge amounts of time to figuring out how we can do better. A constant stream of criminal justice initiatives is brought forward; but there is no simple answer. Short of capital punishment or indefinite detention, no one thing works in

---

[6] Sheldon Krimsky and Tania Simoncelli, *Genetic Justice* (New York: Columbia University Press, 2011), 313.

[7] For a seminal critique, see Richard Danzig, 'Towards the Creation of a Complementary Decentralized System of Criminal Justice', *Stanford Law Review*, 26 (1973), 1.

preventing recidivism; and, even the most severe of sanctions fail to stop the commission of crimes to which they are applied.

In some respects,[8] it is a rather depressing story and nowhere more so than in the lower courts where the futility of the system is most painfully exposed. In this light, consider the following prologue to a policy briefing by the Bow Group.[9]

> A defendant stands in the dock at Camberwell Green magistrates' court in South East London and, in a broken voice, enters a plea of guilty to a charge of theft by shoplifting. The facts are simple. The previous day, making no attempt to hide what he was doing, he stole £60 worth of razor blades from the local supermarket and walked out. He was arrested immediately.
>
> Grey faced and clearly unwell, he has a trembling whisper and unsteady bearing of an old man. He clings to the dock with shaking hands and stares at his feet because he hasn't the strength to hold up his head. Every so often he scratches relentlessly at his arm. The District Judge asks him to confirm his age. Twenty-six.
>
> This is the defendant's twenty-eighth conviction for theft or burglary in the last seven years. It's a certainty that he got away with crimes at the beginning of his career, but now he lacks the skill and insight to get away with anything. Where understanding once influenced his actions, now holes exist. There's no linkage anymore between theft and the consequences of capture. Need comes before caution.
>
> The District Judge invites the defendant's solicitor to speak in mitigation. It's a familiar story. The Court has heard it a thousand times before. Inner City Council-Estate – dysfunctional family background – violent, drunk father – Prozac addicted mother – parental neglect – truancy from school – illiteracy – no qualifications – bad company – and a downward spiral into physical addiction through glue sniffing and cannabis.
>
> Now dependent on heroin, the defendant has become a compulsive thief and burglar, selling the stolen goods to feed his habit. After being abandoned by his family who can no longer cope with his dependency, he has no fixed abode and cannot give the name of anyone willing to take him in. Speaking on his behalf the solicitor says that his client is motivated to kick his habit – *yet again* – but the court is reminded that the defendant has used this excuse on every previous appearance.
>
> Imagine you are the District Judge and you had heard all this before and would hear it all again tomorrow. What sentence should you pass on this once young man?

The author of the briefing, himself having sat as a judge in the criminal courts, concludes that 'much of current and recent court sentencing practice is completely ineffective in dealing with the drug addict criminal'.[10] Moreover, not only

---

[8] It might seem strange to put this in such qualified terms; however, a criminal justice system that is fully effective might itself be pathological. See Roger Brownsword, 'Code, Control, and Choice: Why East is East and West is West', *Legal Studies*, 25 (2005), 1.

[9] Humfrey Malins, 'Crackpot: A Fresh Approach to Drugs Policy' (Bow Group, 27 December 2006), at 4.

[10] *Ibid.*, at 2.

is the system seemingly incapable of correcting such offenders, it only succeeds in detecting their crimes when they are so helpless that they make no attempt to conceal their criminality.

So, what judgement should be made as to the effectiveness of such a system? Should we conclude that modern criminal justice systems simply are not fit for purpose? Is this tantamount to saying that they represent a case of regulatory failure? Or, should we treat regulatory effectiveness and ineffectiveness as a matter of degree?

First, we can agree with Francis Fukuyama[11] that:

> [N]o regulatory regime is ever fully leak-proof, and if one selects a sufficiently long time frame, most technologies end up being developed eventually. But this misses the point of social regulation: no law is ever fully enforced. Every country makes murder a crime and attaches severe penalties to homicide, and yet murders nonetheless occur. The fact that they do has never been a reason for giving up on the law or on attempts to enforce it.[12]

It follows that, if we set the bar for regulatory effectiveness at the level of complete achievement of the regulators' objectives, we will judge that virtually all regulatory interventions are ineffective. On the other hand, if we set the bar at a much lower level, we will find ourselves declaring that some regulatory intervention is effective when the *ex post* state of affairs merely represents an improvement (relative to the regulatory objectives) over the *ex ante* situation. Where, then, should we set the threshold for regulatory effectiveness?

Second, in response to the question where we should set the bar for effectiveness, we suggest that we might do better to focus on the relative effectiveness and ineffectiveness of a particular regulatory intervention. If we adopt such a focus, we can answer the question that actually interests us, namely, whether (for better or worse) the regulatory intervention is actually making a difference.

Third, there might also be a less obvious advantage in thinking about regulatory effectiveness in terms of such a spectrum of effect rather than in all-or-nothing terms. So long as we are thinking about an intervention that is designed to prevent the occurrence of certain conduct, we have a pretty clear idea as to the state of affairs that would reflect complete regulatory effectiveness – namely, a state of affairs in which no conduct of the regulated kind occurs. However, if the intervention is designed to incentivise, encourage and promote certain conduct (for example, in the way that the patent regime is intended to promote innovation), it is not so clear what would count as complete regulatory effectiveness. No doubt, regulators could identify a certain target level of activity to supply the effectiveness threshold (for example, so many small business contractors with a viable online enterprise, so much online consumption, and the like); but, if the regulatory view is that the more of the particular activity the better, an effectiveness ceiling is artificially imposed. Once again, then,

---

[11] Francis Fukuyama, *Our Posthuman Future* (London: Profile Books, 2002).   [12] *Ibid.*, at 189.

we might do better to abandon a simple distinction between regulation that is effective and regulation that is ineffective and treat regulatory effectiveness always as a matter of degree.

If this suggestion for treating regulatory effectiveness as a matter of degree seems plausible, it might be because it presupposes traditional regulatory environments in which the regulatory signals are normative. Where the regulatory strategy becomes more reliant on technological instruments, where the environment is such that desired patterns of conduct are designed in (or undesired patterns designed out), it might be meaningful and appropriate to revert to an all-or-nothing notion of regulatory effectiveness. Perfect (technologically secured) regulatory control implies complete regulatory effectiveness. Even then, though, there is a caveat.

Suppose that regulators decide, for safety reasons, that the maximum speed for lorries should be 56 mph and that drivers should not work for more than ten hours in any 24-hour period. Adopting a technological strategy, regulators prescribe that lorries should be built with the appropriate speed regulators, monitors and immobilisers. So fitted, lorries simply cannot exceed 56 mph and the ten-hour limit cannot be breached. Provided that regulators can also ensure that every lorry that is on the road is compliant with these regulatory requirements, we might judge that this is an effective (100 per cent effective) regulatory intervention. However, lorries and drivers that are so limited can give rise to other problems. For example, it can take a lorry that is flat out at 56 mph several miles to overtake another lorry that is travelling at just short of 56 mph; and this can cause a dangerous tailback on motorways. Or, in emergency situations, when drivers need to be at work for more than ten hours, the immobiliser prevents this happening. In other words, a regulatory intervention might be fully effective in relation to its focal purpose but the effectiveness of the intervention has a collateral cost and these undesired consequences need to be factored into the judgement as to the effectiveness of the intervention.

Lest we should think that factoring in the undesired consequences is relatively straightforward, consider a variation on the above scenarios. Let us suppose that, by and large, motorists think that far too much police time is devoted to detecting road traffic offences. According to popular sentiment, the resources of the criminal justice system should be targeted at 'real crime' and 'real criminals'. If, assisted by new technologies, such as automatic number plate recognition and the like, the policing of the roads becomes even more effective, this might be badly received not only by the motorists whose offences are detected but by the general public; and this might be damaging to the public support and willingness to cooperate that is essential for an effective criminal justice system.[13] As Scott Adams once quipped, if the good news is that the police, aided

---

[13] See Claire Corbett, 'Roads Policing: Current Context and Imminent Dangers', *Policing: A Journal of Policy and Practice*, 2(1) (2008), 131–42; and 'Techno-Surveillance of the Roads: High Impact and Low Interest', *Crime Prevention and Community Safety*, 10 (2008), 1.

by new technologies, will solve 100 per cent of all crimes, then the 'bad news is that we'll realize 100 percent of the population are criminals, including the police'.[14]

Clearly, the possibility of a regulatory intervention having unanticipated consequences is an important consideration and we will return to this question in the fourth part of the chapter.

(b) Regulatory economy and efficiency

Regulation is not costless; and there is sometimes a sense that the bureaucracy of regulation is top-heavy. If savings (with regard to the regulatory inputs) can be made without any loss of regulatory effect, then why not exercise this economy? Equally, if there are levels or mixes of resource input at which we find significant increments in regulatory effect, then why not try to maximise the return that we get on our regulatory investment? After all, whether the regulatory resource is publicly or privately funded, it makes sense to strive for value for money.

Suppose, for example, that regulators, having decided that genetic discrimination by employers is as objectionable as racial or sexual discrimination, prohibit such discriminatory practices and establish a genetic discrimination unit (the GDU) to monitor employers and to enforce the prohibition. Let us suppose further, however, that employers generally see little advantage in the genetic profiling of their employees (prospective and actual) and that, apart from a few exceptional cases, employers make no attempt to discriminate on the basis of genetic information. With regulatees having little interest in flouting the regulation, the GDU might seem to be over-resourced. Accordingly, we might judge that, in the interests of regulatory economy, there should be a reduction in GDU resources. Indeed, we might judge that keeping the GDU lean and mean makes sense not only relative to considerations of economy but also to avoid the GDU using its surplus resources for unintended and possibly counter-productive purposes.

Once we have trimmed the regulatory resource to the point where any further cut will reduce the *effectiveness* of the regulatory intervention, we have taken regulatory *economy* as far as we should. However, this still leaves the consideration of regulatory *efficiency*, understood as the optimal gearing of regulatory input to effective regulatory output. Consider again the example of genetic discrimination by employers. However, let us suppose that the attitude of employers is exactly opposite to that previously hypothesised. Let us suppose, in other words, that employers have for some time been genetically profiling their employees (prospective and actual) and that they believe it is essential for the profitability of their businesses. In such a setting, the GDU, far from

---

[14] Scott Adams, *The Dilbert Future: Thriving on Business Stupidity in the 21st Century* (London: HarperBusiness, 1998), 194.

pushing at an open door, faces widespread and deep resistance to the regulatory prohibition against the practice of genetic discrimination that is already embedded. Given such resistance, regulators anticipate that it will take a major regulatory effort to turn things round. Facing this challenge, let us suppose that regulators commission projections as to the regulatory impact of various levels of regulatory resource. What the projections suggest is that a regulatory input of resource x (say, an annual budget of £10m. for the GDU) will reduce genetic discrimination by 10 per cent, that a regulatory input of resource y (say, an annual budget of £15m. for the GDU) will reduce genetic discrimination by 50 per cent, and that a regulatory input of resource z (say, an annual budget of £20m. for the GDU) will reduce genetic discrimination by 55 per cent. On the basis of such projections, considerations of regulatory efficiency point to resource y. For, although this level of regulatory investment does not do as well in terms of regulatory effectiveness as higher levels of investment, the ratio of input to output is superior at this lower level.

That said, once we try to finesse effectiveness, economy and efficiency in this way, we are normally leaving the real world behind. In the real world, regulatory intelligence is far less sophisticated. If we understood how to deliver effective regulation, we might be able to fine-tune it for economy and efficiency; but, in the present state of the art, this is something of a pipe dream.

To return to one of our introductory remarks, what precisely does it mean to require the HFEA to carry out its functions 'effectively, efficiently and economically'? The demand for regulatory economy is reasonably clear; and, given the very limited budget for the HFEA, it is unlikely to be accused of being wasteful – this is a regulatory agency that operates on the proverbial shoestring. So far as effectiveness and efficiency are concerned, the Cabinet Office guidance would suggest that we should be checking how inputs relate to outputs and how outputs relate to outcomes. However, even if these terms had a clear meaning – which they do not – it is difficult to imagine how they might be applied to the work of an agency, such as the HFEA, which covers a broad range of purposes. Regulatory oversight in relation to an evolving field of science and medicine is scarcely comparable to building so many council houses or reducing the incidence of fatalities caused by heart disease. We might conclude, therefore, that the regulatory environment within which the HFEA operates suffers from a lack of clarity, a significant cause in itself of regulatory failure.[15]

---

[15] The limitations of the underlying ideology of 'better regulation' are neatly captured by Tony Prosser in *The Regulatory Enterprise* (Oxford: Oxford University Press, 2011): 'After all, "better regulation" is not simply a matter of "less is more"; it is a matter of ensuring that, so far as possible, regulators do their best to implement properly the rationale for their work, not only in maximizing efficiency and consumer choice, but also in, for example, protecting the environment, health and safety and patients' rights. The most appropriate approach will differ depending on the rationales, for example for those regulators concerned with protecting human rights the "lifting burdens" approach will be less appropriate than monitoring their effectiveness in achieving such protection' (*ibid.*, at 22).

3 Guidelines for regulatory effectiveness

Gathering together the threads of his study of the regulation of cyberspace, Stuart Biegel proposes twenty regulatory guidelines. This extremely useful exercise helps us to develop our thinking about the factors that make for effective and ineffective regulatory interventions. However, because, these guidelines are generated in the context of the regulation of *cyberspace* and they are not specifically focused on effectiveness, we need to filter out those particular guidelines that are clearly not material for the present discussion. Having done that, we can consider how Biegel's guidelines on effectiveness relate to the three sources of regulatory ineffectiveness that we have identified.

Biegel, *Beyond Our Control?*, 359–64[16]

1. Beware of grand generalizations regarding the current state of cyberspace regulation and the advantages or disadvantages of regulation across the board. Some cyberspaces are, in fact, beyond our control at the present time, but many others are not. For some situations, regulatory solutions make sense, while other problem areas should simply be left alone.
2. When addressing a particular problem area, consider the entire range of regulatory approaches, including litigation, legislation, policy changes, administrative agency activity, international cooperation, architectural changes, private ordering, and self-regulation. In cyberspace, it is reasonable to assume that a creative combination of approaches will be more *effective* than any single regulatory strategy.
3. In order to ensure that the Internet retains its ability to serve as a dramatic and unique marketplace of ideas, it is essential that would-be regulators continue to respect the autonomy of individuals and groups in the online world.
4. The status quo, however, should not necessarily be viewed as inviolable. Certain aspects of the online world can and should be changed. And solutions can be crafted for individual cyberspaces that will not impact other cyberspaces. Beware of all-or-nothing arguments that view any change in the law for a particular situation as the first step down a slippery slope. Cutting back the rights of either the powers-that-be or individual Netizens in certain areas does not have to mean that it will be this way across the board.
5. No analysis of prospective regulatory approaches to specific problems is complete without reviewing the academic journal databases to take advantage of the many creative proposals and recommendations in the cyberspace regulation literature of the past six to eight years.
6. Care must be taken to avoid viewing cyberspace regulation issues in a vacuum, and the classification of problematic activity into one of four categories is an important first step in this process. By determining whether certain online behaviour constitutes dangerous conduct [e.g., cyberterrorism], fraudulent conduct [e.g., in e-commerce], unlawful anarchic conduct [e.g., copying and

---

[16] The italics highlighting the use of the word 'effective' (or 'effectiveness') are ours; and the examples supplied in square brackets in the sixth guideline are the ones discussed by Biegel in the body of the book.

file-sharing] or inappropriate conduct [online hate], patterns can be identified and helpful signposts can be pinpointed within a larger context. In addition, such an approach recognizes that Internet-related problems can be as varied as the range of issues that must be addressed by legislators and policy makers in the offline world.

7. If we are committed to maintaining the present-day version of the Internet, then consensus among the various stakeholders will be an essential component of an *effective* problem-solving approach. Under current conditions, given the highly participatory nature of online activity and the distributed, anarchic design of cyberspace itself, there are a host of ways to get around most restrictions that may be imposed. In addition, new architectural changes can often be countered by other code-based solutions. Thus a proposed regulatory approach may not be possible unless those that have the ability to resist agree to go along with the plan. And the list of such persons and entities would include not just the powers-that-be, but also Internet advocacy groups, virtual communities, and individual Netizens.

8. Any decision regarding how to regulate an online activity must necessarily begin with a determination of just how unique the particular setting and specific behaviour might be. Certain conduct may be no different in cyberspace than it is in the offline world, while other conduct may be so dependent on speed, scale, and anonymity that it may require a very new regulatory approach.

9. The inherent limits of our legal system must always be addressed by would-be regulators of the online world. These limits are especially important in cyberspace, and range from the difficulties of establishing a rule of law in complex territory with many variables to the practical limits of any effort to bring everything and everybody under control.

10. In spite of these limitations, however, both the existing rules and any prospective new strategies that might be developed under the traditional law model should invariably be considered first. Statutes, case decisions, and administrative agency activity have already made a difference in certain key areas. And while no law enforcement operation is ever completely successful, a rule of law that modifies the behaviour of most people can indeed constitute a reasonable solution in the end.

11. Particularly from a US perspective, it is important to note the centrality of the federal regulatory approach. State laws may have value in some areas that are typically regulated on that level, but given the ease with which borders can be crossed in cyberspace, a legal structure that can impact a larger geographic area will often be more *effective*.

12. Even though the United States has continued to dominate both access to cyberspace and the nature of online content, the Internet must inevitably be viewed at least on some level as a global communications medium. Given the fact that at any particular moment persons may be connected to the Internet from anywhere in the world and through servers located across the globe, international agreement and cooperation has become an essential component of any regulatory strategy. As the Internet continues to foster globalization and as nations move toward the identification of international baselines

for certain key areas of the law, the prospects for international cooperation are surprisingly good here.

13. Code-based change at various levels of the Internet architecture has emerged as potentially the single most powerful regulatory strategy available. Especially when combined with one or more of the other models, software solutions can have a dramatic impact in a setting that is in fact comprised solely of binary code. Yet even as caution must be exercised in this area so that the essential nature of cyberspace does not change, it must be recognized that code-based changes in the online world have often been successfully countered by other code-based changes.

14. Private ordering continues to be set forth as a viable regulatory option by many stakeholders, and its potential *effectiveness* either by itself or in creative combination with other approaches should not be overlooked. It is in fact useful to identify two types of private ordering. The first – private architectural adjustment through the use of filtering, firewalls, and other security measures – can serve a protective function for individuals and groups against unlawful or inappropriate activity. The second – private rule-making by networks, content providers, and institutions – will typically dictate what others can and cannot do. While the former is appropriately viewed as a subcomponent of the broad architectural change model, the latter can generally be seen as a type of self-regulation.

15. Whatever strategies or combination of strategies that are ultimately adopted, regulators must set forth guidelines that are clear, direct, and understandable. Intellectual property laws, for example, have proven notoriously difficult for the average online user to comprehend, and the new statutory schemes that were added in the late 1990s have served to further complicate this territory. Everyone benefits from rules that are simple and straightforward.

16. In addition, regulatory approaches must be realistic. While this may seem inherently obvious, we have noted, for example, that the law has not truly come to grips with private personal copying since the advent of the Xerox machine and the widespread availability of audiotaping and video-taping technology. Certain adjustments have been made, but most of the personal day-to-day copying that takes place in the privacy of an individual's own home has remained subject to the vagaries of conflicting legal interpretation.

17. As a related corollary, the importance of the implicit social contract in cyberspace must also be taken into account. Clear and realistic rules are an important beginning, but it must also be recognized that, on some level, our legal system is often based upon an implicit social contract. People must want to follow the law, and if they decide they no longer wish to do so, the implicit social contract breaks down. Particularly in certain cyber spaces, where law-breaking is still very easy, steps must be taken to foster a spirit of cooperation between and among all online users.

18. To this end, regulators must recognize and build on existing social norms. While there has been much debate in the legal and policy literature regarding the extent to which Internet norms can be pinpointed, most commentators agree that – at least for specific areas of the law and in particular cyber spaces – identifiable traditions and clear community standards do exist.

Examples of generally accepted activity that may have already influenced the development of the law in this regard include linking without permission, a commitment to a libertarian view of free speech rights, an ongoing consensus regarding a perceived right to remain anonymous, and a broad acceptance of file sharing technology to create new digital copies of previously protected works.

19. Ultimately, in the area of cyberspace regulation, there is no magic formula and no quick fix. Particularly for certain intractable problems, solutions simply cannot be imminent. In these cases, it is important to identify combinations of approaches that may serve to move things in the right direction. Compromises that may seem unacceptable now could become central features of such new approaches under one or more of the three major regulatory models – traditional national law, international agreement, and code-based change.

20. The Internet today is one of the great achievements of the modern era, and any attempt to adjust its realities for regulatory purposes must proceed slowly and with great caution. Perhaps the most important of all the inherent limits of our legal system is the rule of unintended consequences. Especially in the light of the fact that cyberspace technology will inevitably continue to change, it is essential that we seek to avoid modifications that may have unanticipated effects. While there are no guarantees, since such effects are not always obvious at the time a new strategy is adopted, a regulatory approach that builds upon these twenty principles will begin with a good chance of success.

Four of these guidelines, namely, 2, 7, 11 and 14, explicitly refer to effectiveness; and the implicit reference is strong in thirteen of the other guidelines, namely, 1, 4, 5, 8, 9, 10, 12, 13, 15, 16, 17, 19 and 20. This leaves guidelines 3, 6 and 18. Before we review the guidelines that refer, explicitly or implicitly, to effectiveness, what do we make of the residual three guidelines?

Guidelines 3 and 18 (especially the former) might be read as specific to the regulation of the internet and, moreover, as being concerned with legitimate rather than effective regulation. So interpreted, these guidelines demand that regulators should respect the autonomy of online users and follow the grain of evolving custom and practice. On the other hand, in so far as we think that the effectiveness of regulation depends upon a positive reception by regulatees (which Biegel clearly does), then this guideline speaks to an important indicator of effectiveness. In freedom-loving communities, encroachments on autonomy will be resisted; and, in any kind of community, regulation that tries to override existing social norms will be opposed. In both cases, these guidelines go to the heart of questions of effectiveness.

Guideline 6 gathers up one of the most prominent features of Biegel's analysis. It is not initially clear (at any rate, not from the short summary statement) why Biegel thinks that the classification of the problem in terms of the kind of conduct is so important. Is some kind of regulatory triage being exercised here? Is it that we need to prioritise the application of scarce regulatory resources? If so, this is a guideline that speaks to regulatory economy or efficiency rather than regulatory effectiveness. In fact, the better reading of Biegel's intentions is that he believes that this classificatory exercise facilitates regulatory effectiveness; and that it does so in two respects. First, the classification will help regulators to gauge the level of support for a regulatory intervention; and, second, it will point to those combinations of regulatory instruments that are most likely to work. In both cases, we might think that the utility of the classification exercise could be expressed more directly; but, be this as it may, the point is that, on this reading, guideline 6 also speaks to critical elements of effectiveness.

If we now include guidelines 3, 6 and 18 in our list, how do the various guidelines relate to our three keys to regulatory effectiveness? Which guidelines focus on regulators, which on regulatees, and which on third parties?

First, almost all the guidelines bear on the approach of regulators: above all, regulators need to be 'smart' in just the sense that so-called smart regulatory theorists advocate,[17] thinking about the best mix of regulatory instruments (see guidelines 2, 6, 12, 13, 14 and 19). They also need to act in an intelligent well-advised way (see guidelines 4, 5, 8, 10 and 20), to be realistic (see guidelines 1, 9 and 16), and to have a clarity of purposes (see guideline 15).

Second, considerable attention is given to securing the backing and support of regulatees (see guidelines 3, 6, 7, 17 and 18). In a sense, a key aspect of the regulatory intelligence is to understand that, without a supportive consensus in the part of regulatees, an intervention will struggle to have the intended effect.

Third, there are occasional hints as to externalities, most obviously on the references to the extra-territorial and jurisdictional considerations which were very much to the fore in the early debates about regulating cyberspace (see guidelines 11 and 12).

Each of these is a matter to which we shall return (in Chapters 12–14); but, in the next part of this chapter, we can take a more careful look at what Biegel calls the rule of unintended consequences.

4 Unintended consequences

In traditional regulatory environments, where the signals are normative, the impact of a regulatory intervention will depend upon how regulatees react to the signal. It is possible that they will react in ways that regulators have not anticipated and that the intervention will lead to unintended consequences. Occasionally, those consequences might be welcome – for example (admittedly a somewhat unlikely example), regulatee compliance with a ban on smoking in public places might lead to a heightened sense of responsibility for one's own health which, in turn, might lead to a reduction in the consumption of alcohol. Our principal interest, however, is in interventions that have consequences that

---

[17] See, Chapter 2: in general, Neil Gunningham and Peter Grabosky, *Smart Regulation* (Oxford: Clarendon Press, 1998); and, with regard to cyberspace in particular, Lawrence Lessig, *Code and Other Laws of Cyberspace* (New York: Basic Books, 1999), ch. 7.

are not only unintended but also viewed negatively by regulators (and, quite possibly, by regulatees).

Sometimes, the negative consequences are collateral (as in our earlier example of lorries that are speed-limited); at other times, they turn back on the focal regulatory purpose itself – the regulatory intervention, in other words, sets in train a sequence of events that renders the intervention entirely self-defeating relative to the regulatory purpose.[18] Famously, for example, John Adams suggested that regulatory interventions to improve the safety of motor cars (by building in safety features) have tended to lead drivers to think that they are safer in their vehicles; which, in turn, has encouraged drivers to take more risks; as a result of which overall safety levels have been brought back to where they were prior to the regulatory intervention.[19] Provocatively, Adams argued that, instead of requiring motor manufacturers to fit seatbelts, and air bags, and the like in cars, regulators should require manufacturers to fit a spike in the centre of the steering wheel.[20]

Where a regulatory intervention has an impact on the financial circumstances of regulatees, we might anticipate some adjustment of position. For example, if regulators, with a view to improving public finances, raise the rates of taxation, regulatees might become much more active in seeking out (lawful) tax avoidance options; as a result of which, far from raising more revenue, the intervention leads to a reduction in the overall tax take. Or, if regulators, with a view to improving the stock of rented accommodation, require landlords to spend significant sums on refurbishing their properties, landlords might switch their investments as a result of which there is a shortage in rented accommodation. However, reactions of this kind are far from unpredictable; and regulators need to proceed with an intelligent appreciation that taxpayers and businessmen will be disposed to take reasonable steps to protect their financial interests. In other words, smart regulators will be astute to such responses; they will anticipate consequences of this kind and endeavour to minimise the risk of unintended negative effects.

In what follows, we can consider two cases in which a well-intended regulatory intervention might set in train unintended negative consequences. Whether or not regulators should anticipate such consequences is open to debate; but the more that regulators are attuned to the patterns of regulatee response, the better the chance of avoiding such effects.

(a) Insurers and genetic discrimination

Our first case concerns the prospect that insurance companies might require applicants either to take genetic tests or, where test information is already

---

[18] Compare Cass R. Sunstein, 'Paradoxes of the Regulatory State', *University of Chicago Law Review*, 57 (1990), 407.

[19] John Adams, *Risk* (London: Routledge, 2001).   [20] *Ibid.*, at 143.

available, to disclose that information to prospective insurers. At a time when it was assumed that many disorders would be traceable to single genetic markers, this kind of information was seen as being highly material to any insurers operating in health-related sectors (such as medical insurers). With the realisation that the relationship between genetic markers and disorders is much more complex than this simple one-to-one model suggests, it is not so clear that genetic information has quite such dramatic utility to insurers who, anyway, have access to an applicant's medical history. Although the debate about regulating the insurance market in a way that does not involve an unacceptable form of genetic discrimination has lost some of its early heat, it still offers an interesting study in potential regulatory effectiveness.

In Europe, regulators have responded in a variety of ways to the risk that insurers might unfairly require the disclosure of genetic information. Some regulators have adopted a highly restrictive position (so-called 'total regulation'), prohibiting insurance companies from either requiring genetic tests to be taken or, where test information is already available, requiring disclosure of the results. According to a less restrictive approach (so-called 'partial regulation'), insurers are prohibited from requiring genetic testing as a precondition of insurance but they are permitted to insist upon the disclosure of test information that is already available. These restrictive regulatory regimes may be fine-tuned in various ways, particularly by admitting exceptions for high-value policies. Away from these restrictive regimes, regulation may be permissive, allowing insurance companies to require the disclosure of genetic information in just the way that any other kind of material information must be made known to the insurer. In some cases, the regulation (particularly of the more restrictive kind) is in a hard law form; in other cases, as in the United Kingdom, it is in a soft law form. In some places, regulatory positions have been firmed up; in others, again as in the United Kingdom, regulators are in 'monitoring and reviewing' mode before making up their minds. Our interest is in those restrictive regimes that have opted for total regulation. On paper, they are most protective of whatever interests we have against genetic discrimination; but will they work?

In *Genes and Insurance*,[21] the case against such regulatory regimes is advanced, the authors contending that, far from having the intended effect of shielding those whose genetic make-up would otherwise disadvantage them in the insurance market, this kind of regulatory intervention is likely to induce the collapse of a market that can no longer bear the weight of its high-risk burden. In other words, the thesis is that the consequences of adopting total regulation will be to destroy the very insurance markets that regulators are seeking to maintain for the benefit of those who have high-risk genetic profiles.

Let us assume that the intended purpose of total regulatory regimes is to prevent insurance companies from discriminating against applicants whose

---

[21] Marcus Radetzki, Marian Radetzki and Niklas Juth, *Genes and Insurance* (Cambridge: Cambridge University Press, 2003).

genetic profile shows up as a bad risk and, concomitantly, to protect such applicants against being priced out of, or excluded altogether from, vital insurance or insurance-financed services. In this way, the intention underlying such regulation is that the private insurance market should mimic solidarity-based social insurance. Yet, the authors observe, the regulators seek to do this at just the time that social insurance is being dismantled. Not only this, this particular regulatory approach is adopted in the face of burgeoning information about the human genome and in a context of globalisation. Putting these pieces together, the authors argue that total regulation simply will not work.

To understand why there is a problem with such regulatory regimes, we need to recall a truism about disclosure in contracting situations. In many contractual negotiations (including negotiations for insurance), there is an asymmetry of information. The asymmetry might favour the purchaser or the provider. If the former, then the rational–economic purchaser will disclose the information in question if the effect of disclosure will be to reduce the price. However, if the effect of disclosure will be to increase the price, the rational-economic purchaser will not disclose. Now, imagine the position of an applicant for insurance who has information (asymmetrically) about his own genetic make-up. If disclosure of that information will exert a downward pressure on the premium, the information will be disclosed; but if disclosure would exert an upward pressure, the applicant would not usually wish to disclose. The intended effect of total regulation is to permit the latter kind of applicant to withhold the information and, thus, to enjoy what is in effect a discounted premium (as well as avoiding whatever collateral disadvantages might flow from putting this information into circulation). However, the secondary effect of total regulation is that low-risk applicants, who are willing to disclose, are either not permitted to do so or are not able to profit from doing so. In consequence, lower-risk applicants (unwillingly) subsidise those who are higher-risk and, with this, there is a danger that the pool will be destabilised through the process of 'adverse selection'.

In the first instance, the stability of an insurance pool (comprising both high-risk and low-risk insured parties) subject to a regime of total regulation depends on the attitudes of the three key stakeholders. Those who are high-risk parties will normally wish to sustain the pool on total regulation terms (because it is to their economic advantage to do so); those who are low risk will wish to revise the regulatory terms on which the pool operates so that premiums or contributions paid by individuals more faithfully reflect real risk profiles or, failing this, they will wish to exit the pool in order to join a pool with more favourable terms; and, depending upon a number of economic variables, the insurance companies might or might not prefer the pool to be run under total regulation terms or on terms that allow for premiums to be set on sophisticated differential terms. Given this, although there might be some occasional abuses of a total regulation scheme by those who know that they are high-risk, the major impulse for change (and the most likely source of destabilisation) will come from low-risk stakeholders who would prefer to participate in a pool where premiums are adjusted in line with disclosed risk profiles.[22]

While the authors' thesis that total regulation invites adverse selection is certainly plausible, whether or not low-risk stakeholders actually leave the pool depends upon a number of variables about which we can be rather less certain. For example, the dynamics of this situation depend upon:

- how much genetic information we have and just how informative such information actually is for insurance purposes;
- the availability, and ease of access to, alternative insurance pools that operate in accordance with standard rules for disclosure;
- the degree of inertia, caution, longer-term calculation or loyalty displayed by low-risk parties in sticking with their existing pools; and
- whether insurers who operate in total regulation schemes *and who have an interest in sustaining such schemes*, are able either to impose costs against exits that deter low-risk members from leaving, or to devise incentives for staying within the pool.

Having said this, it seems reasonable to assume that, other things being equal, low-risk members will take their business away from insurance pools that are subject to total regulation. As a pool progressively becomes a club for high-risk members, premiums necessarily will rise – and, indeed, as insurers understand what is happening to the pool, they might well inflate premiums in anticipation of the higher risks that they now realise they are covering. With membership becoming more expensive, even high-risk insured parties might have to drop out; and, in due course, dwindling membership might threaten the viability of the scheme so that the few remaining members are treated as uninsurable.

If total regulation will prove self-defeating, does it follow that regulators should abandon this kind of intervention? Given that the purpose of regulators is to prevent the kind of genetic discrimination that they consider to be unfair, the question is whether they have a better option. Simply to abandon total regulation and permit insurers to require genetic tests to be taken, and the results to be disclosed, would also be self-defeating – and it would not even have the virtue of delaying the inevitable. For smart regulators, the question is whether a mix of instruments, encouraging a culture of solidarity, might be effective in achieving the desired regulatory objective; and, if so, what the optimal mix looks like.

---

[22] In identifying low-risk parties as the key source of instability, we are conscious that we are departing from the view that it will be unconscionable profit-taking by high-risk insured that is the real problem. However, there are various ways that insurers can limit their exposure to this kind of opportunism and, with the appropriate safeguards in place, the real problem then lies with low-risk parties. For an appreciation of both high-risk and low-risk sources of difficulty, see Ronald Dworkin, *Sovereign Virtue* (Cambridge, MA: Harvard University Press, 2000), ch. 13.

(b) Patenting the human genome and patent thickets

As we saw in Chapter 1, there has been a sustained, and still unresolved, debate about the patenting of modern biotechnological processes and products. No aspect of this debate has been more fiercely contested than that relating to the patenting of human gene sequences, or fragments of the human genome. The leading objection is that it is immoral to treat such matter as patentable; and, in Europe, where the patent regimes explicitly permit a moral objection to be taken, objectors have argued that a permissive approach to patentability compromises human dignity. However, objectors also take the non-moral point (a) that patent offices have been too easily satisfied that the work being brought forward for protection is truly inventive and (b) that the patents actually granted to cover work on the human genome are too broad. So, for example, the Nuffield Council on Bioethics,[23] having noted this dual generosity in the approach taken by patent offices, strikes a critical tone:

> In general, the law has, in our view, tended to be generous in granting patents in relation to DNA sequences. Not only are many of the patents broad in scope, but they have been granted when the criteria for inventiveness and utility were weakly applied. Many of these patents are broad because an inventor who successfully makes a claim in relation to a DNA sequence will, in effect, obtain broad protection on *all* uses of the DNA, and sometimes the proteins which the DNA produces. This is because the patent system provides that in the case of patents directed to novel and inventive DNA and other chemical entities, inventors are entitled to property rights not only over the uses of their invention that they anticipated or predicted, but over any new uses that are developed.[24]

Yet, why should we object to such an approach? As the Council itself puts it, 'The overall aim of the patent system is to promote the public interest and to provide a fair reward to inventors by offering protection to inventors in return for disclosure of their inventions.'[25] To be sure, a technical-minded lawyer might complain that the technical tests are being misapplied; but, if the regulatory intention is to incentivise research and development in relation to the human genome, a weak requirement of inventiveness coupled with broad patents seems to be an appropriate approach. The problem, however, is that the race to the patent office can be counter-productive; while some researchers are (over)-protected, others find their work stifled by patent thickets. In other words, if this is the regulatory policy, patent law and its application does not have the intended effect; patents, instead of acting as a spur to innovation, act as a serious impediment to downstream (post-patent) researchers.[26]

---

[23] Nuffield Council on Bioethics, *The Ethics of Patenting DNA* (London, 2002).

[24] *Ibid.*, at para. 5.2.   [25] *Ibid.*, at para. 5.1.

[26] See Michael A. Heller and Rebecca Eisenberg, 'Can Patents Deter Innovation? The Anticommons in Biomedical Research', *Science*, 280 (1998), 698.

In this light, consider the following press release issued jointly by Econexus and Genewatch UK.

Econexus and GeneWatch UK, 'Patenting genes: stifling research and jeopardising health care' April 2001

Every day, new patents are being filed for discoveries about genetic material which are obstructing the progress of science and the development of new or cheaper treatments.

Published on the eve of the World Patent Summit in London, research by GeneWatch UK and Econexus shows that gene patents are already:

- preventing or hindering development of new or improved medicines and treatments;
- limiting access to healthcare by increasing the cost of diagnostics and treatment for certain diseases;
- exploiting information and materials and inhibiting their free exchange between researchers;
- involving unsuspecting parties in extensive and costly legal battles.

The research looks at the battles to control three important human genes – the breast cancer gene(s), the erythropoietin (EPO) gene crucial to blood production, and the AIDS virus receptor gene.

'Our research shows that public science is being hijacked. Companies are claiming to have invented discoveries about nature and are profiting unfairly from research about genes, much of which has taken place in universities', said Dr Ricarda Steinbrecher of Econexus. 'For the best healthcare, discoveries about genes must be freely available, not just exclusively to profit the drug companies.'

'Unless the Government takes action to outlaw the patenting of genes and gene sequences, we will find the whole genome has been privatised', said Dr Sue Mayer of GeneWatch UK. 'Companies are getting greedy and the NHS could be bankrupted by having to pay royalties for gene tests and drugs.'

It should be emphasised that it is not just patents in the area of biotechnologies that can be counter-productive. Focusing on the practice of the US Patent Office, Siva Vaidhyanathan[27] sees the story repeating itself in relation to nanotechnologies:

Imagine if some firm held a patent on the brick. The patent would be drawn so broadly as to cover any baked and/or glazed solid building element that would be used to construct lattice structures for human habitation. That firm would be able to charge royalties for most of the simple edifices in the world. It could designate which buildings would go up first and which would have to wait. There would probably be a rush to invent and patent a substitute for the patented brick that would be just different enough to preclude a lawsuit, yet similar enough to work as easily and dependably as a brick. Some buildings would cost much more than

---

[27] Siva Vaidhyanathan, 'Nanotechnologies and the Law of Patents: A Collision Course', in Geoffrey Hunt and Michael Mehta (eds.), *Nanotechnology: Risk, Ethics and Law* (London: Earthscan, 2006), 225.

they do now. Others might never get built at all. A tremendous amount of time and money would be spent trying to negotiate the brick-patent maze ... we are fortunate that we live in a world in which bricks are in the public domain ...

But at a much smaller scale, we have allowed bricks to be patented. In the ill-defined world of 'nanotechnology', a simple sphericule or rod of carbon – the 'buckyball' or 'nanotube' – has been patented not once, but more than 250 times in slightly different forms. The dream of nanotechnology reveals many of the dangers of an overprotective patent system. Paradoxically, an overprotective patent system threatens the potential benefits of a fully realized nanotechnology industry.[28]

As Vaidhyanathan puts it, the 'patent mania of the past two decades has created a "tragedy of the anti-commons".[29] While, on the one side, the patent office is not sufficiently staffed to handle the sheer number of applications and to conduct a stringent review of the prior art, on the side of applicants, 'the incentive to file for overbroad, frivolous, and well-meaning patents has never been higher'.[30] In this way, '[p]atent paranoia has sparked an alarming increase in the number of patent applications filed per year in the United States. And the resulting increase in the potential to extract rents for licensing has led to the creation of a set of firms devoted to nothing more than harvesting patents for later exploitation. These firms invent nothing yet issue many cease-and-desist letters to restrict actively innovative firms from exploiting the techniques that these patent hoarders might control.'[31]

To return to the case of biotechnologies, the sense that the current liberal approach to patenting is having unintended effects comes through particularly strongly in the Nuffield Council's discussion of diagnostic tests based on DNA sequences.

Nuffield Council on Bioethics, *Ethics of Patenting DNA*, ch. 5

5.12 We have already noted that one of the benefits of the patent system is that scientific knowledge about new inventions is put into the public domain, enabling others to develop further inventions and improvements. For most inventions, it will be possible to invent another product that has a similar function, but which is put together in a different way from the existing inventions, such that it does not infringe the patent. This is known as 'inventing around'. [The vacuum cleaner is a case in point]

5.13 When developing products based on genetic material, however, this concept of 'inventing around' is harder to apply because there may be no alternatives to the naturally-occurring DNA sequences. In the case of diagnostic tests, any test for a gene associated with a disease will need to identify whether one of the many mutations in the relevant sequence is present in the individual being tested and will, therefore, have to involve comparison with the DNA sequence of the normal gene. Moreover, if a patent also claims the products expressed by the gene in question, which would

[28] *Ibid.*   [29] *Ibid.*, at 227.   [30] *Ibid.*, at 232.   [31] *Ibid.*

include the proteins which the gene encodes, any alternative tests developed by others based on identifying the presence of such proteins in an individual would require a licence from the holder of the patent.

5.14 A second problem as regards some patents on diagnostic tests based on DNA sequences is that an excessively broad patent that contains claims to *all* conceivable diagnostic tests creates a monopoly, such that there is little incentive to develop improved tests …

5.15 The difficulty in developing improved alternatives to diagnostic tests based on DNA sequences that do not infringe the original patents, which may assert broad rights over the DNA sequence or its use in all areas in which it can be used in diagnosis, is potentially serious. Indeed, one study in the US indicates that research on genetic testing has been inhibited by patents on DNA sequences: almost half of the research laboratories which were surveyed have ceased to pursue such research because of existing patents. Another US study found that as many as 30% of laboratories have discontinued or not developed genetic testing for haemochromatosis because of exclusive licensing of patents that assert rights over the most common mutations in the gene involved. This state of affairs may create too great a monopoly, inhibiting innovation rather than stimulating it …

5.16 As well as potentially restricting the development of improved diagnostic tests, broad patents in this area could also restrict other forms of research. That genes are involved in common diseases is beyond doubt but there is disagreement as to how useful such genes could be in diagnosis … It is widely acknowledged, however, that understanding the role of a large number of genes in a wide range of common diseases and biological pathways will be of crucial importance for research into new medicines. The possibility that many of these genes, or the SNPs associated with them, will be patented at an early stage of research is likely to limit significantly the freedom of other researchers, particularly those in the pharmaceutical industry. They may be prevented from developing and applying what is essentially scientific knowledge for the purpose of creating new medicines and other products relating to healthcare.

How, then, does the Council propose that the regulatory environment should be adjusted?

5.22 We have argued above that allowing property rights to be asserted over all uses, or even all diagnostic uses, of DNA sequences for diagnostic tests based on DNA sequences gives inventors too great a monopoly in the light of the contribution and inventiveness of their product, may hamper innovation and may not, in fact, satisfy the legal criteria for patenting. We think it likely that, if left unchanged, the patent system as it is currently applied to DNA sequences in the case of diagnostic tests will have a deleterious effect on the development and use of such tests. In view of this conclusion, we consider that the criteria for patenting DNA sequences as they apply to diagnostic tests based on DNA sequences should be applied more stringently or amended. Patent offices should critically assess whether the isolation of DNA sequences, in particular human DNA sequences, can any longer be viewed as inventive … We take the view that in the majority of cases, this criterion will not be met …

5.23 One of the main concerns about asserting rights over a DNA sequence in a product patent is that the patent owner has exclusive rights to all subsequent uses of that sequence. One option that is often suggested as a way to avoid the deleterious effects of this, is to limit patents on diagnostic tests based on DNA sequences to use patents, that is, patents which do not assert rights over the DNA sequence itself. It has been argued that the DNA sequence would be freely available for other researchers to develop new products, without having to negotiate a licence. In contrast, a product patent on a diagnostic test for a gene would allow the patent owner a monopoly on all uses of that sequence for any sort of test or other application. For example, if BRCA 1 [one of the main genetic markers for breast cancer] were found to be linked to heart disease, or cancer of the bladder, the rights of the owner of the product patent would extend to these new diagnostic tests or other applications.

5.24 A broad use patent for a diagnostic test for BRCA 1 that referred specifically to breast cancer, would give the owner rights over all testing for that genetic susceptibility to breast cancer, but not for other diseases. However, the effect of the patent owner having broad property rights over the diagnostic use of the gene for just one disease, would be that the patent owner has a monopoly over all ways of testing for that disease. This is because, even though the use patent does not include the sequence itself in the patent claims, in practice, any other diagnostic test for the disease specified in a use patent would infringe that patent … However, if a use patent could be defined, so that the owner of the patent is entitled to rights only to the use of the DNA sequence for his specific diagnostic test for the disease in question, and not *all* diagnostic tests for the disease involving the use of the sequence, this could, on the one hand, provide sufficient incentive for the company to develop the test, and on the other, result in the development and marketing of a number of different tests for the same gene.

Once the problem of over-broad patents or patent thickets has been spotted, there is more than one way of trying to correct it. In addition to the ideas floated by the Nuffield Council in the extract above, consideration might be given, for example, to the use of compulsory licensing[32] or to the widening of the so-called research exemption.[33] However, for at least two reasons, this is a tricky calculation. First, to some extent, regulators see themselves as being in competition with one another and they will not want to take such a restrictive approach that key businesses move their research operations to regulatory environments that they find more supportive of their business activities. Second, if certain kinds of research cannot be protected by patents, then commercial researchers might

---

[32] For discussion by the Nuffield Council on Bioethics, see *Ethics*, paras. 5.25–5.29.

[33] On the current understanding of this exemption for researchers, see Åsa Hellstadius, 'The Research Exemption in Patent Law and Its Application to hESC Research', in Aurora Plomer and Paul Torremans (eds.), *Embryonic Stem Cell Patents: European Law and Ethics* (Oxford: Oxford University Press, 2009), 323.

resort to reliance on trade secret protection. As an impediment to innovative research, this might be even more of a problem. For, patented innovations, unlike trade secrets, are at least in the public domain; and, while some researchers might be prepared to take their chances in infringing complex patent thickets (by proceeding without a licence), they cannot so easily access vital information that is locked up as a trade secret.[34] In a global regulatory marketplace, local regulators hope to stimulate innovation but they also need to give researchers an incentive for putting their inventive work in the public domain.

5 Summary

Our first look at the challenge of regulatory effectiveness suggests that there is much more to making the regulatory environment fit for purpose than we might suppose. It is not enough that regulators make an intelligent selection of their regulatory instruments, nor that regulatees are primed for compliance; it is essential, too, that regulatory success does not either have damaging side-effects relative to other regulatory objectives or (paradoxically) a reflexive effect that undermines the very objective that regulators are trying to achieve. Nevertheless, it is necessary, if not sufficient, that regulators do approach their work in a smart way and it is to this aspect of regulatory effectiveness that we turn in the next chapter.

---

[34] See Antonina Bakardjieva Engelbrekt, 'Stem Cell Patenting and Competition Law', in Plomer and Torremans, *Embryonic Stem Cell Patents*, at 369.

12

Regulatory effectiveness II: failure by regulators

1 Introduction

We have suggested that there are, so to speak, three hot spots where we can locate the keys to regulatory effectiveness and ineffectiveness. In this chapter, our focus is on the first of these loci, the actions of regulators themselves.

We will recall that, in Stuart Biegel's analysis, we saw the significance of regulators being smart and intelligent. However, this is just one of a number of desiderata. To be sure, we need our regulators to be competent and professional, but also we need them to act with integrity. Accordingly, we start by sketching three pathologies: where regulators are corrupt (section 2), where they are captured (section 3), and where they are incompetent (in a broad and inclusive sense) (section 4).

Having sketched these indicators of regulatory character and capacity, we will focus on two test cases of regulator failure: first, data protection (section 5) and, secondly, nanomaterials (section 6). In the first case, even though regulators have tried to put in place a dedicated regime for data protection in a rapidly developing information society, it is arguable that a lack of clarity of purpose coupled with rapid changes in the underlying technologies has frustrated their efforts to deliver effective regulation. In the latter case, the problem is rather different: here the story of regulatory failure turns on regulatory inaction – that is, regulators have failed to adjust existing provisions for health, safety and the environment in ways that both engage with nanomaterials and recognise the promise of this embryonic sector of technology.

Before we embark on this discussion, however, we should say that there is one important kind of 'failure' by regulators that we do not deal with in this chapter. As we have seen in earlier chapters, regulators are seriously challenged where they operate in a context of either prudential or ethical plurality. Responsible and legitimate regulation demands that regulators engage with the plurality of views and that they do their best to respect reasonable differences of opinion. Where the processes of engagement and accommodation lead to compromises being made, we might congratulate regulators; we might see the granting of concessions as evidence of deliberative democracy in action. However, the resulting regulatory product might be less clear than it would have been if regulators had been able to press ahead with their original regulatory intentions; and, indeed, we might find that the intervention is ineffective relative to the purposes of any of the participants in the regulatory process.[1] If this is to be judged a regulatory failure, we find that legitimacy can come at the price of effectiveness – just one dimension of the complex relationship between these two generic challenges that regulators must face.

2 Regulatory corruption

At all points, regulators might be 'buyable'. Sometimes, this might be quite subtle as when standard-setting regulators are exposed to a range of lobbying; at other times, it will be blatant, as when an enforcement officer is on the 'payroll' of regulatees, receiving payments to turn a blind eye to non-compliance or to issue the required licence or permission.[2]

According to John Braithwaite, 'the pharmaceutical industry is more prone to bribery than any other in international business'.[3] Why so? Braithwaite speculates that this is possibly 'because, like the aerospace companies, pharmaceutical firms deal with big win or lose situations – the new billion dollar product to be approved, the ten million dollar hospital supply contract to be won. Moreover, the multitude of regulatory decisions to which pharmaceutical companies are subjected creates many opportunities for buying off regulators'.[4] Based on the evidence on file with the US Securities and Exchange Commission (the SEC), Braithwaite paints a sobering picture of industry-wide declarations of 'questionable payments'. Thus:

> The welter of documents available in the offices of the SEC confirm the conclusion from the interviews with industry executives: bribery is routine and widespread in the international pharmaceutical industry and large amounts of money are involved. Almost every type of person who can affect the interests of the industry has been the subject of bribes by pharmaceutical companies: doctors, hospital administrators, cabinet ministers, health inspectors, customs officers,

---

[1] For an intervention that possibly misfires in this way, see Andrew Murray, 'The Reclassification of Extreme Pornographic Images', *Modern Law Review*, 72(1) (2009), 73 (concerning the prohibition in section 63 of the Criminal Justice and Immigration Act 2008 of the possession of 'an extreme pornographic image'). After debates and amendments in Parliament, the prohibitionists might feel that the offence, as eventually drafted, misses much of the online pornographic material that was the original target for the intervention; and the anti-prohibitionists might worry that the offence will operate as 'a proxy to crack down on the activities of fetish communities' (*ibid.*, at 90).

[2] See, e.g., Ben Bowling, *Policing the Caribbean* (Oxford: Oxford University Press, 2010), at 5, where the Caribbean islands' illicit drug economy sets the context for 'widespread corruption, ranging from the junior Customs officer paid to "look the other way" when baggage handlers are packing aircraft luggage holds with parcels of cocaine at the international airport, to the senior officials who take a cut of the cash generated on their watch'.

[3] John Braithwaite, *Corporate Crime in the Pharmaceutical Industry* (London: Routledge & Kegan Paul, 1984), 16.

[4] *Ibid.*

tax assessors, drug registration officials, factory inspectors, pricing officials, and political parties.[5]

While it is perhaps one thing for international traders to bribe their way into marketplaces where this is the only way of gaining access, it is a very different matter for companies to buy off regulatory controls that are intended to safeguard human health and the environment.

It is true that it takes a lack of integrity on both sides of the transaction before bribes or other corrupt payments will be made and received. To counteract such practice, the regulatory environment needs to be fortified. In other words, there needs to be a strong regulatory environment within which regulation itself is undertaken. Sadly, as Braithwaite notes, the SEC does not have the resources to chase down each and every case of corruption and, in practice, it settles for recording admissions of questionable payments coupled with an assurance that it will not prosecute. Provided that regulatees admit their offences, the regulators will take no further action; but, as the next section highlights, this might not be the full extent of the regulatory agency's weakness.

3 Regulatory capture

It is commonly said that regulators are prone to 'capture' by their regulatees. However, what does this mean? Or, more accurately, what kind of regulatory environment does this presuppose?

When we introduced the idea of a regulatory environment in Chapter 2, we indicated that, while some (Type 1) regulatory environments are constructed in a top-down hierarchical way, others are constructed heterarchically, or even bottom-up (as is the case with a Type 2 self-regulatory environment). Where the regulatory environment is, indeed, bottom-up in its nature, then there is an analytical sense in which regulators are captured by their regulatees – because, quite simply, in such a self-regulatory environment, agents act as both regulators and regulatees. Moreover, it is the fact that regulatees have 'ownership' of their regulatory environment that is seen as key to its effectiveness. In other words, self-regulation implies ownership/capture; and, whatever the shortcomings of self-regulation with regard to the protection of the public interest, this kind of regulatory capture should not be a problem for the effectiveness of regulation.

In general, then, where there are concerns about regulatory capture, we are presupposing a regulatory environment that is more top-down, in which there is a clear separation between regulators and regulatees and, in which, in all probability, there are conflicting interests on the part of regulators and regulatees. In such a setting, we will talk about regulatory capture where, at one or more stages of the regulatory cycle, regulatees are able to exert undue influence

---

[5] *Ibid.*, at 30–2.

over regulators. Where this happens, the standards set (or their interpretation and application) might not truly reflect the purposes that regulators have (or should have);[6] or, if there is no distortion of the standards set, it might be the monitoring or correcting agencies that are captured, as a result of which regulatees are able to deviate without this being effectively picked up or rectified. Paradigmatically, we have a powerful class of regulatees who are able to 'get away with it' because they have influence in regulatory circles.

Consider the common case of a regulatory agency that is charged with monitoring the various medicines and therapies that are available both in the public health system and in the private marketplace. The mission of the agency is to supervise and license these health care products and services, ensuring that patients and consumers (a) are properly informed and (b) are not exposed to undeclared or unreasonable risks. Braithwaite offers many examples of the way in which dangerous drugs (including Thalidomide) have been able to slip through the regulatory net and cause grievous harm to patients and consumers; and in *Dispensing with the Truth*,[7] Alicia Mundy presents an extended account of how the Fen-Phen diet drug found its way onto the marketplace where it took a heavy toll on its users.

According to Mundy, the personal tragedies brought about by use of Fen-Phen might have been averted had American Home Products (AHP) (through its Wyeth-Ayerst division) not been so economical with the truth in relation to the risks associated with the drug and had the prevailing culture at the regulatory agency (the FDA) been less concerned with assisting the pharmaceutical companies to bring their products to market and more concerned with product safety. Once the lawyers were able to make the right connections between the knowledge of the producers of Fen-Phen, the properties of the drug, and the damage done to the complainants, AHP had little choice but to make massive compensatory settlements with individual and mass tort claimants. Generally speaking, the tort system comes out of Mundy's account rather well and public regulation rather badly. By and large, individual tort litigators shine through as honest and independent operators with honourable intentions. However, so far as the FDA is concerned we have a familiar tale of regulatory capture: put crudely, the agency is either not willing or not able to distance itself from the interests of the pharmaceutical companies (resulting in a failure to take a hard look at the companies' claims) and this arises, in part, from the influence that the companies exert directly over the agency and, in part, from the indirect influence that is exerted via the political branch over, *inter alia*, resourcing for the agency.

---

[6] Compare Peter Drahos with John Braithwaite, *Information Feudalism* (London: Earthscan, 2002), at 158, where a US patent attorney is reported as remarking that the utility requirement for the patentability of modern biotechnology is so weak that 'You get utility if you can spell it.'
[7] (New York: St Martin's Press, 2001).

It is not just dangerous drugs that can slip past the regulatory sentries. There are many instances in which the task of monitoring a product or a state of affairs that is a matter of concern to public health is charged to a public agency, but where a hazard gets through the public health net and, having caused personal injury or damage, it is left to the tort system to sound the alarm bells. That the tort system played a key role in cleaning up after BSE (bovine spongiform encephalopathy), tobacco, asbestos, thalidomide, and the like, seems undeniable.

Nevertheless, we should not place too much faith in tort. We need only recall the often-rehearsed limitations that afflict the general effectiveness of private law actions.[8] Potential claimants will often be unaware of their legal position and they will be deterred from inquiring because of the fear of costs, and the like; one-shot individual litigants will do much less well than repeat players;[9] one-off claims, unless they are class claims, might deliver a remedy for the particular claimant but they do little to remedy a more general problem; and the doctrinal hurdles put in front of claimants are serious – even if the adoption of product liability regimes removes the need for the claimant to prove a lack of reasonable care, here and elsewhere there are causation requirements that are notoriously problematic where there is an asymmetry of information between the parties.[10] Not surprisingly, then, the studies consistently indicate that there is a significant underuse of legal measures that are designed to protect more vulnerable persons against exploitation, discrimination, and deception whether in the workplace, in the housing sector, in the consumer marketplace or even in their own homes.[11] In some cases, the parties concerned have alternative (sometimes more satisfactory) ways of dealing with their disputes and grievances; but, in many instances, the victims of wrongdoing who might be expected to come forward to take legal action simply do not do so.

4 Regulatory competence

In what we have called a first-generation regulatory environment, regulators will rely entirely on normative signals, the standard set by the law being one such signal. As regulators begin to rely on non-normative design and coding, the criteria of regulatory competence will change. However, we can start with

---

[8] Compare, e.g., Stuart Biegel, *Beyond Our Control?* (Cambridge, MA: MIT Press, 2003), ch. 4; and Mauro Cappelletti, 'Alternative Dispute Resolution Processes Within the Framework of the World-Wide Access-to-Justice Movement', *Modern Law Review*, 56(3) (1993), 282.

[9] Famously, see M. Galanter, 'Why the "Haves" Come Out Ahead: Speculation on the Limits of Legal Change', *Law and Society Review*, 9 (1974), 95.

[10] The much-discussed relaxation of standard causation principles in *Fairchild* v. *Glenhaven Funeral Services* [2002] 3 WLR 89, does not assist claimants who need the cooperation of better informed defendants if the right causal link is to be established.

[11] No doubt, there are many appropriate references. A good place to start is Vilhelm Aubert, 'Some Social Functions of Legislation', *Acta Sociologica*, 10 (1966), 99; and, generally, see Bob Roshier and Harvey Teff, *Law and Society in England* (London: Tavistock, 1980).

the criteria of competence that apply to regulatory interventions that rely on normative signals.

In a classic discussion of the ideal of 'legalism', understood as a set of procedural requirements, Lon Fuller proposed that the standards set should be general, promulgated, prospective, clear, non-contradictory, (reasonably) constant and possible (of compliance).[12] He also suggested that it was of the essence of the rule of law that enforcement should be congruent with the standards so promulgated. Where the standards are not promulgated, prospective, clear, non-contradictory and (reasonably) constant, regulatees will simply not know where they stand; even if they wish to comply with the regulatory standard, they will not know what it is. If the standard set requires impossible acts of compliance, regulatees cannot comply. Reliance on highly specific regulations will drain most regulatory resource and, again, it will leave many regulatees unclear about their position. And, if there is a disconnect between the standards set and the enforcement practice, not only will regulatees be unclear about their position, they will lose respect for the regulatory regime. If regulators are to be minimally competent, if they are to implement effective interventions, they need to act on these Fullerian principles of good practice.

For many years, jurists have debated whether the Fullerian principles speak only to the conditions for effective regulation or whether, as Fuller insists, they go to the heart of distinctively *legal* forms of regulation.[13] According to Fuller, there is a critical distinction between legal direction and mere managerial direction. As he puts it, 'law is not, like management, a matter of directing other persons how to accomplish tasks set by a superior, but is basically a matter of providing the citizenry with a sound and stable framework for their interactions with one another, the role of the government being that of standing as a guardian of the integrity of this system'.[14] Although, in the context of debates concerning the essential nature (or concept) of law, there is a fundamental choice between a moralised idea of law (evincing a necessary connection between law and morals) and an idea of law as a by and large effective institution for the direction of social life, in the larger regulatory picture other distinctions loom large. In particular, there is the choice between normative and non-normative ordering, between rules (signalling ought and ought not) and design (signalling can and cannot). For Fuller, as for his critics, law and management alike operate with normative registers; they are traditional regulatory environments. However, what happens when we move into second- and third-generation

---

[12] Lon L. Fuller, *The Morality of Law* (New Haven: Yale University Press, 1969). For an application of the Fullerian principles to particular instances of cyberlaw, see Chris Reed, 'How to Make Bad Law: Lessons from Cyberspace', *Modern Law Review*, 73(6) (2010), 903, esp. at 914–16. As Reed summarises it: 'Complexity makes laws hard to understand, contradictory rules make compliance impossible and frequent change compounds these difficulties' (*ibid.*, at 927).

[13] See, e.g., H. L. A. Hart's review of *The Morality of Law*, in *Harvard Law Review*, 78 (1964–5), 1281.

[14] Fuller, *Morality of Law*, at 210.

regulatory environments, where non-normative signals (speaking only to what is practicable or possible) predominate? In such environments, there are many concerns for the virtues of the rule of law; but what would we make of the Fullerian criteria of competence in such settings?

In non-normative regulatory environments, regulators still need to communicate with their regulatees; crucially, they need to signal that only certain options are practically available. To this extent, *clarity* of transmission is still important. Of course, if the regulatory environment, even a regulatory environment in which the signals are not clear, is designed in such a way that regulatees have no option other than to do x, they will eventually do x. Even so, x should be done with less friction and confusion where the regulatory signal is clearly and decisively transmitted. Similarly, we might think that *constancy* has some value even in a non-normative regulatory environment. In other respects, though, the traditional Fullerian criteria no longer seem to be applicable – or, at any rate, their application takes on a new meaning. For example, the requirement that regulators respect the principle of 'ought implies can' by prescribing only the possible takes on a new significance where regulators are operating in a register that recognises only the possible (regulatory approved courses of action) and the impossible (courses of action that regulators have disallowed). Most strikingly, the Fullerian value of *congruence*, which assumes a gap between the standard as declared and as administered, takes on a quite different significance in a context in which there is no such gap. In an increasingly technological age, the threat to the rule of law is not so much regulators who engage in enforcement practices that deviate from the declared rules but regulators who manage risk by adopting undeclared risk management strategies that necessarily enforce the desired pattern of behaviour.

To return to those regulatory environments that rely on normative signals, it will be recalled that, once the norms have been declared (the rules promulgated), the regulatory work is not yet done. After standard setting, there has to be monitoring and, in the event of non-compliance, a corrective regulatory response. Where regulatory agencies are under-resourced, their monitoring activities might be quite inadequate – they will simply fail to detect non-compliance. Moreover, even if non-compliance is detected it might be on a scale that would overwhelm those agencies that are responsible for correction. For example, according to Ian Walden, when the Internet Watch Foundation identified some 7,200 UK persons who were involved with Landslide (a major child pornography site hosted in Texas), this was a level of offending with which the criminal justice system simply could not cope.[15] Moreover, although the authorities in Texas were able to close down the site, as fast as one site is closed many others are opened. If the criminal justice system cannot cope with the general run of crime, it is hardly surprising that under-resourcing is a problem in

---

[15] Ian Walden, 'Porn, pipes and the state: regulating internet content', inaugural lecture, delivered on 3 February 2010, at Queen Mary University London.

relation to newer kinds of online criminality – and, indeed, we might expect to find a similar story where regulatory agencies have somewhat specialised roles and responsibilities.

From time to time, it has been suggested that the resourcing of the Human Fertilisation and Embryology Authority has inhibited its ability to defend its position when challenged by a determined litigator. However, it is the performance of the data protection authorities that has most commonly raised the resourcing issue. It is the view of Peter Hustinx, the European Data Protection Supervisor, that while the regulatory framework is right to focus enforcement on data protection authorities, this has to be on terms that enable them to be effective.[16] The alternatives, he suggests, are even less attractive:

> The first and perhaps most obvious alternative would have been to limit data protection law to sets of rights and obligations and to leave conflict resolution to *existing mechanisms, such as the court system and civil procedure*. However, this would have had at least three negative consequences. Firstly, it would have put most 'right holders' in a very difficult position, left alone with the 'onus of initiative', without adequate expertise and with a very uneven distribution of interests, mostly limited at the individual side and typically rather large at the data user's end. Secondly, as a result, it would have taken a long time before the meaning of legal norms would have become sufficiently clear to have any preventive impact. Thirdly, the consistency of this impact in various sectors would have been dubious and unpredictable and the value of data protection as a fundamental right would have suffered considerably as a result ...
>
> Relying on the *criminal law* as yet another alternative, would have been hardly more attractive. Firstly, in short, the use of criminal law requires clear and precise legal norms but these are mostly not available in data protection, except in special fields. Secondly, violations of data protection provisions would have to compete in practice with other types of simple or complicated 'ordinary crime' and it would be unlikely that enforcement of data protection law would have a high priority on the list. The lack of expertise to deal with these matters in an integrated fashion would in any case have led to unsatisfactory results.[17]

To some extent, these remarks draw on the special character of data protection; but, in general, they echo very frequently rehearsed reservations about the limitations inherent in both private law remedies and in the criminal law. What, then, is the key to effectiveness?

According to Hustinx, the key is to cultivate the right kind of regulatory environment, with the supervisory authorities co-opting intermediary organisations, such as consumer associations and trade unions.[18] 'Independent authorities', Hustinx says, 'should ... not refrain from entering into appropriate and productive relationships with these *different stakeholders*'[19] – a

---

[16] 'The Role of Data Protection Authorities', in Serge Gutwirth, Yves Poullet, Paul de Hert, Cécile de Terwangne and Sjaak Nouwt (eds.), *Reinventing Data Protection?* (Dordrecht: Springer, 2009) 131.

[17] *Ibid.*, at 134.   [18] *Ibid.*, at 135.   [19] *Ibid.*, at 135–6.

possibility that the Commission now seems to have as one of the items on its reform agenda.[20]

5 The regulation of data protection

Few would argue that European data protection law is fit for purpose. As we mentioned in the previous section, a common complaint is that regulators are not sufficiently resourced to detect non-compliance, added to which they are often accused of holding back on the kinds of sanctions that will have some corrective impact. However, this is by no means the end of the indictment. For, in recent years, it has been recognised that some of the problems go right back to the regulatory framework itself, principally, the Data Protection Directive.[21] Two problems can be highlighted: one is the Directive's lack of connection with the rapidly changing world of information technology; and the other is the lack of clarity in the drafting of the Directive.

We will take up the problem of regulatory connection (and disconnection) in Chapters 15 and 16. However, we can say a few words about it here. From the start, some commentators argued that the Directive mapped badly onto the reality of information technology.[22] Already mainframe computers were being overtaken by personal computers, the internet was bringing a new dimension to information technology, and both computer and information technologies were moving rapidly into a global consumer marketplace. This was no longer a tidy world of data controllers and data subjects.[23]

During the lifetime of the Directive, these doubts about the suitability and sustainability of the regulatory framework have intensified. With most technologies, regulators are operating against a shifting background; and, in the case of information technologies, there is a constant movement in the background that challenges the accuracy and focus of the regulatory gaze.[24] In November

---

[20] European Commission, Communication (A comprehensive approach on personal data protection in the European Union), Brussels, 4 November 2010, COM(2010)609 final, see 9 and 17–18.

[21] The Directive on Data Protection, Directive 95/46/EC, OJ L281 (23 November 1995), 31.

[22] Seminally, see Peter P. Swire and Robert E. Litan, *None of Your Business: World Data Flows, Electronic Commerce and the European Privacy Directive* (Washington, DC: Brookings Institution, 1998).

[23] For a clear description of the problem, see Chris Reed, 'The Law of Unintended Consequences – Embedded Business Models in IT Regulation', *Journal of Information and Technology Law*, 1 (2007) (available online at: www2.warwick.ac.uk/fac/soc/law/elj/jilt).

[24] Compare Kirstie Ball, David Lyon, David Murakami Wood, Clive Norris and Charles Raab, *A Report on the Surveillance Society* (September 2006): 'Neither the data protection principles nor the fragmented condition of regulatory machinery and instruments seem fully capable of meeting challenges that are likely to be posed in the future from public, private and combined sources. The advent of many new information and communication technologies ... including the Internet and mobile telematics, and the coming environment of AmI and ubiquitous computing that integrates many and varied surveillance devices, puts a question-mark over the efficacy of regulatory concepts and instruments that originated to handle issues in the age of the mainframe computer, *or even of the laptop, the mobile telephone, and the Internet*

2010, the Commission responded to these concerns by formally launching a consultation on a fresh attempt to regulate for the effective and comprehensive protection of personal data.[25] Right at the start of the consultation document, the Commission concedes that 'rapid technological developments and globalisation have profoundly changed the world around us, and brought new challenges for the protection of personal data'.[26] It continues:

> Today technology allows individuals to share information about their behaviour and preferences easily and make it publicly and globally available on an unprecedented scale. Social networking sites, with hundreds of millions of members spread across the globe, are perhaps the most obvious, but not the only, example of this phenomenon. 'Cloud computing' – i.e., Internet-based computing whereby software, shared resources and information are on remote servers ('in the cloud') could also pose challenges to data protection, as it may involve the loss of individuals' control over their potentially sensitive information when they store their data with programs hosted on someone else's hardware.[27]

At the same time, the Commission notes that 'ways of collecting personal data have become increasingly elaborated [sic] and less detectable'. Thus:

> the use of sophisticated tools allows economic operators to better target individuals thanks to the monitoring of their behaviour. And the growing use of procedures allowing automatic data collection, such as electronic transport ticketing, road toll collecting, or of geo-location devices make it easier to determine the location of individuals simply because they use a mobile device. Public authorities also use more and more personal data for various purposes, such as tracing individuals in the event of an outbreak of a communicable disease, for preventing and fighting terrorism and crime more effectively, to administer social security schemes or for taxation purposes, as part of their e-government applications etc.[28]

As we have said, this kind of problem of disconnection is endemic in the regulation of emerging technologies and we will consider it in due course. This, however, is not the only criticism of data protection law. For many the problem with the Data Protection Directive and its national implementation is that the law is framed in terms that are unclear and unduly complex – for example, in the *Naomi Campbell* case, one of the first opportunities for the English appeal courts to comment on the local implementing legislation, Lord Phillips MR described the Data Protection Act 1998, as 'cumbersome and inelegant'.[29]

(*ibid.*, para. 44.9; emphasis ours). For a similar point, concerning current data protection regulation and upcoming profiling data sets, see Mireille Hildebrandt, 'A Vision of Ambient Law', in Roger Brownsword and Karen Yeung (eds.), *Regulating Technologies* (Oxford: Hart, 2008), 175.

[25] European Commission, Communication, 4 November 2010, COM(2010)609 final.

[26] *Ibid.*, at 2.   [27] *Ibid.*   [28] *Ibid.*, at 2–3.

[29] *Naomi Campbell* v. *Mirror Group Newspapers Ltd* [2002] EWCA Civ. 1373, at para. 72; similarly, at the trial, Morland J. had already likened the Act to a 'thicket': see [2002] EWHC 499 (QB) (at

Clearly, this is a serious impediment to regulatory effectiveness; if regulatees do not know where they stand, they cannot be expected to comply.

Recognising the importance of both clarity and sustainability, the Commission opens the concluding remarks to its consultation in the following terms:

> Like technology, the way our personal data is used and shared in our society is changing all the time. The challenge this poses to legislators is to establish a legislative framework that will stand the test of time. At the end of the reform process, Europe's data protection rules should continue to guarantee a high level of protection and provide legal certainty to individuals, public administrations and businesses in the internal market alike for several generations. No matter how complex the situation or how sophisticated the technology, clarity must exist on [*sic*] the applicable rules and standards that national authorities have to enforce and that businesses and technology developers must comply with. Individuals should also have clarity about the rights they enjoy.[30]

In response to this challenge, the Commission proposes a comprehensive approach that *inter alia* strengthens the rights of individuals as well as enhancing the internal market dimension. Without doubt, this is indicative of an intention to do better; but how confident can we be that the regulators are on track to legislate a more effective data protection regime? For two reasons, in particular, we might have our doubts.

First, whenever regulators are legislating for rapidly changing technologies, they face a tension between the demand for clarity and the need for flexibility. Information technologies are no different from other technologies in this respect and data protection law is not exempt from this difficulty. In fact, the concept of 'personal data' that is the cornerstone of data protection law is the perfect example of the problem. In the existing law, 'personal data' is understood as being 'any information relating to an identified or identifiable natural person'; and 'an identifiable person is one who can be identified directly or indirectly'.[31] This is amplified by Recital 26 which says that, to determine identifiability, account should be taken of 'all the means likely reasonably to be used either by the controller or by any other person to identify the said person'. According to the Commission, a degree of flexibility was deliberately built into these provisions but, as it admits, 'a consequence of such a broad and flexible approach is that there are numerous cases where it is not always clear, when implementing the Directive, which approach to take, whether individuals enjoy data protection rights and whether data controllers should comply with the obligations imposed by the Directive'.[32]

---

para. 72). On final appeal to the House of Lords, there was no further consideration of the Act, it being agreed between the parties that the DPA claim stood or fell with the main claim for breach of confidence: see [2004] UKHL 22, para. 32 (Lord Nicholls).

[30] European Commission, Communication, 4 November 2010, COM(2010)609 final, at 18.

[31] Article 2(a) Directive 95/46/EC.

[32] European Commission, Communication, 4 November 2010, COM(2010)609 final, at 5.

One such case is that of 'anonymised' data. Given that there are various degrees of 'anonymisation', rendering the identification of the person to whom the data relates more or less difficult, at which point does data protection law recognise that the data in question is no longer personal (linkable) data? The question is not addressed in the operative part of the Directive. However, according to Recital 26, the data protection principles do not apply to 'data rendered anonymous in such a way that the data subject is no longer identifiable'; and the Recital then flags up the possible articulation of guidance to indicate 'the ways in which data may be rendered anonymous and retained in a form in which identification of the data subject is no longer possible'. On the face of it, this presupposes a narrow view of (irreversible) anonymisation. However, some prefer the German view, holding that data is to be treated as anonymised so long as it would take a disproportionate amount of time, expense and labour to identify the relevant data subject; and some might prefer a much looser test that treats anonymised data as beyond the reach of the protective principles so long as those who are processing the data cannot reasonably expect an identifying link back to the data subject to be made. Once there is any such movement away from the narrow view, the qualifying concepts (which are the source of some flexibility) invite interpretation. What constitutes a 'disproportionate' amount of time, expenses and labour? What kind of linking attempts might be 'reasonably' expected? In the particular case of human genetic research, where the research teams are processing anonymised (pseudonymised) data, these are pressing issues. The fact that, somewhere in the research team, linking identifiers are retained, means that it is perfectly possible for some members of the team to connect the data to a particular person. For others in the team, depending upon the security measures that are built into the organisational arrangements, identification might not be a realistic possibility.[33] Even then, though, if data is transferred between teams, or circulated more widely, it is possible that a link will be made. Moreover, because the genetic data relates to the health of a person, the practical implications of an identifying connection being made could be especially serious.

Arguably, however, the flexibility of the Directive, together with its lack of explicit provision on critical issues, does not quite get to the crux of the problem. For, the fundamental questions are about the scope and quality of personal data itself (crucially, the question of what data about an identifiable individual counts as personal data) rather than about the identifiability of individuals, which in turn leads to the second reason for doubting the future effective drafting of data protection law.

The second reason goes right back to the basic approach of the Directive, to its twin objectives: namely, to facilitate the free flow of data in the internal

---

[33] For a thorough discussion of this matter, see Nikolaus Forgó, Regine Kollek, Marian Arning, Tina Kruegel and Imme Petersen, *Ethical and Legal Requirements for Transnational Genetic Research* (Munich and Oxford: Beck with Hart, 2010).

market while, at the same time, respecting the fundamental right of individuals to the protection of their data. Immediately, we see the underlying problem: to the extent that data protection law is designed to facilitate the circulation of data, it surely means that individuals lose some control over their data; but, if individual control is to be restored, this implies some restriction on the circulation of data. The ECJ, in the *Lindqvist* case,[34] sketched the problem as follows:

> According to the seventh recital in the preamble to Directive 95/46, the establishment and functioning of the common market are liable to be seriously affected by differences in national rules applicable to the processing of personal data. According to the third recital of that directive the harmonisation of those national rules must seek to ensure not only the free flow of such data between Member States but also the safeguarding of the fundamental rights of individuals. Those objectives may of course be inconsistent with one another.
>
> On the one hand, the economic and social integration resulting from the establishment and functioning of the internal market will necessarily lead to a substantial increase in cross-border flows of personal data between all those involved in a private or public capacity in economic and social activity in the Member States, whether businesses or public authorities of the Member States. Those so involved will, to a certain extent, need to have access to personal data to perform their transactions or to carry out their tasks within the area without internal frontiers which the internal market constitutes.
>
> On the other hand, those affected by the processing of personal data understandably require those data to be effectively protected.[35]

In 1995, when the Directive was adopted, it was tempting to equate the protection of personal data with the protection of informational privacy; but this was a serious mistake. The online processing of personal data can raise issues about the protection of informational privacy but it always gives rise to issues about the fair and open processing of data. Nowadays, following the separation of privacy from data protection in the EU Charter of Fundamental Rights (where Article 8 recognises a distinctive right to the protection of personal data), there is an invitation to elaborate a regulatory regime that is tailored to two quite different informational interests. One interest is the traditional, rather narrow, interest in privacy, where certain types of information, whether in offline or online contexts, are treated as 'private'. This is an interest in 'opacity';[36] and the individual's right is to control access to that information, typically by granting or withholding consent. The other interest is in open, fair, appropriate and secure processing of data in online contexts. This is an interest in 'transparency'; and the individual's rights centre on being aware that personal data is being processed for certain proper purposes.[37] In its consultation paper, the Commission flags up the need for greater transparency in the way that data is collected and processed online as well as ensuring that data should be processed

[34] Case C-101/01 (Bodil Lindqvist).   [35] *Ibid.*, at paras. 79–81.
[36] See, e.g., Serge Gutwirth and Paul de Hert, 'Privacy, Data Protection and Law Enforcement. Opacity of the Individual and Transparency of Power', in Erik Claes, Antony Duff and Serge Gutwirth (eds.), *Privacy and the Criminal Law* (Antwerp and Oxford: Intersentia, 2006), 61.
[37] *Ibid.*

only for the purposes indicated. It also recognises that it should be easier for individuals to access, rectify and retrieve their personal data (such as pictures) from online service providers. In none of this, however, is there any sense that the regulatory regime needs to be radically overhauled so that the protection of the privacy interest is clearly separated from the general principles of open and fair data processing.

Possibly, the Commission believes that the existing regulatory regime already differentiates between simple data protection interests and special privacy interests. For, Article 8 of the Directive, entitled 'the processing of special categories of data', sets out a heightened level of protection in relation to 'the processing of personal data revealing racial or ethnic origin, political opinions, religious or philosophical beliefs, trade-union membership, and the processing of data concerning health or sex life'. Where this class of personal data is to be processed, the 'explicit consent' of the data subject is usually required. In the *Lindqvist* case, where Mrs Lindqvist set up internet pages on her home computer, giving information about herself and eighteen colleagues in the local church (this being designed to assist parishioners who were preparing for their confirmation), some of the personal data was special but, for the most part, it was not. As the ECJ explained:

> The pages in question contained information about Mrs Lindqvist and 18 colleagues in the parish, sometimes including their full names and in other cases only their first names. Mrs Lindqvist also described, in a mildly humorous manner, the jobs held by her colleagues and their hobbies. In many cases, family circumstances and telephone numbers and other matters were mentioned. She also stated that one colleague had injured her foot and was on half-time on medical grounds.[38]

Giving Article 8(1) of the Directive a broad interpretation, the data about the colleague with an injured foot fell within the category of special personal data.[39] But, was the remaining data, the bulk of the information put up online, within the scope of the Directive? One of the arguments put in support of Mrs Lindqvist was that the mere mention of the names, telephone numbers, hobbies and so on of her colleagues was so trivial and well known that it could not breach the right to private life.[40] So long as we underline 'the right to private life', in other words so long as we treat this as a privacy issue, Mrs Lindqvist surely had a point. However, the question for the ECJ was whether the information given (the health information apart) amounted to personal data. On this point, the ECJ was clear: personal data 'undoubtedly covers the name of a person in conjunction with his telephone coordinates or information about his working conditions or hobbies'.[41] So, although we might think that there is a considerable difference between disclosing a named individual's medical record online and simply naming a person online, for the ECJ both acts of data processing

---

[38] Case C-101/01 (Bodil Lindqvist), para. 13. [39] *Ibid.*, at paras. 49–51.
[40] *Ibid.*, at para. 74. [41] *Ibid.*, at para. 24.

engage the data protection regime (albeit that different provisions are made for justifying the acts in question).

Although the 1995 regime hints at the difference between informational privacy and data protection pure and simple, it leaves too much to interpreters. It needs to be much clearer, not only as a matter of principle, but also for practical reasons. Quite simply, if the free circulation of data is to be restricted only for general reasons of fairness, openness and acceptability, there will be facilitative ground rules for online processing of personal data without individuals having a strong veto of the kind represented by the privacy right. Such facilitative ground rules might find some space for the expression of personal preferences; but they will not be comparable to the power of a right-holder to prevent the circulation of data by declining to give consent to access it in the first place or to its onward transmission. So long as the focus is on the facilitation of the circulation of data, the regulatory controls (for the protection of the interests of data subjects) will primarily be procedural; in other words, the collection and circulation of data will need to be done in the right way. However, where the focus is on respect for the fundamental right of privacy, regulators will largely leave it to the individual to determine whether data can be accessed and circulated. In the one case, individuals who transact or interact online will do so on terms that regulators judge serve the public interest (striking an appropriate balance between the free flow of information and transparency); individuals, thus, will have little control over their personal data. By contrast, in the other case, the regulatory protection of privacy rights puts individuals in a key controlling position.

Unless a revised data protection regime disentangles these issues, it will be pulled in different directions and no amount of clever drafting can overcome this basic tension. So long as the tension is unresolved, while those whose priority is free circulation of data will see the regulatory restrictions as obstructive (particularly if there are heightened restrictions of the kind that one would expect where privacy rights are engaged), those whose priority is the protection of privacy rights will see the regulation as confused and ineffective. It is in this context that we find critics complaining that data protection has become an indiscriminate obsession, failing to check malign and incompetent handling of personal data, but impairing the benign processing of personal data. So, for example, some public health researchers have campaigned hard against what they see as the unnecessary obstacles to accessing the personal data that they need for their research projects. Expressing their concerns most dramatically, these researchers have asserted that compliance with the Act is 'killing patients'.[42]

---

[42] For guidance, see Parliamentary Office of Science and Technology, 'Data Protection and Medical Research' (Postnote No. 235, January 2005). For relevant references and a sober assessment, see Deryck Beyleveld, 'Medical Research and the Public Good', *King's Law Journal*, 18 (2007), 275, at 286–7. For the official response, see P. Boyd, 'The Requirements of the Data Protection

In this context, consider this broadside against the regulatory environment from the Academy of Medical Sciences.

Academy of Medical Sciences, *Personal Data for Public Good: Using Health Information in Medical Research* (London, January 2006), 3–4

The legal framework around the use of personal data in research is a complicated patchwork involving UK legislation, case decisions and European directives, augmented by various guidance documents. There are many areas of imprecision, and the courts have not tested the legislation as it applies to medical research. Those responsible for research approval decisions have made their judgements within this uncertain legal framework. The resulting variable legal interpretations have been a source of great difficulty, delay and disillusionment for researchers.

Legal uncertainty and an undue emphasis on privacy and autonomy have created a conservative culture of research governance, in which regulatory and professional bodies promote a policy of 'consent or anonymise'. The Academy firmly believes that researchers should employ adequate data security policies … where appropriate, and should seek consent where it is feasible and proportionate. However, the 'consent or anonymise' policy advocated by some authorities is **not** a strict legal requirement. The rigid application of this policy has been detrimental to research in terms of financial and time resources, as well as scientific opportunity and value. Measures designed to protect autonomy and privacy must be considered against the societal costs of diminishing the quality of the research, or of not doing the research at all …

Research involving personal data has been damaged by the complexity, inconsistency and length of time involved in the assessment of research proposals. There is an urgent need for a simplified scheme for assessing a research proposal involving personal data that maintains standards but also reduces the number of steps a proposal must take.

There are at least five points of criticism compressed in these remarks. First, that the legal framework relating to data protection (which, in the UK, includes the human rights legislation and the common law of confidentiality) is unclear; second, that the guidance given and the decisions made are inconsistent; third, that the process of getting clearance for research proposals that involve data protection issues is too cumbersome and slow; fourth, that the weight given to privacy and autonomy is disproportionate; and, fifth, that the strict legal requirements are being systematically (and unhelpfully) over-interpreted relative to the protection of privacy and autonomy. While regulators should always try to avoid clutter, confusion and a lack of clarity – desiderata that the Academy of Medical Sciences repeatedly emphasises in its more recent report on the regulation of health research[43] – in the particular case of the data

---

Act 1998 for the Processing of Medical Data', *Journal of Medical Ethics*, (2003), 29, 34; and www.dataprotection.gov.uk/dpr/dpdoc.nsf

[43] The Academy of Medical Sciences, *A New Pathway for the Regulation and Governance of Health Research* (London, January 2011), in which it is proposed that, in the interests of a more efficient and effective regulatory regime, there should be a new health research agency.

Law and the technologies of the twenty-first century

protection regime it is, indeed, the failure to sort out the intersecting demands of informational privacy and fair processing of personal data that prevents regulators from making an effective intervention.

6 Nanomaterials

In the ministerial foreword to a recent UK strategy document, we read that the government is determined 'to develop the nanotechnologies industry while protecting the health of consumers and employees and avoiding damage to the environment'.[44] With a spectacular predicted growth in the global revenue of nanotechnologies, especially in the field of ICT,[45] the government has strong commercial reasons for wanting to see the UK positioned 'at the forefront of nanotechnologies development ... maintain[ing] momentum and keep[ing] pace with the biggest players on the international stage'.[46] The document presents four illustrative case studies: one concerning the development of nanofluids that can be used, with energy-saving effects, in motor car cooling systems; a second concerning the use of a handheld nanosensoring device that will help asthma sufferers to monitor their condition; a third concerning the application of nanoscience to reduce the fat content in ice cream; and the fourth concerning the use of titanium dioxide nanoparticles in third-generation solar cells. If nanotechnologies are developed and applied in ways that are environmentally friendly as well as facilitating healthier lives, all will be well. However, a considerable number of nanoproducts are already in the marketplace, nanoparticles being used in a range of goods from tennis balls to cosmetics and sunscreens, nanofibres being used in clothes, and so on.[47] Have these products been safety checked? If, as some claim, nanoparticles might be the new asbestos, how well would regulators fare if they were to be held to account for their prudential responsibilities?

As we said in an earlier chapter, it is rarely true that a new technology, or technological application, finds itself in a regulatory void. The application of extant regulation might not be altogether clear and comprehensive but this is not a void. In the case of nanomaterials, there is likely to be both *ex ante* and *ex post* regulation that has some possible relevance. *Ex ante*, we would expect to find regulation that is designed to assess the novelty and safety of nanomaterials,

---

[44] *UK Nanotechnologies Strategy: Small Technologies, Great Opportunities*, London, March 2010, at 2.

[45] *Ibid.*, at 12.   [46] *Ibid.*, at 2.

[47] In general, see Brent Blackwelder, 'Nanotechnology Jumps the Gun: Nanoparticles in Consumer Products', in Nigel M. de S. Cameron and M. Ellen Mitchell (eds.), *Nanoscale* (Hoboken, NJ: John Wiley, 2007) 71. According to Ahson Wardak and Michael E. Gorman in, 'Using Trading Zones and Life Cycle Analysis to Understand Nanotechnology Regulation', *Journal of Law, Medicine and Ethics*, 34 (2006), 695, there are already more than 200 nanotechnology-based products in the consumer marketplace; and, more recently, the Royal Commission on Environmental Protection, *Novel Materials in the Environment: The Case of Nanotechnology* (London, November 2008) puts the figure at more than 600.

whether for use in contained laboratory conditions, or for release into the environment, or for use in clinical or commercial settings. So, for example, before nanofluids are used in motor car cooling systems or nanosensors are used by asthma sufferers, we would expect various kinds of risk assessment to be undertaken. *Ex post*, if there are problems with nanofluids in cars, we would expect there to be product liability regimes to regulate the compensatory questions; and, if nanosensors harm asthma sufferers, there might well be product liability issues but we would also expect the doctrine of informed consent to regulate the doctor–patient relationship. So, as nanomaterials come onto the regulatory agenda, one of the questions is whether the extant regulation is fit for purpose.

For the most part, legal commentators have focused on the *ex ante* regulatory apparatus. Here, it is commonly argued that extant regulations will not do because either (a) they assume that materials exhibit the same properties regardless of their scale (when we know that many materials function quite differently at the nanoscale); or (b) they are triggered only when production of the material or substance passes a certain threshold – a threshold that permits nanomaterials to slip under the regulatory radar.[48] For example, Bob Lee and Steven Vaughan,[49] detect weaknesses of this kind – indeed, weaknesses of both coverage and clarity – in the European Regulation on the Registration, Evaluation, Authorisation and Restriction of Chemicals (REACH).[50] According to Lee and Vaughan:

> although, in theory, REACH has great regulatory potential in relation to nanomaterials, it is beset by two main problems. The first is a coverage problem arising because of difficulties of definition, exclusion and thresholds. Among the concerns here are that only a small number of nanosubstances may fall within the main remit of the Regulation due to threshold criteria (despite indications that these thresholds may be amended at some, as yet undisclosed, future date). Coverage issues also arise out of difficulties in classifying nanosubstances (as existing or new chemical substances) and in making judgements about the equivalence of nanosubstances to existing, conventional counterparts.
>
> The second problem concerns the operation of REACH in its main activities of registration (together with risk assessment) and the evaluation, authorisation

---

[48] See Albert C. Lin, 'Size Matters: Regulating Nanotechnology', *Harvard Environmental Law Review*, 31 (2007), 349, at 361–74 (for the view that US regulatory provisions are inadequate); Giorgia Guerra, 'European Regulatory Issues in Nanomedicine', *Nanoethics*, 2 (2008), 87 (for the view that EC regulation does not fit very well with potential nanomedical applications), and, generally, Trudy A. Phelps, 'The European Approach to Nanoregulation', in Cameron and Mitchell, *Nanoscale*, 189.

[49] R. G. Lee and S. Vaughan, 'REACHing Down: Nanomaterials and Chemical Safety in the European Union', *Law Innovation and Technology*, 2 (2010), 193.

[50] Regulation No. 1907/2006 of the European Parliament and of the Council of 18 December 2006 concerning the Registration, Evaluation, Authorisation and Restriction of Chemicals (REACH), establishing a European Chemicals Agency, amending Directive 1999/45/EC and repealing Council Regulation (EEC) No. 793/93 and Commission Regulation (EC) No. 1488/94 as well as Council Directive 76/769/EEC and Commission Directives 91/155/EEC, 93/67/EEC, 93/105/EC and 2000/21/EC – hereafter REACH.

and restriction, as necessary, of nanosubstances using REACH methodologies. In particular, the lack of consensus (within and without the EU) on the appropriateness and applicability of mapping existing chemical evaluation testing methodologies onto nanosubstances (and the potential for new methodologies to be devised in a near future time frame) limits control even where nanosubstances are captured by REACH.[51]

Of course, there is much devil in the regulatory details; but the general picture is clearly one of regulators needing to conduct an urgent stocktake of their coverage of nanotechnologies.

In a seminal article, Albert Lin[52] highlights the deficiencies of key US regulatory schemes for the control of toxic substances, environmental protection, consumer safety, and occupational health and safety. For example, he finds that the Toxic Substances Control Act (TSCA)[53] is deficient in four respects. The first is that products such as cosmetics and sunscreens (perhaps the most controversial of the nanoproducts) simply fall outside the scope of the EPA's competence, the EPA being the regulatory authority for the purposes of the Act. The second is that, before the EPA can limit the manufacture, processing or distribution of a chemical substance, it must demonstrate that the substance presents an unreasonable risk and, moreover, its decision to take regulatory action must be supported by substantial evidence. In the case of untested nanosubstances, the burden on the regulatory authority is too great. Third, as Lin puts it, 'the implicit assumption behind the TSCA is that no information on the risk of a chemical means that there is no risk'.[54] Fourth, there is an exemption for new chemicals or significant new uses of chemicals where production is less than 10,000 kilograms per annum. Most nanomaterials will fall below this threshold; and, although the EPA may disapply the exemption where there are serious acute, chronic or significant environmental effects, the burden is again on the regulatory authority to show that such effects are attributable to the chemical. Lin finds a similar pattern of shortcomings in relation to the Consumer Products Safety Act[55] and the Federal Hazardous Substances Act:[56] many nanoproduct applications (including food and drugs, cosmetics and cars) fall outwith the competence of the regulatory authority; reliance is generally on voluntary standards; and the thresholds for mandatory measures are comparable to those set by the TCSA. Moreover, this is another instance of under-resourcing, the regulatory authority simply lacking the manpower, expertise and money to assess the dangers of nanomaterials in a rapidly growing list of consumer products.

To the extent that nanomaterials are effectively safety-checked under other regulatory provisions, there is no major problem (other than some untidiness in the regulatory array). Can we assume then that those nanoproducts that

---

[51] Lee and Vaughan, 'REACHing Down', at 194–5 (footnotes omitted).
[52] Lin, 'Size Matters', 349.   [53] 15 USC §§ 2601–92.
[54] Lin, 'Size Matters', 365.   [55] 15 USC §§ 2051–84 (2006).
[56] 15 USC §§ 1261–78 (2006).

fall outwith the TSCA and consumer product safety provisions are satisfactorily dealt with under other regulatory arrangements? Lin dispels any such complacency.

> Like pesticides and drugs, cosmetics and sunscreens are the subject of specific statutory authority. The use of nanomaterials in these products nevertheless has become widespread with little actual oversight. The FDA has authority to regulate cosmetics under the Federal Food, Drug and Cosmetic Act (the 'FDCA'), but the Agency has interpreted and exercised that authority in a limited manner … For cosmetics products and ingredients … the FDA does not require premarket approval, with the exception of color additives. The FDA instead places the responsibility on cosmetics manufacturers to determine the safety of their own products and ingredients before marketing. Although cosmetics manufacturers may participate in voluntary programs to file data on ingredients, register manufacturing sites, and report cosmetic-related injuries to the FDA, a cosmetics manufacturer may use any ingredient or market any cosmetic until the FDA demonstrates that it may be harmful – something that rarely occurs.[57]

With sunscreens, too, regulatory oversight is equally weak. The FDA treats sunscreens as drugs – which generally means that premarket approval is required; however, no such approval is required where the drug contains ingredients that are recognised as safe and effective. In 1999, the FDA put nano-sunscreens in the fast track by ruling that titanium dioxide (nanoparticles of which are ground down for sunscreens) is not a new ingredient despite the fact that there are functional differences between it at the nano and the normal scale. Of course, the FDA might change its view, both with regard to its background powers and what it characterises as a novel substance. Were it to do that, the contrast between the TSCA (where the assumption is that substances are safe unless the regulatory authority demonstrates otherwise) and the FDA powers (where the assumption is that substances might be dangerous and need to be tested before they are approved) would become more apparent. As Lin remarks, the TSCA presumption of safety seems inappropriate when there is so much uncertainty about the way that nanomaterials behave and what impacts they might have on human health and the environment; on the other hand, the more restrictive approach that is evident in relation to drugs might inhibit the research and development of beneficial products. According to Lin, the challenge is 'to develop an intermediate approach that addresses health and environmental concerns without crippling this promising industry'.[58]

Having started with the reasonably straightforward question of whether there are regulatory gaps in relation to nanomaterials (which there are), we now find that there is a good deal more to this than simply fixing the holes. The question that now looms up is one of how to fill the gaps. Do we need bespoke regulatory provisions or will ongoing adjustments suffice? More importantly, perhaps, who should bear the burden of risk assessment and how much risk

---

[57] Lin, 'Size Matters', at 373.   [58] *Ibid.*, at 375.

can we tolerate for fear of regulating the nanotechnology industry to a standstill? This conundrum is highlighted by Diana Bowman and Graeme Hodge in their survey of nanotechnology policies in Australia, the UK and the US.[59] They conclude:

> With research pointing to the existence of real fissures in existing regulatory frameworks, there is a clear need for governments ... to take a more proactive approach to governing nanotechnology. This is especially the case as the number of commercial nano-products increases. However, does this requirement denote the need for a comprehensive new, nano-specific framework? Or will other, less sweeping measures be adequate to protect human and environmental health and safety?
>
> With the jury still out on the scientific evidence ... [it is contended] that in the short term, adjustments to current regulatory frameworks will provide increased protection to citizens and the environment, while providing regulators and industry with the flexibility they require as the technology itself develops. This is not to say that there is not a case for a comprehensive new regulatory framework in the longer term, however. Rather, we must allow the technology to develop, while government, regulators, industry and society continually re-evaluate these frameworks in light of the evolving scientific evidence and in light also of citizen concerns.[60]

Or, to put this in terms that hark back to our earlier discussion of regulatory prudence, the question is how to design the regulatory environment in a way that ensures that any risks presented by nanomaterials are 'acceptable'. Unless regulators are clear about the questions that they face here, it is unlikely that they will put in place a regulatory framework that is satisfactory.

7 Conclusion

The first-generic reason for the ineffectiveness of a regulatory environment is that the regulators themselves might have failed to discharge their responsibilities. Sometimes, this might be for reasons that betray a lack of integrity (as where they are corrupt or captured); at other times, it will be for reasons of restricted competence (including a lack of resources) and professionalism.

In the two extended illustrations that we have considered in this chapter, there is no suggestion that regulatory failure resides in corruption or capture. Rather, the problems tend to go back to matters of competence and professionalism. With regard to data protection, even though regulators have tried to put in place a bespoke regime, there is a lack of focus and foresight. The required focus is no longer a predominantly off-line world with privacy concerns that have to be translated into a developing online world; it is the online world that

---

[59] Diana M. Bowman and Graeme A. Hodge, 'Nanotechnology "Down Under": Getting on Top of Regulatory Matters', 4 (2007), 223.

[60] *Ibid.*

is already with us; and the foresight is simply imagining how off-line and online environments will seamlessly become integrated. With regard to nanomaterials, the shortcoming is rather different. Here, the problem is that regulators have not been sufficiently proactive in reviewing the adequacy of existing regulatory arrangements for health, safety and the environment. Even if regulators had done everything that they could and should have done in these cases, however, it would not be any guarantee of regulatory effectiveness. It is important that regulators set things off on the right foot, but we should not make the mistake of thinking that this is sufficient for regulatory effectiveness.

13

Regulatory effectiveness III: resistance by regulatees

1 Introduction

Commentators on the effectiveness of law in particular, and regulation in general, agree that regulators tend to do better when they act with the backing of regulatees (with a consensus rather than without it).[1] If regulatees do not perceive the purpose that underlies a particular regulatory intervention as being in either their prudential or their moral interests (let alone in both their prudential and moral interests), the motivation for compliance is weakened. The use of marijuana as a recreational drug is the textbook example. Thus:

> The fact remains ... that marijuana use continues to be illegal in most parts of the world, even as people continue to break these laws with apparent impunity. And there is no resolution in sight. The persistence of marijuana use remains a prime example of how our legal system is based on an implicit social contract, and how the laws on the books can cease to matter when a large percentage of people decide they want to do something that may not be acceptable under the law.[2]

Similarly, experience (especially in the United States) with regulatory prohibitions on alcohol suggests not only that legal interventions that overstep the mark will be ineffective but pregnant with corrupting and secondary criminalising effects. However, before we can make the most of this insight, we need to understand much more about the roots of regulatee resistance, whether it be economic, cultural, professional or moral in nature.

One of the key factors that will determine the penetration of a law is whether there is any *economic* resistance: quite simply, if regulatees act like rational economic actors, they will tend to view law as a tax on certain kinds of conduct. If non-compliance is the better economic option, the logic for such regulatees is to disobey and (sometimes) pay. For instance, in the days when Sunday trading in

---

[1] The idea that regulators do best when they 'work with the grain' is emphasised in Iredell Jenkins, *Social Order and the Limits of Law* (Princeton, NJ: Princeton University Press, 1980); see, too, Phillipe Sands, *Lawless World* (London: Penguin, 2005), at 56, for the eminently generalisable piece of regulatory wisdom that 'there exists in diplomatic circles a strongly held view that if a treaty cannot be adopted by consensus its long-term prospects are crippled'.

[2] Stuart Biegel, *Beyond Our Control?* (Cambridge, MA: MIT Press, 2003), 105.

the UK was illegal, it made good business sense for large-scale DIY enterprises to open their doors on Sundays and occasionally pay a £2,000 fine. If Sunday trading had damaged the reputation of these businesses, this would have had to have been factored into the economic calculation; but, generally, the public supported the vanguard Sunday traders, and so there was no such risk. Putting the point rather generally, we can say that, where business people believe that compliance makes economic sense, they will comply; but, where compliance does not make economic sense, they will be less ready to comply.[3]

Another key element of resistance is often to be found in the culture of target regulatees, whether popular or professional, occupational or business. Regulators need to reckon with the attitudes of the professions: professional bodies (particularly the legal and the medical professions) tend to be extremely jealous of their autonomy and, not unreasonably, think that they know their own businesses best. Attempts to regulate the professions in a way that runs across the grain of professional culture will almost certainly be ineffective. Similarly, where there is a certain occupational culture ('cop culture', the culture of getting the policing job done, is one of the best examples), regulators will meet with resistance where they try to legislate across the received norms of that culture. And, of course, so long as the culture of business is to maximise profits, attempts by regulators to encourage corporate social responsibility will tend to be more effective where they channel businesses towards win-win practices.[4]

Occasionally, resistance to the law is required as a matter of conscience – witness, for example, the peace tax protesters; physicians who ignore what they see as unconscionable legal restrictions; members of religious groups who defy a legally supported dress code, and the like. Such persons and such examples are probably the exception rather than the rule; but where the law is up against a case of genuine conscientious objection, then it is truly up against it.

In all these cases, the critical point is that regulation does not act on an inert body of regulatees: regulatees will respond to regulation – sometimes by complying with it, sometimes by ignoring it, sometimes by resisting or repositioning themselves, sometimes by relocating, and so on. Sometimes those who oppose the regulation will seek to overturn it by lawful means, sometimes by unlawful means; sometimes the response will be strategic and organised, at other times it will be chaotic and spontaneous. But, regulatees have minds and interests of

---

[3] To a considerable extent, rational economic thinking operates on both sides of the regulatory fence – for example, in both the licit and the illicit drugs market. Compare Nichola Dorn, Tom Bucke and Chris Goulden, 'Traffick, Transit and Transaction: A Conceptual Framework for Action Against Drug Supply', *Howard Journal of Criminal Justice*, 42 (2003), 348, according to whom, it seems likely that 'only interventions causing traffickers to perceive a significant risk of capture leading to imprisonment have a worthwhile deterrent effect, lower-impact interventions providing for traffickers no more than the expected "costs of doing business"' (*ibid.*, at 363).

[4] See John Parkinson, 'Corporate Governance and the Regulation of Business Behaviour', in Sorcha MacLeod (ed.), *Corporate Governance* (Oxford: Hart, 2006), 1.

their own; they will respond in their own way; and the nature of the response will be an important determinant of the effectiveness of the regulation.[5]

Tim Wu, in a helpful discussion, asks readers to imagine regulatees, faced by an unwelcome law (or by some other kind of regulatory intervention) as disciplined prudential calculators.[6] The basic choice for such calculating regulatees is between avoiding the law or trying to change it. Thus:

> [G]roups and individuals face a choice between avoidance and change mechanisms when deciding how to react to burdensome laws. Very simply, if a law is a cost on its subjects, then *avoidance* and *change* mechanisms, the subjects of the compliance and political choice literatures respectively, can be pictured as different directions of reaction ...
>
> [W]ithin each broader category of mechanism, are specific subcategories, such as lobbying or litigation in the case of change mechanisms, and evasion and avoision [*sic*] in the case of avoidance mechanisms.[7]

By evasion, Wu means that regulatees break the law but invest in reducing the chances of being punished, for example, by obscuring their faces during the commission of a crime, by hiring lawyers, or by bribing officials. By 'avoision', he means acts that involve 'efforts to exploit the differences between a law's goals and its self defined limits'.[8] Some tax avoidance schemes might fit this description, as would an example that Wu gives of a pornographer who includes indecent photographs in a work that also includes serious essays about some aspects of sex in marriage; and, later in this chapter, we will meet the case of car drivers ('manipulators') who slow down at speed cameras but then accelerate away once they are clear of the camera-monitored stretch of road.

We can pursue this dimension of regulatory effectiveness by reflecting on four cases of regulatee resistance: the opposition of the UK scientific community to the government's proposed ban on the use of hybrid embryos as research tools; the reaction of citizens to CCTV and the particular case of motorists responding to speed cameras; file-sharers; and students responding to measures designed to prevent the use of cognition-enhancing drugs.

2 Scientists and hybrid embryos

Wu alerts us to the possibility that, faced with a burdensome law, regulatees might seek to change it. This *ex post* scenario also has an *ex ante* correlate: faced

---

[5] For an illuminating account of the illicit GM seed trade in India, bypassing both the local biosafety regulations and Mahyco-Monsanto's premium prices, see Ronald J. Herring and Milind Kandlikar, 'Illicit Seeds: Intellectual Property and the Underground Proliferation of Agricultural Biotechnologies', in Sebastian Haunss and Kenneth C. Shadlen (eds.), *Politics of Intellectual Property* (Cheltenham: Edward Elgar, 2009), 56. The authors remark: 'Stealth seeds reflect the same kind of agency as urban appropriation of pharmaceuticals and software, films and music – the same anarchic capitalism at the grass roots – with similar risks and rewards' (*ibid.*, at 74).
[6] Tim Wu, 'When Code Isn't Law', *Virginia Law Review*, 89 (2003), 679.
[7] *Ibid.*, at 695–6. [8] *Ibid.*, at 692.

with the prospect of a law that would be burdensome or unhelpful, regulatees might invest in lobbying to prevent the law being adopted. Indeed, this was precisely what happened in the UK when the government announced that, even in the context of a permissive regulatory regime, it was not yet ready to authorise the licensing of research using hybrid embryos (or 'cybrids' as some termed them). Regulatees, particularly leading stem cell researchers, were provoked by this announcement into campaigning against the position that the government seemed to be minded to adopt. Famously, a letter of protest signed by some forty-four experts, including three Nobel laureates, was published in *The Times*. With considerable assistance from the House of Commons Science and Technology Committee, the scientists prevailed and legislation was duly adopted that permitted the licensing of research using hybrid embryos.[9]

The story of this example of proactive regulatory resistance centres on the legislative provisions that set the framework for using human embryos for research purposes. The original provisions, in the Human Fertilisation and Embryology Act 1990, reflect three central principles, namely:

1 that the regulatory authority (the HFEA) should license research using human embryos only if it is necessary (the necessity principle);[10]
2 that, if the HFEA is satisfied that such research is necessary (because it cannot be done in any other way), then a licence should be granted only if the particular activity is judged to be necessary or desirable in relation to one of the approved statutory purposes;[11] and
3 that, in no circumstances, should research on embryos run beyond fourteen days or the appearance of the primitive streak.[12]

In the 1990 legislation, five purposes, were listed as approved. These were:

(a) promoting advances in the treatment of infertility,
(b) increasing knowledge about the causes of congenital disease,
(c) increasing knowledge about the causes of miscarriages,
(d) developing more effective techniques for contraception, [or]
(e) developing methods for detecting the presence of gene or chromosome abnormalities in embryos before implantation.

The Act also provided that research may be licensed 'for such other purposes as may be specified in regulations'.[13] However, this enabling provision was limited: the said 'other purposes' needing to be designed to 'increase knowledge about the creation and development of embryos, or about disease, or enable such knowledge to be applied'.[14]

---

[9] For discussion, see, Tony Prosser, *The Regulatory Enterprise* (Oxford: Oxford University Press, 2010), 40–1.
[10] Schedule 2, para. 3(6).   [11] Schedule 2, para. 3(2).
[12] Sections 3(3)(a) and 3(4).   [13] Schedule 2, para. 3(2).
[14] Schedule 2, para. 3(3).

Having consulted and taken advice on the matter, the government was not confident that the five operative statutory purposes as drafted permitted the HFEA to issue licences for human embryonic stem cell research. Accordingly, they put through the Human Fertilisation and Embryology (Research Purposes) Regulations 2001.[15] The new Regulations virtually 'copied out' the terms of the enabling provisions adding the following three new purposes to the original five:

(a) increasing knowledge about the development of embryos,
(b) increasing knowledge about serious disease, or
(c) enabling any such knowledge to be applied in developing treatments for serious disease.

There is much that could be said about this way of proceeding – there were full and informed parliamentary debates before the new regulations were approved but, as drafted, they hardly advertised their principal purpose.[16] No matter, it was accepted that, on the basis of these regulations, the HFEA could license human embryonic stem cell research; and the Authority duly proceeded to do just that.

For stem cell researchers, although the revised regulatory environment supported their work, they soon ran into a serious practical difficulty: their need for human egg cells outstripped the supply. However, there was a ray of hope, for one piece of published research suggested that human embryonic clusters could be formed if, instead of using human eggs cells to host human nuclear DNA, egg cells from cows or rabbits were used. With no shortage of such egg cells, there was the prospect of using these human–animal constructs to practise stimulating the formation of (hybrid) embryonic clusters. Applications (one from researchers at King's College London and the other from a team at Newcastle) for research licences to cover such work were duly made to the HFEA; but, at much the same time, the government was reviewing the 1990 Act and one of the issues for consultation was precisely whether the legislative framework should be amended to permit the creation and use of hybrid embryos for research purposes.

In what became a muddling response to this turn in stem cell science, the HFEA took legal advice on the basis of which it decided that, before licensing such research, it needed to undertake a public consultation on the matter. As for the government, it recognised that the legal position needed to be clarified and declared its intentions as follows:

---

[15] SI 2001 No. 188. When asked to justify the use of regulations rather than primary legislation, Yvette Cooper (the Parliamentary Under-Secretary of State for Health) simply responded that the 1990 Act gave the government the power to extend the approved purposes by regulation, see Hansard (HC) 17 November 2000, col. 1176.

[16] For discussion, see Roger Brownsword, 'Stem Cells, Superman, and the Report of the Select Committee', *Modern Law Review*, 65 (2002), 568.

The Government will propose that the creation of hybrid … embryos in vitro should not be allowed. However, the Government also proposes that the law will contain a power enabling regulations to set out circumstances in which the creation of hybrid … embryos in vitro may in future be allowed under licence, for research purposes only.[17]

This was not well received by the stem cell community, who read this as a proposal not to allow the use of hybrids as research tools rather than as a proposal to put in place the mechanisms for future permission. The government maintained that it had not set its face against the use of hybrids, the prime minister even being quoted as saying that its position was 'in fact the opposite' and that he was 'sure that research that's really going to save lives and improve the quality of life will be able to go forward'.[18] However, there was no assuaging the scientists and their lobbyists.

Eager to support the scientific arguments, the House of Commons Science and Technology Committee undertook a rapid inquiry that focused specifically on the government's declared intentions with regard to hybrids.[19] Witnesses from both the HFEA and the Department of Health were put on the back foot as they were asked to explain themselves. The Committee concurred with the scientists that 'the use of animal eggs in the creation of cytoplasmic hybrid embryos will help to overcome the current shortage of human eggs available for research and that the use of animal eggs is required to enable researchers to develop the practical techniques which may be required for eventual production of cell-based therapy through this method using eggs'.[20] In conclusion, the Committee said:

We have found the Government's published proposals for future regulation in this area to be unacceptable and potentially harmful to UK science. The Minister has strongly protested that the general interpretation of what the Government is seeking to do is mistaken, and also that she is prepared to revise the proposals for inclusion in the forthcoming draft Bill. We urge the Government to take our Report into consideration in preparation of the draft Bill.[21]

By this stage, the government needed little further urging; and the revised Human Fertilisation and Embryology Act 2008 was passed with appropriate provisions for the licensing of this kind of research.[22] A little more surprisingly, perhaps, the HFEA, following its public consultation and still acting under the 1990 legislative framework, granted the licences that the two research teams had applied for.

---

[17] Department of Health, *Review of the Human Fertilisation and Embryology Act: Proposals for Revised Legislation* Cm 6989 (December 2006), para. 2.82.

[18] *The Times*, 10 January 2007.

[19] House of Commons Science and Technology Committee, *Government Proposals for the Regulation of Hybrid and Chimera Embryos* (Fifth Report, Session 2006–7).

[20] *Ibid.*, at para. 60.   [21] *Ibid.*, at para. 116.

[22] Schedule 2 deals with the activities for which licences may be issued; research activities are covered by para. 3; and para. 3(3) deals specifically with creating, keeping, or using, so-called, 'human admixed embryos'.

Cynics say that scientists tend to want more funding for their research, more time to deliver its benefits, and less regulation. In this case, the scientists wanted, and they succeeded in getting, different regulation from that which the government seemed to be about to adopt. As a result of sustained pressure from the scientific community, the HFEA made the decision that the scientists wanted; the government's new legislation incorporated provisions that the scientists wanted; research using hybrid embryos could be licensed; and, once again, the regulatory environment was in line with what the scientists presented as their requirements. Whether hybrids will help scientists to make significant breakthroughs in human embryonic stem cell research remains to be seen

3 CCTV, cameras and cars

Early in 2010, *The Guardian* newspaper led with a story suggesting that the police were 'planning to use unmanned spy drones, controversially deployed in Afghanistan, for the "routine" monitoring of antisocial motorists, protesters, agricultural thieves and fly-tippers in a significant expansion of covert state surveillance'.[23] Evidently, drones of this kind are capable of staying airborne for very long periods, and at a considerable height, such that they are invisible from the ground. The British public has learned to live with extensive CCTV coverage on the ground but what would they make of the prospect of CCTV in the sky? Would the fear of being detected by an invisible camera in the skies improve the manners of motorists or, generally, deter crime?

Some fifty years earlier, the public were persuaded that any attempt to use a television set without a covering TV licence would be detected by one of the high-tech detector vans that patrolled the streets. In fact, the detector vans played little or no part in the detection of TV licence evasion. Rather, what happened was that retailers and rental companies were required to pass on to the TV-licensing authority the names and addresses of persons to whom television sets were sold or rented. The authority then simply checked whether a TV licence had been issued for the address in question; if not, the detector van could make an inspired visit to the address. This, we might say, was a nice example of smart regulation. The criminal law declared the primary offence and set the penalty for evasion; retailers and rental companies had secondary notification obligations; compliance was strongly encouraged by overstating the detecting power of the vans; and detection was actually carried out by cross-checking the paper notifications with the licences actually issued. If the public had not been fooled by the mystique of the detection vans, fewer licences might have been issued; but, provided the notifications were made, this should still have been an effective way of detecting evasion. Even so, the fact that the public

---

[23] Paul Lewis, 'CCTV in the sky: police plan to use military-style spy drones' *The Guardian*, 23 January 2010, 1.

did believe that the detector vans would catch licence evaders was an important feature of this particular regulatory scheme.

In this light, we might wonder whether ground-level CCTV does work and whether the public believes that it works? According to a 2009 internal report by London's Metropolitan Police Service, CCTV is relatively ineffective, only one crime being solved per 1,000 cameras, and only 8 out of 269 suspected robbers per month being caught by the cameras.[24] Against this background, it is not altogether surprising, perhaps, that some of the most public doubts about the effectiveness of CCTV have been expressed (as in the following extract) by senior policemen.

Owen Boycott, 'CCTV boom has failed to slash crime say police', *The Guardian*, 6 May 2008

Massive investment in CCTV cameras to prevent crime in the UK has failed to have a significant impact, despite billions of pounds spent on the new technology, a senior police officer piloting a new database has warned. Only 3% of street robberies in London were solved using CCTV images, despite the fact that Britain has more security cameras than any other country in Europe.

The warning comes from the head of the Visual Images, Identifications and Detections Office (Viido) at New Scotland Yard as the force launches a series of initiatives to try to boost conviction rates using CCTV evidence. They include:

- A new database of images which is expected to use technology developed by the sports advertising industry to track and identify offenders.
- Putting images of suspects in muggings, rape and robbery cases out on the internet from next month.
- Building a national CCTV database, incorporating pictures of convicted offenders as well as unidentified suspects. The plans for this have been drawn up, but are on hold while the technology required to carry out automated searches is refined.

Use of CCTV images for court evidence has so far been very poor, according to Detective Chief Inspector Mick Neville, the officer in charge of the Metropolitan police unit. 'CCTV was originally seen as a preventative measure', Neville told the Security Document World Conference in London. 'Billions of pounds has been spent on kit, but no thought has gone into how the police are going to use the images and how they will be used in court. It's been an utter fiasco: only 3% of crimes were solved by CCTV. There's no fear of CCTV. Why don't people fear it? [They think] the cameras are not working.'

More training was needed for officers, he said. Often they do not want to find CCTV images 'because it's hard work'. Sometimes the police did not bother inquiring beyond local councils to find out whether CCTV cameras monitored a particular street incident.

'CCTV operators need feedback. If you call them back, they feel valued and are more helpful. We want to develop a career path for CCTV [police] inquirers.'

---

[24] OUT-LAW News, 16 December 2009: see www.out-law.com/page-10607 (last accessed 19 May 2010).

The Viido unit is beginning to establish a London-wide database of images of suspects that are cross-referenced by written descriptions. Interest in the technology has been enhanced by recent police work, in which officers back-tracked through video tapes to pick out terrorist suspects. In districts where the Viido scheme is working, CCTV is now helping police in 15–20% of street robberies.

'We are [beginning] to collate images from across London', Neville said. 'This has got to be balanced against any Big Brother concerns, with safeguards. The images are from thefts, robberies and more serious crimes. Possibly the [database] could be national in future.'

The unit is now investigating whether it can use software – developed to track advertising during televised football games – to follow distinctive brand logos on the clothing of unidentified suspects. 'Sometimes you are looking for a picture, for example, of someone with a red top and a green dragon on it', he explained. 'That technology could be used to track logos.' By back-tracking, officers have often found earlier pictures, for example, of suspects with their hoods down, in which they can be identified.

'We are also going to start putting out [pictures] on the internet, on the Met police website, asking "who is this guy?". If criminals see that CCTV works they are less likely to commit crimes.'

Cheshire deputy chief constable Graham Gerrard, who chairs the CCTV working group of the Association of Chief Police Officers, told the Guardian, that it made no sense to have a national DNA and fingerprint database, but to have to approach 43 separate forces for images of suspects and offenders. A scheme called the Facial Identification National Database (Find), which began collecting offenders' images from their prison pictures and elsewhere, has been put on hold.

He said that there were discussions with biometric companies 'on a regular basis' about developing the technology to search digitised databases and match suspects' images with known offenders. 'Sometimes when they put their [equipment] in operational practice, it's not as wonderful as they said it would be', he said. 'I suspect [Find] has been put on hold until the technology matures. Before you can digitise every offender's image you have to make sure the lighting is right and it's a good picture. It's a major project. We are still some way from a national database. There are still ethical and technical issues to consider.'

Asked about the development of a CCTV database, the office of the UK's information commissioner, Richard Thomas, said: 'CCTV can play an important role in helping to prevent and detect crime. However we would expect adequate safeguards to be put in place to ensure the images are only used for crime detection purposes, stored securely and that access to images is restricted to authorised individuals. We would have concerns if CCTV images of individuals going about their daily lives were retained as part of the initiative.'

The charity Victim's Voice, which supports relatives of those who have been murdered, said it supported more effective use of CCTV systems. 'Our view is that anything that helps get criminals off the street and prevents crime is good', said Ed Usher, one of the organisation's trustees. 'If handled properly it can be a superb preventative tool.'

On the face of it, many of the weaknesses of CCTV can be put down to the limitations of the technology itself (presumably, there will be significant improvements in this respect) and the regulators' own failure to make the most of the resource. Moreover, if the public stops believing in the potency of CCTV, we can assume that this will reduce its regulatory effectiveness.

In this chapter, though, our particular focus is on the response of regulatees. To what extent is it regulatees who make life difficult for CCTV-reliant regulators? First, regulatees might take steps to avoid identification – 'hoodies' being the obvious case in point. Regulatees who are so minded, and who read the above extract, will think: 'Do not wear red tops with green dragons or similarly striking clothes.' Or, again, regulatees will try to ensure that, when they commit their crimes, they are out of range of the cameras. These strategies of resistance are apparent not only on the part of young people on the streets or in the town centres, but also in the way that some motorists will respond to speed cameras on the roads.

Claire Corbett and Isabel Caramlau have researched the attitudes that drivers have to speed cameras and how they respond to them.[25] In two studies that were carried out, one in the mid-1990s and the other in 2003, Corbett and Caramlau develop their analysis around four ideal-typical driving styles, namely: (a) 'conformers' (that is, drivers who comply with speed limits regardless of whether speed cameras are present or operational); (b) 'deterred' (that is, drivers who adjust their speed, slowing down where there are cameras); (c) 'manipulators' (that is, drivers who slow down as they travel through a section of road that is monitored by speed cameras but who then accelerate away as they are clear of it); and (d) 'defiers' (that is, drivers who exceed speed limits regardless of whether speed cameras are present or operational). Most drivers fit the description of conformers (for whom the speed cameras are irrelevant) or deterred (for whom, the presence of speed cameras does have the intended regulatory effect). The harder cases are the manipulators (where there is 'avoision' as Wu terms it) and the defiers (where there might well be 'evasion' as Wu puts it).[26] Overall, Corbett and Caramlau believe that the evidence shows quite clearly that the effect of introducing speed cameras is to reduce the number of road traffic accidents (which is not quite the same as achieving compliance with speed limits); but, familiarity leads to a marked shift as some of the drivers who were once deterred become manipulators. In the longer run, it is argued that the better strategy is to deal with risk in a more targeted way, combining educational speed awareness programmes with intelligent in-vehicle speed control technologies.

Summarising their findings from the two studies, Corbett and Caramlau highlight not only the shift in drivers' attitudes and responses (from the earlier

---

[25] Claire Corbett and Isabel Caramlau, 'Gender Difference in Response to Speed Cameras: Typology Findings and Implications for Road Safety', *Criminology and Criminal Justice*, 4 (2006), 411.

[26] See Wu, 'When Code Isn't Law'.

to the later study) but also (not surprisingly) the need to target young male drivers. Among their salient findings, we learn that:

- At the time of the earlier study, men and women responded to speed cameras in much the same way (even though women were more favourably disposed to the idea of speed cameras).
- At that time, the conformers tended to be older, the manipulators, defiers and deterred were in the younger age range.
- By the time of the later study, there was a distinct change in the pattern of behaviour, with fewer classifying themselves as deterred and more seeing themselves as manipulators; and with women more likely than men to classify themselves as conformers and men more likely than women to see themselves as manipulators.
- Men, especially young men, continued to have the least positive views in relation to speed cameras.

Given these findings, Corbett and Caramlau contend that it would be sensible to target educational publicity at men rather than women, and particularly so at those young males who emerged in both studies as the class of drivers who were least likely to be conformers and most likely to be manipulators.

In the larger regulatory environment, the motor insurance industry is already highly risk sensitive, targeting insured drivers in just the way that Corbett and Caramlau argue that speed awareness education should be targeted. In the motor insurance market, conformers are likely to build up substantial 'no claims' discounts on their premiums; some insurance companies only do motoring business with older drivers; and all insurance companies load the premiums for at-risk young male drivers. However, this is not a perfect world. For those young male drivers who are actually conformers, there is no avoiding heavyweight insurance premiums. The only other option is to take a chance, being a defier not only in relation to speed limits and speed cameras but also with regard to the legal requirements for driving with insurance.

4 File-sharers

On the face of it, file-sharing is one of the most egregious examples of the law being flouted. Regulatees seem to have little or no respect for the rights of copyright holders. As David Bollier has observed:

> Despite the troubling trajectory that intellectual property law has taken over the past generation, a new movement to assert the public interest is starting to take shape and gain momentum. Key constituencies such as consumers, artists, librarians, computer professionals, academics, and scientists have become active players in the debates, and partners in advocacy. The general public, too, has become far more attentive. Ever since the Napster controversy dramatized the everyday implications of copyright law, ordinary people are more aware that technological and legal battles can directly affect them. Now that tens of millions of people

use the Internet, networking software, CD burners, iPods, Wifi, and dozens of other innovations, few will knowingly accept a great cultural lockdown without a fight.[27]

While some regulatees campaign for a change in the law (seeking a new copyright compact for the information society) and while others devise imaginative new 'copyleft' formats, others simply break the law. Moreover, because many of these infringements, including the file-sharing of copyrighted material, take place in private and because they (and especially so file-sharing) occur on such a large scale, it is not obvious how the rights of copyright holders could be rendered more effective.

On the face of it, regulators have three options (none of which is mutually exclusive):[28] one is to target individual file-sharers who are in breach of copyright law; a second is to develop the cooperation and support of the general internet service providers (ISPs); and a third is to target the technological innovators who provide the specialist service or software that facilitates file-sharing.

The first option is relatively unattractive. In the absence of an army of enforcement officers, and reliable information, direct claims against individual file-sharers are unlikely to stem the tide. The most that could be achieved would be enforcement against a handful of infringers as a fairly futile example to the rest.[29] Moreover, in all cases, the risk of reputational damage to the copyright-holders would be considerable – especially so if unreliable information led to innocent persons being falsely accused of unlawful activities – and, insofar as the longer-term strategy is to re-educate file-sharers, such a confrontational approach is liable to be counter-productive.

The second option is to focus on the ISPs. For example, where it is clear that the ISP knows that its service is being used to access a significant copyright-infringing website, then the copyright holders might seek a court order requiring the ISP to block such access – in the way that the High Court ordered BT to block access to Newzbin2 (an illegal file-sharing website).[30] A less head-on approach (pioneered by French regulators) is to enlist the ISPs as informers, educators and enforcers, the basic idea being to place ISPs under an obligation to act on notifications received from copyright-holders of alleged illegal file-sharing. Much of the devil is in the detail of such

---

[27] David Bollier, *Brand Name Bullies: The Quest to Own and Control Culture* (Hoboken, NJ: John Wiley, 2005), 245–6.

[28] See, e.g., Cheng Lim Saw, 'The Case for Criminalising Primary Infringements of Copyright: Perspectives from Singapore', *International Journal of Law and Information Technology*, 18 (2010), 95, esp. at 122–6.

[29] For a case in point, see *Capital Records* v. *Thomas Rassett* 579 F Supp 2d 1210 (DC Minnesota 2008); see discussion in Diane Rowland, Uta Kohl and Andrew Charlesworth, *Information Technology Law* (4th edn, London: Routledge, 2011), at 344–5. There have also been some attempts at so-called 'volume litigation' but with limited success: see Andrew Murray, *Information Technology Law* (Oxford: Oxford University Press, 2010), 258–9.

[30] See, Mark Sweney and Josh Halliday, 'Hollywood ending as BT told to block illegal file-sharing site', *The Guardian*, 29 July 2011, 12.

models – for example, what is the threshold for triggering ISP obligations; and what precisely are these obligations once they are triggered? Whereas, in the hardest articulation of this model, ISPs would be required, in cases of repeat infringement, to disconnect customers, in softer versions the obligation of ISPs would simply be to warn customers that they (ISPs) have been notified by copyright-holders that they (the copyright-holders) believe that illegal file-sharing is taking place. Controversially, in the UK, the Digital Economy Act 2010, takes a relatively hard line – or, at any rate, such is the perception of many, including leading ISPs. In a set of provisions implicating the Secretary of State, OFCOM (the sector regulator), copyright owners, ISPs and their subscribers, the 2010 Act lays out the framework for this kind of strategy. Section 3 of the Act, invites copyright owners to set the process in motion in the following terms:

(1) This section applies if it appears to a copyright owner that –
    (a) a subscriber to an internet access service has infringed the owner's copyright by means of the service; or
    (b) a subscriber to an internet access service has allowed another person to use the service, and that other person has infringed the owner's copyright by means of the service.
(2) The owner may make a copyright infringement report to the internet service provider who provided the internet access service if a code in force under section 124C or 124D (an 'initial obligations code') allows the owner to do so.
(3) A 'copyright infringement report' is a report that –
    (a) states that there appears to have been an infringement of the owner's copyright;
    (b) includes a description of the apparent infringement;
    (c) includes evidence of the apparent infringement that shows the subscriber's IP address and the time at which the evidence was gathered;
    (d) is sent to the internet service provider within the period of 1 month beginning with the day on which the evidence was gathered; and
    (e) complies with any other requirement of the initial obligations code.
(4) An internet service provider who receives a copyright infringement report must notify the subscriber of the report if the initial obligations code requires the provider to do so.
(5) A notification under subsection (4) must be sent to the subscriber within the period of 1 month beginning with the day on which the provider receives the report.
(6) A notification under subsection (4) must include –
    (a) a statement that the notification is sent under this section in response to a copyright infringement report;
    (b) the name of the copyright owner who made the report;
    (c) a description of the apparent infringement;
    (d) evidence of the apparent infringement that shows the subscriber's IP address and the time at which the evidence was gathered;

(e) information about subscriber appeals and the grounds on which they may be made;

(f) information about copyright and its purpose;

(g) advice, or information enabling the subscriber to obtain advice, about how to obtain lawful access to copyright works;

(h) advice, or information enabling the subscriber to obtain advice, about steps that a subscriber can take to protect an internet access service from unauthorised use; and

(i) anything else that the initial obligations code requires the notification to include.

(7) For the purposes of subsection (6)(h) the internet service provider must take into account the suitability of different protection for subscribers in different circumstances.

(8) The things that may be required under subsection (6)(i), whether in general or in a particular case, include in particular –

(a) a statement that information about the apparent infringement may be kept by the internet service provider;

(b) a statement that the copyright owner may require the provider to disclose which copyright infringement reports made by the owner to the provider relate to the subscriber;

(c) a statement that, following such a disclosure, the copyright owner may apply to a court to learn the subscriber's identity and may bring proceedings against the subscriber for copyright infringement; and

(d) where the requirement for the provider to send the notification arises partly because of a report that has already been the subject of a notification under subsection (4), a statement that the number of copyright infringement reports relating to the subscriber may be taken into account for the purposes of any technical measures.

(9) In this section 'notify', in relation to a subscriber, means send a notification to the electronic or postal address held by the internet service provider for the subscriber (and sections 394 to 396 do not apply).

So far, it might be thought, so soft. However, section 3(8)(d) foreshadows the possibility of the ISP taking 'technical measures' against the subscriber. In section 9, the potential seriousness of such measures becomes apparent:

(1) The Secretary of State may direct OFCOM to –

(a) assess whether one or more technical obligations should be imposed on internet service providers;

(b) take steps to prepare for the obligations;

(c) provide a report on the assessment or steps to the Secretary of State.

(2) A 'technical obligation', in relation to an internet service provider, is an obligation for the provider to take a technical measure against some or all relevant subscribers to its service for the purpose of preventing or reducing infringement of copyright by means of the internet.

(3) A 'technical measure' is a measure that –

(a) limits the speed or other capacity of the service provided to a subscriber;

(b) prevents a subscriber from using the service to gain access to particular material, or limits such use;

(c) suspends the service provided to a subscriber; or

(d) limits the service provided to a subscriber in another way.

(4) A subscriber to an internet access service is 'relevant' if the subscriber is a relevant subscriber, within the meaning of section 124B(3), in relation to the provider of the service and one or more copyright owners.

(5) The assessment and steps that the Secretary of State may direct OFCOM to carry out or take under subsection (1) include, in particular –

(a) consultation of copyright owners, internet service providers, subscribers or any other person;

(b) an assessment of the likely efficacy of a technical measure in relation to a particular type of internet access service; and

(c) steps to prepare a proposed technical obligations code.

(6) Internet service providers and copyright owners must give OFCOM any assistance that OFCOM reasonably require for the purposes of complying with any direction under this section.

(7) The Secretary of State must lay before Parliament any direction under this section.

(8) OFCOM must publish every report under this section –

(a) as soon as practicable after they send it to the Secretary of State, and

(b) in such manner as they consider appropriate for bringing it to the attention of persons who, in their opinion, are likely to have an interest in it.

(9) OFCOM may exclude information from a report when it is published under subsection (8) if they consider that it is information that they could refuse to disclose in response to a request under the Freedom of Information Act 2000.

To repeat, much of the devil is in the detail of these provisions, in the detail of the Codes that may be approved under the legislation, and in the way that the technical measures are actually used. Nevertheless, there are already question marks about the legality of these provisions, particularly whether they are consistent with tests of proportionality under European law; and, even if the provisions survive legal challenge, there must be a doubt about how far ISPs can be persuaded that it makes business sense to be policing, informing on and possibly disconnecting their own customers.[31]

This leaves the third option, targeting the specialist service or software providers. While this is not self-evidently the most attractive option, there is a string of famous cases around the world in which regulators have adopted precisely this strategy, targeting the likes of Napster,[32] Grokster[33] and the Pirate Bay.[34] However, this assault on technological innovators raises some complex

---

[31] For discussion of this kind of indirect strategy, see Murray, *Information Technology Law*, 254–8.

[32] *A & M Records, Inc* v. *Napster, Inc.* 239 F 3d 1004 (9th Circuit, 2001).

[33] *MGM Studios Inc* v. *Grokster Ltd* 125 S.Ct 2764 (2005); 545 US 913 (2005).

[34] *Sweden* v. *Neij et al.*, Stockholms Tingsrätt, No. B 13301–06, 17 April 2009.

policy calculations that restrict any idea that regulators should go all out for effective copyright protection; for, it occurs in a context in which eager file-sharers are not the only ones who welcome the development of innovative information technologies.

In the *Napster* case, the centralised nature of the technology that facilitated the sharing of copyright-protected material made it fairly easy to hold that Napster had committed both contributory and vicarious copyright infringement. Napster was unable to continue operating within the terms of the injunctions issued by the court and, in July 2001, its service was closed. However, this was by no means the end of the file-sharing story: if a more decentralised version of the technology could be devised – which, of course, it quickly was – then there might yet be a way around the copyright restrictions. The redesigned file-sharing technology was put to the legal test in the *Grokster* proceedings.

In the lower courts, the rulings favoured Grokster; apparently, they had succeeded in designing their way around liability for either contributory or vicarious copyright infringement. However, the US Supreme Court still had to hear the case. On appeal to the Supreme Court, the scale of the file-sharing problem became clear. For, the evidence collected by MGM (the copyright-holders) indicated that some 90 per cent of the files shared by using Grokster's software involved copyright-infringing material. Given that 'well over 100 million copies of the software in question are known to have been downloaded, and billions of files are shared across the ... networks each month, the probable scope of copyright infringement is staggering'.[35]

In response, Grokster argued that, following *Sony Corp. of America* v. *Universal City Studios, Inc.*[36] (which concerned Sony's Betamax VHS recording system), it could not be liable because (a) the software was capable of significant lawful use and (b) given the decentralised nature of the technology, Grokster itself had no direct knowledge of unlawful use. Nevertheless, the Court held that Grokster was liable because the distribution, far from being innocent, was promoted in a way that actively induced copyright infringement. Although this seemed a particularly blatant case of inducement, the Court recognised that it needed to be careful to strike a reasonable balance between copyright protection and facilitation of technological innovation. Thus, defending the inducement rule, Justice Souter said:

> We are, of course, mindful of the need to keep from trenching on regular commerce or discouraging the development of technologies with lawful and unlawful potential. Accordingly, just as *Sony* did not find intentional inducement despite the knowledge of the VCR manufacturer that its device could be used to infringe ... mere knowledge of infringing potential or of actual infringing uses would not be enough here to subject a distributor to liability. Nor would ordinary acts incident to product distribution, such as offering customers technical support or product updates, support liability in themselves. The inducement rule, instead, premises liability on purposeful, culpable

---

[35] 545 US 913 (2005), at 923 (Justice Souter, delivering the Opinion of the Court).
[36] 464 US 417.

expression and conduct, and thus does nothing to compromise legitimate commerce or discourage innovation having a lawful promise.[37]

In a concurring Opinion, Justice Breyer elaborated on why he thought that the basic standard set in *Sony* was about right in providing technological entrepreneurs with the protection that they needed against copyright claimants:

> *Sony's rule is clear.* That clarity allows those who develop new products that are capable of substantial non-infringing uses to know, *ex ante*, that distribution of their product will not yield massive monetary liability. At the same time, it helps deter them from distributing products that have no real function than – or that are specifically intended for – copyright infringement, deterrence that the Court's holding today reinforces ...

> *Sony's rule is strongly technology protecting.* The rule deliberately makes it difficult for courts to find secondary liability where new technology is at issue. It establishes that the law will not impose copyright liability upon the distributors of dual-use technologies (who do not themselves engage in unauthorized copying) unless the product in question will be used *almost exclusively* to infringe copyrights (or unless they actively induce infringements ...). *Sony* thereby recognizes that the copyright laws are not intended to discourage or to control the emergence of new technologies, including (perhaps especially) those that help disseminate information and ideas more broadly or efficiently. Thus *Sony*'s rule shelters VCRs, typewriters, tape recorders, photocopiers, computers, cassette players, compact disc burners, digital video recorders, MP3 players, Internet search engines, and peer-to-peer software ...

> *Sony's rule is forward looking.* It does not confine its scope to a static snapshot of a product's current uses (thereby threatening technologies that have undeveloped future markets). Rather, as the VCR example makes clear, a product's market can evolve dramatically over time. And *Sony* – by referring to a *capacity* for substantial noninfringing uses – recognizes that fact .... .

> *Sony's rule is mindful of the limitations facing judges where matters of technology are concerned.* Judges have no specialized technical ability to answer questions about present or future technological feasibility or commercial viability where technology professionals, engineers, and venture capitalists themselves may radically disagree and where answers may differ depending upon whether one focuses upon the time of product development or the time of distribution.[38]

As in *Napster*, the immediate upshot of *Grokster* was that the site closed down, a note being posted on its home page to advise and to warn visitors that the Supreme Court had ruled that using the service to trade copyright-protected material was illegal.

What should we make of this particular response to regulatee resistance? First, no one is condoning copyright infringement; but there is a realistic recognition that there is a limit to how far infringement can be controlled by direct action against the infringers. No doubt, smart regulators, appreciating that popular culture treats file-sharing of one kind or another as a fair use, will be thinking about how it might be possible to change the file-sharing culture itself. And, if the culture cannot be changed, then perhaps it is the regulation that

---

[37] 545 US 913 (2005), at 937. [38] *Ibid.*, at 957–8.

must yield: as Jessica Litman has remarked: 'If a law is bad enough, even its proponents might be willing to abandon it in favour of a different law that seems more legitimate to the people it is intended to command.'[39] Second, the *Sony* and *Grokster* rules do not tolerate product development and distribution that has no capacity for lawful use or that comes with a clear inducement to violate the law. Those services that clearly fall foul of the rules have to find another way of doing business. Third, it is recognised, nevertheless, that the regulatory environment needs to be conducive to product development and technological innovation. If dual-use products are to attract liability, for the sake of the copyright holders, innovation will grind to a halt. Fourth, and perhaps predictably, commentators reacted to the decision in different ways. On the one side, critics argued that the inducement standard was unclear and would operate as a chill factor in relation to technological development – particularly bearing in mind the high costs of litigation when set alongside the disparity between the considerable resources of the copyright-holding industries and the limited resources of small technology enterprises.[40] On the other side, defenders of the decision argued that there was no reason why the developers of technology should have a special exemption against inducing copyright infringement; provided that developers played the game, there should be no impediment to innovation.

In Europe, there have been a number of important file-sharing cases but the most discussed is the *Pirate Bay*. Stated simply, Pirate Bay was a site that acted as an indexer for file-sharers using the BitTorrent system. In April 2009, the four operators of the Pirate Bay site were convicted of complicity in making copyright material available, the shape of the prosecutor's argument being very much along the lines of the reasoning in *Grokster*. Pending the outcome of the defendants' appeal, Pirate Bay continues to operate but the local position is uncertain. At the same time that the criminal proceedings were taking place in Sweden, courts elsewhere in Europe ordered local ISPs to block access to Pirate Bay; but, as Andrew Murray points out, none of this deals 'with the root of the problem: individuals sharing copyright protected content with other individuals.'[41]

What should we make of this? Having reviewed the leading cases around the world (including *Napster*, *Grokster* and *Pirate Bay*), Matthew Rimmer[42] concludes in the following terms:

> The future of digital copyright remains uncertain. As Antonio Gramsci once wrote in his prison notebooks, 'The old is dying and the new cannot be born; in this interregnum there arises a great diversity of morbid symptoms.' The matrix of copyright protection proposed by record companies and movie studios will be countered by new technological innovations in peer-to-peer networks. Napster,

---

[39] Jessica Litman, *Digital Copyright* (New York: Prometheus Books, 2001), at 195.

[40] Compare the sophisticated commentary in James Boyle, *The Public Domain* (New Haven: Yale University Press, 2008), 71–82 (encompassing *Napster*, *Grokster* and *Sony*).

[41] Murray, *Information Technology Law*, 254.

[42] Matthew Rimmer, *Digital Copyright and the Consumer Revolution* (Cheltenham: Edward Elgar, 2007).

Aimster, Grokster, Streamcast, and Kazaa may have become defunct. However, they leave behind an important legacy. The strategies of resistance pioneered by the peer-to-peer networks will be refined by their rivals and successors. Peer-to-peer networks can be deservedly criticized for their slick marketing and overweening commercial ambitions, but they certainly deserve credit and respect for their ingenious legal and technical defences against copyright owners.[43]

As Gramsci famously tried to instruct fellow Marxists, winning over 'hearts and minds' matters; and, in the context of regulatory effectiveness, it clearly matters a great deal. To which, we might add, so long as there is a widespread demand for file-sharing facilities, there will be a market response: whether, in the longer run, that market is black, grey or white, time alone will tell.

5 Students and cognition enhancers

A great deal of attention has been paid to the *ethics* of human enhancement. Some think that, if new technologies can be applied to enhance human capacities, then it is at least permissible, and maybe even a requirement, to make use of them; others argue for communitarian ideals that are not corrupted by visions of perfection; and others accept that enhancement is permissible so long as human rights are not infringed.[44] Yet, these questions of regulatory legitimacy might be overtaken by events: if technologies for human enhancement that are cheap and reliable are developed, does anyone imagine that regulators could stem the flow of their adoption and use? To take a case in point: there is some evidence that psychoactive drugs such as Ritalin and Modafinil give their users a degree of intellectual edge (improving memory, concentration, and so on) – for example, tasks can be completed in a shorter time (although not always more accurately) and the mind can remain alert for longer periods.[45] Not altogether surprisingly, it is generally believed that such cognition-enhancing drugs are already being used by some university students.[46] In a BMA discussion paper,[47] the present state of play is summarised as follows:

> Research involving these products was undertaken to develop a greater understanding of the mechanisms that control cognition (its neuromodulation) and the way in which different pharmaceutical products affect performance. The research

---

[43] *Ibid.*, at 123.

[44] See, respectively, John Harris, *Enhancing Evolution* (Princeton: Princeton University Press, 2007); Michael Sandel, *The Case against Perfection* (Cambridge, MA: Harvard University Press, 2007); and Roger Brownsword, 'Regulating Human Enhancement: Things Can Only Get Better?', *Law Innovation and Technology*, 1 (2009), 125.

[45] See, e.g., Henry Greely, Barbara Sahakian, John Harris, Ronald C. Kessler, Michael Gazzaniga, Philip Campbell and Martha J. Farah, 'Towards Responsible Use of Cognitive-Enhancing Drugs by the Healthy', *Nature* (2008) (7 December), 702.

[46] A. Frean and P. Foster, 'Cheating students turn to "smart drugs" for edge in exams', *The Times*, 23 June 2007, 16–17.

[47] BMA, *Boosting Your Brainpower: Ethical Aspects of Cognitive Enhancements* (London: BMA Ethics Department, November 2007).

involved healthy volunteers so that the findings would not be confounded by the patient's underlying condition. These studies have led to growing evidence that, in addition to their intended uses, these drugs can also have beneficial effects on some aspects of cognitive functioning in healthy individuals. In effect, they can improve on some aspects of normal functioning and make people 'better than well'. With a structure as complicated as the brain, however, it is not surprising that this is not as straightforward as it might sound. Although the pharmaceutical products produce interesting and promising results in ideal laboratory conditions, their impact in less controlled situations is still to be investigated. In the meantime, there are risks in attempting to extrapolate from small scale studies. There is some suggestion that improvements in one aspect of an individual's performance may be offset by decreased performance in another aspect. It must also be strongly emphasised here that the side-effects of taking the drugs, particularly over a prolonged period, are unknown and may turn out to be problematic. Nevertheless, despite the lack of information about the long-term use of such drugs in healthy individuals, there is already evidence of demand. As our understanding of the way the brain functions in relation to cognition improves, it is likely that more drugs, with fewer side-effects, will be developed and that such demand will increase.[48]

Given this assessment and prognosis, is there any reason to think that regulation could be effective in preventing the use, by healthy individuals, of cognition-enhancing drugs?

If regulating the use of drugs for cognition enhancement is anything like regulating the use of drugs for recreational purposes, we have little reason to think that criminalisation would be an effective intervention. As is well known, in the UK, the Misuse of Drugs Act 1971 identifies a number of psychoactive substances ('controlled substances') that are its target and that are famously classified as Class A, Class B or Class C substances. In relation to these substances, the Act then provides for a raft of offences – the principal offences relating to unauthorised production or (in the case of cannabis) cultivation, possession and supply, allowing premises to be used for the production, supply, or taking of drugs, and trafficking (importing or exporting). Within the regulatory inventory, offences relating to Class A drugs are the most serious; offences relating to Class B drugs are less serious; and, offences relating to Class C drugs are the least serious. On paper, even Class C drug offences, though, are serious crimes – for example, the penalties for dealing in Class C drugs are a custodial sentence of up to fourteen years, or an unlimited fine, or both. There is a great deal that could be said about this regime;[49] but the key point is that, since 1971, recreational drug use has relentlessly risen and, despite occasional enforcement successes, the bigger picture is that the long-running war on drugs is being lost.

[48] *Ibid.*, at 10 (notes omitted).
[49] See, e.g., House of Commons Select Committee on Home Affairs (2002): *The Government's Drugs Policy: Is It Working?* (3rd Report, 2001–2).

What is the state of our regulatory intelligence? In the Foresight report, *Drugs Futures 2025?*[50] it is acknowledged that there is more than one strategic option. One option is to:

> [d]eal with 'recreational' substance use through existing regulations that seek to modify behaviour by making drugs harder to get, increasing the risks associated with their use by criminalising them, and providing information on harms.[51]

The counterpoint to such a predominantly hard law approach is one that focuses on encouraging a longer-term cultural change which, if successful, results in effect in self-regulation. Although this choice does not translate into a straightforward choice between a supply-side and a demand-side strategy, the emphasis of the latter (longer-term) option is on the demand side.

It is also a 'strong message' in the Foresight analysis that 'any change to the legal status of a "recreational" drug could lead to unexpected negative effects if society is not ready for it'.[52] So: '[I]f management of the use of a specific substance is tightened, users may try to find a way around the change, which can lead to other forms of harm.'[53] Moreover, where the use of a particular drug for recreational purposes is socially embedded, there are limited opportunities for heavy-duty legal intervention. From this, the following implication is drawn:

> This means that effective change needs to be preceded by effective engagement with the public. This requires considerable investment and patience, but in the long run it can produce the best result. Such engagement has to work with society's acceptance of the best way to reduce the overall harm.[54]

Not surprisingly, perhaps, the impression is that the war on recreational drug use is not easily won; and that if the law has a part to play in that war, it is not entirely clear where or when it might make a positive contribution. So, if we take this intelligence forward to the use of drugs as cognition enhancers, how should regulators proceed?

Broadly speaking, regulators might adopt a supply-side or a demand-side strategy, or both, and they might rely on a criminal justice or some other (non-criminal justice) mode of regulatory approach.

Where intervention is targeted at the supply side, the idea is to prevent the drug in question from reaching the market. This might involve acting against producers, importers, carriers, coordinators or those who supply directly to users. In fact, in tackling recreational drug use, government has placed considerable emphasis on such supply-side intervention; and, indeed, it is generally agreed that supply-side activity is an important element in any attempt to reduce drug use.[55] Conversely, where the intervention is targeted at the demand

---

[50] Office of Science and Technology, *Drugs Futures 2025?* (London, 2005).
[51] Ibid., Executive Summary, 10.
[52] *Ibid.*, at 8.   [53] *Ibid.*   [54] *Ibid.*, at 42.
[55] See Deborah Brown, Mark Mason, and Rachel Murphy, 'Drug Supply and Trafficking: An Overview', *Howard Journal of Criminal Justice*, 42 (2003), 324.

side, the idea is to reduce the volume or intensity of demand. If people decide to give up smoking or consuming alcohol or using cocaine, there is less urgency about disrupting the supply-side network.

Where the intervention, whether on the supply side or the demand side, is of a criminal justice kind, government relies on the deterrent effect of the criminal law coupled with the activities of the law enforcement agencies and the corrective effects of penal sanctions. However, as the Foresight report recognises, government might also, or alternatively, focus on a non-criminal justice approach – one, for instance that aims to educate and inform users about the harms associated with the targeted drug; or it might adjust the tax and benefit regime with a view to introducing appropriate financial incentives and disincentives, and so on.

The context in which government pursues such a policy of confinement or reduction might be more or less conducive to its regulatory efforts, with regulatees being more or less receptive and responsive to the intervention in question. The least helpful context will be one in which:

1 the use of the drug (for recreational purposes or for cognition-enhancement) is socially embedded;
2 such use is not unlawful;
3 such use is regarded as perfectly acceptable by a majority of the community;
4 use of the drug is addictive;
5 lawful suppliers of the drug are significant employers; and
6 government itself relies on the usage as a source of revenue.

If this checklist is applied to the use of drugs as cognition enhancers, what kind of context is it that regulators would be working in?

First, although the idea that drugs might act as cognition enhancers has not yet caught the imagination of the general population, it might already be embedded in some sections of the population (particularly so in the universities). To the extent that this part of the population is both competitive and ready to experiment, the use of these drugs could spread quite quickly.

Second, unlike tobacco and alcohol, it is likely to be a criminal offence to be found in possession of, or to be supplying, cognition-enhancing drugs. While students will not want to have a criminal record on their CVs, it is hard to imagine that anyone who is simply caught in possession of such drugs (for their personal use) will get more than a caution.

Third, there are likely to be mixed views in student populations as to the acceptability of using cognition-enhancing drugs. Some students will regard this as a form of cheating and this will create a pressure against use of the drugs. However, as with file-sharing, some will see this as perfectly acceptable – in fact, as little different from using coffee or other lawful stimulants. While opinions are forming, the immediate regulatory environment is likely to contain mixed signals. Moreover, the attitude taken by each particular university will be an important element in the regulatory mix.

Fourth, the use of the drugs might not be addictive in the way that we associate with heroin or cocaine; but, if users come to rely on the drugs, it will be more difficult to break the habit.

Fifth, the future of the pharmaceutical, tobacco or alcoholic drinks business does not hinge on the student market for cognition-enhancing drugs. And, nor at this stage has this been seen as an opportunity for organised crime – if that were to happen, the regulatory stakes would be raised enormously. Currently, students are able to access the drugs through internet suppliers and, as we will see in the next chapter, it is not at all easy for domestic regulators to prevent this happening.

Sixth, government is not yet in a position where it treats cognition-enhancing drugs and their users as a source of revenue. But, of course, one strategy might be to try to price students out of a lawful market for such drugs.

Finally, there are two other rather obvious points that have not been mentioned. First, the warrant of police officers runs to all corners of the community. However, in practice, policing by consent militates against a high-profile police presence in supposedly reputable quarters. The idea of the police swamping a university to seek out students in possession of cognition enhancers would not be well received. Just as student file-sharers judged that the chances of detection were low, so too students using cognition-enhancing drugs would not expect to be detected. Second, the use of cognition enhancers is victimless. It is trite that without victims to report crime, detection of crime is more difficult. As the House of Commons Select Committee on Home Affairs once put it:

> While around four million people use illicit drugs each year, most of those people do not appear to experience harm from their drug use, nor do they cause harm to others as a result of their habit.[56]

If this is the case for a range of drugs that are used for recreational purposes, it is likely to be even more so in relation to cognition-enhancing drugs.

If this context already looks too challenging for an effective regulatory intervention, there is another option. Instead of trying to prevent the use of cognition-enhancing drugs, regulators might judge that they would do better to focus on managing the consequences of such use. This is not the end of the problem for the terms on which use would be legalised would need some discussion and imagination.[57] Would such drugs be available across the counter, on prescription, only in certain areas, and so on? Would there be some universities where cognition-enhancers would be permitted and others where their use would be regarded as cheating? Whatever the answer to these questions, if this it to be the strategy, it shifts the phasing of the regulation; and, with that,

---

[56] House of Commons Select Committee on Home Affairs (2002): *Government's Drugs Policy*, at para. 20.

[57] Compare BMA, *Boosting Your Brainpower*, at 34–5.

the question of effectiveness, so to speak, to a second-phase rather than a first-phase intervention.[58]

6 Conclusion

We started this chapter by observing that regulation is likely to encounter least resistance where regulators and regulatees have similar purposes and where the means adopted to achieve those purposes are thought to be appropriate. In Type 2, self-regulating communities, the conditions for generating such an accord between regulators and regulatees are quite good. Or, to put this another way, the greater the 'distance' between regulators and regulatees, the more likely it is that regulatees will resist interventions made by regulators – which might be another way of saying that, where regulation is ineffective, and where the problem can be traced to regulatee resistance, this is more likely to arise in a Type 1 regulatory environment than in a Type 2 environment.

It also seems plausible to suppose that regulatee resistance is more likely to be a problem in first-generation normative regulatory environments than in environments that rely on design. Indeed, where normative strategies are ineffective, as we have seen in this chapter (for example, in relation to road traffic) one option for regulators is to introduce non-normative elements into the regulatory environment.

In this chapter, we have seen that regulatee resistance can be more or less organised; it can be large scale or small scale; it can be embedded or merely occasional; and it can be local or global. Where it is organised (as with the stem cell scientific community) or where the numbers are large (as with file-sharers and car drivers), and where it is embedded (as with the consumption of alcohol), it is difficult for regulators to overcome such resistance. Where resistance is not yet embedded and on a small scale (possibly as with the use of cognition enhancers), intervention might be effective. Finally, where resistance spreads beyond national regulatory boundaries, there is the possibility that local regulatees will be aided and abetted by parties who escape the reach of local regulators. This increases the difficulties for regulators and, in the next chapter, our discussion focuses on third-party interference of this kind.

[58] For elaboration, see Roger Brownsword, *Rights, Regulation and the Technological Revolution* (Oxford: Oxford University Press, 2008), ch. 1.

14

Regulatory effectiveness IV: third-party interference and disruptive externalities

1 Introduction

Where regulators proceed in an informed and competent way, and where regulatees are disposed to comply, is there any reason to suppose that a regulatory intervention might not be effective? Certainly, *other things being equal*, we should expect such an intervention to be relatively effective. However, the world does not stand still; things are rarely equal; and the best-laid regulatory plans can be frustrated by third-party interference and by various kinds of crises and catastrophes.

Some kinds of third-party interference are well known – for example, regulatory arbitrage (which is a feature of company law and tax law) is nothing new. Sadly, much the same can be said about natural disasters. Although externalities of this kind continue to play their part in determining the fate of a regulatory intervention, it is the emergence of the internet that has most dramatically highlighted the possibility of interference from third parties. For this reason, in this chapter, we will focus quite extensively on the implications of cyberspace and online technologies for the challenge of regulatory effectiveness.

We will start (in section 2) by identifying the kinds of externalities that can interfere with the success of a regulatory intervention, after which (in section 3) we will summarise David Johnson and David Post's famous early assessment of the prospects for regulating activities in cyberspace.[1] According to Johnson and Post, national regulators would have little success in controlling extraterritorial online activities, even though those activities have a local impact. Most seriously, what might local regulators do to combat 'cybercrime'? And, how can regulators effectively control local off-line activities where third parties engage in online conduct that cuts across the regulatory objectives – for example, how can local regulators control access to drugs, or alcohol, or gambling or direct-to-consumer genetic-testing services, where internet pharmacies, or online drinks suppliers or casinos, or the like, all hosted on servers that are located beyond the national borders, direct their goods and services at local regulatees?

---

[1] David R. Johnson and David Post, 'Law and Borders: The Rise of Law in Cyberspace', *Stanford Law Review*, 48 (1996), 1367.

Regulatory effectiveness IV

Having set the scene with Johnson and Post, we will pursue these issues for regulatory effectiveness (in sections 4 and 5).

2 Five types of external interference

There are a number of different types of externality that can interfere with a particular regulatory intervention. The origins of the externality are either in human action (sometimes hostile, at other times not so) or non-human natural disasters and disturbances.

First, regulatory capacity might be disrupted by the actions of hostile third parties. War-mongering or terrorist activities can damage, divert and deplete regulatory resources; and, as governments and regulators become ever more reliant on information and communication technologies, new targets for hostile actions present themselves. The distributed denial-of-service (DDoS) attack on Estonia in 2007 is a case in point.[2] In a report on large-scale cybercrime, the House of Lords European Committee described the attack on Estonia and its impact as follows:[3]

> Estonia has the highest broadband connectivity in Europe. In 2007, 98 percent of all bank transactions in Estonia used electronic channels and 82 percent of all Estonian tax declarations were submitted through the Internet. Nearly every school in Estonia uses an e-learning environment, and the use of ID cards and digital signatures has become routine in both public and private sector administrations in Estonia. Estonia has a significant ethnic Russian population, and the movement of a statue of a Soviet soldier commemorating the end of World War II led to civil unrest within Estonia and complaints by the Russian Government. Online DDoS attacks began to target Estonian government and private sector sites, including banking institutions and news sites. The attacks built up over the course of a few weeks and peaked at 11 pm Moscow time on Victory Day, 9 May. The attacks hit many parts of the infrastructure, including the websites of the prime minister, parliament, most ministries, political parties, and three of the biggest news organisations. Members of the Estonian Parliament went for four days without email. Government communications networks were reduced to radio for a limited period. Financial operations were severely compromised, ATMs were crippled, and Hansabank, the largest bank, was forced to close its Internet operations. Most people found themselves effectively barred from financial transactions while the attacks were at their height. Estonia responded by closing large parts of its network to people from outside the country, and a consequence was that Estonians abroad were unable to access their bank accounts.

---

[2] Compare, too, Richard Norton-Taylor, 'Titan rain: how Chinese hackers targeted Whitehall', *The Guardian*, 5 September 2007, 1. One notch down from such incidents are the denial-of-service attacks launched by pro-Wikileaks 'hactivitists' in December 2010: see, e.g., Cahal Milmo and Nigel Morris, 'Prepare for all-out cyber war', *The Independent*, 14 December 2010, 1.

[3] House of Lords European Union Committee, *Protecting Europe Against Large-Scale Cyber-Attacks* (Fifth Report, Session 2009–10), para. 11, box 1.

If Estonian governance and commerce could be disabled in this way, how vulnerable might other European countries be? According to the Committee:

> There are wide differences between the Member States. Some, like Estonia, are very heavily reliant on the Internet but have – or had until very recently – defences wholly inadequate to protect their CII [critical information infrastructures] against even minor attacks. Some, and the United Kingdom is among them, also rely heavily on the Internet, but have sophisticated and well-developed defences to guard against attacks or disruptions. Yet other Member States rely less on the Internet, but their defences are insufficient. We concluded that all Member States have an interest in bringing the defences of the lowest up to those of the highest, and that this is a matter of legitimate concern to the EU as a whole.[4]

Even if defence levels were to be raised in the way that the Committee believes would be desirable, there is a view that nation states are no longer geared to respond to external cyberthreats. According to Susan Brenner, it is not always clear, first, who is responsible for a particular cyberthreat and, second, whether it is an act of cyberwar, cyberterror or even cybercrime – indeed, she maintains that the attacks on Estonia were just such a case.[5] While the importance of identifying the source of the threat is obvious, the relevance of classifying the threat correctly is that responsibility needs to be allocated to the appropriate national agents (the military, the intelligence services or the police).

With an increased concern for the security of both off-line and online critical infrastructures, a tension can develop between the security imperatives and the importance attached by both regulators and regulatees to the values of privacy and data protection.[6] Stefano Rodotà[7] identifies three interacting pressures on privacy as follows:

> Firstly, after 9/11 many reference criteria changed and the guarantees were reduced everywhere in the world, as shown, in particular, by the Patriot Act in the USA and the European decisions on transfer of airline passenger data to the US as well as on the retention of electronic communication data. Secondly, this trend towards downsizing safeguards was extended to sectors that are trying to

---

[4] *Ibid.*, summary.

[5] Susan W. Brenner, *Cyberthreats: The Emerging Fault Lines of the Nation State* (New York: Oxford University Press, 2009).

[6] Compare Nicole van der Meulen, *Fertile Grounds* (Nijmegen: Wolf Legal Publishers, 2010), where it is argued that the burgeoning of accessible online data coupled with increased concerns about security (and, concomitantly, the importance of identification and verification) has created a context that invites various kinds of (particularly financial) identity theft. We might take this forward by imagining two ideal-typical settings: (a) where it is easy to collect personal information and to personate another; and (b) where, because of biometric requirements and the like, it is more difficult to personate another. In the first setting, it will be easy to commit crime unless targets are hardened; in the latter, more effort is required to acquire another's identity but, having done that, crime might be easier to commit (because the biometrics are trusted).

[7] Stefano Rodotà, 'Data Protection as a Fundamental Right', in Serge Gutwirth, Yves Poullet, Paul de Hert, Cécile de Terwangne and Sjaak Nouwt (eds.), *Reinventing Data Protection?* (Dordrecht: Springer, 2009), 77.

benefit from the change in the general scenario – such as those related to business. Thirdly, the new technological opportunities make continuously available new tools for classification, selection, social sorting and control of individuals, which are resulting in a veritable technological drift that national and international authorities are not always capable to adequately counter.[8]

Rodotà's point is that the disruptive effects of events such as 9/11 and the DDoS attacks on Estonia are not limited to their immediate impact; rather, they operate in conjunction with both business initiatives and new technologies to amplify the disruption.[9]

A second type of external interference occurs where third parties, albeit not hostile, compete with local regulators. Even where regulatory arbitrage is not being actively pursued, the effectiveness of local regulators can be reduced as regulatees take up more attractive options that are available elsewhere. Somewhat unusually, in the case of *S. H. and Others* v. *Austria*,[10] there was a suggestion that the restrictiveness of the Austrian IVF rules was *helpfully assisted* by the coexistence of less restrictive regulatory regimes in adjacent European countries. Generally, though, this kind of regulatory competition is unwelcome in the home country. To the several examples of regulatee flight and relocation that we have already encountered, we can add one more. In this instance, in response to a German law that was introduced in August 2007, with the intention of criminalising the creation or distribution of (put simply) tools for hacking into computer systems, it seems that a number of legitimate computer security companies announced their intention to relocate out of Germany.[11] Had the law, which was designed to implement Article 6 of the Convention on Cybercrime (see below section 4), made it clear that no offence was committed where the tools were intended for legitimate security use, all would have been well. However, without this being made clear (a case of regulator failure), regulatees who were not the intended targets of the law took flight; and, it seems that there were no prosecutions against those who were the intended targets.

A third scenario is one in which friendly states act in ways that are damaging to local regulatory effectiveness. For example, even if the recent global financial crisis originated in the lending practices of a friendly state, the impact was felt far and wide. And, where this leads to funds being diverted or regulators being deprived of resources that they were counting on having, then there can be a regulatory failure.

Fourth, where nation states enter into trade or cultural agreements, the obligations that are assumed under such agreements can have an impact on

---

[8] *Ibid.*, at 78.
[9] Compare David Lyon, *Identifying Citizens* (Cambridge: Polity, 2009).
[10] Application no. 57813/00 (1 April 2010).
[11] Mark Rasch, 'German hacker-tool law snares ... no-one', *The Register*, 7 June 2009; available online at www.theregister.co.uk/2009/06/07/germany_hacker_tool_law (last accessed 22 January 2010).

the effectiveness of local regulation. For example, in the *Marper*[12] case that we discussed in Chapter 4, the decision handed down by the European Court of Human Rights placed some limits on the way in which the National DNA Database was being developed in England and Wales. This was not a conspiracy by Convention members to wreck what the local regulators saw as a flagship use of DNA profiling technology for forensic purposes; rather, it was simply the accumulation of different third-party regulatory positions that placed such a large (and decisive) question mark against the proportionality of the local practice. In this chapter, we will spend some time (in section 5) noting how membership of the EU restricts the ability of local regulators to impose their own health and safety or cultural standards. When, in a pre-internet age, members signed up for a single market, they perhaps did not appreciate how difficult it would become (both in practice and as a matter of membership commitments) to control the cross-border supply of goods and services.

Finally, there can be many kinds of natural disasters, earthquakes, floods, fires, and so on that have a similar disabling effect on local regulators and the policies that they are seeking to implement.[13]

3 The prospects for regulating cyberspace

Opening their seminal paper on the regulation of online communications, David Johnson and David Post[14] wrote:

> Global computer-based communications cut across territorial borders, creating a new realm of human activity and undermining the feasibility – and legitimacy – of laws based on geographic boundaries. While these electronic communications play havoc with geographic boundaries, a new boundary, made up of the screens and passwords that separate the virtual world from the 'real world' of atoms, emerges. This new boundary defines a distinct Cyberspace that needs and can create its own law and legal institutions. Territorially based law-makers and law-enforcers find this new environment deeply threatening.[15]

Generally speaking, legal systems as we have traditionally known them map onto geographical territories with clear boundaries.[16] We know when and where we cross from one legal system to another; within each legal system the authorities enjoy a measure of control and legitimacy. However, in cyberspace, matters are quite different:

> Cyberspace radically undermines the relationship between legally significant (online) phenomena and physical location. The rise of the global computer

---

[12] *Case of S. and Marper v. The United Kingdom* (Applications nos. 30562/04 and 30566/04, 4 December 2008).

[13] Compare Philip Bobbitt, *Terror and Consent* (London: Allen Lane, 2008).

[14] Johnson and Post, 'Law and Borders', 1367.   [15] *Ibid.*

[16] Subject, that is, to the increasingly prevalent, but still controversial, effects doctrine in theories of jurisdiction, whereby a state claims jurisdiction in relation to events that have effects on its territory but that neither begin nor end on its territory, nor involve one of its nationals.

network is destroying the link between geographical location and: (1) the *power* of local governments to assert control over online behavior; (2) the *effects* of online behavior on individuals or things; (3) the *legitimacy* of a local sovereign's efforts to regulate global phenomena; and (4) the ability of physical location to give *notice* of which sets of rules apply. The Net thus radically subverts the system of rule-making based on borders between physical spaces, at least with respect to the claim that Cyberspace should naturally be governed by territorially defined rules.[17]

Despite these fundamental differences, traditional regulators respond in ways that assume that business is as usual. Thus:

> The power to control activity in Cyberspace has only the most tenuous connection to physical location. Nonetheless, many governments' first response to electronic communications crossing their territorial borders is to try to stop or regulate that flow of information. Rather than permitting self-regulation by participants in online transactions, many governments establish trade barriers, attempt to tax border-crossing cargo, and respond especially sympathetically to claims that information coming into the jurisdiction might prove harmful to local residents …
>
> But efforts to control the flow of electronic information across physical borders – to map local regulation and physical boundaries onto Cyberspace – are likely to prove futile, at least in countries that hope to participate in global commerce. Individual electrons can easily, and without any realistic prospect of detection, 'enter' any sovereign's territory. The volume of electronic communications crossing territorial boundaries is just too great in relation to the resources available to government authorities. United States Customs officials have generally given up … Banking and securities regulators seem likely to lose their battle to impose local regulations on a global financial marketplace.[18]

The more that regulators try to claim jurisdiction over an online matter, the more difficult it is for there to be any coherent co-ordination. To try to reduce online transactions to 'a legal analysis based in geographic terms', just like '[e]fforts to determine "where" the events in question occur are decidedly misguided, if not altogether futile'.[19]

According to Johnson and Post, the remedy is to treat cyberspace as a place in its own right. This would overcome jurisdictional competition with regard to defamation, professional qualifications, IP, and so on, as well as facilitating the creation of bespoke online law. Moreover, such a response is not unprecedented:

> Perhaps the most apt analogy to the rise of a separate law of Cyberspace is the origin of the Law Merchant – a distinct set of rules that developed with the new, rapid boundary-crossing trade of the Middle Ages. Merchants could not resolve their disputes by taking them to the local noble, whose established feudal law

---

[17] Johnson and Post, 'Law and Borders', at 1370.
[18] *Ibid.*, at 1371–3.   [19] *Ibid.*, at 1378.

mainly concerned land claims. Nor could the local lord easily establish meaningful rules for a sphere of activity that he barely understood and that was executed in locations beyond his control. The result of this jurisdictional confusion was the development of a new legal system – *Lex Mercatoria*. The people who cared most about and best understood their new creation formed and championed this new law, which did not destroy or replace existing law regarding more territorially based transactions (e.g., transferring land ownership). Arguably, exactly the same type of phenomenon is developing in Cyberspace right now.[20]

Concluding their paper, Johnson and Post say:

> Global electronic communications have created new spaces in which distinct rule sets will evolve. We can reconcile the new law created in this space with current territorially based legal systems by treating it as a distinct doctrine, applicable to a clearly demarcated sphere, created primarily by legitimate, self-regulatory processes, and entitled to appropriate deference – but also subject to limitations when it oversteps its appropriate sphere.[21]

Would this entail the end of law? Not at all; to be sure, the relationship between traditional top-down lawmakers and subjects will have to change. Nevertheless, 'Law, defined as a thoughtful group conversation about core values, will persist. But it will not, could not, and should not be the same law as that applicable to physical, geographically-defined territories.'[22] Put slightly differently, Johnson and Post presuppose that online regulatory environments will be modelled on Type 2, rather than Type 1, lines.

To the extent that this seminal piece suggests that regulators will have difficulty in asserting Type 1 control over the online world, it was surely correct – file-sharing (which we reviewed in the previous chapter) is one particular case and we will shortly consider cybercrime more generally. However, to the extent that Johnson and Post envisage a transfer of power from traditional regulators to the largely self-regulating communities that populate cyberspace, we might wonder about both the legitimacy and the effectiveness of these groups. Consider, for example, the following reservations that are expressed about the capacity of the operators of Second Life to regulate the gambling activities of their players:[23]

> According to press reports Linden Lab [the operators of Second Life] was visited by FBI agents and decided to ban gambling in July 2007. Online gambling is largely illegal in the US, where Linden Lab is established. However, an operator of a virtual world established in another jurisdiction where gambling is not regulated may well decide not to ban gambling or even promote the use of the platform for such cross-border activities.

---

[20] *Ibid.*, at 1389–90.   [21] *Ibid.*, at 1400–1.   [22] *Ibid.*, at 1402.

[23] Julia Hörnle and Brigitte Zammit, *Cross-Border Online Gambling Law and Policy* (Cheltenham: Edward Elgar, 2010), 13 (footnotes omitted). Nevertheless, Second Life is precisely the kind of model of a prospectively self-governing community that David Post draws on; see, David G. Post, *In Search of Jefferson's Moose* (Oxford: Oxford University Press, 2009), 178–86.

Enforcement thus takes place on two levels: at the level of the enforcement authorities of a particular state and at the platform level. However, even if a virtual world operator decides to ban gambling, the question arises whether the operator itself is effectively able to enforce the ban on online gambling engaged in by users of the virtual world.

Before the ban, it was estimated that there were hundreds of casinos and virtual poker tables in Second Life. This raises the question whether any are left or whether new ones have developed. The rules of Second Life now state that all forms of online gambling are prohibited and Linden Lab may confiscate any virtual land or other objects used for gambling and may exclude users infringing the rules. Furthermore, in order to prevent users finding virtual casinos, Linden Lab blocks any advertising of gambling opportunities and acts on notifications of gambling activities in its abuse reporting system. In other words, Linden Lab operate a notice and take-down system whereby users report illegal activity and Linden Lab remove any such content and exclude the users engaged in such illegal activity. However, if users do not report such activity, it is hard to see whether the operator can find out about gambling activities. Users may find casinos on external internet blogs and by word of mouth. Hence it is at least questionable how effective a ban is as such. An operator such as Linden Lab would have to constantly search its servers hosting the virtual world to find the code enabling the online gambling … This is not impossible, but it may be time-consuming and expensive to implement.

Even this is not the full story; for there is also the question of how the existence of the internet impacts on the attempts made by regulators to control activities in the off-line world. If, for example, Second Life were hosted outside the US, and if it offered online gambling sites and services that could be accessed by US citizens, how would local regulators defend their no-gambling policy? This is a matter to which we will return in section 5 of the chapter.

4 Cybercrime

Cybercrime, understood broadly as the online commission of a traditional off-line crime (such as fraud or the circulation of pornographic material) or as an entirely novel form of online criminality (such as phishing or spamming), is a problem for regulators. The 'Internet separatists', as Joel Reidenberg calls them,[24] seem to think that the rule of law (and national rules of law) simply do not apply to their online activities. This seems to be the case, for example, when thousands of users of Twitter conspire to disclose the identity of persons in defiance of protective court orders.[25] Hence, as Reidenberg says:

The defenses for hate, lies, drugs, sex, gambling, and stolen music are in essence that technology justifies the denial of personal jurisdiction, the rejection of an

---

[24] Joel R. Reidenberg, 'Technology and Internet Jurisdiction', *University of Pennsylvania Law Review*, 153 (2005), 1951.

[25] See, e.g., Frances Gibb, Anushka Asthana and Alexi Mostrous, 'Paper faces legal threat over picture of footballer', *The Times*, 23 May 2011, 1 (the Ryan Giggs case). See, in general, our discussion of privacy in Chapter 8.

assertion of applicable law by a sovereign state, and the denial of the enforcement of decisions ... In the face of these claims, legal systems engage in a rather conventional struggle to adapt existing regulatory standards to new technologies and the Internet. Yet, the underlying fight is a profound struggle against the very right of sovereign states to establish rules for online activity.[26]

Where cybercrime originates within a regulator's home territory, the challenge of making an effective intervention is of the kind that we have surveyed in the previous two chapters. It might be the case, for example, that regulatory resource, or expertise or prioritisation is simply not adequate; or it might be that regulatees engage in strategies of resistance. However, in this part of our discussion, our interest is in cybercrime that originates outside the regulator's home territory.[27] Specifically, our interest is in third-party cybercriminal interventions that interfere with what would otherwise be an unproblematic relationship between regulators and regulatees.

Consider this scenario. Let us suppose that national regulators believe that it is in the public interest to encourage the development and use of online facilities for the purpose of governance and commerce, as well as for social purposes. Let us also suppose that, other things being equal, regulatees are content to move from off-line to online mechanisms for their transactions and interactions. Provided that regulators make appropriate interventions for the creation of their particular vision of the information society, and provided that regulatees remain willing to inhabit such a society, what can go wrong? What can go wrong is that third parties might intrude in ways that either disable or undermine confidence in the safety, reliability and integrity of online systems. As we mentioned in our introductory remarks, such damage might be done by denial-of-service attacks; but it also might be brought about in many other ways – for example, by hacking into databases that contain sensitive information, or by circulating various kinds of virus, or by devising ever more ingenious and credible online scams, and so on.

For many regulatees the problem with the online environment might be summed up in the one word, spam. As David Wall[28] reminds readers, there is more to spam than the inconvenience of receiving unsolicited e-mails; spam is not just like the off-line junk mail that drops through the letterbox:

[S]pams rarely, if ever, live up to their promises and they degrade the overall quality of virtual life. Unlike terrestrial junk mailings, which support postal services, spamming actively impedes the efficiency of email communications. It chokes up internet bandwidth and reduces access rates and overall efficiency, costing internet service providers and individual users lost time through their having to manage spams and remedy the problems they give rise to ... More importantly, spams

---

[26] Reidenberg, 'Technology', at 1953–4.
[27] We should also recall Susan Brenner's cautionary commentary on the practical difficulties of classifying particular cyberacts as acts of war, terrorism or crime (see *Cyberthreats*).
[28] David S. Wall, *Cybercrime* (Cambridge: Polity, 2007).

introduce new risks to recipients in the form of unpleasant payloads, potent deceptions or harmful computer viruses and worms, and their relentless attack dispirits internet users.[29]

If regulatees become dispirited and begin to defect from the information society, a regulatory response is called for. How is the problem that is created by spam messages, much of which is generated beyond national borders, to be managed? How should regulators respond?

According to Wall, the two leading views are those of the 'legal determinists', who advocate a legal response, and of the 'technological determinists', who argue for a technological response. On the face of it, there is little reason to suppose that a legal response, standing alone, can stem the tide of incoming spam. In both Europe and the United States, there has been legislation directed against spamming,[30] but it seems to have had little impact on the volume of spam.[31] In the case of Europe, this is hardly surprising because a great deal of the world's spam originates beyond the Union's borders. By contrast, the development and use of anti-spam software that checks all incoming emails, does seem to have had some effect – not necessarily in relation to the volume of spam being sent but in relation to the number of spams being received.[32] And, if the main purpose of the regulatory intervention is to arrest the loss of support on the part of dispirited regulatees, this is a move in the right direction. Nevertheless, as Wall points out, this is only a partial solution to the problem; on its own the technological fix does not change the behaviour of the spammers.[33]

Is there any other way in which the regulatory environment might be improved? Regulators might, as Wall, discusses, try to change the culture by encouraging regulatees to be more defensive in the use of their computers or more assertive in pursuing their (legally protected) rights; they might actively support the development of online counter-spam communities; and they might even try to educate the spammers themselves. As we saw in Chapter 2, it is a mistake to underrate the significance and influence of good netizenship. That said, Wall accepts that, 'faced with the choice, most would go for the technological fix'.[34]

Regardless of whether it is agreed that a technological fix is the most *effective* way of dealing with spamming, there are always issues about the *legitimacy* of this kind of regulatory strategy. Moreover, it is not clear that a technological fix is either the most effective or the most legitimate way of responding to

---

[29] *Ibid.*, 134.

[30] See the Directive on Privacy and Electronic Communications, Directive 2002/58/EC, and the US CAN-SPAM Act 2003.

[31] See Wall, *Cybercrime*, 193–5.   [32] *Ibid.*, 195–6.

[33] Compare, Karen M. Bradshaw and Souvik Saha, 'Academic Administrators and the Challenge of Social-Networking Websites', in Saul Levmore and Martha C. Nussbaum (eds.), *The Offensive Internet* (Cambridge, MA: Harvard University Press, 2010), 140, 'Taking away in-class Internet use to prevent cyber-bullying is like unplugging a television set to prevent violence on television: it fails to address the core concern' (*ibid.*, at 146).

[34] Wall, *Cybercrime*, 201.

cybercrime in general. In a global information society, cybercrime is an international problem; and it invites a global response. Although both the United Nations and the European Union have committed to cooperating in the attempt to combat cybercrime,[35] it is the Council of Europe, in its Convention on Cybercrime that has taken the lead. The Convention has been signed by more than forty states, with some two-thirds of the latter (including the US) ratifying it.

We extract below Articles 2–11 of the Convention which identify the principal substantive cybercrimes that are covered together with Articles 23, 25 and 27 which give an indication of the general principles of mutual assistance and cooperation. To the extent that members share the same (pre- or extra-Convention) understanding of which cyber-acts should be treated as criminal, the Convention puts no great strain on the spirit of cooperation. However, where the Convention requires mutual assistance beyond this common core, critics argue that it goes too far. However, any scheme of mutual recognition implies that there will be cooperation notwithstanding differences; the Convention gives some margin in relation to the substantive offences; and, as Andrew Murray has pointed out, the effect of Article 25(4) is that 'the requested state can refuse a mutual assistance request where it exceeds the agreed parameters of the requested state except in specific cases set out, mostly in Article 27, which itself provides safeguards [see Article 27(4)]'.[36]

> Convention on Cybercrime (Budapest 23.XI.2001)
> Chapter II – Measures to be taken at the national level
> Section 1 – Substantive criminal law
>
> Title 1 – Offences against the confidentiality, integrity and availability of computer data and systems
>
> Article 2 – Illegal access
>
> Each Party shall adopt such legislative and other measures as may be necessary to establish as criminal offences under its domestic law, when committed intentionally, the access to the whole or any part of a computer system without right. A Party may require that the offence be committed by infringing security measures, with the intent of obtaining computer data or other dishonest intent, or in relation to a computer system that is connected to another computer system.
>
> Article 3 – Illegal interception
>
> Each Party shall adopt such legislative and other measures as may be necessary to establish as criminal offences under its domestic law, when committed intentionally, the interception without right, made by technical means, of non-public transmissions of computer data to, from or within a computer

---

[35] UN Resolution 55/63. On the European Union, see Marco Gercke, 'Europe's Legal Approaches to Cybercrime', *ERA Forum*, 10 (2009), 409.

[36] Andrew Murray, *Information Technology Law* (Oxford: Oxford University Press, 2010), 406.

system, including electromagnetic emissions from a computer system carrying such computer data. A Party may require that the offence be committed with dishonest intent, or in relation to a computer system that is connected to another computer system.

Article 4 – Data interference

1 Each Party shall adopt such legislative and other measures as may be necessary to establish as criminal offences under its domestic law, when committed intentionally, the damaging, deletion, deterioration, alteration or suppression of computer data without right.

2 A Party may reserve the right to require that the conduct described in paragraph 1 result in serious harm.

Article 5 – System interference

Each Party shall adopt such legislative and other measures as may be necessary to establish as criminal offences under its domestic law, when committed intentionally, the serious hindering without right of the functioning of a computer system by inputting, transmitting, damaging, deleting, deteriorating, altering or suppressing computer data.

Article 6 – Misuse of devices

1 Each Party shall adopt such legislative and other measures as may be necessary to establish as criminal offences under its domestic law, when committed intentionally and without right:

a the production, sale, procurement for use, import, distribution or otherwise making available of:

  i a device, including a computer program, designed or adapted primarily for the purpose of committing any of the offences established in accordance with Articles 2 through 5;

  ii a computer password, access code, or similar data by which the whole or any part of a computer system is capable of being accessed,

    with intent that it be used for the purpose of committing any of the offences established in Articles 2 through 5; and

b the possession of an item referred to in paragraphs a.i or ii above, with intent that it be used for the purpose of committing any of the offences established in Articles 2 through 5. A Party may require by law that a number of such items be possessed before criminal liability attaches.

2 This article shall not be interpreted as imposing criminal liability where the production, sale, procurement for use, import, distribution or otherwise making available or possession referred to in paragraph 1 of this article is not for the purpose of committing an offence established in accordance with Articles 2 through 5 of this Convention, such as for the authorised testing or protection of a computer system.

3 Each Party may reserve the right not to apply paragraph 1 of this article, provided that the reservation does not concern the sale, distribution or otherwise making available of the items referred to in paragraph 1 a.ii of this article.

Title 2 – Computer-related offences

Article 7 – Computer-related forgery

Each Party shall adopt such legislative and other measures as may be necessary to establish as criminal offences under its domestic law, when committed intentionally and without right, the input, alteration, deletion, or suppression of computer data, resulting in inauthentic data with the intent that it be considered or acted upon for legal purposes as if it were authentic, regardless whether or not the data is directly readable and intelligible. A Party may require an intent to defraud, or similar dishonest intent, before criminal liability attaches.

Article 8 – Computer-related fraud

Each Party shall adopt such legislative and other measures as may be necessary to establish as criminal offences under its domestic law, when committed intentionally and without right, the causing of a loss of property to another person by:
a any input, alteration, deletion or suppression of computer data,
b any interference with the functioning of a computer system,
   with fraudulent or dishonest intent of procuring, without right, an economic benefit for oneself or for another person.

Title 3 – Content-related offences

Article 9 – Offences related to child pornography

1 Each Party shall adopt such legislative and other measures as may be necessary to establish as criminal offences under its domestic law, when committed intentionally and without right, the following conduct:
   a producing child pornography for the purpose of its distribution through a computer system;
   b offering or making available child pornography through a computer system;
   c distributing or transmitting child pornography through a computer system;
   d procuring child pornography through a computer system for oneself or for another person;
   e possessing child pornography in a computer system or on a computer-data storage medium.
2 For the purpose of paragraph 1 above, the term 'child pornography' shall include pornographic material that visually depicts:
   a a minor engaged in sexually explicit conduct;
   b a person appearing to be a minor engaged in sexually explicit conduct;
   c realistic images representing a minor engaged in sexually explicit conduct.
3 For the purpose of paragraph 2 above, the term 'minor' shall include all persons under 18 years of age. A Party may, however, require a lower age-limit, which shall be not less than 16 years.

4 Each Party may reserve the right not to apply, in whole or in part, paragraphs 1, sub-paragraphs d. and e, and 2, sub-paragraphs b. and c.

Title 4 – Offences related to infringements of copyright and related rights

Article 10 – Offences related to infringements of copyright and related rights

1 Each Party shall adopt such legislative and other measures as may be necessary to establish as criminal offences under its domestic law the infringement of copyright ... where such acts are committed wilfully, on a commercial scale and by means of a computer system.
2 Each Party shall adopt such legislative and other measures as may be necessary to establish as criminal offences under its domestic law the infringement of related rights ... where such acts are committed wilfully, on a commercial scale and by means of a computer system.
3 A Party may reserve the right not to impose criminal liability under paragraphs 1 and 2 of this article in limited circumstances, provided that other effective remedies are available and that such reservation does not derogate from the Party's international obligations ...

Title 5 – Ancillary liability and sanctions

Article 11 – Attempt and aiding or abetting

1 Each Party shall adopt such legislative and other measures as may be necessary to establish as criminal offences under its domestic law, when committed intentionally, aiding or abetting the commission of any of the offences established in accordance with Articles 2 through 10 of the present Convention with intent that such offence be committed.
2 Each Party shall adopt such legislative and other measures as may be necessary to establish as criminal offences under its domestic law, when committed intentionally, an attempt to commit any of the offences established in accordance with Articles 3 through 5, 7, 8, and 9.1.a and c. of this Convention.
3 Each Party may reserve the right not to apply, in whole or in part, paragraph 2 of this article.

Chapter III – International co-operation

Section 1 – General principles

Title 1 – General principles relating to international co-operation

Article 23 – General principles relating to international co-operation

The Parties shall co-operate with each other, in accordance with the provisions of this chapter, and through the application of relevant international instruments on international co-operation in criminal matters, arrangements agreed on the basis of uniform or reciprocal legislation, and domestic laws, to the widest extent possible for the purposes of investigations or proceedings concerning criminal offences related to computer systems and data, or for the collection of evidence in electronic form of a criminal offence.

Title 3 – General principles relating to mutual assistance

Article 25 – General principles relating to mutual assistance

1 The Parties shall afford one another mutual assistance to the widest extent possible for the purpose of investigations or proceedings concerning criminal offences related to computer systems and data, or for the collection of evidence in electronic form of a criminal offence.

2 Each Party shall also adopt such legislative and other measures as may be necessary to carry out the obligations set forth in Articles 27 through 35.

3 Each Party may, in urgent circumstances, make requests for mutual assistance or communications related thereto by expedited means of communication, including fax or e-mail, to the extent that such means provide appropriate levels of security and authentication (including the use of encryption, where necessary), with formal confirmation to follow, where required by the requested Party. The requested Party shall accept and respond to the request by any such expedited means of communication.

4 Except as otherwise specifically provided in articles in this chapter, mutual assistance shall be subject to the conditions provided for by the law of the requested Party or by applicable mutual assistance treaties, including the grounds on which the requested Party may refuse co-operation. The requested Party shall not exercise the right to refuse mutual assistance in relation to the offences referred to in Articles 2 through 11 solely on the ground that the request concerns an offence which it considers a fiscal offence.

5 Where, in accordance with the provisions of this chapter, the requested Party is permitted to make mutual assistance conditional upon the existence of dual criminality, that condition shall be deemed fulfilled, irrespective of whether its laws place the offence within the same category of offence or denominate the offence by the same terminology as the requesting Party, if the conduct underlying the offence for which assistance is sought is a criminal offence under its laws.

Article 27 – Procedures pertaining to mutual assistance requests in the absence of applicable international agreements

1 Where there is no mutual assistance treaty or arrangement on the basis of uniform or reciprocal legislation in force between the requesting and requested Parties, the provisions of paragraphs 2 through 9 of this article shall apply. The provisions of this article shall not apply where such treaty, arrangement or legislation exists, unless the Parties concerned agree to apply any or all of the remainder of this article in lieu thereof.

2a. Each Party shall designate a central authority or authorities responsible for sending and answering requests for mutual assistance, the execution of such requests or their transmission to the authorities competent for their execution.

b. The central authorities shall communicate directly with each other;

c. Each Party shall, at the time of signature or when depositing its instrument of ratification, acceptance, approval or accession, communicate to the Secretary General of the Council of Europe the names and addresses of the authorities designated in pursuance of this paragraph;

d. The Secretary General of the Council of Europe shall set up and keep updated a register of central authorities designated by the Parties. Each Party shall ensure that the details held on the register are correct at all times.

3 Mutual assistance requests under this article shall be executed in accordance with the procedures specified by the requesting Party, except where incompatible with the law of the requested Party.

4 The requested Party may, in addition to the grounds for refusal established in Article 25, paragraph 4, refuse assistance if:

a the request concerns an offence which the requested Party considers a political offence or an offence connected with a political offence, or

b it considers that execution of the request is likely to prejudice its sovereignty, security, *ordre public* or other essential interests.

5 The requested Party may postpone action on a request if such action would prejudice criminal investigations or proceedings conducted by its authorities.

6 Before refusing or postponing assistance, the requested Party shall, where appropriate after having consulted with the requesting Party, consider whether the request may be granted partially or subject to such conditions as it deems necessary.

7 The requested Party shall promptly inform the requesting Party of the outcome of the execution of a request for assistance. Reasons shall be given for any refusal or postponement of the request. The requested Party shall also inform the requesting Party of any reasons that render impossible the execution of the request or are likely to delay it significantly.

8 The requesting Party may request that the requested Party keep confidential the fact of any request made under this chapter as well as its subject, except to the extent necessary for its execution. If the requested Party cannot comply with the request for confidentiality, it shall promptly inform the requesting Party, which shall then determine whether the request should nevertheless be executed.

9a. In the event of urgency, requests for mutual assistance or communications related thereto may be sent directly by judicial authorities of the requesting Party to such authorities of the requested Party. In any such cases, a copy shall be sent at the same time to the central authority of the requested Party through the central authority of the requesting Party.

b. Any request or communication under this paragraph may be made through the International Criminal Police Organisation (Interpol).

c. Where a request is made pursuant to sub-paragraph a. of this article and the authority is not competent to deal with the request, it shall refer the request to the competent national authority and inform directly the requesting Party that it has done so.

d. Requests or communications made under this paragraph that do not involve coercive action may be directly transmitted by the competent authorities of the requesting Party to the competent authorities of the requested Party.

e. Each Party may, at the time of signature or when depositing its instrument of ratification, acceptance, approval or accession, inform the Secretary General of the Council of Europe that, for reasons of efficiency, requests made under this paragraph are to be addressed to its central authority.

5 Online interference with off-line regulation

In the global information society, how precisely are local regulators to maintain their domestic policies and purposes (which may involve restrictions on access to certain kinds of information, or goods or services) against uninvited third-party interveners, particularly extra-jurisdictional internet providers? If the political and social culture is authoritarian, the state will control the internet at all key layers and, in this context, it will be possible for local regulators to establish Chinese walls and filters that enable it to determine the content that is available to users.[37] However, where the culture is more liberal, direct control of this kind is not feasible.

Nevertheless, liberal states are not entirely powerless. One option is to rely in an ad hoc fashion on measures that target relevant third parties, or their assets, where such persons or their assets are physically within the jurisdiction. So, for example, when a Paris court (acting on a complaint made by LICRA, the League Against Racism and Antisemitism, against Yahoo) ordered the removal of Nazi memorabilia from Yahoo's French auction sites, it was able to enforce its judgment by targeting Yahoo's assets in France.[38] Another option is to enter into systematic (reciprocal) cooperative arrangements with other local regulators. Lawrence Lessig[39] has proposed such a scheme under which online users would carry passports that declared their citizenship; an international table would be drawn up in which nation states declared their local restrictions; and, local regulators would require servers within their jurisdiction to respect the restrictions as laid out in the international table. All being well, the servers would know which restrictions to apply to which users because of the required declaration of citizenship. Hence:

> The pact would look like this. Each state would promise to enforce on servers within its jurisdiction the regulations of other states for citizens from those other states, in exchange for having its own regulations enforced in other jurisdictions. New York would require that servers within New York keep Minnesotans away

---

[37] For a helpful review, see Ronald J. Deibert and Nart Villeneuve, 'Firewalls and Power: An Overview of Global State Censorship of the Internet', in Mathias Klang and Andrew Murray (eds.), *Human Rights in the Digital Age* (London: Cavendish Glasshouse, 2005), 111.

[38] For one of the best renditions of the Yahoo story, see Jack Goldsmith and Tim Wu, *Who Controls the Internet?* (Oxford: Oxford University Press, 2006), ch 1.

[39] Lawrence Lessig, *Code Version 2.0* (New York: Basic Books, 2006), ch. 15.

from New York gambling servers, in exchange for Minnesota keeping New York citizens away from privacy-exploiting servers. Utah would keep EU citizens away from privacy-exploiting servers, in exchange for Europe keeping Utah citizens away from European gambling sites.[40]

This is an elegant exercise in reciprocity and, as Lessig remarks:

> Such a regime would return geographical zoning to the Net. It would re-impose borders on a network built without those borders. It would give the regulators in Hungary and Thailand the power to do what they can't do just now – control their citizens as they want. It would leave citizens of the United States or Sweden as free as their government has determined they should be.[41]

A further option, at any rate if local regulators know in which internet haven the third-parties are based, is to turn the technology back on the host country. As Joel Reidenberg[42] puts the idea, if an extraterritorial operator will not comply with local rules, why not disable the offending site, or official sites in the host jurisdiction,[43] by denial-of-service measures, or the like?

There are fairly obvious practical limitations on the first of these strategies (which depends on the target regulatees or their assets being in the right jurisdictional place at the right time); and the third might be eschewed as likely to escalate technological warfare. However, the idea of international cooperation that underlies Lessig's proposal – and which is in the same regulatory family as the cooperative response to cybercrime – is a strategy that has some appeal. Is this a possible response to concerns about the online supply of direct-to-consumer genetic tests, medicines, and the like?

In the UK, the Human Genetics Commission has published a set of principles for the provision of direct-to-consumer genetic tests, with a view to promoting 'high standards and consistency in the provision of genetic tests amongst commercial providers at an international level in order to safeguard the interests of people seeking genetic testing and their families'.[44] These principles articulate stringent standards of consumer protection, placing test providers under a multiplicity of obligations with regard to the marketing and advertising of services, the scientific validity of the test, the information both general and specific to be provided about a long list of matters, counselling and support, consent, data protection, the handling of samples, the laboratory processes, the interpretation and provision of the test results, and complaints procedures. It is a formidable set of requirements, as one would expect in a culture of strong

---

[40] *Ibid.*, at 308.   [41] *Ibid.*, at 309.

[42] Joel R. Reidenberg, 'Technology and Internet Jurisdiction', *University of Pennsylvania Law Review*, 153 (2005), 1951.

[43] The thinking here is that action against official sites might encourage the host regulators to clamp down on the offending activity. One is reminded of the denial-of-service attacks, allegedly originating from Russia, that disabled Estonian government sites in 2007. Compare, too, Norton-Taylor, 'Titan rain', 1.

[44] Human Genetics Commission, *A Common Framework of Principles for Direct-To-Consumer Genetic Testing Services* (London, 2010), 1.

consumer protection. Even if these requirements are accepted by local regulators, they will have problems enforcing them against local regulatees who regard them as over-demanding; and, this applies as fortiori where regulators are trying to control extraterritorial online suppliers.[45]

There is a further complication. It might be thought that local regulators in Europe have reasonable prospects for agreeing to a scheme for regional cooperation. However, modern Europe is based on the single market project and cooperation is predicated on acceptance of the principles of free trade and free movement (including the free movement of information society services). It follows that any attempt by one member state to close its market to a third-party internet provider who is based in another member state has to be consistent with the market's free trade ground rules. In the *DocMorris* case that is extracted below, we see how the ECJ handled just such a dispute between Germany and an internet pharmacy (supplying into Germany) that was based in the Netherlands.

(a) Case C-322/01 Deutscher Apothekerverband eV v. 0800 DocMorris NV and Jacques Waterval

The claimant, the Apothekerverband, is an association whose aim is to protect and promote the economic and social interests of pharmacists in Germany; the defendant, DocMorris, is a Dutch company that carries on a traditional pharmacy business as well as offering for sale, at the internet address 0800 DocMorris, prescription and non-prescription medicines for human use, in languages including German, for end consumers in Germany. The claimants, referring to German law, challenged the legality of the defendant supplying medicines in this way. In response, the defendants argued *inter alia* that a prohibition on the sale of medicinal products by mail order is incompatible with Community law. The extract that follows picks up the story with the German court referring a number of questions for the opinion of the European Court of Justice.

The first question

45   By its first question, the national court is asking essentially whether the principle of the free movement of goods under Articles 28 EC to 30 EC is infringed by national legislation, such as that at issue in the main proceedings, whereby medicinal products for human use the sale of which is restricted to pharmacies in the Member State concerned may not be imported commercially by way of mail order through pharmacies approved in other Member States in response to individual orders placed by consumers over the internet.

46   In the light of the arguments put forward, particularly by the defendants in the main proceedings, it is appropriate to examine this question, first, in relation to medicinal products which have not been authorised in Germany. The question

---

[45] Compare, the Nuffield Council on Bioethics, *Medical Profiling and Online Medicine* (London, 2010), paras. 7.19–7.20.

will then be examined in relation to products which are authorised there. The latter category can be further subdivided into non-prescription and prescription-only medicines.

Medicinal products which are not authorised in Germany

47 Of the national provisions at issue in the main proceedings, Paragraph 73(1) of the AMG prohibits, as a general rule, the importation of medicinal products subject to authorisation or registration within the national territory on the sole ground that they have not been authorised or registered for being placed on the market there. Consequently, the importation of such products into German territory is precluded for the sole reason that they have not been authorised, irrespective of the method of sale.

48 If a provision such as Paragraph 73(1) of the AMG is compatible with Community law, it will not be necessary to consider whether, in respect of this category of medicines, Articles 28 EC to 30 EC preclude national legislation which prohibits the sale by mail order of medicinal products the sale of which is restricted to pharmacies.

...

The Court's reply [to observations submitted]

52 As the German and Greek Governments and the Commission rightly observe, the general prohibition imposed by Paragraph 73(1) of the AMG corresponds to the prohibition, at Community level, on placing on the market medicinal products which have not been authorised in the Member State concerned, which was laid down in Article 3 of Directive 65/65, now replaced by Article 6(1) of the Community Code. According to those provisions, medicinal products, even if they are authorised in one Member State, must also, if they are to be placed on the market of another Member State, have been authorised either by the competent authority of that State or under the Community rules referred to in those provisions.

53 Consequently, a national rule such as Paragraph 73(1) of the AMG, whereby a Member State discharges its obligations under Directive 65/65 and the Community Code, cannot be characterised as a measure having equivalent effect to a quantitative restriction on imports within the meaning of Article 28 EC ... Accordingly, Articles 28 EC to 30 EC cannot be relied on in order to circumvent the system of national authorisation provided for by Directive 65/65 and the Community Code, which is implemented in national law by Paragraph 73(1) of the AMG.

54 It follows from that finding that, as regards medicinal products which are subject to, but which have not obtained, authorisation there is no need to consider whether the national provisions at issue in the main proceedings are precluded by Articles 28 EC to 30 EC.

Medicinal products which are authorised in Germany

55 The first question is more germane as regards medicinal products which have obtained marketing authorisations for the German market. More specifically, this question seeks to ascertain whether the prohibition on the sale by mail order of medicinal products which may be sold only in pharmacies in the Member State concerned, such as the prohibition laid down in Paragraph 43(1) of the AMG, is compatible with the principle of the free movement of goods. That question is divided into three parts, which must be dealt with separately.

Is the national prohibition on mail-order sales a measure having equivalent effect within the meaning of Article 28 EC? (Question 1(a))

...

Law and the technologies of the twenty-first century

The Court's reply [to observations submitted]

63   It must be stated at the outset that the prohibition laid down in Paragraph 43(1) of the AMG falls within the scope of Directive 97/7. Article 14 of the directive allows Member States to introduce or maintain, in the area covered by this Directive, more stringent provisions compatible with the Treaty, to ensure a higher level of consumer protection. Article 14 also states that such provisions shall, where appropriate, include a ban, in the general interest, on the marketing of certain goods or services, particularly medicinal products, within their territory by means of distance contracts, with due regard for the Treaty.

64   A national measure in a sphere which has been the subject of exhaustive harmonisation at Community level must be assessed in the light of the provisions of the harmonising measure and not those of the Treaty (see Case C-37/92 *Vanacker and Lesage* [1993] ECR I-4947, paragraph 9, and Case C-324/99 *DaimlerChrysler* [2001] ECR I-9897, paragraph 32). However, the power conferred on Member States by Article 14(1) of Directive 97/7 must be exercised with due regard for the Treaty, as is expressly stated in that provision.

65   Such a provision does not, therefore, obviate the need to ascertain whether the national prohibition at issue in the main proceedings is compatible with Articles 28 EC to 30 EC.

66   In that regard, there is settled case-law to the effect that all measures which are capable of hindering directly or indirectly, actually or potentially, intra-Community trade are to be regarded as measures having equivalent effect to quantitative restrictions and, on that basis, as prohibited by Article 28 EC (see Case 8/74 *Dassonville* [1974] ECR 837, paragraph 5, and Case C-420/01 *Commission* v. *Italy* [2003] ECR I-6445, paragraph 25).

67   Even if a measure is not intended to regulate trade in goods between Member States, the determining factor is its effect, actual or potential, on intra-Community trade. By virtue of that factor, in the absence of harmonisation of legislation, obstacles to the free movement of goods which are the consequence of applying, to goods coming from other Member States where they are lawfully manufactured and marketed, rules that lay down requirements to be met by such goods constitute measures of equivalent effect prohibited by Article 28 EC, even if those rules apply to all products alike, unless their application can be justified by a public-interest objective taking precedence over the requirements of the free movement of goods (Case 120/78 *Rewe-Zentral* (*Cassis de Dijon*) [1979] ECR 649, paragraphs 6, 14 and 15; *Keck and Mithouard*, paragraph 15, and *Familiapress*, paragraph 8).

68   Furthermore, as the Court held in *Keck and Mithouard*, even if commercial rules do not relate to the actual characteristics of the products but govern the arrangements for their sale, they may constitute measures of equivalent effect for the purposes of Article 28 EC if they fail to meet two conditions. Those conditions are that such rules must apply to all relevant traders operating in national territory and must affect in the same manner, in law and in fact, the marketing of both domestic products and those from other Member States (see *Keck and Mithouard*, paragraph 15; *Hünermund*, paragraph 21, and Case C-412/93 *Lerclerc-Siplec* [1995] ECR I-179, paragraph 21).

69   As regards the first condition in the preceding paragraph, the prohibition in Paragraph 43(1) of the AMG applies to all the traders concerned, whether German or not, with the result that the first condition is fully met.

70   As to the second condition in paragraph 68 of this judgment, it must be borne in mind that the marketing of a product on a domestic market may entail a

number of stages between the time when the product is manufactured and the time when it is ultimately sold to the end consumer.

71 In order to ascertain whether a particular measure affects in the same manner the marketing of both domestic products and those from other Member States, the scope of the restrictive measure concerned must be ascertained. Thus, the Court has found that a prohibition on pharmacists from advertising quasi-pharmaceutical products outside the pharmacy, which they were authorised to offer for sale, did not affect the ability of traders other than pharmacists to advertise those products (see *Hünermund*, paragraph 19). Similarly, the prohibition on broadcasting the advertising at issue in *Leclerc-Siplec* was not extensive, since it covered only one particular form of promotion (television advertising) of one particular method of marketing products (distribution) (see *Leclerc-Siplec*, paragraph 22).

72 By contrast, the Court has accepted the relevance of the argument that a prohibition on television advertising deprived a trader of the only effective form of promotion which would have enabled it to penetrate a national market (see *De Agostini and TV-Shop*, paragraph 43). Furthermore, the Court has found that in the case of products such as alcoholic beverages, the consumption of which is linked to traditional social practices and to local habits and customs, prohibiting all advertising directed at consumers in the form of advertisements in the press, on the radio and on television, the direct mailing of unsolicited material or the placing of posters on the public highway is liable to impede access to the market for products from other Member States more than it impedes access for domestic products, with which consumers are instantly more familiar (see Case C-405/98 *Gourmet International Products* [2001] ECR I-1795, paragraphs 21 and 24).

73 As regards a prohibition such as that laid down in Paragraph 43(1) of the AMG, it is not disputed that the provision contains both a requirement that certain medicines be sold only in pharmacies and a prohibition on mail-order sales of medicines. It is true that such a prohibition on mail-order sales may be regarded as merely the consequence of the requirement for sales to be made exclusively in pharmacies. However, the emergence of the internet as a method of cross-border sales means that the scope and, by the same token, the effect of the prohibition must be looked at on a broader scale than that suggested by the Apothekerverband, by the German, French and Austrian Governments and by the Commission (see paragraphs 56 to 59 of this judgment).

74 A prohibition such as that at issue in the main proceedings is more of an obstacle to pharmacies outside Germany than to those within it. Although there is little doubt that as a result of the prohibition, pharmacies in Germany cannot use the extra or alternative method of gaining access to the German market consisting of end consumers of medicinal products, they are still able to sell the products in their dispensaries. However, for pharmacies not established in Germany, the internet provides a more significant way to gain direct access to the German market. A prohibition which has a greater impact on pharmacies established outside German territory could impede access to the market for products from other Member States more than it impedes access for domestic products.

75 Accordingly, the prohibition does not affect the sale of domestic medicines in the same way as it affects the sale of those coming from other Member States.

76 The answer to Question 1(a) is therefore that a national prohibition on the sale by mail order of medicinal products the sale of which is restricted to pharmacies in the Member State concerned, such as the prohibition laid down in Paragraph 43(1) of the AMG, is a measure having an effect equivalent to a quantitative restriction for the purposes of Article 28 EC.

Whether there is any justification for the prohibition on mail-order sales (Question 1(b))

77 By its first question, under subparagraph (b), the national court is asking essentially whether the prohibition on the sale by mail order of medicines the sale of which is restricted to pharmacies can be justified under Article 30 EC where, before prescription medicines are supplied, a doctor's original prescription must have been produced to the pharmacy dispatching the medicines. On that point, the national court wonders what requirements should be placed on that pharmacy as regards control of orders, packaging and receipt.

…

The Court's reply [to observations submitted]

102 As is maintained by the parties to the main action, the Member States which have submitted observations to the Court and the Commission, Article 30 EC continues to apply in relation to the manufacture and marketing of specialised pharmaceutical products as long as harmonisation of national rules has not been fully achieved in those areas (see *Schumacher*, paragraph 15; *Delattre*, paragraph 48; *Eurim-Pharm*, paragraph 26; *Commission* v. *Germany*, paragraph 10; and *Ortscheit*, paragraph 14). In that regard, it should be noted that the sale of medicinal products to end consumers has not been subject to full Community harmonisation.

103 It is settled case-law that the health and life of humans rank foremost among the assets or interests protected by Article 30 EC and it is for the Member States, within the limits imposed by the Treaty, to decide what degree of protection they wish to assure (see *Schumacher*, paragraph 17; *Eurim-Pharm*, paragraph 26; and *Ortscheit*, paragraph 16).

104 However, national rules or practices likely to have a restrictive effect, or having such an effect, on the importation of pharmaceutical products are compatible with the Treaty only to the extent that they are necessary for the effective protection of health and life of humans. A national rule or practice cannot benefit from the derogation provided for in Article 30 EC if the health and life of humans may be protected just as effectively by measures which are less restrictive of intra-Community trade (*Schumacher*, paragraphs 17 and 18; *Delattre*, paragraph 53; *Eurim-Pharm*, paragraph 27; *Commission* v. *Germany*, paragraphs 10 and 11; and *Ortscheit*, paragraph 17).

105 In the case before the national court, no doubt is cast on the fact that the virtual pharmacy is subject to supervision by the Netherlands authorities, with the result that the arguments put forward by the Apothekerverband to assert generally that the supervision to which such a pharmacy is subject is inadequate, in comparison with that to which a traditional pharmacy is subject, cannot be accepted.

106 The only arguments which are capable of providing adequate reasons for prohibiting the mail-order trade in medicinal products are those relating to the need to provide individual advice to the customer and to ensure his protection when he is supplied with medicines and to the need to check that prescriptions are genuine and to guarantee that medicinal products are widely available and sufficient to meet requirements.

107 Looked at generally, most of those reasons are based on the possible dangers posed by medicinal products and, accordingly, on the care which must be taken with all aspects of the marketing of those products, objectives which are also those of the Community legislation in the pharmaceuticals field. Thus, and in any event, consideration of the reasons put forward to justify the prohibition on the sale by mail order of medicinal products must take into account the various provisions of Community law which may affect that issue.

...

111 In the light of the foregoing, the reasons advanced by the Apothekerverband by way of justification must be examined in relation to non-prescription medicines, on the one hand, and prescription medicines, on the other hand.
Non-prescription medicines

112 None of the reasons which the Apothekerverband advances by way of justification can provide a valid basis for the absolute prohibition on the sale by mail order of non-prescription medicines.

113 First, as regards the need to provide the customer with advice and information when a medicinal product is purchased, it is not impossible that adequate advice and information may be provided. Furthermore, as the defendants in the main proceedings point out, internet buying may have certain advantages, such as the ability to place the order from home or the office, without the need to go out, and to have time to think about the questions to ask the pharmacists, and these advantages must be taken into account.

114 As to the argument that virtual pharmacists are less able to react than pharmacists in dispensaries, the disadvantages which have been mentioned in this regard concern, first, the fact that the medicine concerned may be incorrectly used and, second, the possibility that it may be abused. As regards incorrect use of the medicine, the risk thereof can be reduced through an increase in the number of on-line interactive features, which the customer must use before being able to proceed to a purchase. As regards possible abuse, it is not apparent that for persons who wish to acquire non-prescription medicines unlawfully, purchase in a traditional pharmacy is more difficult than an internet purchase.

115 Second, as regards non-prescription medicines, considerations relating to their delivery do not justify an absolute prohibition on their sale by mail order.

116 Third, as regards the reasons based on the need to guarantee that medicinal products are widely available and sufficient to meet requirements, the Court notes that, in the submission of the defendants in the main proceedings (see paragraph 100 of this judgment), the Netherlands virtual pharmacy is subject to public-service obligations such as those mentioned by the Apothekerverband, with the result that it is not, in that respect, in a better position than German pharmacies. Furthermore, the APO, which sets the ultimate selling price of medicinal products, applies solely to prescription-only medicines and thus is not a reason for prohibiting mail-order sales of non-prescription medicines, the prices of which may be set freely by German pharmacies.
Prescription medicines

117 The supply to the general public of prescription medicines needs to be more strictly controlled. Such control could be justified in view of, first, the greater risks which those medicines may present (see Article 71(1) of the Community Code) and, second, the system of fixed prices which applies to them and which forms part of the German health system.

118 As regards the first consideration, the fact that there might be differences in the way those medicines are classified by the Member States, so that a particular

medicinal product may be subject to prescription in one Member State but not in another, does not mean that the first Member State forfeits the right to take more stringent action with regard to that type of medicinal product.

119   Given that there may be risks attaching to the use of these medicinal products, the need to be able to check effectively and responsibly the authenticity of doctors' prescriptions and to ensure that the medicine is handed over either to the customer himself, or to a person to whom its collection has been entrusted by the customer, is such as to justify a prohibition on mail-order sales. As the Irish Government has observed, allowing prescription medicines to be supplied on receipt of a prescription and without any other control could increase the risk of prescriptions being abused or inappropriately used. Furthermore, the real possibility of the labelling of a medicinal product bought in a Member State other than the one in which the buyer resides being in a language other than the buyer's may have more harmful consequences in the case of prescription medicines.

120   The Apothekerverband has also put forward arguments concerning the integrity of the German health system, arguing that, since German pharmacies are obliged by the APO to sell prescription medicines at fixed prices, allowing the cross-border sale of those medicines at uncontrolled prices would jeopardise the existence of those pharmacies and thus the integrity of the German health system.

121   That argument requires an examination of the rationale for the system set up by the APO, which sets the selling price of prescription medicines.

122   Although aims of a purely economic nature cannot justify restricting the fundamental freedom to provide services, it is not impossible that the risk of seriously undermining the financial balance of the social security system may constitute an overriding general-interest reason capable of justifying a restriction of that kind (see *Kohll*, paragraph 41; *Vanbraekel*, paragraph 47; *Smits and Peerbooms*, paragraph 72; and Case C-358/99 *Müller-Fauré and Van Riet* [2003] ECR I-4509, paragraphs 72 and 73). Moreover, a national market for prescription medicines could be characterised by non-commercial factors, with the result that national legislation fixing the prices at which certain medicinal products are sold should, in so far as it forms an integral part of the national health system, be maintained.

123   However, neither the Apothekerverband nor the Member States which have submitted observations to the Court have put forward any arguments as to the necessity of the APO. Therefore, in the absence of any such arguments, the Court cannot find that, as regards prescription medicines, the prohibition on mail-order sales in Germany may be justified on grounds of the financial balance of the social security system or the integrity of the national health system.

124   In the light of the foregoing, the answer to Question 1(b) must be that Article 30 EC may be relied on to justify a national prohibition on the sale by mail order of medicinal products the sale of which is restricted to pharmacies in the Member State concerned in so far as the prohibition covers medicinal products subject to prescription. However, Article 30 EC cannot be relied on to justify an absolute prohibition on the sale by mail order of medicinal products which are not subject to prescription in the Member State concerned.

...

THE COURT,

in answer to the questions referred to it by the Landgericht Frankfurt am Main by order of 10 August 2001, hereby rules:

1 (a)   A national prohibition on the sale by mail order of medicinal products the sale of which is restricted to pharmacies in the Member State concerned, such as the prohibition laid down in Paragraph 43(1) of the Arzneimittelgesetz (Law on medicinal products) in the version of 7 September 1998, is a measure having an effect equivalent to a quantitative restriction for the purposes of Article 28 EC.

(b)   Article 30 EC may be relied on to justify a national prohibition on the sale by mail order of medicinal products which may be sold only in pharmacies in the Member State concerned in so far as the prohibition covers medicinal products subject to prescription. However, Article 30 EC cannot be relied on to justify an absolute prohibition on the sale by mail order of medicinal products which are not subject to prescription in the Member State concerned.

(c)   Questions 1(a) and 1(b) do not need to be assessed differently where medicinal products are imported into a Member State in which they are authorised, having been previously obtained by a pharmacy in another Member State from a wholesaler in the importing Member State.

2.   Article 88(1) of Directive 2001/83/EC of the European Parliament and of the Council of 6 November 2001 on the Community code relating to medicinal products for human use precludes a national prohibition on advertising the sale by mail order of medicinal products which may be supplied only in pharmacies in the Member State concerned, such as the prohibition laid down in Paragraph 8(1) of the Heilmittelwerbegesetz (Law on the advertising of medicinal products), in so far as the prohibition covers medicinal products which are not subject to prescription.

Stated simply, the effect of *DocMorris* is to shield local regulators against cross-border internet suppliers only where there are compelling reasons for doing so (in this case, health-related reasons associated with prescription drugs). It is an open question, however, whether the ECJ has taken a consistent approach in determining how much margin is to be accorded to Member States. Commentators on the jurisprudence might ask, for example, whether *Gambelli*,[46] on the provision of internet gambling services, gives too much margin to local regulators[47] and, conversely, whether *Klas Rosengren and Others v. Riksåklagaren*[48] (where the ECJ ruled against the Swedish prohibition on alcohol imports outside the state monopoly) gives too little margin.[49]

6 Conclusion

In the preceding chapters, we have seen that, where regulators are not competent, or where regulatees are not disposed to comply, there is likely to be some degree of regulatory failure. We can add that, in such circumstances, the prospects for regulatory effectiveness can be even more damaged by external

---

[46] Case C-243/01, 6 November 2003.
[47] For comment on the jurisprudence, see Niall A. O'Connor, 'From *Schindler* to *Placanica* and Beyond'; available online at www.bettingmarket.com/eurolaw222428.htm (last accessed 3 May 2007).
[48] Case C-170/4; [2007] ECR 1–04071 (5 June 2007).
[49] For critical commentary on the Swedish case, see Julia Hörnle and Brigitte Zammit, *Cross-Border Online Gambling Law and Policy* (Cheltenham: Edward Elgar, 2010), at 154–5.

interference and disruption. However, it also needs to be said that, even where regulators are competent and regulatees compliant, such third-party intervention can contribute to regulatory failure.

Before the development of the information society, in a pre-digital world, there were various kinds of external risks – there were hostile third parties, there was regulatory arbitrage, and there were natural disasters, and so on. However, with the coming of the information society, when online business is largely business as usual, the scale and impact of third-party interventions are quite different. Local regulators and their regulatees are now exposed to a range of cybercrimes that can target both critical infrastructures and everyday online transactions and interactions. Moreover, where local regulators are members of information society clubs, such as the EU, the club rules can tie their hands in imposing their preferred local policies. Johnson and Post were right in foreseeing that local regulators would have difficulties in controlling online content and conduct. This is a challenge in itself. However, what we now know is that online content and conduct can interfere, too, with the policies that local regulators seek to implement for the *off-line* world. Globalisation in the twenty-first century, in conjunction with cheap and convenient online technologies, is not just about the lowering of national borders; it is as much about lowering the border between the online and the off-line worlds – and, with that, for better or for worse, bringing about some reduction in the capacity for regulatory effectiveness.

Part V
Regulatory connection

15

Regulatory connection I: getting connected

1 Introduction

One of the distinctive challenges presented to regulators by rapidly developing modern technologies is, quite simply, the pace of their development. How do regulators get connected to these technologies, and how do they stay connected? As John Perry Barlow famously remarked:

> Law adapts by continuous increments and at a pace second only to geology in its stateliness. Technology advances in ... lunging jerks, like the punctuation of biological evolution grotesquely accelerated. Real world conditions will continue to change at a blinding pace, and the law will get further behind, more profoundly confused. This mismatch is permanent.[1]

If Barlow is correct, at any rate in the context of emerging technologies, regulators will be challenged as they attempt to make and then to sustain the connection between the regulatory environment, the technology in question, and its applications.

Where a technology or a novel application emerges, it will sometimes be lamented that there is, so to speak, a regulatory void, this meaning that there is no *bespoke legal* guidance on the issue. However, even if there is no *bespoke* legal guidance, and even though regulatees might be unclear as to their *legal* position, we should not overstate the problem. First, the regulatory environment might have clear default signals as to the appropriate action where the legal position is unclear; in some cases, the signal might be that, without clear legal authorisation, one should not proceed; or, to the contrary, it might be that it is permissible to proceed in such circumstances. Second, even in the absence of *dedicated* and *specific* legal guidance, there are likely to be various *legal* provisions that have some application. For example, there are likely to be some *ex ante* safety provisions in place (although, quite possibly, needing some adjustment); and, there will be *ex post* general doctrines such as product liability and informed consent that will provide some protection to those who might be

---

[1] John Perry Barlow, 'The Economy of Ideas: Selling Wine without Bottles on the Global Net'; available online at www.eff.org/~barlow/EconomyOfIdeas.html, and extracted in Yee Fen Lim, *Cyberspace Law* (Oxford: Oxford University Press, 2002), 398, at 402.

injured by dangerous goods or procedures.[2] Hence, if nanoparticles in cosmetics or nanofibres in clothes and sports equipment should prove to be a new kind of asbestos, or if GM crops cross-pollinate to create a nuisance, then those consumers who are injured or non-GM farmers who are affected would not make their compensatory claims in a regulatory void. Similarly, if medical procedures that make use of novel genetic therapies, nanomaterials, or nanodevices should prove injurious to participants in research trials or to patients, then the injured parties would not make their compensatory claims in a void; once again, such claims would engage existing legal standards.[3]

Having said this, we have no reason for regulatory complacency. Few legal regimes will bring together *ex ante* and *ex post* provision in a coherent scheme of protective and corrective regulation; new technologies will expose a number of weaknesses in existing provision as a result of which some fine-tuning, clarification and gap-filling will be necessary;[4] and, if regulators are to be fully informed as to the technology that they are dealing with, they cannot afford to sit on their hands and hope for the best. To take up this last-mentioned point, as a particular technology emerges, regulators need to be actively taking steps to ensure that its risk profile is understood as well as orchestrating debate as to any ethical and social issues. Moreover, as a technology matures, regulators need to maintain a regulatory position that comports with a community's view of its acceptable use. In the present chapter, the focus of discussion will be on getting connected, especially where the technology raises concerns about safety; and, in the next chapter, we will focus on strategies for staying connected, particularly where regulators have to judge the moral mood of the community.

The present chapter is in six principal sections. First, the nature of the problem is sketched. Our purpose here is largely to underline that connection is a generic challenge for regulators ranging across a sweep of emerging technologies. Second, we pick out some elements in the connection puzzle that enable us to focus more clearly on the nature of the challenge. These elements are:

---

[2] In general, see Brent Blackwelder, 'Nanotechnology Jumps the Gun: Nanoparticles in Consumer Products', in Nigel M. de S. Cameron and M. Ellen Mitchell (eds.), *Nanoscale* (Hoboken, NJ: John Wiley, 2007), 71. According to Ahson Wardak and Michael E. Gorman in, 'Using Trading Zones and Life Cycle Analysis to Understand Nanotechnology Regulation', *Journal of Law, Medicine and Ethics*, 34 (2006), 695, there are already more than 200 nanotechnology-based products in the consumer marketplace; and, more recently, the Royal Commission on Environmental Protection, *Novel Materials in the Environment: The Case of Nanotechnology* (London, November 2008) puts the figure at more than 600.

[3] Compare Roger Brownsword, 'Human Dignity as the Basis for Genomic Torts', *Washburn Law Journal*, 42 (2003), 413.

[4] See Albert C. Lin, 'Size Matters: Regulating Nanotechnology', *Harvard Environmental Law Review*, 31 (2007), 349, at 361–74 (for the view that US regulatory provisions are inadequate); Giorgia Guerra, 'European Regulatory Issues in Nanomedicine', *Nanoethics*, 2 (2008), 87 (for the view that EU regulation does not fit very well with potential nanomedical applications), and, generally, Trudy A. Phelps, 'The European Approach to Nanoregulation', in Cameron and Mitchell, *Nanoscale*, 189.

1 the type of regulatory environment and regulatory modality;
2 the developmental trajectory of a technology from a primitive to a mature and established state;
3 whether the technologies in question elicit concerns about human health and safety or harm to the environment; and
4 whether the technologies in question elicit ethical concerns.

In the four sections that follow, we speak to each of these elements. However, by far, our most extensive discussion is in relation to the second and (particularly) the third of these elements, where we review the challenge facing regulators who seek to get connected to early stage technologies (nanotechnologies and synthetic biologies being obvious cases in point) about which there is considerable uncertainty but also major health, safety and environmental concerns.[5]

2 The nature of the problem

Although, in most parts of the United States, gambling is illegal (Atlantic City and Las Vegas being notable exceptions), the Indian Gaming Regulatory Act (25 USC 2701) upholds the right of tribes to conduct gaming on their land. However, with the development of the internet and the availability of online gambling sites, what would be the legal position if Indian online gambling operations could be accessed from States where gambling was prohibited? In *State ex rel Nixon* v. *Coeur d'Alene Tribe*,[6] the State of Missouri argued that such an online gambling site was not within the terms of the statutory exception. Without answering the fundamental substantive question, the Court ruled that, if the gambling was conducted on Indian land, then the exception applied and the statute pre-empted Missouri's challenge. The case was sent back to the District Court for determination but, before a decision was given, it was settled. While settlement put an end to this particular dispute, the more general problem of aligning old law with new technologies remains to be resolved.

Whether one looks at the regulation of information technology or the regulation of biotechnology[7] – or, for that matter, at the future regulation of

---

[5] For seminal analysis, see Gregory N. Mandel, 'Nanotechnology Governance', *Alabama Law Review*, 59 (2008), 1323, and 'Regulating Emerging Technologies', *Law, Innovation and Technology*, 1 (2009), 75. See, too, R. Wilson, 'Nanotechnology: The Challenge of Regulating Unknown Unknowns', *Journal of Law, Medicine and Ethics*, 34 (2006), 704.

[6] 164 F. 3d 1102 (8th Cir. 1999).

[7] Compare Robert G. Lee and Derek Morgan, 'Regulating Risk Society: Stigmata Cases, Scientific Citizenship and Biomedical Diplomacy', *Sydney Law Review*, 23 (2001), 297: 'Increasingly, developments will be funded, findings unveiled, possibilities mooted, results replicated and then (and only then) regulatory responses sought. Previous structures of cooperative and corporatist workings may fall under the competitive pressures of a global market. Regulation within domestic markets will become more problematic as providers of services can engage in regulatory arbitrage and operate from their chosen base in an increasingly global market' (*ibid.*, at 305).

nanotechnology[8] or the technologies associated with the new brain sciences[9] – there seems to be ample support for Barlow's thesis. Indeed, it is arguable that the pace of technological development, already too fast for the law, is accelerating. While this is not an easy matter to measure,[10] there are at least two respects in which modern information technology, in addition to being significant in its own right, plays a key enabling role relative to other technologies – facilitating basic research in biotechnology (spectacularly so in the case of sequencing the human genome) as well as the commercial exploitation of the products of other technologies. Whether or not this amounts to a further technological 'revolution' is hardly worth arguing about. If the wheels of technology are spinning faster, this suggests that Barlow's prognosis is correct – legal provisions will lag further and further behind the technology in question.

Technology is capable of leaving the law behind at any phase of the regulatory cycle: namely, before regulators have anything resembling an agreed position, before the terms of the regulation are finalised, and once the regulatory scheme is in place. For example, a new technology might emerge very quickly, catching regulators (at any rate, national legislators) cold; or it might be that a controversial new technology (nanotechnology perhaps being a case in point) develops and circulates long before regulators are able to agree upon the terms of their regulatory intervention. While regulators are getting up to speed, or pondering their options and settling their differences, the technology moves ahead, operating in what for the time being at least amounts to, if not a regulatory void, at least a space in need of regulatory attention.[11] Sometimes a new and unanticipated technological development can appear to disrupt the negotiation of a more general regulatory instrument. In Europe, this happened when the rapid development of the internet overtook the drafting of the Directive on Distance Contracts;[12] and it happened again when the drafting of the Directive on the Legal Protection of Biotechnological Inventions[13] was overtaken (and all but extinguished) by developments concerning the identification and isolation of human gene sequences.

Even (or especially) when regulatory frameworks have been put in place, they enjoy no immunity against technological change. For example, the Human Fertilisation and Embryology Act 1990 was overtaken by developments in embryology (in particular, the ability to carry out genetic engineering in eggs which are

---

[8] See Glenn Harlan Reynolds, 'Nanotechnology and Regulatory Policy: Three Futures', *Harvard Journal of Law and Technology*, 17 (2003), 179.

[9] See, e.g., Dai Rees and Steven Rose (eds.), *The New Brian Sciences: Perils and Prospects* (Cambridge: Cambridge University Press, 2004). For the state of the neuro art, see David Nutt, Trevor W. Robbins, Gerald W. Stimson, Martin Ince and Andrew Jackson (eds.), *Drugs and the Future* (London: Academic Press, 2007).

[10] Compare the thoughtful remarks in Monroe E. Price, 'The Newness of New Technology', *Cardozo Law Review*, 22 (2001), 1885.

[11] Cloning is perhaps a case in point: see Richard A. Merrill and Bryan J. Rose, 'FDA Regulation of Human Cloning: Usurpation or Statesmanship?', *Harvard Journal of Law and Technology*, 15 (2001), 85.

[12] Directive 97/7/EC, [1997] OJ L144.   [13] Directive 98/44/EC.

then stimulated without fertilisation rather than in embryos).[14] Similarly, modern information technology has outstripped a straightforward reading of legislation such as the Protection of Children Act 1978[15] and the Video Recordings Act 1984;[16] and, in another island community, that of Hawai'i, the local peeping-Tom laws were found wanting when 'Tyler Takehara, a voyeur who shot video up the skirts of unsuspecting women at [a shopping mall] in Honolulu ... managed to escape conviction because of a legal loophole – at the time, Hawai'i law prohibited only the installation of tiny cameras in private places, such as bathrooms.'[17] Famously, the mismatch created by rapidly developing information technology (specifically that between European data protection law[18] and computing) has been vividly highlighted by Peter Swire and Robert Litan:[19]

> In both the United States and Europe, debates are being driven by fears that computers pose a threat to privacy. That is, computers are *the key reason* for data protection rules. But changing computer technology also makes the Directive's rules seem badly matched to the reality of information flows.
>
> The Directive's approach is designed for the regulation of mainframe computers in which one expects a relatively small number of hierarchical systems. Information technology, however, has shifted radically to new configurations such as client-server systems and the internet. Today there is a much larger number of systems organized into distributed networks rather than simple

[14] See, e.g., House of Commons Science and Technology Committee, *Human Reproductive Technologies and the Law* (Fifth Report of Session 2004–5), vol. 1 (London: Stationery Office Limited, 2005), ch. 4. Early in the report, the Committee recall that, some three years earlier, they had 'concluded that it was necessary to "reconnect the Act with modern science"' (*ibid.*, at para. 2).

[15] Under the Act, it is an offence, *inter alia*, to take, distribute, or show indecent 'photographs' of children, or to possess such 'photographs' with a view to their being distributed or shown by oneself or others. But, what is a 'photograph'? Does it, for example, include indecent images (scanned from conventional photographs) that are stored on a computer hard disk, and that are available via the Internet to be shown on a monitor screen but that are never actually printed out? (See *R* v. *Fellows and Arnold* [1997] 2 All ER 548.) Or images recorded directly onto a disk by a digital camera before being transferred to a computer and viewed on-screen? For discussion, see Lilian Edwards, 'Pornography and the Internet', in Lilian Edwards and Charlotte Waelde (eds.), *Law and the Internet* (2nd edn, Oxford: Hart, 2000), 275, 283ff.; and Ian J. Lloyd, *Information Technology Law* (3rd edn, London: Butterworths, 2000), 276–9.

[16] This Act targets so-called 'video nasties'. In *Meechie* v. *Multi-Media Marketing*, 94 LGR 474, there was a question whether a video product, front-ended by a game successful completion of which prompted the display of a series of erotic images, fell within the terms of the legislation. In particular, was this product (with its series of images) a 'video work' as defined by section 1 of the Act (where 'a moving picture' was contemplated); and was the product a video game so as to come within the exempting provisions of section 2? See Lloyd, *Information Technology Law*, 279–81.

[17] Aimee Jodoi Lum, 'Don't Smile, Your Image Has Just Been Recorded on a Camera-Phone: The Need for Privacy in the Public Sphere', *University of Hawai'i Law Review*, 27 (2005), 377, at 398. Even the Takehara case does not reflect state-of-the-art video voyeurism: Lum highlights the use of camera-enabled mobile phones, coupled with posting of the shots on the Internet.

[18] As in the Directive on Data Protection, Directive 95/46/EC, OJ L281 (23 November1995), 31.

[19] On the latter, see the seminal analysis in Peter P. Swire and Robert E. Litan, *None of Your Business: World Data Flows, Electronic Commerce and the European Privacy Directive* (Washington, DC: Brookings Institution, 1998).

hierarchies. The data protection regime designed for mainframes performs much less well when applied to the many and the distributed.

The language of the Directive evokes its mainframe, top-down assumptions. Consider the terms 'controller' and 'data subject'. A controller is at the top of the hierarchy, the person in command of a unified computer system. One expects a 'controller' to have many minions, who carry out commands. A data subject is clearly much less powerful – acted upon and subject to manipulation by one who controls.

This language is far less apt in a world of personal computers and the Internet. The entity running a Web site is often an individual or a small company – hardly worthy of the term 'controller'. The persons browsing may be equipped with a large variety of tools for protecting their privacy. For instance, they might be able to browse anonymously, use software to disable a site's 'cookies', or submit false information on any forms that the site employs. Such people are no longer passive and powerless. They instead may be more sophisticated than the operators of the Web site and will often be employed by major corporations.[20]

As the authors go on to suggest, data protection regimes are designed for large visible 'elephants' rather than highly mobile 'mice' that scurry hither and thither.[21] And, so it is more generally: the technological landscape is a shifting scene, what we see today might be gone by tomorrow, constantly challenging the accuracy and focus of the regulatory gaze.[22]

3 A framework for analysis

In order to focus our thinking about the challenge of regulatory connection, we can develop a matrix that builds on the answers that we have to the following four questions:

[20] *Ibid.*, at 50–1.

[21] *Ibid.*, at 200ff. Europe sought to catch up with the 'mice' by enacting Directive 2002/58/EC (the Directive on privacy and electronic communications). But, even then, the world of technology does not stand still. See, e.g., the discussion in Daniel B. Garrie and Rebecca Wong, 'Regulating Voice Over Internet Protocol: An EU/US Comparative Approach', *American University International Law Review*, 22 (2007), 549, where it is concluded that 'as technology is evolving with respect to VoIP and oral Internet communications [the regulatory position] is becoming progressively greyer' (*ibid.*, at 580); and, for a particular case arising with Web2 technologies, see Giovanni Sartor and Mario Viola de Azevedo Cunha, 'The Italian Google-case: Privacy, Freedom of Speech and Responsibility of Providers for User-Generated Contents', *International Journal of Law and Information Technology*, 18 (2010), 356.

[22] Compare Kirstie Ball, David Lyon, David Murakami Wood, Clive Norris and Charles Raab, *A Report on the Surveillance Society* (September 2006): 'Neither the data protection principles nor the fragmented condition of regulatory machinery and instruments seem fully capable of meeting challenges that are likely to be posed in the future from public, private and combined sources. The advent of many new information and communication technologies … including the Internet and mobile telematics, and the coming environment of AmI and ubiquitous computing that integrates many and varied surveillance devices, puts a question-mark over the efficacy of regulatory concepts and instruments that originated to handle issues in the age of the mainframe computer, *or even of the laptop, the mobile telephone, and the Internet*' (*ibid.*, at para. 44.9; emphasis ours). For a similar point, concerning current data protection regulation and upcoming profiling data sets, see Mireille Hildebrandt, 'A Vision of Ambient Law', in Roger Brownsword and Karen Yeung (eds.), *Regulating Technologies* (Oxford: Hart, 2008).

1 What type of regulatory environment and what kind of regulatory modality are we assuming?
2 At which point is the technology on the developmental pathway from a primitive to a mature and established state?
3 Is the concern elicited by the technology that it might be harmful to human health and safety or to the environment?
4 Is it ethical concerns that are elicited by this technology?

Broadly speaking, we can expect the problems of regulatory connection to be more difficult as we assume a Type 1 (hierarchical) regulatory environment with law as the key regulatory modality. For, all the difficulties that we have encountered so far concern the initial setting and then the maintaining of the *legal* position. On these assumptions, we can find the problems of connection and disconnection arising at different stages in the development of the technology; and we can pinpoint whether our difficulties stem from an uncertain or a shifting understanding of the risk profile presented by the technology or from an awakening to its ethical implications. In what follows, we can speak to each of these variables.

4 The type of regulatory environment and regulatory modality

So long as regulators are employing normative registers, there is a sense that regulatory connection is a greater challenge in Type 1 than in Type 2 regulatory environments. Essentially, this is because, in the latter, there is likely to be a double flexibility – in the articulation of the standards themselves as well as in the capacity of self-regulating groups to change their standards. In Type I environments, the principles of legality – we need only recall the Fullerian desiderata of clarity and relatively constancy – militate against vagueness in drafting; and, of course, there is much more pressure on regulatory resources.

In a helpful paper, with the regulation of nanotechnology as its focus, Bärbel Dorbeck-Jung and Marloes van Amerom[23] draw out the relative strengths and weaknesses of 'hard' and 'soft' law interventions in a way that supports the sense that it is Type I environments that are particularly problematic. Having reviewed the literature, Dorbeck-Jung and van Amerom identify soft law as having the following strengths:

1 It can cope with situations of uncertainty, which may demand constant experimentation and adjustment in allowing minimum levels of adherence to be established and formalize progressive advancement towards higher standards. By experimentation progressively more coherent regulation can be developed.

---

[23] Bärbel Dorbeck-Jung and Marloes van Amerom, 'The Hardness of Soft Law in the United Kingdom: State and Non-State Regulatory Activities Related to Nanotechnological Development', in Hanneke van Schooten and Jonathan Verschuuren (eds.), *International Governance and Law* (Cheltenham: Edward Elgar, 2008), 129.

2 It is capable of responding to the demands for frequent change of norms to achieve optimal results ('flexibility').

3 Its capacity of adaptation to changing circumstances makes it more suited to the unification of law.

4 It allows a range of possibilities for interpretation and trial and error processes without the constraints of uniform rules and threat of sanction. This makes soft law relatively resistant to symbolic destruction in the case of deviance ...

5 It allows for diversity in regulation, tailored to the needs of specific circumstances (since the forms of soft law are not strictly fixed).

6 It allows for simplicity and speed of regulation (since the procedure for establishing soft law is simple and not formalized).

7 It allows for regulatory sovereignty and autonomy and it supports the internalisation of norms, as actors usually will accept rules of conduct they agreed upon, making it easier to achieve support for its implementation ('social basis of legitimacy').

8 It reduces negotiation costs, because non-binding norms lower the stakes for the parties involved.[24]

It is apparent from these points in favour of soft law that it is not only connection that might be eased; in particular, point 7 in the list underlines what has already been said about the prospects for regulatory effectiveness where regulatees have some ownership of the code. However, as we have also seen, the flexibility of self-regulation can give rise to concerns about the tension between self-interest and the public interest, that is, about the legitimacy of the regulatory norms. The following are perceived to be the weaknesses of soft law (which, to some extent, might be corrected by hard law):

1 Soft law lacks the clarity and precision needed to provide predictability and a reliable framework for action that is essential for investment and innovation.

2 Soft law is not robust in its ability to constrain behaviour through credible threats of enforcement.

3 Soft law cannot forestall 'races to the bottom' in social policy. Compromises will lead to lower quality, efficacy and safety standards.

4 Soft law bypasses basic requirements of legitimacy of regulation (among them the requirements of legality, due process and accountability).

5 Soft law implies high transaction costs because of the constant adaptation and change of rules of conduct.[25]

This prompts the thought that regulators should strive for a smart mix of soft law with hard law – and, possibly, the thought that the mix changes (becoming harder) as the technology develops, as more is known about it, and as its risk profile becomes clearer. Relative to such an approach, Dorbeck-Jung and van Amerom see the UK as relying on a predominantly soft-law strategy for dealing with nanotechnologies, this being well suited to an initial phase of 'evidence gathering, standardization, public dialogue, funding of research and

[24] *Ibid.*, at 133–4.   [25] *Ibid.*, at 134.

development, and international and national collaboration'.[26] The subsequent challenge is to achieve a smart 'hybridization of soft and hard law'.[27] Although this has yet to be accomplished in relation to nanotechnologies, there are many examples of soft law codes of practice that are nested within hard law statutory frameworks – as is the case, for example, with the regulation of human fertilisation and embryology.

This leaves one other point. So far, the contrast has been between harder and softer forms of the normative registers. However, what is the position where regulators rely on non-normative signalling (as they do in second- and third-generation regulatory environments)? While such use of non-normative techniques eliminates the challenge of regulatory connection in the way that we currently understand it, it does not eliminate the possibility of regulatees applying their technological ingenuity to find ways round the regulatory designs. In second- and third-generation regulatory environments, it seems that the challenge will not be to keep the normative standards connected to technological developments but to develop technological standards that render regulatory designs and coding resistant to counter-technologies. To this extent, the regulatory challenge of the future seems to be more one of effectiveness than of connection.

5 The trajectory of technological development

James Moor has suggested that the development pathway for a new technology involves three stages – the stage of introduction, that of permeation, and that of what Moor terms the 'power' stage.[28] In Moor's elaboration of these stages, we see that, with each stage, there is an increasing penetration of the technology:[29]

> We can understand a technological revolution as proceeding through three stages: (1) the introduction stage, (2) the permeation stage ... and (3) the power stage ... Of course, there are not sharp lines dividing the stages any more than there are sharp lines dividing children, adolescents, and adults. In the first stage, the *introduction stage*, the earliest implementations of the technology are esoteric, often regarded as intellectual curiosities or even as playthings more than as useful tools. Initially, only a few people are aware of the technology, but some are fascinated by it and explore its capabilities. Gradually, the devices improve and operate effectively enough to accomplish limited goals. Assuming that the technology is novel and complex, the cost in money, time, and resources to use the technology will typically be high. Because of these limitations, the technology's integration into society will be minor and its impact on society will be marginal.

---

[26] *Ibid.*, at 143.   [27] *Ibid.*, at 146.

[28] James H. Moor, 'Why We Need Better Ethics for Emerging Technologies', in Jeroen van den Hoven and John Weckert (eds.), *Information Technology and Moral Philosophy* (Cambridge: Cambridge University Press, 2008), 26.

[29] *Ibid.*, at 27–8.

In the second stage, the *permeation stage*, the technological devices are standardized. The devices are more conventional in design and operation. The number of users grows. Special training classes might be given to educate more people in the use of the technology. The cost of application drops, and the development of the technology begins to increase as the demand for its use increases. The integration into society will be moderate, and its overall impact on society becomes noticeable as the technological devices are adopted more widely.

Finally, in the third stage, the *power stage*, the technology is firmly established. The technology is readily available and can be leveraged by building upon existing technological structures. Most people in the culture are affected directly or indirectly by it. Many understand how to use it or can benefit from it by relying on people who do understand and use it. Economy of scale drives down the price, and wide application provides pressure and incentive for improvements. The integration into society will be major, and its impact on society, if it is truly a revolutionary technology, will be significant.

At which stage should regulators make a bespoke intervention? Perhaps, no such intervention is necessary at any stage. There are, after all, fall-back general purpose regulatory doctrines such as product liability regimes and the requirement of informed consent. However, if a dedicated intervention is to be made, regulators are confronted by the so-called Collingridge dilemma[30] – according to which regulators tend to find themselves in a position such that either they do not know enough about the (immature) technology to make an appropriate intervention or they know what regulatory intervention is appropriate but they are no longer able to turn back the (now mature) technology. In Moor's terms, we would expect regulators to experience the former aspect of the dilemma when the technology is in the introduction stage and the latter aspect of the dilemma when it is in the power stage. Possibly, this suggests that the permeation stage is the time for serious regulatory action. However, much depends upon what it is that concerns regulators about the particular technology.

6 HSE concerns

In the introductory stage of a technology's development, it might be unclear whether there are any reasons for regulatory concern and, if so, what they might be. Generally, the first concern is that the technology might be dangerous, presenting HSE risks. If so, what does responsible regulation require? How is it to get connected in a way that addresses those concerns? Should regulators take an ultra-precautionary approach and prohibit all development of the technology or should they simply wait until the risks have been properly characterised? Echoing the views of the Royal Commission on Environmental Pollution,[31]

---

[30] See David Collingridge, *The Social Control of Technology* (New York: Francis Pinter, 1980).

[31] Royal Commission on Environmental Pollution, *Novel Materials in the Environment: The Case of Nanotechnology* (London, November 2008). See, too, the ideas of responsible stewardship and prudent vigilance that are put forward in the Presidential Commission for the Study of

whose approach we considered in Chapter 5, Gregory Mandel argues that, in the early stage of a technology's development, neither approach is appropriate. Instead, he outlines a six-point approach to flexible upstream governance.

Mandel, 'Regulating Emerging Technologies', 75

The new governance recommendations presented here are directed at developing a reliable, efficient, adaptive, transparent, and participatory management system. The new governance model for emerging technologies seeks to achieve a number of goals that would likely receive relatively universal support for any technology governance system: protecting human health, safety, and the environment; not unduly hindering the development of a nascent technology; advancing scientific understanding of the technology and its risks; governance that is adaptable as the technology and scientific understanding advance; allowing for widespread participation in management; and maintaining public confidence in the emerging technology and its governance. The proposal seeks these goals through regulatory agency, industry, and public interest group cooperation and management incentives rather than relying primarily on conventional command and control regulation.

Emerging technology governance must traverse a fine line. Insufficient protection could lead to excessive or unknown human health and environmental risks and undercut public confidence. Excessive regulation could limit the development of an extremely promising technology and foreclose potentially great social, health, environmental, and economic benefits. This combination of vast potential benefits and uncertain risks presents unique and difficult challenges. All stakeholders, however, have significant incentives to develop a protective and well-defined governance structure.

Because of the variation and uncertainties in emerging technology development, there are inherent limitations in how precise a universal or *ex ante* governance structure can be developed. These limitations, however, do not prevent the identification of substantial parts of a general governance system, with details that can be worked out for particular technologies and specifications that can be identified as a technology develops and its risks become better understood. A general management structure can provide a kind of best practice for emerging technology governance. Such a structure would provide needed assurance and protection for the public, greater certainty for industry, and resource and time savings for the government.

The new governance proposal developed below includes a variety of recommendations, focused on six areas: (1) improving data gathering and sharing in the face of limited resources; (2) filling newly exposed or created regulatory gaps; (3) incentivizing strong corporate stewardship beyond regulatory requirements; (4) enhancing agency expertise and coordination; (5) providing for regulatory adaptability and flexibility; and, (6) achieving substantial, diverse stakeholder involvement. The result of these proposals would be a system that is more protective of human health and the environment, more efficient for industry and taxpayers, and better geared for responsible technology

Bioethical Issues, *New Directions: The Ethics of Synthetic Biology and Emerging Technologies* (Washington, DC, December 2010).

development. The governance recommendations are detailed in the following sections.

2.1. Data Gathering

One of the greatest challenges facing emerging technology governance is scientific uncertainty concerning the potential human health and environmental impacts of a technology … . A primary focus of governance should be on gathering all available data, developing as much new useful information as possible, and providing incentives for data reporting and development. Greater data will provide the government, scientists, and the public with a better understanding of the types and risks presented by a technology.

At a basic level, the public, citizen groups, and industry should place pressure on public sources to increase funding for studies on the human and environmental exposure and risk posed by emerging technology products. Often, exposure and risk research is substantially underfunded by the government in relation to the funding available for technology development. Many commentators agree that this has been the case for nanotechnology, although funding for research into nanotechnology hazards has been increased more recently. Public agencies also should take a lead role in identifying research needs.

Regulatory agencies, of course, should take advantage of any existing authority to encourage or require the development and production of scientific information. Agencies also can develop voluntary consultation programs even where they lack authority to mandate reporting. Such policies can provide firms with strong incentives to comply or risk consumer backlash. For example, although consultation with the FDA on the commercialization of most genetically modified food products is voluntary, the FDA believes that it has been consulted prior to the introduction of all new genetically modified products.

More innovative approaches to improve data gathering also are available, such as a model proposed for nanotechnology. Nanotechnology substances and uses could be classified as having negligible, low, medium, or high concern. The classification would be based on the substance's size, structure, coating, solubility, ease of transport in the body, toxicity characteristics, expected human or environmental exposure, and other relevant factors. For any given nanotechnology product or use, the extent of both pre- and post-commercialization data gathering and reporting requirements could vary according to the level of concern. If a nanomaterial manufacturer believed that certain nanomaterials had been misclassified or demonstrated to be safe, the manufacturer would be able to apply for re-classification. This classification proposal could operate as a default, information-forcing system that would provide industry with the incentive to develop greater data concerning nanotechnology risks, but avoid command and control dictates that prescribe exactly how to act or impose unduly burdensome requirements on low risk activities. Such a system could also provide substantial flexibility to adapt governance to new understandings of risk as greater information develops.

Regulatory agencies also should consider incentives they can provide to industry to promote data gathering and reporting. One option would be to create fast-track review of applications under various statutes where data beyond that required is developed and submitted by the applicant, or where the applicant commits to post-commercialization data gathering and reporting that is not required. Industry would thus be able to get their new technology products to market more rapidly, agencies could conduct the same level of review to achieve adequate protection, and more data on the emerging technology would be developed. Great Britain, for example, has instituted a voluntary reporting system with certain of these characteristics for those involved in developing new engineered nanotechnology materials.

2.2. *Filling Regulatory Gaps*

Statutes and regulations, almost by definition, are designed to handle regulatory concerns existing at the time of promulgation. It is not surprising that emerging technologies often exacerbate regulatory gaps or introduce new concerns that create new regulatory lacunae …

New technologies, particularly technology as revolutionary as biotechnology and nanotechnology, disrupt existing regulatory systems. These disruptions can exacerbate problems with existing systems, such as regulatory gaps, but can also provide the opportunity to fix such deficiencies. Regulatory agencies must get beyond the hurdles created by scientific uncertainty and bureaucratic and status quo inertia to respond more proactively to these challenges. Closing regulatory gaps expeditiously can provide certainty for industry and comfort for the public.

2.3. *Industry Stewardship*

Many of the emerging technology governance goals identified above can be advanced by developing incentives for industry to act in a socially responsible manner. Such incentives can include economic, public relations, social values, and legal mechanisms.

The largest companies generally have strong incentives to maintain robust public confidence in their technological field across the board. These companies have the largest economic stake in a particular technology industry, and will be harmed the most by any perceived adverse event, whether traced to their company or another in the same industry …

In addition to the public relations and fast-track opportunities identified in this and the preceding sections, emerging technology industry can be encouraged to engage in activities beyond those mandated through other incentives, such as potential penalty avoidance. A firm that agrees to conduct regular auditing and self-reporting of regulatory agency-determined practices, for example, could be exempted from certain regulatory fines for minor violations that are not intentional or the result of gross negligence. Firms thus can be incentivized to go beyond what is legally required to address unregulated matters, adopt preventive measures, and help regulatory agencies gather greater data.

Under this model, regulatory rules are not intended to set the ideal standard for behavior, but serve as a mandatory back-stop that applies only if firms do not achieve alternative arrangements that provide greater protection. In this manner, greater protection than mandated can be accomplished, at a lower cost to both taxpayers and industry, by offering industry flexibility to achieve more efficient protection and by highlighting the importance of public confidence in emerging technology development.

A broad system of industry stewardship, as outlined here, could also have substantial long-run returns. Such a system could help develop more of an industry ethic of responsibility and a goal of teamwork between the government, industry, and consumer organizations. This teamwork can also help build commitment among various stakeholders to the governance structure and to cooperation itself, instead of each entity constantly challenging the program and each other over every perceived deficiency.

2.4. Agency Expertise and Coordination

Emerging technologies often exacerbate enduring problems with regulatory agency staffing, funding, lack of scientific expertise, and coordination. For example, in the United States, the EPA, Food and Drug Administration (FDA), Unites States Department of Agriculture (USDA), and Office of Safety and Health Administration (OSHA) each have been identified as understaffed, underfunded, and lacking personnel properly trained to handle pertinent emerging technologies. Similar concerns exist for European regulatory agency oversight of emerging technologies as well.

The problems of agency inexperience will be great for most emerging technologies due to the technological complexity and forefront-of-science issues involved, but it may be particularly severe for nanotechnology. Nanotechnology represents a strikingly interdisciplinary field. Depending on the particular technology or product in question, advanced understanding in materials science, chemistry, physics, and biology all may be required to analyze risks. There are few scientists with sufficient training in the multiple necessary areas, let alone those who work for government agencies. This problem is exacerbated by the disparity between the remuneration such scientists could receive in the private nanotechnology sector versus their opportunities at government agencies.

Emerging technologies also often raise particular challenges for interagency coordination. The regulation of genetically modified plants and animals in the United States, for example, implicates as many as twelve different statutes and five different agencies and services. The multiplicity of statutes and agencies has created confusion among regulated industry and the public, reduced clarity regarding scientific standards and requirements, and retarded the efficiency of biotechnology development and regulation. There have even been instances of inconsistencies in regulation between the FDA, EPA, and USDA. Regulatory agency coordination for nanotechnology has been identified as a critical need as well.

Regulatory coordination and consistency for emerging technologies is important on a number of fronts. First, coordination can offer significant cost savings. In a system where agencies are understaffed and underfunded, coordination allows a pooling of personnel, data, and other resources, rather than wasteful duplication. Second, because scientific uncertainty rates as one of the most significant problems facing emerging technology regulation, coordinating research concerning human health and environmental risks can allow scarce agency research resources to be stretched further. Finally, a coordinated approach to regulation and requirements can provide efficiency benefits for both government and industry. New governance systems for emerging technologies should include a focus on promoting both intra- and inter- agency coordination.

2.5. Governance Adaptability

Emerging technologies develop rapidly. It is often impossible to predict what products and risks will need to be governed even a short time into the future ...

One method for achieving adaptability and flexibility is for emerging technology governance to include mechanisms that allow for incremental changes in governance as the need arises. Such an approach simultaneously provides flexibility in governance and limits the likelihood of quickly upsetting settled expectations for industry. Emerging technology governance should be an iterative process at early stages of technological development and commercialization. A particular system of governance should be developed, followed by data gathering, followed by result evaluation, followed by modifications to the system as warranted, in a continuing cycle until industry and scientific understanding has matured ...

Governmental agencies also should work with firms to permit flexibility in how regulatory requirements are satisfied to the extent practicable while still protecting human health and the environment. Flexibility will allow industry to experiment with economic or technical feasibility and various control approaches, while still ensuring adequate protection. Such experimentation also may help develop additional information on technology risks and the relative advantages of various governance approaches.

2.6. Stakeholder Involvement

Critical to this proposal for emerging technology governance is wide and diverse stakeholder involvement. This involvement will require regular communication with and workshops among a variety of stakeholders, including regulatory agencies, industry representatives, research scientists, environmental organizations, public interest groups, academics, and others. Broad stakeholder outreach and dialogue can bring credibility, new ideas, current information, continual feedback, and public trust to a governance system.

The communication should include information on the known and unknown risks and benefits of an emerging technology (provided in a form accessible to a broad cross-section of lay individuals), disclosure of new scientific information concerning the technology as it arises, and further encouragement of public involvement. Such communication is particularly important at the early stages of a technology's development because of the public's limited knowledge and awareness of the technology. A well-informed public, in turn, can allow consumers to 'vote with their dollars' to try to affect industry decisions. Of course, there also must be a high level of transparency in regulatory decision-making and activity.

The communication efforts must include specialized outreach to smaller technology companies. Current health and environmental regulatory programs generally evolved around existing, mature industries, at times when there were relatively fewer and larger companies. Larger companies are generally more aware of and able to respond to regulatory requirements. Emerging technology governance, on the other hand, will evolve with an industry itself. In order to be effective, start-up and small companies, including many that are not familiar or sophisticated with respect to existing health and environmental regulations, will need to be made aware of, and in some cases receive assistance with, regulatory requirements. Training and technical assistance on compliance for start-ups and small companies should be provided.

As noted, public trust in an emerging technology and its governance is critical to the success of the technology. The failure to provide for adequate stakeholder involvement and public communication, in particular, has been identified by some as one reason for some of the public backlash against biotechnology. The potential for a public reaction against emerging technologies is elevated by the complex science involved, the high level of uncertainty concerning risk, and the potential for interest group polarization. Perhaps recognizing this concern, there are growing efforts to more proactively incorporate discussion of ethical, legal, and social implications of synthetic biology into its research and development in Europe and the United States.

Communication will not resolve all concern or potential for conflict, but it can go a long way towards establishing broad public trust. Implementing these measures in concert with those above can produce a framework for emerging technology governance that could simultaneously better protect against health and environmental risks, develop greater information about a technology, permit the technology industry to continue to rapidly advance, and maintain public confidence in the governance system.

Mandel concedes that this is an optimistic proposal. Nevertheless, as we have remarked, his thinking finds considerable echoes in the approach of the Royal Commission on Environmental Pollution;[32] and it also chimes in with the approach favoured by the House of Lords Science and Technology Committee in its more recent report entitled *Nanotechnologies and Food*.[33] Stated shortly, the tenor of this latter report is precisely that regulatory gaps should be closed, that government should take steps actively to increase our understanding of the risk profile of nanotechnologies, that cooperative data sharing should be encouraged during the pre-competitive period, and that consumers should be properly engaged and informed with regard to the use of nanotechnologies in the food sector. In this light, from the Committee's thirty-two recommendations, we can note the following:

- That Government should take steps to ensure the establishment of research collaborations between industry, academia and other relevant bodies at the pre-competitive stage in order to promote the translation of basic research into commercially viable applications of nanotechnologies in the food sector (recommendation 2).
- That the Research Councils should establish more proactive forms of funding to encourage the submission of research bids to address the severe shortfalls

---

[32] Royal Commission on Environmental Pollution, *Novel Materials in the Environment: The Case of Nanotechnology* (London, November 2008).

[33] 1st Report of Session 2009–10, HL Paper 22-I, 8 January 2010.

in research required for risk assessment of nanomaterials, particularly relating to the harm caused by such materials that lodge in the gut (recommendations 5 and 6).

- That Government should take steps to address the shortage of trained toxicologists (recommendation 8).
- That Government should work more closely with European and international partners on research related to the health and safety risks of nanomaterials to ensure that knowledge gaps are filled quickly and without duplication (recommendation 9).
- That the Food Standards Agency should develop, in collaboration with the food industry, a confidential database of information about nanomaterials being researched within the food sector to inform the development of appropriate risk assessment procedures, and to assist in the prioritisation of research (recommendation 10).
- That the Government should work within the European Union to promote the amendment of current legislation to ensure that all nanomaterials used in food products, additives, or supplements fall with the scope of current legislation (recommendation 11).
- That the Government, in collaboration with relevant stakeholders, should support the development of voluntary codes of conduct for nanotechnologies, ensuring that such codes are transparent, are of high standard, and are subject to effective monitoring processes (recommendation 19).
- That the Government should continue to push for international dialogue and information exchange on appropriate approaches to regulating the application of nanotechnologies in the food sector (recommendation 25).
- That the Food Standards Agency should create and maintain an accessible list of publicly-available food and food packaging products that contain nanomaterials that have been approved by the European Food Safety Authority (recommendation 26).
- That, rather than labelling of nanomaterials on food packaging, there should be a public register of foods containing nanomaterials (recommendation 30).
- That the Government should establish an open discussion group, along the lines of the DEFRA-sponsored Nanotechnology Stakeholder Forum, to discuss issues surrounding the application of nanotechnologies in the food sector, this group including representatives from government, academia, and industry, as well as consumers and NGOs (recommendation 32).

Interestingly, the possibility is recognised that nanofoods might be offered for sale by internet suppliers who fall outside the safe and secured regulatory regime that is envisaged by the Committee.[34] In response to this concern (a concern about a disruptive third-party effect of just the kind that we discussed in Chapter 14), the Committee relies on its general strategy of

---

[34] *Ibid.*, at para. 6.14.

ensuring that consumers are properly informed about the use of nanomaterials in the food sector.

7 Broader concerns

With technologies still in their introductory stage, or possibly as they move into the permeation stage, the concern might not be as to the safety of the technology but as to its social and ethical acceptability. How are regulators to respond to this kind of concern, some of which might be expressed in evocative but less than helpful terms (as with concerns about 'Frankenfoods')?

Where regulators initiate public debate about an emerging technology, this seems like a move in the right direction. However, to repeat the reservation that we entered in Chapter 5, if the debate focuses on HSE risks, there is a danger that the ethical concerns might not get a fair hearing. The obvious risk is that the HSE risks will simply dominate the discussion so that broader concerns get marginalised.[35] There is also, though, a more insidious risk, one which might arise where the debate is staged in such a way that the HSE issues are fully addressed before attention turns to any further concerns. While this might seem like an efficient way of organising the agenda, it can operate in a way that weakens the significance of the ethical concerns such that they become, not just second stage, but secondary. In other words, if the outcome of the first-stage, HSE debate is that the risks are judged to be acceptable, then the broader concerns will be debated in a context in which the technology already has been pronounced 'safe'. Where this is so, it will be difficult for regulators to counter the presumption that the technology should be given the go-ahead.

In this light, consider UK policy discussions of nanotechnologies.[36] Here, the recurrent theme is that there is considerable potential for commercial exploitation but that there needs to be proper assessment and regulation of any HSE risks. So, in the Ministerial Foreword to a recent UK strategy document, we read that the government is determined 'to develop the nanotechnologies industry while protecting the health of consumers and employees and avoiding damage to the environment'.[37] With a spectacular predicted growth in the global revenue of nanotechnologies, especially in the field of ICT,[38] the government has strong commercial reasons for wanting to see the UK positioned 'at the forefront of nanotechnologies development ... maintain[ing] momentum

---

[35] See, especially, Maria Lee, 'Beyond Safety? The Broadening Scope of Risk Regulation', *Current Legal Problems*, 62 (2009), 242.

[36] Starting with the seminal Royal Society and the Royal Academy of Engineering, *Nanoscience and Nanotechnologies: Opportunities and Uncertainties* (London: Royal Society, 2004) (RS Policy document 19/04), this HSE framing runs through the Royal Commission on Environmental Pollution's report, *Novel Materials in the Environment: The Case of Nanotechnology* (London, November, 2008) and the House of Lords Science and Technology Committee's report, *Nanotechnologies and Food*.

[37] *UK Nanotechnologies Strategy: Small Technologies, Great Opportunities*, London, March 2010, at 2.

[38] *Ibid.*, at 12.

and keep[ing] pace with the biggest players on the international stage'.[39] In itself, this is perfectly sensible but the danger is that any social and ethical concerns about nanotechnologies are neither elicited nor debated. How are regulators to avoid this happening?

One counter-strategy is to task a high-profile body with putting ethical concerns into the public domain. This is precisely the role of the European Group on Ethics in Science and New Technologies (the EGE). So, when the EGE considered the issues raised by nanomedicine, in its *Opinion on the Ethical Aspects of Nanomedicine* (2007), it identified the following ethical questions:

> How should the dignity of people participating in nanomedicine research trials be respected? How can we protect the fundamental rights of citizens that may be exposed to free particles in the environment? How can we promote responsible use of nanomedicine which protects both human health and the environment? And what are the specific ethics issues, such as justice, solidarity and autonomy, that have to be considered in this scientific domain?[40]

To be sure, the EGE Opinion, like the UK strategy document, expresses concern about matters of human health, safety and the environment; but it also senses that there are issues relating to fundamental rights, justice, solidarity and autonomy – and, at the start of its list, the EGE voices a concern about the dignity of humans. No doubt, this is not the only way in which regulators might seek to protect the integrity of the cultural debate, but they will not get properly connected unless ethical concerns are fairly and fully debated.

The development of powerful new brain-imaging technologies – technologies that facilitate both structural and functional neuroimaging – is an interesting test case. Some of these technologies do give rise to safety concerns but the big talking point is not safety; rather it is that, with this technology, researchers have a window into the brains and, possibly, into a deeper understanding of the mental lives, of their participants.[41] Already the latest work in the brain sciences has figured in legal argument;[42] and it is easy to imagine a future in which

---

[39] *Ibid.*, at 2. [40] At para. 4.1.

[41] Some, however, doubt that even the most sophisticated understanding of the brain's biology can challenge, change or engage with our social understanding of our thoughts, acts and self-perception. On this view, it is one thing to understand how the brain works, but quite another to understand the social significance of our mental lives. For one such view, see Roger Smith, *Being Human* (Manchester: University of Manchester Press, 2007): 'Knowledge of differential activity of the brain during different kinds of mental activity is one kind of knowledge. In itself, however, it says nothing about either what causes mental activity or what that activity is about. Different knowledge is needed to answer such questions, and in the latter case this certainly requires knowledge of language. It may also well be that we will not understand the causes of consciousness independently of knowledge of the causes of language and hence of people as social beings ... The argument leads to the conclusion that there are different kinds of knowledge, different kinds of science – different kinds of rational understanding. There are human sciences as well as natural sciences' (*ibid.*, at 114).

[42] The highest-profile example is *Roper* v. *Simmons* 543 US 551 (2005); see, for an impressive survey and analysis, O. Carter Snead, 'Neuroimaging and the "Complexity" of Capital Punishment', *New York University Law Review*, 82 (2007), 1265.

various scanning and imaging technologies will present a range of opportunities in many spheres of social life – not only in the criminal and civil justice systems, but also, for example, in health care, employment, business contexts, and so on.[43]

Nevertheless, we are still at a relatively early stage of the development of imaging technology and its penetration into everyday life is still fairly modest. In terms of Moor's three developmental stages, we seem to be somewhere between the first and the second stages, that is, between the stage of introduction (when the technology is expensive, known about only by a few specialists, and not in general circulation) and that of permeation (when the costs start to drop, circulation spreads, and demand increases). At this relatively early stage, we do not have dedicated legal provision for brain imaging; but, it is not being conducted in a regulatory void. There are, for example, well-developed rules about the admissibility of new scientific evidence in the courtroom and it might be decided, generally as is the position with polygraph testing, that functional magnetic resonance imaging (fMRI) evidence is not sufficiently reliable to help the court ascertain whether a party is telling the truth or telling a lie. Of course, although polygraph evidence might not be admissible in the courtroom, it might be routinely used by the police during the course of their investigation of crime; and, if fMRI has a similar future, the regulatory environment in which such imaging is used will need to be developed. Similarly, in clinical and research settings, fMRI is not 'unregulated'; the usual principles of informed consent apply. However, as brain imaging becomes a more important research tool, the regulatory environment will again need to be developed. In particular, there are already ethical concerns about whether, when, and if so how, researchers should feed back information based on brain scans to their participants. For example, if UK Biobank were to invite some of its participants to undergo MRI scans, what would be the protocol in relation to feeding back results to individual participants? As the Ethics and Governance Council poses the questions:

> What feedback, if any, ought participants to receive as a result of their MRI scans? What information, if any, ought participants [to] receive if the MRI shows an unexpected finding (e.g., a lesion on the brain)? When performing an MRI scan, what is the likelihood of making a false positive finding (i.e., a scan that is erroneously showing a problem when a situation is normal) or making a false negative finding (i.e., a scan that appears to show no problem when in fact there is a problem)?[44]

Clearly, these are questions that need to be debated generally as well as specifically with participants.

---

[43] See, e.g., Henry T. Greely, 'The Social Effects of Advances in Neuroscience: Legal Problems, Legal Perspectives', in Judy Illes (ed.), *Neuroethics* (Oxford: Oxford University Press, 2006), 245; and 'Law and the Revolution in Neuroscience: An Early Look at the Field', *Akron Law Review*, 42 (2009), 687 (where the focus is on prediction, mind reading, responsibility, treatment and enhancement); and Jeffrey Rosen, 'The brain on the stand', *New York Times*, 11 March 2007.

[44] UK Biobank Ethics and Governance Council, *Annual Review 2008*, 13.

As the ethical issues relating to brain imaging can be stated with more confidence, and as a consensus begins to emerge, is this the time to make a more dedicated regulatory connection? One of the things that we should caution against is a repetition of the kind of mistake that regulators made when they first addressed the issues of privacy and data protection in an age of big mainframe computers. So long as the technology is large, visible and expensive, it might be tempting to think that we can operate with a regulatory scheme that is based on registration, inspection, and institutional responsibility. However, as technologies assume much less expensive and more widely distributed formats, we might find that the regulation has become disconnected, leaving a regulatory environment that is deficient.[45] Imagine, for example, a world in which scanners are routinely incorporated into pillows so that, when we awake from our sleep, we (or, more problematically, others) are able to access the results of our overnight scan. In such a world, where the technology is both widely distributed and accepted, one would expect a very different culture with, quite possibly, rather different attitudes towards, and expectations of, privacy.

In the absence of safety concerns about fMRI scanning, a number of broader concerns have been brought into focus. At a very deep level, there is the worry that brain imaging might threaten our self-perception as agents – that is, as beings who act on the basis of 'free will', who are 'in control' of their actions, and who are rightly answerable for the choices they make and the actions they take. To the extent that the criminal law presupposes this model of agency, can it survive? Stephen Morse, who is a particularly robust defender of the view that neuroscience is no threat to our criminal justice practices, captures the essential legal presuppositions (which, it should be emphasised, do *not* presuppose the existence of free will) in the following way:[46]

> Law guides human conduct by giving citizens prudential and moral reasons for conduct. Law would be powerless to achieve its primary goal of regulating human interaction if it did not operate through the practical reason of the agents it addresses and if agents were not capable of rationally understanding the rules and their application under the circumstances in which the agent acts.
>
> Responsibility is a normative condition that law and morality attribute only to human beings. We do not ascribe responsibility to inanimate natural forces or to other species. Holding an agent responsible means simply that it is fair to require the agent to satisfy moral and legal expectations and to bear the consequences if he or she does not do so; holding an agent non-responsible means simply that we do not believe the agent was capable in the context in question of satisfying moral and legal expectations. The central reason why an agent might not be able to be guided by moral and legal expectations is that the agent was not capable of being guided by reason.[47]

[45] Compare Henry T. Greely, 'The Social Effects of Advances in Neuroscience: Legal Problems, Legal Perspectives', in Illes, *Neuroethics*, 245, 254–5.

[46] Stephen J. Morse, 'Uncontrollable Urges and Irrational People', *Virginia Law Review*, 88 (2002), 1025.

[47] *Ibid.*, at 1065–6.

On this analysis, neuroscience will be fundamentally disruptive if it can show that we do not have the capacity to respond to regulatory signals (legal or otherwise); but, short of this, neuroscientific findings are likely only to pose questions as to the details of our practice of holding law-breakers responsible (subject to excuse and mitigation).[48] Morse concludes that 'until currently unimaginable [neuro]scientific advances convince us otherwise, we are fully entitled to believe that we are ordinarily conscious, intentional, and potentially rational creatures' and that determinism gives us no reason 'to abandon current responsibility criteria and practices'.[49] There is, so to speak, 'always a story' but the narrative that comes with modern brain science does not mechanically translate into an excusing or mitigating story.[50]

Others take a rather different view. Famously, Joshua Greene and Jonathan Cohen[51] argue that, while Morse is correct in believing that the 'law provides a coherent framework for the assessment of criminal responsibility that is not threatened by anything that neuroscience is likely to throw at it',[52] nevertheless neuroscience is likely to challenge the broader intuitions of society that underpin the perceived fairness and appropriateness of punishing offenders in accordance with their deserts. They conclude:

> Neuroscience is unlikely to tell us anything that will challenge the law's stated assumptions. However, we maintain that advances in neuroscience are likely to change the way people think about human action and criminal responsibility by vividly illustrating lessons that some people appreciated long ago. Free will as we ordinarily understand it is an illusion generated by our cognitive architecture. Retributivist notions of criminal responsibility ultimately depend on this illusion, and, if we are lucky, they will give way to consequentialist ones, thus radically transforming our approach to criminal justice. At this time, the law deals firmly but mercifully with individuals whose behaviour is obviously the product of forces that are ultimately beyond their control. Some day, the law may treat all convicted criminals this way. That is, humanely.[53]

---

[48] For example, what should we do if we find that a psychopath simply lacks any capacity to respond to moral signals (but has the capacity to respond to prudential signals)? Should we condemn or excuse? For discussion, see Nicole A. Vincent, 'Madness, Badness, and Neuroimaging-Based Responsibility Assessments', in Michael Freeman (ed.), *Law and Neuroscience* (Oxford: Oxford University Press, 2011), 79.

[49] Stephen J. Morse, 'Moral and Legal Responsibility and the New Neuroscience', in Illes, *Neuroethics*, 33, at 47.

[50] See, e.g., Stephen J. Morse, 'Lost in Translation? An Essay on Law and Neuroscience', in Michael Freeman (ed.), *Law and Neuroscience* (Oxford: Oxford University Press, 2011), 529: 'All behaviour is the product of the necessary and sufficient causal conditions without which the behaviour would not have occurred, including brain causation, which is always part of the causal explanation for any behaviour. If causation were an excusing condition per se, then no one would be responsible for any behaviour' (*ibid.*, at 534).

[51] Joshua Greene and Jonathan Cohen, 'For the Law, Neuroscience Changes Nothing and Everything', *Philosophical Transactions of the Royal Society B: Biological Sciences*, 359 (2004), 1775.

[52] *Ibid.*, at 1778.   [53] *Ibid.*, at 1784.

Whatever we make of the proposition that retributivist thinking is misconceived, the way in which the criminal law deals with arguments based on various kinds of mental pathology is surely likely to change as brain imaging and the accompanying neuroscientific understanding becomes more sophisticated. Where scanners can detect abnormalities in the morphology of the brain, this might be connected to abnormal conduct – as can be seen, for example, where tumours create pressures on the brain.[54] Similarly, even if the brain structure seems normal, with the development of fMRI, it might be possible to detect abnormal *functioning* of the brain. And, in both cases, this might be treated as relevant to some reshaping of such doctrines as that of diminished responsibility, automatism, and so on.[55] Of course, whether or not the overall result of an increased reliance on neuroscience will be that offenders are treated more humanely or fairly, time alone will tell.[56]

Away from the sphere of criminal law, the moral concerns elicited by brain imaging tend to be that privacy and respect for human dignity are threatened by this development. If we focus on privacy, how should we formulate our concern?

Currently, much thinking about privacy proceeds on the basis that there is only an infringement where a balance of reasonableness so indicates. In the common law world, this idea is expressed by asking whether the complainant has a 'reasonable expectation' of privacy – as Lord Nicholls put it in the *Naomi Campbell* case:[57] '[e]ssentially the touchstone of private life is whether in respect of the disclosed facts the person in question had a reasonable expectation of privacy'.[58] Typically, in the case law, this will involve some balancing of the interests of a celebrity complainant against the interests of the media in publishing some story and pictures of the celebrity. Thus, in the J. K. Rowling case,[59] Sir Anthony Clarke MR said:

> As we see it, the question whether there is a reasonable expectation of privacy is a broad one, which takes account of all the circumstances of the case. They include the attributes of the claimant, the nature of the activity in which the claimant was engaged, the place at which it was happening, the nature and purpose of the

---

[54] As in the much discussed case of Oft (the teacher who developed paedophilic tendencies): see Morse, 'Lost in Translation?', at 559–62.

[55] For some redrafting of the notion of diminished responsibility in English law, see section 52 of the Coroners and Justice Act 2009. See, further, Lisa Claydon, 'Law, Neuroscience, and Criminal Culpability', in Michael Freeman (ed.), *Law and Neuroscience* (Oxford: Oxford University Press, 2011), 141, 168–9.

[56] For some concerns about the longer-term impact of neuroscientific evidence, see Carter Snead, 'Neuroimaging'.

[57] *Campbell* v. *Mirror Group Newspapers Limited* [2004] UKHL 22.

[58] *Ibid.*, at para. 21. Compare the seminal case of *Katz* v. *United States* 389 US 347 (1967), at 361, where Justice Harlan set out a famous two-part test: first, the complainant must have exhibited a subjective expectation of privacy; and, second, the complainant's expectation must be one that society is prepared to recognise as reasonable.

[59] *Murray* v. *Express Newspapers plc* [2007] EWHC 1908 (Ch); [2008] EWCA Civ. 446 (reversing the trial court decision).

intrusion, the absence of consent and whether it was known or could be inferred, the effect on the claimant and the circumstances in which and the purposes for which the information came into the hands of the publisher.[60]

Although high-profile disputes of this kind are determined very much on a case-by-case basis, it is important to keep an eye on the benchmark or reference point for a judgment that a particular expectation of privacy is reasonable. Frequently, the judgments that are made take their lead from what seems to be reasonable in the light of prevailing custom and practice. However, practice is a shifting scene; and particularly so where new technologies not only make possible ever more remote and undetectable observation but also encourage netizens to be carefree about their personal data.[61] Somewhat bizarrely, if we apply this flexible conception in such conditions we find that the more that there is pressure to push back the line of privacy, the less that it is infringed – because our reasonable expectation has been adjusted (i.e., lowered) by the practice. Accordingly, as brain imaging becomes more widespread and accepted, arguments that there has been an infringement of privacy are liable to look less compelling.

What seems to be required is a more robust notion of privacy. One thought is that an agent may be related to certain information in such a way that the agent's privacy interest is engaged. Just as an agent may claim a controlling interest over an object by asserting, 'This is my property; this is mine', so an agent may claim a controlling interest over information by asserting, 'This is my information; it is private'. Or, 'Keep out! These are my thoughts. They are private.' On this conception, a privacy claim is analogous to a property claim; in both cases, the reasonableness of the claim is irrelevant – it matters not one jot, for example, that some third-party might make better use of the property or information, or that the third party has greater needs than the agent with the controlling interest. If the information is private, it is mine to control.[62]

If some information is to be protected in the way implied by the robust conception, how could this be justified? Such information, surely, would need to be pretty important if it were to be safeguarded in this 'beyond questions of reasonableness' haven. One possible answer is suggested by Christian Halliburton.[63] Writing with reference to US constitutional jurisprudence, Halliburton has argued that we should recognise an interest in 'personal informational property'. Distinctively, this interest would target 'information which is closely bound up with identity, or necessary to the development of the fully

---

[60] [2008] EWCA Civ. 446, para. 36.

[61] Compare our discussion of privacy in Chapter 9.

[62] For elaboration of this approach, see Roger Brownsword, 'Regulating Brain Imaging: Questions of Privacy and Informed Consent', in Sarah J. L. Edwards, Sarah Richmond and Geraint Rees (eds.), *I Know What You Are Thinking: Brain Imaging and Mental Privacy* (Oxford: Oxford University Press, 2012).

[63] Christian Halliburton, 'How Privacy Killed *Katz*: A Tale of Cognitive Freedom and the Property of Personhood as Fourth Amendment Norm', *Akron Law Review*, 42 (2009), 803.

realized person, [and which] like certain types of property, is deserving of the most stringent protection'.[64] Elaborating this idea, Halliburton says:[65]

> I think it is easy to see (and rather difficult to dispute) that our thoughts, our internal mental processes, and the cognitive landscape of our ideas and intentions are so closely bound up with the self that they are essential to our ongoing existence and manifestation of a fully developed personal identity. As such, they are inherently and uncontrovertibly personal information property deserving absolutist protections because any interference with these informational assets cannot be tolerated by the individual. Many would therefore argue that capturing thoughts, spying on mental processes, and invading cognitive landscapes with [brain-imaging technologies] deprive the individual not only of property related to personhood, but of personhood altogether.

Needless to say, the mingling of property, privacy, and the notoriously difficult concept of personal identity, makes this a complex mix. Still, a privacy concept of this kind might be what is required if there is to be real resistance to a burgeoning practice of brain imaging.

In practice, any concept of privacy is liable to be overridden by more compelling interests and there is always the possibility that an agent will authorise an act that would otherwise infringe his or her privacy. That said, we would not expect the more robust notion to be easily overridden; after all, if privacy is treated as akin to a property interest, it will take a conflicting interest of some significance before privacy yields. Moreover, we would expect the conditions for a valid consent (including whether consent is by opt-in or opt-out) to be stringently applied where the robust notion is in play.

If this is how the land lies, then the first question for regulators, relative to brain imaging technologies, is which conception of privacy they should adopt. Possibly, regulators will find that their regulatees are relatively sanguine about a loss of informational privacy; and they might also see no convincing argument for the need to protect some inner sanctum of informational interests. In this case, regulators will see no reason to depart from the standard more flexible conception. However, where the loss of privacy is treated as a serious matter, and in the light of the above analysis, then the more robust conception might well be preferred; but we can anticipate a number of objections to such a regulatory choice.

One question is whether we can express and apply this conception in a convincing way. For example, can we coherently map the brain in a way that fits with this conception, treating some parts of the brain as open for examination and some parts as private? Are there some sections of the brain (for example, the pre-frontal cortex area, which researchers treat as the 'blackboard of the mind'[66] where we deliberate and plan), that we should treat as per se 'off-limits'? Given the apparent interconnectedness and plasticity of the brain, and given

---

[64] *Ibid.*, at 864.   [65] *Ibid.*, at 868.
[66] Matt Grist, *Steer* (London: Royal Society of Arts, 2010), at 53.

the current level of technological competence, this is perhaps not a promising thought. Alternatively, if we focus not so much on regions of the brain but on protected types of information and the areas of the brain with which such information seems to be associated, we are still in difficulty. Initially, there is the challenge of identifying the relevant type of information and then locating the relevant hot spots in the brain. Once again, though, the complexity of the brain, in conjunction with the current level of technological competence, suggests that this is beyond our reach. Accordingly, if privacy (in line with the robust conception) is to be protected, the appropriate regulatory response must be to treat the brain, in its entirety, and the thoughts therein as private. This, however, leads right into another objection.

If any kind of brain imaging amounts to a per se infringement of privacy, in practice, this means that those who wish to conduct scans will need the clear and explicit consent of the person in question. No doubt, a regulatory move in this direction will provoke objection from those who argue that this is an unwarranted inconvenience. What should regulators say to this?

Insofar as the objection is backed by utilitarian reasons, and where regulators are committed to respect for a range of (human or agency) rights, including privacy, the response is straightforward. Quite simply, utilitarian reasons are not recognised as legitimate counters to the application of rights. However, if the objection is rights based, then regulators need to engage with this view in order to assess the strength of the rights arguments for preferring the standard flexible conception of privacy (or a less demanding requirement of informed consent). Even so, regulators might reasonably expect objectors to bear the burden of justification.

Finally, it might be objected that it is all very well having strong paper protection of privacy but little use if, in practice, it will be observed in the breach or compliance will be perfunctory. How might regulators respond? One possibility is to instate professional training and education in order to develop an understanding of how to process consent (or refusal) and why it matters; or perhaps consents should have to be procured and issued by a trusted third party (which is clearly a major design challenge); or, possibly, brain scans should be used only in the most exceptional of circumstances where we can be confident that no rational person would refuse consent (which will severely limit the strides that are made in the brain sciences). Regulators might also suggest that the use of privacy-enhancing technologies (PETs) should be investigated. Even if it is not immediately obvious how the filters and privacy settings that are available for use in ICTs could be transferred to brain imaging technologies, advocates of a technological fix will want to explore whatever options there are.

8 Conclusion

It is in the nature of innovation that new technologies tend to emerge in regulatory environments that have not been set up specifically for their development and application. The connection between existing regulatory provisions and the new technology can be far from ideal. Accordingly, there needs to be an early identification of the kinds of concerns to which the technology gives rise. Where the concerns are about health, safety or the environment, there needs to be as much pooling of information as possible; and, where the concerns are of a broader social and ethical kind, the process of public engagement and debate needs to be commenced. In some cases, it might be sufficient to operate with a Type 2 regulatory environment, retaining a degree of flexibility and capacity for rapid adjustment of the regulatory position. However, where the concerns are of an ethical kind, it might be difficult to avoid picking these up in a Type I regulatory intervention. At all events, once a Type I regulatory connection has been made, it becomes more difficult to change the regulatory position and there is then the risk of disconnection as the technology or its application moves on (the challenge to be discussed in the next chapter). For this reason, regulators should not think that a Type I intervention that is made while the technology is still developing is likely to be the last word on the matter.

16

Regulatory connection II: disconnection and sustainability

1 Introduction

Recommendation 16 of the House of Lords Science and Technology Committee's report *Nanotechnologies and Food*[1] reads as follows:

> Given the pace at which novel technologies develop we recommend that, in addition to its on-going monitoring of the state of the science, the Food Standards Agency should formally review the suitability of legislation every three years to ensure that regulatory oversight and risk assessment keeps pace with the development of these technologies.

While this shows an admirable awareness of the challenge, we might wonder whether regular review and revision is the best that we can do to maintain connection. Is there no better way?

Ideally, we want regulation to bind to the technology and to evolve with it. In pursuit of this ideal, regulators (at any rate, regulators in first-generation environments) seem to face a choice between taking a traditional hard law approach or leaving it to self-regulation and, concomitantly, a softer form of law.[2] Where the former approach is taken, the hard edges of the law can be softened in various ways – for example, by adopting a 'technology neutral' drafting style,[3] by delegating regulatory powers to the relevant minister and by encouraging a culture of purposive interpretation in the courts. Conversely, where self-regulation and softer law is preferred, the regime can be hardened up by moving towards a

---

[1] 1st Report of Session 2009–10, HL Paper 22-I, 8 January 2010.

[2] Compare Christopher Slobogin, 'Technologically-Assisted Physical Surveillance: The American Bar Association's Tentative Draft Standards', *Harvard Journal of Law and Technology*, 10 (1997), 383, 425 (for the view that the pace of technological development renders regulation obsolete) and 426 (for the, predictable, response that guidelines have a better chance than rules of staying connected).

[3] As advocated, for instance, in relation to electronic signatures (see e.g., Pamela Samuelson, 'Five Challenges for Regulating the Global Information Society', in Christopher T. Marsden (ed.), *Regulating the Global Information Society* (London: Routledge, 2000), 316, at 320–1) and electronic money. For a comprehensive analysis of technological neutrality, see Bert-Jaap Koops, 'Should ICT Regulation Be Technology-Neutral?', in Bert-Jaap Koops, Miriam Lips, Corien Prins and Maurice Schellekens (eds.), *Starting Points for ICT Regulation – Deconstructing Prevalent Policy One-Liners* (The Hague: TMC Asser Press, 2006), 77.

form of co-regulatory strategy.[4] However, no matter which approach is adopted, there is no guarantee that it will be effective and the details of the regulatory regime will always reflect a tension between the need for flexibility (if regulation is to move with the technology) and the demand for predictability and consistency (if regulatees are to know where they stand).

Even if there are no simple prescriptions for effective and legitimate regulatory connection, there is a growing awareness that there is a serious problem that requires attention. So, for example, it has been proposed that 'the Chief Scientific Advisor should establish a group that brings together the representatives of a wide range of stakeholders to look at new and emerging technologies and identify at the earliest possible stage areas where potential health, safety, environmental, social, ethical and regulatory issues may arise and advise on how these might be addressed.'[5] Such a group should ensure, not only that regulators are forewarned but also, as experience is gathered, that regulators are forearmed.

In this chapter, where our focus is on strategies for maintaining connection, our discussion is in four principal parts. First, we look again at the nature of, and the reasons for, disconnection. It is as well to be clear about precisely what it is that we are trying to avoid. In the following parts, we consider three strategies upon which regulators might rely: intelligent, anticipatory, drafting; an approach that is technologically neutral; and judicial assistance through purposive and flexible interpretation of the regulation.

2 The nature of and the reasons for the disconnection

We can identify the following three kinds of mismatch:

1 A mismatch between the description of the technology in the regulation and the characteristics of the technology as now constituted (arising from technological development).
2 A mismatch between the assumptions underlying the regulation as to the range of uses of the technology and the uses that are now made of the technology (arising from a changing use of the technology).
3 A mismatch between the presumed business model on which the regulation was predicated and the model of business that actually obtains.

In each case, there is a disconnection between the regulation and the technology. However, the reasons for the disconnection are different and each case merits independent consideration.

---

[4] As advocated, for instance, in relation to nanotechnologies: see, Bärbel Dorbeck-Jung and Marloes van Amerom, 'The Hardness of Soft Law in the United Kingdom: State and Non-State Regulatory Activities Related to Nanotechnological Development', in Hanneke van Schooten and Jonathan Verschuuren (eds.), *International Governance and Law* (Cheltenham: Edward Elgar, 2008), 129.

[5] Royal Society and the Royal Academy of Engineering, *Nanoscience and Nanotechnologies: Opportunities and Uncertainties* (London: Royal Society, 2004) (RS Policy document 19/04), para. 9.7.

(a) A mismatch between the description of the technology in the regulation and the characteristics of the technology as now constituted (arising from technological development)

In the previous chapter, we saw that, right across the sweep of emerging technologies, it is common to find that legislation is framed in terms that no longer correspond to the current state of the technology. Indeed, one of the great regulatory ironies is that, where regulators (in an attempt to let regulatees know where they stand) try their utmost to establish an initial set of standards that are clear, detailed and precise, then the more likely it is that the regulation will lose connection with its technological target (leaving regulatees unclear as to their position).

Later in this chapter, we will consider some problems of this kind that have been caused by the rapid developments in embryology and its associated techniques. In this area, the technology has moved on since 1990 when the framework legislation, the Human Fertilisation and Embryology Act, was enacted. One such technological advance has been in relation to cell nuclear replacement (CNR), where an embryonic mass is not produced, in the way that the drafting of the 1990 Act assumes, by a process of fertilisation.[6] This leaves a yawning gap between the language of the legislation and the actuality of the technology, a gap that the appeal courts tried to close by adopting a purposive approach.[7]

(b) A mismatch between the assumptions underlying the regulation as to the range of uses of the technology and the uses that are now made of the technology (arising from a changing use of the technology)

A technology might be developed for use in one context and then applied in another – for example, the early form of the internet was developed for use in a military or intelligence context but then was applied ubiquitously; and some technologies that are developed for use in medical contexts might be taken up in a forensic context. There is no suggestion yet that the migration of a technology from one context to another is undesirable; it is simply that it has not been fully anticipated by the regulation. Where the new use is not seen as problematic, regulators will be under no great pressure to clean up the regulation; but, where the use is controversial, there will be pressure to address the arguments and to re-connect the regulation. In what follows, we give two examples of controversial new uses that invite regulatory connection.

The first example is that of radio frequency identification (RFID) technologies. Currently, RFID chips or tags are widely used to identify and track vehicles, containers and products in the supply chain. So long as RFID technologies are employed to track products from the point of production to the

---

[6] Human Fertilisation and Embryology Act 1990, section 1(1).

[7] *R v. Secretary of State for Health ex parte Quintavalle (on behalf of Pro-Life Alliance)* [2001] EWHC 918 (Admin.) (Crane J.); [2002] EWCA Civ. 29; [2003] UKHL 13.

point of retail sale, they clearly have some considerable utility without eliciting any great moral concern. However, if the use of RFID chips moves from inanimate objects to living things, say to cattle and domestic pets, some might have concerns; and these concerns would be considerably amplified if it were proposed to introduce RFID implants into humans. In fact, without any general discussion and without explicit regulatory provision, this already seems to have happened, with several thousand people being chipped.[8] Consider these four examples that Jeroen van den Hoven gives:[9]

1 In Japan, school children are chipped subcutaneously and are traced by a computer at school and to and from school.
2 The Baya Beach Club in Rotterdam and Barcelona offers people the possibility of having a chip for payments in the club to be placed under their skin by a doctor who is present in the club.
3 At the Ministry of Justice in Mexico 160 people received a chip under their skin to make it easier to trace them in case of kidnapping.
4 Millions of pets in the United States have implanted chips to make it easier to find them when they run away.[10]

While each of these instances might be justified by appealing to arguments of benign paternalism and (in the case of the clubbers) informed consent, the trajectory of this extended use is a matter for concern. What might we make, for example, of the involuntary chipping of convicted sex offenders (as a condition for parole or release)?[11] Possibly, the majority will think that this is a reasonable idea but, then, does this move us one notch closer towards a surveillance society? Whatever we think, regulators need to be aware of our views.

The second example is that of the use of embryo-testing technologies in the context of assisted reproduction. Stated simply, it is possible to remove a cell from an embryonic mass in order to screen it for genetic markers for particular diseases. This procedure can be carried out without harming the developmental prospects of the embryo. So, for example, if beta thalassaemia is prevalent in a family, there is the possibility of screening embryos for that condition; and then, if the test is positive, not implanting the embryo in question. The concerns that have arisen in relation to the screening of embryos have been accentuated by the proposed use of the same kind of technology for the additional purpose of tissue-typing an embryo. The object of this additional exercise is to identify an embryo as a potential bone-marrow donor for the benefit of an already born, but sick, sibling. The donor child has been dubbed as a 'saviour sibling'. In the United Kingdom, nothing of this kind was anticipated in the Human Fertilisation and Embryology Act 1990; there was

---

[8] See Isaac B. Rosenberg, 'Involuntary Endogenous RFID Compliance Monitoring as a Condition of Federal Supervised Release: Chips Ahoy?, *Yale Journal of Law and Technology*, 10 (2008), 331.
[9] Jeroen van den Hoven, 'Nanotechnology and Privacy: Instructive Case of RFID', in Fritz Allhoff, Patrick Lin, James Moor, and John Weckert (eds.), *Nanoethics* (Hoboken, NJ: Wiley, 2007) 253.
[10] *Ibid.*, at 256.
[11] See Rosenberg, 'Involuntary Endogenous RFID Compliance Monitoring'.

no explicit connection between the regulation of assisted conception and the use of tissue-typing technologies. In the extract that follows, Lord Hoffmann sets out the background and poses the question as to the legality of such a procedure.

R (Quintavalle on behalf of Comment on Reproductive Ethics) v. *Human Fertilisation and Embryology Authority* [2005] UKHL 28 (Lord Hoffmann)

2. Zain Hashmi is a little boy, now aged 6, who suffers from a serious genetic disorder called beta thalassaemia major. His bone marrow does not produce enough red blood cells and in consequence he is often very poorly and needs daily drugs and regular blood transfusions to keep him alive. But he could be restored to normal life by a transplant of stem cells from a tissue compatible donor.

3. The problem is to find compatible tissue which Zain's immune system will not reject. The chances of finding a compatible donor who is not a sibling are extremely low. Even in the case of siblings, the chances are only one in four. None of Zain's three elder siblings is compatible. In addition, the donor must be free of the same disorder. That lengthens the odds even more. Zain's mother, Mrs Hashmi, has twice conceived in the hope of giving birth to a child whose umbilical blood could provide stem cells for Zain. Once the foetus was found to have beta thalassaemia major and she had an abortion. On the second occasion she gave birth to a child whose tissue turned out not to be compatible.

4. There is a way to save the Hashmi family from having to play dice with conception. For 30 years it has been possible to produce a human embryo by fertilisation of egg and sperm outside the body and then to implant that embryo in the womb. In vitro fertilisation (IVF) has enabled many couples who could not achieve natural fertilisation to have children. More recently, it has become possible to perform a biopsy upon the newly fertilised IVF embryo and remove a single cell to test it for genetic disorders. This is called pre-implantation genetic diagnosis (PGD). It provides a woman with information about the embryo proposed to be implanted in her body so that she may decide whether or not to proceed. Mrs Hashmi, for example, would have been spared having to have her foetus carrying beta thalassaemia major aborted if the embryo had been created by IVF and the disorder diagnosed by PGD.

5. Still more recently, and so far only in the United States, it has become possible to use the same single cell biopsy technique to test for tissue compatibility. This involves examination of the human leukocyte antigens (HLA) and is known as HLA typing. That means that if Mr and Mrs Hashmi's sperm and eggs are used to create IVF embryos which are then tested for beta thalassaemia major by PGD and for tissue compatibility with Zain by HLA typing, they can know that the child Mrs Hashmi conceives will have stem cells which could cure Zain. The question in this appeal is whether this can lawfully be done in the United Kingdom.

In the event, the House of Lords ruled that it was within the powers of the regulatory body to license the procedure; but this did not put an end to the matter. Pressure to review the 1990 legislative framework was already building and, in due course, the reconnection had to be made by legislation. We will review the reasoning of the House later in this chapter.

(c) A mismatch between the presumed 'business' model on which the regulation was predicated and the practice that actually obtains

The way that business is organised or actually practised can deviate significantly from the assumptions on which the law is predicated. For example, bodies of contract law that were adopted in the nineteenth century no longer map onto the networked approaches that are characteristic of many modern transactional practices (such as franchising). To the extent that the regulators can delay acting until the practice has stabilised, the better the chance that there will be a decent match; but, a waiting game is not always possible; and, even with a delayed approach, practice evolves and a mismatch can arise.

In a helpful paper, Chris Reed argues that it is particularly important that regulators who are intervening in the fast-moving field of information and communication technologies, should have a clear and appropriate view of the business models that are operative or likely to develop.[12] A failure to get this right can lead to a mismatch in the way that Reed contends has happened with the European regulation of databases,[13] e-signatures[14] and e-money.[15] Assuming that regulators are sensitised to the importance of the underlying business model, what else can regulators do to prevent disconnection? Reed suggests that regulators should aim to put in place a scheme that is, so to speak, business model neutral. In the following extract, Reed identifies four ways in which this can be facilitated.

> First, it is essential to identify and enunciate the regulatory objectives. It is surprising how seldom this is done in any depth, and how easy it is to assume that controlling some aspect of the business model will achieve the intended result without questioning that assumption. Two examples from the EU IT regulation … illustrate this particularly clearly.
>
> The Data Protection Directive does not explain what it aims to achieve by the prohibition in art. 25 on transferring personal data outside the EU. Is it the transfer itself which is the problem, or is the aim to ensure that personal data originating within the EU does not lose the privacy protections set out in the Directive when it is processed in a third country? Assuming the latter to have been the regulatory aim, then if this had been expressed it would have been clear that data whose storage remained within the EU, but was processed outside, presented a potential problem. The difficulty could have been resolved either by defining 'transfer' to include such remote processing or by imposing an obligation on the controller to ensure that any processing outside the EU did not deprive the data of those protections unless the place of processing also provided adequate protection. The latter would have been preferable because it addresses the aim more directly, and should thus work for future technologies or business models which might fall outside a revised definition of 'transfer'.

---

[12] Chris Reed, 'The Law of Unintended Consequences: Embedded Business Models in IT Regulation', *Journal of Information & Technology Law (JILT)*, (1) (2007), pt 3.1; see www2.warwick.ac.uk/fac/soc/law/elj/jilt

[13] Directive 1996/29/EC.   [14] Directive 1999/93/EC.   [15] Directive 2000/46/EC.

The regulatory objective of the liability regime set out in the e-Signatures Directive appears to have been to give a remedy to a relying party who suffers loss as a consequence of inaccurate information in a signature certificate. However, this is not stated anywhere in the legislative history of the Directive, which simply and without comment sets out a minimum level of liability for certification-service-providers. Had the regulatory aim been enunciated, it should have alerted the legislators to the possibility that this information might in practice be verified by persons other than the certification-service-providers and a consequent recognition that the verifying person might more appropriately bear the liability. This would have been a more nearly optimum solution because (a) it is the person who verified the information who was negligent and is therefore responsible for the loss, and (b) this approach regulates the behaviour of the verifier rather than the person who merely has the status of certification-service-provider, the quality of whose processes may play no role in determining whether the verification is accurate.

This leads us to the second technique, which is for the regulation to address human behaviour directly, rather than indirectly by regulating institutions, structures or status. The latter approach contains an implicit assumption that the institution, structure or person of that status actually undertakes the behaviour in question, and thus embeds part of the underlying business model. As we have seen, this assumption is often falsified by changes in business model: Registration Authorities take over functions which in the e-signatures model were performed by certification-service-providers, individual staff members take decisions about personal data processing which the data protection model presumed would be the preserve of the employer, non-financial institutions identify a business case for providing ancillary e-payment services, and so on. Even when business models change the behaviours usually continue, and thus regulating behaviour alone tends towards business model-neutrality.

The third requires regulators to recognise that the behaviours addressed by the regulation may not always be carried out in the manner anticipated in their original business models. A failure to notice this can lead to the unintentional embedding of a business model by limiting the scope of the regulation to those behaviours envisaged in the model. The drafters of the Databases Directive defined 'making' a database in terms of 'obtaining, verification or presentation' of its contents, and therefore granted sui generis protection where there had been a substantial investment in those activities. Had they resisted the temptation to explain 'making' and merely required there to have been a substantial investment in that making … the original intention of the Directive would have been preserved.

Finally, IT regulation should be undertaken at the most general level which is likely to achieve its objectives. The more detail included in regulation about the precise behaviours which are to be regulated, the more likely the regulation is to become outdated. For the same reasons, there is likely to be an inverse relationship between the volume of detail and the regulation's business model-neutrality.

If regulators are able to avoid the problem of embedded business models, are there any other steps that they can take to reduce the risk of disconnection? We can consider three such strategies, namely: intelligent, anticipatory, drafting; an approach that is technologically neutral; and judicial assistance through purposive and flexible interpretation of the regulation.

3 Intelligent (anticipatory) drafting

Regulators are waking up to the fact that sustainability is a problem and there are encouraging signs of imaginative solutions being sought. So, for example, in the House of Commons Science and Technology Select Committee's report on hybrid and chimera embryos,[16] it was suggested that the regulatory agency should be given a broad licensing power to authorise the use of inter-species embryos as research tools but that, if a particularly controversial use or wholly uncontemplated type of embryo were to be proposed, the regulatory framework should 'contain a provision to enable the secretary of state to put a stop to the procedure for a limited period while deciding whether or not to make regulations'.[17] Such an idea contemplates a constructive exercise in joint regulation, with the breadth of the agency's licensing powers being geared for flexibility and connection, and the Secretary of State's stop-and-review powers designed for both clarity and legitimacy.

In the event, this particular suggestion was not taken forward. Nevertheless, the drafters of the Human Fertilisation and Embryology Act 2008 endeavoured to incorporate in the regulatory framework a number of anti-disconnection measures. Most strikingly, section 1(5) of the Act provides for a new inserted sub-section as follows:

> If it appears to the Secretary of State necessary or desirable to do so in the light of developments in science or medicine, regulations may provide that in this Act ... 'embryo', 'eggs', 'sperm' or 'gametes' includes things specified in the regulations which would not otherwise fall within the [relevant] definition.

In addition to the limitations that are specified in the express terms of this regulation-making power, the Act stipulates that regulations 'may not provide for anything containing any nuclear or mitochondrial DNA that is not human to be treated as an embryo or as eggs, sperm or gametes'. In other words, even if it were to appear necessary or desirable to do so, the Secretary of State's powers do not extend to changing the relevant statutory definitions in a way that would encompass hybrid or chimera embryos. A further example of an attempt to maintain connection is found in section 26 of the Act which authorises the

---

[16] House of Commons Science and Technology Select Committee, *Government Proposals for the Regulation of Hybrid and Chimera Embryos* (Fifth Report of Session 2006–7) (HC 272-I, 5 April 2007).

[17] *Ibid.*, at para. 100. Compare, too, Academy of Medical Sciences, *Inter-Species Embryos* (London, July 2007), at 39; and the House of Lords, House of Commons Joint Committee on the Human Tissue and Embryos (Draft) Bill, *Human Tissue and Embryos (Draft) Bill*, HL Paper 169-I, HC Paper 630-I (London: Stationery Office, 1 August 2007), where a regime of 'devolved regulation' is favoured.

making of regulations to cover procedures for mitochondrial donation such that human embryos are created by using genetic material provided by two women. What should we make of such forward-looking measures?

On the face of it, such provisions are a welcome attempt to come to terms with one of the key facts of regulatory life, namely that there will be technological developments that legislatures simply cannot foresee. In the case of the power to broaden the statutory definitions, no attempt is made to second-guess what the nature of the developments in science or medicine might be. We know from recent experience that embryology is a rapidly developing field; but the particular way in which it might develop is less predictable – hence, the absence of any particular triggering circumstances in the terms of the regulation-making powers. By contrast, the powers given by section 26 represent a response to a rather particular technological development, indeed one that has been foreshadowed for some time.

Before we embrace particular measures of this kind, we need to be satisfied on two related matters. First, we need to be confident that the scenarios and powers in question have been fully debated and authorised at the time of enactment – otherwise the advance authorisation will fail to satisfy the criteria of legitimacy. Second, we need to be sure that the scenarios and the scope of the powers are sufficiently clear to enable the debate to be adequately informed – otherwise, a well-intended effort to try to be ahead of the game will prove to be a false regulatory economy. In the light of these provisos, we might have some reservations about the section 1(5) power, certainly more so than with regard to the section 26 power. Granted, the former has been circumscribed so that hybrids and chimeras are excluded; even so, unlike the section 26 power, there is no knowing what kind of developments in science and medicine might prompt the secretary of state to invoke the section 1(5) regulation-making power.

There is no guarantee, of course, that advance measures of this kind will be effective when they are activated. To some extent, it might make a difference whether the purpose of the regulatory intervention is to *prohibit* some conduct or to *permit* it. Consider, for example, clause 65(2) of the (subsequently abandoned) draft Human Tissue and Embryos Bill 2007, a clause that gave the secretary of state prior authorisation to regulate against (i.e. to prohibit) the selling, supplying or advertising of DIY sperm sorting kits (if and when such kits become available). While the joint parliamentary committee that scrutinised the draft Bill expressed sympathy with the intention behind this clause, it judged that the provision would be unenforceable in practice[18] – and the committee might well have been right in its assessment. For, had couples not accepted the legitimacy of this restriction, they might have tried to source the kits on the black market; and we can be fairly confident that they would have been assisted by overseas internet suppliers. This does not mean that activating

---

[18] *Human Tissue and Embryos (Draft) Bill*, HL Paper 169-I, HC Paper 630-I, para. 284.

such regulatory powers will always be a complete waste of time; but regulators should have fairly modest expectations about the likely effectiveness of their intervention.[19] By contrast, where regulation declares some activity (such as egg donation for mitochondrial replacement only) to be *permitted*, then there is perhaps less of an issue about effectiveness – or, at any rate, this is so unless the intention is not merely to permit but to permit *and to promote*. Nevertheless, a permissive provision of this kind might agitate the dignitarians (i.e., those who hold that we have a categorical duty not to act in any way that compromises human dignity);[20] and, although the signals from the appeal courts have hardly given this constituency any encouragement,[21] we should not discount the possibility that the exercise of such new-style powers might be tested through judicial review.[22]

In the field of nanotechnology, as in that of embryology, there is a concern that rapid technological developments might raise questions about the powers of regulators where those powers are tied to particular (rather precisely drawn) legislative definitions. In the following extract, we see this underlying concern in the definitional recommendations made by the House of Lords Science and Technology Committee.

House of Lords Science and Technology Committee Report, *Nanotechnologies and Food*, 1st Report of Session 2009–10, HL Paper 22-I, 8 January 2010, paras. 8.11–8.14

8.11. Given the uncertainty about the potential risks of nanomaterials, it is essential that any nanomaterial used in a food product (with the exceptions set out in paragraph 5.32) should to be subject to a formal risk assessment process through the European Food Safety Authority. We recommend, therefore, that the Government should work within the European Union to promote the amendment of current legislation to ensure that all nanomaterials used in food products, additives or supplements fall within the scope of

---

[19] See Chapter 14; and Roger Brownsword, 'Red Lights and Rogues: Regulating Human Genetics', in Han Somsen (ed.), *The Regulatory Challenge of Biotechnology* (Cheltenham: Edward Elgar, 2007), 39.

[20] See Chapter 8. For discussions of dignitarian thinking, see e.g., Roger Brownsword, 'Bioethics Today, Bioethics Tomorrow: Stem Cell Research and the "Dignitarian Alliance"', *University of Notre Dame Journal of Law, Ethics and Public Policy*, 17 (2003), 15; 'Three bioethical approaches: a triangle to be squared', paper presented at international conference on the patentability of biotechnology organised by the Sasakawa Peace Foundation, Tokyo, September 2004 (available online at www.ipgenethics.org/conference/transcript/session3.doc); 'Stem Cells and Cloning: Where the Regulatory Consensus Fails', *New England Law Review*, 39 (2005), 535; and *Rights, Regulation and the Technological Revolution* (Oxford: Oxford University Press, 2008), esp. ch. 2.

[21] Notably, *R* v. *Secretary of State for Health ex parte Quintavalle (on behalf of Pro-Life Alliance)* [2001] EWHC 918 (Admin.) (Crane J.); [2002] EWCA Civ. 29; [2003] UKHL 13 and *R (Quintavalle on behalf of Comment on Reproductive Ethics)* v. *Human Fertilisation and Embryology Authority* [2002] EWHC 2785 (Admin.); [2003] EWCA 667; [2005] UKHL 28.

[22] By way of comparison, in EU law, there tends to be strict scrutiny and restrictive interpretation of provisions that authorise the Commission to amend legislation in the light of scientific and technical progress: see, e.g., *European Parliament and Denmark* v. *Commission* [2008] ECR-I-1649; and, for comment, see Alexander H. Türk, *Common Market Law Review*, 46 (2009), 1293.

current legislation. We recommend in particular that the legislation should, for the avoidance of uncertainty, include workable definitions of nanomaterials and related concepts (paragraph 5.19). (Recommendation 11)

8.12. We recommend that the Government should work towards ensuring that any regulatory definition of nanomaterials proposed at a European level, in particular in the Novel Foods Regulation, should not include a size limit of 100nm but instead refer to 'the nanoscale' to ensure that all materials with a dimension under 1000nm are considered. A change in functionality, meaning how a substance interacts with the body, should be the factor that distinguishes a nanomaterial from its larger form within the nanoscale (paragraph 5.24). (Recommendation 12)

8.13. We recommend that Government should work within the European Union to clarify the phrase 'properties that are characteristic to the nanoscale' through the inclusion in the Novel Foods Regulation of a more detailed list of what these properties comprise. This list should be regularly reviewed, as the understanding of nanomaterials develops, to ensure it provides comprehensive and up-to-date coverage of relevant properties (paragraph 5.26). (Recommendation 13)

8.14. We recommend that, for regulatory purposes, any definition of 'nanomaterials' should exclude those created from natural food substances, except for nanomaterials that have been deliberately chosen or engineered to take advantage of their nanoscale properties. The fact that they have been chosen for their novel properties indicates that they may pose novel risks (paragraph 5.32). (Recommendation 14)

4 Technological neutrality

In July 1997 the US government published its *Framework for Global Electronic Commerce*, in which it was stated that 'rules should be technology neutral (i.e., the rules should neither require nor assume a particular technology) and forward looking (i.e., the rules should not hinder the use or development of technologies in the future)'. Rapidly, this became a mantra for regulators worldwide. For example, in the Recitals to the proposed EU electronic money Directive,[23] we read that the intention is to introduce 'a technology-neutral legal framework that harmonises the prudential supervision of electronic money institutions'.[24] However, as has been highlighted by both Bert-Jaap Koops[25] and Chris Reed,[26] 'technological neutrality' has several meanings, most of which are not

---

[23] Proposal for a European Parliament and Council Directive on the taking up, the pursuit and the prudential supervision of the business of electronic money institutions, COM(1998)0461 final, OJ C317, 15 October 1998.

[24] *Ibid.*, at 7.

[25] Bert-Jaap Koops, 'Should ICT Regulation be Technology-Neutral?', in Bert-Jaap Koops, Miriam Lips, Corien Prins and Maurice Schellekens (eds.), *Starting Points for ICT Regulation: Deconstructing Prevalent Policy One-Liners* (The Hague: TMC Asser Press, 2006), 77.

[26] Chris Reed, 'Taking Sides on Technology Neutrality', *SCRIPTed*, 4 (2007), 263; and, for a related paper that is valuable in its own right, see Chris Reed, 'Online and Offline Equivalence: Aspiration and Achievement', *International Journal of Law and Information Technology*, 18 (2010), 248.

actually relevant to the question of regulatory connection – for example, a call for 'technological neutrality' might be another way of expressing the demand that the regulation of online transactions and interactions should be equivalent to their off-line correlates; or, that regulation should not directly or indirectly discriminate (unfairly) in favour of one technology (and its commercial stakeholders) over another. If, however, we apply the idea of technology neutrality to a particular regulatory (especially legislative) technique, what might it mean and how far might it respond to the problem of regulatory connection?

The basic idea is that the regulation is drafted in such a way that, given a particular purpose, it does not matter which technological instrument is employed. As Reed explains:[27]

> Some laws and regulations apply in identical ways, whatever the technology. The law of murder is an obvious example. Professor Plum's liability is unaffected by her choice between strangling the victim with the rope in the conservatory or bludgeoning him with the lead pipe in the drawing room. Such laws are *indifferent* to the technology involved, because they apply to behaviour of the actors involved and the effects of that behaviour and not to the means through which the actors behave or by which those effects come about.

Even if the regulation is not indifferent in quite this sweeping way, it might allow for a range of technologies to suffice for a particular purpose (as, say, with various kinds of biometric identifiers). Where the regulation is technology neutral in this way, it is proof against new technologies being developed and applied for the given purpose. However, there is nothing in this that guarantees that the regulation stays connected where it is not the technology that is new but the purposes to which the technology is applied. To maintain connection in such a scenario, the regulators need to aim for purpose neutrality so that it does not matter for which purpose the technology is applied. However, this is a tall order because many regulatory initiatives are defined precisely by the limited range of purposes that they are willing to approve.

5 Purposive interpretation

In two major judicial reviews, the *Pro-Life Alliance* case[28] and *Comment on Reproductive Ethics*[29] (the CORE case, also referred to as *Quintavalle*), the English courts were called upon to rescue a legislative scheme, the Human Fertilisation and Embryology Act 1990, that seemed to be seriously disconnected. In the former, the disconnection arose precisely because the Act had failed to define the key concept of an 'embryo' in a technology-neutral way; and,

---

[27] Reed, 'Taking Sides'.
[28] *R* v. *Secretary of State for Health ex parte Quintavalle (on behalf of Pro-Life Alliance)* [2001] EWHC 918 (Admin.) (Crane J.); [2002] EWCA Civ. 29; [2003] UKHL 13.
[29] *R (Quintavalle on behalf of Comment on Reproductive Ethics)* v. *Human Fertilisation and Embryology Authority* [2002] EWHC 2785 (Admin.); [2003] EWCA 667; [2005] UKHL 28.

in the latter, which was a 'saviour sibling' case, it was the unanticipated application of PGD that caused the disconnection.

In both cases, the High Court took a fairly literal approach, holding that the Act was now disconnected from the technology, only to be reversed by the Court of Appeal; and, in both cases, the House of Lords unanimously affirmed the decisions made by the Court of Appeal. However, the effect of treating the Act as disconnected was not identical in the two cases. In the *Pro-Life Alliance* case, if CNR embryos (that is, embryos developed from egg cells whose nuclear DNA had been replaced) fell outwith the jurisdiction of the regulatory Authority, and if they were not otherwise covered by the Act, then the residual regulatory position seemed to be that research on CNR embryos (including reproductive cloning) was permitted. In the CORE case, if PGD (pre-implantation genetic diagnosis) and PTT (pre-implantation tissue-typing) fell within the jurisdiction of the regulatory Authority but outwith its licensing powers, then such procedures were not permitted. If the result of disconnection in the former case was to generate a moral panic and a rush to prohibition (lest the UK should become a haven for aspiring human reproductive cloners),[30] in the latter it was to generate pressure to permit these newly developed techniques to be applied (lest the life of a young boy should be lost).

In the extract that follows, there is a critical assessment of the way in which, in the *Pro-Life Alliance* case, the House of Lords rewrites the key sections of the Act in order to reconnect it.

Roger Brownsword, *Rights, Regulation and the Technological Revolution* (2008), 169–72 (footnotes omitted)

When the Human Fertilisation and Embryology Act was enacted, the science as it stood encouraged Parliamentarians to make two relevant assumptions. One assumption was that a human embryo would necessarily be the product of a process of fertilisation (of a human egg by human sperm); and the second was that, if there was to be cell nuclear replacement for the purposes of cloning, then it would involve manipulation of an *embryo* (rather than replacement of the nucleus of an *egg*). In line with the first of these assumptions, section 1(1) of the Act provides:
'In this Act, except where otherwise stated –

(a) embryo means a live human embryo where fertilisation is complete, and
(b) references to an embryo include an egg in the process of fertilisation, and, for this purpose, fertilisation is not complete until the appearance of a two cell zygote'.

In line with the second assumption, section 3(3)(d) of the Act provides that no licence may authorise 'replacing a nucleus of a cell of an embryo with a nucleus taken from a cell of any person, embryo or subsequent development of an embryo.'

---

[30] See the Human Reproductive Cloning Act 2001. The Bill was introduced just six days after the High Court decision and it became law about two weeks later.

However, as embryologists developed processes for engineering eggs and then stimulating eggs to divide and develop into embryonic clusters, two nice questions of legal interpretation arose. One question was whether the 1990 Act applied to such embryonic clusters (to what were the functional equivalents of embryos produced by fertilisation); and the other was how the prohibition in section 3(3)(d) related to such developments. In the *Pro-Life Alliance* case, these two questions were put to the test.

At first instance, Crane J, taking a literal approach, held that the Act applied only to human embryos produced by a process involving fertilisation. However, the Court of Appeal and the House of Lords, taking a more purposive approach, arrived at the different view that such embryos, albeit not produced by fertilisation but by CNR and stimulation, fell within the terms of section 1(1). Moreover, it was also the view of the Court of Appeal and the House of Lords that the prohibition against CNR in an embryo, as provided for by section 3(3)(d), did not cover CNR in an egg. This led to the convenient conclusion that the Act did not leave a worrying loophole in relation to human reproductive cloning – although, ironically, by the time that the appeal courts had finally confirmed this, Parliament had rushed through legislation [the Human Reproductive Cloning Act 2001] to create a new criminal offence to cover the maverick cloners.

To deal, first, with the interpretation of section 1(1): in order to achieve a semblance of congruence, the appeal courts effectively read into the definition section the additional phrase '[if it is produced by fertilisation]'. With the benefit of this addition, section 1(1)(a) defined an embryo in terms of 'a live human embryo where [if it is produced by fertilisation] fertilisation is complete.' So transformed, section 1(1) simply specified what counted as an embryo for the purposes of the Act where the embryo in question happened to be the product of fertilisation. However, this was no longer an exhaustive definition; for section 1(1) did not presume to exclude the possibility that an embryo might be produced by some process other than fertilisation – indeed, by just such a process as that of CNR and stimulation that became headline news almost a decade after section 1(1) was drafted. Clearly, such a creative reading of the section is driven by considerations other than the ordinary meaning of the text and the deeper question is whether it is backed by intelligent purposivism.

Delivering the leading judgment, Lord Bingham asserts that the references to fertilisation in section 1(1) cannot have been intended to signal a material distinction between 'live human embryos produced by fertilisation of a female egg and live human embryos produced without such fertilisation'; for, 'Parliament was unaware that the latter alternative was physically possible.' Rather, continues Lord Bingham:

> [t]he crucial point … is that this was an Act passed for the protection of live human embryos created outside the human body. The essential thrust of section 1(1)(a) was directed to such embryos, not the manner of their creation, which Parliament (entirely understandably on the then current state of scientific knowledge) took for granted.

Let us suppose that this is a plausible reconstruction of the regulatory intentions of Parliament – that is to say, let us suppose that it is plausible to treat Parliament as intending to regulate live human embryos, whether such embryos were produced by fertilisation or by some other technique, not yet contemplated and, necessarily, yet to be developed. We might even go as far as Lord Millett and say that any other reading would 'not only defeat the evident purpose of Parliament … but would produce an incoherent and irrational regulatory code.' And, more generally, we might agree that, while such an irrational code 'could be the inevitable result of legislation enacted at the time of rapid technological development, a construction which leads to this result should not be adopted where it can be avoided.'

Fine. But, now, what would such an approach suggest about the application of section 3(3)(d)? Clearly, it implies that no licence may authorise cell nuclear replacement in a human embryo, whether that embryo is produced by sperm-fertilisation of an egg or by a technique other than fertilisation (such as CNR). The question dramatically raised by the *Pro-Life Alliance* case, though, is whether a licence may authorise cell nuclear replacement in a human egg when, as we have just inferred, no licence may authorise cell nuclear replacement in a human embryo that itself has been developed by CNR techniques. If Parliamentarians in 1990 saw fit to prohibit cloning at the embryonic stage, would they not also intend to prohibit cloning at the earlier egg stage? Copying across Lord Bingham's language as applied to section 1(1), we would say that the essential thrust of section 3(3)(d) was directed to cloning, not the particular technique of cloning, which Parliament (entirely understandably on the then current state of scientific knowledge) took for granted as involving *embryonic* manipulation. Yet, quite to the contrary, Lord Bingham reads section 3(3)(d) as having a very restricted ambit, literally to cell nuclear replacement in the human embryo and to nothing else.

The conjunction of the broad approach to section 1(1) with the narrow approach to section 3(3)(d) is highlighted by one of Lord Steyn's remarks on the latter point. Referring back to the similar approach taken by the Court of Appeal, Lord Steyn says:

> The Master of the Rolls observed that he could see no basis for arguing that an unfertilised egg, prior to the insertion of the nucleus by the cell nuclear replacement process, is required to be treated under the Act as if it is an embryo: para. 51. I agree.

However, this only serves to highlight the layering of the interpretive tensions. On a literal reading of the provisions, a CNR embryo is not an embryo produced by fertilisation (so section 1(1) decrees that the Act has no application to CNR embryos); and an egg is not an embryo (so the prohibition in section 3(3)(d) does not apply to CNR manipulation of an egg). The first tension is that it is wholly unclear why the appeal courts adopt the latter literalism but not the former. Why say (literally) that an egg is not an embryo (for the purposes of section 3(3)(d)) but (non-literally) that a stimulated CNR egg can count as an embryo (for the purposes of section 1(1))? A second tension crystallises when we consider how the failure to anticipate developments in embryology impacts on the interpretation. In the one case, Parliamentarians are excused from not anticipating such developments; in the other case they are not. In the one case, the gist of what Parliament intended to cover is relied on; in the other case (the intention to ban cloning), it is not even allowed to make an entry.

[That said] Lord Bingham is right in recognising 'the difficulty of legislating against a background of fast-moving medical and scientific development', and he might have gone on to note the difficulties that are created for the courts when 'Parliament has to frame legislation apt to apply to developments at the advanced cutting edge of science.' Even so, we might wonder whether the courts might rise more convincingly to the challenge of regulatory connection than we find in the *Pro-Life Alliance* appeals.

If the stakes in the *Pro-Life Alliance* case were high, they were even higher in the CORE case because (as the earlier extract from Lord Hoffmann's speech spelled out), young Zain Hashmi's life depended on finding a tissue-compatible donor. In the two extracts that follow, we have, first, the key parts of Lord Hoffmann's reasoning and then a critical assessment of that reasoning.

R (Quintavalle on behalf of Comment on Reproductive Ethics) v. Human Fertilisation and Embryology Authority [2005] UKHL 28 (Lord Hoffmann)

10. In this case we are particularly concerned with the activities which may be authorised to be done in the course of providing treatment services. 'Treatment services' are defined by section 2(1) to mean, among other things, medical services provided to the public for the purpose of assisting women to carry children. IVF is of course such a service; the proposal is to assist Mrs Hashmi to carry a child conceived by the implantation of an IVF embryo. So the question is whether PGD and HLA typing are activities which the authority can authorise to be done 'in the course' of providing her with IVF treatment.

11. To find the answer, one must look at the list of activities in para. 1 of Schedule 2. Para. 1(3) provides that the authority may licence an activity on the list only if it appears to the authority to be 'necessary or desirable for the purpose of providing treatment services'. The activities include:

    '(d) practices designed to secure that embryos are in a suitable condition to be placed in a woman or to determine whether embryos are suitable for that purpose'.

12. The authority's case is that both PGD and HLA typing are to determine whether an embryo would be suitable for the purpose of being placed in Mrs Hashmi. The definition of treatment services focuses upon the woman as the person to whom the services are provided. The authority says that Mrs Hashmi is entitled to regard an embryo as unsuitable unless it is both free of abnormality and tissue compatible with Zain. Without such testing, she cannot make an informed choice as to whether she wants the embryo placed in her body or not. The authority considers it desirable for the purpose of providing her with treatment services, ie IVF treatment, that she should be able to make such a choice. Mr Pannick QC, who appeared for the authority, pointed out that the Act does not require that PGD or HLA typing should *constitute* treatment services. They must be activities *in the course* of such services, ie in the course of providing IVF treatment.

13. The claimant, on the other hand, says that this gives far too wide a meaning to the notion of being suitable. It would enable the authority to authorise a single cell biopsy to test the embryo for whatever characteristics the mother might wish to know: whether the child would be male or female, dark or blonde, perhaps even, in time to come, intelligent or stupid. Suitable must therefore have

a narrower meaning than suitable for that particular mother. Maurice Kay J thought that suitable meant only that the embryo would be viable. That would rule out a good deal of PGD, because many genetic abnormalities do not affect the viability of the foetus. The abnormality manifests itself after birth. Before your Lordships Lord Brennan QC, for the claimant, disavowed so narrow a construction. I think that he was right to do so. The narrower meaning is particularly difficult to support when paragraph 3(2)(e) lists, among the research projects which may be licensed, 'developing methods for detecting the presence of gene or chromosome abnormalities in embryos before implantation'. It would be very odd if Parliament contemplated research to develop techniques which could not lawfully be used. So Lord Brennan accepts that suitable means more than viable. Building on paragraph 3(2)(e), he says that an embryo is suitable if it is capable of becoming a healthy child, free of abnormalities. PGD to establish that the embryo is free from genetic abnormalities is therefore acceptable. But not HLA typing. A baby which is not tissue compatible with Zain would not be in any way abnormal. It just would not answer the particular needs of the Hashmi family.

14. 'Suitable' is one of those adjectives which leaves its content to be determined entirely by context. As my noble and learned friend Lord Scott of Foscote put it in argument, a suitable hat for Royal Ascot is very different from a suitable hat for the Banbury cattle market. The context must be found in the scheme of the 1990 Act and the background against which it was enacted. In particular, one is concerned to discover whether the scheme and background throw light on the question of whether the concept of suitability includes taking into account the particular wishes and needs of the mother. If so, the authority may authorise tests to determine whether the embryo is in that sense suitable for implantation in her womb. It may, but of course it is not obliged to do so. It may consider that allowing the mother to select an embryo on such grounds is undesirable on ethical or other grounds. But the breadth of the concept of suitability is what determines the breadth of the authority's discretion.

[paras. 15–22 omitted]

23. The structure of the 1990 Act reflects the scheme foreshadowed in the White Paper. Section 3(3)(a) prevents, as the Warnock Committee recommended, the development of the foetus in vitro by providing that a licence may not authorise the keeping or use of an embryo after the appearance of the primitive streak. Nor may the authority authorise the placing of an embryo in an animal (subsection (3)(b)) or the cloning of an embryo (subsection (3)(d)). By para. 1(4) of Schedule 2, a licence may not authorise altering the genetic structure of any cell while it forms part of an embryo. These activities are all clearly prohibited. In addition, section 3(3)(c) enables the Secretary of State and Parliament by affirmative resolution to add other activities involving the keeping or using of embryos to the prohibited list.

24. Subject to these prohibitions, the licensing power of the authority is defined in broad terms. Paragraph 1(1) of Schedule 2 enables it to authorise a variety of activities (with the possibility of others being added by regulation) provided only that they are done 'in the course of' providing IVF services to the public and appear to the authority 'necessary or desirable' for the purpose of providing those services. Thus, if the concept of suitability in sub-paragraph (d) of 1(1) is broad enough to include suitability for the purposes of the particular mother, it seems to me clear enough that the activity of determining the genetic characteristics of the embryo by way of PGD or HLA typing would be 'in the course of' providing the mother with IVF services and that the authority would

be entitled to take the view that it was necessary or desirable for the purpose of providing such services.

25. The chief argument of Lord Brennan against interpreting suitability in this sense was that, once one allowed the mother's choice to be a legitimate ground for selection, one could not stop short of allowing it to be based upon such frivolous reasons as eye or hair colour as well as more sinister eugenic practices. It was, he said, inconceivable that Parliament could have contemplated the possibility of this happening.

26. Let it be accepted that a broad interpretation of the concept of suitability would include activities highly unlikely to be acceptable to majority public opinion. It could nevertheless be more sensible for Parliament to confine itself to a few prohibitions which could be clearly defined but otherwise to leave the authority to decide what should be acceptable. The fact that these decisions might raise difficult ethical questions is no objection. The membership of the authority and the proposals of the Warnock Committee and the White Paper make it clear that it was intended to grapple with such issues.

27. In this case, as I have said, Maurice Kay J thought that suitable meant no more than suitable to produce a viable foetus but Lord Brennan, understandably unwilling to argue that Parliament might have outlawed PGD, said that it meant suitable to produce a healthy foetus, free of genetic defects. But this definition is itself not free from difficulty. What amounts to a genetic defect? Marie Stopes, an enthusiastic believer in eugenics, cut off relations with her son because she considered that the woman he chose to marry suffered from a genetic defect: she was short-sighted and had to wear spectacles. Surely it would be more sensible to concentrate on whether choice on such grounds was ethically acceptable rather than to argue over whether it counted as a genetic defect. The great advantage which Parliament would have seen in using broad concepts to define the remit of the authority is that it would avoid sterile arguments over questions of definition and focus attention upon the ethical issues.

28. Even in cases in which one could clearly say that the ground for selection was not a genetic defect, a total prohibition might exclude cases which many people would think ethically acceptable. Mr Pannick drew attention to the facts of *Leeds Teaching Hospitals NHS Trust* v. *A* [2003] 1 FLR 1091. In the course of providing IVF treatment to a husband and wife, the hospital mixed up the sperm provided by the husband with that of another man. As a result, a woman gave birth to twins, the father of whom was a stranger. But they suffered from no genetic defects and Mr Pannick points out that if the muddle had been suspected before implantation of the embryo, Lord Brennan's construction of suitability would have prevented any tests to check the embryo's DNA. Likewise, many people might agree with the authority that the tests proposed to be conducted in the present case would be ethically acceptable. It often seemed that an unstated assumption in Lord Brennan's argument was that the authority was likely to authorise anything that it was not positively prohibited from authorising or that it could not be trusted to make proper ethical distinctions. But these assumptions are in my opinion illegitimate. The authority was specifically created to make ethical distinctions and, if Parliament should consider it to be failing in that task, it has in reserve its regulatory powers under section 3(3)(c).

29. Perhaps the most telling indication that Parliament did not intend to confine the authority's powers to unsuitability on grounds of genetic defects is, as Mance LJ pointed out [2004] QB 168, 209, para. 143, the absence of any reference in the Act to selection on grounds of sex. It could be said that the Act made no reference to HLA typing because neither the Warnock Committee nor Parliament

in 1990 foresaw it as a possibility. But there was intense discussion, both in the report and in Parliament, about selection for sex on social grounds. If ever there was a dog which did not bark in the night, this was it. It is hard to imagine that the reason why the Act said nothing on the subject was because Parliament thought it was clearly prohibited by the use of the word 'suitable' or because it wanted to leave the question over for later primary legislation. In my opinion the only reasonable inference is that Parliament intended to leave the matter to the authority to decide. And once one says that the concept of suitability can include gender selection on social grounds, it is impossible to say that selection on the grounds of any other characteristics which the mother might desire was positively excluded from the discretion of the authority, however unlikely it might be that the authority would actually allow selection on that ground.

[paras. 30–4 omitted]

35. I would therefore accept Mr Pannick's argument and hold that both PGD and HLA typing could lawfully be authorised by the authority as activities to determine the suitability of the embryo for implantation within the meaning of paragraph 1(1)(d).

Brownsword, *Rights*, 177–80 (footnotes omitted)

In argument before the House, the critical interpretive question becomes what one makes of Schedule 2, paragraph 1 of the 1990 Act when it provides that, in the course of providing treatment services (treatment services being equated, broadly speaking, with medical services that are designed to assist women to carry children), the Authority may license '(d) practices designed to secure that embryos are in a suitable condition to be placed in a woman or to determine whether embryos are suitable for that purpose.' This opaque drafting invites the following two questions:

(i) in what sense might reproductive service providers be checking to ensure that an embryo is 'in a suitable condition' for implantation; and

(ii) in what sense might reproductive service providers be checking to determine whether an embryo is, in the statutory language, 'suitable for that purpose'?

The answer to the first question is tolerably clear. Or, at any rate, it is not difficult to think of activities that fit the statutory description – for example, checking the condition of an embryo that, having been frozen and stored, is now unfrozen with a view to implantation. However, the answer to the second question is much less clear. Assuming that the activity is not concerned with checking the condition of the embryo, it seems that the check here is, as it were, for fitness for purpose rather than as to basic implantable quality. But, the fundamental question remains: relative to which or whose purposes is an embryo to be judged fit – or, to which or whose purpose does the phrase 'that purpose' refer?

In response to this question, both the Court of Appeal and the House of Lords took the relevant reference point to be that of the woman to whom treatment services are being supplied. In other words, it is *the particular reproductive purposes of the particular client woman* that are treated as the governing reference point. On this view, the range of licensable activities covers checking the suitability of the embryo relative to the particular purposes (*whatever those purposes*) of the particular woman in question. How did the House account for this quite extraordinary reading of the legislation?

The central feature of Lord Hoffmann's leading speech (supported by Lord Brown) is to make and to reiterate the point that the word 'suitable' is an adjective that is context-sensitive, that it 'is an empty vessel which is filled with meaning by context and background.' So, for instance, as Lord Scott apparently put it in argument, 'a suitable hat for Royal Ascot is different from a suitable hat for the Banbury cattle market.' No doubt, this is the case. However, it is not the word 'suitable' that is the key to cracking the legislative code. Rather, the key is the phrase 'that purpose'. *If* 'that purpose' translates as 'whatever reproductive purpose the particular woman specifies' then suitability is indeed an empty vessel waiting to be filled by the particular context and background – namely, the particular context and background supplied by the particular reproductive purposes declared by the particular woman; and it might well be the case that the racing aristocracy at Ascot might have rather different criteria of suitability (both in relation to their hats and their offspring) from the country folk in Banbury let alone the Hashmis from Leeds. On the other hand, if 'that purpose' refers generically to assisting women to have children (or healthy children), the context and background for suitability is already set; and for the women of Ascot, Banbury and Leeds alike, the criteria are the same. It follows that the judgment handed down by the House passes legal muster only if it convincingly explains why 'that purpose' is to be read in the former (woman specific) rather than the latter (generic) way. Effectively, three arguments are directed against the latter interpretation.

First, once it is conceded that the Authority may license PGD not only to check the viability of an embryo (as Maurice Kay J held) but also to check its health prospects (as the challengers eventually conceded), it would be difficult to draw a line between those serious conditions for which PGD may be authorised and those less serious conditions that would fall beyond the Authority's licensing remit. Echoing Lord Hoffmann's reservations, Lord Brown says:

> The fact is that once the concession is made ... that PGD itself is licensable to produce not just a viable foetus but a genetically healthy child, there can be no logical basis for construing the authority's power to end at this point. PGD with a view to producing a healthy child assists a woman to carry a child only in the sense that it helps her decide whether the embryo is 'suitable' and whether she will bear the child.

But, to the contrary, once the concession is made, while there is a margin of interpretive doubt about the bounds of health (as in a healthy child), this does not entail that a generic reading of 'that purpose' must be abandoned. What this concession signifies is simply that the terms of the generic reading must be qualified so that the purpose in question is not simply to help women to have children but to do so in a way that avoids implanting an embryo that carries a serious disease. As Lord Brown said when rehearsing the gist of the challenge, '[i]t is one thing to enable a woman to conceive and bear a child which will itself be free of genetic abnormality; quite another to bear a child specifically selected for the purpose of treating someone else'. And, similarly, it is one thing to modify the generic purpose as indicated and quite another to claim that this entails accepting that the governing purpose is supplied by whatever particular purpose the particular woman specifies.

Secondly, if the only purpose for which embryos may be screened is to avoid an implantation that cannot result in the birth of a genetically healthy child, then this would seem to mean that it would not be lawful for the Authority to license PGD to check an embryo where a mix up of some sort is suspected. However, there is nothing in this point. If it is agreed that the legislation must allow for PGD to be used to confirm that the embryo to be implanted is that of the couple in question then it is easy enough to modify the generic purpose. To read 'that purpose' as covering such cases in no way assists the argument that 'that purpose' hinges on the particular reproductive purposes of the particular woman.

Thirdly, Lord Hoffmann argues that the absence from the legislation of any reference to the use of PGD for sex selection is a telling indicator of the legislative intention to confer upon the Authority very broad licensing powers. 'It is hard to imagine', suggests Lord Hoffmann, 'that the reason why the Act said nothing on the subject was because Parliament thought it was clearly prohibited by the use of the word 'suitable' or because it wanted to leave the question over for later primary legislation.' Indeed, this is so: it surely is implausible to suppose that Parliament thought that the word 'suitable' would signal that PGD for sex selection was prohibited. However, it is entirely plausible to suppose that Parliament thought that 'that purpose', by referring back to the general generic objectives of the legislation, signalled that PGD for sex selection was off limits. On this analysis, the regulatory tilt is against conferring this discretion on the Authority; and, if PGD for sex selection is to be licensable, it needs to be explicitly so declared by Parliament.

Whatever we make of the merits of their Lordships' reasoning, the upshot of their decision, as Lord Hoffmann freely admits, is that the legislative scheme is to be understood as conferring on the Authority a much wider licensing remit than previously appreciated. As the challengers put it, and as Lord Hoffmann accepted, 'once one allowed the mother's choice to be a legitimate ground for selection, one could not stop short of allowing it to be based upon such frivolous reasons as eye or hair colour as well as more sinister eugenic practices'. Yet, the House was not deterred. If particular women came along with preposterous reproductive purposes, the Authority would be expected not to license such activities; and, failing that, the Secretary of State would intervene by invoking the regulatory powers reserved under section 3(3)(c) of the Act.

What *Quintavalle* boils down to, therefore, is a choice between two institutional designs. One design is that favoured by the House, under which the Authority has a broad discretion to deal with a wide range of controversial reproductive choices subject to Parliamentary reserve powers; the other design is one that confers upon the Authority a limited licensing discretion with Parliament having to expressly authorise each significant extension of the Authority's remit. The House does not take us into the kind of debate that might stake out the relevant considerations that bear on making a rational choice between these alternatives. If it were not for the fact that the Government cut across the process by reviewing the legislation and bringing forward proposals that are relatively restrictive in relation to the use of PGD, we might have thought that *Quintavalle* presaged a period during which the Authority would be invited to flex its full licensing powers.

6 Conclusion

Where a regulatory framework becomes disconnected, there is no denying that this might be undesirable relative to considerations of regulatory effectiveness and/or regulatory economy. With regard to the former (regulatory effectiveness) the problem is that, once regulation becomes disconnected, regulatees cannot be quite sure where they stand – and this will create difficulties irrespective of whether the regulatory environment is intended to support and promote certain activities (for example, human embryonic stem cell research) or to prohibit them (for example, human reproductive cloning). With regard to regulatory economy, the point is that, where regulation becomes formally disconnected, it is wasteful to expend either legislative or judicial resources simply to declare, albeit expressly and for the avoidance of doubt, that the regulatory position is as it was clearly intended to be. That said, we should not assume that (*ex post*) regulatory disconnection is necessarily and inevitably a bad thing and that, when it happens, every effort should be made to close the gap. Sometimes, in the interests of regulatory legitimacy and democracy, it is important to take time out to debate the developments that have taken place and to determine how the regulatory framework should be adjusted.

In the larger picture, two things are clear: first, the challenge of connection characteristically arises where first generation normative regulatory approaches are employed; and, second, the problem is more acute in Type 1 than in Type 2 regulatory environments (where it is easier to make ongoing adjustments to the regulatory framework). As second and third generation approaches evolve, the regulatory environment becomes a very different place. There is no longer a gap between regulatory norms and regulatee actions; provided that the design is reliable, compliance is warranted. Effectiveness and connection become problems of another era. However, the movement from law and norms to designs and codes is not wholly unproblematic. Crucially, where the regulatory environment moves in this direction, there are questions about the fate of moral communities, about agents and autonomy, and about what happens to the rule of law and its virtues. In such technologically controlled environments, the challenge of regulatory legitimacy assumes new dimensions; and it is to questions of this kind that we turn in our concluding chapter.

Concluding overview

17

From law to code: the surveillance society and *Marper* revisited

1 Introduction

In Chapter 4, we reviewed the *Case of S. and Marper* v. *The United Kingdom*,[1] the leading case in Europe on the taking (and retention) of DNA samples and the banking of DNA profiles for criminal justice purposes. The main point at issue, it will be recalled, was whether the authorising legislative provisions were compatible with the UK's Convention commitments, particularly whether they were compatible with the privacy right protected under Article 8 of the ECHR. The view of the Grand Chamber in Strasbourg was that the legal provisions were far too wide and disproportionate in their impact on privacy. But, this, of course, was not the end of the matter. How did the UK react to the Strasbourg ruling?

The story after *Marper* can be told quite shortly.[2] Predictably, the Labour administration did not welcome this setback to what it regarded as its flagship criminal justice strategy and it made little secret that it would not rush to implement the Strasbourg ruling. Moreover, there were indications that, when UK law was revised, it would be with a view to adopting no more than a minimally compliant position. There was a period of consultation before proposals (including, perhaps surprisingly, the destruction of all samples that were taken from persons who were not convicted) were published. However, before the new legislative provisions were put into effect, there was a general election, following which a new (Conservative–Liberal Democrat) coalition government took office. The new administration took a rather different view to its predecessor, announcing that it would fully implement the Strasbourg ruling. At the same time, it declared that it would address concerns about the spread of CCTV surveillance. These significant attempts to control the tide of regulatory technologies are set out in the coalition's Protection of Freedoms Act 2012.[3]

---

[1] (2009) 48 EHRR 50. For the domestic UK proceedings, see [2002] EWCA Civ. 1275 (Court of Appeal), and [2004] UKHL 39 (House of Lords).

[2] For a full account, see the joined appeals in *R (on the application of GC) (FC)* v. *Commissioner of Police of the Metropolis*, and *R (on the application of C) (FC)* v. *Commissioner of Police of the Metropolis* [2011] UKSC 21, Lord Dyson, at paras. 7–11.

[3] However, there might yet be some devil in the regulatory detail, the profiles of innocent persons apparently still being retained albeit in an anonymised form (such that the profiles could only be

In this final chapter, we broach four large issues, each of which questions the legitimacy of the turn to emerging technologies as regulatory instruments. As a set, these issues invite reflection on the moral limits that should be imposed on such regulatory reliance, on the impact of such technological instruments on moral community, and on the prospects for law itself. The first issue focuses on the principles for legitimate uses of DNA in law enforcement as advocated by Sheldon Krimsky and Tania Simoncelli.[4] Second, we review the post-*Marper* judicial attitudes to the acceptable limits of the use of surveillance technologies. Here, we focus on the Court of Appeal's thinking in *Wood* v. *Commissioner of Police for the Metropolis*.[5] Third, we present some reflections on, so to speak, the changing complexion of the regulatory environment when technologies are deployed as various kinds of regulatory tools. In particular, we are interested in the way in which moral signals (and, concomitantly, moral reasons for compliance) can be superseded, first, by amplified prudential signals (by signals that appeal to self-interested reasons for compliance) and then by non-normative technological management. It is easy to overlook the potential significance of such changes but Beatrice von Silva-Tarouca Larsen[6] has put her finger on precisely this point, saying:

> Another reason speaks against pervasive recording in public space as a strategy for crime prevention. Increasing the threat of punishment does not deprive punishment of its moral message, and highlighting the detection risk of offending does not have to dilute the deontological condemnation expressed in punishment. *Nevertheless, one should not rule out the possibility that an over-reliance on CCTV, with its emphasis on the instrumental appeal to desist from crime in order to avoid paying the cost, might entail a dilution of the moral reasons for desistence.* This could become a problem, for it is not possible to record and monitor people all the time. It is important that policy makers realise that CCTV can only ever be a small part of the solution for enforcing the criminal law, and that instrumental obedience is no substitute for moral endorsement of criminal prohibitions. Strengthening, communicating and convincing people of the normative reasons for desistence should always remain a priority.[7]

Finally, we take up the question of how the virtues of legality might be retained when regulators resort to design (that is, when we are acting in what we have previously called second and third generation regulatory environments).[8]

---

reidentified by processes that would involve a breach of data protection law): see www.telegraph.co.uk/news/uknews/law-and-order/8660821/Innocent-peoples-D (last accessed 11 August 2011).

[4] Sheldon Krimsky and Tania Simoncelli, *Genetic Justice* (New York: Columbia University Press, 2011), ch. 18.

[5] [2009] EWCA Civ. 414.

[6] Beatrice von Silva-Tarouca Larsen, *Setting the Watch: Privacy and the Ethics of CCTV Surveillance* (Oxford: Hart, 2011).

[7] *Ibid.*, at 153–4 (emphasis ours).

[8] See Chapter 2.

2 Fair and responsible use of biometric data

In the UK, the effect of the Protection of Freedoms Act 2012 is to follow the guidance from Strasbourg and restore proportionality to the legal provisions that authorise the retention of DNA profiles. Broadly speaking, under the new legislative scheme, the DNA profiles (and fingerprints) that have been taken from persons who have been arrested for a minor offence will be destroyed following either a decision not to charge or following an acquittal. Where a person is charged in connection with a serious offence but not then convicted, the DNA profiles (and fingerprints) may be retained for three years. For the most part, then, the retention of DNA profiles (and fingerprints) will be restricted to cases where there has been a conviction.

Although we might say that, relative to European human rights standards, the UK's reliance on DNA evidence has been brought back into line, the burgeoning use of DNA is an international phenomenon. For example, in the United States, the FBI-coordinated database holds more than 8 million profiles. Typically, such databases have grown without any clear overarching principles for the fair and responsible collection, retention and use of DNA evidence. In an attempt to rectify this position, Sheldon Krimsky and Tania Simoncelli[9] advance a set of ten axioms (or guiding principles) that 'seek to balance the concept of justice for victims of crime with the ideals of justice for the presumed innocent and convicted felons who seek to prove "actual innocence" through postconviction DNA testing'.[10] Moreover, these axioms strive 'to bring the medical and forensic systems into greater concordance by adopting the principle that all people have an expectation of privacy in their genetic information'.[11] The ten principles are as follows:[12]

1 Genetic information collected in the law-enforcement context should be protected in a manner that is consistent with the protection afforded to medical information.
2 People have an expectation of privacy in the informational content of their DNA regardless of where it has been obtained or acquired (on their person, shed, within medical records).
3 People have a prima facie but not fundamental right to withhold their identity.
4 The taking of DNA constitutes a search. Therefore, in order for the police to forcibly collect DNA from an individual suspected of a crime, they must have a warrant supported by probable cause.
5 DNA data banks should be limited to DNA profiles from persons who are convicted of felonies.
6 Written informed-consent procedures and proper protections against coercion should be in place for warrantless searches of nonsuspect DNA samples when police engage in voluntary DNA dragnets.

---

[9] Sheldon Krimsky and Tania Simoncelli, *Genetic Justice* (New York: Columbia University Press, 2011).
[10] *Ibid.*, at 330. [11] *Ibid.* [12] *Ibid.*, at 330–5.

7 Police seeking to acquire and analyse the DNA of family members of an individual identified through a partial match must obtain a warrant.
8 Surreptitious taking, testing, or storing of DNA from suspects or their relatives is a violation of a person's privacy and should be prohibited.
9 The analysis of crime-scene DNA should be limited to identity and to those externally perceptible traits whose DNA markers have been scientifically validated.
10 Offender or suspect biological samples should be destroyed after DNA profiling so that the encoded information cannot be accessed for information beyond the DNA profile.

Such protective principles, albeit inviting some interpretation, fit nicely with the thinking that underlies human rights instruments and a charter of this kind would make a significant contribution to the regulatory environment. We should not forget, however, that it is not only the use of DNA evidence that puts the privacy of citizens at risk, it is also the burgeoning technology of surveillance. If potential crime scenes are under constant surveillance, individuals who pass by might well be recognised quite independently of analysing their DNA traces. Accordingly, in the next part of the chapter, we turn to the larger impact of *Marper*, specifically to matters of surveillance.[13]

3 Surveillance

The UK coalition government's Protection of Freedom Act 2012 is not concerned simply to rebalance the legal position in relation to the use of DNA evidence. It also makes provision to increase the protection of citizens against overbearing surveillance technologies such as CCTV and ANPR. Accordingly, the Secretary of State is required to publish a code of practice in respect of the development and use of surveillance camera systems; and there is to be a surveillance camera commissioner who will be responsible for monitoring the operation of the code.

In the courts, too, there are already signs that the impact of *Marper* has gone beyond DNA databases to embrace questions of surveillance. We see this in the case of *Wood* v. *Commissioner of Police for the Metropolis*,[14] where the Court of Appeal, guided by the approach set out in *Marper*, took an altogether tougher line in determining the proportionality of police action in interfering with the claimant's privacy right.

Stated shortly, in *Wood*, the claimant complained that, in April 2005, the police had taken and retained photographs of him as he was leaving Reed Elsevier plc's annual general meeting (AGM) in London. The claimant, who was employed by a group that campaigned against the arms trade (CAAT), had

---

[13] Compare, Ian Brown, 'Communications Data Retention in an Evolving Internet', *International Journal of Law and Information Technology*, 19 (2011), 95.
[14] [2009] EWCA Civ. 414.

attended the AGM in order to find out more about Reed's indirect involvement in the arms trade (one of Reed's subsidiary companies organised trade fairs for various industries, including the arms industry). The claimant had no criminal convictions; he had never been arrested; and he had committed no offences at the AGM. As the claimant walked away from the AGM, he was followed by a number of police officers who sought to establish his identity. The central question was whether the actions of the police, in taking and retaining the photographs, violated the claimant's right to privacy under Article 8 of the ECHR.

At first, instance, McCombe J. dismissed the application for judicial review of the police actions.[15] However, on appeal, the majority of the Court of Appeal held (a) (unanimously) that the police actions engaged the claimant's privacy right and (b) (by a majority: Dyson LJ and Lord Collins, with Laws LJ dissenting) that the retention of the photographs could not be justified under Article 8(2) because, on the facts, this was not a proportionate action. Accordingly, the appeal was allowed.

In the extract that follows, we start with that part of Laws LJ's judgment (Dyson LJ and Lord Collins agreeing with this part) that deals with the question of whether the taking and retaining of photographs of a person in a public place engages the privacy right under Article 8(1). Then, we set out the judgments of the majority, in which the question is whether the police actions were proportionate relative to the privacy interest.

Wood v. *Commissioner of Police for the Metropolis* [2009] EWCA Civ. 414

(1) Is Article 8(1) engaged?

JUSTICE LAWS:

INTRODUCTION

ARTICLE 8

15. The principal issue in the case as the argument has developed is whether the appellant's right to respect for his private life, guaranteed by ECHR Article 8, was violated by the police taking and retaining photographs of him on 27 April 2005.

(1) The Scope of Article 8

16.   Article 8 is one of the provisions of the ECHR most frequently resorted to in our courts since the HRA came into force. It falls to be considered most often in immigration cases, where the nature of the actual or putative interference with private and family life is plain enough: the claimant complains that if he is removed or deported he will be separated from family members, often a spouse and children, settled in the United Kingdom. In this present case, however, the nature of the claimed interference is more elusive. So is the nature of the private or family life interest which is said to be assaulted. It is useful therefore

---

[15] [2008] EWHC Admin. 1105.

to have in mind the many facets of the Article 8 right acknowledged by the European Court of Human Rights, and – if it can be ascertained – what it is that links them.

17. The leading case of *Von Hannover* v. *Germany* (2005) 40 EHRR 1 concerned the publication of photographs of Princess Caroline of Monaco engaged in various everyday activities such as horse riding, shopping, dining in a restaurant with a companion, on a skiing holiday, leaving her Paris home with her husband and tripping over an obstacle at a private beach club in Monaco. The Strasbourg court held that there had been a violation of Article 8, even though all the photographs were taken when the Princess was in a public place except those, taken at long range, when she was at the private beach club. I should cite the following passages from the judgment …

[para. 18 summarising and quoting from *Marper* v. *UK* omitted]

19. These and other cases show that the content of the phrase 'private and family life' is very broad indeed. Looking only at the words of the Article, one might have supposed that the essence of the right was the protection of close personal relationships. While that remains a core instance, and perhaps the paradigm case of the right, the jurisprudence has accepted many other facets; so many that any attempt to encapsulate the right's scope in a single idea can only be undertaken at a level of considerable abstraction. But it is an endeavour worth pursuing, since we need if possible to be armed at least with a sense of direction when it comes to disputed cases at the margin.

20. The phrase 'physical and psychological integrity' of a person (*Von Hannover* paragraph 50, *Marper* paragraph 66) is with respect helpful. So is the person's 'physical and social identity' (*Marper* paragraph 66 and other references there given). These expressions reflect what seems to me to be the central value protected by the right. I would describe it as the personal autonomy of every individual. I claim no originality for this description. In *Murray* v. *Big Pictures (UK) Ltd* [2008] EWCA Civ. 446 Sir Anthony Clarke MR, giving the judgment of the court, referred at paragraph 31 to Lord Hoffmann's emphasis, at paragraph 51 of *Campbell* v. *MGN Ltd* [2004] 2 AC 457, upon the fact that 'the law now focuses upon the protection of human autonomy and dignity – "the right to control the dissemination of information about one's private life and the right to the esteem and respect of other people"'.

21. The notion of the personal autonomy of every individual marches with the presumption of liberty enjoyed in a free polity: a presumption which consists in the principle that every interference with the freedom of the individual stands in need of objective justification. Applied to the myriad instances recognised in the Article 8 jurisprudence, this presumption means that, subject to the qualifications I shall shortly describe, an individual's personal autonomy makes him – should make him – master of all those facts about his own identity, such as his name, health, sexuality, ethnicity, his own image, of which the cases speak; and also of the 'zone of interaction' (*Von Hannover* paragraph 50) between himself and others. He is the presumed owner of these aspects of his own self; his control of them can only be loosened, abrogated, if the State shows an objective justification for doing so.

22. This cluster of values, summarised as the personal autonomy of every individual and taking concrete form as a presumption against interference with the individual's liberty, is a defining characteristic of a free society. We therefore need to preserve it even in little cases. At the same time it is important that this core right protected by Article 8, however protean, should not be read so widely that its claims become unreal and unreasonable. For this purpose I think

there are three safeguards, or qualifications. First, the alleged threat or assault to the individual's personal autonomy must (if Article 8 is to be engaged) attain 'a certain level of seriousness'. Secondly, the touchstone for Article 8(1)'s engagement is whether the claimant enjoys on the facts a 'reasonable expectation of privacy' (in any of the senses of privacy accepted in the cases). Absent such an expectation, there is no relevant interference with personal autonomy. Thirdly, the breadth of Article 8(1) may in many instances be greatly curtailed by the scope of the justifications available to the State pursuant to Article 8(2). I shall say a little in turn about these three antidotes to the overblown use of Article 8.

[paras. 23–8 omitted]

(2) Article 8(1) – Was There a Prima Facie Violation?

29. Against that background I turn to the issues in this appeal. It is useful first to refer to the respondent Commissioner's case. Mr Grodzinski on his behalf contends that the actions of the police in taking and retaining the pictures did not touch the appellant's right under Article 8: there was no *prima facie* violation of Article 8(1), and therefore nothing for the respondent to justify by reference to any of the considerations set out in Article 8(2). In the course of his submissions he drew a distinction between the *taking* of the photographs and the *retention* of the images. His case is that neither involved any *prima facie* violation of Article 8(1). The learned judge below agreed. Although for reasons I shall explain I consider that this distinction is in the end unhelpful (at least in the present case) for the purpose of ascertaining the reach of the Convention right, it is nevertheless convenient first to consider whether Article 8(1) was engaged by the mere taking of the photographs.

(2a) Is Article 8(1) Engaged by the Mere Taking of the Photographs?

30. Mr Grodzinski supports his position as regards the taking of the photographs principally by reference to two propositions given by the authorities, one broad, the other narrow. I have already introduced the broad proposition. It recalls that the ECHR is concerned with the protection of fundamental rights and freedoms; and is to the effect that the facts said to constitute an interference with the right guaranteed by Article 8 must attain 'a certain level of seriousness'. This is supported by a wealth of authority; Mr Grodzinski cites *R (Gillan)* v. *Commissioner of Police for the Metropolis* [2006] 2 AC 307, *per* Lord Bingham of Cornhill at paragraph 28, a passage which I have set out above at paragraph 22.

31. I have also foreshadowed the second, and narrower, proposition advanced by Mr Grodzinski. It is that ordinarily the taking of photographs in a public street involves no element of interference with anyone's private life and therefore will not engage Article 8(1), although the later publication of such photographs may be a different matter. Here I should again cite *Campbell* v. *MGN Ltd*. The facts in barest outline were that a well-known fashion model was photographed in a public street leaving a narcotic addiction therapy session, and the photographs (or some of them) were later published. The House of Lords was divided as to the outcome of Miss Campbell's privacy/confidence claim, albeit on a very narrow aspect of the case …

32. In the present case there was, of course, no question of the photographs being published. Mr Grodzinski says there are no aspects of the facts that could elevate the case to 'a certain level of seriousness': the fact that more than one

430   Law and the technologies of the twenty-first century

picture was taken, or that the police followed the appellant down Duke St, cannot suffice. He submits that in the end this is no more than an instance of photographs being taken in a public street and there can be no Article 8 complaint.

33. It is clear that the real vice in *Campbell* (and also *Von Hannover* and *Big Pictures*, which concerned the covert photographing of a well known author, J K Rowling, her husband and young child in a public street in Edinburgh) was the fact or threat of publication in the media, and not just the snapping of the shutter. Can Mr Westgate for the appellant sustain a claim that the mere taking of the pictures, irrespective of the use made of them (a claim he vigorously pursued), engages Article 8(1)?

34. I would certainly acknowledge that the circumstances in which a photograph is taken in a public place may of themselves turn the event into one in which Article 8 is not merely engaged but grossly violated. The act of taking the picture, or more likely pictures, may be intrusive or even violent, conducted by means of hot pursuit, face-to-face confrontation, pushing, shoving, bright lights, barging into the affected person's home. The subject of the photographers' interest – in the case I am contemplating, there will usually be a bevy of picture-takers – may be seriously harassed and perhaps assaulted. He or she may certainly feel frightened and distressed. Conduct of this kind is simply brutal. It may well attract other remedies, civil or criminal, under our domestic law. It would plainly violate Article 8(1), and I can see no public interest justification for it under Article 8(2). But scenarios of that kind are very far from this case. I accept Mr Grodzinski's submission that the fact that more than one picture was taken, or that the police followed the appellant down Duke St, cannot turn this episode into anything remotely so objectionable.

35. The core of Mr Westgate's case is however that it was the police – and thus the State – who took the pictures. As I have stated (paragraph 28), the paradigm case of Article 8's application is where the putative violation is by the State. Can that make all the difference, simply as regards the taking of the photographs and nothing more? In my judgment it cannot. It is no surprise that the *mere taking* of someone's photograph in a public street has been consistently held to be no interference with privacy. The snapping of the shutter of itself breaches no rights, unless something more is added.

36. Accordingly I conclude that the bare act of taking the pictures, by whoever done, is not of itself capable of engaging Article 8(1) unless there are aggravating circumstances. I have already referred (paragraph 34) to the case where the subject of the photographer's attention is harassed and hounded, and perhaps assaulted. As I have said that is plainly not this case. And as for this particular case, I have already rejected (again paragraph 34) the suggestion that the fact that more than one picture was taken, or that the police followed the appellant down Duke St, could give rise to a *prima facie* violation of the Article. I would add that notwithstanding the appellant's apprehensions, there is in my view every reason to accept Mr Williams' evidence that he was generally at pains 'to keep a safe distance from the subject and try not to invade their "personal space"', for reasons he gives at paragraph 5 of his statement. It is also obvious that the new material I have described, based on Superintendent Hartshorn's interview, cannot advance the case as regards the bare act of taking the pictures.

37. I should note that Mr Westgate also submits, somewhat more generally, that the use of overt photography by the police has actually become an intimidating feature of London life. He relies on a second witness statement from Mr Gask,

an employee of Liberty, for whose introduction in evidence we gave permission at the hearing. Mr Gask gives particulars of three press publications on the subject. One of these (the Guardian, 30 May 2008) describes an operation by Essex police involving intensive surveillance of youths (including repeated photography) in a bid to curb anti-social behaviour; an operation which was welcomed by some very muscular observations by the Secretary of State. In my view all this puts the matter far too high. None of Mr Gask's instances suggests, far less demonstrates, that the snapping of the shutter by the police in a public place is capable without more of engaging Article 8(1), or that the facts of this case (so far as they concern only the taking of the pictures) do so.

38. The real issue is whether the taking of the pictures, along with their actual and/or apprehended use, might amount to a violation.

(2b) Article 8(1): The Taking of the Photographs and their Use

39. It might be thought that if (as I would hold) the mere taking of the pictures does not engage Article 8(1), there follows a wholly separate question: whether their retention and intended use might do so. But I do not think this is the right way to analyse the case. I stated earlier (paragraph 29) that the supposed distinction between the taking of the photographs and the retention of the images is in the end unhelpful for the purpose of ascertaining the reach of the Article 8 right. We have seen that the respondent's policy is that 'cameras are deployed overtly … officers should clearly identify themselves as police officers or police staff and not hide the fact that they are filming'. This is certainly as it should be; if it were done covertly, there would be other very substantial arguments to consider which in this case do not arise. As it is, the subject – here, the appellant – observes who is taking his picture and knows it is a police photographer. He is bound to assume that the picture will be kept, and that it will, or at least might, be used for a police purpose. Mr Grodzinski submitted that if the taking of the pictures is not itself any interference with the appellant's Article 8(1) right, it cannot become so by reason of the pictures' potential use; but this I think is too simplistic. The subject's complaint – absent any question of intimidation or harassment – is that his image is being recorded by State authorities, an act to which he does not consent, which he believes to be unjustified, and whose precise purpose is unknown to him. The police operation, from the taking of the pictures to their actual and intended retention and use, must in my opinion be judged as a whole. Accordingly I am inclined to agree with Mr Westgate's submission recorded by the learned judge below as follows:

> 24 … It is impossible … to 'compartmentalise' the taking of the photographs without regard to the circumstances in which they were taken, the purposes of their retention, whether, for example, it is intended thereby to identify the individual and whether there is proper and certain legal control over the photography as a whole. He submits that here the Claimant's identity was discovered and there was a degree of systematic gathering of information about CAAT activity and its members. He pointed also to evidence from the Claimant's solicitor of other occasions when members of CAAT have been similarly photographed.'

[paras. 40–4 referring to two decisions of the Strasbourg Commission omitted]

42. What, then, of the Article 8(1) issue on the facts of the present case? In his first witness statement the appellant says:

> 9 … I was … confused as to why this was happening to me, as I knew I had not done anything wrong …

11. I felt threatened and uncomfortable throughout this. At no point would any of the officers explain why we were being photographed or questioned. It was my unease at this and my knowledge that I had not done anything wrong which meant that I chose not to give them my identity …

…

15. The knowledge that I have nothing to hide in terms of my own actions does not make this situation any easier for me. Instead it makes me more anxious that the photographs were taken when there did not seem to be any reasonable explanation as to why there was a need to do so.

16. I feel that I do not know how any information might be used by the police in the future, and that I had no control over the photographs being taken. I feel very uncomfortable that the information might be kept on my file by police indefinitely …

43. The appellant has not been cross-examined, and his witness statement has of course been crafted, perfectly properly, by his solicitor. But the essential point being made is clearly right: he found himself being photographed by the police, and he could not and did not know why they were doing it and what use they might make of the pictures. The case is in my judgment quite different from *X v. UK*, in which the photographs were taken on and after the applicant's arrest, when the police might well have been expected to do just that. It is possibly closer to *Friedl*, but in that case there had been a demonstration – a sit-in – where again the taking of police photographs could readily have been expected. In *R (Gillan)* v. *Commissioner of Police for the Metropolis*, which I have cited at paragraph 23, Lord Bingham referred to 'an ordinary superficial search of the person and an opening of bags, of the kind to which passengers uncomplainingly submit at airports': another instance in which the putative violation of Article 8 (if any violation were suggested) consists in something familiar and expected. In cases of that kind, where the police or other public authority are acting just as the public would expect them to act, it would ordinarily no doubt be artificial and unreal for the courts to find a *prima facie* breach of Article 8 and call on the State to justify the action taken by reference to Article 8(2).

44. I do not of course suggest that there is a rigid class of case in which, once it is shown that the State actions complained of (such as taking photographs) are expected and unsurprising, Article 8 cannot be engaged; nor likewise that where they are surprising and unexpected, Article 8 will necessarily be applicable. The Strasbourg court has always been sensitive to each case's particular facts, and the particular facts must always be examined. And the first two limiting factors affecting Article 8's application – a certain level of seriousness and a reasonable expectation of privacy – are not sharp-edged.

45. But in my judgment it is important to recognise that State action may confront and challenge the individual as it were out of the blue. It may have no patent or obvious contextual explanation, and in that case it is not more apparently rational than arbitrary, nor more apparently justified than unjustified. In this case it consists in the taking and retaining of photographs, though it might consist in other acts. The Metropolitan Police, visibly and with no obvious cause, chose to take and keep photographs of an individual going about his lawful business in the streets of London. This action is a good deal more than the snapping of the shutter. The police are a State authority. And as I have said, the appellant could not and did not know why they were doing it and what use they might make of the pictures.

46. In these circumstances I would hold that Article 8 is engaged. On the particular facts the police action, unexplained at the time it happened and carrying as it

did the implication that the images would be kept and used, is a sufficient intrusion by the State into the individual's own space, his integrity, as to amount to a *prima facie* violation of Article 8(1). It attains a sufficient level of seriousness and in the circumstances the appellant enjoyed a reasonable expectation that his privacy would not be thus invaded. Moreover I consider with respect that this conclusion is supported by the judgment of the Strasbourg court in *Marper*. It will be recalled that the first sentence of paragraph 67 reads:

> The mere storing of data relating to the private life of an individual amounts to an interference within the meaning of Article 8 …

And at paragraph 121 the court said:

> The Government contend that the retention could not be considered as having any direct or significant effect on the applicants unless matches in the database were to implicate them in the commission of offences on a future occasion. The Court is unable to accept this argument and reiterates that the mere retention and storing of personal data by public authorities, however obtained, are to be regarded as having direct impact on the private-life interest of an individual concerned, irrespective of whether subsequent use is made of the data (see paragraph 67 above).

However the impact of these observations on the present case is I think weakened by the fact that the appellant's image was not placed on the CO11 database, which I have described in dealing with the new material arising from the Guardian article, nor on any other database. And I should make clear my view that this new material does not assist the appellant in any respect. The fact that the CO11 database exists cannot conceivably support the appellant's contention that his Article 8 rights have been interfered with, since his image was never placed upon it; and he has no proper business advancing any arguments – if this is what he seeks to do – to assault the practice or procedure of the respondent (as regards the storage and use of information) in circumstances where any such arguments cannot actually bear on his claim.

47. In arriving at this conclusion on the application of Article 8(1) I intend no criticism of the police. Their action's merits will be for consideration under Article 8(2). Their subjection to the discipline of Article 8 means that the fair balance which falls to be struck throughout the Convention provisions between the rights of the individual and the interest of the community has to be struck on the facts of this case. That I think is as it should be.

(2) Was the police action proportionate under Article 8(2)?

Lord Justice Dyson:

64. I gratefully adopt the account of the facts and issues set out so fully by Laws LJ. I agree with his valuable analysis of the article 8(1) issue and his reasons for concluding that article 8 is engaged on the facts of this case. For the reasons that follow, however, I have reached a different conclusion on the article 8(2) issue …

[paras. 65–78 detailing the relevant facts omitted]

Article 8(2)

Legitimate aim

79. I agree with Laws LJ that the taking and retention of the photographs were in pursuit of a legitimate aim, namely 'for the prevention of disorder or crime' or 'for the protection of the rights and freedoms of others': article 8(2). The

phrase 'prevention of disorder or crime' includes the detection of disorder or crime: see, for example, *Marper* v. *UK* (Application 30562/04 and 30566/04, judgment of ECtHR 4 December 2008, BAILII: [2008] ECHR 1581). The contrary was not argued by Mr Westgate.

'In accordance with the law'

80. The next question is whether the interference with the appellant's article 8 rights was 'in accordance with the law'. In view of the conclusion that I have reached on the issue of proportionality, I do not find it necessary to express a view on this question. I do, however, wish to express one reservation about Laws LJ's analysis.

81. At [53], Laws LJ attaches particular importance to the nature of the intrusion said to violate article 8 and suggests that, broadly, the more intrusive the act complained of, the more precise and specific must be the law said to justify it. I would merely say that I have some doubt as to whether [56] of the speech of Lord Hope in *Gillan* supports such a proposition or that, if it does, it is supported by the concluding words of [67] of the decision in *Malone* v. *UK* (1985) 7 EHRR 14. In any event, I see no support for this proposition in the speech of Lord Bingham in *Gillan*. It is to be noted that all the other members of their Lordships' House (including Lord Hope himself) agreed with the reasoning of Lord Bingham.

'Necessary in a democratic society': proportionality

82. The phrase 'necessary in a democratic society' has been considered and applied by the ECtHR on many occasions. In *Marper* at [101], the court said:
    > An interference will be considered 'necessary in a democratic society' for a legitimate aim if it answers a 'pressing social need' and, in particular, if it is proportionate to the legitimate aim pursued and if the reasons adduced by the national authorities to justify it are 'relevant and sufficient'.

83. In deciding whether the interference is necessary, the court must have regard to the nature of the Convention right in issue, its importance for the individual, the nature of the interference and the object pursued by the interference: see *Marper* at [102]. At [103], the court went on to say that the protection of personal data is of fundamental importance to a person's enjoyment of his or her article 8 rights and the domestic law must afford appropriate safeguards to prevent any such use of personal data as may be inconsistent with the guarantees of article 8. The need for such safeguards is all the greater where the protection of personal data undergoing automatic processing is concerned, not least when such data are used for police purposes.

84. In other words, the court is required to carry out a careful exercise of weighing the legitimate aim to be pursued, the importance of the right which is the subject of the interference and the extent of the interference. Thus an interference whose object is to protect the community from the danger of terrorism is more readily justified as proportionate than an interference whose object is to protect the community from the risk of low level crime and disorder. The importance of the former was emphasised by the House of Lords in *R (Gillan)* v. *Commissioner of Police of the Metropolis* [2006] UKHL 12, [2006] 2 AC 307: see per Lord Bingham of Cornhill at [29] and Lord Scott of Foscote at [62].

85. I agree that *Marper* is wholly distinguishable on the facts. Whether an interference with a Convention right is proportionate is a fact-sensitive question. I accept that the retention of the photographs by the police was not an

interference of the utmost gravity with the appellant's article 8 rights. Nor, however, should it be dismissed as of little consequence. The retention by the police of photographs taken of persons who have not committed an offence, and who are not even suspected of having committed an offence, is always a serious matter. I say this notwithstanding the fact that I accept that the retention of the photographs in this case was tightly controlled and that there is a qualitative difference between photographic images on the one hand and fingerprints and DNA on the other. It should also be recorded that the evidence is that, had these proceedings not been commenced, the photographs would have been destroyed after the DSEi fair. That is because the appellant did not attend that event and there was no intelligence suggesting that he had prior to that event (and after the AGM) participate in any other unlawful activities: see para. 13 of the statement of Superintendent Gomme.

86. The retention by the police of photographs of a person must be justified and the justification must be the more compelling where the interference with a person's rights is, as in the present case, in pursuit of the protection of the community from the risk of public disorder or low level crime, as opposed, for example, to protection against the danger of terrorism or really serious criminal activity.

87. I return to the facts of this case. Within a few days of the AGM, the retention of the photographs could not rationally be justified as furthering the aim of detecting the perpetrators of any crime that may have been committed during the meeting. There was no realistic possibility that evidence that a crime had been committed at the meeting would only be obtained weeks or months after the event. The meeting was well attended. There were Reed officers and private security officials present who were on the look-out for trouble-makers and who did indeed eject two of them (although there is no evidence that even they committed any offence). I repeat that the principal object of the evidence-gathering operation was to obtain evidence about possible disorder and criminal conduct at the AGM and/or in the vicinity of the hotel and the sole reason given by the officer who instructed the photographer to take the photographs was to obtain evidence which would be of value if offences had been committed at the AGM.

88. The fact that the appellant had been seen briefly in the company of EA after the AGM may have provided further justification for retaining the photographs for a few days after 27 April. But thereafter, in my judgment, neither the brief association with EA nor anything else relating to the AGM provided any justification for retaining the photographs any longer.

89. It follows that the only justification advanced by the police for retaining the photographs for more than a few days after the meeting was the possibility that the appellant might attend and commit an offence at the DSEi fair several months later. But in my judgment, even if due allowance is made for the margin of operational discretion, that justification does not bear scrutiny. First, the DSEi fair was not the principal focus of the evidence-gathering operation. The principal concern of the police was what might happen at the AGM and/ or in the vicinity of the hotel. But for that concern, the evidence would suggest that the operation would not have taken place in the first place. Secondly, the sole reason why the photographs were taken was to obtain evidence in case an offence had been committed at the AGM. Thirdly, once it had become clear that, notwithstanding his brief association with EA, the appellant had not committed any offence at the AGM, there was no reasonable basis for fearing that, even if he went to the DSEi fair, he might commit an offence there. His behaviour on 27 April was beyond reproach, even though he was subjected to what

he considered to be an intimidating experience. There was no more likelihood that the appellant would commit an offence if he went to the fair than that any other citizen of good character who happened to go to the fair would commit an offence there.

90. It is for the police to justify as proportionate the interference with the appellant's article 8 rights. For the reasons that I have given, I am of the opinion that they have failed to do so. I would allow this appeal.

Lord Collins of Mapesbury:

[paras. 91–5 omitted]

96. I agree with Laws and Dyson LJJ that Article 8(1) was engaged, but that the taking and retention of the photographs were in pursuance of a legitimate aim, namely 'for the prevention of disorder or crime' or 'for the protection of the rights and freedoms of others' for the purposes of Article 8(2).

97. But I agree with Dyson LJ that the interference was not proportionate. He has referred to the crucial facts, of which it seems to me that the following are the most important. First, the main object of the evidence gathering operation was to obtain evidence about possible disorder and criminal conduct at the AGM and/or in the vicinity of the hotel, and the sole reason given by PS Dixon who instructed the photographer to take the photographs was to obtain evidence which would be of value if offences had been committed at the AGM. Second, the retention of the photographs for more than a few days could not be justified as furthering the aim of detecting the perpetrators of any crime that may have been committed during the meeting. Third, a possible brief association between Mr Wood and EA on the day did not provide any justification for a lengthy retention of the photographs. Fourth, the suggestion that retention of the photographs was justified by the possibility that Mr Wood might attend and commit an offence at the DSEi fair several months later is plainly an afterthought and had nothing to do with the decision to take the photographs.

98. Like Dyson LJ, I prefer to express no concluded view on the question whether the interference was 'in accordance with the law' …

[para. 99 omitted]

100. Nevertheless, it is plain that the last word has yet to be said on the implications for civil liberties of the taking and retention of images in the modern surveillance society. This is not the case for the exploration of the wider, and very serious, human rights issues which arise when the State obtains and retains the images of persons who have committed no offence and are not suspected of having committed any offence.

There is no doubt that *Wood* is a very different kind of case to *Marper*. In part, this is because of the differences between the respective technologies of photography and DNA databases. More significantly, though, it is because, whereas *Marper* is concerned with the compatibility of the background regulation (relative to respect for privacy), *Wood* is simply concerned with whether a particular police action in a particular context sufficiently respected the privacy rights of the complainant. The decision in *Wood*, standing alone, would not signal a significant shift in the regulatory position; but, *Wood*, in conjunction with *Marper* – together with, it should be said, the Protection of Freedom Act – is a clear rebalancing of basic values and it represents a major change in the regulatory environment.

4 The changing complexion of the regulatory environment

In this part of the chapter, we are interested in the cumulative effect of reliance on technologies as regulatory instruments. The changes that take place to the regulatory environment are subtle and their impact is uncertain. Essentially, there are two significant changes in the complexion of the regulatory environment that we need to monitor: the first is the use of technologies (such as CCTV, DNA profiling, RFID chips, and the like) that serve to amplify prudential signals (by impressing upon regulatees that there is a heightened likelihood of offenders being detected and punished, thereby highlighting that compliance is the rational self-interested option); and the second is the use of technologies that replace normative signals with non-normative controls.[16] Each of these changes might be a watershed and we will review them one at a time.[17]

(a) Technologies that amplify prudential signals

If we are to assess the significance of technological instruments that amplify the prudential noise, we need to identify the impact on both individual decision-making and the overall environment for moral community. Having elaborated on these two points of potential impact, we introduce the idea of a regulatory margin (designed to highlight the overall significance of regulators moving away from a moral register and to facilitate review of the legitimacy of such a movement).

(i) The impact on the individual
If the prudential signal is amplified, how does this affect the way that individual agents reason and act? For example, if speed cameras are fixed to a section of highway, or if CCTV covers a public square, how does this impact on the reasons and actions of regulatees? Here, we are not thinking about the effectiveness of the technologies in the way that we discussed in Chapters 11–14. Rather, the focal question is whether the use of regulatory technologies that amplify prudential signals comes at any cost to moral community. Specifically, how does such use impact on the moral life of individual regulatees?

To pursue such an inquiry, we might imagine four ideal-typical agents as follows:

1 Type 1 agents who act only and always on moral reasons.
2 Type 2 agents who act only and always on prudential reasons.

---

[16] On the first of these watersheds, compare Silva-Tarouca Larsen, *Setting the Watch*; and, on the second, note Antoinette Rouvray, 'Technology, Virtuality and Utopia', in Mireille Hildebrandt and Antoinette Rouvray (eds.), *Law, Human Agency and Autonomic Computing* (London: Routledge, 2011), 119, esp. at 128.

[17] In this and the final part of the chapter, we are drawing on Roger Brownsword, 'Lost in Translation: Legality, Regulatory Margins, and Technological Management', *Berkeley Technology Law Journal*, 26 (2011), 1321.

3 Type 3 agents who act on a mix of moral and prudential reasons.
4 Type 4 agents who are erratic, sometimes acting on moral reasons, sometimes on prudential reasons, and sometimes on mixed reasons.

Broadly speaking, for Type 1 agents, the amplification of prudential signals is
irrelevant unless there are choices that are morally optional. For Type 2 agents
(whose prudential mindset will be treated as pathological in an aspirant moral
community), the amplification of prudential signals will not change the general way that they reason but, in some cases, it might alter their conduct. For
example, motorists who reason in this prudential way might slow down on a
road when speed cameras are introduced, reasoning that the introduction of
cameras tips the balance of self-interested considerations towards compliance.
However, while this would be relevant to understanding the effectiveness of
particular regulatory technologies, it would not speak to concerns about damage to moral community. The remaining categories, Type 3 and Type 4 agents,
are probably characteristic of many agents in an aspirant moral community. In
principle, there could be some significant alterations in both the reasoning and
the conduct of such agents; and, if there were serious concern about such alterations, there would need to be an inquiry to establish their prevalence and their
significance.

That said, if the amplification of prudential signals does change the conduct of Type 2 agents so that they cause less harm to the morally protected
interests of other agents, there is an element of moral gain without any offsetting loss – or, at any rate, this is so provided that Type 2 agents are incorri-
gible prudentialists. In the case of Type 3 and 4 agents, the moral trade-off is
more complex. As with Type 2 agents, the amplification of prudential signals
might lead to a reduction in the harm caused to the protected moral interests
of others; but, if there is also a switch from moral to prudential reason in the
thinking of these agents (even though their conduct is unaltered) this suggests
some corrosion of moral community – that is, even though these agents might
do what is generally thought to be the right thing, they now do so for prudential
rather than moral reasons.

Without further inquiry, we cannot be confident about the impact of the
amplification of prudential signals that comes with an increased reliance
on some regulatory technologies. So long as such technologies operate at the
fringes of a traditional criminal justice system, there is probably little, if any,
overall cost to moral community. However, where the regulatory environment
features pervasive surveillance and monitoring technologies, aspirant moral
communities should not be so complacent.

(ii) The impact on the prospects for moral community
In an aspirant moral community, the regulatory environment should declare
the community's commitment to doing the right thing and it should express its
understanding of the guiding principles. At some times and in some places, the

process of articulating the community's moral commitments might have been left to an elite group; the commitments so articulated might have been seen as a durable statement (in a world of little change); and the substantive principles articulated might have been viewed with epistemic certainty. However, this will not do in the twenty-first century – the moral project today needs to be inclusive (implying comprehensive public engagement), constantly under review (implying that decisions made are to be treated as provisional), and undertaken with a degree of uncertainty (and humility).

To the extent that the public life of such a community focuses on constructing an appropriate regulatory environment, it follows that we cannot assess the impact of an amplification of prudential signals simply by checking the impact on regulatees. For, as members of the community, regulatees have a role to play in debating the regulatory purposes and agreeing the public rules and standards. In other words, before we set aside any concerns about the amplification of prudential signals, we need to check not only whether there is an impact on regulatees at the point of compliance but also on their ability to participate as members of the political (and aspirant moral) community. However, to do this, they must have the capacity to engage in moral discourse and debate – which is to say, there must be no impairment of their moral development. Unless the amplification of prudential signals clearly has no negative impact on any part of the community's moral project, regulators should proceed with care.

(iii) The regulatory margin

Regulators might interpret their responsibilities in relation to the complexion of the regulatory environment in a weak or strong sense. In a weak sense, the responsibility is to ensure that the moral life of the community is not altogether extinguished; in a strong sense, the role of regulators is to ensure that there is, at worst, no reduction in the moral life of the community and, at best, some promotion of moral community. On the former interpretation, regulators would not be concerned that the amplification of prudential signals encroached on and reduced the space for moral reason, provided that there was (in the spirit of the Lockean proviso) still sufficient and plenty of opportunity for the moral life. By contrast, on the latter interpretation, such encroachment and reduction would be unacceptable. While the former evokes a community that is trying to preserve something of its moral project, the latter fits with a community that sees itself on a trajectory towards the completion of its moral project. In the light of what we have said about the inclusiveness of moral community, it should be for the community as a whole to debate whether it defines itself as undertaking the weak or the strong version of the moral project.

Whether the community's aspiration is to retain some part of its moral life or to push forward towards a more complete moral life, there needs to be some kind of regulatory margin that serves as a benchmark for decisions involving the use of technologies that amplify prudential signals. On the weak interpretation of stewardship, the margin will represent a minimal zone for moral life to be protected at all costs; on the strong interpretation, the margin will mark the present level of moral life. The function of this margin would be twofold: first, for the *ex ante* guidance of regulators (the marginal question would be one that they should ask themselves); and, secondly, as a focus for *ex post* review.

What might be the relevant marginal considerations? One consideration is whether the amplification of prudential signals might interfere with the development of moral reason and the capacity to participate in the life of the community as a moral agent. No doubt, the foreground regulatory environment for children and young persons is that found in the family, at school and in the neighbourhood – and we should not assume that the larger public regulatory environment aligns with these most proximate environments. Nevertheless, regulators need to be sensitive to the possibility that the amplification of prudential signals in the background environment might carry over to the foreground. A second consideration concerns the importance of the moral interest served by prudential amplification. For example, if amplified prudential signals serve to protect essential infrastructural conditions for the community or to prevent life-threatening harm, this might be seen overall as an acceptable measure – and, of course, it would be much easier to justify such measures where the weak interpretation of moral stewardship is invoked. Clearly, there is a considerable jurisprudence waiting to be developed here; but, it will not get under way unless there is an appropriate doctrinal and institutional opening.

Briefly, to earth this point, imagine that in the *Marper* case the objection was not that the legal position was incompatible with respect for privacy but that it foreshadowed an unacceptable change in the complexion of the regulatory environment. Imagine that it had been argued that the use of DNA evidence in conjunction with a raft of other modern technologies went too far in amplifying prudential signals at the cost of moral community. Even the most creative lawyer would have difficulty in finding a peg in the Convention on which to hang such an argument. To get such a claim off the ground there would need to be something analogous to a (moral) regulatory margin, relative to which the objection could be assessed. On this analysis, other contracting states, limiting the use of DNA profiling to the most serious criminal offences, would seem more respectful of privacy but, arguably, also more sensitive to the need to maintain a moral margin (where prudential signals do not drown out the moral). In other words, what would be seen as disproportionate would be, not the infringement on privacy, but the encroachment on the moral margin. The outcome of the case would be the same but the issues and the reasoning would be quite different.

(b) Technologies that replace normative signals

When regulators rely on technological instruments, they can go beyond the amplification of prudential signals to design in a desired pattern of conduct or to design out conduct that is not desired. Sometimes, the technology will not replace normative signals; the regulatory environment, although employing technologies, will still speak to the moral and prudential interests of regulatees. However, the technology might go a step further and replace any normative signals with an entirely non-normative register. Such techno-regulatory strategies might focus on products, places or persons.[18]

The impact of non-normative regulation is that regulatees lose some degree of control and choice, specifically in relation to their prudential and moral reasoning and action. If the variables in the non-normative forms of regulation are significant, it is because of the particular way that they impact on prudential and moral action. Accordingly, we can start by reviewing the significance of non-normative regulatory interventions with regard to prudential reason and the pursuit of self-interest; and then we can return to the implications for moral community.

(i) Prudential interests

To reason prudentially is to make a judgement about one's own best interests (short term or long term). So long as we have the capacity for prudential reason, we will probably want to make our own prudential judgements. The sentiment will be that, if anyone is to judge what is in my interest, it should be me. At all events, let us suppose that this is how agents tend to think.

We can assess the impact of non-normative technologies on prudential reason in four steps: first, by considering how such technologies might operate where an agent self-regulates (and prudentially elects a certain level of technological regulation); second, by reviewing the imposition of non-normative regulatory environments in products and places; third, by thinking about the significance of in-person technological management; and, finally, by revisiting the idea of a regulatory margin.

Self-regulation

Let us suppose that some products (motor cars, for example) are marketed with the following three design options (each reflecting a different level of technological control over the user's self-interested decision-making):

1 Level 0 (that is, no) technological assistance or constraint: the user is on his or her own in driving the car.
2 Level 1 technological assistance or constraint: this is what, as we have seen in an earlier chapter, Mireille Hildebrandt terms a 'regulative' technology;[19] it is an amber light alert: it is a motor car fitted with sensors that detect the presence of alcohol or drugs and that cautions against driving under the influence; the technological signal is normative.

---

[18] See Roger Brownsword, 'Code, Control, and Choice: Why East Is East and West Is West', *Legal Studies*, 25 (2005), 1, 12.

[19] Mireille Hildebrandt, 'Legal and Technological Normativity: More (and Less) than Twin Sisters', *Techné*, 12(3) (2008), 169.

3 Level 2 technological assistance or constraint: again, in Mireille Hildebrandt's terms, this is a 'constitutive' technology; it is red light control: it is the car that is immobilised when its sensors detect the presence of drink or drugs; the technological signal is non-normative.

For the individual who elects level 0, there is no technological impingement on prudential reason and action; and, with level 1 features, the technology simply advises the user – the technology is a partner in prudential decision-making; and the user remains in control in the sense that the advice can be ignored. With level 2, though, the technology takes on a non-normative character. For the individual who elects level 2, the power of prudential decision is transferred to the technology. However, the election itself is a strategic prudential decision. For example, an individual might be prone to acting on short-term considerations which lead to actions that are subsequently regretted. To minimise this risk, the individual elects level 2 technological features.[20] Granted, this does involve a transfer of control. However, the transfer is selected and accepted because the individual makes a background prudential judgement that, all things considered, this is the way to advance his or her self-interest. Moreover, provided that the decision is reversible (either by replacing the product or, in some sophisticated designs, by virtue of an override feature), there is no loss of prudential independence.

Perhaps we should not be too sanguine about consumer choices being enhanced by products that offer a range of options of the kind just outlined. After all, consumer preferences can be manipulated and, in markets that use sophisticated profiling and advertising technologies, individuals might be less in control of their prudential judgements than they assume. Still, in principle, prudential self-regulatory election of non-normative technological management is much less problematic than the imposition of such management systems by others.

Non-normative regulation imposed by others

If we put self-regulation to one side, the question is: where non-normative technological features are introduced into the regulatory environment without this being the (self-regulating) choice of each regulatee, is this at a cost to valued prudential independence? Is the community losing something that it values?

As we have said, in the marketplace, mass-produced goods might not be designed as one would choose. If this means that the better off have a better chance of realising their preferences, there is an obvious concern about the fairness and equity of access to various technological options; but the concern is not about the loss of prudential reason from the life of the community. In the same way, if one market player is in a position to impose a technological

---

[20] For discussion of how different conceptions of autonomy are implicated in these technological designs, see Roger Brownsword, 'Autonomy, Delegation, and Responsibility: Agents in Autonomic Computing Environments', in Hildebrandt and Rouvroy, *Autonomic Computing*, 64.

restriction on the other (as with DRM technologies and Monsanto's supposed terminator gene in seeds), there is an imbalance of contractual power, with producers using the technology to advance their commercial self-interest against the preferences of purchasers. These facts of market life might give rise to some concern; but the concern is not about the loss of opportunities for prudential reason so much as the legitimacy of this kind of transactional power play.

Away from the market, what should we make of public impositions of non-normative technologies? For example, what should we make of the non-normative regulatory environments that are characteristic of many aspects of public transport systems? Suppose that it were proposed that, instead of conventional driver-controlled motor cars, there should be a fully technologically managed road transport system. Even with the best deliberative, democratic, and participatory processes, there is no guarantee that the outcome will be in line with each participant's judgement of their own personal prudential interest. Once the new transport system is in operation, there is some loss of opportunity for prudential action – drivers will no longer ponder the best route for getting from A to B. However, there has been no loss of prudential reason in the debates about the adoption of the system; and, indeed, there might be further prudential arguments about possible modifications to the system, or even its abandonment and the restoration of the old system. So, provided that there is the opportunity to apply prudential reason in public debates, for the public to vote its preferences, we are not losing it from public life – even if the ensuing regulatory environments are non-normative.

Again, we should not be too sanguine about this. In practice, how often are there public debates about the adoption of managed environments – rather, how often are there simply incremental changes which just seem to happen? And, even if there are public debates, how often are they framed in terms of a shift from a normative to a non-normative regulatory environment? For a community that values prudential reason and the possibility of acting on one's own prudential judgements, the public imposition of non-normative regulatory environments needs to be preceded by an inclusive public debate that flags up the replacement of normative with non-normative signals. Moreover, such communities need to be careful that what start out as level 1 technological regulatory features (as might happen with some 'nudges') do not morph into level 2 features without the community having the opportunity to vote its preferences on the matter.

Technology in the person

Are non-normative regulatory technologies that are embedded in persons rather than in their surrounding environments an exceptional case? Does the locating of such technologies in the person present a special challenge to the community that values prudential independence?

Suppose that an individual suffers from depression. There are two options: either to take a course of drugs or to work out regularly at the local fitness club.

Whichever option is taken, the biochemistry is the identical; serotonin levels are raised; and the depression lifts. It is a simple choice: which option, prudentially, is preferred? Some (perhaps many)[21] will prefer the latter because they are suspicious of drugs for mental health, or they think that their recovery will be more authentic if unaided by drugs, or the like. Others elect to take the drugs. So far as the prudential life of the community is concerned, there seems to be nothing exceptional about any of this. Whichever option is taken, it is the result of the individual's prudential preference, their own independent judgement as to what is in their self-interest.

In some cases, the initial decision to use an in-person regulatory technology is suspect. For example, we might debate whether an offender's election to be chipped or tagged (for parole or early release or to avoid a custodial disposition) is in any relevant sense 'unfree'. Is this really an unforced choice? Or we might argue about the morality of such measures.[22] However, there is no loss of prudential community here. Similarly, we might debate the merits of tagging children or elderly people for their own health and safety. To the extent that such technological interventions are backed by paternalistic reasoning that takes no account of the capacity of these persons for making their own prudential decisions, there is a problem – although by no means a problem that is limited to, or driven by, regulatory technologies. So long as our question is about the preservation of prudential self-determination, we have not yet hit a nerve.

What would hit such a nerve? Imagine, in the way that Bruce Ackerman once did,[23] that there are master geneticists who can code persons in a way that they have particular talents and, concomitantly, associated preferences. No doubt, for each of us, the way in which we perceive our self-interest, as well as our tendency towards short-term or longer-run calculation, owes something to our genetic inheritance. However, it has not been designed into us in the self-conscious way that we are imagining would happen if we employed the services of the master geneticist. So long as this coding is a somatic fix, which we select for ourselves, it fits the self-regulatory pattern. However, where others (the state, our parents, or others) are specifying the coding for us, this raises a host of *moral* concerns: for liberals, it violates the person's right to an open future;[24] and for dignitarians, it wrongly treats persons as commodities.[25] Does it also impinge upon prudential community? In a sense, there is no loss of the community's aggregate capacity for prudential reason, but the individuals who are

---

[21] See Academy of Medical Sciences, *Brain Science, Addiction, and Drugs* (London 2008).

[22] Compare, e.g., Jeroen van den Hoven, 'Nanotechnology and Privacy: Instructive Case of RFID', in Fritz Allhoff, Patrick Lin, James Moor and John Weckert (eds.), *Nanoethics* (Hoboken, NJ: Wiley, 2007), 253; and Rosenberg, 'Involuntary Endogenous RFID Compliance Monitoring', 331.

[23] Bruce A. Ackerman, *Social Justice in the Liberal State* (New Haven: Yale University Press, 1980).

[24] See, e.g., Dena S. Davis, 'Genetic Dilemmas and the Child's Right to an Open Future', *Rutgers Law Journal*, 28 (1997), 549, esp. at 561–7 (arguing that a reflexive application of autonomy values will set limits to parents' reproductive autonomy).

[25] Deryck Beyleveld and Roger Brownsword, *Human Dignity in Bioethics and Biolaw* (Oxford: Oxford University Press, 2001).

coded for a particular kind of prudence do not enjoy the independence that is integral to valuing prudential decision-making. Put bluntly, when I judge that x is in my self-interest, I want that to be my judgement not the judgement that has been designed into me by others. Where it is my interests that are at issue, I want to be speaking and deciding for myself.

If there is anything exceptional about *imposed* in-person regulatory technologies, it is that they might not be transparent and they might not be reversible. In both respects, there seems to be a diminution in prudential community.

A regulatory margin

We have said already that there needs to be a regulatory margin to facilitate deliberation about, and review of, changes to the complexion of the regulatory environment – in this case concerning the tuning down of prudential signals in favour of non-normative signals.

If there is to be a prudential regulatory margin, what kind of considerations would it highlight? First, provided that regulatory technologies are self-consciously adopted by individuals who reason prudentially that this kind of management advances their self-interest, and provided that these decisions are reversible, there seems to be little cause for concern – although, of course, there might be concerns that are not related to the prudential margin. Second, where non-normative regulatory technologies are imposed by public bodies, there needs to be an opportunity for prudential and inclusive deliberation before such measures are adopted; the fact that the character of the regulatory environment will change should be highlighted for discussion; and, if the decision cannot be reversed, a great deal of care needs to be taken before proceeding. Stated shortly, regulators need to ensure that imposed technological management is in line with general prudential preferences.[26] Finally, any attempt to design out a person's capacity for prudential reason, or to design in a particular kind of prudential pathway for a person should be prohibited.

(ii) Moral community

If the amplification of prudential signals can be a problem for moral community, then we might expect the problems to be accentuated where the change in the regulatory environment is from normative to non-normative signals. As with our discussion of the impact on prudential reason, we can start with self-regulatory choices and then turn to the imposition of techno-regulation.

Self-regulation

Let us suppose that we are dealing with an aspirant moral agent. When this person is offered a choice of product design, such as a car, he or she will be thinking about how the technological management secures his or her own safety but

---

[26] Compare Danielle Keats Citron, 'Technological Due Process', *Washington University Law Review*, 85 (2008), 1249, esp. at 1312.

also about how this safeguards the legitimate interest of others. So, for example, while a purely prudential agent might elect level 1 technology that reminds the driver about his or her own safety, a moral agent might elect similar technology that expresses the caution in moral rather than prudential terms, reminding the driver about the safety of other road users. Indeed, being aware of their own shortcomings, moral agents might choose something stronger than an advisory message and choose level 2 technology. Would this be problematic?

For moral reasons, the agent has elected technological non-normative management that guarantees that the legitimate interests of other road users will be respected. Although this seems to be in line with the aspirations of moral community, there are three questions that we might raise about the agent's choice. These concern, respectively, the authenticity of the agent's moral performance, the possibility of expressing human dignity and the constraints on dealing with moral emergencies.

First, as the motorist proceeds in a way that the level 2 technological management ensures causes no harm to other road users, one might say that this is not an authentic moral performance; for it is the on-board technology, not the agent, that does all the work. Clearly, this latter point has to be conceded. However, moral reason lies at the root of the technology that has been selected and, arguably, this is good enough.

Second, when the car is in motion, observing the interests of other road-users, the driver cannot proceed otherwise (assuming no facility for overriding the technological controls). There is no possibility of the driver expressing his or her human dignity by turning away from doing the wrong thing. A car with level 2 technological management never confronts the choice between doing the right thing and doing wrong. Again, though, the driver is where he or she is only because the earlier design choice was made. If that choice was made freely, then that seems to be the moment at which human dignity is expressed.

Third, en route from A to B, the smart car might encounter an emergency in which, without the technological controls, the driver would have deviated to assist another (as in the stock example of a motorist who exceeds the speed limit in order to get a pregnant woman to hospital).[27] No doubt, the really smart car will have an override that allows the moral agent to do the right thing in such an emergency. Failing this, when the moral agent elects level 2 technological management, he or she must calculate the potential moral cost of subjecting their conduct to the governance of the technology. Still, this does not signify a loss of moral community.

However, what if the product were not a car with a specific range of managed compliance but, rather, a broad sweep moral drug, operating either by tuning up the moral (normative) signals or by repressing the prudential will to defect? Intuitively, we might find this problematic. If the drug simply serves

---

[27] For discussion of just such a case, see Karen Yeung, 'Can We Employ Design-Based Regulation While Avoiding *Brave New World*', *Law, Innovation and Technology*, 3 (2011), 1.

to amplify the moral signals, it might be seen as problematic, but not because of any non-normative characteristics. If the drug functions by repressing any harmful desires, the agent finds it easy to respect others – and, aside from its broad sweep, this seems to be akin to the car with level 2 technological management. For the individual agent who elects to take this short cut to moral performance, there might be some costs (such as the loss of authenticity[28] or dignity). However, unless the project of moral community requires that moral action be unaided – or, perhaps, unless it becomes so easy for agents to do the right thing that they lose the sense that they face a choice between right and wrong – there is no real problem.

Imposed regulation

Let us suppose that the regulatory environment takes on non-normative features after a full and inclusive public debate; and let us suppose that the rationale for adopting techno-regulation is that this is more effective in protecting relevant moral interests. Let us suppose, moreover, that there is general agreement that the interests to be protected are important and that a managed environment is the right regulatory strategy. Once this non-normative regulatory environment is in place, regulatees lose the opportunity to do wrong by violating the protected interests of others – which, of course, is precisely the point of making this particular regulatory move. However, it also means that regulatees cannot demonstrate in such an environment that they do the right thing for the right reason. How serious a price is this to pay? How serious is it for moral community that agents, in techno-regulated environments, think only about what is practicable or possible rather than what morally is required?

Recalling our earlier specification of four ideal-typical agents, how might a regulatory environment coded for moral reason impact on such agents? While type 1 agents can remind themselves that they do what they do for moral reasons, they cannot openly demonstrate that this is the case – which a moral community might or might not judge to be problematic. For type 2 agents, there is no loss. These agents, who always act on prudential reasons, are steered by the technological management system towards a moral course of action. To be sure, they lose the opportunity to do the right thing for the right reason; but, if they are never going to do the right thing anyway, this seems to be no loss – and, of course, there is an offsetting moral gain.

What about type 3 and type 4 agents? Some of these all-too-human agents will be quite badly conflicted, experiencing weakness of the will as prudential gains trump moral arguments as well as exhibiting a tendency to rationalise self-serving acts as actually being in line with moral requirements. In short, for such agents, the prudential parts of their practical reason can often defeat their moral aspirations. If a managed regulatory environment prevents

---

[28] Authenticity is by no means a straightforward idea: see, e.g., Neil Levy, *Neuroethics* (Cambridge: Cambridge University Press, 2007), esp. chs. 2 and 3.

this happening, keeping regulatees on the right moral tracks, this seems to be a positive for moral community. The fact that, once agents are set on the right tracks, there is no getting off does not seem too serious a price to pay. Granted, there is no possibility of demonstrating that one is freely doing the right thing for the right reason; but, provided that the right reasons were present when the management system was initiated, this seems good enough. Moreover, for some of these type 3 and type 4 agents, the problem was always that, when presented with the opportunity, they did not do the right thing.

Having said this, there might be a dual concern that, where techno-regulation is widely employed, type 3 and type 4 agents (a) rarely encounter situations where their moral resolve is put to the test and (b) begin to lose a sense of responsibility for their acts. If the former means that the capacity of agents for moral reflection and judgement is impaired, this becomes a serious matter for moral community. For, as we saw in our earlier discussion (concerning the amplification of prudential signals), moral communities need to keep debating their commitments. In such a community, it is fine to be a passive techno-managed regulatee, but active moral citizenship is also required. If there are any such 'demoralising' effects, they would need to be carefully monitored; for, they are clearly corrosive of moral community.

In-person moral coding

We said earlier that the coding of persons for prudential preferences could be problematic both for prudential and moral community. Imagine, now, the coding of persons for moral action. In an aspirant moral community, this gives rise to a clutch of concerns, three of which we can highlight.

First, there is the question of whether the coding is an act of self-regulation. If it is, then what is the difference between this and taking a daily dose of soma or whatever it is that keeps the agent on the moral tracks? Provided that the coding is reversible, then the cases might be comparable and it is for each agent to make a choice about whether, all things considered, this kind of fix is the best way to lead a moral life. If, however, the coding is imposed, we might want to distinguish between coding before or at birth (which might be seen in a negative or a positive light) and the enforced coding of mature agents who have perhaps shown themselves to be otherwise incapable of respecting the moral interests of others. We might also want to differentiate between coding that amplifies moral signals (or strengthens moral resolve) and that which simply suppresses harmful or dangerous instincts. Whereas, in the former case, we seem to be designing for the moral life, in the latter it seems to be an exercise in risk management. Clearly, there is much devil in the details of such fixes.

Second, as we saw earlier, a moral community will be greatly concerned that technologies are not employed in ways that interfere with the development of a capacity for moral reason and an agent's appreciation of morality as a normative code. Here, we need only recall the concerns famously expressed by the President's Council on Bioethics with regard to the administration of methylphenidate (Ritalin) and amphetamine (Adderall) to children whose conduct is outside the range of acceptability.[29] If we rely on biotechnological or neurotechnological interventions to respond to (or manage) our social problems, there is a danger that, as the President's Council puts it, 'we may weaken our sense of responsibility and agency'.[30]

Third, once a coding intervention is made, is it capable of responding to changes in the community's interpretation of their moral commitments and the way in which fundamental principles should be applied? If the coding simply represses antisocial instincts, or if it strengthens the signal to do the right thing, it might continue to be functional even as the substance of morality changes. However, so long as the moral project is understood as an ongoing one, the community will want to take a hard look at in-person measures lest they should inappropriately freeze morals.

The regulatory margin

We have already sketched the idea of a moral margin in the context of the amplification of prudential signals. This sketch continues to apply where the questions for moral community arise, not from the amplification of prudential signals but from non-normative regulatory approaches.

Consider the case where a techno-regulatory intervention precludes certain kinds of harmful acts, whether those acts are intentional or unintentional – for example, where products (such as surgical instruments),[31] or complexes of products (such as transport systems) are designed for safety. Primarily, the purpose of such safety measures will be to safeguard users or passengers – for example, by phasing out trains with slam door carriages,[32] or by making it impossible for trains to pass through signals on red. Given that such measures are designed to make routine activities (such as the journey to work) less risky, it is reasonable to assume that most interested parties judge them to be in their prudential interests; and, if public engagement has indeed shown this to be the case, then all well and good. However, the effect of these measures is not only to replace prudential norms with non-normative design but also to impact on the opportunity to display a moral performance. For example, commuters opening railway train doors might want to show that they do so with due regard for the safety of fellow passengers and persons standing on station platforms. Likewise, train drivers might want to show that they exercise due care by stopping at red signals. Once the train is designed for safety, these displays of due care and concern for others cannot be made in this way. However, assuming

---

[29] President's Council on Bioethics, *Beyond Therapy* (Washington, DC: Dana Press, 2003), esp. at 105–6.

[30] *Ibid.*, at 106.

[31] Compare Karen Yeung and Mary Dixon-Woods, 'Design-Based Regulation and Patient Safety: A Regulatory Studies Perspective', *Social Science and Medicine*, 71 (2010), 540.

[32] See Jonathan Wolff, 'Five Types of Risky Situation', *Law, Innovation and Technology*, 2 (2010), 151.

that such displays of moral virtue are valued by the community, do regulators have a short answer to these 'objections'?

One thought is that regulators might be able to say that, where their primary purpose is the safety of passengers, they do not have to answer for any secondary effects – that they are shielded by a doctrine akin to that of double effect. Surely, though, this will not do. Otherwise, this would involve accepting that, because Robert Moses's bridges were built with safety in mind, there is no need for regulators to answer for their secondary (and racially discriminatory) effects.[33] This is quite contrary to one of the main points in our discussion, namely that regulators need to be much more sensitive to the impact of relying on architecture, product design, and the like as features of the regulatory repertoire.

The other thought is that there is no real loss of moral community when such safety features are introduced because, insofar as the intervention targets acts that are harmful to others, its focus is on unintentional rather than intentionally harmful acts. If the technology only prevented non-negligent unintentionally harmful acts, there might be something in this thought. However, it also blocks negligent acts as well as intentionally harmful acts. Now, as we have indicated already, in a moral community, it is important not only to eschew intentionally violating the protected interests of others but also to respect such interests by taking reasonable care not to cause harm to others. To be sure, even a dog might know the difference between being kicked intentionally and unintentionally; but a smart dog will also distinguish between an owner that takes reasonable care not to kick it and one that takes no such care. At all events, for the sake of argument, let us suppose that it is conceded that regulators do not have to answer for any impingement on unintentional acts (even negligent acts); but the crucial point is that regulators must not interfere with opportunities for intentional wrongdoing. On the face of it, this is a very strange view: what it amounts to is that regulators, whatever other good they may do by using non-normative controls, must not deprive those agents who might intentionally harm others of the opportunity to do so if this means that, when such agents do not harm others, they cannot then demonstrate that they are freely doing the right thing. Hence, train drivers must not be prevented from passing through signals when they are on red lest this prevents the driver from showing that he does the right thing by stopping on red. This seems such a strange view that one wonders whether any moral community could reasonably attach such importance to preserving the opportunity to do wrong in order to demonstrate that one does right. Having said that, a moral community might perfectly reasonably attach importance to there being some such opportunities and the question then would be whether train drivers or their passengers need this

---

[33] On value-sensitive design, see Noëmi Manders-Huits and Jeroen van den Hoven, 'The Need for Value-Sensitive Design of Communication Infrastructures', in Paul Sollie and Marcus Düwell (eds.), *Evaluating New Technologies* (Heidelberg: Springer Science, 2009), 51.

particular opportunity more than they need the design-in safety features – a question for the regulatory margin.

5 Sustaining legality in second- and third-generation regulatory environments

How much of law survives in regulatory environments that have transitioned to techno-management? To be sure, there might still be some laws in the background; but all the foreground work is done by techno-regulation. If the regulatory environment retains some normative signals they are so weak as to be irrelevant. This, however, is not the real issue. What really matters is whether the processes that lead to the particular techno-regulatory features are compatible with the ideal of legality.

Famously, Lon Fuller argued that law should be viewed 'as the product of an interplay of purposive orientations between the citizen and his government [and not] as a one-way projection of authority, originating with government and imposing itself upon the citizen'.[34] Legality implies reciprocity and is to be distinguished from managerial direction. Thus:

> The directives issued in a managerial context are applied by the subordinate in order to serve a purpose set by his superior. The law-abiding citizen, on the other hand, does not apply legal rules to serve specific ends set by the lawgiver, but rather follows them in the conduct of his own affairs, the interests he is presumed to serve in following legal rules being those of society generally. The directives of a managerial system regulate primarily the relations between the subordinate and his superior and only collaterally the relations of the subordinate with third persons. The rules of the legal system, on the other hand, normally serve the primary purpose of setting the citizen's relations with other citizens and only in a collateral manner his relations with the seat of authority from which the rules proceed. (Though we sometimes think of the criminal law as defining the citizen's duties towards his government, its primary function is to provide a sound and stable framework for the interactions of citizens with one another.)[35]

As Fuller concedes, these remarks need 'much expansion and qualification';[36] and he tries to give more substance to them by characterising the relationship, in a legal order, between government and citizens in terms of 'reciprocity' and 'intendment'.[37] Perhaps, Fuller's most evocative observation is that 'the functioning of a legal system depends upon a cooperative effort – an effective and responsible interaction – between lawgiver and subject'.[38]

No doubt, these seminal Fullerian ideas are open to many interpretations. However, for our purposes, it is the association of legal ordering with a two-way reciprocal process that is most fruitful. For, in the larger context of the regulatory environment, it implies that the legal approach – an approach to be

---

[34] Lon L. Fuller, *The Morality of Law* (rev. edn, New Haven: Yale University Press, 1969), at 204.
[35] *Ibid.*, at 207–8. [36] *Ibid.*, at 208. [37] *Ibid.*, at 209ff. [38] *Ibid.*, at 219.

valued – is one that embeds participation, transparency, due process, and the like. Hence, if we take our lead from Fuller, we will surely reason that, as the translation is made from a normative to a non-normative regulatory environment, we certainly need to hold on to the idea that what we value is a reciprocal enterprise, not just a case of management by some regulatory elite.

Accordingly, while various kinds of self-regulation that adopt measures of technological control might be fine, even empowering, the imposed public ordering of the community needs to respect the values of legality. This means that there needs to be a comprehensively transparent and democratic relationship between regulators and regulatees.

How far should that relationship extend? If we try to tease out an answer to this question by scrutinising Fuller's text, we will surely think that regulators should engage with the prudential preferences of their regulatees; however, we might be less sure about how far Fuller sees legal order as a community's best expression of its moral commitments. Cutting through this, we can say that, for those who take a morally driven view of law, then it is not just the prudential preferences of regulatees that matter; there is more to law than assisting regulatees to know where they stand so that they can maximise their self-interested preferences. A moral community is an interpretive community; and the regulatory environment at any one time should reflect the community's best understanding of its moral project. It is critical for such an aspirant moral community that there is no technological interference with the moral development of agents; that technological interventions should be reviewable and reversible; and that there is, at minimum, a clear and protected margin for moral action.

It follows that one of the challenges for legal forms of ordering in the twenty-first century is to construct regulatory environments that enable moral community to flourish, even though the normativity of the foreground signals might have given way to non-normative coding and design. Provided that the character and content of the regulatory environment flows from a reciprocal engagement with regulatees, and provided that the background discourse continues to be informed by prudential and moral reason, the things that we value about law will not have been lost. As Fuller rightly says, whether or not we have a regulatory environment of this kind, is far from being a matter of moral indifference – to which we might add: if we are indifferent to the kinds of questions raised in this part of the chapter, the regulatory environment that we have will be, at best, no more than we deserve.

Index

abortion 191, 193
Academy of Medical Sciences 312
access to justice, right of 215–16, 261–2
accountability 4–179, 261–2
Ackerman, Bruce 444
Adams, John 286
Adams, Scott 278–9
agencies
  coordination between 384–5
  need for expertise 384–5
agonism 267–8
agriculture 113
alcohol
  (attempted) prohibition 318
  ban on imports 367
Allhoff, Fritz *et al.*, *What Is Nanotechnology?*
  165
American Home Products 299
amphetamines 448–9
Angell, Marcia 138
arbitrage, regulatory 342, 345
architecture, regulatory 28, 35
Arendt, Hannah 202
Argentina 124
  patent law 17
asthma, treatments 313
asymmetry of information *see* information
Australia
  nanotechnology regulation 316
  property cases 220–1
Austria
  IVF legislation 106–7
  reproductive technology law 241
  stance on GM crops 127
autonomy
  human dignity as 192, 194–6, 201, 205, 243
  personal, right to 428–9
'avoision', tactics of 320, 327

Baldwin, Robert 40
Barlow, John Perry 42–371, 373
Bazelon, David 49
Bentham, Jeremy 186
Berlin, Isaiah 266
beta thalassaemia, testing of embryos for
  401–2
bicycles, regulation of 112
Biegel, Stuart 272, 281–5, 296
Bignami, Francesca 175
bioethics 227
  'bioethical triangle', 184–5, 227
biology *see* bioethics; biotechnology; synthetic
  biology
biotechnology 4–5, 178, 250–1, 373–4
  agricultural use 183
  competing ethical approaches 17
  ethical debates 6–19, 184–5, 204
  global nature of developments 256
  'green' vs. 'red' 154
  pace of developments 170–1
  property, as boundary marker 220–3
  WTO regulation 268
  see also bioethics
Bismarck, Otto von 235–6
BitTorrent 335
Black, Julia 26, 40, 157–157
Blair, Tony 104, 323
BMA (British Medical Association) 336–7
Bollier, David 328–9
boundary-marking concepts 173, 188–224,
  228–33, 268
  defined 231
  enabling/prohibitive uses 189
  fundamental nature 188–9
  mutual incompatibility 266, 267
  normative framework 190
  principal types of 191

Index

boundary-marking concepts (*cont.*)
  setting of outer limits 189–90
Bow Group 276–7
Bowcott, Owen 325–6
Bowman, Diana 316
brain-imaging technology 4, 66
  broader concerns raised by 391–3
  detection of abnormalities, implications for
    criminal justice 393
  disclosure of results 390
  ethical implications 37, 389–93
  legitimacy 60–1
  limitations 389
  practicalities of regulatory response 396
  and privacy rights 394, 395–6
  proposed limitation of areas 395–6
  regulatory environment 390
  regulatory use 5
  threats to self-perception 391–3
Braithwaite, John 30–1, 297
Brake, Tom, MP 274–5
Brandeis, Louis 235
breast cancer 294
Brenner, Susan 70, 111–13, 344, 350
Breyer, Justice 334
Brown, Gordon 292
Brownsword, Roger
  'Biotechnology and Rights' 208
  'Red Lights and Rogues' 189
  *Rights, Regulation and the Technological
    Revolution* 184–5, 207, 410–13, 416–18
  'What the World Needs Now' 194
BT 208–9
Buchanan, Allen 210–11, 215, 244
burden of proof
  and the precautionary principle 150–151
  reversal 150–151
Burgess, Adam 47
Bush, George W. 197

Cabrera, Laura 195
Cameron, David 293
Campbell, Alan, MP 274–5
Campbell, Naomi 305, 393, 429–30
Campbell, Tom 195
Canada 124
  DNA sampling 86
Caramlau, Isabel 328
Caribbean islands 297
Caroline of Monaco, Princess 175, 428
Carrasco de Paula, Ignacio, Bishop 188
Cassavetes, Nick 172

catastrophes, medical/environmental 113, 155
  and the precautionary principle 165
Catholic Church
  Catechism 197
  stance on biotechnological issues 188,
    189–90, 197, 199, 212
CCTV (closed-circuit television) 5, 320, 324–8
  avoidance strategies 327
  critiqued by police officers 325–6
  inefficacy 325–7
  response of regulatees 327–8
  technological limitations 327
cell nuclear replacement (CNR) 400
censorship 112–13
child pornography 302, 375
  banning of access to 208–9
China, internet access restrictions 209
chipping 444
  see also RFID
Cicero, M. Tullius 194
civil law *see* tort system
civil society 251, 254, 257
  see also NGOs
clarity, requirement of 302, 406
  conflict with flexibility 306–7
Clarke, Sir Anthony MR 393–4
cloning, human
  reproductive, prohibition on 4, 14, 159–160,
    226
  therapeutic 14
Codex Alimentarius 182–3
Cohen, Jonathan 392
Cohen, Julie 219
'Collingridge dilemma', 132, 380
common good, as aim of society 250
communication technology *see* information/
    communication technology
communitarianism 185
compliance
  culture of 61–2
  designed-in 75
  impossibility of 301
  tendency towards 74–5
  see also non-compliance
congruence, requirement of 301, 302
consent 11, 172, 196, 238–41, 243
  and brain-imaging technology 390, 396
  to chipping/tagging 401
  location of boundary 240
  and personal data 309
  role in governmental legitimacy 248
consistency, principle of 147, 148

Index

constancy, requirement of 302
contract law 403
Cooper, Yvette 322
copyright infringement, inducement to 333–4
see also file-sharing; intellectual property
Corbett, Claire 327–8
corporate social responsibility 319
  incentives to 383–4
cosmopolitanism 6
cost–benefit analysis (economic)
  role in precautionary principle 149
courts
  lower, nature of case law 276–7
  positive attitude to technology 73–4
crime prevention strategies 34
  failure 275–6
  see also CCTV; criminal law; DNA; speed
    cameras; surveillance
criminal law/justice 29–30, 74–5, 275, 303,
  339
  agency model 391–3
  retributivist thinking 393
  system failure 275–6, 277
cruel and unusual punishments 9
Cuijpers, Colette 223–4
cybercrime 20, 163–164, 343–4, 349–58, 368
  global extent/response 352–8
  originating in regulator's home territory 350
cyberspace 272, 281–5, 342, 346–9
  classification of problematic activities
    281–2, 284–5
  impossibility of local control 347
  inapplicability of traditional legal systems
    346–7
  jurisdiction 347–8
  as place in its own right 347–8
  see also cybercrime; internet

data protection 296, 304–12, 316–17, 376
  criticisms 312
  regulatory connection 304–5
  regulatory lack of clarity 305–6, 310,
    311–12, 391
  resourcing 303–4
  see also personal data
data storage, as interference with privacy 433
deafness, discrimination on grounds of 213
decision-making, location of 256–7
see also individual decision-making
defective implementation, regulatory focus on
  111–13
de Hert, Paul 107

Deibert, Ronald 264
deliberative–constitutive regulatory approach
  151–2
  application of precautionary principle 152–152
  flexibility of framework 152
deliberative democracy 58–9, 128–9
  problems of 59
della Mirandola, Pico 199
Demissie, Hailemichael T. 178–9
democracy/ies 250
  electoral mechanisms 252
  importance of participation 251
  supplementary mechanisms 250
  see also deliberative democracy
'democratic deficit,' protests against 183
denial-of-service measures 343–4, 359
deontology 185–6, 208
depression, sufferers from 443–4
design, regulatory 28, 424
  intent, role of 31
detection rates, impact of technology on 73
digital photography
  development 236
  permanence of record 236
disability, genetic testing for 211–15
disconnection 419
  findings in case law 410
  forms of/reasons for 399–405
  measures designed to avoid 405–6
  (occasional) benefits 419
  between presumed and actual business
    model 399, 403–5
  between presumed and actual nature of
    technology 399–400
  between presumed and actual uses of
    technology 399, 400–2
discrimination
  genetic (hypothetical) 279–80
  prohibition, between WTO members 125
  as regulatory outcome 30–1, 211–15,
    450
  systematic 178
  in taking of DNA samples 103, 107–8
  see also non-discrimination
disruptive externalities 62–3, 342–3
  types of 343–6
  see also unintended consequences
DNA (deoxyribonucleic acid) samples 72, 75,
  102–8, 423, 440
  age of person taken from 104
  (alleged) public unease over 76
  cellular samples 103

DNA (deoxyribonucleic acid) samples (*cont.*)
circumstances of taking 104
discriminatory use of 107
duration of retention 105
effectiveness in crime detection 274–5
familial searching 77, 107
forms to be retained 102–3
guidelines on retention 80–1
methods of collection 107
power of taking 75
profiling 5, 77, 103
proposed guiding principles 425–6
purpose of taking 104
sequencing, diagnostic tests based on 292–4
UK national database 73–4, 75, 104, 274–5,
326, 346;
accessibility 104;
racial composition 103
use in law enforcement 424
whose samples to be retained 104
Dorbeck-Jung, Bärbel 377–9
double effect, doctrine of 450
Douzinas, Costas 231
Down's syndrome 212–13
Drachten (Netherlands), traffic policy 297
drugs (illicit/recreational)
changes in legal status 338
classification system 337
dependence on 276–7
difficulty of suppression 318, 337
illicit trade in 297, 319
see also pharmaceuticals; psychoactive drugs
dwarf throwing, prohibition of 196
Dworkin, Ronald 171, 176–7, 188, 203–4, 205,
210, 211–12, 213, 216–17, 229

eBay 24, 36, 40–2
ethical stance 317; reversal of policy 41–2
inception 40
role of user community 25
e-commerce, regulatory environment 40–1
Econexus 291
education (public), required levels of 264–6
Edwards, Robert 188, 189–90
effects doctrine 346
embryos, human
definition 410–11; absence of 409–10
destruction 12–14
freezing 238–43
hybrid 320–4, 405–7; construction 322;
licensing of research 323
industrial/commercial use 13

numbers created/stored 222
potential for suffering 208
principles for use 304–21
public consultation on 322–4
research on 11–14, 65, 207, 374–5; pace of
advance 400
selection 212–15,
see also (gender); for organ donation172–3
testing for genetic markers 401–2
theological arguments 197, 199
US policy on 197
endangered species 216–17
enhancement, human 209–10, 336–7
ethics of 336
as moral obligation 206–7
environment, protection of 274, 113–14, 129–32
links with international trade 140–1
long-term 148–148
national obligations 137
public opinion 142
role of precautionary principle 139–41,
147, 154, 162–162; excessive reliance on
159–159
see also endangered species; nature
EPA (Environmental Protection Agency, US),
314, 384
equality 210–16
Estonia
denial-of-service attack on (2007), 343–4, 359
reproductive technology law 241
European Commission 7, 51, 127, 142–154,
156–156, 303–6
reform proposals 306
European Court of Human Rights 226
European Court of Justice
case law *see* Table of cases
Grand Chamber, composition 102
jurisdiction 145–146
European Group on Ethics in Science and New
Technologies (EGE) 389–90
European Patent Office (EPO) 8
European Scientific Technology Observatory
144
European Union
application of precautionary principle
153–154
criticisms 183
data protection regime 174–5, 304–12
decision-making structures 257
e-commerce regulation 408
GMO regulatory framework 169, 174, 180;
criticisms 169–70; legitimacy 169–70;

licensing procedure 256
internet regulation 335, 403–5
Member State variations 84–5, 106–7, 127, 169, 241, 287
nanotechnology regulation 313–14
patent law 7–14, 290
reaffirmation of international position 151–151
restrictions on local regulators 346
stance on GM crops 15–16, 124, 125, 127–9, 156, 218–19; internal controversy 172
'evasion', tactics of 320, 327
evidence, rules on admissibility 390
experts *see* scientists

Facebook 233–4
Facial Identification National Database (FIND) 326
fair trial, right to 235
family life, right to 242
FDA (Food and Drug Administration, US), 265, 299, 315, 382, 384
Fen-Phen (slimming drug) 299
fertility treatments 237–43
file-sharing 320, 328–36, 340, 348
  closure of offending sites 334
  culture of, aims to change 334–5
  regulatory options 329–35
  reporting procedure 330–1
  responses to court decisions 335
  standards set by case law 334
  targeting of individual offenders 329, 334
  targeting of software providers 329, 332–5
fingerprints, storing of 103
Fisher, Elizabeth 137, 141, 151–154, 161
food, right to 232
Food Standards Agency (UK), 263, 387, 398
Ford, Henry 111
Foresight programme 252, 338
Fox, Tom 255–6
France
  bioethical legislation 214
  internet regulation 329
Franck, Thomas 180
'Frankenfoods' 388
fraud, online 40–1
free movement of goods, principle of 360–7
freedom of assembly, right of 262
freedom of association, right of 180, 262
freedom of expression, right of 180, 215, 262–3
  clash with other rights 234–7, 244

Fukuyama, Francis 19–20, 200, 201, 204, 208, 277
Fuller, Lon 61, 301–2, 377, 451–2
future generations
  conflicts of interest with present 155
  protection of interests 142, 148–148, 208

Galligan, Denis 250–1, 253
gambling
  legality 373
  online 349, 367, 373
Garland, David 34
Gasser, Urs 224
Gavaghan, Colin 213
Geldof, Bob 41
gender, selection on grounds of 213–14
genetic engineering 200–3, 290–5, 374
  distribution of harms and benefits 210–11
  hypothetical future developments 444–5
  see also GMOs
genetic profiling, for insurance use 119
genetic testing 211–12, 286–9, 359–60
  limits on research 293
  partial regulation 287
  permissive regulation 287
  proposed reforms to regulatory environment 293–4
  see also embryos; total regulation
Genewatch UK 291
Germany
  data retention 307
  internet regulation 345, 360
  IVF legislation 106
  privacy law 235–6
  social security system 366
  view on human dignity 196
Gerrard, Graham, DCC 326
Gettysburg Address 246
Gibb, John 20–1
Gibbons, Susan 39
global financial crisis (2007–9) 345
GMOs (genetically modified organisms) 4, 10–11, 15–18, 22, 115, 117, 122–9, 169, 183, 218, 372
  consumer perceptions 119–20, 132–3
  ethical/cultural divides 16, 17, 170
  illicit trade in 320
  individual choice 111
  licensing procedure 255–6
  moral consensus, role of 11
  moral objections 128, 171–2, 218–19
  NGOs' role in debates 254

Index

GMOs (genetically modified organisms) (*cont.*)
  product vs. process, as focus of safety debates 15
  prudential vs. precautionary judgements 16
  public comprehension 265
  public protests against 169
  reasons for objecting to 128
  refusal to license 169
  risk assessment 17, 156–156
  scientific disagreements 15
God, humankind as made in image of 48
  relationship between humankind and creator 199
  as support for technological advancement 198
Goldsmith, Jack 40–1
governance 26, 49
  adaptability 385
  democratic, right to 180, 249
  distinguished from government 181
  move from government to 180–2
  online facilities 350
governments
  attempts at cyberspace regulation 347
  exercise of power 176
  illegitimate 177–8
  legitimacy 176, 180
  (perceived) responsibility for non-state actions 184
  responsibility to citizens 176, 177–8
  sources of authority 173, 179, 180
Grabosky, Peter 276,
Gramsci, Antonio 335–6
Greene, Joshua 392
Greenfield, Susan, Baroness 45
Griffin, James 231
Gunningham, Neil 275
Gutmann, Amy 58–9

Habermas, Jürgen 200–3, 266, 267
Haines, Fiona 181
Hale, Lady 76–7
Halliburton, Christian 394–5
harm, definitions of 208–10
  culturally specific 209–10
harm–benefit analysis 205–10
  biotechnical 8, 48
  and human rights 243
  legislative provisions 205
  need for ethical perspectives alongside 207–8
Harmon, Shawn H. E. 52

Harris, John 206–7
Harvard Onco-mouse 6–7, 8, 9, 10–11, 51, 209
Hashmi, Zain 402, 413–16
Hawai'i, privacy laws 375
health/safety 113–14
  application of precautionary principle 137, 141, 147, 154, 162–162
  call for openness of data 310
  chipping/tagging on grounds of 444
  concerns raised by new technology 380–9, 397
  identification of antithetical factors 163–163
  minimum requirements 163
  non-normative technological enforcement 449–50
  product monitoring 299
  threats to 164
Heidegger, Martin 200
Hildebrandt, Mireille 35, 441–2
Hiroshima, nuclear attack on 200
Hodge, Graeme 316
Hoffmann, Lord 105, 402, 413–16
House of Commons Science and Technology Select Committee 67–8, 154, 205–6, 207–8, 321, 323, 405
House of Commons Select Committee on Home Affairs 340
House of Lords European Committee 343–4
House of Lords Science and Technology Committee 247–8, 252, 254–5, 261, 263, 265–6, 268, 386–8, 398, 407–8
Howse, Robert 128–9
human dignity 4, 10–12, 23, 172, 178, 191–205, 290, 389, 393
  as absolute 196, 232
  empowering/constraining functions 194; used both ways in same discussion 193–4
  function of appeals to 192–4
  history 192–4
  moving of boundaries 220–3
  relationship with human rights 195–6, 229, 243
  relationship with utilitarianism 190–1
  as root of other moral claims 191–2
  specifically technological application 192
  as stemming from intrinsic human qualities 194–5
  theological perspectives 189–90, 192, 196–9, 205, 266, 267
  as ultimate boundary marker 191–2
  see also autonomy; human nature

Human Fertilisation and Embryology
Authority (HFEA, UK), 272, 280, 303,
322–4
Human Genetics Commission (UK) 359–60
human genome, manipulation of *see* genetic
engineering; patentability
Human Genome Project 18
human nature 192, 199–205
distinguished from human dignity 201–2
technological capacity to destroy 199–205
see also nature
human rights 225–45
alternatives to 227
as boundary markers 173, 191, 228–33
case law 226
claims against non-state actors 230
conflicts between 244; between two aspects
of the same right 240
core elements 228–31, 232
defined 228
domination of moral debate 226
dualism 230, 232
foundational ideology 195
group-based 229
history 228, 231
indeterminacy 231, 232, 237, 244–5
in international agreements 225–6, 227
lack of legal standing 232
as legal entitlements 232
limits 237
local application 241
as minimum guarantee 229–30
new, creation of 244
as normative framework 243–4
outrunning of established definitions
230–1, 244
relationship with human dignity
195–6
relationship with technology regulation
226–7, 243–4
relative importance 185
role in legitimacy 177–8
technological challenges to 227
tension with other values 243
as tools of empowerment 237–43
trumping of policy considerations 229
universality 228–9; challenges to 231–2
violations 208
Hungary, reproductive technology law 241
Hustinx, Peter 303–4
Huxley, Aldous 208
Brave New World 200

Ida, Ryuichi 209–10
identity theft 344
India, bioethical legislation 214
indigenous peoples, involvement in decision-
making 255
individual decision-making, impact of
technologies on 437–8
ideal-typical forms 437–8, 447–8
moral choices, forestalled by technology
449–51
moral coding 448–9
information
asymmetry of 288, 300
decisions on supplying public with 145
freedom of 179, 263; distinguished from
transparency 263–4
Information Commissioner (UK) 72–3
information/communication technology 18,
19–21, 142, 304–5, 368, 373–6
business models 403–5
convergence with other technologies 21
enabling of other technologies 374
ethical concerns 20–1
prudential concerns 112–13
state control/deployment of 20–1
infrastructure 162–3
generic vs. specific features 163–4
inputs, role in regulatory theory/process
273–4, 280
instrumentalism 249–50
insurance 286–9
'adverse selection' 288–9
high-risk insured 289
motor 328
variables 289
intellectual property 179, 219–20
intention, role in legitimacy 176–7
internet 19–21
access to: denial of 1544, ; as fundamental
right 215
code-based change 283
complexity of regulation 284
criminal activity on 163–4
and data protection 376
emergence 342, 374, 400
filtering 264
global reach 282–3
lawlessness 20, 63, 349–50
nanofood sales 387–8
social networking sites 233–4
specific regulatory requirements 284
see also cyberspace; eBay; *Wikipedia*

Internet Watch Foundation 302
'inventing around' 292–3
Islam 198
ISPs (internet service providers), mobilisation against file-sharing 329–32
  recourse to 'technical measures' 331–2
Israel, reproductive technology law 241
Italy, reproductive technology law 241
IVF (in vitro fertilisation) treatment 106–7, 188, 189–90, 413–18

Japan, bioethical theory 185, 209–10, 212–13, 216
Jasanoff, Sheila 120
Johnson, David 342, 346–8, 368
Jones, Judith 137
Joy, Bill 22–3
Judaism 198
Judge, Lord 233
justice
  as boundary marker 173, 191–2
  denied by nature/circumstance 212
  distinguished from legitimacy 176–7

Kafka, Franz 21, 108
Kant, Immanuel 186, 192–3, 194, 196
Karpowicz, Phillip 201
Kay, W. D. 49
Kirby, Michael 66
Klang, Mathias 18–19
Koops, Bert-Jaap 3, 223–4, 408–9
Kornhauser, Lewis 51
Krimsky, Sheldon 275, 424, 425–6

La Rue, Frank 215
law
  alternative sources 181
  challenges facing 23
  defined 97
  distinguished from managerial regulation 301, 451
  hard vs. soft 377–9
  need for restraints 22–3
  need to evolve in cyberspace 348
  relationship with regulatory environment 24, 25–6, 34–5, 45, 451–2
  situations inappropriate to invocation of 60
  traditional systems 346
  as two-way reciprocal process 451–2
  universal application 177–8
  see also courts; rule of law

Lee, Bob 313–14
Lee, Maria 16–17, 114, 129
legal determinism 351
legal exclusivity, mistake of 28
legalism 300–4
legitimacy 171–2, 419
  boundaries of 173
  of cyberspace regulation 348–51
  degrees of 177
  dimensions of 173
  and 'ethical oversight' 207–8
  of EU GMO regime 169–70
  'input' vs. 'output', 182, 253
  of non-state actors 182–4
  and online regulation 284
  at price of effectiveness 297
  range of approaches 226
  relationship with regulator's identity 184
  varying standards of 178–9
  see also governments; procedural legitimacy; source legitimacy; substantive legitimacy
Lessig, Lawrence 28, 33, 34, 358–9
Levmore, Saul 41–4
lex mercatoria (merchant law) 347–8
libel/slander, laws of 235
liberalism 185–7
  cyberspace regulation 358–9
  as normative framework 190
LICRA (League Against Racism and Antisemitism) 358
life, right to 242
Lin, Albert 314–15
Lincoln, Abraham 246, 248
Lindon, Vincent 175
Litan, Robert 375–6
Littman, Jessica 335
Live8 concert (June 2005) 287
Locke, John 248, 439

mail order, sale of goods by 358–60
Mandel, Gregory N. 380–6
Manson, Neil 138
marginalised groups, involvement in decision-making 255
'margin of appreciation' doctrine 105, 239, 246–7
marijuana 318
Marlowe, Christopher, *Doctor Faustus* 199
Marx, Gary T. 68–70
Max Planck Institute 6, 11
Mayer, Sue, Dr 291
medicine

ethics of 227
innovative procedures 372
medicines, online sales 360–7
  advertising 363
  fears of misuse/abuse 365
  non-prescription 365
  obligation to inform customer 365
  prescription 365–6
  risks attached to 366
Mill, John Stuart 116, 186, 249–52
miscarriages of justice, reluctance to reopen
    107
misuse, regulatory focus on 111–13
mobile phones, risks of 47, 115–16, 121–2
Modafinil 336
Monsanto 133
Moor, James 66, 379–80, 390
moral community 437, 438–9, 445–51, 452
  impact of non-normative regulatory
      technologies 447–8
  regulatory responsibilities towards 439–40
  self-regulation and 445–7
morality *see* GMOs; patentability;
    precautionary principle
Morse, Stephen 391–2
Moses, Robert 30, 450
motor vehicles 111
  cooling systems 313
  (hypothetical) design options 441–2
  self-defeating safety features 286
  'smart' 445–7; handling of emergencies 446
  see also bicycles; speed cameras; speed
      limits; traffic offences
Mundy, Alicia 299
murder, justification for 191
Murphy, Thérèse 226–7
Murray, Andrew 33–4, 41–2, 335
My Sister's Keeper (2009), 172–3

nanoparticles 113, 130–2
  contradictory evidence on 131
  (feared) toxicity 129, 130, 312, 372
  novel features 130
  presence in marketplace 130, 312, 372
  range of regulatory approaches 131
  use in cosmetics 47, 48, 314–15
nanotechnology 4, 18, 49, 113, 114, 121,
    129–32, 253–4, 291–2, 312–16, 373, 374,
    382, 386–9, 398, 407–8
  absence of premarket approval requirement
      315
  ex ante/ex post regulation 312–13

exemptions from regulation 314
legal commentaries 313–16
presumption of safety 315
public consultation exercises 261, 265–6,
    387
public register 387
regulatory failure 296, 317
regulatory lacunae 314
research trials 389
responsibility for decision-making 254
natality 202
national legal systems 23
  cooperative/reciprocal arrangements 360
  maintenance in face of online threats 358
  problems in cyberspace 282, 346–7
  standards of legitimacy 178–9
natural disasters 342, 346
natural rights/justice, doctrine of 172
nature
  as boundary marker 216–19
  desire to live in harmony with 216–18
  technology ruled 'unnatural' 218–19
  see also human nature
Nazi memorabilia (prohibited) sale of 358
Netherlands
  GM debate 254
  regulation of technology 154, 223–4
neuroscience, relationship with criminal
    justice 391–3
  see also brain-imaging technology
neurotechnology 18, 45
Neville, Mick, DCI 325–6
new technology/ies 45
  adaptation of existing concepts 172,
      312
  adaptive regulatory approach 132, 136, 372,
      383
  application of existing legal provisions
      371–2; *ex ante* 371–2; *ex post* 371–2
  challenge posed to regulatory connection
      372–3
  data gathering 382–3
  development pathway 377, 379–80, 390
  disruptive impact 18–19
  ethical concerns 377, 388–97
  exposure of gaps in law 371, 372, 374,
      396–7, 400
  flexible governance guidelines 381–6
  'hard' vs. 'soft' regulation 377–9, 398–9
  HSE concerns 377, 380–9, 397
  individuals' protective measures 111
  industry stewardship 383–4

Index

new technology/ies (*cont.*)
  introduction stage 379, 390
  pace of development 170–1, 371, 374–6, 385, 398
  permeation stage 380, 390
  popularity with citizens 113
  power stage 380
  precautionary approach to 161–2
  public consultation process 48–9, 388–9, 406
  public information 136
  regulatory environment 108
  regulatory focus 111–13
  risk–benefit assessment 64, 111, 115–22, 136
  stage requiring regulatory intervention 380
  stakeholder involvement 385–6
  unforeseen developments 406
New York
  parkway bridges 30–1, 450
  traffic code 112
Newzbin2 329
NGOs (non-governmental organisations), 155, 254
  Northern domination 257
Nicholls, Lord 393
Nickel, James 228–30
Nobel Prize for Medicine 189–90
non-compliance
  strategies for dealing with 62, 302
  on undefeatable scale 302–3
non-discrimination, principle of 147, 148
non-normative regulatory technologies 437, 440–51
  consultation process 445, 447
  embedded in the person 443–5, 448–9
  imposed from outside 442–3, 447–8
  prevention of harmful acts 449–50;
    intentional vs. accidental 450–1
  regulatory margin 449–51
  self-regulatory 441–2
normative exclusivity, mistake of 28
Norrie, Alan 29–30
North Carolina, traffic code 112
North–South divide (in global power/ economic structures), 256, 257
Northern Ireland
  DNA sampling/profiling 81
Novartis 156
Nozick, Robert 194–5, 266
Nuffield Council on Bioethics 81–2, 138, 274, 290, 292

OECD (Organization for Economic Cooperation and Development) 134–5
OFCOM 330, 331–2
Office of Safety and Health Administration (OSHA, US) 384
Omidyar, Pierre 40
O'Neill, Onora 133–4, 135
organ donation *see* 'saviour siblings'
O'Rourke, P. J. 233
Orwell, George 21, 107, 108
  1984, 31–3, 177–8
outcomes
  relationship with legitimacy 177
  role in regulatory theory/process 273–5
outputs, role in regulatory theory/process 273–4

Pahuja, Sundhya 230
Palfrey, John 224
parenthood, right to 227, 241–3
Parfitt, Derek
participation 48–9, 179–80, 248–52
  actors warranting special consideration 255
  attitudinal types 50–1
  background conditions 262–6
  deferral to expert opinion 253–4
  direct form 252
  format 257–62
  in governance, defined 249, 251
  and human dignity 192
  identity of participants 253–6
  importance to state–people relationship 251
  increasing use in technology regulation 268
  key features 252–66
  legislative provisions 261
  liberal model 252, 261
  means of representation 257
  moves towards 172
  and precautionary principle 147
  problems of 49–51, 180
  range of approaches 250–1
  requirement of public understanding 264–6
  stakeholder model 255–6
patentability of biotechnology 6–14, 218, 294
  compulsory licensing 294
  counter-productivity of standards 290–5
  human genome 272, 290–5
  moral boundaries 10, 14, 290
  non-moral arguments against 290
  research exemption 294
  utility requirement 299
personal copying 283

personal data
  'anonymised', 307, 423–4
  contradictory objectives 307–10
  defined 306, 307; scope of definition
    309–10
  distinguished from privacy issues 308–10
  protection 304–5
  special categories 309–10
Pettit, Philip 180
PGD (pre-implantation genetic diagnosis)
    technology 154, 417–18
pharmaceutical industry 297–8
see also medicines
Phillips, Lord MR 305
photographs
  of deceased public figures 235–6
  retention, as breach of rights 435–6
  unauthorised taking of 426–36; as intrusive
    430; as no breach of rights 430–1
phytosanitary measures
  key distinction 127
  national obligations 141
  risk assessment 126–7, 149–50
Picoult, Jodi 172–3
plants, relationship of humans to 217–18
pluralism
  ethical 58–9, 266, 296–7; impossibility of
    reconciliation 267; open/closed types 59
  prudential 59, 115–16, 296–7
police
  constraints on 340
  criticisms of CCTV 325–6
  resistance to outside regulation 319
  unauthorised surveillance activities 426–36
pornography
  avoidance strategies 320, 375
  'extreme' 297
  see also child pornography
Porter, Gerard 7–8
positivism, legal 171–2
Post, David 342–3, 346–8, 368
precautionary principle 137–166, 205, 208
  arguments for 166
  burden of proof 150–1
  as coherent regulatory response 161–5
  common-sense precaution 164
  constituent parts 143
  context-specific justifications 155–6
  costs of application 161–2
  criticisms 137–8
  decision on whether to act 142, 145, 151

defined 140
deliberative precaution 154, 157–8, 160
determination of appropriate action 146
as enabling principle 159–60; in
  reproductive technologies 160–1
EU case law 153–4, 158
examination of scientific developments
  147, 149
fact-finding precaution 156–7, 158, 160
forms of 148
general principles of application 147
guidelines for application 146–51
health care applications 154
identification of negative effects 143, 148
implementation 146
increased focus on 151
key functions 140
legislative provisions 138–41, 155
maintenance of status quo 159–60
measures resulting from application 143,
  145, 151
misuse 159
moral precaution 164–6
national obligations 139–40
'precautionary creep' 156
'pure prudential' precaution 164–5
range of actions available 145
relationship with regulatory environment
  162–4
risk–benefit analysis 147, 149, 165
rival readings 152–3
scientific evaluation 144, 146
trigger factors 143–5, 146–7
variety of formulations 138
printing, development of technology 112–13
prior arrival, principle of 150
privacy 4, 74, 75–7, 104, 223–4, 233–7, 308–10,
  393–6, 426–36
  authorised infringements 395
  and brain-imaging technology 394, 395–6
  changing conceptions of 224
  clash with freedom of expression
    235–7, 244
  clash with security concerns 344–5
  compared with property rights 394–5
  European standard of 176
  move to more robust conception of 394–5
  overemphasis at expense of other concerns
    311
  'physical and psychological integrity'
    criterion 428–9

privacy (*cont.*)
  private life, right to 236, 239–40
  of public figures 175–6
  'reasonable expectation' criterion 393
  regulatory flaws 391
  UK legislative provisions 234
procedural legitimacy 172, 179–81, 183, 246–8
  defined 179
  as embodied in act of participation 248–9
  importance to technology regulation 247, 268
'procrastination principle' 131
professions, resistance to outside regulation 319
Project on Emerging Nanotechnologies (US) 263
Prometheus (mythical figure) 204
property 219–23, 394–5
  human body viewed as 220–3, 242
  rights created by lawful exercise of skill 221
  see also intellectual property
proportionality principle 105, 147–8, 433–6
Prosser, Tony 280
protectionism 128–9
prudential calculation 115–22, 452
  complicating factors 119–20
  divergence of popular and expert views 122
  impact of non-normative technologies on 441–5
  individual choices 115–16, 136
  likelihood of variations 116, 119, 121–2
  mode of operation 116–22
  simplest form 115–19
  trumping of moral choices 447–8
psychoactive drugs 320, 336–41
  addictiveness 340
  administration to children 448–9
  criminalisation 339
  (hypothetical) amplification of moral signals 446–7
  low share of market 340
  management (as alternative to prohibition) 340–1
  mixed views among regulatees 339
  as (projected) source of government revenue 340
  regulatory options 338–9
  social embeddedness 339
  student use 336–7, 339–40
  supply-side vs. demand-side strategies 338–9
  victimless nature of use 340

psychopathy 392
public interest, balancing against individual rights 104, 105, 142, 234–5
publicity 233

Radetzki, Marcus *et al.*, *Genes and Insurance* 60–2, 287–9
railway systems 163, 163
rational–instrumental regulatory approach 141, 151–4
  in EU case law 153–4
  official endorsement 153–4
  relationship with precautionary principle 152–3
  role of scientific opinion 153
  structured framework 152
Rawls, John 266–8
Raz, Joseph 226
Reed, Chris 403–5, 408–9
regulatees
  as active participants 319–24
  attempts to change law/regulations 320, 329
  avoidance strategies 320, 327–8
  economic impact of measures on 286, 318–19
  lobbying to prevent proposed law changes 320–4
  need for cooperation 282, 283–4, 285, 318, 339–41, 378, 439
  prudential calculations 320
  resistance to regulatory measures 271, 319, 341; on grounds of conscience 319
  uncertainty as to position 301
  undue influence on regulators 298–9
regulation
  adequacy of, focus on 64
  alternative visions 25
  challenges 46, 70–1
  checklist 68–70
  complexity 22, 25, 39
  contextualisation 6
  defined 83
  direct public involvement 252
  distinction between components 164
  levels of 16–17
  normative outlook 3–4
  precautionary approach 115, 136
  preventive 161–2, 406–7
  'red light' *see* total regulation
  role of knowledge 3–4
  self-defeating 286
  types of 3–4

see also disruptive externalities; regulators; regulatory connection; regulatory effectiveness; regulatory environment; regulatory failure; regulatory legitimacy; regulatory margin; regulatory modalities; regulatory prudence; regulatory strategy; regulatory use of technology; smart regulation; unintended consequences

regulators
- agreed competences 51
- 'capture', 298–300, 316
- corruption 297–8, 316
- inaction 296
- incompetence 271–2, 316–17, 367–8
- integrity 61–2

regulatory connection 5, 46, 63–8, 70, 71, 304–5, 371–3
- analytical framework 376–7
- challenge of new technologies to 372–3, 399
- complexity 67–8
- drafting strategies 399, 405–18; intelligent (anticipatory) drafting 405–8; 'purpose neutral' 409; purposive interpretation 409–18; 'technology neutral' 408–9
- establishment 64–5
- failure of 65, 67; acceptability 67
- means of maintaining 65–6, 398–9
- through rewriting of legislation 410–13
- *see also* disconnection

regulatory economy 67, 272, 273–5, 279, 280, 419
- nature of measures 273–4

regulatory effectiveness 5, 46, 61, 67, 70, 71, 131–2, 271–2, 273–9, 295, 419
- clarification of concept 272, 275–9
- criteria 277–8
- degrees of 277–8
- guidelines 272, 273, 281–5
- importance of regulatees' response 62, 378
- key factors 273, 285, 296
- markers of competence 300–4
- nature of measures 273–4
- online 282, 283, 284–5, 348–9
- 'perfect', impracticability of 278–9

regulatory efficiency 272, 273–5, 279–80
- nature of measures 273–4

regulatory environment(s) 5–6, 27–31, 108
- changing nature 437–51
- compatibility with law 54
- complexity 27
- constitutive division 65
- defective 112

fortification against corruption 298
ideal-typical regimes 33
illustrative examples 36–44
impact of technological change 374–6
ingredients 26, 27
lack of clarity 280
maximisation of positive effects 64–5
minimisation of negative effects 64
non-normative 379
range of instruments 27–9, 31, 64–5
'red light' *see* regulation, total
and regulatory connection 377–9
regulatory intention/effect 27, 30–1
relationship with precautionary principle 162–4
suited to moral community 452
three generations of 28–9, 74–5
first-generation 300, 419; second/third-generation 301–2, 379, 424, 451–2
'top-down' vs. 'bottom-up' structure 298
'Type 1', 27, 31, 36, 63, 341, 377, 397, 419; regulatee resistance 341
'Type 2', 27, 31, 36, 341, 348, 377, 397
see also regulatory strategy

regulatory failure 61, 62–3, 345
- causes 271–2, 296–7, 316–17, 367–8
- *see also* disruptive externalities

regulatory legitimacy 5, 46, 48–61, 70, 71, 132
- (limited) role of scientists 49
- procedural 48–51
- of regulatory means 60–1
- reviewability of decisions 59
- *see also* participation; standards, regulatory

regulatory margin 439–40, 445
- impact of non-normative technologies 449–51
- relevant considerations 440

regulatory modalities 31–5
- components 34–5
- optimal mix 34, 60–1

regulatory prudence 5, 46, 47–8, 70–1, 111, 165–6, 316
- determination of acceptable risk 113–15
- need for balance 47–8
- *see also* precautionary principle; prudential calculation

regulatory standards set by 301
regulatory strategy 27, 29–30
- direct vs. indirect 80
- moral register 29–30
- prudential register 29–30

Index

regulatory strategy (*cont.*)
  register of practicability 29–30
regulatory use of technology 5, 72–108, 173, 424–52
  accuracy 74
  amplification of prudential signals 437–40; excessive 440
  concerns regarding 74–5
  correct functioning 74
  depth of technical reliance 74–5
  excessive reliance on 278–9
  impact on regulatory environment 424
  replacement of normativity *see* non-normative regulatory technologies
  unintended effects 74
Reichman, Nancy 181
Reidenberg, Joel 20, 349–50, 359
religion, as source of legitimacy 174
see also Catholic Church; God; human dignity; Islam; Judaism
reproductive technologies 154, 160–61, 205–6, 401–2
see also cloning; IVF treatment
republican theory of citizenship 180
research
  collaborations 386–7
  difficulty of verification 135
  disciplines 4
  frame of inquiry 4
  funding 145, 386–7
  nature of questions 4
  pressure to falsify results 134–5, 136
  purpose 149
  regulatory environment 134–5
responsible stewardship, principle of 132
RFID (radio frequency identification) technology 400–1
Ridley, Matt 22
Rimmer, Matthew 335–6
risk, categories of 119
  hypothetical 119
  probabilistic 119
  speculative 119
  see also risk assessment; risk communication; risk management
risk assessment 142
  in absence of full information 143
  accommodation of uncertainty factors 144–5
  components 144
  long-term 148
  role of precautionary principle 143

risk communication 142
risk management 142
  accommodation of uncertainty factors 145, 149–50
  general principles 147
  role of precautionary principle 143, 156–7, 158
  state involvement 156
Ritalin 336, 448–9
robotics 178
Rodotà, Stefano 344
Roman thought/ethics 192
Rosenau, James 181
Rothstein, Mark 108
Rousseau, Jean-Jacques 248, 251–2, 253
Rowling, J. K., 393–4, 430
Royal Academy of Engineering 50–1, 60–1, 129–30
Royal Commission on Environmental Pollution 130–2, 380–1, 386
Royal Society 60, 129–30
Rule of Law 23, 301–2, 419
  in cyberspace 349–50
Russia, denial-of-service attack on Estonia 343–4, 359

sacred, explorations of 216–19
Sandel, Michael 171, 203–4, 266
Sandler, Ronald 49
Sassen, Saskia 181
'saviour siblings', 157, 172–3, 401–2
scepticism, distinguished from cynicism 138
Schneider, Carl 226
Schomberg, René von 137, 154, 157–8
science/scientists
  disagreements among 124, 147, 161
  divergences from public opinion 180, 266–5
  neutrality, problems of 124–5, 267
  overestimation of powers 131
  place in RI framework 153
  public trust in 132–4; breakdown of 133–4; (lack of) alternatives 134
  regulatory environment 134–5
  'sound' 132–5
  vested political/economic interests 132–3
  see also research
Scotland
  DNA sampling/profiling 81
Scott, Colin 33–4, 181, 182
seatbelts, wearing of 73
Seattle protests (1999), 183, 184
Second Life 348–9

Securities and Exchange Commission (US) 297-8
Sedley L. J., 76, 234
self-determination, right to 248
self-regulation 441-2, 452
   and moral community 445-6
   online 348-9; problems of 348-9
September11 attacks 344-5
sex offenders, RFID chipping 401
Shakespeare, William, *Hamlet* 203
Shimazono, Susumu 212-13
'Shoe Rapist' case 77
Simoncelli, Tania 275, 424, 425-6
Skogstad, Grace 169-70, 179, 182, 183
slander *see* libel
smart meters 223-4
smart regulation 35, 296, 324-5, 334-5
   beneficial impacts 31
   flexibility of approach 39
   online 285
Smith, Roger 389
soccer 60
soft law
   strengths 377-8
   weaknesses 378
Solove, Daniel 21, 236
Somsen, Han 141, 154
source legitimacy 174-6, 179, 183
   defined 173
   relevance to technological regulation 174
Souter, Justice 333-4
South Africa, apartheid regime 178
spam 350-1
   legislation directed against 351
   software designed to combat 351
speed cameras 72, 437
   motorists' responses to 320, 327-8
speed limits 171, 278
sperm
   confusion of two samples 415
   DIY sorting kits (anticipated) 406-7
   property rights over 220-2
spy drones 324
stakeholders
   involvement in emerging technologies 385-6
   and participation processes 255-6, 261-2
   regulators' actions on behalf of 162
standards 51-9
   ethical viability 51
   of legality 63
states

application of precautionary principle 156
authoritarian, internet control 358
diffusion of authority 181-2
diminution of powers 156, 181-2, 256-7
ethical responsibilities 210
friendly, accidentally disruptive acts by 345
rights claimed against 229-30, 232
trade/cultural agreements 345-6
vulnerability to cyber-attacks 344
see also governments; national legal systems
Steinbrecher, Ricarda, Dr 291
stem cell research 11-14, 22, 197, 207, 256, 321-4
   permissibility under UK law 322
   theological support for 198
Steyn, Lord 73, 76
Stirling, Andy 49-50
substantive legitimacy 176-9
   defined 176
   intent vs. outcome 176-7
   overlap with procedural legitimacy 179-80
   relevance to technological regulation 178-9
Sunday trading 318-19
sunscreens, use of nanoparticles in 314-15
Sunstein, Cass R., 47-8, 157
super-injunctions 233, 234, 237
surveillance society 31-3, 72-3, 304-6, 376
   moves towards 401, 426-36
   as unavoidable in modern world 73
SWAMI (Safeguards in a World of Ambient Intelligence) project 21
Swire, Peter 375
Swiss Federal Committee on Non-Human Biotechnology 217-18
synthetic biology, debate on 50-1, 113, 129

tagging 444
Takehara, Tyler 375
Talbott, Meghan 108
taxation 286
technological determinism 351-2
technology
   beneficial impacts 22, 47-8
   'constitutive' 442
   courts' positive attitude to 73-4
   failure to develop, harmful effects of 208
   and human rights 227
   innovativeness 3
   location 3
   migration from one context to another 400-2
   need for regulation 5, 22

technology (*cont.*)
  'out of control' 233–4
  rapidity of developments 3
  'regulative' 441–2
  risks of 4
  supranational regulation 174
  time dimension 3
  types of 3
  see also new technology/ies; regulatory use of technology
'technology neutral' drafting style 65–6, 398, 408–9
ten Have, Henk 5
Tennessee, treatment of privacy/property 240
Thalidomide 177, 299
third parties
  competition with local regulators 345
  hostile acts in cyberspace 343–5, 350, 367–8
  interventions, as cause of regulatory failure 301
Thomas, Richard 326
titanium dioxide 315
Titian 294
tobacco advertising 51
tort system 300
  limitations 300
total regulation 60–2, 287–9
  abandonment, arguments for/against 289
  objections to 287–9
  purpose 287–8
  secondary effects 288–9
  see also genetic testing
trade secrets 294–5
traffic offences
  police time (allegedly) wasted on 278–9
  predominance of young male offenders 327–8
Transfigura affair 234
transparency, need for 128–9, 147, 151, 179, 263–4, 308–9
transport system, technologically managed 443
Tully, James 267
Turkle, Sherry, *Alone Together* 178
TV licensing 324–5
Twitter 233–4, 237, 349

UK Biobank 24, 36
  adherence to ethical commitments 129
  disclosure of results 37, 390
  Ethics and Governance Council (EGC), 36–7, 38–9

Ethics and Governance Framework (EGF), 37–8
  participants' role 36
  regulatory environment, critiqued 39
  scale of operations 36
uncertainty 115, 122–4, 161, 373
  categories 144
  causes 144
  created by new technologies 9, 47, 50, 113, 129
  mapping of nature/extent 123–4
  public comprehension 265
  range of scenarios 123
  role in risk analysis 143, 144–5, 165
under-resourcing, problem of 302–26, 384
UNESCO (United Nations Educational, Scientific and Cultural Organization)
  Bioethics Committee 52, 160–1
unintended consequences (of regulation), 278–9, 284, 285–95
United Kingdom
  Cabinet Office guidelines on regulatory effectiveness 273–4
  compliance with EU standards 246–7
  criminal justice strategy 423
  data protection 311–12
  DNA sampling, compared with EU standards 85, 105, 423, 425
  domestic politics 430
  drug law 337
  embryo selection 213–14
  genetic testing 359–60
  GM food debate 120, 122, 219
  identity card scheme 63
  incorporation of right to privacy 234
  internet regulation 330–2
  misinformation of public 133
  nanotechnology policy 114, 129–30, 215–16, 253–4, 312, 316, 388–9; soft law strategy 378–9
  participation processes 257–61
  privacy debate 233–4
  protection against surveillance technologies 426–36
  regulation of genetic testing 287
  regulatory connection, steps to improve 67–8
United Nations
  divisions 64
  Food and Agricultural Organization (FAO) 182

Human Rights Committee 252
see also UNESCO
United States
  abortion debate 191
  alcohol regulation 318
  constitutional jurisprudence 394–5
  criminal law 9
  cyberspace regulation 282
  Department of Agriculture (USDA) 384
  DNA database 425
  e-commerce regulation 408
  embryo research policy 197
  gambling law 373
  GM food policy/disputes 124
  internet regulation 333–5; failure of 347
  nanotechnology regulation 314–16
  patent law 7
  Patent Office 291–2
  Presidential Commission for the Study of
    Bioethical Issues 58–9, 132
  President's Council on Bioethics 18, 448–9
  see also names of individual States
Usher, Ed 326
utilitarianism 9, 185–6, 190–1, 206–7, 243,
  266, 396
  rejection 186

Vaidhyanathan, Siva 291–2
van Ameroom, Marloes 377–9
van Asselt, Marjolein 255–6
van den Hoven, Jeroen 401
van der Daele, Wolfgang 207
van der Meulen, Nicole 344

Vatican *see* Catholic Church
Vaughan, Steven 313–14
verkeerspordvrij (sign-free) traffic policy 298
Victim's Voice 326
Villeneuve, Nart 264
von Silva-Tarouca Larsen, Beatrice 430
Vos, Ellen 255–6

Walden, Ian 302
Wall, David 350–1
Warnock, Mary, Baroness 8–9, 11, 48, 51, 170,
  240
Warren, Samuel D. 235
WHO (World Health Organization) 182
Wikileaks 343
Wikipedia 24, 36, 42–4
  Counter-Vandalism Unit 44
  evolving nature 44
  extent of central control 44
  regulatory environment 42–4
  role of user community 44
  vandalism 44
Woodrow Wilson International Center for
  Scholars 263
Woolf, Lord CJ 73, 75–6
World Summit on the Information Society 225
WTO (World Trade Organization), 174,
  182–3, 230, 257
  protests against 183
Wu, Tim 40, 320, 327

Yahoo 358

Zittrain, Jonathan 20, 42–4

For EU product safety concerns, contact us at Calle de José Abascal, 56–1°, 28003 Madrid, Spain or eugpsr@cambridge.org.

www.ingramcontent.com/pod-product-compliance
Ingram Content Group UK Ltd.
Pitfield, Milton Keynes, MK11 3LW, UK
UKHW050054090825
461487UK00036B/1733